Lecture Notes in Computer Science 8723

Advanced Research in Computing and Software Science

Subline of Lectures Notes in Computer Science

Markus Müller-Olm Helmut Seidl (Eds.)

Static Analysis

21st International Symposium, SAS 2014
Munich, Germany, September 11-13, 2014
Proceedings

Springer

Volume Editors

Markus Müller-Olm
Westfälische Wilhelms-Universität Münster
Institut für Informatik, FB 10
Einsteinstr. 62
48149 Münster, Germany
E-mail: markus.mueller-olm@wwu.de

Helmut Seidl
Technische Universität München
Institut für Informatik, 12
Boltzmannstr. 3
85748 Garching, Germany
E-mail: seidl@in.tum.de

ISSN 0302-9743 e-ISSN 1611-3349
ISBN 978-3-319-10935-0 e-ISBN 978-3-319-10936-7
DOI 10.1007/978-3-319-10936-7
Springer Cham Heidelberg New York Dordrecht London

Library of Congress Control Number: 2014946920

LNCS Sublibrary: SL 1 – Theoretical Computer Science and General Issues

Typesetting: Camera-ready by author, data conversion by Scientific Publishing Services, Chennai, India

Printed on acid-free paper

Springer is part of Springer Science+Business Media (www.springer.com)

Preface

Static analysis is increasingly recognized as a fundamental tool for program verification, bug detection, compiler optimization, program understanding, and software maintenance. The series of Static Analysis Symposia has served as the primary venue for presentation of theoretical, practical, and application advances in the area.

This volume contains the proceedings of the 21st International Static Analysis Symposium, SAS 2014, which was held during September 11–13 in Munich, Germany. Previous symposia were held in Seattle, Deauville, Venice, Perpignan, Los Angeles, Valencia, Kongens Lyngby, Seoul, London, Verona, San Diego, Madrid, Paris, Santa Barbara, Pisa, Aachen, Glasgow, and Namur. Three workshops were affiliated with SAS 2014 that took place in parallel on September 10: the 6th Workshop on Numerical and Symbolic Abstract Domains (NSAD 2014), the 5th Workshop on Static Analysis and Systems Biology (SASB 2014), and the 5th Workshop on Tools for Automatic Program Analysis (TAPAS 2014).

We received 53 papers. Each submission was reviewed – with the help of external subreviewers – by at least three Program Committee members. Out of the 53 submissions the Program Committee selected 20 papers for presentation at the conference and inclusion in the proceedings. As last year, we encouraged the authors to submit virtual machine images (VMs) containing artifacts and evaluations presented in their submission. While these VMs were not formally evaluated, they were used as an additional source of information during the evaluation of the papers. Overall, we received 23 VMs among them 12 accompanying accepted papers. The latter will be made available for future reference on http://www.staticanalysis.org, subject to approval by the respective authors.

Besides presentations of the contributed papers the program of SAS 2014 comprised three invited talks by Patrice Godefroid (Microsoft Research, Redmond) on Dynamic Program Verification, Luke Ong (University of Oxford) on Higher-Order Model Checking: From Theory To Practice, and Tomáš Vojnar (Brno University of Technology) on Fully Automated Shape Analysis Based on Forest Automata with Data Constraints.

We would like to thank the Program Committee members and the external reviewers for their dedicated work in the program selection. We acknowledge the support by Microsoft, CEA, and itestra that sponsored SAS 2014. We thank Manuel Hermenegildo for his support in hosting the VMs and Andreij Voronkov and his team for providing EasyChair that was of indispensable help in managing the paper submission and selection process as well as the compilation of the proceedings.

June 2014

Markus Müller-Olm
Helmut Seidl

Organization

Program Comittee

Ahmed Bouajjani	LIAFA, University Paris Diderot, France
Michele Bugliesi	Università Ca' Foscari, Italy
Vijay D'Silva	University of California at Berkeley, USA
Johannes Kinder	Royal Holloway, University of London, UK
Andy King	University of Kent, UK
Laura Kovács	Chalmers University of Technology, Sweden
Viktor Kuncak	EPFL Lausanne, Switzerland
Francesco Logozzo	Microsoft Research, USA
Isabella Mastroeni	Università degli Studi di Verona, Italy
Alan Mycroft	Cambridge University, UK
Anders Møller	Aarhus University, Denmark
Markus Müller-Olm	Universität Münster, Germany
Aditya Nori	Microsoft Research, India
Madhusudan Parthasarathy	University of Illinois at Urbana-Champaign, USA
Sylvie Putot	CEA, LIST & École Polytechnique, Palaiseau, France
Xavier Rival	Inria Paris-Rocquencourt, France
Sriram Sankaranarayanan	University of Colorado at Boulder, USA
Helmut Seidl	TU München, Germany
Gregor Snelting	Karlsruher Institut für Technologie, Germany
Eran Yahav	Technion, Israel

Additional Reviewers

Albarghouthi, Aws
Amtoft, Torben
Atig, Mohamed Faouzi
Ben Sassi, Mohamed Amin
Blanchette, Jasmin Christian
Bono, Viviana
Botincan, Matko
Bouissou, Olivier
Bucur, Stefan
Calzavara, Stefano
Chawdhary, Aziem
Cox, Arlen
Crafa, Silvia
Dalla Preda, Mila
David, Yaniv
Dillig, Işil
Dinsdale-Young, Thomas
Dolan, Stephen
Drăgoi, Cezara
Dräger, Klaus
Emmi, Michael
Enea, Constantin
Genaim, Samir
Giacobazzi, Roberto
Gurfinkel, Arie
Hack, Sebastian
Halder, Raju
Hardekopf, Ben

Jiang, Liu
Jobstmann, Barbara
Katz, Omer
Kerneis, Gabriel
Khedker, Uday
Kneuss, Etienne
Konnov, Igor
Lal, Akash
Le Gall, Tristan
Lin, Zhiqiang
Madhavan, Ravichandhran
Marin, Andrea
Midtgaard, Jan
Mimram, Samuel
Miné, Antoine
Monniaux, David
Myreen, Magnus
Müller, Peter
Partush, Nimrod
Peleg, Hila
Ramalingam, Ganesan
Ranzato, Francesco
Spoto, Fausto
Surendran, Rishi
Tiwari, Ashish
Vafeiadis, Viktor
Vojnar, Tomáš
Védrine, Franck
Wickerson, John
Zanardini, Damiano
Zuleger, Florian

Invited Talks

Dynamic Program Verification

Patrice Godefroid

Microsoft Research
pg@microsoft.com

Abstract. Static analysis is not the only way to verify universal (for-all-paths) properties of programs: program verification can also be performed *dynamically*. As a recent milestone, we were able to prove, for the first time in 2013, attacker memory safety of an entire operating-system image parser, namely the ANI Windows image parser, using compositional exhaustive testing (implemented in the dynamic test generation tool SAGE and using the Z3 SMT solver), i.e., *no static analysis whatsoever*. However, several key verification steps were performed manually, and these verification results depend on assumptions regarding input-dependent loop bounds, fixing a few buffer-overflow bugs, and excluding some code parts that are not memory safe by design. This talk will discuss dynamic program verification, and its strengths and weaknesses.

Higher-Order Model Checking: From Theory To Practice

C.-H. Luke Ong

University of Oxford

Higher-order model checking is the problem of model checking trees generated by *higher-order recursion schemes*, or equivalently the $\lambda\mathbf{Y}$-calculus (i.e. simply-typed λ-calculus with fixpoint combinators). With respect to monadic second-order properties, the model checking of trees generated by higher-order recursion schemes was first proved to be decidable in 2006 [11], using game semantics [6]. A variety of semantic and algorithmic techniques and models of computation have since been employed to study higher-order model checking, notably, intersection types [9], collapsible pushdown automata [5] and Krivine machines [15]. Algorithmic properties that refine and extend the monadic second-order decidability result have also been introduced, such as *logical reflection* [2], *effective selection* [4] and *transfer theorem* [16]. A recent advance [18] generalises higher-order model checking to the model checking of ($\lambda\mathbf{Y}$-definable) higher-type Böhm trees, based on a compositional analysis.

Higher-order model checking has been applied to the verification of higher-order programs [7]. Higher-order recursion schemes / $\lambda\mathbf{Y}$-calculus are an appealing abstract model for model checking higher-order programs: not only do they have rich and decidable logical theories, they accurately model higher-order control flow [5, 17] and are highly expressive [12]. Indeed, in a precise sense, recursion schemes are the higher-order analogue of Boolean programs, which have played a successful rôle in the model checking of first-order, imperative programs [1]. Techniques such as predicate abstraction and CEGAR have been incorporated into higher-order model checking, enabling the automatic verification of higher-order programs that use infinite data domains [10] and pattern-matching algebraic data types [13]. At the same time, despite the severe worst-case complexity of the problem, there has been significant progress in algorithm design [8, 3, 14] with the aim of solving the higher-order model checking problem for many "practical" instances.

In this talk, I will provide a survey of higher-order model checking, and discuss further directions.

References

1. Ball, T., Rajamani, S.K.: Bebop: A symbolic model checker for boolean programs. In: Havelund, K., Penix, J., Visser, W. (eds.) SPIN 2000. LNCS, vol. 1885, pp. 113–130. Springer, Heidelberg (2000)

2. Broadbent, C.H., Carayol, A., Ong, C.-H.L., Serre, O.: Recursion schemes and logical reflection. In: LICS, pp. 120–129 (2010)
3. Broadbent, C.H., Kobayashi, N.: Saturation-based model checking of higher-order recursion schemes. In: CSL (2013)
4. Carayol, A., Serre, O.: Collapsible pushdown automata and labeled recursion. In: LICS, pp. 165–174 (2012)
5. Hague, M., Murawski, A.S., Ong, C.-H.L., Serre, O.: Collapsible pushdown automata and recursion schemes. In: LICS, pp. 452–461 (2008)
6. Hyland, J.M.E., Ong, C.-H.L.: On full abstraction for PCF: I, II, and III. Inf. Comput. 163(2), 285–408 (2000)
7. Kobayashi, N.: Types and higher-order recursion schemes for verification of higher-order programs. In: POPL, pp. 416–428 (2009)
8. Kobayashi, N.: A practical linear time algorithm for trivial automata model checking of higher-order recursion schemes. In: Hofmann, M. (ed.) FOSSACS 2011. LNCS, vol. 6604, pp. 260–274. Springer, Heidelberg (2011)
9. Kobayashi, N., Ong, C.-H.L.: A type system equivalent to the modal mu-calculus model checking of higher-order recursion schemes. In: LICS, pp. 179–188 (2009)
10. Kobayashi, N., Sato, R., Unno, H.: Predicate abstraction and CEGAR for higher-order model checking. In: PLDI, pp. 222–233 (2011)
11. Ong, C.-H.L.: On model-checking trees generated by higher-order recursion schemes. In: LICS, pp. 81–90 (2006)
12. Ong, C.-H.L.: Models of higher-order computation: Recursion schemes and collapsible pushdown automata. In: Logics and Languages for Reliability and Security, pp. 263–299 (2010)
13. Ong, C.-H.L., Ramsay, S.J.: Verifying higher-order functional programs with pattern-matching algebraic data types. In: POPL, pp. 587–598 (2011)
14. Ramsay, S.J., Neatherway, R.P., Ong, C.-H.L.: A type-directed abstraction refinement approach to higher-order model checking. In: POPL, pp. 61–72 (2014)
15. Salvati, S., Walukiewicz, I.: Krivine machines and higher-order schemes. In: Aceto, L., Henzinger, M., Sgall, J. (eds.) ICALP 2011, Part II. LNCS, vol. 6756, pp. 162–173. Springer, Heidelberg (2011)
16. Salvati, S., Walukiewicz, I.: Using models to model-check recursive schemes. In: Hasegawa, M. (ed.) TLCA 2013. LNCS, vol. 7941, pp. 189–204. Springer, Heidelberg (2013)
17. Tobita, Y., Tsukada, T., Kobayashi, N.: Exact flow analysis by higher-order model checking. In: Schrijvers, T., Thiemann, P. (eds.) FLOPS 2012. LNCS, vol. 7294, pp. 275–289. Springer, Heidelberg (2012)
18. Tsukada, T., Ong, C.-H.L.: Compositional higher-order model checking via ω-regular games over Böhm trees". In: CSL/LICS (to appear, 2014)

Fully Automated Shape Analysis Based on Forest Automata with Data Constraints

Tomáš Vojnar

FIT, Brno University of Technology, IT4Innovations Centre of Excellence
Božetěchova 2, 612 66 Brno, Czech Republic
e-mail: vojnar@fit.vutbr.cz

Dealing with programs that use complex dynamic linked data structures belongs to the most challenging tasks in formal program analysis. The reason is a necessity of coping with infinite sets of reachable heap configurations that have a form of complex graphs. Representing and manipulating such sets in a sufficiently general, efficient, and automated way is a notoriously difficult problem. Moreover, the problem becomes even harder when program correctness depends on relationships between data values that are stored in the dynamically allocated structures.

In this talk, we present an approach to shape analysis based on the notion of *forest automata* (FAs) that were proposed for representing sets of reachable configurations of programs with complex dynamic linked data structures in [2]. FAs have a form of tuples of *tree automata* (TAs) that encode sets of heap graphs decomposed into tuples of *tree components* whose leaves may refer back to the roots of the components.

Alongside the notion of FAs, a shape analysis applying FAs in the framework of *abstract regular tree model checking* (ARTMC) was proposed in [2] and implemented in the open source tool called Forester[1], which has a form of a gcc plugin. ARTMC accelerates the computation of sets of reachable program configurations represented by FAs by abstracting their component TAs, which is done by collapsing some of their states.

In order to allow for representing complex heap graphs, the notion of FAs allowed one to *hierarchically structure* the automata and to provide user-defined FAs—called *boxes*—that encode *repetitive graph patterns* of shape graphs to be used as alphabet symbols of other, higher-level FAs. Later, a technique of automatically learning the FAs to be used as boxes was proposed in [3], which rendered the approach fully automated. Finally, in [1], the framework was extended with constraints between data elements of nodes in the heaps represented by FAs, allowing one to verify programs depending on *ordering relations* among data values.

Both of the above extensions have been implemented in the Forester tool and experimentally evaluated on a number of small but—from the point of view of

[1] http://www.fit.vutbr.cz/research/groups/verifit/tools/forester

automated shape analysis—highly challenging programs manipulating different flavours of lists (singly/doubly linked, circular, nested, ...), trees, skip lists, and their combinations. The experiments showed that the approach is not only fully automated, rather general, but also quite efficient.

Acknowledgement. The works on which the talk is based were supported by the Czech Science Foundation (projects P103/10/0306, 102/09/H042, and P14-11384S), the Czech Ministry of Education (projects COST OC10009 and MSM 0021630528), as well as the EU/Czech IT4Innovations Centre of Excellence project CZ.1.05/1.1.00/02.0070.

References

1. Abdulla, P.A., Holík, L., Jonsson, B., Lengál, O., Trinh, C.Q., Vojnar, T.: Verification of Heap Manipulating Programs with Ordered Data by Extended Forest Automata. In: Van Hung, D., Ogawa, M. (eds.) ATVA 2013. LNCS, vol. 8172, pp. 224–239. Springer, Heidelberg (2013)
2. Habermehl, P., Holík, L., Rogalewicz, A., Šimáček, J., Vojnar, T.: Forest Automata for Verification of Heap Manipulation. In: Gopalakrishnan, G., Qadeer, S. (eds.) CAV 2011. LNCS, vol. 6806, pp. 424–440. Springer, Heidelberg (2011)
3. Holík, L., Lengál, O., Rogalewicz, A., Šimáček, J., Vojnar, T.: Fully Automated Shape Analysis Based on Forest Automata. In: Sharygina, N., Veith, H. (eds.) CAV 2013. LNCS, vol. 8044, pp. 740–755. Springer, Heidelberg (2013)

Table of Contents

Block Me If You Can!*
Context-Sensitive Parameterized Verification

Parosh Aziz Abdulla[1], Frédéric Haziza[1], and Lukáš Holík[2]

[1] Uppsala University, Sweden
[2] Brno University of Technology, Czech Republic

Abstract. We present a method for automatic verification of systems with a parameterized number of communicating processes, such as mutual exclusion protocols or agreement protocols. To that end, we present a powerful abstraction framework that uses an efficient and precise symbolic encoding of (infinite) sets of configurations. In particular, it generalizes *downward-closed* sets that have successfully been used in earlier approaches to parameterized verification. We show experimentally the efficiency of the method, on various examples, including a fine-grained model of Szymanski's mutual exclusion protocol, whose correctness, to the best of our knowledge, has not been proven automatically by any other existing methods.

1 Introduction

We consider the verification of safety properties for *parameterized systems*: systems that consist of an arbitrary number of components (processes) organized according to a certain predefined topology. In this paper, we consider the case where the system has a linear topology (the processes form an array). Our method can be easily extended to other topologies such as rings, trees, or multisets (the latter are systems where the processes are entirely anonymous, e.g. Petri nets). Processes can perform two types of transitions, namely *local* and *global* transitions. In the former, the process does not need to check the states of the rest of the processes in the system. A global transition is either *universal* or *existential*. For example, in a universal transition, a process (at position i) may perform a transition only if *all* processes to its left (i.e. with index $j < i$) satisfy a property φ. In an existential transition, it is required that *some* (rather than *all*) processes satisfy φ. Parameterized systems arise naturally in the modeling of mutual exclusion algorithms, bus protocols, distributed algorithms, telecommunication protocols, and cache coherence protocols. The task is to perform *parameterized verification*, i.e. to verify correctness regardless of the number of processes. This amounts to the verification of an infinite family; namely one for each possible size of the system. We consider *safety properties*, i.e. properties that forbid reachability of bad configurations. For instance, mutual exclusion protocols must guarantee that no reachable configuration contains two processes in the critical section.

* supported by the Uppsala Programming for Multicore Architectures Research Center (UPMARC), the Czech Science Foundation (13-37876P, 14-11384S), Brno University of Technology (FIT-S-12-1, FIT-S-14-2486).

M. Müller-Olm and H. Seidl (Eds.): SAS 2014, LNCS 8723, pp. 1–17, 2014.

An important line of research in parameterized verification has been based on the observation that such systems may have invariants that are *downward-closed* wrt. a natural ordering on the set of configurations (e.g. the subword ordering for systems with linear topologies, or the multiset ordering on Petri nets). The existence of downward-closed invariants allows the employment of well quasi-ordered transition systems [2,1]. In particular, a downward-closed set D can be characterized by a finite set of counter-examples. This set contains the configurations that are the minimal elements of the complement of D (notice the complement of D is upward-closed). This characterization gives compact symbolic representations leading to very efficient implementations. This observation has resulted in several powerful frameworks such as the "Expand, Enlarge, and Check" method [26], monotonic abstraction [6], and small model based verification [4]. Although these frameworks are applicable to a wide range of parameterized systems, there are several classes of systems that are beyond their applicability. The reason is that such systems do not allow good downward-closed invariants, and hence over-approximating the set of reachable configurations by downward-closed sets will give false counter-examples. In this paper, we propose a method that targets a class of invariants which are needed in many practical cases and cannot be expressed as downward-closed sets, hence cannot be inferred by the above-mentioned methods. Specifically, we express invariants as quantified formulae over process indices and states within a configuration. The formulae are of the form:

$$\phi = \forall i_1,\ldots,i_n\ \exists i_{n+1},\ldots,i_{n+m} : \psi(i_1,\ldots,i_{n+m})$$

where $i_1,\ldots,i_{n+m}$ are pairwise distinct *position variables* and $\psi(i_1,\ldots,i_{n+m})$ is a boolean formula that relates the process positions, their local states and the topological constraints at those positions. We call these properties *almost downward-closed* (henceforth $\forall_\exists$-formulae), since they are a generalization of downward-closed sets. Observe that downward-closed properties correspond to the special case where the formulae solely have universal quantification.

Let us illustrate the notion of an almost downward-closed good invariant with the example of a barrier implementation (see Fig. 1). All processes start in the state B before the barrier. The first process at the barrier moves to state P and acts as a *pivot*. All other arriving processes must wait in state W as long as there is a pivot. When all processes have arrived at the barrier, the pivot can proceed to the state A after the barrier, which in turn releases the waiting processes.

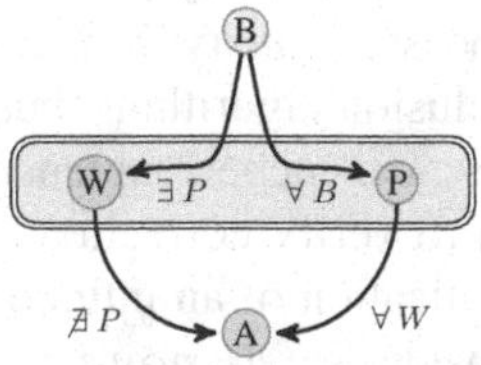

Fig. 1. Barrier

The system is correct if there cannot be at the same time a process in the state B and a process in the state A. A waiting process W trying to move to the state A counts on the fact that *if* there is a process in B, *then* there is also a process in P. If this implication did not hold, the barrier would be incorrect, because the move from W to A could be performed under presence of B. The weakest good invariant must reflect this implication, and state that (i) A and B never coexist, and (ii) if W and B appear together then P is present. The first condition denotes a downward-closed set, any configuration that does not contain both A and B satisfies it. On the contrary, the second condition is not downward-closed. It is an implication of the form "contains W and B" ⇒

"must contain P", which can be characterized using the disjunction of a downward-closed set (the antecedent) and an upward-closed set (the consequent). (Recall $A \Rightarrow B \Leftrightarrow \neg A \vee B$ and when A is upward-closed, $\neg A$ is downward-closed). This example illustrates an almost downward-closed property, and also a situation where inferring such properties is needed. The system does not indeed have any good downward-closed invariant.

We propose a method that can fully automatically infer *almost downward-closed* invariants through the creation of *small models*. This allows to carry out parameterized verification *fully automatically* through analyzing, in an abstract domain, only a small number of processes (rather than the whole family). To define the abstraction, we will first introduce a new symbolic encoding, called *context-sensitive views*, that allows to characterize almost downward-closed sets. Context-sensitive views are generalizations of minimal elements used for characterizing downward-closed sets. They retain enough information in order to *disable* (or *block*) universal transitions, which would have been otherwise enabled without the presence of contexts. We show that our abstract predicate transformer is exact, so the method is guaranteed to find the weakest almost downward-closed good invariant (if it exists).

To simplify the presentation, we will assume in the first part of the paper that global transitions are performed atomically. However, in reality, such transitions are implemented as a for-loop ranging over process indices and do not assume atomicity. Moreover, any number of processes may be performing a for-loop simultaneously. This makes the model of fine-grained systems and the verification task significantly harder, since it requires to distinguish intermediate states of such for-loops. We show that our method retains its simplicity and efficiency when instantiated to the (more complicated) case of fine-grained parameterized systems where the atomicity assumption is dropped. To the best of our knowledge, it is the only method which combines the ability to infer almost downward-closed invariants with the support of fine-grained modeling. We have used it to fully automatically verify several systems which were not previously verified automatically. Among these, we highlight the *fully automatic* verification of the fine-grained and complete version of Szymanski's mutual exclusion protocol, which has been considered a challenge in parameterized verification.

Outline. We first consider a basic model in Section 2 which only allows atomically checked global conditions and instantiate the abstract domain for such systems in Section 4. We present our verification procedure in Section 5 and introduce in Section 6 how the settings are adapted to cope with non-atomicity. We report on our experimental results in Section 7, describe related work in Section 8 and conclude the paper in Section 9.

2 Parametrized Systems

We introduce a standard model [31,13,6,30] of parameterized systems operating on a linear topology, where processes may perform local or global transitions. Formally, a *parameterized system* is a pair $\mathcal{P} = (Q, \Delta)$ where Q is a finite set of process *local states* and Δ is a set of *transition rules* over Q. A transition rule is either *local* or *global*. A local rule is of the form $s \rightarrow s'$, where the process changes its local state from s to s' independently from the local states of the other processes. A global rule is either *universal* or *existential*. It is of the form: $\mathbf{if}\, \mathbb{Q}\, j \circ i : S\ \mathtt{then}\ s \to s'$, where $\mathbb{Q} \in \{\exists, \forall\}$, $\circ \in \{<, >, \neq\}$ and $S \subseteq Q$. We call s the *source*, s' the *target*, $\mathbb{Q}$ the *quantifier* and $\circ$ the *range*. S represents a set of *witness* process states. Here, the ith process checks the local states of the other processes before it makes the move. For the sake of presentation, we only consider, in this section, a version where each process checks atomically the other processes. The more realistic and more difficult case, where the atomicity assumption is dropped, will be introduced in Section 6. For instance, the condition $\forall j < i : S$ means that "every process j, with a lower index than i, should be in a local state that belongs to the set S"; the condition $\forall j \neq i : S$ means that "the local state of all processes, except the one at position i, should be in the set S".

A *configuration* in $\mathcal{P}$ is a word over the alphabet Q. We use $\mathcal{C}$ to denote the set of all configurations and $c[i]$ to denote the state of the ith process within the configuration c. We use $[\![a;b]\!]$ to denote the set of integers in the interval $[a;b]$ (i.e. $[\![a;b]\!] = [a;b] \cap \mathbb{N}$). For a configuration c, a position $i \leq |c|$, and a transition $\delta \in \Delta$, we define the immediate successor $\delta(c,i)$ of c under a δ-move of the ith process (evaluating the condition) such that $\delta(c,i) = c'$ iff $c[i] = s$, $c'[i] = s'$, $c[j] = c'[j]$ for all $j : j \neq i$ and either (i) δ is a local rule $s \to s'$, or (ii) δ is a global rule of the form $\mathbf{if}\, \mathbb{Q}\, j \circ i : S\ \mathtt{then}\ s \to s'$, and one of the following two conditions is satisfied:
- $\mathbb{Q} = \forall$ and for all $j \in [\![1;|c|]\!]$ such that $j \circ i$, it holds that $c[j] \in S$
- $\mathbb{Q} = \exists$ and there exists some $j \in [\![1;|c|]\!]$ such that $j \circ i$ and $c[j] \in S$.

For a set of configurations $X \subseteq \mathcal{C}$, we define the *post-image* of X as the set $post(X) = \{\delta(c,i) \mid c \in X, i \leq |c|, \delta \in \Delta\}$.

An instance of the *reachability problem* is defined by a parameterized system $\mathcal{P} = (Q, \Delta)$, a set $I \subseteq Q^+$ of *initial configurations*, and a set $\mathcal{B} \subseteq Q^+$ of *bad configurations*. We say that $c \in \mathcal{C}$ is *reachable* iff there are $c_0, \ldots, c_l \in \mathcal{C}$ such that $c_0 \in I$, $c_l = c$, and for all $0 \leq i < l$, there are $\delta_i \in \Delta$ and $j \leq |c_i|$ such that $c_{i+1} = \delta_i(c_i, j)$. We use $\mathcal{R}$ to denote the set of all reachable configurations (from I). We say that the system $\mathcal{P}$ is *safe* with respect to I and $\mathcal{B}$ if no bad configuration is reachable, i.e. $\mathcal{R} \cap \mathcal{B} = \emptyset$.

The set I of initial configurations is usually a regular set. In order to define the set $\mathcal{B}$ of bad configurations, we use the usual *subword relation* $\sqsubseteq$, i.e., $u \sqsubseteq s_1 \ldots s_n$ iff $u = s_{i_1} \ldots s_{i_k}, 1 \leq i_1 < \ldots < i_k \leq n$. We assume that $\mathcal{B}$ is the upward-closure $\{c \in \mathcal{C} \mid \exists b \in \mathcal{B}_{min} : b \sqsubseteq c\}$ of a given *finite* set $\mathcal{B}_{min} \subseteq Q^+$ of *minimal bad configurations*. This is a common way of specifying bad configurations which often appears in practice.

3 Example: Szymanski's Protocol

We illustrate the notion of a parameterized system with the example of Szymanski's mutual exclusion protocol [33]. The protocol ensures exclusive access to a shared resource in a system consisting of an unbounded number of processes organized in an array. The transition rules of the parameterized system are given in Fig. 3 and the source code in Fig. 2. The state of the ith process is modelled with a number, which reflects the values of the program location and the local variable *flag*$[i]$. A configuration of the induced transition system is a word over the alphabet $\{⓪, \ldots, ⑪\}$ of local process states. The task is to check that the protocol guarantees exclusive access to the shared resource regardless of the number of processes. A configuration is considered to be bad if it

```
(0)  flag[i] = 1;
(1)  for(j=0;j<N;j++){ if(flag[j]≥3) goto (1); }
(2)  flag[i] = 3;
(3)  for(j=0;j<N;j++){
         if (flag[j] = 1) {
(4)          flag[i] = 2;
(5)          for(j=0;j<N;j++){ if(flag[j]==4) goto (7); }
(6)          goto (5);
         }
     }
(7)  flag[i] = 4;
(8)  for(j=0;j<i;j++){ if(flag[j]≥2) goto (8); }
(9)  /* Critical Section */
(10) for(j=i+1;j<N;j++){ if(flag[j]==2||flag[j]==3) goto (10); }
(11) flag[i] = 0; goto (0);
```

Fig. 2. Szymanski's protocol implementation (for process i)

contains two occurrences of state (9) or (10), i.e., the set of minimal bad configurations $\mathcal{B}_{min}$ is {(9 9), (9 10), (10 9), (10 10)}. Initially, all processes are in state (0), i.e. $I = (0)^+$.

Many techniques [4,3,7,13,30,8,12] have been used to verify automatically the safety property of Szymanski's mutual exclusion protocol but only in restricted settings. They either assume atomicity of the global conditions and/or only consider a more compact variant of the protocol (i.e. where the invariant can be expressed solely by a downward-closed set). The full and fine-grained version has been considered a challenge in the verification community. To the best of our knowledge, this paper presents the first technique to address the challenge of verifying the protocol fully automatically without atomicity assumption.

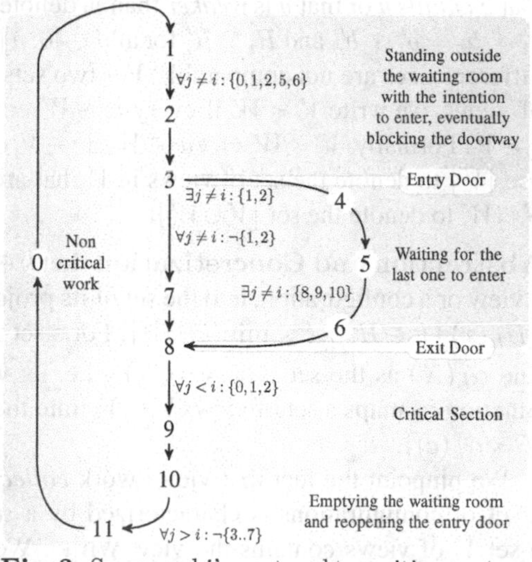

Fig. 3. Szymanski's protocol transition system

4 Views and $\forall_\exists$-Formulae

We introduce our symbolic encoding and show how it corresponds to $\forall_\exists$-formulae.

Context-Sensitive Views. A *context-sensitive view* (henceforth only called *view*) is a pair $(b_1 \ldots b_k, R_0 \ldots R_k)$, often written as $R_0 b_1 R_1 \ldots b_k R_k$, where $b_1 \ldots b_k$ is a configuration and $R_0 \ldots R_k$ is a *context*, such that $R_i \subseteq Q$ for all $i \in [\![0;k]\!]$.

We call the configuration $b_1 \ldots b_k$ the *base* of the view where k is its *size* and we call the set R_i the ith *context*. We use $\mathcal{V}_k$ to denote the set of views of size up to k. For $k,n \in \mathbb{N}, k \leq n$, let H_n^k be the set of strictly increasing injections $h\colon [\![0;k+1]\!] \to [\![0;n+1]\!]$, i.e. $1 \leq i < j \leq k \implies 1 \leq h(i) < h(j) \leq n$. Moreover, we require that $h(0) = 0$ and $h(k+1) = n+1$.

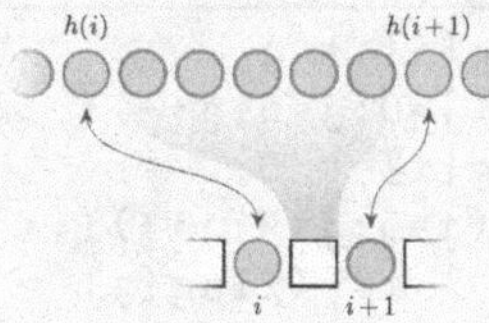

Fig. 4. Projection

Projections. We define the projection of a configuration. For $h \in H_n^k$ and a configuration $c = q_1 \ldots q_n$, we use $\Pi_h(c)$ to denote the view $v = R_0 b_1 R_1 \ldots b_k R_k$, obtained in the following way (see Fig. 4):
(i) $b_i = q_{h(i)}$ for $i \in [\![1;k]\!]$, (ii) $R_i = \{q_j \mid h(i) < j < h(i+1)\}$ for $i \in [\![0;k]\!]$. Intuitively, respecting the order, k elements of c are retained as the base of v, while all other elements are collected into contexts as sets in the appropriate positions.

We also define projections of views. For a view $v = R_0 b_1 R_1 \ldots b_n R_n$ and $h \in H_n^k$, we overload the notation for the projection of configurations and use $\Pi_h(v)$ to denote the view $v' = R'_0 b'_1 R'_1 \ldots b'_k R'_k$, such that (i) $b'_i = b_{h(i)}$ for $i \in [\![1;k]\!]$ and (ii) $R'_i = \{b_j \mid h(i) < j < h(i+1)\} \cup (\bigcup_{h(i) \leq j < h(i+1)} R_j)$ for all $i \in [\![0;k]\!]$ (see Fig. 5).

We define an *entailment relation* on views of the same size. Let $u = R_0 b_1 R_1, \ldots, b_n R_n$ and $v = R'_0 b'_1 R'_1, \ldots, b'_n R'_n$ be views of the same size n. We say that v *entails* u or that u is *weaker* than v, denoted $u \preccurlyeq v$, if $b_1 \cdots b_n = b'_1 \cdots b'_n$ and $R_i \subseteq R'_i$ for all $i \in [\![0;n]\!]$. Views of different sizes are not comparable. For two sets V and W of views, we write $V \preccurlyeq W$ if every $w \in W$ entails some $v \in V$. Formally, $V \preccurlyeq W \Leftrightarrow \forall w \in W, \exists v \in V, v \preccurlyeq w$. We use $\lfloor V \rfloor$ to denote the set of views in V that are *weakest*, i.e. minimal w.r.t. $\preccurlyeq$. We use $V \sqcup W$ to denote the set $\lfloor V \cup W \rfloor$.

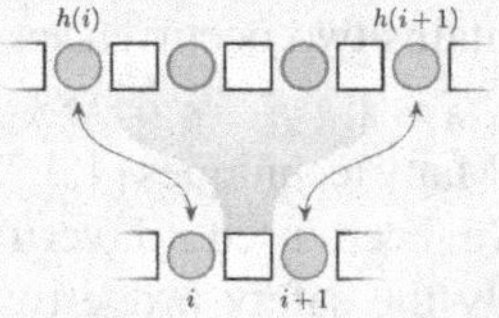

Fig. 5. View Projection

Abstraction and Concretization. Let $k \in \mathbb{N}$. The *abstraction function* α_k maps x, a view or a configuration, into the set of its projections of the size k or smaller: $\alpha_k(x) = \{\Pi_h(x) \mid h \in H_{|x|}^{\ell}, \ell \leq \min(k,|x|)\}$. For a set X of views or of configurations, we define $\alpha_k(X)$ as the set $\lfloor \cup_{x \in X} \alpha_k(x) \rfloor$, i.e. its weakest projections. The *concretization* function γ_k maps a set of views $V \subseteq \mathcal{V}_k$ into the set of configurations $\gamma_k(V) = \{c \in \mathcal{C} \mid V \preccurlyeq \alpha_k(c)\}$.

We pinpoint the fact that views work *collectively*, rather than individually. That is, a set of configurations is characterized by a *set* of views. Consider for example that a set V of views contains the view WB[P]. We write contexts in square brackets and we omit empty contexts for brevity. Then, in order to characterize the configuration WBP, it must *also* contain the views [W]BP and W[B]P (or weaker). The three views together characterize the configuration, while the view WB[P] alone cannot. Abstraction and concretization are illustrated on a larger example in Fig. 6.

Lemma 1. *For any $k \in \mathbb{N}$, $V \subseteq \mathcal{V}$ and $X \subseteq \mathcal{C}$, $X \subseteq \gamma_k(V) \iff V \preccurlyeq \alpha_k(X)$, i.e. the pair (α_k, γ_k) forms a Galois connection.*

For any set $X \subseteq \mathcal{C}$ and $k \in \mathbb{N}$, it is clear that $\gamma_k(\alpha_k(X)) \supseteq X$. In fact, we can observe that the precision of the abstraction increases with k, i.e. $\gamma_1(\alpha_1(X)) \supseteq \gamma_2(\alpha_2(X)) \supseteq$

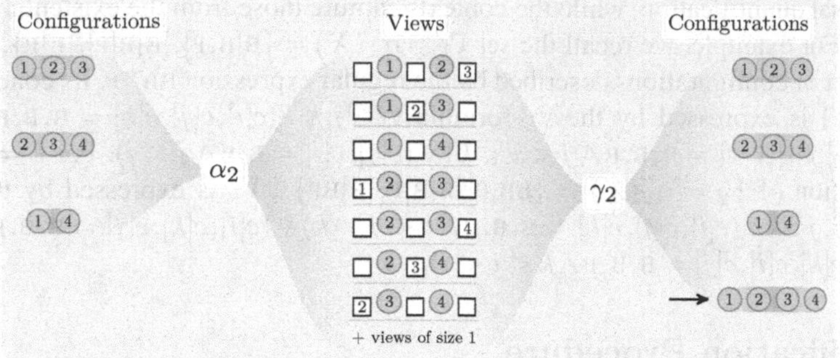

Fig. 6. Abstraction and Concretization

$\gamma_3(\alpha_3(X)) \supseteq \ldots \supseteq X$. We illustrate this property with the following example. Consider the set X of configurations of the barrier protocol from Fig. 1 described by the regular expression $\mathtt{BB}^{+}\mathtt{P}$. Its abstraction with $k=1$ is the set of views $V_1 = \alpha_1(X) = \{\mathtt{B}[\mathtt{B},\mathtt{P}], [\mathtt{B}]\mathtt{B}[\mathtt{P}], [\mathtt{B}]\mathtt{P}\}$.The concretization $\gamma_1(V_1)$ is the set of configurations following the regular expression $\mathtt{B}(\mathtt{B}|\mathtt{P})^*\mathtt{B}(\mathtt{B}|\mathtt{P})^*\mathtt{P}$ (i.e. the information preserved is that configurations begin by B, end by P, and there are at least two Bs). With $k=2$, we get $V_2 = \alpha_2(X) = \{\mathtt{BB}[\mathtt{P}], \mathtt{B}[\mathtt{B}]\mathtt{P}, [\mathtt{B}]\mathtt{BP}\} \cup V_1$. Its concretization is $\gamma_2(V_2) = \mathtt{BB}^{+}\mathtt{P}$ which is equal to the original set X. The role of contexts may be seen already with $k=1$: the concretization of V_1 preserves the information that there is at least one P and at least two Bs present in every configuration. This set is not downward-closed.

Views vs $\forall_\exists$-formulae. An $\forall_\exists$-*formula* is a formula of the form:

$$\phi = \forall i_1,\ldots,i_n\ \exists i_{n+1},\ldots,i_{n+m} : \psi(i_1,\ldots,i_{n+m})$$

where $i_1,\ldots,i_{n+m}$ are pairwise distinct *position variables* and $\psi(i_1,\ldots,i_{n+m})$ is a boolean combination of *basic formulae*. A basic formula is either (i) a *topological predicate* of the form $i_j < i_k$ or (ii) a *state predicate* of the form $c[i_j] = q$, where $j,k \in [\![1;n+m]\!]$ and $q \in Q$.

The notion of satisfaction by a configuration c of a basic formula $\psi(i_1,\ldots,i_\ell)$ is defined in the natural way. More precisely, an assignment ρ is a function that maps the indices $i_1,\ldots,i_\ell$ to pairwise different positions within the configuration c (i.e. $\rho(i_j) \in [\![0;|c|]\!]$ and $\rho(i_j) \neq \rho(i_k)$ for all $j,k \in [\![1;\ell]\!]$). We write $c \models_\rho \psi$, if c satisfy the formula $\psi(i_1,\ldots,i_\ell)$ under the assignment ρ. We say that c satisfies ϕ and write $c \models \phi$, if for every assignment ρ of $i_1,\ldots,i_n$, there exists an assignment ρ' of $i_{n+1},\ldots i_{n+m}$ such that $c \models_{\rho\cup\rho'} \psi$. We use $[\![\phi]\!]$ to denote the set $\{c \in C \mid c \models \phi\}$ of all configurations that satisfy ϕ.

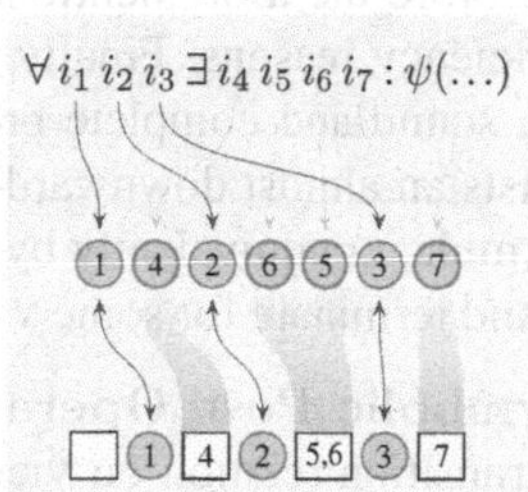

Fig. 7. view ↔ $\forall_\exists$-formula

Lemma 2. *For any set C of configurations, there exists an $\forall_\exists$-formula ϕ such that $C = [\![\phi]\!]$ iff there exists a finite set of views V and $k \in \mathbb{N}$ such that $C = \gamma_k(V)$.*

Lemma 2 shows that the $\forall_\exists$-formulae correspond to sets of views. Intuitively, the base of a view captures the predicates in an $\forall_\exists$-formula relating the position variables from the universal quantification, while the contexts capture those from the existential quantification. For example, we recall the set $V_1 = \alpha_1(X) = \{\mathrm{B}[\mathrm{B},\mathrm{P}], [\mathrm{B}]\mathrm{B}[\mathrm{P}], [\mathrm{B}]\mathrm{P}\}$, where X is the set of configurations described by the regular expression $\mathrm{BB}^+\mathrm{P}$. Its concretization $\gamma_1(V_1)$ is expressed by the $\forall_\exists$-formula $\forall i\ \exists j,k : (c[i],c[j],c[k] = \mathrm{B},\mathrm{B},\mathrm{P} \wedge i < j,k) \vee (c[j],c[i],c[k] = \mathrm{B},\mathrm{B},\mathrm{P} \wedge j < i < k) \vee (c[j],c[i] = \mathrm{B},\mathrm{P} \wedge j < i)$. For $k = 2$, the concretization of $V_2 = \alpha_2(X) = \{\mathrm{BB}[\mathrm{P}], \mathrm{B}[\mathrm{B}]\mathrm{P}, [\mathrm{B}]\mathrm{BP}\} \cup V_1$ is expressed by the $\forall_\exists$-formula $\forall i,j\ \exists k : (c[i],c[j],c[k] = \mathrm{B},\mathrm{B},\mathrm{P} \wedge i < j < k) \vee (c[i],c[k],c[j] = \mathrm{B},\mathrm{B},\mathrm{P} \wedge i < k < j) \vee (c[k],c[i],c[j] = \mathrm{B},\mathrm{B},\mathrm{P} \wedge k < i < j)$.

5 Verification Procedure

We present our verification method for the class of parameterized systems described in Section 2. We fix a parameterized system $\mathcal{P} = (Q, \Delta)$ for the rest of the section. We use the abstract domain from Section 4. For $k \in \mathbb{N}$, the abstract post-image of a set of views V is defined, as usual, as $\alpha_k \circ post \circ \gamma_k(V)$. The core of our verification procedure consists in checking whether there is a $k \in \mathbb{N}$ such that the least fixpoint of $\alpha_k \circ post \circ \gamma_k$ is a set of views with the following properties: its concretization (i) covers the set I of initial configurations and (ii) is disjoint from the set $\mathcal{B}$ of bad configurations. More precisely, the precision of the abstraction increases with k, so we iterate the fixpoint computation $\mu X.\alpha_k(I) \sqcup \alpha_k \circ post \circ \gamma_k(X)$ for increasing values of k starting from $k = 1$, until point (ii) holds.

We present our procedure in a stepwise manner. Since $\gamma_k(V)$ is in general infinite, we need to compute the abstract post-image symbolically. First, we introduce a symbolic abstract transformer and show that it precisely corresponds to the abstract post. Although we show that is possible to compute the abstract transformer precisely (and therefore the aforementioned fixpoint), we also introduce an over-approximation for efficiency reasons. Finally, we stitch the different components together and describe the sound and complete procedure. Since the symbolic transformer is exact, if there exists an almost downward-closed invariant (i.e., good invariant expressible by an $\forall_\exists$-formula, or equivalently by a set of views), then the iteration is guaranteed to discover it and terminate for some value of k [14].

Symbolic Post Operator. To define the symbolic post operator, we first define a transition relation on views. For a view $v = (\mathtt{base}, \mathtt{ctx})$, $i \leq |\mathtt{base}|$, and a transition $\delta \in \Delta$, we define the symbolic immediate successor of v under a δ-move of the ith process from base, denoted $\delta^{\#}(v,i)$. Informally, the moving process checks the other processes from the base. In addition, if δ is a universal transition, the moving process checks as well the processes in the contexts. If the transition is enabled, the moving process from base changes its state according to the δ-transition, otherwise it is blocked. The contexts do not change. In fact, we can here observe the role played by a context: it retains enough information in a view to *disable* (or *block*) universal transitions, which would have been otherwise enabled without the presence of contexts. This reduces the risk of running a too coarse over-approximation.

Formally, for a view $v = R_0 b_1 R_1 \ldots b_n R_n$ and $i \leq n$, $\delta^{\#}(v,i) = R_0 b'_1 R_1 \ldots b'_n R_n$ iff $b_i = s$, $b'_i = s'$, $b_j = b'_j$ for all $j : j \neq i$ and either (i) δ is a local rule $s \to s'$, or (ii) δ is a global rule of the form $\mathbf{if}\, \mathbb{Q}\ j \circ i : S\ \mathbf{then}\ s \to s'$, and one of the following two conditions is satisfied: (a) $\mathbb{Q} = \forall$ and it holds both that $b_j \in S$ for all $j \in \llbracket 1;n \rrbracket$ such that $j \circ i$ and that $R_j \subseteq S$ for all $j \in \llbracket 0;n \rrbracket$ such that $j \circ i$, or (b) $\mathbb{Q} = \exists$ and there exists $j \in \llbracket 1;n \rrbracket$ such that $j \circ i$ and $b_j \in S$. Note that we do not need to check the contexts in the latter case. Indeed, this is supported by the fact that the views work collectively. If there is a view where a process appears in a context, then there is always another view where it appears in the base, while the others are in a context. Finally, for a set of views V, we define $\mathit{spost}(V) = \{\delta^{\#}(v,i) \mid v \in V, i \leq |v|, \delta \in \Delta\}$.

We now explain how we define the *symbolic post* operating on views. It is based on the observation that a process needs *at most one* other process as a witness in order to perform its transition (cf. existential transitions). A moving process can appear either (i) in the base of a view, or (ii) in a context. *Extending adequately* the view with one extra process is enough to determine whether the moving process, in case (i), can perform its transition. However, in case (ii), since *spost* only updates processes of the base, a first extension with one process "materializes" the moving process into the base and a second extension by one process considers its witness. Therefore, it is sufficient to extend the views with two extra processes to determine if a transition is *enabled*, whether the moving process belongs to the base or a context of a view. Formally, for a set V of views of size k and for $\ell > k$, we define the *extensions* of V of size ℓ as the set of views $\int_k^\ell(V) = \alpha_l(\gamma_k(V))$. Finally, we define the *symbolic post* as $\alpha_k \circ \mathit{spost} \circ \int_k^{k+2}(V)$. Lemma 3 allows us to conclude that the symbolic post is the best abstract transformer.

Lemma 3. *For any k and set of views V of size up to k,*

$$V \sqcup \alpha_k \circ \mathit{post} \circ \gamma_k(V) = V \sqcup \alpha_k \circ \mathit{spost} \circ \int_k^{k+2}(V)$$

The definition of $\int_k^\ell(V)$ still involves the potentially infinite set $\gamma_k(V)$, so it cannot be computed in a straightforward manner. We show how $\int_k^\ell(V)$ can be computed via a translation to finite automata, consisting of three steps, sketched here and described in details in the technical report [5]:

1. Translate V into an $\forall_\exists$-formula ϕ such that $\llbracket \phi \rrbracket = \gamma_k(V)$ (by Lemma 2)
2. Translate ϕ into a finite automaton A_ϕ such that $L(A_\phi) = \llbracket \phi \rrbracket$
3. Compute $\alpha_\ell(L(A_\phi))$

Approximation. The described automata-theoretic procedure to compute $\int_k^\ell(V)$ comes at some cost. Step 2 involves internally the complementation of an intermediate automaton, which is at worst exponential, both in time and space. We therefore introduce an over-approximation and compute $\iint_k^\ell(V) = \{v \in \mathcal{V} \mid \alpha_k(v) \succcurlyeq V, |v| \leq \ell\}$, i.e. the set of views of size ℓ that can be generated from V, without inspecting its concretization first. By lemma 4 (below), it follows that the views in $\iint_k^\ell(V)$ over-approximate the views in $\int_k^\ell(V)$ and may enable more universal transitions than they should. Indeed, views in $\iint_k^\ell(V)$ have (at least) the same bases as the views in $\int_k^\ell(V)$, but they might have smaller contexts (and are therefore weaker). Consider for example the case where $k = 2$, $\ell = 3$ and the set of views $V = \{ab, bc, ac[e], ce[f], ae, be, af, bf, cf, ef\}$. The set $\iint_2^3(V)$ contains the view $abc[e]$ but $\int_k^\ell(V)$ contains the view $abc[e,f]$ because the smallest configuration in $\gamma_2(V)$ that has abc as a subword is $abcef$ (this is due to the view $ce[f]$

which enforces the presence of f). Another example is $V = \{ab, bc, ac[e], a[c]e, [a]ce\}$. Here, $\not\oint_2^3(V)$ contains $abc[e]$, however, there is no view with the base abc in $\oint_2^3(V)$ since there is no configuration with the subword abc in $\gamma_2(V)$.

Lemma 4. *For any $\ell \geq k$ and $V \subseteq \mathcal{V}$, $\not\oint_k^\ell(V) \preccurlyeq \oint_k^\ell(V)$*

Sound and Complete Algorithm. We combine the fixpoint computation of the symbolic post with a systematic state-space exploration in order to find a bad configuration. The algorithm (described succintly in Alg. 1) proceeds by iteration over configurations and views of size up to k, starting from $k = 1$ and increasing k after each iteration. Every iteration consists in two computations in parallel: (i) Using the exact post-image, we compute the set $\mathcal{R}_k$ of configurations reachable from the initial configurations, involving only configurations of size k (line 2). Note that there are only finitely many such configurations and that we consider, in this paper, length-preserving transitions,[1] so this step terminates and (ii) the fixpoint computation of the symbolic post over views of size up to k.

Alg. 1: Verification Procedure

```
1 for k := 1 to ∞ do
2     if bad(R_k) then return Unsafe
3     V := μX . α_k(I) ⊔ α_k ∘ spost ∘ ∮_k^{k+2}(X)
4     if ¬bad(V) then return Safe
```

A reachable bad configuration of some size must be reachable through a sequence of transitions involving configurations of some maximal size, so it will be eventually discovered. By lemma 4, it is sound to replace the fixpoint computation of the symbolic post with the approximated set of views $\not\oint_k^{k+2}$ (line 3). Finally, the termination criteria on line 2 and 4 require the use of the function bad which returns either if a set of configurations contains a bad configuration or whether a set of views characterizes a bad configuration. The function bad is implemented by checking whether any configuration from $\mathcal{B}_{min}$ appears in its input set either (i) as a subword of a configuration or (ii) within the base of a view. We do not inspect any context, because the views work collectively and there is always another view in the set which contains this context in its base.

The resulting verification algorithm is sound and terminates for some k if and only if there is a reachable bad configuration or if there is a good almost downward-closed invariant. It uses the property of small models, that is, most behaviors are captured with small instances of the systems, either in the form of configurations and views.

Acceleration. The fixpoint computation on line 3 can be accelerated by leveraging the entailment relation. It is based on the observation that $\mathcal{R}_k$ contains configurations of size up to k, which can be used as initial input for the fixpoint computation (rather than I). All views of size k in $\alpha_k(\mathcal{R}_k)$ have empty contexts (i.e. they are weakest).

[1] Although, in this paper, there is no process deletion nor creation, our method works with non length-preserving transitions. The set $\mathcal{R}_k$ is not anymore computed by simply searching through the state-space, since a sequence of transitions from a configuration of size k might lead to arbitrarily many configurations of larger sizes. The alternative definition of $\mathcal{R}_k$ is configurations that may be reached via sequences of transitions involving configurations of the size up to k. This again defines a finite search space, and it holds that every reachable configuration is within $\mathcal{R}_j$ for some j.

They avoid the computations of the symbolic post on any stronger views. A similar argument can be used to see that it is not necessary to apply *spost* on the views in $\text{∯}_k^{k+2}(X)$ that are stronger than the views in $\alpha_{k+2}(\mathcal{R}_{k+2})$. We therefore seed the fixpoint computation with a larger set than $\alpha_k(I)$, namely $\alpha_k(\mathcal{R}_k \cup \mathcal{R}_{k+1} \cup \mathcal{R}_{k+2})$, and cache the set of views $\alpha_{k+2}(\mathcal{R}_{k+2})$.

6 Non-atomically Checked Global Conditions

We extend our model and method to handle parameterized systems where global conditions are *not* checked atomically. We replace both existentially and universally guarded transition rules by the following variant of a for-loop rule:

$$\textbf{if foreach } j \circ i : S \textbf{ then } s \to s' \textbf{ else } s \to e$$

where $e \in Q$ is an *escape* state and the other s, s', $\circ$ and S are named as in Section 2. For instance, line 3 of Szymanski's protocol is be replaced by **if foreach** $j \neq i : \neg\{1,2\}$ **then** $3 \to 7$ **else** $3 \to 4$. Essentially, for a configuration with linear topology, a process at position i inspects the state of another process at position j, *in-order*. Without loss of generality, we will assume that the for-loops iterate through process indices in increasing order. If the state of the process at position j is not a reason for the process i to escape, process i moves on to inspect the process at position $j+1$, unless there is no more process to inspect in which case process i completes its transition.

We extend the semantics of a system with for-loop rules from transition systems of Section 2 in the following way: A configuration is now a pair $c = (q_1 \cdots q_n, \checkmark)$ where $q_1 \cdots q_n \in Q^+$ is as before and where $\checkmark : [\![1;n]\!] \to [\![0;n]\!]$ is a total map which assigns to every position i of c the last position which has been inspected by the process i. Initially, $\checkmark(i)$ is assigned 0.

We fix a rule $\delta =$ **if foreach** $j \circ i : S$ **then** $s \to t$ **else** $s \to e$ from Δ, a configuration c with $|c| = n$, and $i \in [\![1;n]\!]$. We first define the position $next(i)$ which the process at position i is expected to inspect next. Formally, $next(i) = min\{j \in [\![1;n]\!] \mid j > \checkmark(i), j \circ i\}$ is the smallest position larger than than $\checkmark(i)$ which satisfies $next(i) \circ i$. Notice that if process i has already inspected the right-most position j which satisfies $j \circ i$, then (and only then) $next(i)$ is undefined.

We distinguish three types of δ-move on c by the process at position i: (i) $\delta_i(c,i)$ for a loop iteration, (ii) $\delta_e(c,i)$ for escaping and (iii) $\delta_t(c,i)$ for termination. Each type of move is defined only if $q_i = s$.

– $\delta_i(c,i)$ is defined if $next(i)$ is defined and $q_{next(i)} \in S$. It is obtained from c by only updating $\checkmark(i)$ to $next(i)$. Intuitively, process i is only *ticking* position $next(i)$.

– $\delta_e(c,i)$ is defined if $next(i)$ is defined and $q_{next(i)} \notin S$. It is obtained from c by changing the state of the process i to e and resetting $\checkmark(i)$ to 0. Intuitively, process i has found a reason to escape.

– $\delta_t(c,i)$ is defined if $next(i)$ is undefined, and it is obtained from c by changing the state of the process i to t and resetting $\checkmark(i)$ to 0. Intuitively, process i has reached the end of the iteration and terminates its transition (i.e. moves to its target state).

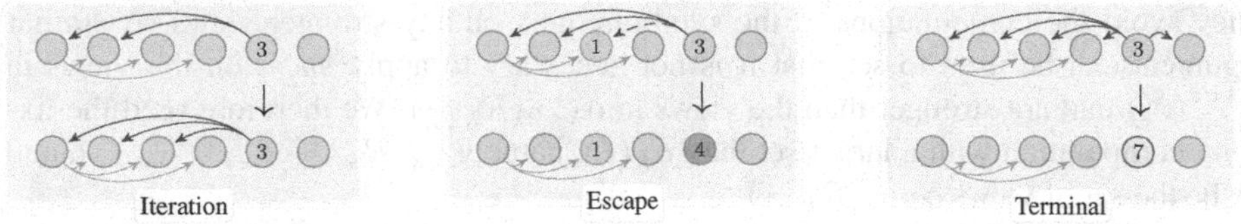

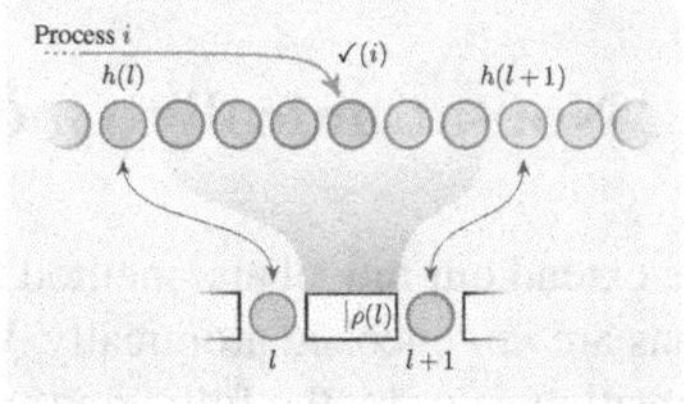

Fig. 8. Projection with non-atomicity. The blue states have been inspected by process i, the green states have not.

We now instantiate the abstract domain by adapting the notion of views from Section 4. A view is now of the form $(R_0 q_1 R_1 \ldots q_n R_n, \checkmark, \rho)$, where $(q_1 \cdots q_n, \checkmark)$ is a configuration called the *base*, and $(R_0, \cdots, R_n, \rho)$ is a *context*, such that $R_0, \ldots, R_n \subseteq Q$ and $\rho : [\![1;n]\!] \to 2^Q$ is a total map which assigns a subset of Q to every $i \in [\![1;n]\!]$. Intuitively, the role of $\rho(i)$ is to keep track of the processes that process i has not yet inspected in case they get mixed up in a context with other already inspected processes. This will be the case, as depicted in Fig.8, for one context only, say R_ℓ (in fact, R_ℓ is the context where $\checkmark(i)$ is projected to). It is trivial to see that contexts of higher (resp. lower) indices than ℓ contain processes that are not (resp. are) inspected by process i.

The projection of a configuration into a view is defined similarly as in Section 5. For $h \in H_n^k, k \leq n$, and a configuration $c = (q_1 \cdots q_n, \checkmark)$, $\Pi_h(c) = (\Pi_h(q_1 \cdots q_n), \checkmark', \rho')$ where $\checkmark'$ and ρ' are defined as follows. For all $i \in [\![1;k]\!]$, there exists ℓ such that $h(\ell) \leq \checkmark(i) < h(\ell+1)$. Then, $\checkmark'(i) = \ell$ and $\rho'(i) = \{q_j \mid \checkmark(i) < j < h(\ell+1)\}$. The projection of views is defined analogously. Note that this definition also implies that the concretization of a set of views is precise enough and reconstructs configurations with in-order ticks.

The entailment relation between the views $v = (R_0 q_1 R_1 \ldots q_n R_n, \checkmark, \rho)$ and $v' = (R'_0 q'_1 R'_1 \ldots q'_n R'_n, \checkmark', \rho')$ (of the same size) is defined such that $v \preccurlyeq v'$ iff (i) both have the same base, i.e. $(q_1 \cdots q_n, \checkmark) = (q'_1 \cdots q'_n, \checkmark')$, (ii) $R_i \subseteq R'_i$ for all $i \in [\![0;n]\!]$, and (iii) $\rho(i) \subseteq \rho'(i)$ for all $i \in [\![1;n]\!]$. This intuitivelly reflects that the more unticked states within a context the likelier it is for a transition to be blocked, and the larger contexts are the likelier they retain non-ticked states.

Finally, abstraction, concretization, and *spost* (and therefore symbolic post) are then adapted using the new definition of projection, entailment and *post*. This also implies that the contexts are inspected in-order and all processes in a context at once. Lemma 1, 3 and 4 hold in the same wording. The symbolic post with contexts and non-atomicity is precisely the abstract post and we use a similar over-approximation than in Section 5.

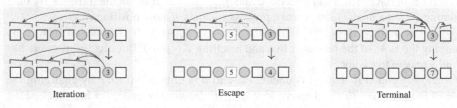

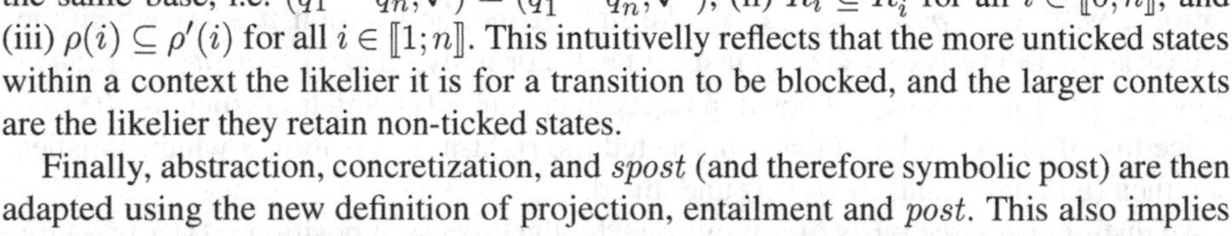

7   Experiments

We have implemented a prototype in OCaml based on our method to verify the safety property of numerous protocols.

We report the results running on a 3.1 GHz computer with 4GB memory. Table 1 displays, for various protocols with linear topology (over 2 lines), the running times (in seconds) and the final number of views generated ($|V|$). The first line is the result of the atomic version of the protocol, while the second line corresponds to the non-atomic version. The complete descriptions of the experiments can be found the technical report [5]. In most cases, the method terminates almost immediately illustrating the *small model property*: all patterns occur for small instances of the system.

Table 1. Linear topologies ± Atomicity

Protocol	Time	$|V|$	
$\forall_\exists$-example*	0.005	22	✓
	0.006	-	✗
Burns	0.004	34	✓
	0.011	64	✓
Dijkstra	0.027	93	✓
	0.097	222	✓
Szymanski*	0.307	168	✓
	1.982	311	✓
Szymanski (compact)*	0.006	48	✓
	0.557	194	✓
Szymanski (random)	1.156	-	✗
Bakery	0.001	7	✓
	0.006	30	✓
Gribomont-Zenner*	0.328	143	✓
	32.112	888	✓
Simple Barrier*	0.018	61	✓
(as array)	1.069	253	✓

* contexts needed ✓: Safe ✗: Unsafe

For the first example of Table 1 in the case of non-atomicity, our tool reports the protocol to be *Unsafe* (✗). The method is sound. It is indeed a real error and not an artifact of the over-approximation. In fact, this is also the case when we intentionally tweak the implementation of Szymanski's protocol and force the for-loops to iterate randomly through the indices, in the non-atomic case. The tool reports a trace, that is, a sequence of configurations — here involving only 3 processes — as a witness of an (erroneous) scenario that leads to a violation of the mutual exclusion property.

The method is not limited to linear topologies. We also used the method to verify several examples with a multiset topology: Petri nets with inhibitor arcs. Inhibitor places should retain some content (therefore creating a context) in order to not fire the transition and potentially make the over-approximation too coarse. The bottom part of Table 2 lists examples where the contexts were necessary to verify the protocol, while the top part lists examples that did not require any.

Table 2. Petri Net with Inhibitor Arcs

Protocol	Time	$|V|$	
Critical Section with lock	0.001	42	✓
Priority Allocator	0.001	33	✓
Barrier with Counters	0.001	22	✓
Simple Barrier	0.001	8	✓
Light Control	0.001	15	✓
List with Counter Automata	0.002	38	✓

Heuristics. If $\alpha_2(\mathcal{R}_2 \cup \mathcal{R}_3) = \alpha_2(\mathcal{R}_2 \cup \mathcal{R}_3 \cup \mathcal{R}_4)$, it is likely the case that the computation in Alg. 1 (line 3) is already at fixpoint for $k = 2$ and discovered all the bases of the system in the sets from the above equation. It is therefore interesting to inspect whether a new base could be discovered by

Table 3. Leveraging the heuristics

Protocol		Time	$|V|$	it.
Agreement	insertion heuristic	8.247	199	28
	all contexts	3.950	216	1
	contexts discovery	166.893	121	4
Gribomont-Zenner	insertion heuristic	0.328	143	7
	all contexts	0.808	317	1
	contexts discovery	50.049	217	3
Szymanski, non-atomic	insertion heuristic	2.053	311	26
	all contexts	48.065	771	1
	contexts discovery	732.643	896	7

the symbolic post, while ignoring contexts (to consider the weakest views). If not, a fixpoint is indeed discovered and the invariant is strong enough to imply safety. If so, we can stop the computations, detect which views led to the new inserted base and remember their contexts for the next round of computations. This heuristic happen to be very successful in the case of Szymanski's protocol (in its non-atomic full version). On the other hand, this idea can be used in general: Do not remember any contexts, therefore considering the weakest views, and if the procedure discovers a counter-example, we trace the views that generated it and remember their contexts for the next round of computations, in a CEGAR-like fashion. It is however inefficient if all views most likely need a context (as shown with the ring agreement example). Table 3 presents the results of using the insertion and context discovery heuristics. The time is given in seconds and `it.` represents the number of iteration to terminate.

8 Related Work

An extensive amount of work has been devoted to regular model checking, e.g. [29,15]; and in particular augmenting regular model checking with techniques such as widening [11,34], abstraction [12], and acceleration [8]. All these works rely on computing the transitive closure of transducers or on iterating them on regular languages. There are numerous techniques less general than regular model checking, but they are lighter and more dedicated to the problem of parameterized verification. The idea of *counter abstraction* is to keep track of the number of processes which satisfy a certain property [27,22,16,17,32]. In general, counter abstraction is designed for systems with unstructured or clique architectures, but may be used for systems with other topologies too.

Several works reduce parameterized verification to the verification of finite-state models. Among these, the *invisible invariants* method [9,31] and the work of [30] exploit cut-off properties to check invariants for mutual exclusion protocols. In [10], finite-state abstractions for verification of systems specified in WS1S are computed on-the-fly by using the weakest precondition operator. The method requires the user to provide a set of predicates to compute the abstract model. *Environment abstraction* [13] combines predicate abstraction with the counter abstraction. The technique is applied to Szymanski's algorithm (with atomicity assumption).

The only work we are aware of that attempts to automatically verify systems with non-atomic global transitions is [7]. It applies the recently introduced method of *monotonic abstraction* [6], which combines regular model checking with abstraction in order to produce systems that have monotonic behaviors wrt. a well quasi-ordering on the state-space. The verification procedure in this case operates on unbounded abstract graphs, and thus is a non-trivial extension of the existing framework. The method of [26,25] and its reformulated, generic version of [24] come with a complete method for well-quasi ordered systems which is an alternative to backward reachability analysis based on a forward exploration, similarly to our recent work [4].

Constant-size cut-offs have been defined for ring networks in [21] where communication is only allowed through token passing. More general communication mechanisms such as guards over local and shared variables are described in [20]. However, the cut-offs are linear in the number of states of the components, which makes the verification task intractable on most of our examples. The work in [28] also relies on dynamic detection of cut-off points. The class of systems considered in [28] corresponds essentially to Petri nets.

Most of the mentioned related works can verify only systems with good downward-closed invariants, up to several exceptions: Regular model checking can express even more complicated properties of states with the word topology. Our method is significantly simpler and more efficient. The data structure [23] extends the data structures discussed in [18,19] so that they are able to express almost downward-closed sets of states with multiset topology. The work [3] allows to infer almost downward-closed invariants using an extension of backward reachability algorithm with CEGAR. Last, in [30], the need of inferring almost downward-closed invariants may be sometimes circumvent by manually introducing auxiliary variables.

The only two works we are aware of that support handling non-atomic global transitions are [4] and [3].

Our method is simpler and more efficient than most of the mentioned methods, but what distinguishes it most clearly is that it is the only one that combines handling non-atomic global transitions and automatic inference of almost downward-closed properties.

9 Conclusion and Future Work

We have presented a method for automatic verification of parameterized systems which alleviates the lack of precision from [4] that it exhibits on systems without fully downward-closed invariants. This is a unique method that combines the feature of discovering non downward-closed invariants while allowing to model systems with fine-grained transitions.

The method performs parameterized verification by only analyzing a small set of instances of the system (rather than the whole family) and captures the reachability of bad configurations to imply safety. Our algorithm relies on a very simple abstraction function, where a configuration of the system is approximated by breaking it down into smaller pieces. This gives rise to a finite representation of infinite sets of configurations while retaining enough precision. We showed that the presented algorithm is complete for systems with almost downward-closed invariants. Based on the method, we have implemented a prototype which performs efficiently on a wide range of benchmarks.

We are currently working on extending the method to the case of multi-threaded programs running on machines with different memory models. These systems have notoriously complicated behaviors. Showing that verification can be carried out through the analysis of only a small number of threads would allow more efficient algorithms for these systems.

References

1. Abdulla, P.A.: Well (and better) quasi-ordered transition systems. Bulletin of Symbolic Logic 16(4), 457–515 (2010)
2. Abdulla, P.A., Čerāns, K., Jonsson, B., Tsay, Y.K.: General decidability theorems for infinite-state systems. In: LICS 1996, pp. 313–321 (1996)

3. Abdulla, P.A., Delzanno, G., Rezine, A.: Approximated context-sensitive analysis for parameterized verification. In: Lee, D., Lopes, A., Poetzsch-Heffter, A. (eds.) FMOODS 2009. LNCS, vol. 5522, pp. 41–56. Springer, Heidelberg (2009), http://dx.doi.org/10.1007/978-3-642-02138-1_3
4. Abdulla, P.A., Haziza, F., Holík, L.: All for the price of few (parameterized verification through view abstraction). In: Giacobazzi, R., Berdine, J., Mastroeni, I. (eds.) VMCAI 2013. LNCS, vol. 7737, pp. 476–495. Springer, Heidelberg (2013)
5. Abdulla, P.A., Haziza, F., Holík, L.: Block me if you can (context-sensitive parameterized verification). Technical Report FIT-TR-2014-03, Brno University of Technology (2014)
6. Abdulla, P.A., Delzanno, G., Ben Henda, N., Rezine, A.: Regular model checking without transducers (on efficient verification of parameterized systems). In: Grumberg, O., Huth, M. (eds.) TACAS 2007. LNCS, vol. 4424, pp. 721–736. Springer, Heidelberg (2007)
7. Abdulla, P.A., Ben Henda, N., Delzanno, G., Rezine, A.: Handling parameterized systems with non-atomic global conditions. In: Logozzo, F., Peled, D.A., Zuck, L.D. (eds.) VMCAI 2008. LNCS, vol. 4905, pp. 22–36. Springer, Heidelberg (2008)
8. Abdulla, P.A., Jonsson, B., Nilsson, M., d'Orso, J.: Regular model checking made simple and efficient. In: Brim, L., Jančar, P., Křetínský, M., Kučera, A. (eds.) CONCUR 2002. LNCS, vol. 2421, pp. 116–130. Springer, Heidelberg (2002)
9. Arons, T., Pnueli, A., Ruah, S., Xu, J., Zuck, L.D.: Parameterized verification with automatically computed inductive assertions. In: Berry, G., Comon, H., Finkel, A. (eds.) CAV 2001. LNCS, vol. 2102, pp. 221–234. Springer, Heidelberg (2001)
10. Baukus, K., Lakhnech, Y., Stahl, K.: Parameterized verification of a cache coherence protocol: Safety and liveness. In: Cortesi, A. (ed.) VMCAI 2002. LNCS, vol. 2294, pp. 317–330. Springer, Heidelberg (2002)
11. Boigelot, B., Legay, A., Wolper, P.: Iterating transducers in the large. In: Hunt Jr., W.A., Somenzi, F. (eds.) CAV 2003. LNCS, vol. 2725, pp. 223–235. Springer, Heidelberg (2003)
12. Bouajjani, A., Habermehl, P., Vojnar, T.: Abstract regular model checking. In: Alur, R., Peled, D.A. (eds.) CAV 2004. LNCS, vol. 3114, pp. 372–386. Springer, Heidelberg (2004)
13. Clarke, E., Talupur, M., Veith, H.: Environment abstraction for parameterized verification. In: Emerson, E.A., Namjoshi, K.S. (eds.) VMCAI 2006. LNCS, vol. 3855, pp. 126–141. Springer, Heidelberg (2006)
14. Cousot, P., Cousot, R.: Systematic design of program analysis frameworks. In: POPL 1979, pp. 269–282. ACM, New York (1979), http://doi.acm.org/10.1145/567752.567778
15. Dams, D., Lakhnech, Y., Steffen, M.: Iterating transducers. In: Berry, G., Comon, H., Finkel, A. (eds.) CAV 2001. LNCS, vol. 2102, pp. 286–297. Springer, Heidelberg (2001)
16. Delzanno, G.: Automatic verification of cache coherence protocols. In: Emerson, E.A., Sistla, A.P. (eds.) CAV 2000. LNCS, vol. 1855, pp. 53–68. Springer, Heidelberg (2000)
17. Delzanno, G.: Verification of consistency protocols via infinite-state symbolic model checking. In: FORTE 2000. IFIP Conference Proceedings, vol. 183, pp. 171–186. Kluwer (2000)
18. Delzanno, G., Raskin, J.F., Begin, L.V.: Csts (covering sharing trees): Compact data structures for parameterized verification. In: Software Tools for Technology Transfer (2001)
19. Delzanno, G., Raskin, J.-F.: Symbolic representation of upward-closed sets. In: Graf, S. (ed.) TACAS 2000. LNCS, vol. 1785, pp. 426–441. Springer, Heidelberg (2000)
20. Emerson, E.A., Kahlon, V.: Reducing model checking of the many to the few. In: McAllester, D. (ed.) CADE-17. LNCS (LNAI), vol. 1831, pp. 236–254. Springer, Heidelberg (2000)
21. Emerson, E., Namjoshi, K.: Reasoning about rings. In: POPL 1995, pp. 85–94 (1995)
22. Esparza, J., Finkel, A., Mayr, R.: On the verification of broadcast protocols. In: LICS 1999. IEEE Computer Society (1999)

23. Ganty, P.: The Interval Sharing Tree Data Structure (1999), https://github.com/pierreganty/mist/wiki/The-Interval-Sharing-Tree-Data-Structure
24. Ganty, P., Raskin, J.-F., Van Begin, L.: A Complete Abstract Interpretation Framework for Coverability Properties of WSTS. In: Emerson, E.A., Namjoshi, K.S. (eds.) VMCAI 2006. LNCS, vol. 3855, pp. 49–64. Springer, Heidelberg (2006)
25. Geeraerts, G., Raskin, J.-F., Van Begin, L.: Expand, enlarge and check... made efficient. In: Etessami, K., Rajamani, S.K. (eds.) CAV 2005. LNCS, vol. 3576, pp. 394–407. Springer, Heidelberg (2005)
26. Geeraerts, G., Raskin, J.F., Begin, L.V.: Expand, enlarge and check: New algorithms for the coverability problem of wsts. J. Comput. Syst. Sci. 72(1), 180–203 (2006)
27. German, S.M., Sistla, A.P.: Reasoning about systems with many processes. Journal of the ACM 39(3), 675–735 (1992)
28. Kaiser, A., Kroening, D., Wahl, T.: Dynamic cutoff detection in parameterized concurrent programs. In: Touili, T., Cook, B., Jackson, P. (eds.) CAV 2010. LNCS, vol. 6174, pp. 645–659. Springer, Heidelberg (2010)
29. Kesten, Y., Maler, O., Marcus, M., Pnueli, A., Shahar, E.: Symbolic model checking with rich assertional languages. Theoretical Computer Science 256, 93–112 (2001)
30. Namjoshi, K.S.: Symmetry and completeness in the analysis of parameterized systems. In: Cook, B., Podelski, A. (eds.) VMCAI 2007. LNCS, vol. 4349, pp. 299–313. Springer, Heidelberg (2007)
31. Pnueli, A., Ruah, S., Zuck, L.: Automatic deductive verification with invisible invariants. In: Margaria, T., Yi, W. (eds.) TACAS 2001. LNCS, vol. 2031, pp. 82–97. Springer, Heidelberg (2001)
32. Pnueli, A., Xu, J., Zuck, L.D.: Liveness with (0,1,infinity)-counter abstraction. In: Brinksma, E., Larsen, K.G. (eds.) CAV 2002. LNCS, vol. 2404, pp. 107–122. Springer, Heidelberg (2002)
33. Szymanski, B.K.: A simple solution to lamport's concurrent programming problem with linear wait. In: Proceedings of the 2nd International Conference on Supercomputing, ICS 1988, pp. 621–626. ACM, New York (1988), http://doi.acm.org/10.1145/55364.55425
34. Touili, T.: Regular Model Checking using Widening Techniques. Electronic Notes in Theoretical Computer Science 50(4) (2001); Proc. of VEPAS 2001

Peak Cost Analysis of Distributed Systems

Elvira Albert[1], Jesús Correas[1], and Guillermo Román-Díez[2]

[1] DSIC, Complutense University of Madrid, Spain
[2] DLSIIS, Technical University of Madrid, Spain

Abstract. We present a novel static analysis to infer the *peak cost* of distributed systems. The different locations of a distributed system communicate and coordinate their actions by posting tasks among them. Thus, the amount of work that each location has to perform can greatly vary along the execution depending on: (1) the amount of tasks posted to its queue, (2) their respective costs, and (3) the fact that they may be posted in parallel and thus be pending to execute *simultaneously*. The peak cost of a distributed location refers to the maximum cost that it needs to carry out along its execution. Inferring the peak cost is challenging because it increases and decreases along the execution, unlike the standard notion of *total cost* which is cumulative. Our key contribution is the novel notion of *quantified queue configuration* which captures the worst-case cost of the tasks that may be simultaneously pending to execute at each location along the execution. A prototype implementation demonstrates the accuracy and feasibility of the proposed peak cost analysis.

1 Introduction

Distributed systems are increasingly used in industrial processes and products, such as manufacturing plants, aircraft and vehicles. For example, many control systems are decentralized using a distributed architecture with different processing locations interconnected through buses or networks. The software in these systems typically consists of concurrent tasks which are statically allocated to specific locations for processing, and which exchange messages with other tasks at the same or at other locations to perform a collaborative work. A decentralized approach is often superior to traditional centralized control systems in performance, capability and robustness. Systems such as control systems are often critical: they have strict requirements with respect to timing, performance, and stability. A failure to meet these requirements may have catastrophic consequences. To verify that a given system is able to provide the required quality, an essential aspect is to accurately predict *worst-case costs*. We develop our analysis for a generic notion of cost that can be instantiated to the number of executed instructions (considered as the best abstraction of time for software), the amount of memory created, the number of tasks posted to each location, or any other *cost model* that assigns a non-negative cost to each instruction.

Existing cost analyses for distributed systems infer the *total* resource consumption [3] of each distributed location, e.g., the total number of instructions

M. Müller-Olm and H. Seidl (Eds.): SAS 2014, LNCS 8723, pp. 18–33, 2014.

that it needs to execute, the total amount of memory that it will need to allocate, or the total number of tasks that will be added to its queue. This is unfortunately a too pessimistic estimation of the amount of resources actually required in the real execution. An important observation is that the *peak* cost will depend on whether the tasks that the location has to execute are pending *simultaneously*. We aim at inferring such peak of the resource consumption which captures the maximum amount of resources that the location might require along any execution. In addition to its application to verification as described above, this information is crucial to dimensioning the distributed system: it will allow us to determine the size of each location *task queue*; the required size of the location's memory; and the processor execution speed required to execute the peak of instructions and provide a certain response time. It is also of great relevance in the context of software *virtualization* as used in cloud computing, as the peak cost allows estimating how much processing/storage capacity one needs to buy in the host machine, and thus can greatly reduce costs.

This paper presents, to the best of our knowledge, the first static analysis to infer the peak of the resource consumption of distributed systems, which takes into account the type and amount of tasks that the distributed locations can have in their queues simultaneously along any execution, to infer precise bounds on the peak cost. Our analysis works in three steps: (1) *Total cost analysis.* The analysis builds upon well-established analyses for total cost [9,3,18]. We assume that an underlying total cost analysis provides a *cost* for the tasks which measures their efficiency. (2) *Queues configurations.* The first contribution is the inference of the *abstract queue configuration* for each distributed component, which captures all possible configurations that its queue can take along the execution. A particular queue configuration is given as the sets of tasks that the location may have pending to execute at a moment of time. We rely on the information gathered by a *may-happen-in-parallel* analysis [7,1,11,5] to define the abstract queue configurations. (3) *Peak cost.* Our key contribution is the notion of *quantified queue configuration*, which over-approximates the peak cost of each distributed location. For a given queue configuration, its quantified configuration is computed by removing from the total cost inferred in (1) those tasks that do not belong to its configuration, as inferred in (2). The peak for the location is the maximum of the costs of all configurations that its queue can have.

We demonstrate the accuracy and feasibility of the presented cost analysis by implementing a prototype analyzer of peak cost within the SACO system [2], a static analyzer for distributed concurrent programs. In preliminary experiments on some typical applications for distributed programs, the peak cost achieves gains up to 70% w.r.t. a total cost analysis. The tool can be used on-line from a web interface available at `http://costa.ls.fi.upm.es/web/saco`.

2 The Distributed Model

We consider a distributed programming model with explicit locations. Each location represents a processor with a procedure stack and an unordered queue

$$\frac{t = tsk(tid, m, l, \langle x = \mathsf{newLoc}; s\rangle, c),\ \mathrm{fresh}(lid_1)\ ,\ l' = l[x \rightarrow lid_1]}{loc(lid, tid, \{t\}\cup\mathcal{Q}) \leadsto loc(lid, tid, \{tsk(tid, m, l', s, c{+}cost(\mathsf{newLoc}))\}\cup\mathcal{Q}) \| loc(lid_1, \bot, \{\})}\ (\textsc{newLoc})$$

$$\frac{l(x) = lid_1,\ \mathrm{fresh}(tid_1),\ l_1{=}buildLocals(\bar{z}, m_1),\ l' = l[f \rightarrow tid_1]}{\begin{array}{c} loc(lid, tid, \{tsk(tid, m, l, \langle f{=}x!m_1(\overline{z}); s\rangle, c)\} \cup \mathcal{Q}) \ \|\ loc(lid_1, \_, \mathcal{Q}') \leadsto \\ loc(lid, tid, \{tsk(tid, m, l', s, c + cost(f{=}x!m_1(\overline{z})))\}\cup\mathcal{Q}) \ \| \\ loc(lid_1, \_, \{tsk(tid_1, m_1, l_1, body(m_1), 0) \cup \mathcal{Q}'\}) \end{array}}\ (\textsc{async})$$

$$\frac{t = tsk(tid, m, l, \langle \mathsf{await}\ f?; s\rangle, c), l(f) = tid_1, tsk(tid_1, \_, \_, s_1, \_) \in \mathsf{Locs}, s_1 = \tau}{loc(lid, tid, \{t\} \cup \mathcal{Q}) \leadsto loc(lid, tid, \{tsk(tid, m, l, s, c + cost(\mathsf{await}\ f?))\} \cup \mathcal{Q})}\ (\textsc{await-t})$$

$$\frac{t = tsk(tid, m, l, \langle \mathsf{await}\ f?; s\rangle, c), l(f) = tid_1, tsk(tid_1, \_, \_, s_1, \_) \in \mathsf{Locs}, s_1 \neq \tau}{loc(lid, tid, \{t\} \cup \mathcal{Q}) \leadsto loc(lid, \bot, \{tsk(tid, m, l, \langle \mathsf{await}\ f?; s\rangle, c)\} \cup \mathcal{Q})}\ (\textsc{await-f})$$

$$\frac{\begin{array}{c} select(\mathcal{Q}){=}tid, \\ t{=}tsk(tid, \_, \_, s, c){\in}\mathcal{Q}, s{\neq}\tau \end{array}}{loc(lid, \bot, \mathcal{Q}) \leadsto loc(lid, tid, \mathcal{Q})}\ (\textsc{select}) \qquad \frac{t = tsk(tid, m, l, \langle \mathsf{return}; \rangle, c)}{\begin{array}{c} loc(lid, tid, \{t\} \cup \mathcal{Q}) \leadsto \\ loc(lid, \bot, \{tsk(tid, m, l, \tau, c{+}cost(\mathsf{return}))\}\cup\mathcal{Q}) \end{array}}\ (\textsc{return})$$

Fig. 1. (Summarized) Cost Semantics for Distributed Execution

of pending tasks. Initially all processors are idle. When an idle processor's task queue is non-empty, some task is selected for execution. Besides accessing its own processor's global storage, each task can post tasks to the queues of any processor, including its own, and synchronize with the completion of tasks. When a task completes or when it is awaiting for another task to terminate, its processor becomes idle again, chooses the next pending task, and so on.

2.1 Syntax

The number of distributed locations needs not be known a priori (e.g., locations may be virtual). Syntactically, a location will therefore be similar to an *object* and can be dynamically created using the instruction newLoc. The program is composed by a set of methods defined as $M{::=}T\ m(\bar{T}\ \bar{x})\{s\}$ where $s{::=}\ s; s \mid x{=}e \mid \mathsf{if}\ e\ \mathsf{then}\ s\ \mathsf{else}\ s \mid \mathsf{while}\ e\ \mathsf{do}\ s \mid \mathsf{return} \mid b{=}\mathsf{newLoc} \mid f{=}b!m(\bar{e}) \mid \mathsf{await}\ f?$. The notation $\bar{T}$ is used as a shorthand for $T_1, \ldots, T_n$, and similarly for other names. The special location identifier *this* denotes the current location. For the sake of generality, the syntax of expressions e and types T is left open. The semantics of future variables f and concurrency instructions is explained below.

2.2 Semantics

A *program state* has the form $loc_1\| \ldots \|loc_n$, denoting the currently existing distributed locations. Each *location* is a term $loc(lid, tid, \mathcal{Q})$ where *lid* is the location identifier, *tid* is the identifier of the *active task* which holds the location's lock or $\bot$ if the lock is free, and $\mathcal{Q}$ is the set of tasks at the location. Only one task, which holds the location's *lock*, can be *active* (running) at this location.

All other tasks are *pending*, waiting to be executed, or *finished*, if they terminated and released the lock. Given a location, its set of *ready* tasks is composed by the tasks that are pending and the one that it is active at the location. A *task* is a term $tsk(tid, m, l, s, c)$ where tid is a unique task identifier, m is the name of the method executing in the task, l is a mapping from local variables to their values, s is the sequence of instructions to be executed or $s = \tau$ if the task has terminated, and c is a positive number which corresponds to the cost of the instructions executed in the task so far. The cost of executing an instruction i is represented in a generic way as $cost(i)$.

The execution of a program starts from a method m in an initial state S_0 with a single (initial) location of the form $S_0{=}loc(0, 0, \{tsk(0, \mathsf{m}, l, body(\mathsf{m}), 0)\})$. Here, l maps parameters to their initial values and local references to null (standard initialization), and $body(m)$ refers to the sequence of instructions in the method m. The execution proceeds from the initial state S_0 by selecting *non-deterministically* one of the locations and applying the semantic rules depicted in Fig. 1. The treatment of sequential instructions is standard and thus omitted. The operational semantics $\rightsquigarrow$ is given in a rewriting-based style where at each step a subset of the state is rewritten according to the rules as follows. In NewLoc, an active task tid at location lid creates a location lid_1 which is introduced to the state with a free lock. Async spawns a new task (the initial state is created by *buildLocals*) with a fresh task identifier tid_1 which is added to the queue of location lid_1. The case $lid{=}lid_1$ is analogous, the new task tid_1 is simply added to $\mathcal{Q}$ of lid. The future variable f allows synchronizing the execution of the current task with the termination of created task. The association of the future variable to the task is stored in the local variables table l'. In Await-t, the future variable we are awaiting for points to a finished task and await can be completed. The finished task t_1 is looked up at all locations in the current state (denoted by Locs). Otherwise, Await-f yields the lock so that any other task of the same location can take it. Rule Select returns a task that is not finished, and it obtains the lock of the location. Return releases the lock and it will never be taken again by that task. Consequently, that task is *finished* (marked by adding τ). For brevity, we omit the return instructions in the examples.

3 Peak Cost of Distributed Systems

The aim of this paper is to infer an *upper bound* on the *peak cost* for all locations of a distributed system. The peak cost refers to the maximum amount of resources that a given location might require along any execution. The over-approximation consists in computing the sum of the costs of all tasks that can be simultaneously ready in the location's queue. Importantly, as the number of ready tasks in the queue can increase and decrease along the execution, in order to define the notion of peak cost, we need to observe all intermediate states along the computation and take the maximum of their costs.

Example 1. Figure 2 shows to the left a method m that spawns several tasks at a location referenced from variable x (the middle code can be ignored by now).

```
1  m (C x, int n){
2    x!r();
3    while(n>0){
4      x!p(n);
5      f=x!q(n);
6      await f?;
7      n = n−1;
8    }
9    x!s();
10 }

11 main (int i){
12 ⓐ C x=newLoc;
13 ⓑ C y=newLoc;
14     z=this!m(x,i);
15     await z?;
16     this!m(y,i−1);
17 }
18 r (){...}
19 p (int i){...}
20 q (int i){...}
21 s (){...}
```

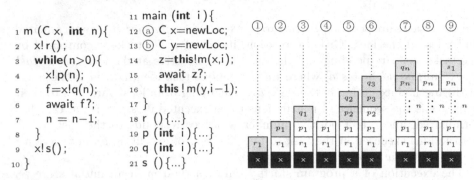

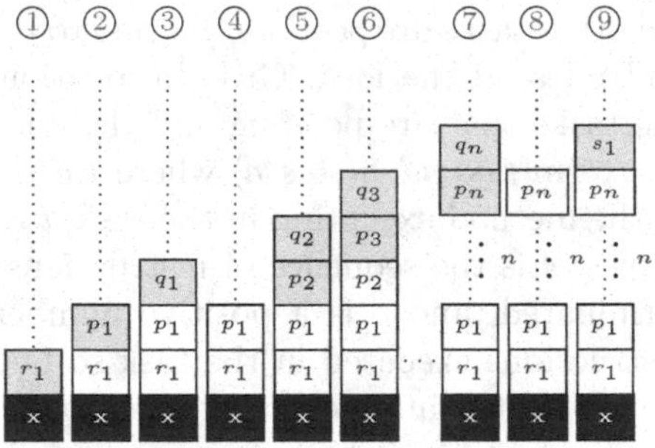

Fig. 2. Running example

To the right of the figure, we depict the tasks that are ready in the queue of location x at different states of the execution of m. For instance, the state ① is obtained after invoking method r at line 2 (L2 for short). The first iteration of the while loop spawns a task p (state ②) and then invokes q (state ③). The important observation is that q is awaited at L6, and thus it is guaranteed to be finished at state ④. The same pattern is repeated in subsequent loop iterations (states ⑤ to ⑦). The last iteration of the loop, captured in state ⑦, accumulates all calls to p, and the last call to q. Observe that at most one instance of method q appears in the queue at any point during the execution of the program. Finally, state ⑧ represents the exit of the loop (L8) and ⑨ when method s is invoked at L9. The await at L6 ensures that methods q and s will not be queued simultaneously.

We start by formalizing the notion of peak cost in the concrete setting. Let us provide some notation. Given a state $S{\equiv}loc_1 \| \ldots \| loc_n$, we use $loc \in S$ to refer to a location in S. The set of ready tasks at a location lid at state S is defined as $ready\_tasks(S, lid) = \{tid \mid loc(lid, \_, \mathcal{Q}) \in S, tsk(tid, \_, \_, s, \_){\in}\mathcal{Q}, s{\neq}\top\}$. Note that we exclude the tasks that are finished. Given a finite trace $t \equiv S_0{\rightarrow}\ldots{\rightarrow}S_N$, we use $\mathcal{C}(lid, tid)$ to refer to the accumulated cost c in the final state S_N by the task $tsk(tid, \_, \_, \_, c){\in}\mathcal{Q}$ that executes at location $loc(lid, \_, \mathcal{Q}){\in}S_N$, and $\mathcal{C}(S_i, lid)$ to refer to the accumulated cost of all active tasks that are in the queue at state S_i for location lid: $\mathcal{C}(S_i, lid) = \sum_{tid \in ready\_tasks(S_i, lid)} \mathcal{C}(lid, tid)$. Now, the peak cost of location lid is defined as the *maximum* of the addition of the costs of the tasks that are simultaneously ready at the location at any state: $peak\_cost(t, lid) = \max(\{\mathcal{C}(S_i, lid) \mid S_i \in t\})$. Observe that the *cost* always refers to the cost of each task in the *final* state S_N. This way we are able to capture the cost that a location will need to carry out at each state S_i with $i \leq N$ in which we have a set of ready tasks in its queue but they have (possibly) not been executed yet.

Since execution is non-deterministic in the selection of tasks, given a program $P(x)$, multiple (possibly infinite) traces may exist. We use $executions(P(\overline{x}))$ to denote the set of all possible traces for $P(\overline{x})$.

Definition 1 (peak Cost). *The peak cost of a location with identifier lid in a program P on input values $\overline{x}$, denoted $\mathcal{P}(P(\overline{x}), lid)$, is defined as:*

$$\mathcal{P}(P(\overline{x}), lid) = max(\{peak\_cost(t, lid) \mid t \in executions(P(\overline{x}))\})$$

Example 2. Let us reason on the peak cost for the execution of m. We use $\ddddot{m}$ to refer to the concrete cost of a task executing method m. We use subscripts $\ddddot{m}_j$ to refer to the cost of the j-th task spawned executing method m. As the cost often depends on the parameters, in general, we have different costs $\ddddot{m}_1$, $\ddddot{m}_2$,... for the multiple executions of the same method. The queue of x in states ② and ④ accumulates the cost $\ddddot{r}_1 + \ddddot{p}_1$. At ⑥, it accumulates $\ddddot{r}_1 + \ddddot{p}_1 + \ddddot{p}_2 + \ddddot{p}_3 + \ddddot{q}_3$. The peak cost corresponds to the maximum among all states. Note that it is unknown if the cost at ⑦ is larger than the cost at ③-⑤-⑥-.... This is because at each state we have a different instance of q running, and it can be that $\ddddot{q}_1$ is larger than the whole cost of the next iterations. Only some states can be discarded (for instance ① and ② are subsumed by ③, and ⑧ by ⑨).

The above example reveals several important aspects that make the inference of the peak cost challenging: (1) We need to infer all possible queue configurations. This is because the peak cost is non-cumulative, and any state can require the maximum amount of resources and constitute the peak cost. This contrasts with the total cost in which we only need to observe the final state. (2) We need to track when tasks terminate their execution and eliminate them from the configuration (the await instructions will reveal this information). (3) We need to know how many instances of tasks we might have running and bound the cost of each instance, as they might not all have the same cost.

4 Basic Concepts: Points-to, Cost, and MHP Analyses

Our peak cost analysis builds upon well-established work on points-to analysis [14,13], total cost analysis [9,18,3] and may-happen-in-parallel (MHP) analysis [11,5]. As regards the points-to and may-happen-in-parallel analyses, this section only reviews the basic concepts which will be used later by our peak cost analysis. As for the total cost analysis, we need to tune several components of the analysis in order to produce the information that the peak cost analysis requires.

Points-to Analysis. Since locations can be dynamically created, we need an analysis that abstracts them into a *finite* abstract representation, and that tells us which (abstract) location a reference variable is pointing-to. Points-to analysis [14,13,16] solves this problem. It infers the set of memory locations that a reference variable can *point-to*. Different abstractions can be used and our method is parametric on the chosen abstraction. Any points-to analysis that provides the following information with more or less accurate precision can be used (our implementation uses [13]): (1) $\mathcal{O}$, the set of abstract locations; (2) $\mathcal{M}(o)$, the set of methods executed in tasks at the abstract location $o \in \mathcal{O}$; (3) a function $pt(pp, v)$ which for a given program point pp and a variable v returns the set of abstract locations in $\mathcal{O}$ to which v may point to.

Example 3. Consider the main method shown in Fig. 2, which creates two new locations x at program point ⓐ (abstracted as o_1) and y at ⓑ (abstracted as o_2) and passes them as parameters in the calls to m (at L14, L16). By using the points-to analysis we obtain the following relevant information, $\mathcal{O}=\{\epsilon, o_1, o_2\}$ where ϵ is the location executing main, $\mathcal{M}(o_1)=\{r,p,q,s\}$, $\mathcal{M}(o_2)=\{r,p,q,s\}$, $pt(L14,x)=\{o_1\}$ and $pt(L16,y)=\{o_2\}$. Observe that the abstract task executing p at location o_1 represents multiple instances of the tasks invoked at L4.

Cost Analysis. The notion of *cost center* (CC) is an artifact used to define the granularity of a cost analyzer. In [3], the proposal is to define a CC for each distributed location, i.e., CCs are of the form $c(o)$ where $o \in \mathcal{O}$. In essence, the analyzer every time that accounts for the cost of executing an instruction b at program point pp, it also checks at which locations it is executing. This information is provided by the points-to analysis as $O_{pp}=pt(pp, this)$. The cost of the instruction is accumulated in the CCs of all elements in O_{pp} as $\sum c(o)*cost(b), \forall o \in O_{pp}$, where $cost(b)$ expresses in an abstract way the cost of executing the instruction. If we are counting steps, then $cost(b) = 1$. If we measure memory, $cost(b)$ refers to memory created by b. Then, given a method $m(\bar{x})$, the cost analyzer computes an *upper bound* for the total cost of executing m of the form $\widehat{\mathcal{C}}_m(\bar{x})=\sum_{i=1}^{n} c(o_i)*C_i$, where $o_i \in \mathcal{O}$ and C_i is a cost expression that bounds the cost of the computation carried out by location o_i when executing m. We omit the subscript in $\widehat{\mathcal{C}}$ when it is clear from the context. Thus, CCs allow computing costs at the granularity level of the distributed locations. If one is interested in studying the computation performed by one particular location o_j, denoted $\widehat{\mathcal{C}}_m(\bar{x})|_{o_j}$, we simply replace all $c(o_i)$ with $i \neq j$ by 0 and $c(o_j)$ by 1. The use of CCs is of general applicability and different approaches to cost analysis (e.g., cost analysis based on recurrence equations [17], invariants [9] or type systems [10]) can trivially adopt this idea so as to extend their frameworks to a distributed setting. In principle, our method can work in combination with any analysis for total cost (except for the accuracy improvement in Sec. 5.3).

Example 4. By using the points-to information obtained in Ex. 3, a cost analyzer (we use in particular [2]) would obtain the following upper bounds on the cost distributed at the locations o_1 and o_2 (we ignore location ϵ in what follows as it is not relevant): $\widehat{\mathcal{C}}_{main}(i)=c(o_1)*\widehat{r_1} + c(o_1)*i*\widehat{p_1} + c(o_1)*i*\widehat{q_1} + c(o_1)*\widehat{s_1} + c(o_2)*\widehat{r_2} + c(o_2)*(i-1)*\widehat{p_2} + c(o_2)*(i-1)*\widehat{q_2} + c(o_2)*\widehat{s_2}$. There are two important observations: (1) the analyzer computes the *worst-case* cost $\widehat{p_1}$ for all instances of tasks spawned at L4 executing p at location o_1 (note that it is multiplied by the number of iterations of the loop "i"); (2) the upper bound at location o_2 for the tasks executing p is $\widehat{p_2}$, and it is different from $\widehat{p_1}$ as the invocation to m at L16 has different initial parameters. By replacing $c(o_1)$ by 1 we obtain the cost executed at the location identified by o_1, that is, $\widehat{\mathcal{C}}_{main}|_{o_1}=\widehat{r_1} + i*\widehat{p_1} + i*\widehat{q_1} + \widehat{s_1}$.

Context-Sensitive Task-Level Cost Centers. Our only modification to the total cost analysis consists in using *context-sensitive task-level* granularity by means of appropriate CCs. Let us first focus on the task-level aspect. We want to distinguish the cost of the tasks executing at the different locations. We define task-level cost centers, $\overline{\mathcal{T}}$, as the set $\{o{:}m \in \mathcal{O} \times \mathcal{M} \mid o \in pt(pp, this) \wedge pp \in m\}$, which contains all methods combined with all location names that can execute them. In the example, $\overline{\mathcal{T}}=\{\epsilon{:}m, o_1{:}r, o_1{:}p, o_1{:}q, o_1{:}s, o_2{:}r, o_2{:}p, o_2{:}q, o_2{:}s\}$. Now, the analyzer every time that accounts for the cost of executing an instruction *inst*, it checks at which location it is executing (e.g., o) and to which method it belongs (e.g., m), and it accumulates $c(o{:}m)*cost(b)$. Thus, it is straightforward to modify an existing cost analyzer to include task-level cost centers. The context-sensitive aspect refers to the fact that the whole cost analysis can be made context-sensitive by considering the calling context when analyzing the tasks [15]. As usual, the context is the *chain of call sites* (i.e., the program point in which the task is spawned and those of its ancestor calling methods). The length of the chains is up to a maximum k which is a fixed parameter of the analysis. For instance, for k=2, we distinguish 14:4:p the task executing p from the first invocation to m at L14 and 16:4:p the one arising from L16. Their associated CCs are then o_1:14:4:p and o_2:16:4:p. In the formalization, we assume that the context (call site chain) is part of the method name m and thus we write CCs simply as $c(o{:}m)$. Then, given an entry method $p(\bar{x})$, the cost analyzer will compute a *context-sensitive task-level upper bound* for the cost of executing p of the form $\widehat{\mathcal{C}}_p(\bar{x})=\sum_{i=1}^{n} c(o_i{:}m_i)*C_i$, where $o_i{:}m_i \in \overline{\mathcal{T}}$, and C_i is a cost expression that bounds the cost of the computation carried out by location o_i executing method m_i, where m_i contains the calling context. The notation $\widehat{\mathcal{C}}_p(\bar{x})|_{o:m}$ is used to obtain the cost associated with $c(o{:}m)$ within $\widehat{\mathcal{C}}_p(\bar{x})$, i.e., the one obtained by setting to zero all $c(o'{:}m')$ with $o'{\neq}o$ or $m'{\neq}m$ and to one $c(o{:}m)$.

Example 5. For the method main shown in Fig. 2, the cost expression obtained by using task-level CCs and k=0 (i.e., making it context insensitive) is the following: $\widehat{\mathcal{C}}(i){=}c(o_1{:}r)*\widehat{r_1}+c(o_1{:}p)*i*\widehat{p_1}+c(o_1{:}q)*i*\widehat{q_1}+c(o_1{:}s)*\widehat{s_1}+c(o_2{:}r)*\widehat{r_2}+c(o_2{:}p)*(i{-}1)*\widehat{p_2}+c(o_2{:}q)*(i{-}1)*\widehat{q_2}+c(o_2{:}s)*\widehat{s_2}$. To obtain the cost carried out by o_1 when executing q, we replace $c(o_1{:}q)$ by 1 and the remaining CCs by 0, resulting in $\widehat{\mathcal{C}}(i)|_{o_1:q}{=}i*\widehat{q_1}$. For $k{>}0$, we simply add the call site sequences in the CCs, e.g., $c(o_1{:}14{:}4{:}p)$.

May-Happen-in-Parallel Analysis. We use a MHP analysis [11,5] as a black box and assume the same context and object-sensitivity as in the cost analysis. We require that it provides us: (1) The set of MHP pairs, denoted $\tilde{\mathcal{E}}_P$, of the form $(o_1{:}p_1, o_2{:}p_2)$ which indicates that program point p_1 running at location o_1 and program point p_2 running at location o_2 might execute in parallel. (2) A function $nact(o{:}m)$ that returns 1 if only one instance of m can be active at location o or ∞ if we might have more than one ([5] provides both 1 and 2).

Example 6. An MHP analysis [5] infers for the main method in Fig. 2, among others, the following set of MHP pairs at location o_1, $\{(o_1{:}18, o_1{:}19), (o_1{:}18, o_1{:}20), (o_1{:}18, o_1{:}21), (o_1{:}19, o_1{:}20), (o_1{:}19, o_1{:}21)\}$. In essence, each pair is capturing that the corresponding methods might happen in parallel, e.g., $(o_1{:}18, o_1{:}19)$ implies that methods r and p might happen in parallel. The MHP analysis learns information from the await to capture that only one instance of q can be active at location o_1, thus $nact(o_1{:}q)=1$. On the contrary, the number of active calls to p is greater than 1, then $nact(o_1{:}p)=\infty$.

5 Peak Cost Analysis

In this section we present our framework to infer the peak cost. It consists of two main steps: we first infer in Sec. 5.1 the configurations that the (abstract) location queue can feature (we use the MHP information in this step); and in a second step, we compute in Sec. 5.2 the cost associated with each possible queue configuration (we use the total cost in this step). Finally, we discuss in Sec. 5.3 an important extension of the basic framework that can increase its accuracy.

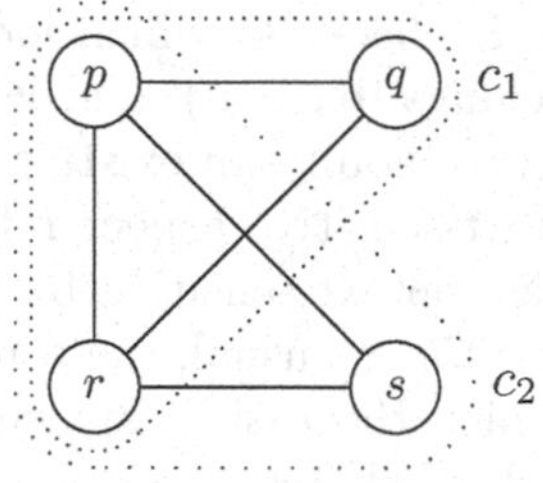

Fig. 3. $\mathcal{G}_t(o_1)$ for Fig 2

5.1 Inference of Queue Configurations

Our goal now is to infer, for each abstract location in the program, all its *non-quantified* configurations, i.e., the sets of method names that can be executing in tasks that are simultaneously ready in the location's queue at some state in the execution. Configurations are non-quantified because we ignore how many instances of a method can be pending in the queue and their costs.

Definition 2 (Tasks Queue Graph). *Given a program P, an abstract location* $o \in \mathcal{O}$ *and the results of the MHP analysis* $\tilde{\mathcal{E}}_P$, *the* tasks queue graph *for o* $\mathcal{G}_t(o)=\langle V_t, E_t\rangle$ *is an undirected graph where* $V_t = \mathcal{M}(o)$ *and* $E_t = \{(m_1, m_2) \mid (p_1, p_2) \in \tilde{\mathcal{E}}_P, p_1{\in}m_1, p_2{\in}m_2, m_1{\neq}m_2\}$.

It can be observed in the above definition that when we have two program points that may-happen-in-parallel in the location's queue, then we add an edge between the methods to which those points belong.

Example 7. By using the MHP information for location o_1 in Ex. 6, we obtain the tasks queue graph $\mathcal{G}_t(o_1)$ shown in Fig. 3 with the following set of edges $\{(r,p),(r,q),(r,s),(p,s),(p,q)\}$ (dotted lines will be explained later).

The tasks queue graph allows us to know the sets of methods that may be ready in the queue simultaneously. This is because, if two methods might be queued at the same time, there must be an edge between them in the tasks queue graph. It is then possible to detect the subsets of methods that can be queued at the same: those that are connected with edges between every two nodes that represent such subset, i.e., they form a *clique*. Since we aim at finding the maximum number of tasks that can be queued simultaneously, we need to compute the *maximal cliques* in the graph. Formally, given an undirected graph $\mathcal{G}=\langle V, E\rangle$, a *maximal clique* is a set of nodes $C{\subseteq}V$ such that every two nodes in C are connected by an edge, and there is no other node in $V \backslash C$ connected to every node in C.

Example 8. For $\mathcal{G}_t(o_1)$ in Fig. 3, we have two maximal cliques: $c_1 = \{p, q, r\}$ and $c_2 = \{p, r, s\}$, which capture the states ⑦ and ⑨ of the queue of o_1 (see Fig. 2). Observe that the maximal cliques subsume other states that contain subsets of a maximal clique. For instance, states ①-⑥ are subsumed by c_1.

```
1  Unit m1 () {
2    fa =x!a();
3    fb=x!b();
4    await fa ?;
5    fc =x!c();
6    await fb ?;
7    await fc ?;
8  }
9  Unit m2 () {
10   x! d();
11   x! e();
12 }
```

```
13 Unit ex1 () {
14   ff =this!m1();
15   await ff ?;
16   this ! m2();
17 }

18 Unit ex2 () {
19   ff =this!m2();
20   await ff ?;
21   this ! m1();
22 }
```

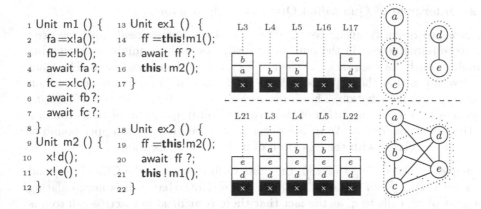

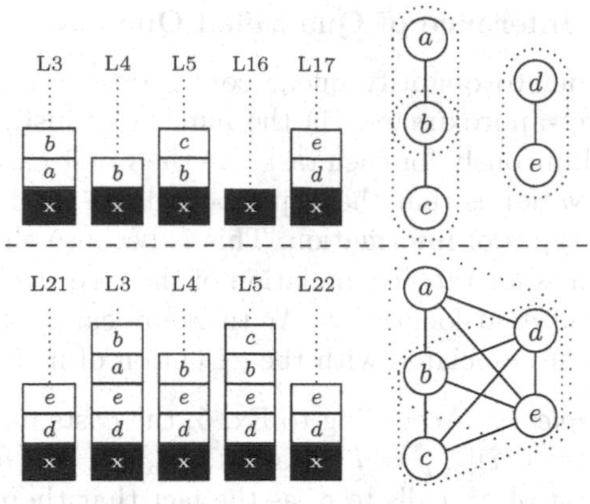

Fig. 4. Queue Configurations Example

Definition 3 (Queue Configuration). *Given a location o, we define its queue configuration, denoted by $\mathcal{K}(o)$, as the set of maximal cliques in $\mathcal{G}_t(o)$.*

Therefore, a queue configuration is a set of sets, namely each element in $\mathcal{K}(o)$ is a set of method names which capture a possible configuration of the queue. Clearly, all possible (maximal) configurations must be considered in order to obtain an over-approximation of the peak cost.

Example 9. Let us see a more sophisticated example for queue configurations. Consider the methods in Fig. 4 which have two distinct entry methods, ex1 and ex2. They both invoke method m1, which spawns tasks a, b and c. m1 guarantees that a, b and c are completed when it finishes. Besides, we know that b and c might run in parallel, while the await instruction in L4 ensures that a and c cannot happen in parallel. Method m2 spawns tasks d and e and does not await for their termination. We show in the middle of Fig. 4 the different configurations of the queue of x (at the program points marked on top) when we execute ex1 (above) and ex2 (below). Such configurations provide a graphical view of the results of the MHP analysis (which basically contains pairs for each two elements in the different queue states). In the queue of ex1, we can observe that the await instructions at the end of m1 guarantee that the queue is empty before launching m2 (see queue at L16). To the right of the queue we show the resulting tasks queue graph for ex1 obtained by using the MHP pairs which correspond to the queues showed in the figure. Then, we have $\mathcal{K}(x)=\{\{a,b\},\{b,c\},\{d,e\}\}$. Note that these cliques capture the states of the queue at L3, L5 and L17, respectively. As regards ex2, the difference is that m2 is spawned before m1. Despite the await at L21, m2 is not awaiting for the termination of d nor e, thus at L21 the queue might contain d and e. As for m1, we have a similar behaviour than before, but now we have to accumulate also d and e along the execution of m1. The resulting tasks queue graph is showed to the right. It can be observed that it is densely connected, and now $\mathcal{K}(x)=\{\{d,e,a,b\},\{d,e,b,c\}\}$. Such cliques correspond to the states of the queue at L3 and L5, respectively.

5.2 Inference of Quantified Queue Configurations

In order to quantify queue configurations and obtain the peak cost, we need to over-approximate: (1) the number of instances that we might have running simultaneously for each task, (2) the worst-case cost of such instances. The main observation is that the upper bounds on the total cost in Sec. 4 already contain both types of information. This is because the cost attached to the CC $c(o{:}m)$ accounts for the accumulation of the resource consumption of *all* tasks running method m at location o. We therefore can safely use $\widehat{\mathcal{C}}(\overline{x})|_{o:m}$ as upper bound of the cost associated with the execution of method m at location o.

Example 10. According to Ex. 5, the costs accumulated in the CCs of $o_1{:}q$ and $o_1{:}p$ are $\widehat{\mathcal{C}}(i)|_{o_1:p} = i * \widehat{p}$ and $\widehat{\mathcal{C}}(i)|_{o_1:q} = i * \widehat{q}$. Note that $o_1{:}q$ is accumulating the cost of *all* calls to q, as the fact that there is at most one active call to q is not taken into account by the total cost analysis. This is certainly a sound but imprecise over-approximation that will be improved in Sec. 5.3.

The key idea to infer the *quantified queue configuration*, or simply *peak cost*, of each location is to compute the total cost for each element in the set $\mathcal{K}(o)$ and stay with the maximum of all of them. Given an abstract location o and a clique $k \in \mathcal{K}(o)$, we have that $\widehat{\mathcal{C}}(\overline{x})|_k = \sum_{m \in k} \widehat{\mathcal{C}}(\overline{x})|_{o:m}$ is the cost for the tasks in k.

Definition 4. *Given a program $P(\overline{x})$ and an abstract location o, the peak cost for o, denoted $\widehat{\mathcal{P}}(P(\overline{x}), o)$, is defined as $\widehat{\mathcal{P}}(P(\overline{x}), o) = \max(\{\widehat{\mathcal{C}}(\overline{x})|_k \mid k \in \mathcal{K}(o)\})$.*

Intuitively, as the elements of $\mathcal{K}$ capture all possible configurations that the queue can take, it is sound to take the maximum cost among them.

Example 11. Following Ex. 8, the quantified queue configuration, that gives the peak cost, accumulates the cost of all nodes in the two cliques, $\widehat{\mathcal{C}}(i)|_{c_1} = \widehat{r} + i * \widehat{p} + i * \widehat{q}$ and $\widehat{\mathcal{C}}(i)|_{c_2} = \widehat{r} + i * \widehat{p} + \widehat{s}$. The maximum between both expressions captures the peak cost for o_1, $\widehat{\mathcal{P}}(main(i), o_1) = max(\ \{\widehat{r} + i * \widehat{p} + i * \widehat{q}, \widehat{r} + i * \widehat{p} + \widehat{s}\})$.

The following theorem states the soundness of our approach.

Theorem 1 (Soundness). *Given a program P with arguments $\overline{x}$, a concrete location lid, and its abstraction o, we have that $\mathcal{P}(P(\overline{x}), lid) \leq \widehat{\mathcal{P}}(P(\overline{x}), o)$.*

5.3 Number of Tasks Instances

As mentioned above, the basic approach has a weakness. From the queue configuration, we might know that there is at most one task running method m at location o. However, if we use $\widehat{\mathcal{C}}(\overline{x})|_{o:m}$, we are accounting for the cost of all tasks running method m at o. We can improve the accuracy as follows. First, we use an instantiation of the cost analysis in Sec. 4 to determine how many instances of tasks running m at o we might have. This can be done by defining function *cost* in Sec. 4 as follows: $cost(inst) = 1$ if *inst* is the entry instruction to a method, and 0 otherwise. We denote by $\widehat{\mathcal{C}^c}(\overline{x})$ the upper bound obtained using such cost model that counts the number of tasks spawned along the execution, and $\widehat{\mathcal{C}^c}(\overline{x})|_{o:m}$ the number of tasks executing m at location o.

Example 12. The expression that bounds the number of calls from main is $\widehat{\mathcal{C}}^c(i) = c(o_1{:}r) + i{*}c(o_1{:}p) + i{*}c(o_1{:}q) + c(o_1{:}s) + c(o_2{:}r) + (i{-}1){*}c(o_2{:}p) + (i{-}1){*}c(o_2{:}q) + c(o_2{:}s)$. It can be seen that CCs are the same as the ones used in Ex. 5. The difference is that when inferring the number of calls we do not account for the cost of each method but rather count 1. Then, $\widehat{\mathcal{C}}^c(i)|_{o_1:q} = i$ and $\widehat{\mathcal{C}}^c(i)|_{o_2:q} = i{-}1$.

Let us assume that the same cost analyzer has been used to approximate $\widehat{\mathcal{C}}$ and $\widehat{\mathcal{C}}^c$, and that the analysis assumed the worst-case cost of m for *all* instances of m. Then, we can gain precision by obtaining the cost as $\widetilde{\mathcal{C}}(\overline{x})|_{o:m} = \widehat{\mathcal{C}}(\overline{x})|_{o:m} / \widehat{\mathcal{C}}^c(\overline{x})|_{o:m}$ if $nact(o{:}m) = 1$ and $\widetilde{\mathcal{C}}(\overline{x})|_{o:m} = \widehat{\mathcal{C}}(\overline{x})|_{o:m}$, otherwise. Intuitively, when the MHP analysis tells us that there is at most one instance of m (by means of *nact*) and, under the above assumptions, the division is achieving the desired effect of leaving the cost of one instance only.

Example 13. As we have seen in Ex. 6, the MHP analysis infers $nact(o_1{:}p) = \infty$ and $nact(o_1{:}q) = 1$. Thus, by the definition of $\widetilde{\mathcal{C}}$, the cost for p is $\widetilde{\mathcal{C}}(i)|_{o_1:p} = i * \widehat{p}$ (the same obtained in Ex. 10). However, for q we can divide the cost accumulated by all invocations to q by the number of calls to q, $\widetilde{\mathcal{C}}(i)|_{o_1:q} = i * \widehat{q}/i = \widehat{q}$.

Unfortunately, it is not always sound to make such division. The problem is that the cost accumulated in a CC for a method m might correspond to the cost of executions of m from different calling contexts that do not necessarily have the same worst-case cost. If we divide the expression $\widehat{\mathcal{C}}(\overline{x})|_{o:m}$ by the number of instances, we are taking the average of the costs, and this is not a sound upper bound of the peak cost, as the following example illustrates.

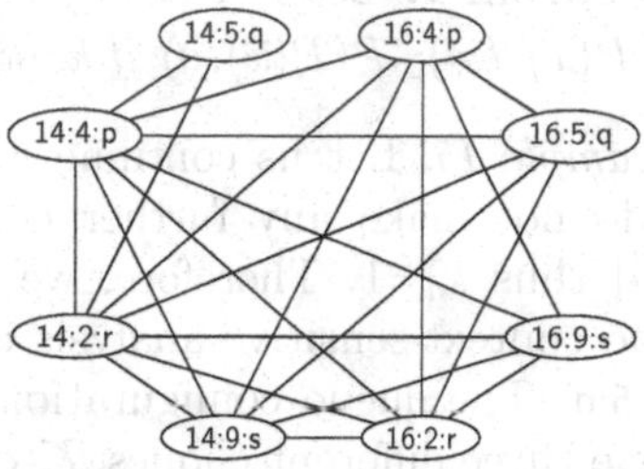

Fig. 5. Queue Config. for Fig. 2

Example 14. Consider a method main′ which is as main of Fig. 2 except that we replace L16 by this!m(x, i − 1), i.e., while main uses two different locations, x and y, in main′ we only use x. Such modification affects the precision because it merges o_1 and o_2 in a single queue, o_1. Now, in main′, s, launched by the first call to m, might run in parallel with q, spawned in the second call to m. Therefore, in Fig. 3 a new edge that connects q and s appears, and consequently, the new queue configuration contains all methods in just one clique $\{p, q, r, s\}$. Moreover, CCs $o_1{:}q$ with $o_2{:}q$ are merged in a single CC $o_1{:}q$. For main′, the cost of $\widehat{q}$ is $\widehat{\mathcal{C}}(i)|_{o:q} = i{*}\widehat{q} + (i{-}1){*}\widehat{q}$, and the number of calls is $\widehat{\mathcal{C}}^c(i)|_{o:q} = i + (i{-}1)$. Assume that the cost of q is $\widehat{q} = n * 5$ which is a function on the parameter n. The worst-case cost for $\widehat{q}$ depends on the calling context: in the context at L14, we have $\widehat{q} = i{*}5$ while in L16, we have $\widehat{q} = (i{-}1){*}5$. Then, the cost that we obtain for main′ is $\widehat{\mathcal{C}}(i)|_{o:q} = i{*}i{*}5 + (i{-}1){*}((i{-}1){*}5)$. The division of $\widehat{\mathcal{C}}(i)$ by $\widehat{\mathcal{C}}^c(i)$ is not sound because it computes the average cost of all calls to q, rather than the peak.

Importantly, we can determine when the above division is sound in a static way. The information we are seeking is within the *call graph* for the program: (1) If there are not convergence nodes in the call graph (i.e., the call graph is a tree), then it is guaranteed that we do not have invocations to the same method from different contexts. In this case, if there are multiple invocations, it is because we are invoking m from the same context within a loop. Typically, automated cost analyzers assume the same worst-case cost for all loop iterations and, in such case, it is sound to make the division. Note that if the total cost analysis infers a different cost for each loop iteration, the accuracy improvement in this section cannot be applied; (2) If there are convergence nodes, then we need to ensure that the context-sensitive analysis distinguishes the calls that arise from different points, i.e., we have different CCs for them. This can be ensured if the length of the chains of call sites used in the context by the analysis, denoted k, is larger than k_d, the depth of the subgraph of the call graph whose root is the first convergence node encountered. Note that, in the presence of recursive methods, we will not be able to apply this accuracy improvement since the depth is unbounded. Theorem 1 holds for $\widetilde{\mathcal{C}}$ if the context considered by the analysis is greater than k_d.

Theorem 2. *Let $\widetilde{\mathcal{P}}(P(\overline{x}),o)$ be the peak cost computed using $\widetilde{\mathcal{C}}$. We have that $\mathcal{P}(P(\overline{x}),lid) \leq \widetilde{\mathcal{P}}(P(\overline{x}),o)$ if $k > k_d$, where k is the length of the context used.*

Example 15. Let us continue with main′ of Ex. 14. Assuming that p, q, r and s do not make any further call, the call graph has m as convergence node, and thus k_d=1. Therefore, we apply the context-sensitive analysis with k=2. The context-sensitive analysis distinguishes 14:4:p, 16:4:p, and, in q, 14:5:q and 16:5:q. The queue configuration is showed in Fig. 5. In contrast to Ex. 14 we have three different cliques, $\mathcal{K}(o_1)$={{14:4:p, 14:2:r, 14:5:q}, {14:4:p, 14:2:r, 14:9:s, 16:4:p, 16:2:r, 16:5:q}, {14:4:p, 14:2:r, 14:9:s, 16:4:p, 16:2:r, 16:9:s}}, which capture more precisely the queue states (e.g., we know that 16:5:q cannot be in the queue with 16:9:s but it might be with 14:9:s). Besides, we have two different CCs for q, 14:5:q and 16:5:q, which allow us to safely apply the division as to obtain the cost of a single instance of q for the two different contexts. We obtain $\widehat{\mathcal{C}}(i)|_{\mathsf{14:5:q}}=i*i*5$ and $\widehat{\mathcal{C}}(i)|_{\mathsf{16:5:q}}=(i-1)*((i-1)*5)$, and for the number of calls, $\widehat{\mathcal{C}}^c(i)|_{\mathsf{14:5:q}}=i$ and $\widehat{\mathcal{C}}^c(i)|_{\mathsf{16:5:q}}=i-1$. Using such expressions we compute $\widetilde{\mathcal{C}}(i)|_{\mathsf{14:5:q}} = i*5$ and $\widetilde{\mathcal{C}}(i)|_{\mathsf{16:5:q}} = (i-1)*5$ which are sound and precise over-approximations for the cost due to calls to q.

6 Experimental Evaluation

We have implemented our analysis in SACO [2] and applied it to some typical examples of distributed systems: BBuffer, a bounded-buffer for communicating producers and consumers; MailS, a client-server distributed system; Chat, a chat application; DistHT, a distributed hash table; and P2P, a peer-to-peer network. Experiments have been performed on an Intel Core i5 (1.8GHz, 4GB RAM), running OSX 10.8. Table 1 summarizes the results obtained. Columns Bench.

Table 1. Experimental results (times in seconds)

				Context Insensitive					Context Sensitive				
Bench.	loc	$\#_\mathsf{c}$	T	$\#_\mathsf{q}$	$\%_{\overline{q}}$	$\%_m$	$\%_M$	$\%_{\widehat{\mathcal{P}}}$	$\#'_\mathsf{q}$	$\%'_{\overline{q}}$	$\%'_m$	$\%'_M$	$\%_{\widetilde{\mathcal{P}}}$
BBuffer	107	6	2.0	9	66.7%	50.0%	100%	78.1%	10	52.2%	17.6%	100%	31.6%
MailS	97	6	2.8	8	75.1%	71.6%	100%	81.7%	8	73.3%	71.6%	100%	81.7%
DistHT	150	4	2.5	8	69.4%	53.7%	100%	88.0%	8	69.4%	46.4%	100%	88.0%
Chat	328	10	2.4	16	66.0%	50.0%	100%	90.8%	16	66.0%	7.5%	100%	90.8%
P2P	259	9	28.0	26	52.9%	91.1%	100%	97.3%	32	32.3%	44.6%	100%	64.7%
Mean					66.0%	62.3%	100%	87.1%		58.6%	37.46%	100%	71.3%

and loc show, resp., the name and the number of program lines. Column $\#_\mathsf{c}$ shows the number of locations identified by the analysis. Columns T and $\#_\mathsf{q}$ show, resp., the time to perform the analysis and the number of cliques.

We aim at comparing the gain of using peak cost analysis w.r.t. total cost. Such gain is obtained by evaluating the expression that divides the peak cost by the total cost for 15 different values of the input parameters, and computing the average. The gain is computed at the level of locations, by comparing the peak cost for the location with the total cost for such location in all columns except in $\%_{\overline{q}}$, where we show the average gain at the level of cliques. Columns $\%_m$ and $\%_M$ show, resp., the greatest and smallest gain among all locations. Column $\%_{\widehat{\mathcal{P}}}$ shows the average gain weighted by the cost associated with each location (locations with higher resource consumption have greater weight). Columns $\#'_\mathsf{q}$, $\%'_{\overline{q}}$, $\%'_m$, $\%'_M$, and $\%_{\widetilde{\mathcal{P}}}$ contain the same information for the context-sensitive analysis. As we do not have yet an implementation of the context-sensitive analysis, we have replicated those methods that are called from different contexts. DistHT and Chat do not need replication. The last row shows the arithmetic mean of all results.

We can observe in the table that the precision gained by considering all possible queue states ($\%_{\overline{q}}$ and $\%'_{\overline{q}}$) is significant. In the context-insensitive analysis, it ranges from a gain of 53% to 75% (on average 66%). Such value is improved in the context sensitive analysis, resulting in an average gain of 58.6%. This indicates that the cliques capture accurately the cost accumulated in the different states of the locations' queues. The gain of the context sensitive analysis is justified by the larger number of cliques ($\#'_\mathsf{q}$) in BBuffer and P2P. The maximal gains showed in columns $\%_m$ (and $\%'_m$) indicate that the accuracy can be improved on average 62.3% (and 37.46%). The minimal gains in $\%_M$ and $\%'_M$ are always 100%, i.e., no gain. This means that in all benchmarks we have at least one state that accumulates the cost of all methods executed at its location (typically because await is never used). Columns $\%_{\widehat{\mathcal{P}}}$ and $\%_{\widetilde{\mathcal{P}}}$ show, in BBuffer and P2P, that $\widetilde{\mathcal{P}}$ significantly outperforms $\widehat{\mathcal{P}}$. Such improvement is achieved by a more precise configuration graph that contains more cliques, and by the division on the number of calls in methods that require a significant part of the resource consumption. However, in MailS, $\widetilde{\mathcal{P}}$ does not improve the precision of $\widehat{\mathcal{P}}$. This is because the methods that contain one active instance are not part of the cliques that lead to the peak cost of the location. Despite of the NP-completeness of the clique problem, the time spent performing the clique computation is irrelevant in comparison with the time taken by the upper bound computation (less than 50ms for all benchmarks). All in all, we argue that our experiments demonstrate the accuracy of the peak cost analysis, even in its context insensitive version, with respect to the total cost analysis.

7 Conclusions, Related and Future Work

To the best of our knowledge, our work constitutes the first analysis framework for peak cost of distributed systems. This is an essential problem in the context of distributed systems. It is of great help to dimension the distributed system in terms of processing requirements, and queue sizes. Besides, it paves the way to the accurate prediction of response times of distributed locations. The task-level analysis in [4] is developed for a specific cost model that infers the peak of tasks that a location can have. There are several important differences with our work: (1) we are generic in the notion of cost and our framework can be instantiated to measure different types of cost, among them the task-level; (2) the distributed model that we consider is more expressive as it allows concurrent behaviours within each location (by means of instruction await), while [4] assumes a simpler asynchronous language in which tasks are run to completion; (3) the analysis requires the generation of non-standard recurrence equations, while our analysis benefits from the upper bounds obtained using standard recurrence equations for total cost, without requiring any modification. Indeed, the analysis in [4] could be reformulated in our framework using the MHP analysis of [11,12].

Also, the peak heap consumption in the presence of garbage collection is a non cumulative type of resource. The analysis in [6] presents a sophisticated framework for inferring the peak heap consumption by assuming different garbage collection models. As before, in contrast to ours, the analysis is based on generating non-standard equations and for a specific type of resource. In this case, the differences are even more notable as the language in [6] is sequential. Analysis and verification techniques of concurrent programs seek finite representations of the program traces which avoid the exponential explosion in the number of traces (see [8] and its references). In this sense, our queue configurations are a coarse representation of the traces. As future work, we plan to further improve the accuracy of our analysis by splitting tasks into fragments according to the processor release points within the task. Intuitively, if a task contains an await instruction we would divide into the code before the await and the code after. This way, we do not need to accumulate the cost of the whole task if only the fragment after the await has been queued.

Acknowledgments. This work was funded partially by the EU project FP7-ICT-610582 ENVISAGE: Engineering Virtualized Services (`http://www.envisage-project.eu`) and by the Spanish projects TIN2008-05624 and TIN2012-38137.

References

1. Agarwal, S., Barik, R., Sarkar, V., Shyamasundar, R.K.: May-happen-in-parallel analysis of x10 programs. In: Yelick, K.A., Mellor-Crummey, J.M. (eds.) PPOPP, pp. 183–193. ACM (2007)
2. Albert, E., Arenas, P., Flores-Montoya, A., Genaim, S., Gómez-Zamalloa, M., Martin-Martin, E., Puebla, G., Román-Díez, G.: SACO: Static Analyzer for Concurrent Objects. In: Ábrahám, E., Havelund, K. (eds.) TACAS 2014. LNCS, vol. 8413, pp. 562–567. Springer, Heidelberg (2014)
3. Albert, E., Arenas, P., Genaim, S., Gómez-Zamalloa, M., Puebla, G.: Cost Analysis of Concurrent OO programs. In: Yang, H. (ed.) APLAS 2011. LNCS, vol. 7078, pp. 238–254. Springer, Heidelberg (2011)
4. Albert, E., Arenas, P., Genaim, S., Zanardini, D.: Task-Level Analysis for a Language with Async-Finish parallelism. In: Proc. of LCTES 2011, pp. 21–30. ACM Press (2011)
5. Albert, E., Flores-Montoya, A.E., Genaim, S.: Analysis of May-Happen-in-Parallel in Concurrent Objects. In: Giese, H., Rosu, G. (eds.) FMOODS/FORTE 2012. LNCS, vol. 7273, pp. 35–51. Springer, Heidelberg (2012)
6. Albert, E., Genaim, S., Gómez-Zamalloa, M.: Heap Space Analysis for Garbage Collected Languages. Science of Computer Programming 78(9), 1427–1448 (2013)
7. Barik, R.: Efficient computation of may-happen-in-parallel information for concurrent java programs. In: Ayguadé, E., Baumgartner, G., Ramanujam, J., Sadayappan, P. (eds.) LCPC 2005. LNCS, vol. 4339, pp. 152–169. Springer, Heidelberg (2006)
8. Farzan, A., Kincaid, Z., Podelski, A.: Inductive data flow graphs. In: POPL, pp. 129–142. ACM (2013)
9. Gulwani, S., Mehra, K.K., Chilimbi, T.M.: Speed: Precise and Efficient Static Estimation of Program Computational Complexity. In: Proc. of POPL 2009, pp. 127–139. ACM (2009)
10. Hoffmann, J., Aehlig, K., Hofmann, M.: Multivariate Amortized Resource Analysis. In: Proc. of POPL 2011, pp. 357–370. ACM (2011)
11. Lee, J.K., Palsberg, J.: Featherweight x10: A core calculus for async-finish parallelism. SIGPLAN Not. 45(5), 25–36 (2010)
12. Lee, J.K., Palsberg, J., Majumdar, R.: Complexity results for may-happen-in-parallel analysis (2010) (manuscript)
13. Milanova, A., Rountev, A., Ryder, B.G.: Parameterized Object Sensitivity for Points-to Analysis for Java. ACM Trans. Softw. Eng. Methodol. 14, 1–41 (2005)
14. Shapiro, M., Horwitz, S.: Fast and Accurate Flow-Insensitive Points-To Analysis. In: Proc. of POPL 1997, Paris, France, pp. 1–14. ACM (January 1997)
15. Smaragdakis, Y., Bravenboer, M., Lhoták, O.: Pick your Contexts Well: Understanding Object-Sensitivity. In: Proc. of POPL 2011, pp. 17–30. ACM (2011)
16. Sridharan, M., Bodík, R.: Refinement-based context-sensitive points-to analysis for Java. In: PLDI, pp. 387–400 (2006)
17. Wegbreit, B.: Mechanical Program Analysis. Communications ACM 18(9), 528–539 (1975)
18. Zuleger, F., Gulwani, S., Sinn, M., Veith, H.: Bound analysis of imperative programs with the size-change abstraction. In: Yahav, E. (ed.) Static Analysis. LNCS, vol. 6887, pp. 280–297. Springer, Heidelberg (2011)

Backward Analysis via over-Approximate Abstraction and under-Approximate Subtraction

Alexey Bakhirkin[1], Josh Berdine[2], and Nir Piterman[1]

[1] University of Leicester, Department of Computer Science
[2] Microsoft Research

Abstract. We propose a novel approach for computing weakest liberal safe preconditions of programs. The standard approaches, which call for either under-approximation of a greatest fixed point, or complementation of a least fixed point, are often difficult to apply successfully. Our approach relies on a different decomposition of the weakest precondition of loops. We exchange the greatest fixed point for the computation of a least fixed point above a recurrent set, instead of the bottom element. Convergence is achieved using over-approximation, while in order to maintain soundness we use an under-approximating logical subtraction operation. Unlike general complementation, subtraction more easily allows for increased precision in case its arguments are related. The approach is not restricted to a specific abstract domain and we use it to analyze programs using the abstract domains of intervals and of 3-valued structures.

1 Introduction

Forward static analyses usually compute program invariants which hold of executions starting from given initial conditions, e.g., over-approximations of reachable states. Conversely, backward static analyses for universal properties compute program invariants which ensure given assertions hold of all executions, e.g., under-approximations of safe states. Forward analysis of programs has been a notable success, while such backward analysis has seen much less research and is done less frequently (a notable example is [17]).

The standard formulation of forward analyses involves over-approximating a least fixed point of a recursive system of equations (transformers) that over-approximate the forward semantics of commands. Conversely, backward analyses for universal properties usually involve under-approximating a greatest fixed point of under-approximate equations.

The over-approximating abstractions used by forward analyses are far more common and well-developed than the under-approximations used by backward analyses. One approach to under-approximation is via over-approximate abstraction and under-approximate complementation $\overline{(\cdot)}$. For example, lower widening $p \mathbin{\underline{\triangledown}} q$ may be seen as $\overline{\overline{p} \triangledown \overline{q}}$. However, computing the complement is, in many cases, infeasible or impractical (e.g., for 3-valued structures [22], separation logic [8], or polyhedra [12]).

Here, we suggest an alternative backward analysis approach that uses least fixed-point approximation, and an *under-approximate logical subtraction* operation in lieu

M. Müller-Olm and H. Seidl (eds.): SAS 2014, LNCS 8723, pp. 34–50, 2014.

of complementation. (Logical subtraction can also be understood as *and with complement* or *not implies*.) We show how to extend a computation of a recurrent set of a program with a least fixed-point approximation to obtain an under-approximation of the safe states from which *no* execution can lead to a failure (such as violating an assertion, dividing by zero, or dereferencing a dangling-pointer – i.e., an event that causes program execution to immediately abort and signal an error). Soundness is ensured by subtracting an over-approximation of the unsafe states.

Using subtraction instead of complementation has several advantages. First, it is easier to define in power set domains for which complementation can be hard or impractical. Second, as the approximations of safe and unsafe states are the results of analyzing the same code, they are strongly related and so subtraction may be more precise than a general under-approximate complementation.

Our approach is not restricted to a specific abstract domain and we use it to analyze numeric examples (using the domain of intervals) and examples coming from shape analysis (using the domain of 3-valued structures).

2 Preliminaries

Let $\mathcal{U}$ denote the set of program *memory* states and $\epsilon \notin \mathcal{U}$ a *failure* state. The concrete domain for our analysis is the power set $\mathcal{P}(\mathcal{U})$ ordered by $\subseteq$, with least element $\varnothing$, greatest element $\mathcal{U}$, join $\cup$, and meet $\cap$.

We introduce an abstract domain $\mathcal{D}$ (with $\sqsubseteq$, $\bot$, $\top$, $\sqcup$, and $\sqcap$) and a concretization function $\gamma : \mathcal{D} \to \mathcal{P}(\mathcal{U})$. For an element of an abstract domain, $d \in \mathcal{D}$, $\gamma(d)$ is the set of states represented by it. For example, for a program with two variables x and y, an element of the interval domain $d = \langle x : [1; 2], y : [3; 4]\rangle$ represents all states satisfying $(1 \le x \le 2) \wedge (3 \le y \le 4)$, i.e., $\gamma(d) = \{(x, y) \mid 1 \le x \le 2 \wedge 3 \le y \le 4\}$.

For a lattice $\mathcal{L}$, we define *complementation* as a function $\overline{(\cdot)} : \mathcal{L} \to \mathcal{L}$ such that for every $l \in \mathcal{L}$, $\gamma(\overline{l}) \cap \gamma(l) = \varnothing$ (i.e., they represent disjoint sets of states – but we do not require that $\gamma(\overline{l}) \cup \gamma(l) = \mathcal{U}$). For example, if $d \in \mathcal{D}$ over-approximates the unsafe states, then $\overline{d}$ under-approximates the safe states. For our concrete domain $\mathcal{P}(\mathcal{U})$ (and similarly, for every power set of atomic elements), we can use standard set-theoretic complement: $\overline{S} = \mathcal{U} \setminus S$.

We define *subtraction* as a function $(\cdot - \cdot) : \mathcal{L} \to \mathcal{L} \to \mathcal{L}$ such that for $l_1, l_2 \in \mathcal{L}$ we have $\gamma(l_1 - l_2) \subseteq \gamma(l_1)$ and $\gamma(l_1 - l_2) \cap \gamma(l_2) = \varnothing$. For example, given a domain $\mathcal{D}$, we can define subtraction for the power set domain $\mathcal{P}(\mathcal{D})$ as

$$D_1 - D_2 = \{d_1 \in D_1 \mid \forall\, d_2 \in D_2.\, \gamma(d_1) \cap \gamma(d_2) = \varnothing\} \qquad (1)$$

This way, subtraction can be defined in e.g., the domain of 3-valued structures that does not readily support complementation. We claim that a useful subtraction is often easier to define than a useful complementation. We also note that for every $l_0 \in \mathcal{L}$, the function $\lambda l.(l_0 - l)$ is a complementation. However, for a given l, the accuracy of this complement depends on the actual choice of l_0.

2.1 Programming Language Syntax and Semantics

We consider a simple structured programming language. Given a set of *atomic statements* A ranged over by a, statements C of the language are constructed as follows:

$C ::= a$	atomic statement
$\mid C_1 \,;\, C_2$	sequential composition: executes C_1 and then C_2
$\mid C_1 + C_2$	branch: non-deterministically branches to either C_1 or C_2
$\mid C^*$	loop: iterated sequential composition of ≥ 0 copies of C

We assume A contains: the empty statement `skip`, an assertion statement `assert` φ (for a state formula φ), and an assumption statement $[\varphi]$. Informally, an assertion immediately aborts the execution and signals an error if φ is not satisfied, and we consider that there are no *valid* executions violating assumptions. Standard conditionals `if`(φ) C_1 `else` C_2 can be expressed by $([\varphi]; C_1) + ([\neg\varphi]; C_2)$. Similarly, loops `while`($\varphi$) C can be expressed by $([\varphi]; C)^* \,;\, [\neg\varphi]$.

A state formula φ denotes a set of non-failure states $[\![\varphi]\!] \subseteq \mathcal{U}$ that satisfy φ. The semantics of a statement C is a relation $[\![C]\!] \subseteq \mathcal{U} \times (\mathcal{U} \cup \{\epsilon\})$. For $s, s' \in \mathcal{U}$, $[\![C]\!](s, s')$ means that executing C in state s *may* change the state to s'. Then, $[\![C]\!](s, \epsilon)$ means that s is unsafe: executing C from state s may result in failure (may cause the program to immediately abort). Let $\Delta_{\mathcal{U}}$ be the diagonal relation on states $\Delta_{\mathcal{U}} = \{(s, s) \mid s \in \mathcal{U}\}$. Let composition of relations in $\mathcal{U} \times (\mathcal{U} \cup \{\epsilon\})$ be defined as $S \fatsemi R = (R \cup \{(\epsilon, \epsilon)\}) \circ S$ where $\circ$ is standard composition of relations. Fixed points in $\mathcal{U} \times (\mathcal{U} \cup \{\epsilon\})$ are with respect to the subset order, where $\operatorname{lfp} \lambda X.\, F(X)$ denotes the least fixed point of $\lambda X.\, F(X)$, and similarly, $\operatorname{gfp} \lambda X.\, F(X)$ denotes the greatest fixed point of $\lambda X.\, F(X)$. For an atomic statement a, we assume that $[\![a]\!]$ is a predefined left-total relation, and the semantics of other statements is defined as follows:

$$[\![\mathtt{skip}]\!] = \Delta_{\mathcal{U}} \qquad [\![C_1 \,;\, C_2]\!] = [\![C_1]\!] \fatsemi [\![C_2]\!]$$
$$[\![[\varphi]]\!] = \{(s, s) \mid s \in [\![\varphi]\!]\} \qquad [\![C_1 + C_2]\!] = [\![C_1]\!] \cup [\![C_2]\!]$$
$$[\![\mathtt{assert}\,\varphi]\!] = \{(s, s) \mid s \in [\![\varphi]\!]\} \cup \{(s, \epsilon) \mid s \in \mathcal{U} \wedge s \notin [\![\varphi]\!]\} \qquad [\![C^*]\!] = \operatorname{lfp} \lambda X.\, \Delta_{\mathcal{U}} \cup ([\![C]\!] \fatsemi X)$$

Note that the assumption that atomic statements denote left-total relations excludes statements that affect control flow such as `break` or `continue`. In what follows, we constrain considered programs in the following way. Programs cannot have nested loops and assumption statements $[\varphi]$ are only allowed to appear at the start of branches and at the entry and exit of loops (they cannot be used as normal atomic statements):

$$C ::= a \mid C_1 \,;\, C_2 \mid ([\varphi] \,;\, C_1) + ([\psi] \,;\, C_2) \mid ([\psi] \,;\, C)^* \,;\, [\varphi]$$

We require that for branches and loops, $\varphi \vee \psi = 1$ (i.e., $[\![\varphi]\!] \cup [\![\psi]\!] = \mathcal{U}$). That is, for a loop-free statement, the domain of its semantics is $\mathcal{U}$. We also require that the language of state formulas is closed under negation.

2.2 Fixed-Point Characterizations of Safe and Unsafe States

Given a statement C and a set of states $S \subseteq \mathcal{U}$, we define:

- $pre(C, S) = \{s \in \mathcal{U} \mid \exists s' \in S.\ [\![C]\!](s, s')\}$. The states that may lead to S after executing C.
- $fail(C) = \{s \in \mathcal{U} \mid [\![C]\!](s, \epsilon)\}$. The *unsafe* states: those that may cause C to fail.
- $wp(C, S) = \{s \in \mathcal{U} \mid \forall s' \in \mathcal{U} \cup \{\epsilon\}.\ [\![C]\!](s, s') \Rightarrow s' \in S\}$. The *weakest liberal precondition* that ensures safety [7] – safe states that must lead to S if execution of the statement terminates.

We abbreviate $pre(C, S) \cup fail(C)$ to $pre{+}fail(C, S)$.

Lemma 1. *For a statement C and a set of states $S \subseteq \mathcal{U}$, $wp(C, S) = \mathcal{U} \setminus pre{+}fail(C, \mathcal{U} \setminus S)$.*

The proof is a direct calculation based on the definitions. See the companion technical report [3] for proofs.

For a program C, our goal is to compute (an under-approximation of) $wp(C, \mathcal{U})$, and (an over-approximation of) its complement $fail(C)$. If we are interested in termination with specific postcondition φ, we add an `assert` φ statement to the end of the program. We characterize these sets (as is standard [9,10]) as solutions to two functionals P and N that associate a statement C and a set of states S (resp., V) $\subseteq \mathcal{U}$ with a predicate $P(C, S)$, resp., $N(C, V)$. $P(C, S)$ (the *positive side*) denotes the states that must either lead to successful termination in S or cause non-termination, and $N(C, V)$ (the *negative side*) denotes the states that may lead to failure or termination in V.

$$
\begin{aligned}
P(a, S) &= wp(a, S) & N(a, V) &= pre{+}fail(a, V)\\
P([\varphi], S) &= [\![\neg\varphi]\!] \cup S & N([\varphi], V) &= [\![\varphi]\!] \cap V\\
P(\texttt{assert}\,\varphi, S) &= [\![\varphi]\!] \cap S & N(\texttt{assert}\,\varphi, V) &= [\![\neg\varphi]\!] \cup V\\
P(C_1; C_2, S) &= P(C_1, P(C_2, S)) & N(C_1; C_2, V) &= N(C_1, N(C_2, V))\\
P(C_1 + C_2, S) &= P(C_1, S) \cap P(C_2, S) & N(C_1 + C_2, V) &= N(C_1, V) \cup N(C_2, V)\\
P(C^*, S) &= \text{gfp}\,\lambda X.\, S \cap P(C, X) & N(C^*, V) &= \text{lfp}\,\lambda Y.\, V \cup N(C, Y)
\end{aligned}
$$

Lemma 2. *For a statement C and set of states $S \subseteq \mathcal{U}$, $P(C, S) = \mathcal{U} \setminus N(C, \mathcal{U} \setminus S)$.*

The proof is by structural induction.

Lemma 3. *For a statement C and sets of states $S, V \subseteq \mathcal{U}$, $P(C, S) = wp(C, S)$, and $N(C, V) = pre{+}fail(C, V)$.*

The proof is by structural induction, relying on continuity of *pre+fail*.

3 Least Fixed-Point Characterization of Safe States

The direct solution of the positive side is by under-approximating a greatest fixed point. This can be problematic since most domains are geared towards over-approximating least fixed points. Hence, we are not going to approximate the greatest fixed point for the positive side directly. Instead, we restate the problem for loops such that the resulting characterization leads to a least fixed point computation where termination is ensured by using an appropriate over-approximate abstraction.

In this section, we focus on the looping statement:

$$C_{\text{loop}} = ([\psi]\ ;\ C_{\text{body}})^*\ ;\ [\varphi] \tag{2}$$

where C_{body} is the *loop body*; if ψ holds the execution may enter the loop body; and if φ holds the execution may exit the loop. To simplify the presentation, in what follows, we assume that the semantics of C_{body} is directly known. Since C_{body} is itself loop-free, $[\![C_{\text{body}}]\!]$ does not induce fixed points, and the transformers for the loop body can be obtained, e.g., by combining the transformers for its sub-statements.

3.1 Recurrent Sets

We reformulate the characterizations of safe states in terms of least fixed points with the use of recurrent sets. For the loop in (2), an *existential recurrent set* is a set $R_\exists$, s.t.

$$\begin{aligned} &R_\exists \subseteq [\![\psi]\!] \\ &\forall s \in R_\exists.\ \exists s' \in R_\exists.\ [\![C_{\text{body}}]\!](s, s') \end{aligned}$$

These are states that may cause non-termination (i.e., cause the computation to stay inside the loop forever). For the loop in (2), a *universal recurrent set* is a set $R_\forall$, s.t.

$$\begin{aligned} &R_\forall \subseteq [\![\neg\varphi]\!] \\ &\forall s \in R_\forall.\ \big(\forall s' \in \mathcal{U} \cup \{\epsilon\}.\ [\![C_{\text{body}}]\!](s, s') \Rightarrow s' \in R_\forall\big) \end{aligned}$$

These are states that must cause non-termination. For practical reasons discussed later in Sect. 4.2, we *do not* require these sets to be maximal.

Lemma 4. *For the loop* $C_{\text{loop}} = ([\psi]\ ;\ C_{\text{body}})^*\ ;\ [\varphi]$*, and a set of states* $S \subseteq \mathcal{U}$

$$R_\forall \subseteq P(C_{\text{loop}}, S) \qquad\qquad R_\exists \smallsetminus N(C_{\text{loop}}, \mathcal{U} \smallsetminus S) \subseteq P(C_{\text{loop}}, S)$$

For $R_\forall$, the proof correlates universal recurrence and *wp*, relying on monotonicity of $P(C_{\text{loop}}, \cdot)$. For $R_\exists$, the result follows from Lemma 2.

3.2 Positive Least Fixed Point via Recurrent Sets

We begin with an informal explanation of how we move from a greatest fixed point formulation to a least fixed point one. Observe that for the loop in (2), the positive and negative sides (following the definition in Sect. 2.2) are characterized by:

$$\begin{aligned} P(C_{\text{loop}}, S) &= \text{gfp}\,\lambda X.\,([\![\neg\varphi]\!] \cup S) \cap \big([\![\neg\psi]\!] \cup P(C_{\text{body}}, X)\big) \\ N(C_{\text{loop}}, V) &= \text{lfp}\,\lambda Y.\,([\![\varphi]\!] \cap V) \cup \big([\![\psi]\!] \cap N(C_{\text{body}}, Y)\big) \end{aligned} \tag{3}$$

Then, since loops only occur at the top level, a program C_{prg} that contains the loop C_{loop} can be expressed as $C_{\text{init}}\ ;\ C_{\text{loop}}\ ;\ C_{\text{rest}}$ (where C_{init} or C_{rest} may be `skip`). Let:

- $P_{\text{rest}} = P(C_{\text{rest}}, \mathcal{U})$ – the safe states of the loop's continuation.
- $N_{\text{rest}} = N(C_{\text{rest}}, \varnothing)$ – states that may cause failure of the loop's continuation. Note that $N_{\text{rest}} = \mathcal{U} \smallsetminus P_{\text{rest}}$.

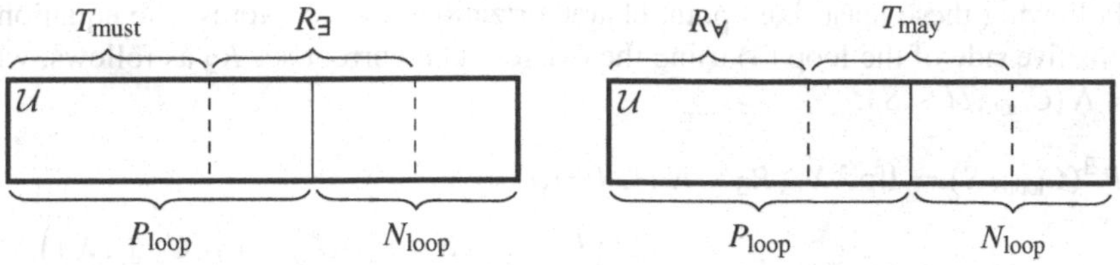

(a) Partitioning with existential recurrence. (b) Partitioning with universal recurrence.

Fig. 1. Partitioning of the states at the loop entry

- $P_{\text{loop}} = P(C_{\text{loop}}, P_{\text{rest}})$ – the safe states of the loop and its continuation.
- $N_{\text{loop}} = N(C_{\text{loop}}, N_{\text{rest}})$ – states that may cause failure of the loop or its continuation. Note that $N_{\text{loop}} = \mathcal{U} \smallsetminus P_{\text{loop}}$.

For the loop in (2), Fig. 1 shows how the states entering the loop can be partitioned. In the figure, by T_{must}, we denote the states that must cause successful termination *of the loop* (in a state belonging to P_{rest}), and by T_{may}, we denote states that may cause successful termination.

Fig. 1a shows that the positive side for the loop in (2) can be partitioned into the following two parts:

- $R_{\exists} \smallsetminus N_{\text{loop}}$ – states that may cause non-termination but may not fail;
- T_{must} – states that must cause successful termination of the loop.

T_{must} can be characterized as the least fixed point:

$$T_{\text{must}} = \text{lfp}\, \lambda X.\, (\llbracket \neg\psi \rrbracket \cap P_{\text{rest}}) \cup \Big(\big((\llbracket \psi \rrbracket \cap P_{\text{rest}}) \cup \llbracket \neg\varphi \rrbracket \big) \cap wp(C_{\text{body}}, X) \Big)$$

Intuitively, the states in $\llbracket \neg\psi \rrbracket \cap P_{\text{rest}}$ cause the loop to immediately terminate (such that the rest of the program does not fail), those in $((\llbracket \psi \rrbracket \cap P_{\text{rest}}) \cup \llbracket \neg\varphi \rrbracket) \cap wp(C_{\text{loop}}, \llbracket \neg\psi \rrbracket \cap P_{\text{rest}})$ can make one iteration through the loop, and so on.

Fig. 1b shows that the positive side can also be partitioned in another way:

- $R_{\forall}$ – states that must cause non-termination of the loop;
- $T_{\text{may}} \smallsetminus N_{\text{loop}}$ – states that may cause successful termination but may not fail.

In a way similar to [10], T_{may} can be characterized as the least fixed point:

$$T_{\text{may}} = \text{lfp}\, \lambda X.\, (\llbracket \varphi \rrbracket \cap P_{\text{rest}}) \cup (\llbracket \psi \rrbracket \cap pre(C_{\text{body}}, X))$$

Intuitively, from states $\llbracket \varphi \rrbracket \cap P_{\text{rest}}$, the loop *may* immediately terminate in a state safe for C_{rest}, from states $\llbracket \psi \rrbracket \cap pre(C_{\text{body}}, \llbracket \varphi \rrbracket \cap P_{\text{rest}})$ the loop may make one iteration and terminate, and so on. From this, it can be shown that

$$T_{\text{may}} \smallsetminus N_{\text{loop}} = \text{lfp}\, \lambda X.\, \big((\llbracket \varphi \rrbracket \cap P_{\text{rest}}) \smallsetminus N_{\text{loop}}\big) \cup \big((\llbracket \neg\varphi \rrbracket \cap pre(C_{\text{body}}, X)) \smallsetminus N_{\text{loop}}\big)$$

We replace ψ with $\neg\varphi$, since the states in $\llbracket \psi \rrbracket \cap \llbracket \varphi \rrbracket \cap pre(C_{\text{body}}, X)$ are either already included in the first disjunct (if belonging to P_{rest}), or are unsafe and removed by subtraction.

Following these least fixed point characterizations, we re-express the equation for the positive side of the loop (3) using the existential recurrent set $R_\exists$ as follows, where $N = N(C_{\text{loop}}, \mathcal{U} \smallsetminus S)$:

$$\begin{aligned} P^{\exists}(C_{\text{loop}}, S) = \operatorname{lfp} \lambda X.\, &(R_\exists \smallsetminus N) \cup (\llbracket \neg\psi \rrbracket \cap S) \\ &\cup \Big(((\llbracket \psi \rrbracket \cap S) \cup \llbracket \neg\varphi \rrbracket) \cap \mathit{wp}(C_{\text{body}}, X) \Big) \end{aligned} \tag{4}$$

or using the universal recurrent set $R_\forall$ as follows:

$$\begin{aligned} P^{\forall}(C_{\text{loop}}, S) = \operatorname{lfp} \lambda X.\, &R_\forall \cup ((\llbracket \varphi \rrbracket \cap S) \smallsetminus N) \\ &\cup \Big((\llbracket \neg\varphi \rrbracket \cap \mathit{pre}(C_{\text{body}}, X)) \smallsetminus N \Big) \end{aligned} \tag{5}$$

Theorem 1. *The alternative characterizations of the positive side of the loop:* (4) *and* (5) *– under-approximate the original characterization* (3)*. That is, for a set $S \subseteq \mathcal{U}$,*

$$P^{\exists}(C_{\text{loop}}, S) \subseteq P(C_{\text{loop}}, S) \qquad P^{\forall}(C_{\text{loop}}, S) \subseteq P(C_{\text{loop}}, S)$$

4 Approximate Characterizations

In Sects. 2.2 and 3.2, we characterized both the negative and the positive sides as least fixed points. For the negative side, our goal is to over-approximate the least fixed point, and we can do that using standard tools. That is, we move to an abstract domain $\mathcal{D}(\sqsubseteq, \bot, \top, \sqcup, \sqcap, \triangledown)$ where widening $\triangledown$ and join $\sqcup$ may coincide for domains that do not allow infinite ascending chains. For the positive side our goal is to under-approximate the least fixed point, and to do so, we build an increasing chain of its approximations and use the previously computed negative side and subtraction to ensure soundness.

As before, since we do not allow nested loops, we assume that abstract transformers for loop bodies are given. For a loop-free statement C and $d \in \mathcal{D}$, we assume: over- and under-approximating transformers $\mathit{pre}^\sharp(C, d)$ and $\mathit{wp}^\flat(C, d)$, over-approximating operation $\mathit{fail}^\sharp(C)$; and for assumption statements $[\varphi]$: under- and over-approximate transformers $[\varphi, d]^\flat$ and $[\varphi, d]^\sharp$ such that:

$$\begin{aligned} &\gamma(\mathit{pre}^\sharp(C, d)) \supseteq \mathit{pre}(C, \gamma(d)) && \gamma(\mathit{fail}^\sharp(C)) \supseteq \mathit{fail}(C) \\ &\gamma(\mathit{wp}^\flat(C, d)) \subseteq \mathit{wp}(C, \gamma(d)) && \gamma([\varphi, d]^\flat) \subseteq \llbracket \varphi \rrbracket \cap \gamma(d) \subseteq \gamma([\varphi, d]^\sharp) \end{aligned}$$

We abbreviate $[\varphi, \top]^\flat$ to $[\varphi]^\flat$ and $[\varphi, \top]^\sharp$ to $[\varphi]^\sharp$.

Note that the above includes both over-approximating and under-approximating operations. In section 4.1, we relax the requirements and obtain an analysis where subtraction is the only under-approximating operation.

For a statement C and $n \in \mathcal{D}$, the approximate negative side $N^\sharp(C, n)$, which over-approximates $N(C, \gamma(n))$, is (non-recursively) defined as follows:

$$\begin{aligned} N^\sharp(a, n) &= \mathit{pre{+}fail}^\sharp(a, n) \\ N^\sharp(C_1\,;\, C_2, n) &= N^\sharp(C_1, N^\sharp(C_2, n)) \end{aligned}$$

$$N^{\sharp}\big(([\varphi];C_1)+([\psi];C_2),n\big) = [\varphi, N^{\sharp}(C_1,n)]^{\sharp} \sqcup [\psi, N^{\sharp}(C_2,n)]^{\sharp}$$

$$N^{\sharp}\big(([\psi];C_{\text{body}})^{*};[\varphi],n\big) = \text{the first } n_j \in \{n_i\}_{i\geq 0} \text{ such that } n_{j+1} \sqsubseteq n_j \text{ where}$$
$$n_0 = [\varphi,n]^{\sharp} \text{ and } n_{i+1} = n_i \,\triangledown\, [\psi, N^{\sharp}(C_{\text{body}},n_i)]^{\sharp}$$

For a statement C and a pair of elements $p, n \in \mathcal{D}$ that are disjoint ($\gamma(p) \cap \gamma(n) = \varnothing$), we define the approximate positive side $P^{\flat}(C,p,n)$ such that it under-approximates $P(C, \mathcal{U} \smallsetminus \gamma(n))$. $P^{\flat}(C,p,n)$ is defined mutually with an auxiliary $Q^{\natural}(C,p,n)$ by induction on the structure of C. Optimally, $Q^{\natural}(C,p,n)$ represents a tight under-approximation of $P(C,\gamma(p))$, but actually need not be an under-approximation. Also, note how n is used to abstractly represent the complement of the set of interest.

For loop-free code, $P^{\flat}$ and $Q^{\natural}$ are (non-recursively) defined as follows:

$$P^{\flat}(C,p,n) = Q^{\natural}(C,p,n) - N^{\sharp}(C,n)$$
$$Q^{\natural}(a,p,n) = wp^{\flat}(a,p)$$
$$Q^{\natural}(C_1\,;C_2,p,n) = P^{\flat}\big(C_1, P^{\flat}(C_2,p,n), N^{\sharp}(C_2,n)\big)$$
$$Q^{\natural}\big(([\varphi];C_1)+([\psi];C_2),p,n\big) = \big(P^{\flat}(C_1,p,n) \sqcap P^{\flat}(C_2,p,n)\big) \sqcup [\neg\psi, P^{\flat}(C_1,p,n)]^{\flat} \sqcup [\neg\varphi, P^{\flat}(C_2,p,n)]^{\flat}$$

For a loop $C_{\text{loop}} = ([\psi];C_{\text{body}})^{*};[\varphi]$, we define a sequence $\{q_i\}_{i\geq 0}$ of approximants to $Q^{\natural}(C_{\text{loop}},p,n)$, where $q_{i+1} = q_i \,\triangledown\, \tau(q_i)$ and the initial point q_0 and the transformer τ are defined following either the characterization (4) using an approximation $R^{\natural}_{\exists} \in \mathcal{D}$ of an existential recurrent set of the loop:

$$q_0 = \big(R^{\natural}_{\exists} - N^{\sharp}(C_{\text{loop}},n)\big) \sqcup [\neg\psi, p]^{\flat}$$
$$\tau(q_i) = \big([\psi,p]^{\flat} \sqcap wp^{\flat}(C_{\text{body}},q_i)\big) \sqcup [\neg\varphi, wp^{\flat}(C_{\text{body}},q_i)]^{\flat}$$

or the characterization (5) using an approximation $R^{\natural}_{\forall} \in \mathcal{D}$ of a universal recurrent set:

$$q_0 = R^{\natural}_{\forall} \sqcup \big([\varphi,p]^{\flat} - N^{\sharp}(C_{\text{loop}},n)\big)$$
$$\tau(q_i) = \big([\neg\varphi, pre^{\sharp}(C_{\text{body}},q_i)]^{\flat} - N^{\sharp}(C_{\text{loop}},n)\big)$$

As for loop-free commands, $Q^{\natural}$ can be computed first, and $P^{\flat}$ defined using the result. That is, define $Q^{\natural}(C_{\text{loop}},p,n) = q_j$ where p_j is the first element such that $q_{j+1} \sqsubseteq q_j$, and then define $P^{\flat}(C_{\text{loop}},p,n) = Q^{\natural}(C_{\text{loop}},p,n) - N^{\sharp}(C_{\text{loop}},n)$.

Alternatively, $P^{\flat}$ and $Q^{\natural}$ can be computed simultaneously by also defining a sequence $\{p_i\}_{i\geq 0}$ of safe under-approximants of $P^{\flat}(C_{\text{loop}},p,n)$, where $p_0 = q_0$ and $p_{i+1} = (p_i \,\triangledown\, \tau(q_i)) - N^{\sharp}(C_{\text{loop}},n)$. Then $P^{\flat}(C_{\text{loop}},p,n) = p_j$ where p_j is the first element such that $q_{j+1} \sqsubseteq q_j$ or $p_{j+1} \not\sqsupseteq p_j$. In this case, we may obtain a sound $P^{\flat}$ before the auxiliary $Q^{\natural}$ has stabilized. While we have not yet done rigorous experimental validation, we prefer this approach when dealing with coarse subtraction.

When analyzing a top-level program C_{prg}, the analysis starts with $N^{\sharp}(C_{\text{prg}},\bot)$ and precomputes $N^{\sharp}$ (an over-approximation of unsafe states) for all statements of the program. Then it proceeds to compute $P^{\flat}(C_{\text{prg}},\top,\bot)$ (an under-approximation of safe input states) reusing the precomputed results for $N^{\sharp}$.

Note that we are using join and widening on the positive side which means that $Q^\natural$ may not under-approximate the positive side of the concrete characterization. The use of widening allows for the ascending chain to converge, and subtraction of the negative side ensures soundness of $P^\flat$. In other words, while the alternate concrete characterizations (4) and (5) are used to guide the definition of the approximate characterizations, soundness is argued directly rather than by using (4) and (5) as an intermediate step.

Theorem 2. *For a statement* C *and* $p, n \in \mathcal{D}$ *s.t.* $\gamma(p) \cap \gamma(n) = \varnothing$, $N^\sharp(C, n) \supseteq N(C, \gamma(n))$ *and* $P^\flat(C, p, n) \subseteq P(C, \mathcal{U} \smallsetminus \gamma(n))$. *Hence, for a top-level program* C_{prg}, $\gamma(N^\sharp(C_{\text{prg}}, \bot)) \supseteq N(C_{\text{prg}}, \varnothing)$ *(i.e., it over-approximates input states that may lead to failure), and* $\gamma(P^\flat(C_{\text{prg}}, \top, \bot)) \subseteq P(C_{\text{prg}}, \mathcal{U})$ *(i.e., it under-approximates safe input states).*

The argument for $N^\sharp$ proceeds in a standard way [11]. Soundness for $P^\flat$ then follows due to the use of subtraction.

4.1 Optimizations of Constraints

Use of over-approximate operations Since we are subtracting $N^\sharp(C, n)$ anyway, we can relax the right-hand side of the definition of $Q^\natural(C, p, n)$ without losing soundness. Specifically, we can replace under-approximating and must- operations by their over-approximating and may- counterparts. This way, we obtain an analysis where subtraction is the only under-approximating operation.

- For a loop-free statement C, always use $\mathit{pre}^\sharp(C, p)$ in place of $\mathit{wp}^\flat(C, p)$ (note that we *already* use $\mathit{pre}^\sharp$ on the positive side for loop bodies when starting from a universal recurrent set). This can be handy, e.g., for power set domains where $\mathit{pre}^\sharp$ (unlike $\mathit{wp}^\flat$) can be applied element-wise. Also, these transformers may coincide for deterministic loop-free statements (if the abstraction is precise enough). Later, when discussing Example 2, we note some implications of this substitution.
- For a state formula φ, use $[\varphi, \cdot]^\sharp$ in place of $[\varphi, \cdot]^\flat$. Actually, for some combinations of an abstract domain and a language of formulas, these transformers coincide. For example, in a polyhedral domain, conjunctions of linear constraints with non-strict inequalities have precise representations as domain elements.
- For branching statements, use $[\varphi, P^\flat(C_1, p, n)]^\sharp \sqcup [\psi, P^\flat(C_2, p, n)]^\sharp$ in place of the original expression.
- In the definition of $Q^\natural$, an over-approximate meet operation $\sqcap^\sharp$ suffices.

The result of these relaxations is:

$$\begin{aligned}
Q^\natural(a, p, n) &= \mathit{pre}^\sharp(a, p) \\
Q^\natural(C_1\,; C_2, p, n) &= P^\flat\big(C_1, P^\flat(C_2, p, n), N^\sharp(C_2, n)\big) \\
Q^\natural\big(([\varphi]; C_1) + ([\psi]; C_2), p, n\big) &= [\varphi, P^\flat(C_1, p, n)]^\sharp \sqcup [\psi, P^\flat(C_2, p, n)]^\sharp
\end{aligned}$$

$$\begin{aligned}
q_0 &= \big(R^\natural_\exists - N^\sharp(C_{\text{loop}}, n)\big) \sqcup [\neg\psi, p]^\sharp \\
\tau(q_i) &= \big([\psi, p]^\sharp \sqcap^\sharp \mathit{pre}^\sharp(C_{\text{body}}, q_i)\big) \sqcup [\neg\varphi, \mathit{pre}^\sharp(C_{\text{body}}, q_i)]^\sharp
\end{aligned}$$

or

$$q_0 = R^{\natural}_{\forall} \sqcup \big([\varphi, p]^{\#} - N^{\#}(C_{\text{loop}}, n)\big)$$
$$\tau(q_i) = \big([\neg\varphi, pre^{\#}(C_{\text{body}}, q_i)]^{\#} - N^{\#}(C_{\text{loop}}, n)\big)$$

No subtraction for $\mathbf{Q}^{\natural}$ For a similar reason, subtraction can be removed from the characterization of $Q^{\natural}$ without affecting soundness of $P^{\flat}$.

Bound on the positive side Another observation is that for a loop C_{loop} as in (2), the positive side $P(C_{\text{loop}}, S)$ is bounded by $[\![\neg\varphi]\!] \cup S$, as can be seen from the characterization (3). This can be incorporated into a specialized definition for loops, defining $P^{\flat}(C_{\text{loop}}, p, n) = \big(Q^{\natural}(C_{\text{loop}}, p, n) \sqcap ([\neg\varphi]^{\#} \sqcup p)\big) - N^{\#}(C_{\text{loop}}, n)$ or by performing the meet during computation of $Q^{\natural}$ by defining $q_{i+1} = \big(q_i \triangledown \tau(q_i)\big) \sqcap ([\neg\varphi]^{\#} \sqcup p)$.

4.2 Approximating the Recurrent Set

When approximating the positive side for a loop, the computation is initialized with an approximation of the recurrent set induced by the loop. Our analysis is able to start with either an existential or a universal recurrent set depending on what search procedure is available for the domain. The instantiation of our approach for numerical domains uses the tool E-HSF [5] that is capable of approximating both existential and universal recurrence. Other tools for numeric domains are described in [13,24]. The instantiation of our approach for the shape analysis with 3-valued logic uses a prototype procedure that we have developed to approximate existential recurrent sets.

Normally, the search procedures are incomplete: the returned sets only imply recurrence, and the search itself might not terminate (we assume the use of timeouts in this case). For this reason, in Sect. 3, we prefer not to define the recurrent sets to be maximal. This incompleteness leaves room for our analysis to improve the approximation of recurrence. For example, sometimes the solver produces a universal recurrence that is closed under forward propagation, but is not closed under backward propagation. In such cases, our analysis can produce a larger recurrent set.

5 Examples

In this section, we demonstrate our approach on several examples: first for a numeric domain, and then for the shape analysis domain of 3-valued structures. We note that numeric programs are considered here solely for the purpose of clarity of explanation, since the domain is likely to be familiar to most readers. We do not claim novel results specifically for the analysis of numeric programs, although we note that our approach may be able to complement existing tools. Detailed explanations of Examples are included in the companion technical report [3].

Example 1 aims at describing steps of the analysis in detail (to the extent allowed by space constraints). Example 2 is restricted to highlights of the analysis and includes a pragmatic discussion on using $pre^{\#}$ on the positive side. Examples 3 and 4 consider programs from a shape analysis domain and we only report on the result of the analysis.

```
1  while x ≥ 1 do
2    if x = 60 then
3      x ← 50
4    end
5    x ← x + 1
6    if x = 100 then
7      x ← 0
8    end
9  end
10 assert 0
```

(a) With syntactic sugar.

$$
\begin{aligned}
&{}_1([x \geq 1];\\
&\quad {}_2(([x = 60]; {}_3x \leftarrow 50) + ([x \neq 60]; \mathsf{skip}));\\
&\quad {}_5x \leftarrow x + 1;\\
&\quad {}_6(([x = 100]; {}_7x \leftarrow 0) + ([x \neq 100]; \mathsf{skip}));\\
&)^*; [x \leq 0];\\
&{}_{10}\,\mathsf{assert}\,0
\end{aligned}
$$

(b) Desugared.

Fig. 2. Example program 1

Example 1. In this example, we consider the program in Fig. 2: Fig. 2a shows program text using syntactic sugar for familiar while-language, and Fig. 2b shows the corresponding desugared program. We label the statements that are important for the analysis with the corresponding line numbers from Fig. 2a (like in ${}_3x \leftarrow 50$).

We assume that program variables (just x in this case) take *integer* values. For the abstract domain, we use disjunctive refinement over intervals allowing a bounded number of disjuncts (e.g., [2]). Recall that $\langle x : [a; b], y : [c; d] \rangle$ denotes a singleton abstract state of a program with two variables x and y, representing the set of concrete states, satisfying $(a \leq x \leq b) \wedge (c \leq y \leq d)$. Note that for this abstract domain and the formulas, appearing in the program, $[\cdot]^\flat$ and $[\cdot]^\sharp$ coincide, and we write $[\cdot]^\natural$ to denote either. To emphasize that the analysis can produce useful results even when using a coarse subtraction function, we use subtraction as defined in (1). That is, we just drop from the positive side those disjuncts that have a non-empty intersection with the negative side. For example, $\{\langle x : [1; 3] \rangle, \langle x : [5; 7] \rangle\} - \langle x : [6; 8] \rangle = \langle x : [1; 3] \rangle$. The analysis is performed mechanically by a prototype tool that we have implemented.

To simplify the presentation, in this example, we bound the number of disjuncts in a domain element by 2. Also to simplify the presentation, we omit the $\sharp$- and $\flat$-superscripts, and write, e.g., *pre+fail* for *pre+fail*$^\sharp$. For a statement labeled with i, we write N_i^j to denote the result of the j-th step of the computation of its negative side, and N_i to denote the computed value (similarly, for P).

We start with the analysis of the negative side. For the final statement,

$$N_{10}^1 = \mathit{pre\text{+}fail}(\mathsf{assert}\,0, \bot) = \top$$

then, we proceed to the first approximation for the loop (for clarity, we compute *pre* of the body in steps),

$$
\begin{aligned}
N_1^1 &= [x \leq 0, N_{10}^1]^\natural = \langle x : (-\infty; 0] \rangle\\
N_7^1 &= \mathit{pre\text{+}fail}(x \leftarrow 0, N_1^1) = \top\\
N_6^1 &= [x = 100, N_7^1]^\natural \sqcup [x \neq 100, N_1^1]^\natural = \{\langle x : (-\infty; 0] \rangle, \langle x : [100] \rangle\}\\
N_5^1 &= \mathit{pre\text{+}fail}(x \leftarrow x + 1, N_6^1) = \{\langle x : (-\infty; -1] \rangle, \langle x : [99] \rangle\}
\end{aligned}
$$

$$N_3^1 = \mathit{pre{+}fail}(x \leftarrow 50, N_5^1) = \bot$$
$$N_2^1 = [x = 60, N_3^1]^\natural \sqcup [x \neq 60, N_5^1]^\natural = \{\langle x : (-\infty; -1]\rangle, \langle x : [99]\rangle\}$$
$$N_1^2 = N_1^1 \sqcup [x \geq 1, N_2^1]^\natural = \{\langle x : (-\infty; 0]\rangle, \langle x : [99]\rangle\}$$

then, repeating the same similar sequence of steps for the second time gives

$$N_1^2 = N_1^2 \sqcup [x \geq 1, N_2^2]^\natural = \{\langle x : (-\infty; 0]\rangle, \langle x : [98, 99]\rangle\}$$

at which point we detect an unstable bound. The choice of widening strategy is not our focus here, and for demonstration purposes, we proceed without widening, which allows to discover the stable bound of 61. In a real-world tool, to retain precision, some form of widening *up to* [14] or landmarks [23] could be used. Thus, we take

$$N_1 = \{\langle x : (-\infty; 0]\rangle, \langle x : [61; 99]\rangle\}$$
$$N_2 = \{\langle x : (-\infty; -1]\rangle, \langle x : [61; 99]\rangle\} \quad N_6 = \{\langle x : (-\infty; 0]\rangle, \langle x : [61; 100]\rangle\}$$
$$N_3 = \bot \qquad N_7 = \top$$
$$N_5 = \{\langle x : (-\infty; -1]\rangle, \langle x : [61; 99]\rangle\} \quad N_{10} = \top$$

To initialize the positive side for the loop, we use a universal recurrent set obtained by three calls to E-HSF with different recurrent set templates. The result is $R_\forall = \{\langle x : [4; 60]\rangle, \langle x : [100; +\infty)\rangle\}$. Note that in this example, universal recurrence and safety coincide, and our analysis will be able to improve the result by showing that the states in $\langle x : [1; 3]\rangle$ are also safe. Since we are using a power set domain, we choose to use *pre* instead of *wp* for the final statement (as described in Sect. 4.1), not just for the loop (where we need to use it due to starting with $R_\forall$). We start with

$$P_{10}^1 = \mathit{pre}(\texttt{assert}\,0, \top) - N_{10} = \bot - N_{10} = \bot$$

then proceed to the loop (again, computing *pre* of its body in steps),

$$P_1^1 = R_\forall \sqcup [x \leq 0, P_{10}^1]^\natural - N_1 = \{\langle x : [4; 60]\rangle, \langle x : [100; +\infty)\rangle\}$$
$$P_7^1 = \mathit{pre}(x \leftarrow 0, P_1^1) - N_7 = \bot$$
$$P_6^1 = [x = 100, P_7^1]^\natural \sqcup [x \neq 100, P_1^1]^\natural - N_6$$
$$= \{\langle x : [4 : 60]\rangle, \langle x : [101; +\infty)\rangle\} - N_6$$
$$= \{\langle x : [4 : 60]\rangle, \langle x : [101; +\infty)\rangle\}$$
$$P_5^1 = \mathit{pre}(x \leftarrow x + 1, P_6^1) - N_5 = \{\langle x : [3 : 59]\rangle, \langle x : [100; +\infty)\rangle\}$$
$$P_3^1 = \mathit{pre}(x \leftarrow 50, P_5^1) - N_3 = \top$$
$$P_2^1 = [x = 60, P_3^1]^\natural \sqcup [x \neq 60, P_5^1]^\natural - N_2$$
$$= \{\langle x : [3; 59]\rangle, \langle x : [60]\rangle, \langle x : [100; +\infty)\rangle\} - N_2$$
$$= \{\langle x : [3; 60]\rangle, \langle x : [100; +\infty)\rangle\}$$
$$P_1^2 = (P_1^1 \sqcup ([x \geq 1, P_2^1]^\natural - N_2)) - N_2 = \{\langle x : [3; 60]\rangle, \langle x : [100; +\infty)\rangle\}$$

at which point we detect an unstable bound, but we again proceed without widening and are able to discover the stable bound of 1. Also note that (as observed in Sect. 4.1),

P_1 is bounded by $P_{10} \sqcup [\neg x \leq 0]^{\natural} = \langle x : [1; +\infty) \rangle$. This bound could be used to improve the result of widening. Thus, we take

$$
\begin{aligned}
P_1 &= \{\langle x : [1;60] \rangle, \langle x : [100;+\infty)] \rangle\} & & \\
P_2 &= \{\langle x : [0;60] \rangle, \langle x : [100;+\infty)] \rangle\} & P_6 &= \{\langle x : [1;60] \rangle, \langle x : [101;+\infty)] \rangle\} \\
P_3 &= \top & P_7 &= \bot \\
P_5 &= \{\langle x : [0;59] \rangle, \langle x : [100;+\infty)] \rangle\} & P_{10} &= \bot
\end{aligned}
$$

Thus, in this example, our analysis was able to prove that initial states $\{\langle x : [1;60] \rangle, \langle x : [100;+\infty)] \rangle\}$ are safe, which is a slight improvement over the output of E-HSF.

Example 2. In this example, we consider the program in Fig. 3. In the program, $*$ stands for a value non-deterministically chosen at runtime. All the assumptions made for Example 1 are in effect for this one as well, except that we increase the bound on the size of the domain element to 4. The analysis is able to produce the following approximation of the safe entry states:

$$
\begin{aligned}
&\{\langle x : [100;+\infty), y : \top \rangle, \langle x : (-\infty;0], y : (-\infty;-1] \rangle, \\
&\langle x : (-\infty;0], y : [1;+\infty) \rangle, \langle x : [1;99], y : [1;+\infty) \rangle\}
\end{aligned}
$$

This example also displays an interplay between coarse subtraction and the use of over-approximate operations (especially, *pre*) on the positive side. In order to retain precision when coarse subtraction is used, it seems important to be able to keep the positive side partitioned into a number of disjuncts. In a real-world analysis, this can be achieved, e.g., by some form of trace partitioning [16]. In this example, we employ a few simple tricks, one of those can be seen from Fig. 3. Observe that we translated the non-deterministic condition in lines 3-7 of the syntactically sugared program (Fig. 3a) into equivalent nested conditions (statement 3 of the desugared program in Fig. 3b) which allows the necessary disjuncts to emerge on the positive side.

Shape Analysis Examples In what follows, we demonstrate our approach for a shape analysis domain. We treat two simple examples using the domain of 3-valued structures, and we claim that our approach provides a viable decomposition of backward analysis (for this domain and probably for some other shape analysis domains). For background information on shape analysis with 3-valued logic, please refer to [22] and accompanying papers, e.g., [19,1,25]. To handle the examples, we use a mechanized procedure built on top of the TVLA shape analysis tool (`http://www.cs.tau.ac.il/~tvla/`).

Example 3. In this example, we consider the program in Fig. 4. The program manipulates a pointer variable x, and the heap cells each have a pointer field n. We compare x to *nil* to check whether it points to a heap cell. We write $x \to n$ to denote access to the pointer field n of the heap cell pointed to by x. The program in Fig. 4 just traverses its input structure in a loop.

The analysis identifies that both cyclic and acyclic lists are safe inputs for the program – and summarizes them in eight and nine shapes respectively. Figures 6 and 7 show examples of the resulting shapes.

```
1  while x ≥ 1 do
2    if x ≤ 99 then
3      if y ≤ 0 ∧ * then
4
5        assert 0
6
7      end
8      if * then
9        x ← −1
10     end
11   end
12   x ← x + 1
13 end
14 assert y ≠ 0
```

(a) With syntactic sugar.

```
1([x ≥ 1];
  2(([x ≤ 99];
    3(([y ≤ 0]; 4(5 assert 0 + skip))
      + ([y ≥ 1]; skip));
    8(9x ← −1 + skip)
  ) + ([x ≥ 100]; skip));
  12x ← x + 1
)*; [x ≤ 0];
14 assert y ≠ 0
```

(b) Desugared.

Fig. 3. Example program 2

```
while x ≠ nil do
  x ← (x → n)
end
```

Fig. 4. Example program 3

```
1 while x ≠ nil do
2   x ← (x → n)
3   x ← (x → n)
4 end
```

Fig. 5. Example program 4

Example 4. In this example, we consider the program in Fig. 5. In this program, the loop body makes two steps through the list instead of just one. While the first step (at line 2) is still guarded by the loop condition, the second step (at line 3) is a source of failure. That is, the program fails when given a list of odd length as an input. The abstraction that we employ is not expressive enough to encode such constraints on the length of the list. The analysis is able to show that cyclic lists represent safe inputs, but the only acyclic list that the analysis identifies as safe is the list of length exactly two.

6 Related Work

In [15], a backward shape analysis with 3-valued logic is presented that relies on the correspondence between 3-valued structures and first-order formulas [25]. It finds an over-approximation of states that may lead to failure, and then (as 3-valued structures do not readily support complementation) the structures are translated to an equivalent quantified first-order formula, which is then negated. This corresponds to approximating the negative side in our approach and then taking the complement, with the exception that the result is not represented as an element of the abstract domain. At least in principle, the symbolic abstraction $\hat{\alpha}$ of [20] could map back to the abstract domain.

For shape analysis with separation logic [21], preconditions can be inferred using a form of abduction called bi-abduction [6]. The analysis uses an over-approximate

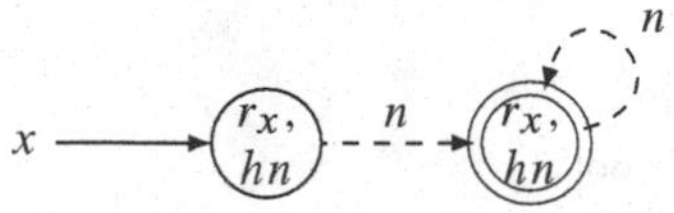

Fig. 6. Example of a safe structure causing non-termination

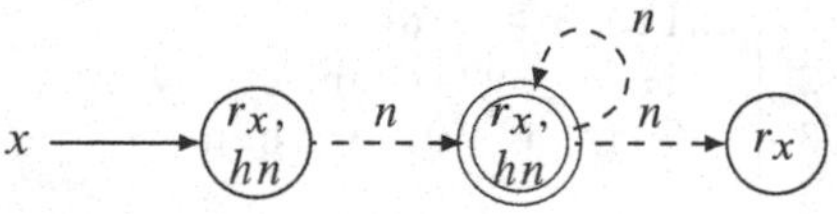

Fig. 7. Example of a safe structure leading to successful termination

abstraction, and it includes a filtering step that checks generated preconditions (by computing their respective postconditions) and discards the unsound ones. The purpose of the filtering step – keeping soundness of a precondition produced with over-approximate abstraction – is similar to our use of the negative side.

For numeric programs, the problem of finding preconditions for safety has seen some attention lately. In [18], a numeric analysis is presented that is based primarily on over-approximation. It simultaneously computes the representations of two sets: of states that may lead to successful termination, and of states that may lead to failure. Then, meet and generic negation are used to produce representations of states that cannot fail, states that must fail, etc. An under-approximating backward analysis for the polyhedral domain is presented in [17]. The analysis defines the appropriate under-approximate abstract transformers and to ensure termination, proposes a lower widening based on the generator representation of polyhedra. With E-HSF [5], the search for preconditions can be formulated as solving ∀∃ quantified Horn clauses extended with well-foundedness conditions. The analysis is targeted specifically at linear programs, and is backed by a form of counterexample-guided abstraction refinement.

7 Conclusion and Future Work

We presented an alternative decomposition of backward analysis, suitable for domains that do not readily support complementation and under-approximation of greatest fixed points. Our approach relies on an under-approximating subtraction operation and a procedure that finds recurrent sets for loops – and builds a sequence of successive under-approximations of the safe states. This decomposition allowed us to implement a backwards analysis for the domain of 3-valued structures and to obtain acceptable analysis results for two simple programs.

For shape analysis examples, we employed quite a simplistic procedure to approximate a recurrent set. One direction for future research is into recurrence search procedures for shape analysis that are applicable to realistic programs.

Another possible direction is to explore the settings where non-termination counts as failure. This is the case, e.g., when checking abstract counterexamples for concrete feasibility [4].

Acknowledgements. We thank Andrey Rybalchenko for helpful discussion and assistance with E-HSF, and Mooly Sagiv and Roman Manevich for sharing the source code of TVLA. A. Bakhirkin is supported by a Microsoft Research PhD Scholarship.

References

1. Arnold, G., Manevich, R., Sagiv, M., Shaham, R.: Combining shape analyses by intersecting abstractions. In: Emerson, E.A., Namjoshi, K.S. (eds.) VMCAI 2006. LNCS, vol. 3855, pp. 33–48. Springer, Heidelberg (2006)
2. Bagnara, R., Hill, P.M., Zaffanella, E.: Widening operators for powerset domains. STTT 9(3-4), 413–414 (2007)
3. Bakhirkin, A., Berdine, J., Piterman, N.: Backward analysis via over-approximate abstraction and under-approximate subtraction. Tech. Rep. MSR-TR-2014-82, Microsoft Research (2014)
4. Berdine, J., Bjørner, N., Ishtiaq, S., Kriener, J.E., Wintersteiger, C.M.: Resourceful reachability as HORN-LA. In: McMillan, K., Middeldorp, A., Voronkov, A. (eds.) LPAR-19 2013. LNCS, vol. 8312, pp. 137–146. Springer, Heidelberg (2013)
5. Beyene, T.A., Popeea, C., Rybalchenko, A.: Solving existentially quantified Horn clauses. In: Sharygina, N., Veith, H. (eds.) CAV 2013. LNCS, vol. 8044, pp. 869–882. Springer, Heidelberg (2013)
6. Calcagno, C., Distefano, D., O'Hearn, P.W., Yang, H.: Compositional shape analysis by means of bi-abduction. In: Shao, Z., Pierce, B.C. (eds.) POPL, pp. 289–300. ACM (2009)
7. Calcagno, C., Ishtiaq, S.S., O'Hearn, P.W.: Semantic analysis of pointer aliasing, allocation and disposal in Hoare logic. In: PPDP, pp. 190–201 (2000)
8. Calcagno, C., Yang, H., O'Hearn, P.W.: Computability and complexity results for a spatial assertion language for data structures. In: APLAS, pp. 289–300 (2001)
9. Clarke, E.M.: Program invariants as fixed points (preliminary reports). In: FOCS, pp. 18–29. IEEE Computer Society (1977)
10. Cousot, P.: Semantic foundations of program analysis. In: Muchnick, S.S., Jones, N.D. (eds.) Program Flow Analysis: Theory and Applications, pp. 303–342. Prentice-Hall (1981)
11. Cousot, P., Cousot, R.: Abstract interpretation and application to logic programs. J. Log. Program. 13(2&3), 103–179 (1992)
12. Cousot, P., Halbwachs, N.: Automatic discovery of linear restraints among variables of a program. In: Aho, A.V., Zilles, S.N., Szymanski, T.G. (eds.) POPL, pp. 84–96. ACM Press (1978)
13. Gupta, A., Henzinger, T.A., Majumdar, R., Rybalchenko, A., Xu, R.G.: Proving non-termination. In: Necula, G.C., Wadler, P. (eds.) POPL, pp. 147–158. ACM (2008)
14. Halbwachs, N., Proy, Y.E., Roumanoff, P.: Verification of real-time systems using linear relation analysis. Form. Method. Syst. Des. 11(2), 157–185 (1997)
15. Lev-Ami, T., Sagiv, M., Reps, T., Gulwani, S.: Backward analysis for inferring quantified preconditions. Tech. Rep. TR-2007-12-01, Tel Aviv University (December 2007)
16. Mauborgne, L., Rival, X.: Trace partitioning in abstract interpretation based static analyzers. In: Sagiv, M. (ed.) ESOP 2005. LNCS, vol. 3444, pp. 5–20. Springer, Heidelberg (2005)
17. Miné, A.: Inferring sufficient conditions with backward polyhedral under-approximations. Electr. Notes Theor. Comput. Sci. 287, 89–100 (2012)
18. Popeea, C., Chin, W.N.: Dual analysis for proving safety and finding bugs. Sci. Comput. Program. 78(4), 390–411 (2013)

19. Reps, T., Sagiv, M., Loginov, A.: Finite differencing of logical formulas for static analysis. In: Degano, P. (ed.) ESOP 2003. LNCS, vol. 2618, pp. 380–398. Springer, Heidelberg (2003)
20. Reps, T., Sagiv, M., Yorsh, G.: Symbolic implementation of the best transformer. In: Steffen, B., Levi, G. (eds.) VMCAI 2004. LNCS, vol. 2937, pp. 252–266. Springer, Heidelberg (2004)
21. Reynolds, J.C.: Separation logic: A logic for shared mutable data structures. In: LICS, pp. 55–74. IEEE Computer Society (2002)
22. Sagiv, S., Reps, T.W., Wilhelm, R.: Parametric shape analysis via 3-valued logic. ACM Trans. Program. Lang. Syst. 24(3), 217–298 (2002)
23. Simon, A., King, A.: Widening polyhedra with landmarks. In: Kobayashi, N. (ed.) APLAS 2006. LNCS, vol. 4279, pp. 166–182. Springer, Heidelberg (2006)
24. Velroyen, H., Rümmer, P.: Non-termination checking for imperative programs. In: Beckert, B., Hähnle, R. (eds.) TAP 2008. LNCS, vol. 4966, pp. 154–170. Springer, Heidelberg (2008)
25. Yorsh, G., Reps, T.W., Sagiv, M., Wilhelm, R.: Logical characterizations of heap abstractions. ACM Trans. Comput. Log. 8(1) (2007)

SawjaCard: A Static Analysis Tool for Certifying Java Card Applications

Frédéric Besson, Thomas Jensen, and Pierre Vittet

Inria, Rennes, France

Abstract. This paper describes the design and implementation of a static analysis tool for certifying *Java Card* applications, according to security rules defined by the smart card industry. *Java Card* is a dialect of Java designed for programming multi-application smart cards and the tool, called *SawjaCard*, has been specialised for the particular *Java Card* programming patterns. The tool is built around a static analysis engine which uses a combination of numeric and heap analysis. It includes a model of the *Java Card* libraries and the *Java Card* firewall. The tool has been evaluated on a series of industrial applets and is shown to automate a substantial part of the validation process.

1 Introduction

Security plays a prominent role in the smart card industry, due to their extensive use in banking and telecommunication. Hence, certification of smart cards has become accepted industrial practice. Traditional certifications (*e.g.*, against the Common Criteria [1]) focus primarily on the protection mechanisms of the card's hardware and operating system. More recently, attention has been drawn to the increasing number of applications that execute on the cards and the smart card industry has elaborated a set of secure coding guidelines [20,12] that apply to *basic* applications. Basic applications are granted limited privileges and the goal of the guidelines is to ensure that they do not interfere with more sensitive (*e.g.*, banking) applications. The verification of these guidelines is done by an independent authority that analyses the code and issues a certificate of conformance (or pinpoints failures of compliance). In collaboration with a company from the smart card industry we have developed the static analysis tool *SawjaCard* that can significantly simplify and automate the validation of smart card *basic* applications.

We consider applications written in the *Java Card* language – a dialect of Java dedicated to smart cards. To be validated, an application must respect a series of secure coding rules. *SawjaCard* is designed for the certification procedure proposed by AFSCM, the French industry association for Near Field Communication (NFC) technology providers, which consists of around 65 rules in total. These rules impose requirements on how an application is programmed, how it uses the resources of the card, and what kind of exceptions are acceptable.

Our main contribution is the implementation of the first static analysis tool able to automate the validation of *basic* applications according to AFSCM rules.

M. Müller-Olm and H. Seidl (Eds.): SAS 2014, LNCS 8723, pp. 51–67, 2014.

Our experiments show that *SawjaCard* proves automatically 87% of the properties. This work also demonstrates that precise but informal security guidelines can be mapped to formal properties that can be checked by harvesting a static analysis result. The design of the static analysis engine is a contribution of its own: we exploit the characteristics of *Java Card* but also constraints imposed by guidelines to get a precise yet efficient analyser. In terms of static analysis, the main contribution is a novel abstract domain for identifying a variant of the object-oriented *singleton object* pattern, where the nullity of a field is used to control the execution of an allocation instruction (Section 4.2).

We first present *Java Card*, highlighting the features relevant for security validation such as the *Java Card* firewall. The security requirements are described, and we explain how they can be verified on the model obtained through static analysis. We then present the main features of the analysis engine that is at the core of the tool. This includes the above-mentioned domain for detecting singleton objects and the use of trace partitioning for identifying file accesses. The tool has been evaluated against a series of industrial applications. We explain how the tool has significantly improved the certification procedure by automating a large part of the code verification.

2 Java Card

Java Card is a software development framework dedicated to multi-application smart cards. It includes a reduced version of *Java*, and has its own binary code format dedicated to devices with limited memory and processing capabilities. Like in *Java*, a *Java Card* application or library is written as a set of packages containing classes. After a standard *Java* compilation, *Java Card* converts all the classes belonging to the same package into a so-called CAP file. The CAP file is optimised to be small and meet smart card constraints, *e.g.*, fields, methods and classes are referred via *token* integers in order to reduce the size of the file.

Java Card keeps the class-based object oriented model of *Java*. Class inheritance, interfaces and the resolution mechanism for virtual and static calls is the same as in *Java*. Primitive types are restricted to the *Java* boolean, byte, short and optionally integer (might not be supported by every platform and the use of integer is also forbidden in some security guidelines). Arrays are limited to single-dimensional arrays. Strings are not available, neither as a primitive type, nor as a provided library class. Garbage collection is not required by the *Java Card* specification and it is still common not to have a garbage collector in a smart card. As memory is precious, application are expected to allocate data only during their installation phase and as parsimoniously as possible. Security guidelines emphasise this aspect (*e.g.*, allocation in a loop is forbidden).

The bytecode language is close to the *Java* bytecode language but with some noticeable differences. It is still a stack-based language with basically a reduced instruction set. However there are some differences which makes the *Java Card* bytecode more than a strict subset. For example, the operand stack contains 16 bits values and the standard operations work on such short values. Hence, each arithmetical operation is semantically different from its Java counterpart.

2.1 Modelling the *Java Card* Runtime and Its Libraries

Our static analysis tool performs a whole program analysis. It takes a single application CAP file but also expects additional CAP files representing all the used libraries. The core *Java Card* libraries are usually not available for analysis. They are i) proprietary; ii) card dependent; iii) and (partly) implemented using native code. To get a portable and card independent whole program, we have implemented the core *Java Card* libraries and standard extensions such as *GlobalPlatform* or ETSI standard UICC [10] using pure *Java Card* code extended by specification methods that are built-ins of the analyser: `RANDOM`, `ASSUME` and `ASSERT`. As we are not interested in proving functional correctness but security properties, the model of a method is usually simple and is based on the informal specification of the libraries. The model initialises system resources of the *Java Card* runtime. For instance, it allocates singleton exceptions objects that are owned by the Java Card runtime or global system input/output buffers. The model is also responsible for simulating the different phases of the applet life cycle. The *install* phase consists in initialising the applet state. The applet is also assigned its Application IDentifier (AID) and is registered within the *Java Card* runtime. The *process* phase is an infinite event loop where the applet processes commands. Eventually, the applet enters the *uninstall* phase where it is removed from the card.

2.2 Modelling the *Java Card* Firewall

The *Java Card* security architecture relies on a *firewall* which strongly limits inter-applet communication. The firewall mechanism guarantees that an inter-applet communication triggers a dynamic run-time check whose success depends on the *owner* of the object and the running *context* of the code. Every created object is assigned an owner, which is the context of the applet performing the object allocation. Each method is assigned the context of its enclosing applet. At runtime, the virtual machine ensures that an applet can only manipulate objects in its context and raises a *SecurityException* otherwise.

Communication between applets is achieved through *Shareable* interfaces. Using a specific method of the runtime, an applet A receives a shareable request from an explicitly identified applet B. The applet A can accept the request depending on the identity of B and return an object *o* implementing a *Shareable* interface. When applet B calls a method of object *o*, a context switch occurs and the method runs with the context of A.

Our Java model makes explicit the security checks performed by the Firewall using built-in API calls to obtain the owner of objects `GET_OWNER` or the running contexts `GET_CALLER_CONTEXT` (see Fig. 1). The owner/context properties are directly modelled by the abstract domains: each abstract object in the heap is assigned a owner and the abstract call stack is tagged by running contexts. This precise modelling of the Firewall is necessary to rule out security exceptions. Needless to say that the validation of applets strictly forbids security exceptions.

```
/* @API javacard.framework.AID: "Throws: SecurityException
 *      - if anObject object is not accessible in the caller's
    context" */
public final boolean equals(Object anObject){
  short caller_ctx = GET_CALLER_CONTEXT();
  if(!JCRESystem.accessible_in_caller_context(anObject, caller_ctx))
    throw JCRESystem.securityException;
  if (anObject==null || !(anObject instanceof AID)) return false;
  return [...] }
```

Fig. 1. Example of API performing a Firewall check

3 Validation of Java Card Applications

The validation of *Java Card* applications is based on several sets of coding guidelines, edited by industrial stakeholders. The main source of guidelines comes from the AFSCM [20], a French association of companies working in the area of NFC and contact-less smart cards. The AFSCM guidelines consists of 65 coding rules that specify properties that an applet must obey in order to be validated. Rules from the Global Platform [12] initiative have also been integrated. Some rules (such as "*The interactions between different interfaces must be clearly defined.*") are not amenable to automatic verification. Others are not considered because they concern the Java source ("*A switch statement must always include a default case.*"). Eliminating duplicates, we extracted 55 verifiable rules from the guidelines mentioned above, and classified them as shown in Fig. 2.

The rules vary significantly in granularity and type of property. Some properties are purely syntactic ("*An application must not contain a* `nop` *instruction*", or "*An application shall not use an AID already registered.*") whereas others require information about the dynamic behaviour of the application ("*no null pointer exceptions*" or "*no array-out-of bounds exceptions*"). Some rules specify restrictions on how library methods can be called, and with what arguments. Most of these rules cannot be verified *as is*, exactly due to the undecidability of

Type	Number	Examples
syntactical	20	Strictly forbidden methods, no Nop, package name checking
constant values	6	Constant array size, Proactive commands and events
call graph	6	Allocation only in specific part of the code.
exceptions	10	Ensure that various exceptions will never occur
file system	4	Report read or written files, ensure deletion of created file.
termination	1	No recursive code.
other	8	Applet instance should not be placed in static field.
total	55	

Fig. 2. Classification of the rules (from AFSCM [20] and Global Platform [12])

the underlying semantic property, and approximations are called for. As mentioned above, an important feature of these rules is that certain rules simplify the verification of others. *E.g.*, knowing that the rules "*Recursive code is forbidden*" and "*Arrays must be allocated with a determined size*" are satisfied means that the analyser can strive for more precision without running into certain complexity and computability issues. In the following, we explain how the validation of the rules can be done by mining the static analysis result.

Numeric Values: In *Java Card*, resources are often accessed using integer identifiers and managed by calling methods with a fixed set of flags. Many rules specify that those integers must be constant or range over a set of legitimate values. Our analyser is computing an abstraction of numeric values and therefore of method arguments. The abstraction of the method arguments is checked for compliance with the rules.

Array Values: Some resources can be coded by arrays of integers. For instance, files are identified by an array $[\mathtt{i}_1;\ldots;\mathtt{i}_n]$ which represents the file name $\mathtt{i}_1/\ldots/\mathtt{i}_n$. Menu entries (*i.e.*, strings) are coded by arrays of bytes. As with numeric values, validation rules often require those arrays to be constant. Files are an exception. File names are constructed by a sequence of calls $\mathtt{fh.select(d_1)} \ldots \mathtt{fh.select(d_n)}$ where `fh` is a `FileView` object and the $\mathtt{d}_i$ are typically constants, identifying directories. Our analyser does not track sequences of events but our model of the class `FileView` is an array representing the current working directory that is updated by calls to the `select` method. Our analyser models arrays and provides for each index a numeric abstraction of the content. This abstraction is queried in order to validate rules about resources encoded as arrays.

Control-Flow: The validation rules impose constraints on the control-flow graph of the application—especially during the installation phase. For instance, most memory allocations are required only to take place during the *install* phase, identified by a call to the `install` method. The analysis is constructing an abstract control-flow graph corresponding to the inlined control-flow graph of the application. Constraints over the control-flow graph can therefore be checked by exploring the abstract control-flow graph. For the particular case of memory allocation, we traverse the graph and make sure that memory allocation primitives *e.g.*, `new` statement, are only accessible from the `install` method.

Exceptional Behaviour: Validation rules are strict about exception handling. Run-time exceptions such as *ArrayOutOfBounds*, *NullPointerException* and *ClassCastException* are strictly forbidden. In our bytecode intermediate representation, run-time exceptions correspond to explicit instructions and we generate verification conditions for all those instructions. For obvious reasons, security exceptions (*SecurityException*) are also forbidden. The abstraction of the heap is designed to model object ownership and can be used to ensure that the security checks performed by the *Java Card* Firewall do no raise *SecurityException*. There are other rules about exceptional behaviours which can be interpreted as coding guidelines. The analysis is precisely modelling the flow of exceptions. In particular, it collects for each handler the caught exception and for each method call the escaping exceptions. This information is sufficient for checking all the rules regarding exceptions.

4 Overview of the Static Analysis Engine

Our static analysis engine is designed specifically for *Java Card* and its particular programming style. Existing general purpose analysis frameworks for *Java* *e.g.*, [32,19,17] cannot be applied directly to *Java Card*. Firstly, existing frameworks do not provide a CAP front-end – this is a non-negligible engineering issue. Although CAP files are compiled from class files, the inverse transformation is far from obvious. For instance, the instruction set is different and dynamic method lookup is compiled using explicit virtual tables. Secondly, our static analysis engine exploits fully the fact that *Java Card* programs are relatively small, forbid recursion and allocate few objects. Standard *Java* analyses designed to scale for object-oriented programs cannot exploit this. Finally, the *Java Card* firewall which has no *Java* counterpart is also modelled directly at the analysis level.

Our analyser operates on a 3-address code intermediate bytecode representation A3Bir [7] that is obtained by pre-processing the binary CAP file. This representation is adapted from the *Sawja* framework [17] and has the advantage of making explicit the different runtime checks performed by the *Java Card* Virtual Machine. An example of such intermediate code is given Fig. 4.

The static analysis engine implements an inter-procedural scheme which consists in a dynamic inlining of method calls. The benefit is a precise inter-procedural scheme that mimics the behaviour of a concrete interpreter. In terms of abstract domains, the domain of the inter-procedural analysis is D^* given that D is the domain for the intra-procedural analysis. This approach is effective for two reasons that are specific to *Java Card*: recursion is forbidden and the programs are relatively small.

4.1 Combining Intervals, Constant Sets and Symbolic Equalities

To abstract numeric values, the analyser is using a combination of three abstract domains: intervals, finite sets and symbolic equalities. The code snippet of Fig 3 illustrates their collaboration. The abstract domain of intervals *Int* is very popular but is not precise enough if used alone. At Line 4 of Fig. 3, the interval [0;5] is used to abstract the non-consecutive values 0 and 5. As many *Java Card* methods take as arguments integer flags or return integer flags that are in general not consecutive, this is a common source of imprecision. To deal with this issue, we use a domain $\mathit{Fin} = \mathcal{P}(\mathit{Cst}) \cup \{\top\}$ where *Cst* is the set of constants that appear in the program text. For efficiency, information about these constants is lost after arithmetic operations and reductions with the interval domain are limited to the cases of $\bot$ and singletons *i.e.*, abstract elements with represent a single concrete value. For Line 4, the product $\mathit{Int} \times \mathit{Fin}$ gives a precise invariant but would still be unable to infer that at Line 6 the value of `i` can only be 5. To get this result, it is necessary to propagate through the test `j==0` the knowledge

```
1  byte i = 0;          /*i:[0;0] & {0}*/
2  if(RANDOM_BOOL()){
3   i = 5;              /*i:[5;5] & {5}*/
4  }                    /*i:[0;5] & {0;5} */
5  byte j = i;          /*i:[0;5] & {0,5} j:[0;5] & {0,5} with j == i */
6  i = (j==0) ? (byte)(i+5) : i; /*i:[5;5] & {5} j:[0;5] & {0,5} */
```

Fig. 3. Collaboration between numeric abstract domains

that j equals i. This is a known weakness of *non-relational* domains which compute an abstraction for each variable independently. There are well-known numeric relational domains *e.g.*, convex polyhedra [6], octagons [24]. These domains are very expressive but are also computationally costly. Our analyser is using a more cost-effective weakly relational domain [25] computing for each program point and each local variable x an equality $x = e$ where e is a side-effect free expression of our intermediate representation *i.e.*, an expression built upon variables, arithmetic operators and field accesses. At Line 5, we have the equality `j==i`. Hence, when `j==0`, `i` is also 0 and when `j != 0`, `j` have value 5 and so has `i`. Combined, the three domains are able to compute the precise invariant of Line 6.

Symbolic expressions improve the precision of numeric abstractions but also significantly contribute to ruling out spurious null pointers. This is illustrated by Fig. 4. Our goal is to verify that **bar** is called with a non-null argument. At source level, this property is obvious. However, the cumulative effect of Java compilation, CAP conversion and the re-construction of our analyser intermediate representation introduces temporary variables. Without symbolic expressions, at Line 3, we only know that the temporary variable `t0` is not null but this variable is not used anymore. Symbolic expressions keep track of equalities between variables `t0`, `t1`, `t2`, the constant **null** and the value of field **this.foo**. Using the theory of equality, we can deduce at Line 2 that **this.foo** is not null. This information is propagated at Line 4 where we deduce that **t2** is also not null. Therefore, at the call in Line 5, **t2** is still not null.

4.2 Points-to Analysis with Detection of Singleton Objects

Our heap abstraction is *flow-sensitive* and takes the form of a *points-to* graph [15]. A node in the graph is an abstract object identified by a call-stack and the

```
1  void baz(){
2   if(foo!=null)
3    bar(foo);}
```

```
1  t0=this.foo; t1=null; if (t0==t1) goto 5;
2  /* t0==this.foo & t1==null */
3  t2=this.foo; checknotnull (this!=null);
4  /* t0==this.foo & t1==null & t2==this.foo */
5  this.bar(t2);  return;
```

Fig. 4. Left: Source code Right: A3Bir representation

creation point of the `new` statement, or a special node representing the `null` value. Object creation is done with parsimony in *Java Card*, and most `new` statements only ever allocate *one* object. In other words, most abstract objects are singletons representing a single concrete object. If an abstract object is a *singleton*, the analyser can precisely model side effects and perform *strong updates*.

Abstract counting of the number of allocations of an abstract object $o \in AO$ is a standard technique for identifying singletons objects. The properties "not allocated", "allocated at most once" and "allocated many times" are encoded by the numeric domain $\{0, 1, \infty\}$. Our domain is therefore $Cnt = AO \to \{0, 1, \infty\}$. In *Java Card* most objects are allocated during the *install* phase. This phase is loop-free and abstract counting therefore precisely identifies singleton objects. However, abstract counting fails at identifying singleton objects that are allocated during the *process* command loop.

To improve precision we propose a novel abstract domain able to capture variants of the so-called object-oriented singleton pattern. The idea behind the singleton pattern is that a field *fd* is either i) `null` and the singleton object is not allocated or ii) not `null` and the singleton object is allocated. To capture such conditional invariants, our singleton domain maps each field to a valuation of the abstract allocation counters. The abstract domain is therefore $Sgton = Field \to Cnt$. Consider $sgton \in Sgton$ and a field *fd*. The intuition is that $sgton(fd)$ only provides information about abstract counters under the condition that the field *fd* is null. When the points-to ensures that a field *fd* is definitely not `null`, the condition does not holds and $sgton(fd)$ can be set arbitrarily, in particular it can be strengthened to $\bot$. When the points-to ensures that a field *fd* is definitely `null`, the condition holds and $sgton(fd)$ can be used to strengthen the current abstract counters. If the condition cannot be decided, the information $sgton(fd)$ remains dormant but becomes useful after *e.g.*, a test $fd = null$ or would be updated after an assignment to the field *fd*.

Formally, given a concretisation $\gamma_{Cnt} : Cnt \to \mathcal{P}(Heap)$ for the *Cnt* domain, the concretisation $\gamma : Sgton \to \mathcal{P}(Heap)$ is defined by:

$$h \in \gamma(sgton) \text{ iff } \bigwedge_{fd} h(fd) = null \Rightarrow h \in \gamma_{Cnt}(sgton(fd)).$$

Fig. 5 illustrates how the reduced product [4] of a points-to, *Sgton* and *Cnt* analyses can ensure the singleton property. Before the loop (Line 1), the object *o* is not allocated, the field *fd* is definitely `null` and the conditional property ($\mathtt{fd} = \mathtt{null} \Rightarrow (\mathtt{o} \mapsto \mathtt{0})$) holds. At the head of the loop (Line 4), the object *o* is a singleton, the field *fd* is either `null` or points to the object *o*. The singleton domain holds the key invariant: the object *o* is not allocated when the field *fd* is `null`. After the test `fd == null` (Line 6), we refine our points-to and conclude that *fd* is definitely `null`. Therefore, the conditional property of the singleton domain holds: we can exploit the right hand side of the condition and refine the abstract counter ($o \mapsto 0 \sqcap o \mapsto 1 = o \mapsto 0$) and conclude that the object *o* is not allocated. After the allocation of *o* (Line 8), the object *o* is a singleton ($o \mapsto 1$) and *fd* points to *o*. Hence, *fd* is definitely not `null`. This is where the conditional

```
1   /* fd = null & (fd = null ⇒ (o ↦ 0)) & o ↦ 0 */
2   [...]
3   while(true){
4     /* fd ∈ {null, o} & (fd = null ⇒ (o ↦ 0)) & o ↦ 1 */
5     if (fd == null)
6     /* fd = null & (fd = null ⇒ (o ↦ 0)) & o ↦ 0 */
7     fd = new o();
8     /* fd = o & (fd = null ⇒ ⊥) & o ↦ 1 */        }
```

Fig. 5. Singleton pattern

singleton domain becomes useful. Because the condition $fd = null$ now no longer applies, the abstract counters can be strengthened to $\bot$. For simplicity, say that the abstract state after the (empty) `else` branch is the abstract state of the loop head of Line 4. At the end of the conditional, after the join, we get the same abstract state as at the loop head, which is therefore a fixpoint.

In practice, our *Sgton* domain also maintains conditions over instance fields and numeric fields (`false` plays the role of `null`). For our *Java Card* applications, those enhancements allow a precise identification of all singleton objects.

5 File System Access: A Case for Trace Partitioning

Trace partitioning [27] is a generic technique for locally improving the precision of a static analysis. It consists in partitioning an abstract state depending on a history of events. Suppose that the original abstract state is $D^\sharp$, after trace partitioning, the abstract state is $(Event^* \times D^\sharp)^*$ where *Event* is an arbitrary set of syntactic events (*e.g.*, a call to a specific method) or semantic events (*e.g.*, the variable x has value v). We have successfully used trace partitioning for precisely determining the files accessed by an application.

As explained in Section 3, *Java Card* comes with a hierarchical file system. In our model, the current directory $\mathtt{i}_1\mathtt{/.../i}_n$ is coded by an array of short $\mathtt{[i}_1\mathtt{;...;i}_n\mathtt{]}$ that is stored in the `path` field of a file handler object `fh` implementing the `FileView` interface. Moving to the $\mathtt{i}_{n+1}$ directory is done by the method call $\mathtt{fh.select(i}_{n+1}\mathtt{)}$. Therefore, determining the accessed files requires a precise analysis of the array content.

Consider the code of Fig. 6 that is representative of how files are accessed in *Java Card*. Suppose that before calling the `cd` method, the field `fh` is either `null` or points to an object `ofh` such that $\forall \mathtt{i}, \mathtt{ofh.path}[\mathtt{i}] = 0$. At the method return, with our base abstraction, the effect of the three paths is merged. We loose precision and get $\mathtt{res} = \mathtt{fh} \in \{\mathtt{null}; \mathtt{ofh}\} \wedge \mathtt{ofh.path}[0] \in [0; 1] \wedge \mathtt{ofh.path}[1] \in [0; 20]$. However, the precise post-condition of the `cd` method is $\mathtt{P}_1 \vee \mathtt{P}_2 \vee \mathtt{P}_3$ where each P_i models the effect of a particular execution path.

$$\mathtt{P}_1 \triangleq \mathtt{res} = \mathtt{null} \wedge \mathtt{fh} = \mathtt{null} \wedge \mathtt{ofh.path}[0] = 0 \wedge \mathtt{ofh.path}[1] = 0$$
$$\mathtt{P}_2 \triangleq \mathtt{res} = \mathtt{null} \wedge \mathtt{fh} = \mathtt{ofh} \wedge \mathtt{ofh.path}[0] = 1 \wedge \mathtt{ofh.path}[1] = 0$$
$$\mathtt{P}_3 \triangleq \mathtt{res} = \mathtt{ofh} \wedge \mathtt{fh} = \mathtt{ofh} \wedge \mathtt{ofh.path}[0] = 1 \wedge \mathtt{ofh.path}[1] = 20$$

```
1 public static FileView cd(){
2  if (fh!=null){
3   fh.select((short)1);
4   if(RANDOM_BOOL()){return null;}
5   fh.select((short)20); }
6  return fh; }
```

Fig. 6. Typical code for accessing files

Even for *Java Card*, the disjunctive completion [4] of our base abstract domain does not scale. Trace partitioning [27] offers a configurable trade-off between efficiency and precision. In particular, it allows a fine-grained control of when abstract states should be merged or kept separate. Our trace partitioning strategy is attaching to abstract states the trace of the encountered `select` calls. A trace event is therefore of the form $\texttt{select}_i$ where i identifies uniquely the method call in the control-flow graph. At the end of the `cd` method, we obtain: $[] : P_1 \quad [\texttt{select}_3] : P_2 \quad [\texttt{select}_3; \texttt{select}_5] : P_3$. The security guidelines mandate that the applet *install* phase and the processing of a single command of the *process* phase should terminate. We exploit this information and merge traces at those specific events. This strategy is precise and terminating for all the *Java Card* applications we have analysed.

6 Experimental Evaluation

We have evaluated *SawjaCard* on 8 industrial *Java Card* applets. For confidentiality reasons, we are required to keep them anonymous. The applications are representative of basic applications. There are loyalty applets but also phone applications. They require few privileges but access nonetheless certain non-sensitive part of the file system. The characteristics of the applets can be found in Fig. 7. For each applet, we provide the number of instructions of the application and the number of instructions taking into account the libraries used by the application. To give a finer estimate of the complexity of the code, we also provide the number of nodes in the inlined control-flow graph constructed by *SawjaCard*. However, this is still a coarse-grained measure of code complexity which is weakly correlated with the analysis time. For instance, applet A1 executes more instructions than applet A2, has fewer CFG nodes but takes longer

Applet	A1	A2	A3	A4	A5	A6	A7	A8
Instrs (app)	2769	2835	1823	1399	636	752	1245	230
Instrs (+ libs)	5824	5236	4301	5643	2834	3044	3402	2040
CFG	3435	6096	1491	1247	825	999	842	487
Time	29min	19min	6min	2min	32s	18s	4s	2s

Fig. 7. Applet characteristics

to analyse. The analysis time is obtained using a laptop with a Intel Core i7 processor and 8 GB of memory.

Fig. 8 summarises the analysis results for the 8 applets. We made a selection of the properties that can be evaluated in a fully automatic way *i.e.*, the result is either boolean or can be expressed as a percentage of alarms. An entry in Fig. 8 reads as follows. A ✓ denotes a fully verified property. A property is marked × if it is a true violation according to our manual inspection of the code. A ? denotes a false positive. A number denotes a percentage. For instance, 90 means that the property holds for 90% of the program points relevant for the property – percentages are rounded from below. If it is in bold red, the remaining alarms are true violation. Otherwise, we could not ascertain the absence of false positives. For 75% of the properties, *SawjaCard* reports no alarm and thus those properties are automatically validated. We have investigated the remaining alarms manually. For 12% of the properties, we have concluded that the alarms were all genuine violations of the properties. Therefore, the verdict of *SawjaCard* is precise for 87% of the properties. For the remaining 13%, there are false positives. For instance, we identified that certain *ArrayOutOfBounds* alarms were due to a lack of precision of the analysis. However, on average, *SawjaCard* validates nonetheless about 87% of array accesses. For the remaining alarms, there are false positives but also real alarms. In the following, we explain in more details a selection of the properties of Fig 8.

Alarms	A1	A2	A3	A4	A5	A6	A7	A8
NullPointerException	94	98	**99**	99	**97**	**98**	97	**99**
ArrayOutOfBounds	71	88	92	87	92	98	90	98
CatchIndividually	**46**	**23**	**82**	**31**	**32**	**67**	**57**	**53**
CatchNonISOException	×	×	×	×	×	×	×	×
HandlerAccess	×	✓	×	×	×	✓	✓	✓
AllocSingleton	✓	✓	✓	✓	✓	×	✓	✓
SDOrGlobalRegPriv	×	✓	✓	✓	✓	✓	✓	✓
SWValid	?	✓	✓	✓	✓	✓	✓	✓
ReplyBusy	?	✓	✓	✓	✓	✓	✓	✓
ClassCastException	✓	✓	✓	✓	✓	✓	✓	✓
NegativeArraySize	✓	✓	✓	✓	✓	✓	✓	✓
ArrayStoreException	✓	✓	✓	✓	✓	✓	✓	✓
SecurityException	✓	✓	✓	✓	✓	✓	✓	✓
AppletInStaticFields	✓	✓	✓	✓	✓	✓	✓	✓
ArrayConstantSize	✓	✓	✓	✓	✓	✓	✓	✓
InitMenuEntries	✓	✓	✓	✓	✓	✓	✓	✓

Fig. 8. Analysis results – selected properties

NullPointerException[1] The precision of our null pointer analysis is satisfactory as *SawjaCard* validates 98% of reference accesses. Moreover, for 4 of the applets,

[1] From AFSCM rules: A basic application shall not include any code that leads to NullPointerException, whatever this exception is caught or not.

we could conclude after manual inspection that the remaining alarms were real errors. For the other 4, the reasoning is more intricate and there might still be false positives. A typical error we found consists in ignoring that certain APIs can (according to the official specification) return a null pointer in some unusual cases. For instance, the method `getEntry` of the class **uicc.toolkit.ToolkitRegistrySystem** may return null *if the server does not exist or if the server returns null.* None of the analysed application performs the necessary defensive check to protect itself against such a null pointer.

ArrayOutOfBounds[2] *SawjaCard* validates 87% of array accesses. The remaining accesses are sometimes false positives. In particular, we have identified an access whose verification would require a relational numeric analysis. However, a simple rewrite of the code would also resolve the problem. Other array accesses rely on invariants that are not available to the analyser. For instance, certain array indexes are read from files. More precisely, when reading a file, certain applications first read a special segment, which is the file status. The full size of the file is a field of this file status. As the content of the file cannot be known, it is impossible to track this length.

CatchIndividually[3] This rule corresponds to a strict coding discipline that is almost syntactic: each type of exception should be caught by a different handler. This property is responsible for numerous alarms. All the reported alarms correspond to true violations of the rule. For instance, the following not compliant code snippet catches all the different exceptions with a single handler.

```
try{buffer =
     JCSystem.makeTransientByteArray((short)140,CLEAR_ON_RESET);}
catch (Exception e) {buffer = new byte[(short)140];}
```

CatchNonISOException[4] All the applets trigger alarms for this property. The alarms correspond to violations of the property. The exceptions that are ignored correspond to exceptions that are not thrown by the application itself but escape from library code. It might very well be that the proprietary implementations never raise these exceptions. Nonetheless, their possibility is reflected by our model of the API which is based on the *Java Card* API specification.

Other properties. The AFSCM rules forbid the classic *Java* exceptions: *ClassCastException*, *NegativeArraySize* and *ArrayStoreException*. For all the applets,

[2] From AFSCM rules: An application must not include any code that leads to ArrayOutOfBoundException, caught or not.

[3] From Global Platform rules: The Application should catch each exception defined by the used APIs individually in the application code and should explicitly rethrow the exception to the card runtime environment if needed.

[4] From AFSCM rules: All exceptions thrown during the execution from any defined entry point must be caught by the application, except *ISOException* that are thrown in response to a command.

SawjaCard proves their absence. Thanks to our modelling of *Java Card* Firewall, *SawjaCard* is also able to rule out *SecurityExceptions*. The rule *AppletInStaticFields* specifies that applet objects should not be stored in static fields. This property is validated for all the applets. The next two rules concern values that should be constant: array sizes and menu entries. Those rules are also validated for all the applets. The rule *SDOrGlobalRegPriv* is about privileges that should be granted to access certain APIs. Applet 1 requires certain privileges and therefore raises an alarm. The rules *SWValid* and *ReplyBusy* specify the range of the status word return by applets. The rule is verified for all the applets except applet 1. This is probably a false alarm given that the applet is using a non-standard way of computing the status word. The last rule concerns certain method calls returning handlers that should be protected by try-catch blocks. *SawjaCard* raises an alarm for all the applets. This rule is indeed violated.

DeadCode[5] For all the applets, *SawjaCard* detects some dead code which is due to the Java compilation. Consider the following method which unconditionally throws an exception. The *return* instruction is not reachable but is required by the *Java* compiler.

```
void dead_code (short val){ SystemException.throwIt(1); return; }
```

The *Java* compiler also enforces that method should list the exceptions they *might* raise using a *throws* clause. However, the algorithm for checking this clause is purely syntactic. To make *Java Card* compile, a defensive approach consists in adding handlers for all the *potential* exceptions. For certain calls, *SawjaCard* proves that certain exceptions are never thrown and that the handlers are therefore dead code. For compliance with the rule, a workaround would be to remove the useless handlers and add to the *throws* clause of the method all the exceptions that are proved impossible.

File handling[6] There is a significant number of properties concerning files. Some of them are simple and do not lead to false positives (such as *CreateFile*, *CreateFilesAtInstall*, *FileResizing* which only require to check arguments for specific method calls). Other properties are more complex and require a precise identification of the files that are read or written. Using trace partitioning (see Section 5), we can precisely identify files paths that are constructed by a sequence of select instructions with constant arguments. However, certain applets make the assumption that the AID of a particular application is stored at a specific position in a system file. The AIDs is thereafter used to access the root of the sub file system owned by the application AID. Our model of the file system is too coarse to encode this assumption and therefore we cannot handle this pattern.

[5] From AFSCM rules: dead code must be deleted/removed from the code.

[6] From AFSCM rules: The file system provides access to files that are under the control of the Mobile Network Operator. These files shall not be accessed by applications, except for a few exceptions.

Allocation[7] The alarms are real violations. Most applets allocate objects after the *install* phase. Yet, more relaxed rules allow the allocation of singleton objects. This rule is still violated by applet 6 which repeatedly tries to get a handler. In our model of the library, each unsuccessful try allocates an intermediate object and is therefore responsible for a memory leak. For the other applets, our singleton domain is precise and ensures that memory allocation is finite.

7 Related Work

For analysing Java programs, there are mature static analysis frameworks such as Soot [32] and Wala [19]. Based on Wala, the Joana tool [13] is able to prove security properties based on information-flow. Information-flow analyses would probably benefit from the *Java Card* restrictions. Currently, AFSCM guidelines do not consider such properties and are limited to safety properties.

Algorithms tuned for Java are usually not well-fitted for the constraints of *Java Card*. In particular, state-of-the-art algorithms for constructing control-flow graphs of Java programs are based on context-sensitive flow-insensitive points-to analyses [22,29]. For *Java Card*, our analyser demonstrates that a context-sensitive flow-sensitive points-to analysis is viable. It dynamically inlines methods calls and therefore literally computes an ∞-CFA. The *Astree* analyser is using a similar strategy for handling function calls [5]. In their context, the programs are large and function calls are rare. *Java Card* programs are comparatively tiny but method calls are ubiquitous.

For Java, Hubert *et al.*, [16] show how to infer the best `@NonNull` annotations for Fähnrich and Leino type system [11]. The static analyser Julia [30,31] implements a more costly but also more precise null pointer analysis that can be efficiently implemented using BDDs. Because our objects are singletons, our flow-sensitive points-to analysis performs *strong updates* and is therefore precise enough to precisely track null pointers and rule out *NullPointerExceptions*.

Might and Shivers [23] show how to improve abstract counting of objects using abstract garbage collection. Their analysis can prove that an abstract object corresponds to a single *live* concrete object. Our singleton domain is based on a different program logic and can ensure that an abstract object is only allocated once. As *Java Card* usually does not provide garbage collection, we really need to prove that there are only a finite number of allocated objects.

Semantics [28,9] and analyses [14,8] have been proposed for *Java Card*. Huisman *et al.*, [18] propose a compositional approach to ensure the absence of illicit applet interactions through *Shareable* interfaces. For *basic* applications such interactions are simply forbidden. Our tool verifies that applets do not expose *Shareable* interfaces and therefore enforces a simpler but stronger isolation property. A version of the Key deductive verification framework [2] has been successfully applied

[7] From Global Platform rules: A basic application should not perform instantiations in places other than in install() or in the applet's constructor.

to *Java Card* [26]. JACK [3] is another deductive verification tool dedicated to *Java Card* that is based on the specification language JML [21]. However, deductive verification is applied at the source level and requires annotations of the code with pre-(post-)conditions. This methodology is not applicable in our validation context which needs to be fully automatic for binary CAP files.

8 Conclusions

The validation process for smart card applications written in *Java Card* involves around 55 rules that restrict the behaviour of the applications. This process can benefit substantially from static analysis techniques, which can automate most of the required verifications, and provide machine-assistance to the certifier for the rest. The SawjaCard validation tool contains a static analysis which combines analysis techniques for numeric and heap-based computations, and which is further enhanced by specific domain constructions dedicated to the handling of the file system and *Java Card* firewall. A substantial part of building such a validation tool involves the modelling of libraries for which we propose to build a series of stubs whose behaviour approximates the corresponding APIs sufficiently well for the analysis to be accurate. Benchmarks on a series of industrial application shows that the tool can analyse such applications in a reasonable time and eliminate more than 80% of the required checks automatically.

The development of the tool suggests several avenues for further improvements. The properties for which the tool could be improved are *ArrayOutOfBoundException* and file properties. The numeric analysis is only weakly relational, and it would be possible to increase its precision by using a full-blown relational domains such as polyhedra or octagons. An effective alternative to significantly reduce the number of alarms would be to impose stricter coding rules (for example defensive checks for narrowing down the range of non constant indexes). Our model of the file system could also be improved. To get a precise and scalable analysis, our assessment is that file system specific abstract domains should be designed. Certain properties are also simply not provable because they depend on invariants that are established by the *personalisation* phase of the application. This phase happens after the *install* phase and corresponds to commands issued, in a secure environment, by the card manufacturer. Currently, the end of this phase has no standard specification and cannot be inferred from the applet code. For the others properties we have satisfactory results: when the tool emits an alarm, it corresponds to a real error in the application. The tool has been recently transferred to industry where it will be used as part of the validation process.

Acknowledgements. We thank Delphine Demange, Vincent Monfort and David Pichardie for their contributions to the development of SawjaCard.

References

1. Common Criteria for Information Technology Security Evaluation (2012)
2. Ahrendt, W., et al.: The KeY system: Integrating Object-Oriented Design and Formal Methods. In: Kutsche, R.-D., Weber, H. (eds.) FASE 2002. LNCS, vol. 2306, pp. 327–330. Springer, Heidelberg (2002)
3. Barthe, G., Burdy, L., Charles, J., Grégoire, B., Huisman, M., Lanet, J.-L., Pavlova, M.I., Requet, A.: JACK - A Tool for Validation of Security and Behaviour of Java Applications. In: de Boer, F.S., Bonsangue, M.M., Graf, S., de Roever, W.-P. (eds.) FMCO 2006. LNCS, vol. 4709, pp. 152–174. Springer, Heidelberg (2007)
4. Cousot, P., Cousot, R.: Systematic Design of Program Analysis Frameworks. In: POPL, pp. 269–282. ACM Press (1979)
5. Cousot, P., Cousot, R., Feret, J., Mauborgne, L., Miné, A., Monniaux, D., Rival, X.: The ASTRÉE Analyzer. In: Sagiv, M. (ed.) ESOP 2005. LNCS, vol. 3444, pp. 21–30. Springer, Heidelberg (2005)
6. Cousot, P., Halbwachs, N.: Automatic Discovery of Linear Restraints Among Variables of a Program. In: POPL, pp. 84–96. ACM Press (1978)
7. Demange, D., Jensen, T., Pichardie, D.: A Provably Correct Stackless Intermediate Representation for Java Bytecode. In: Ueda, K. (ed.) APLAS 2010. LNCS, vol. 6461, pp. 97–113. Springer, Heidelberg (2010)
8. Éluard, M., Jensen, T.P.: Secure Object Flow Analysis for Java Card. In: CARDIS, pp. 97–110. USENIX (2002)
9. Éluard, M., Jensen, T., Denne, E.: An Operational Semantics of the Java Card Firewall. In: Attali, S., Jensen, T. (eds.) E-smart 2001. LNCS, vol. 2140, pp. 95–110. Springer, Heidelberg (2001)
10. ETSI Project Smart Card Platform. Smart Cards; UICC Application Programming Interface (UICC API) for Java Card™
11. Fähndrich, M., Leino, K.R.M.: Declaring and checking non-null types in an object-oriented language. In: OOPSLA, pp. 302–312. ACM (2003)
12. GlobalPlatform Inc. GlobalPlatform Card Composition Model Security Guidelines for Basic Applications (2012)
13. Graf, J., Hecker, M., Mohr, M.: Using JOANA for Information Flow Control in Java Programs - A Practical Guide. In: ATPS 2013. LNI, vol. 215, pp. 123–138. GI (2013)
14. Hansen, R.R., Siveroni, I.: Towards Verification of Well-Formed Transactions in Java Card Bytecode. Electr. Notes Theor. Comput. Sci. 141(1), 145–162 (2005)
15. Hind, M.: Pointer Analysis: Haven't We Solved This Problem Yet? In: PASTE 2001, pp. 54–61. ACM (2001)
16. Hubert, L.: A non-null annotation inferencer for Java bytecode. In: PASTE, pp. 36–42. ACM (2008)
17. Hubert, L., Barré, N., Besson, F., Demange, D., Jensen, T., Monfort, V., Pichardie, D., Turpin, T.: Sawja: Static Analysis Workshop for Java. In: Beckert, B., Marché, C. (eds.) FoVeOOS 2010. LNCS, vol. 6528, pp. 92–106. Springer, Heidelberg (2011)
18. Huisman, M., Gurov, D., Sprenger, C., Chugunov, G.: Checking Absence of Illicit Applet Interactions: A Case Study. In: Wermelinger, M., Margaria-Steffen, T. (eds.) FASE 2004. LNCS, vol. 2984, pp. 84–98. Springer, Heidelberg (2004)
19. IBM. The T.J. Watson Libraries for Analysis (Wala), `http://wala.sourceforge.net`
20. Le Pallec, P., Diallo, S., Simon, T., Saif, A., Briot, O., Picard, P., Bensimon, M., Devisme, J., Eznack, M.: Cardlet Development Guidelines. AFSCM (2012)

21. Leavens, G.T., Kiniry, J.R., Poll, E.: A JML Tutorial: Modular Specification and Verification of Functional Behavior for Java. In: Damm, W., Hermanns, H. (eds.) CAV 2007. LNCS, vol. 4590, p. 37. Springer, Heidelberg (2007)
22. Lhoták, O., Hendren, L.J.: Evaluating the benefits of context-sensitive points-to analysis using a BDD-based implementation. ACM Trans. Softw. Eng. Methodol. 18(1) (2008)
23. Might, M., Shivers, O.: Improving flow analyses via GammaCFA: abstract garbage collection and counting. In: ICFP, pp. 13–25. ACM (2006)
24. Miné, A.: The octagon abstract domain. Higher-Order and Symbolic Computation 19(1), 31–100 (2006)
25. Miné, A.: Symbolic Methods to Enhance the Precision of Numerical Abstract Domains. In: Emerson, E.A., Namjoshi, K.S. (eds.) VMCAI 2006. LNCS, vol. 3855, pp. 348–363. Springer, Heidelberg (2006)
26. Mostowski, W.: Formalisation and Verification of Java Card Security Properties in Dynamic Logic. In: Cerioli, M. (ed.) FASE 2005. LNCS, vol. 3442, pp. 357–371. Springer, Heidelberg (2005)
27. Rival, X., Mauborgne, L.: The trace partitioning abstract domain. ACM Trans. Program. Lang. Syst. 29(5) (2007)
28. Siveroni, I.: Operational semantics of the Java Card Virtual Machine. J. Log. Algebr. Program. 58(1-2), 3–25 (2004)
29. Smaragdakis, Y., Bravenboer, M., Lhoták, O.: Pick your contexts well: understanding object-sensitivity. In: POPL, pp. 17–30. ACM (2011)
30. Spoto, F.: The Nullness Analyser of julia. In: Clarke, E.M., Voronkov, A. (eds.) LPAR-16 2010. LNCS, vol. 6355, pp. 405–424. Springer, Heidelberg (2010)
31. Spoto, F.: Precise null-pointer analysis. Software and System Modeling 10(2), 219–252 (2011)
32. Vallée-Rai, R., Co, P., Gagnon, E., Hendren, L.J., Lam, P., Sundaresan, V.: Soot - a Java bytecode optimization framework. In: CASCON, p. 13. IBM (1999)

Cyclic Abduction of Inductively Defined Safety and Termination Preconditions

James Brotherston[1] and Nikos Gorogiannis[2]

[1] Dept. of Computer Science, University College London
[2] Dept. of Computer Science, Middlesex University London

Abstract. We introduce *cyclic abduction*: a new method for automatically inferring safety and termination preconditions of heap-manipulating `while` programs, expressed as inductive definitions in separation logic. Cyclic abduction essentially works by searching for a *cyclic proof* of the desired property, abducing definitional clauses of the precondition as necessary in order to advance the proof search process.

We provide an implementation, CABER, of our cyclic abduction method, based on a suite of heuristically guided tactics. It is often able to automatically infer preconditions describing lists, trees, cyclic and composite structures which, in other tools, previously had to be supplied by hand.

1 Introduction

Whether a given pointer program is *memory-safe*, or eventually *terminates*, under a given precondition, are well-known (and undecidable) problems in program analysis. In this paper, we consider the even more difficult problem of *inferring* reasonable safety / termination preconditions, in *separation logic* [21] with inductive definitions, for such heap-aware programs.

Analyses of heap-manipulating programs based upon separation logic now extend, in some cases, to substantial code bases (see e.g. [22,20]), and rely on the use of *inductive predicates* to specify the shape of data structures stored in memory. However, such predicates are typically hard-coded into these analyses, which must therefore either give up or ask the user for advice when they encounter a data structure not described by the hard-coded predicates. For example, the well known SPACEINVADER [22] and SLAYER [5] analysers perform accurately on programs using combinations of linked lists, but report a false bug if they encounter a tree. Thus automatically inferring, or *abducing*, the inductive predicates needed to analyse individual procedures has the potential to greatly boost the automation of such verifiers.

The abduction of safety or termination preconditions is a highly non-trivial problem. At one end of the scale, the *weakest (liberal) precondition* (cf. Dijkstra [14]) can straightforwardly be extracted from a program P, but is useless for analysis: Deciding which program states satisfy this precondition is as hard as deciding from which states P runs safely / terminates! At the other end, many correct preconditions are too strong in that they rule out the execution

M. Müller-Olm and H. Seidl (Eds.): SAS 2014, LNCS 8723, pp. 68–84, 2014.

of some or all of the program. Thus we are required to perform a fine balancing act: find the weakest precondition that is at least somewhat "natural". Unfortunately, for fundamental computability reasons, we cannot hope to obtain such a precondition in general, so we must instead look for reasonable approximating heuristics.

Our main contribution is a new method, *cyclic abduction*, for inferring safety and/or termination preconditions, expressed as inductive definitions in separation logic, for heap-manipulating `while` programs. Our approach is based upon heuristic search in a formal system of *cyclic proofs*, adapted from the cyclic termination proofs in [8]. A cyclic proof is a derivation tree possibly containing *back-links*, which identify leaves of the tree with arbitrary interior nodes. This can create potentially unsound cycles in the reasoning, and so a (decidable) global soundness condition must be imposed upon these derivations to qualify them as genuine proofs. In fact, we can consider cyclic proofs of memory safety or of termination as desired, simply by imposing two different soundness conditions.

Given a program, cyclic abduction aims to simultaneously construct an inductively defined precondition in separation logic and a cyclic proof of safety or termination for the program under this precondition. Broadly speaking, we search for a cyclic proof that the program has the desired property, and when the proof search gets stuck, we abduce (i.e., guess) part of the precondition in order to proceed. Approximately, the main abduction principles are:

- symbolically executing *branching commands* in the derivation leads to *conditional disjunction* in the definitions;
- symbolically executing *dereferencing commands* in the derivation forces us to include *pointer formulas* in the definitions;
- forming *back-links* in the derivation leads to the instantiation of *recursion* in the definitions; and
- encountering a *loop* in the program alerts us to the possibility that we may need to *generalise* the precondition.

We have implemented our abduction procedure as an automatic tool, CABER, that builds on the generic cyclic theorem prover CYCLIST [11]. CABER is able to automatically abduce safety and/or termination preconditions for a fairly wide variety of common small programs, including the majority of those tested in the MUTANT tool, where the (list-based) preconditions previously had to be supplied by hand [2]. CABER can abduce definitions of a range of data structures such as lists, trees, cyclic structures, or composites such as trees-of-lists.

The remainder of this paper is structured as follows. Section 2 introduces the programming language and our language of logical preconditions. Section 3 presents our formal system of cyclic safety/termination proofs on which our abduction technique is based. In Section 4 we present our cyclic abduction strategy in detail, and Section 5 describes the implementation of CABER and its experimental evaluation. Section 6 examines related work and Section 7 concludes.

Due to space limitations, we have had to omit quite a few details. These can be found in an earlier technical report [10].

2 Programs and Preconditions

In this section we present a basic language of `while` programs with heap pointers, and the fragment of separation logic we use to express program preconditions. We often use vector notation to abbreviate tuples or lists, e.g. $\mathbf{x}$ for $(x_1, \ldots, x_k)$, and we write $\mathbf{x}_i$ for the ith element of the tuple $\mathbf{x}$.

Syntax of Programs. We assume infinite sets Var of *variables* and Fld of *field names*. An *expression* is either a variable or the constant nil. *Branching conditions* B and *command sequences* C are defined as follows, where x, y range over Var, f over Fld and E over expressions:

$$\begin{aligned} B &::= \star \mid E = E \mid E \neq E \\ C &::= \epsilon \mid x := E;\, C \mid y := x.f;\, C \mid x.f := E;\, C \mid \\ &\quad\ \mathtt{free}(x);\, C \mid x := \mathtt{new}();\, C \mid \\ &\quad\ \mathtt{if}\, B\, \mathtt{then}\, C\, \mathtt{else}\, C\, \mathtt{fi};\, C \mid \mathtt{while}\, B\, \mathtt{do}\, C\, \mathtt{od};\, C \end{aligned}$$

where $y := x.f$ and $x.f := E'$ respectively read from and write to field f of the heap cell with address x, and $\star$ represents a non-deterministic condition. A *program* is simply a list of field names followed by a command sequence: $\mathtt{fields}\ f_1, \ldots, f_k;\ C$.

Program Semantics. We use a RAM model employing heaps of records. We fix a set Val of *values* and an infinite subset $\mathsf{Loc} \subset \mathsf{Val}$ of *locations*, i.e., addresses of heap cells. The "nullary" value $nil \in \mathsf{Val} \setminus \mathsf{Loc}$ will not be the address of any heap cell. A *stack* is a function $s : \mathsf{Var} \to \mathsf{Val}$. The semantics $[\![E]\!]s$ of expression E in stack s is defined by $[\![x]\!]s =_{\text{def}} s(x)$ for $x \in \mathsf{Var}$, and $[\![\mathsf{nil}]\!]s =_{\text{def}} nil$.

A *heap* is a partial function $h : \mathsf{Loc} \rightharpoonup_{\text{fin}} (\mathsf{Val\ List})$ mapping finitely many locations to tuples of values (i.e. records); we write $dom(h)$ for the *domain* of heap h, i.e. the set of locations on which h is defined, and e for the empty heap that is undefined everywhere. If h_1 and h_2 are heaps with $dom(h_1) \cap dom(h_2) = \emptyset$, we define $h_1 \circ h_2$ to be the union of h_1 and h_2; otherwise, $h_1 \circ h_2$ is undefined.

We write $s[x \mapsto v]$ to denote the stack defined exactly as s except that $(s[x \mapsto v])(x) = v$, and adopt a similar update notation for heaps.

We employ a standard small-step operational semantics of our programs. A *(program) state* is either a triple (C, s, h) where C is a command sequence, s a stack and h a heap, or the special state *fault*, used to catch memory errors. Given a program $\mathtt{fields}\ f_1, \ldots, f_k;\ C$, we map the field names $f_1, \ldots, f_k$ onto elements of heap records by $\overline{f_j} =_{\text{def}} j$. The semantics of programs is then standard, given by a relation $\leadsto$ on states (omitted here for space reasons, but see [10]). We write $\leadsto^n$ for the n-step variant of $\leadsto$, and $\leadsto^*$ for its reflexive-transitive closure. A state (C, s, h) is *safe* if there is no computation $(C, s, h) \leadsto^* fault$, and *terminating* if it is safe and there is no infinite $\leadsto$-computation starting from (C, s, h).

As in [23,8], extending the heap memory cannot lead to new memory faults under our semantics, and so the following proposition holds:

Proposition 1. *If (C, s, h) is safe (resp. terminating) and $h \circ h'$ is defined then $(C, s, h \circ h')$ is also safe (terminating).*

Syntax of Preconditions. We express preconditions using the *symbolic heap* fragment of separation logic [3] extended with inductive definitions. We assume an infinite set of *predicate symbols*, each with associated arity.

Definition 1. *Formulas* are given by the following grammar:

$$F ::= \top \mid \bot \mid E = E \mid E \neq E \mid \mathsf{emp} \mid x \mapsto \mathbf{E} \mid P(\mathbf{E}) \mid F * F$$

where $x \in \mathsf{Var}$, E ranges over expressions, P over predicate symbols and $\mathbf{E}$ over tuples of expressions (matching the arity of P in $P(\mathbf{E})$). We write $F[E/x]$ for the result of replacing all occurrences of variable x by the expression E in formula F. Substitution is extended pointwise to tuples; but when we write $F[E/\mathbf{x}_i]$, we mean that E should be substituted for the ith component of $\mathbf{x}$ *only*.

We define $\equiv$ to be the least equivalence on formulas closed under associativity and commutativity of $*$ and $F * \mathsf{emp} \equiv F$.

Definition 2. An *inductive rule set* is a finite set of *inductive rules* each of the form $F \overset{\mathbf{z}}{\Rightarrow} P(\mathbf{E})$, where F and $P(\mathbf{E})$ are formulas and $\mathbf{z}$ (often suppressed) is a tuple listing the set of all variables appearing in F and $\mathbf{E}$. If Φ is an inductive rule set we define Φ_P to be the set of all *inductive rules for* P in Φ, i.e. those of the form $F \Rightarrow P(\mathbf{E})$. We say P is *undefined* if Φ_P is empty.

Semantics of Preconditions. Satisfaction $s, h \models_\Phi F$ of the formula F by stack s and heap h under inductive rule set Φ is defined by structural induction:

$$\begin{array}{lcl}
s,h \models_\Phi \top & \Leftrightarrow & \text{always} \\
s,h \models_\Phi \bot & \Leftrightarrow & \text{never} \\
s,h \models_\Phi E_1 = E_2 & \Leftrightarrow & [\![E_1]\!]s = [\![E_2]\!]s \text{ and } h = e \\
s,h \models_\Phi E_1 \neq E_2 & \Leftrightarrow & [\![E_1]\!]s \neq [\![E_2]\!]s \text{ and } h = e \\
s,h \models_\Phi \mathsf{emp} & \Leftrightarrow & h = e \\
s,h \models_\Phi E \mapsto \mathbf{E} & \Leftrightarrow & \mathit{dom}(h) = \{[\![E]\!]s\} \text{ and } h([\![E]\!]s) = [\![\mathbf{E}]\!]s \\
s,h \models_\Phi P(\mathbf{E}) & \Leftrightarrow & (h, [\![\mathbf{E}]\!]s) \in [\![P]\!]^\Phi \\
s,h \models_\Phi F_1 * F_2 & \Leftrightarrow & h = h_1 \circ h_2 \text{ and } s,h_1 \models_\Phi F_1 \text{ and } s,h_2 \models_\Phi F_2
\end{array}$$

Note that we interpret (dis)equalities as holding in the empty heap. The semantics $[\![P]\!]^\Phi$ of the predicate P under Φ is defined as follows:

Definition 3. Assume that Φ defines predicates $P_1, \ldots, P_n$ with respective arities $a_1, \ldots, a_n$. We let each Φ_{P_i} be indexed by j, and for an inductive rule $\Phi_{P_i,j}$ of the form $F \Rightarrow P_i\mathbf{x}$, we define an operator $\varphi_{i,j}$ by:

$$\varphi_{i,j}(\mathbf{X}) =_{\text{def}} \{(s(\mathbf{x}), h) \mid s, h \models_{\mathbf{X}} F\}$$

where $\mathbf{X} = (X_1, \ldots, X_n)$ and each $X_i \subseteq \mathsf{Val}^{a_i} \times \mathsf{Heaps}$, and $\models_{\mathbf{X}}$ is the satisfaction relation above, except that $[\![P_i]\!]^{\mathbf{X}} =_{\text{def}} X_i$. We then define

$$[\![\mathbf{P}]\!]^\Phi =_{\text{def}} \mu\mathbf{X}.\ (\textstyle\bigcup_j \varphi_{1,j}(\mathbf{X}), \ldots, \bigcup_j \varphi_{n,j}(\mathbf{X}))$$

We write $[\![P_i]\!]^\Phi$ for the ith component of $[\![\mathbf{P}]\!]^\Phi$.

For any inductive rule set, the *satisfiability* of a formula in our fragment is decidable [9], which is very helpful in evaluating abduced preconditions. On the other hand, *entailment* between formulas in the fragment is undecidable [1].

3 Formal Cyclic Safety/Termination Proofs

Here we present our formal cyclic proof system, adapted from the cyclic termination proofs in [8], for proving memory safety and/or termination of programs. We can consider memory safety rather than termination simply by imposing an alternative soundness condition on proofs.

A *proof judgement* is given by $F \vdash C$, where C is a command sequence and F is a formula. The proof rules for judgements are given in Fig. 1. By convention, the primed variables x', x'' etc. appearing in the premises of rules are chosen *fresh*, and we write $\overline{B}$ to mean $E \neq E'$ if B is $E = E'$, and vice versa. The rule (Frame) can be seen as a special case of the general *frame rule* of separation logic (cf. [23]), where the postcondition is omitted; its soundness depends on Proposition 1. We also include a rule for unfolding a formula of the form $P(\mathbf{E})$ according to the definition of P in a given inductive rule set Φ. (Predicate folding is a special case of *lemma application*, handled by the (Cut) rule.)

Definition 4. The judgement $F \vdash C$ is *valid* (resp. *termination-valid*) w.r.t. inductive rule set Φ if $s, h \models_\Phi F$ implies (C, s, h) is safe (resp. terminating).

Lemma 1. *Suppose the conclusion $F \vdash C$ of an instance of a rule R from Figure 1 is invalid w.r.t. Φ, i.e. $s, h \models_\Phi F$ but $(C, s, h) \leadsto^n$ fault for some stack s, heap h and $n \in \mathbb{N}$. Then there is a premise $F' \vdash C'$ of this rule instance and stack s', heap h' and $m \in \mathbb{N}$ such that $s', h' \models_\Phi F'$, but $(C', s', h') \leadsto^m$ fault. Moreover, $m \leq n$, and if R is a symbolic execution rule then $m < n$.*

Definition 5. A *pre-proof* of $F \vdash C$ is a pair $(\mathcal{D}, \mathcal{L})$, where $\mathcal{D}$ is a finite derivation tree with $F \vdash C$ at its root, and $\mathcal{L}$ is a "*back-link*" function assigning to every open leaf ℓ of $\mathcal{D}$ a node $\mathcal{L}(\ell)$ of $\mathcal{D}$ such that the judgements at ℓ and $\mathcal{L}(\ell)$ are identical. A pre-proof $(\mathcal{D}, \mathcal{L})$ can be seen as a graph by identifying each open leaf ℓ of $\mathcal{D}$ with $\mathcal{L}(\ell)$; a *path* in $\mathcal{P}$ is then understood as usual.

Definition 6. A pre-proof $\mathcal{P}$ is a *cyclic (safety) proof* if there are infinitely many symbolic execution rule applications along every infinite path in $\mathcal{P}$.

We can treat termination rather than safety by replacing the soundness condition of Defn. 6 with the condition in [8], which essentially demands that some inductive predicate is unfolded infinitely often along every infinite path in the pre-proof. Thus, by a simple adaptation of the soundness result in [8]:

Theorem 7. *For any inductive rule set Φ, if there is a cyclic safety (resp. termination) proof of $F \vdash C$, then $F \vdash C$ is valid (resp. termination-valid) w.r.t. Φ.*

Proof. We just consider safety here, and refer to [8] for the termination case. Suppose $F \vdash C$ has a cyclic safety proof $\mathcal{P}$ but is invalid. By Lemma 1, there is an infinite path $(F_k \vdash C_k)_{k\geq 0}$ in $\mathcal{P}$, and an infinite sequence $(n_k)_{k\geq 0}$ of natural numbers such that $n_{k+1} < n_k$ whenever $F_k \vdash C_k$ is the conclusion of a symbolic execution rule instance, and $n_{k+1} = n_k$ otherwise. Since $\mathcal{P}$ is a cyclic safety proof, there are infinitely many symbolic executions along $(F_k \vdash C_k)_{k\geq 0}$. Thus $(n_k)_{k\geq 0}$ is an infinite descending chain of natural numbers, contradiction. □

Symbolic execution rules:

$$\frac{x = E[x'/x] * F[x'/x] \vdash C}{F \vdash x := E;\, C} \qquad \frac{}{F \vdash \epsilon}$$

$$\frac{x = \mathbf{E}_{\overline{f}}[x'/x] * (y \mapsto \mathbf{E} * F)[x'/x] \vdash C}{y \mapsto \mathbf{E} * F \vdash x := y.f;\, C}\ |\mathbf{E}| \geq \overline{f} \qquad \frac{x \mapsto \mathbf{E}[E/\mathbf{E}_{\overline{f}}] * F \vdash C}{x \mapsto \mathbf{E} * F \vdash x.f := E;\, C}\ |\mathbf{E}| \geq \overline{f}$$

$$\frac{x \mapsto (x'_1, \ldots, x'_k) * F[x'/x] \vdash C}{F \vdash x := \mathtt{new}();\, C} \qquad \frac{F \vdash C}{x \mapsto \mathbf{E} * F \vdash \mathtt{free}(x);\, C}$$

$$\frac{B * F \vdash C;\, C''}{B * F \vdash \mathtt{if}\, B\, \mathtt{then}\, C\, \mathtt{else}\, C'\, \mathtt{fi};\, C''} \qquad \frac{B * F \vdash C;\, \mathtt{while}\, B\, \mathtt{do}\, C\, \mathtt{od};\, C'}{B * F \vdash \mathtt{while}\, B\, \mathtt{do}\, C\, \mathtt{od};\, C'}$$

$$\frac{\overline{B} * F \vdash C';\, C''}{\overline{B} * F \vdash \mathtt{if}\, B\, \mathtt{then}\, C\, \mathtt{else}\, C'\, \mathtt{fi};\, C''} \qquad \frac{\overline{B} * F \vdash C'}{\overline{B} * F \vdash \mathtt{while}\, B\, \mathtt{do}\, C\, \mathtt{od};\, C'}$$

$$\frac{F \vdash C;\, C'' \qquad F \vdash C';\, C''}{F \vdash \mathtt{if} \star \mathtt{then}\, C\, \mathtt{else}\, C'\, \mathtt{fi};\, C''} \qquad \frac{F \vdash C;\, \mathtt{while}\, B\, \mathtt{do}\, C\, \mathtt{od};\, C' \qquad F \vdash C'}{F \vdash \mathtt{while} \star \mathtt{do}\, C\, \mathtt{od};\, C'}$$

Logical rules:

$$\frac{F \vdash C}{F * G \vdash C}\ \text{(Frame)} \qquad \frac{F \vdash C}{F[E/x] \vdash C}\ x \text{ not in } C\ \text{(Subst)} \qquad \frac{F' \vdash C}{F \vdash C}\ F \equiv F'\ \text{(Equiv)}$$

$$\frac{(t_1 = t_2 * F)[t_2/x, t_1/y] \vdash C}{(t_1 = t_2 * F)[t_1/x, t_2/y] \vdash C}\ (=) \qquad \frac{G' * F \vdash C}{G * F \vdash C}\ G \vdash G'\ \text{(Cut)}$$

$$\frac{}{t_1 = t_2 * t_1 \neq t_2 * F \vdash C}\ (\neq) \qquad \frac{}{x \mapsto \mathbf{E} * x \mapsto \mathbf{E}' * F \vdash C}\ (\mapsto)$$

Predicate unfolding rule:

$$\frac{(\mathbf{E} = \mathbf{E_j}[\mathbf{x_j}/\mathbf{z_j}] * F_j[\mathbf{x_j}/\mathbf{z_j}] * F \vdash C)_{1 \leq j \leq k}}{P(\mathbf{E}) * F \vdash C}\ \begin{array}{l} \Phi_P = \{F_1 \overset{\mathbf{z_1}}{\Rightarrow} P(\mathbf{E_1}), \ldots, F_k \overset{\mathbf{z_k}}{\Rightarrow} P(\mathbf{E_k})\} \\ \forall x_j \in \{\mathbf{x_j}\}.\ x_j \text{ is fresh} \end{array}\ (P)$$

Fig. 1. Hoare logic rules for proof judgements

4 Cyclic Abduction: Basic Strategy and Tactics

We now turn to the main contribution of this paper: our *cyclic abduction* method for inferring inductive safety and/or termination preconditions of programs. Here, we first explain the high-level strategy for abducing such preconditions, and then develop a number of automatic *tactics* implementing this strategy.

4.1 Overview of Abduction Strategy

The typical initial problem we are faced with is: given a program with code C and input variables $\mathbf{x}$, find an inductive definition set Φ such that the judgement $P(\mathbf{x}) \vdash C$ is (termination-)valid wrt. Φ, where P is a predicate symbol.

Our strategy for finding such a Φ is to *search for a cyclic proof* of the judgement $P(\mathbf{x}) \vdash C$, abducing inductive rules as necessary to enable the search to progress. We now set out informally the main principles governing this process.

Principle 1. *The first priority of the search procedure is to close the current branch of the derivation tree, preferably by* applying an axiom, *or else by* forming a back-link *to some other node. (The formation of back-links must respect the relevant soundness condition on cyclic proofs.)*

If closing the branch is not possible, the second priority is to apply the symbolic execution rule *for the (foremost) command appearing at the current subgoal.*

Principle 2. *We may abduce inductive rules and/or deploy the logical rules as "helper functions" to serve the priorities laid out in Principle 1, i.e., in order to form a back-link or to apply the symbolic execution rule for a command.*

We may abduce inductive rules only *for predicate symbols that are in the current subgoal, and currently undefined. When we abduce inductive rules for a predicate, we always immediately unfold that predicate in the current subgoal.*

Principle 3. *Before symbolically executing a* `while` *loop, one can attempt to generalise the precondition F appearing at the subgoal in question. That is to say, we can try to find a formula F' such that $F' \vdash F$ is a valid entailment, and, by applying (Cut), proceed with the proof search using the precondition F' in place of F. If necessary, we may abduce inductive rules in order to obtain F'.*

4.2 Tactics

A *tactic* in our setting, as is standard in automated theorem proving, is simply a transformer on *proof states*. However, since we employ cyclic proofs with back-links joining leaves to arbitrary proof nodes, our proof state must reflect the entire pre-proof rather than just the current subgoal. Furthermore, since we are allowed to abduce new inductive rules in the proof search, the current inductive rule set must also form part of the proof state. Thus our proof states are comprised of the following elements:

$\mathcal{P}$: A partial pre-proof, representing the portion of proof constructed so far. Some of the leaves of $\mathcal{P}$ may be open; we call these the *open subgoals* of $\mathcal{P}$.

Φ: The set of inductive rules abduced so far in the proof search.
ℓ: The open subgoal of $\mathcal{P}$ on which to operate next.

Example 1. Figure 2 shows an abductive cyclic proof of a program that non-deterministically traverses l and r fields of pointer x until it reaches nil; as expected, the abduced predicate defines binary trees. We will often refer to this proof, which satisfies both the safety *and* the termination soundness condition, as a running example in order to illustrate our abductive tactics.

4.3 Abductive Tactic for Branching Commands

Our proof rules for deterministic `if` and `while` commands (Fig. 1) require the precondition to determine the status of the branching condition. We introduce an abductive tactic, `abduce_branch`, that fires whenever the symbolic execution of such a rule fails.

Suppose `abduce_branch` is applied to the proof state $(\mathcal{P}, \Phi, \ell)$ where the command sequence C in the judgement appearing at the current subgoal ℓ is of the form $\texttt{while}\, B\, \texttt{do}\, C\, \texttt{od}; C'$ or $\texttt{if}\, B\, \texttt{then}\, C\, \texttt{else}\, C'\, \texttt{fi}; C''$ (where $B \neq \star$). For simplicity we assume B is an equality or disequality between two program variables x, y (the case where one of the two terms is nil is very similar). First, `abduce_branch` selects a subformula of the form $P(\mathbf{E})$ appearing in ℓ such that P is undefined in Φ, and x and y occur in the tuple $\mathbf{E}$. Thus, we may write the judgement appearing at ℓ as $F * P(\mathbf{E}) \vdash C$ where $x = \mathbf{E}_k$ and $y = \mathbf{E}_j$ (and $k \neq j$). Then, `abduce_branch` adds the following inductive rules for P to Φ:

$$B[\mathbf{z}_k/x, \mathbf{z}_\ell/y] * P'(\mathbf{z}) \Rightarrow P(\mathbf{z})$$
$$\overline{B}[\mathbf{z}_k/x, \mathbf{z}_\ell/y] * P''(\mathbf{z}) \Rightarrow P(\mathbf{z})$$

where P', P'' are fresh predicate symbols and $\mathbf{z}$ is a tuple of appropriately many arbitrary variables. `abduce_branch` then unfolds the indicated occurrence of $P(\mathbf{E})$ in ℓ, and applies the appropriate symbolic execution rule for C to each of the new subgoals (this step is now guaranteed to succeed).

The proof in Figure 2 begins by applying `abduce_branch` in order to symbolically execute the `while` command, abducing a suitable definition of predicate P_0.

4.4 Abductive Tactic for Dereferencing Assignments

The symbolic execution rules for commands that dereference a memory address (Fig. 1) require the precondition to guarantee that this address is indeed allocated. The tactic `abduce_deref` enables the symbolic execution of such commands by abducing the allocation of the appropriate address.

Formally, suppose `abduce_deref` is applied to the proof state $(\mathcal{P}, \Phi, \ell)$, where the first command C in the judgement at ℓ is of the form $\texttt{free}(x)$ or $x.f := E$ or $y := x.f$. First, `abduce_deref` selects a subformula of the form $P(\mathbf{E})$ appearing

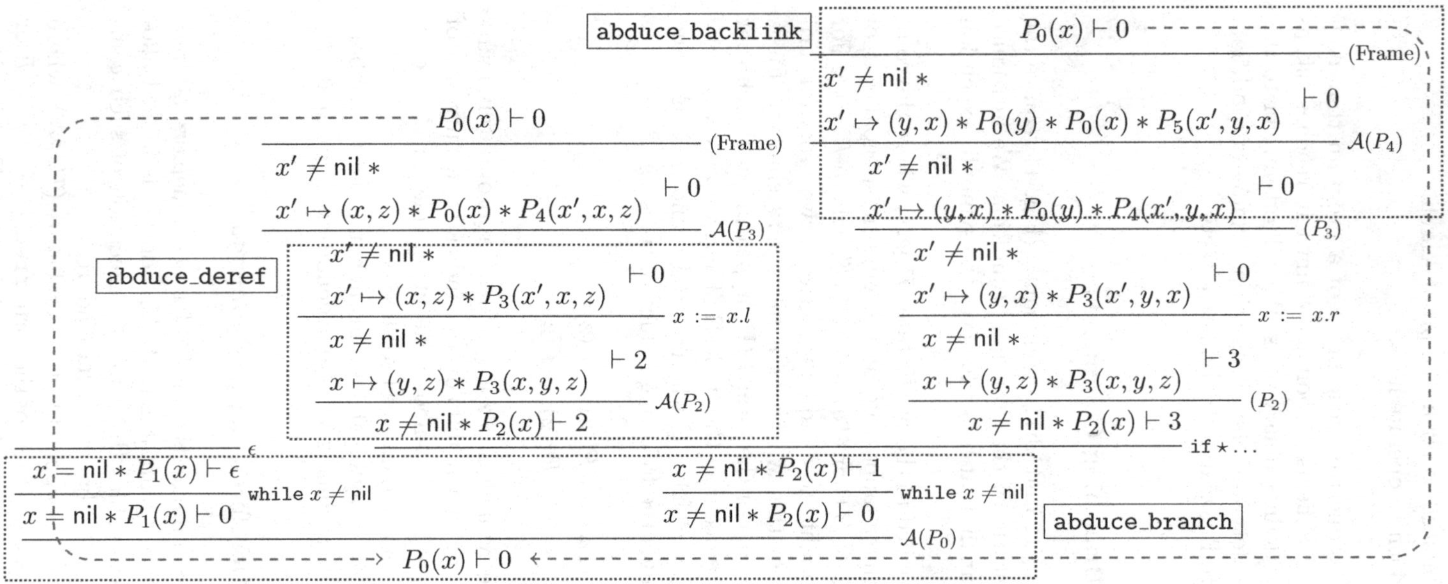


```
     fields l, r;
0 :  while x ≠ nil do
1 :    if ⋆ then
2 :      x := x.l
       else
3 :      x := x.r
       fi od
```

$$x = \mathsf{nil} * P_1(x) \Rightarrow P_0(x)$$
$$x \neq \mathsf{nil} * P_2(x) \Rightarrow P_0(x)$$
$$x \mapsto (y,z) * P_3(x,y,z) \Rightarrow P_2(x)$$
$$P_0(y) * P_4(x,y,z) \Rightarrow P_3(x,y,z)$$
$$P_0(z) * P_5(x,y,z) \Rightarrow P_4(x,y,z)$$

$$x = \mathsf{nil} * \mathsf{emp} \Rightarrow P_0(x)$$
$$x \neq \mathsf{nil} * x \mapsto (y,z) * P_0(y) * P_0(z) \Rightarrow P_0(x)$$

Fig. 2. Top: abductive proof for a binary tree search program (shown bottom left). Note that judgements refer to the indices attached to program commands; and we write $\mathcal{A}(P)$ to indicate a combined abduction-and-unfolding proof step. Bottom centre: inductive rules abduced during the proof. Bottom right: simplified inductive rules.

at ℓ, where P is undefined in Φ, and x occurs in the tuple $\mathbf{E}$ at position k (i.e., $x = \mathbf{E}_k$). Then, the inductive rule below is added to Φ:

$$P'(\mathbf{x} \sqcup \mathbf{y}) * x_k \mapsto \mathbf{y} \Rightarrow P(\mathbf{x})$$

where $\sqcup$ is tuple concatenation, P' is a fresh predicate symbol, and $\mathbf{x}$ and $\mathbf{y}$ are tuples of distinct, fresh variables such that $|\mathbf{x}| = |\mathbf{E}|$, and $|\mathbf{y}|$ is the number of fields in the program. abduce_deref then unfolds the selected occurrence of $P(\mathbf{E})$ in ℓ (introducing fresh variables as appropriate), and applies the symbolic execution rule for $\mathcal{C}$ to the resulting subgoal (which will now succeed).

In the case of the proof in Figure 2, we apply abduce_deref when attempting to symbolically execute the command $x := x.l$ on the middle branch at line 2, abducing a suitable definition for P_2 in the process. A similar situation arises when we attempt to symbolically execute the command $x := x.r$ on the right hand branch, with the crucial difference that here the only predicate in the precondition, P_2, has already been defined. In this case, abduce_deref is able to succeed by unfolding $P_2(x)$ according to its existing definition.

4.5 Abductive Tactic for Forming Back-Links

In principle, we may attempt to form a back-link from an open subgoal labelled by $F \vdash C$ to any other proof node labelled by $F' \vdash C$, provided that: (a) $F \vdash F'$ is a valid entailment; and (b) the addition of this back-link does not violate the soundness condition on cyclic proofs. Here we present a tactic, abduce_backlink, that attempts to form such back-links automatically during the proof search.

Formally, suppose that abduce_backlink is applied to proof state $(\mathcal{P}, \Phi, \ell)$. First, the tactic non-deterministically selects a node ℓ' of $\mathcal{P}$, distinct from ℓ, such that the command sequences at ℓ' and ℓ are identical. Then it tries to manipulate ℓ using logical rules so as to obtain a precondition identical to the one at ℓ'. More precisely, for any predicate P in ℓ that is undefined in Φ, abduce_backlink attempts to abduce inductive rules for P such that after unfolding P, the logical rules (Frame) and (Subst) can be used to obtain an identical copy of ℓ'.

We write ℓ as $F_1 * P(\mathbf{E}) \vdash C$, where P is undefined in Φ, and ℓ' as $F_2 \vdash C$. Then abduce_backlink abduces an inductive rule of the form $F' * P'(\mathbf{z}) \Rightarrow P(\mathbf{z})$ where P' is a fresh predicate, and F' is chosen so as to satisfy

$$F_2[\theta] \subseteq_{\text{multiset}} F_1 * F'[\mathbf{E}/\mathbf{z}]$$

for some substitution θ of expressions for *non-program variables* only (here we view formulas as *-separated multisets). Providing we can find suitable F' (which is essentially a unification problem), abduce_backlink transforms $\mathcal{P}$ by applying rules to ℓ and inserting a new back-link to ℓ' as follows:

$$
\begin{array}{c}
\vdots \\[4pt]
\dfrac{}{F_2 \vdash C} \;\dashleftarrow \\[4pt]
\vdots
\end{array}
\qquad
\cfrac{
\cfrac{
\cfrac{
\overline{F_2 \vdash C}
}{F_2[\theta] \vdash C} \;(\text{Subst})
}{F_1 * F'[\mathbf{E}/\mathbf{z}] * P'(\mathbf{E}) \vdash C} \;(\text{Frame})
}{F_1 * P(\mathbf{E}) \vdash C} \;(P)
$$

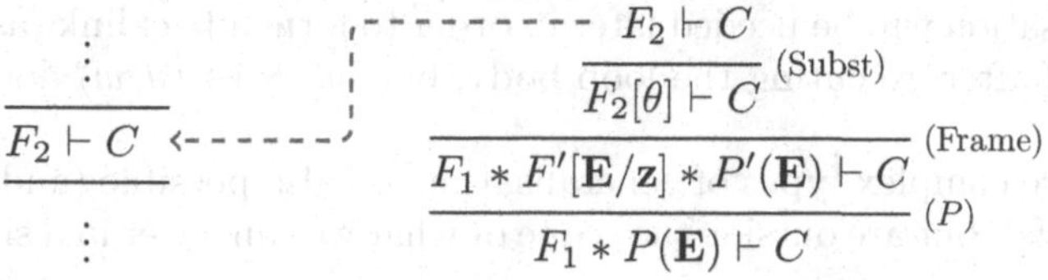

As with our other tactics, `abduce_backlink` is also allowed to try unfolding a defined predicate in the subgoal ℓ if no undefined predicates are available. Finally, `abduce_backlink` ensures that the proposed back-link does not violate the relevant soundness condition on cyclic proofs by calling a model checker.

In the middle branch of the proof in Figure 2, we call `abduce_backlink` after symbolically executing $x := x.l$. The tactic proceeds by abducing a suitable definition for P_3 and applying (Frame), allowing a back-link to the root of the proof. For the similar goal on the rightmost branch, `abduce_backlink` instead unfolds P_3 and then abduces a suitable inductive rule for the undefined P_4.

We observe that `abduce_backlink` is "forgetful" in that it uses (Frame) to discard parts of the precondition. An alternative would be to use (Cut) with an entailment theorem prover to establish the required logical entailment $F \vdash F'$ (such steps are needed for some proofs). We did implement such a tactic, calling on the separation logic entailment prover in CYCLIST [11], but found the costs to be prohibitive in the absence of a sophisticated lemma speculation mechanism.

4.6 Tactic for Existential Generalisation

Symbolically executing `while` loops creates a potentially infinite branch of the proof search, unless it can be closed either by an axiom or, more commonly, by forming a back-link. However, naive attempts to back-link to a target judgement often fail because the judgement specifies a too-precise relationship between program variables which is not preserved by the loop body. One solution, typical of inductive theorem proving in general, is to *generalise* the precondition of a `while` loop so as to "forget" such variable relationships. The tactic `ex_gen` implements this principle.

Formally, suppose `ex_gen` is applied to the proof state $(\mathcal{P}, \Phi, \ell)$, where the judgement labelling current subgoal ℓ is of the form $F \vdash \texttt{while}\ B\ \texttt{do}\ C\ \texttt{od};\ C'$. Then for every program variable x modified by the loop body C, `ex_gen` replaces every occurrence of x in a subformula of F of the form $E = E'$, $E \neq E'$ or $y \mapsto \mathbf{E}$ by a fresh (existentially quantified) variable w. (This step uses (Cut), and is easily seen to be sound.) This tactic may generalise over *any* subset of variables modified by the loop body and present in F.

Example 2. Figure 3 shows the proof of a program with two nested `while` loops; the outer loop traverses *next* pointers while the inner loop traverses *down* pointers. Here, the abduced precondition defines a list of lists.

Consider the goal $x \neq \mathsf{nil} * x \mapsto (y, z) * P_3(x, y, z) \vdash 2$ in Figure 3. Since z is modified by the inner loop body, and the precondition contains $x \mapsto (y, z)$, we call `ex_gen`, which replaces $x \mapsto (y, z)$ by $x \mapsto (y, w)$, where w is a fresh variable. This generalisation will be needed later in order to form a backlink (as $x \mapsto (y, z)$ does not hold after executing the loop body, but $\exists w.\ x \mapsto (y, w)$ does).

Other, more complex types of generalisation are also possible (and are needed for some proofs), but are outside the scope of what we can cover in a single paper.

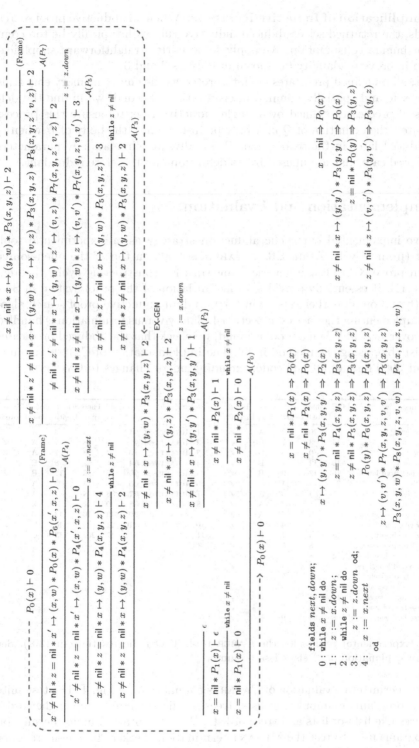

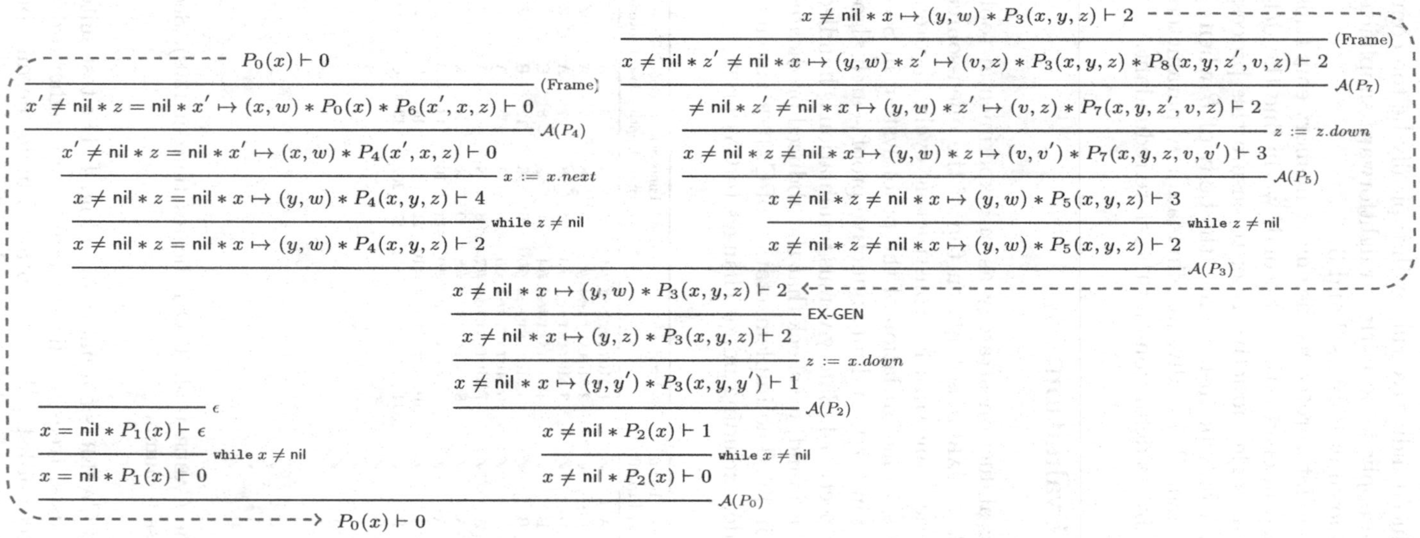

```
    fields next, down;
0 : while x ≠ nil do
1 :    z := x.down;
2 :    while z ≠ nil do
3 :       z := z.down  od;
4 :    x := x.next
    od
```

$$x = \mathsf{nil} * P_1(x) \Rightarrow P_0(x)$$
$$x \neq \mathsf{nil} * P_2(x) \Rightarrow P_0(x)$$
$$x \mapsto (y, y') * P_3(x, y, y') \Rightarrow P_2(x)$$
$$z = \mathsf{nil} * P_4(x, y, z) \Rightarrow P_3(x, y, z)$$
$$z \neq \mathsf{nil} * P_5(x, y, z) \Rightarrow P_3(x, y, z)$$
$$P_0(y) * P_6(x, y, z) \Rightarrow P_4(x, y, z)$$
$$z \mapsto (v, v') * P_7(x, y, z, v, v') \Rightarrow P_5(x, y, z)$$
$$P_3(x, y, w) * P_8(x, y, z, v, w) \Rightarrow P_7(x, y, z, v, w)$$

$$x = \mathsf{nil} \Rightarrow P_0(x)$$
$$x \neq \mathsf{nil} * x \mapsto (y, y') * P_3(y, y') \Rightarrow P_0(x)$$
$$z = \mathsf{nil} * P_0(y) \Rightarrow P_3(y, z)$$
$$z \neq \mathsf{nil} * z \mapsto (v, v') * P_3(y, v') \Rightarrow P_3(y, z)$$

Fig. 3. Top: abductive proof for list-of-lists traversal. Bottom, left to right: program; predicates found; simplified predicates.

4.7 Simplification of Inductive Rule Sets. When an abductive proof search succeeds, the returned set of abduced inductive rules will typically be too complex for human consumption. We apply some fairly straightforward simplifications to improve readability (as shown in Figures 2 and 3).

First, all undefined predicates are interpreted as the empty memory emp (this being a safe and spatially minimal interpretation). Second, we in-line the definitions of predicates defined by a single inductive rule; to ensure this process terminates, the definition of Q may only be in-lined into the body of P when Q was abduced later in the search than P. Finally, we eliminate any parameters from a predicate that are unused by its definition and therefore redundant.

5 Implementation and Evaluation

We have implemented our cyclic abduction strategy as an experimental tool, CABER (from "Cyclic ABducER"). CABER is built on top of the open-source theorem prover CYCLIST, a generic framework for constructing cyclic theorem provers [11]. It essentially provides an instantiation of the proof system in Section 3 (based on an earlier version in [11]), and an abductive proof search algorithm implementing the tactics in Section 4. Safety versus termination is handled via a prover switch. When a proof is found, we check that the abduced predicates are satisfiable, using the method in [9]. The implementation of CABER amounts to about 3000 lines of OCaml code, excluding minor changes to CYCLIST.

#	Program	LOC	Time (ms)	Search Depth	Defs. Class	Term. Proved
1	List traverse	3	20	3	A	✓
2	List insert	14	8	7	B	✓
3	List copy	12	0	8	B	✓
4	List append	10	12	5	B	✓
5	Delete last from list	16	12	9	B	✓
6	Filter list	21	48	11	C	✓
7	Dispose list	5	4	5	A	✓
8	Reverse list	7	8	7	A	✓
9	Cyclic list traverse	5	4	5	A	✓
10	Binary tree search	7	8	4	A	✓
11	Binary tree insert	18	4	7	B	✓
12	List of lists traverse	7	8	5	B	✓
13	Traverse even-length list	4	8	4	A	✓
14	Traverse odd-length list	4	4	4	A	✓
15	Ternary tree search	10	8	5	A	✓
16	Conditional diverge	3	4	3	B	×
17	Traverse list of trees	11	12	6	B	✓
18	Traverse tree of lists	17	68	7	A	✓
19	Traverse list twice	8	64	9	B	✓

#	Program	LOC	Time (ms)	Search Depth	Defs. Class	Term. Proved
1	MUTANT test #1	4	4	3	A	✓
2	MUTANT test #2	6	8	5	A	✓
3	MUTANT test #3	6	8	7	A	✓
4	MUTANT test #4	11	52	8	C	✓
5	MUTANT test #5	16	16	12	B	✓
6	MUTANT test #6	6	4	5	A	✓
7	MUTANT test #7	8	4	7	A	✓
8	MUTANT test #8	30	×	×	×	×
9	MUTANT test #9	13	16	13	B	✓
10	MUTANT test #10	21	4	13	C	✓
11	MUTANT test #11	17	292	13	C	T/O

Fig. 4. Experimental results for the CABER tool. T/O indicates timeout (30s). See below for explanation of "Defs. Class" column.

Our experimental evaluation of CABER is summarised in Fig. 4. The test suite includes programs manipulating lists, trees, cyclic structures and higher-order structures like lists-of-lists and trees-of-lists. We also obtained under permission the programs used to test the MUTANT termination checker [4]. These are loops extracted from the Windows kernel that manipulate list-like structures of varying complexity. Our tests were performed on a x64 Linux system with an Intel i5 CPU at 3.4GHz and 4Gb of RAM. Run-times were generally very low, with no test taking more than 300 ms, apart from MUTANT test #11 whose termination proof times out. The definitions abduced by the safety- and termination-proving runs on each program were identical, except on test #16 and MUTANT test #11.

Evaluating the quality of abduced definitions is not trivial. In principle, definitions could be partially ordered by entailment (cf. [12]) but for our language this is known to be undecidable [1]. Instead, we manually classify solutions into three categories. A solution is rated "A" if it is syntactically equal to the standard precondition for that example, "B" if it is at least *provably* equal to the standard precondition, and "C" if it is strictly stronger than the standard precondition.

Out of 30 tests in total, 14 tests (47%) produce predicates rated "A", 11 tests (37%) produce predicates rated "B", and 4 tests (13%) produce predicates rated "C", with one test (3%) failing entirely. Categories A and B include cyclic list traversal (program 9 in Fig. 4), list of lists traversal (12), searching binary and ternary search trees (10, 15) and traversal of even- and odd-length lists (13, 14). The last four programs typically cannot be handled by (safety-checking) tools such as SPACEINVADER and SLAYER. Test #6 and MUTANT tests #4, #10, #11 produce C-rated definitions, and MUTANT test #8 fails altogether. The common cause behind these (partial) failures is essentially the need for better abstraction and lemma speculation techniques, as discussed briefly in Section 4.6.

6 Related Work

Our approach to the abduction of inductive definitions is close in spirit, if not so much in execution, to *inductive recursion synthesis* in AI (for a survey see [16]). The main novelties of our approach, compared to this technique, are: (a) that we abduce Hoare-style preconditions for imperative programs in separation logic, rather than inputs to functional programs in first-order logic; and (b) that we employ a cyclic proof search to abduce induction schemas.

Our abductive tactics for symbolic execution are similar to the approach taken in [12], which performs abduction for separation logic over a *fixed* signature of (higher-order) lists. In a different setting, Dillig et al. [15] abduce loop invariants as Boolean combinations of integer inequalities. In contrast, we directly abduce the inductive definitions of arbitrary data structures on-the-fly, by refining the meaning of predicate symbols during proof search.

There have also been a number of previous efforts to synthesise inductive predicates of separation logic for use in program analysis. Lee et al. present a shape analysis using an abstract domain of shape graphs based on a grammar of heaps [19]. The main limitation of the technique is the restriction of the inferred predicates to at most two parameters. Later, Berdine et al. developed a shape analysis employing a higher-order list predicate, from which various list-like data structures can be synthesised [2]. Again, the choice of abstract domain limits the class of predicates that can be discovered; for example, predicates defining trees cannot be expressed in this domain. Guo et al. leverage inductive recursion synthesis to infer inductive loop invariants in a shape analysis based on separation logic [17]. Chang and Rival propose a shape analysis whose abstract domain is parameterised by "invariant checkers", which are essentially inductive definitions provided by the user [13]. Finally, He et al. build on the bi-abductive techniques proposed in [12] to infer procedure specifications based on user-defined predicates [18]. The main differences between these works and our own is that they only consider safety and not termination; and they are generally based upon pre-defined recursion schemas or abstract domains, rather than inferring predicate definitions directly as we do. Guo et al. [17], based on inductive recursion synthesis techniques, is a notable exception to the latter rule.

Recently, Brockschmidt et al. developed a termination prover for Java programs based on term rewriting [7] that also performs some inference of heap predicates during analysis. In contrast to our work, their analysis assumes memory safety, while we guarantee it. Several authors have also considered the problem of inferring termination preconditions for integer programs (e.g., [6]). The heap is not usually considered, and the abduced preconditions are generally linear combinations of inequalities between integer expressions.

7 Conclusions and Future Work

In this paper we lay the foundations of a new technique, cyclic abduction, for inferring the inductive definitions of data structures manipulated by `while` pointer programs. This problem is far more challenging than the already difficult one of inferring pre/postconditions based on fixed predicates. Presently, our prototype tool Caber infers correct preconditions for small programs manipulating data structures such as lists, trees, cyclic lists and compositions of these. In particular, Caber abduces the correct termination preconditions, previously supplied by hand, for over 90% of the tests reported for Mutant in [4].

We note that cyclic abduction is subject to the same fundamental limitation as most static analyses: For computability reasons, there is no general solution to the abduction problem, and thus *we cannot do better than a heuristic search.*

The main avenue for future work is to improve the abduction heuristics in order to cover larger and more difficult examples than Caber is currently able to handle automatically. In particular, the `while` language in this paper does not feature procedure calls. There is no difficulty in extending the proof system in Section 3 to programs with procedures, adding postconditions to judgements to capture the effect of procedure calls. However, the abduction problem becomes much more difficult, as preconditions and postconditions must be abduced simultaneously. We know how to achieve this for some simple examples, but have not yet implemented it. For more complicated examples, we need to establish inductive entailments between formulas at procedure call sites, again highlighting the need for good lemma speculation techniques.

Current limitations of the implementation, which are however not fundamental, include: search space explosion in the presence of too many record fields and/or temporary variables in the program; the absence of heuristics for abducing information not explicitly manipulated by the program (e.g. numerical information [20]) and difficulty in abducing suitably segmented structures when several pointers traverse the same data structure.

Our approach is very "pure" in that the only source of information for abduction is the text of the program itself. Thus the recursion in the abduced predicates will typically reflect the manipulation of data structures by the program. In principle, one could compare abduced predicates to a "library" of known structures using a suitable inductive theorem prover for separation logic.

Although by no means a silver bullet, we believe that cyclic abduction offers a promising and natural approach to automatic specification inference.

References

1. Antonopoulos, T., Gorogiannis, N., Haase, C., Kanovich, M., Ouaknine, J.: Foundations for decision problems in separation logic with general inductive predicates. In: Muscholl, A. (ed.) FOSSACS 2014. LNCS, vol. 8412, pp. 411–425. Springer, Heidelberg (2014)
2. Berdine, J., Calcagno, C., Cook, B., Distefano, D., O'Hearn, P.W., Wies, T., Yang, H.: Shape analysis for composite data structures. In: Damm, W., Hermanns, H. (eds.) CAV 2007. LNCS, vol. 4590, pp. 178–192. Springer, Heidelberg (2007)
3. Berdine, J., Calcagno, C., O'Hearn, P.W.: Symbolic execution with separation logic. In: Yi, K. (ed.) APLAS 2005. LNCS, vol. 3780, pp. 52–68. Springer, Heidelberg (2005)
4. Berdine, J., Cook, B., Distefano, D., O'Hearn, P.W.: Automatic termination proofs for programs with shape-shifting heaps. In: Ball, T., Jones, R.B. (eds.) CAV 2006. LNCS, vol. 4144, pp. 386–400. Springer, Heidelberg (2006)
5. Berdine, J., Cook, B., Ishtiaq, S.: Slayer: Memory safety for systems-level code. In: Gopalakrishnan, G., Qadeer, S. (eds.) CAV 2011. LNCS, vol. 6806, pp. 178–183. Springer, Heidelberg (2011)
6. Bozga, M., Iosif, R., Konečný, F.: Deciding conditional termination. In: Flanagan, C., König, B. (eds.) TACAS 2012. LNCS, vol. 7214, pp. 252–266. Springer, Heidelberg (2012)
7. Brockschmidt, M., Musiol, R., Otto, C., Giesl, J.: Automated termination proofs for Java programs with cyclic data. In: Madhusudan, P., Seshia, S.A. (eds.) CAV 2012. LNCS, vol. 7358, pp. 105–122. Springer, Heidelberg (2012)
8. Brotherston, J., Bornat, R., Calcagno, C.: Cyclic proofs of program termination in separation logic. In: Proc. POPL-35. ACM (2008)
9. Brotherston, J., Fuhs, C., Gorogiannis, N., Navarro Pérez, J.: A decision procedure for satisfiability in separation logic with inductive predicates. In: Proceedings of CSL-LICS. ACM (2014) (to appear)
10. Brotherston, J., Gorogiannis, N.: Cyclic abduction of inductively defined safety and termination preconditions. Technical Report RN/13/14, University College London (2013)
11. Brotherston, J., Gorogiannis, N., Petersen, R.L.: A generic cyclic theorem prover. In: Jhala, R., Igarashi, A. (eds.) APLAS 2012. LNCS, vol. 7705, pp. 350–367. Springer, Heidelberg (2012)
12. Calcagno, C., Distefano, D., O'Hearn, P., Yang, H.: Compositional shape analysis by means of bi-abduction. Journal of the ACM 58(6) (December 2011)

13. Chang, B.-Y.E., Rival, X.: Relational inductive shape analysis. In: Proc. POPL-35. ACM (2008)
14. Dijkstra, E.W.: A Discipline of Programming. Prentice-Hall (1976)
15. Dillig, I., Dillig, T., Li, B., McMillan, K.: Inductive invariant generation via abductive inference. In: Proceedings of OOPSLA. ACM (2013)
16. Flener, P., Yilmaz, S.: Inductive synthesis of recursive logic programs: achievements and prospects. The Journal of Logic Programming 41(2-3), 141–195 (1999)
17. Guo, B., Vachharajani, N., August, D.I.: Shape analysis with inductive recursion synthesis. In: Proc. PLDI-28 (June 2007)
18. He, G., Qin, S., Chin, W.-N., Craciun, F.: Automated specification discovery via user-defined predicates. In: Groves, L., Sun, J. (eds.) ICFEM 2013. LNCS, vol. 8144, pp. 397–414. Springer, Heidelberg (2013)
19. Lee, O., Yang, H., Yi, K.: Automatic verification of pointer programs using grammar-based shape analysis. In: Sagiv, M. (ed.) ESOP 2005. LNCS, vol. 3444, pp. 124–140. Springer, Heidelberg (2005)
20. Magill, S., Tsai, M.-H., Lee, P., Tsay, Y.-K.: Automatic numeric abstractions for heap-manipulating programs. In: Proc. POPL-37. ACM (2010)
21. Reynolds, J.C.: Separation logic: A logic for shared mutable data structures. In: Proc. LICS-17. IEEE Computer Society (2002)
22. Yang, H., Lee, O., Berdine, J., Calcagno, C., Cook, B., Distefano, D., O'Hearn, P.W.: Scalable shape analysis for systems code. In: Gupta, A., Malik, S. (eds.) CAV 2008. LNCS, vol. 5123, pp. 385–398. Springer, Heidelberg (2008)
23. Yang, H., O'Hearn, P.: A semantic basis for local reasoning. In: Nielsen, M., Engberg, U. (eds.) FOSSACS 2002. LNCS, vol. 2303, pp. 402–416. Springer, Heidelberg (2002)

Expectation Invariants for Probabilistic Program Loops as Fixed Points

Aleksandar Chakarov and Sriram Sankaranarayanan

Department of Computer Science
University of Colorado, Boulder, CO
{firstname.lastname}@colorado.edu

Abstract. We present static analyses for probabilistic loops using *expectation invariants*. Probabilistic loops are imperative while-loops augmented with calls to random variable generators. Whereas, traditional program analysis uses Floyd-Hoare style invariants to over-approximate the set of reachable states, our approach synthesizes invariant inequalities involving the expected values of program expressions at the loop head. We first define the notion of expectation invariants, and demonstrate their usefulness in analyzing probabilistic program loops. Next, we present the set of expectation invariants for a loop as a fixed point of the pre-expectation operator over sets of program expressions. Finally, we use existing concepts from abstract interpretation theory to present an iterative analysis that synthesizes expectation invariants for probabilistic program loops. We show how the standard polyhedral abstract domain can be used to synthesize expectation invariants for probabilistic programs, and demonstrate the usefulness of our approach on some examples of probabilistic program loops.

1 Introduction

Inductive loop invariants are commonly used in program verification to prove properties of loops in (non-deterministic) programs. Abstract interpretation provides a powerful framework to synthesize inductive invariants automatically from the given program text [7]. In this paper, we provide a static analysis framework for probabilistic loops that can call random number generators to sample from pre-specified distributions such as *Bernoulli*, *uniform* and *normal*. Probabilistic programs arise in a variety of domains ranging from biological systems [16] to randomized algorithms [21]. In this paper, we present an abstract interpretation framework for deriving *expectation invariants* of probabilistic loops. Expectation invariants are expressions whose expectations *at any given iteration of the loop* exist, and are always non-negative.

Proving expectation invariants often requires approximating the distribution of states after n steps of loop execution (see [2,18,20,9,15] for techniques that approximate distributions in a sound manner). However, even simple programs, such as the program shown in Figure 1, can exhibit complex distributions of reachable states after just a few steps of loop execution (see Figure 2). Extrapolating from a few to arbitrarily many loop iterations requires the notion of "inductive invariants" for probabilistic programs. In this paper, we build upon the standard notion of *quantitative invariants* originally considered by McIver and Morgan [17]. First we extend quantitative invariants from single expressions to a set of expressions that are mutually invariant: multiple expressions

M. Müller-Olm and H. Seidl (Eds.): SAS 2014, LNCS 8723, pp. 85–100, 2014.

whose expectations are nonnegative simultaneously. Next, we characterize invariants as a fixed point, making them amenable to automatic approximation using abstract interpretation. We demonstrate polyhedral analysis over numerical probabilistic programs that manipulate real- and integer-valued state variables.

Our approach first defines the notion of inductive invariants using the pre-expectation operator, along the lines of McIver and Morgan [17]. We lift the pre-expectation operator to a cone of expressions, and subsequently construct a monotone operator over finitely generated cones. Any pre-fixed point of this monotone operator is shown to correspond to expectation invariants. We then use the descending abstract Kleene iteration starting from the cone $\top$ of all affine (or fixed degree polynomial expressions) to iteratively apply the monotone operator to this cone and obtain a pre-fixed point. A (dual) widening operator is used to accelerate this process.

We apply our technique to some small but complex examples of probabilistic programs and demonstrate the power of our approach to synthesize expectation invariants that are otherwise hard to realize manually. We also compare our approach with the tool PRINSYS that synthesizes quantitative invariants using a constraint-based approach by solving constraints on the unknown coefficients of a template invariant form [13,11].

Related Work. The broader area of probabilistic program analysis has seen much progress over the recent past. Our previous work combining symbolic execution of probabilistic programs with volume computation, provides an extensive review of approaches in this area [22]. Therefore, we restrict ourselves to very closely related works.

McIver and Morgan were among the first to consider deductive approaches for probabilistic programs using the concept of *quantitative invariants* [17]. Their work focuses on programs where the stochastic inputs are restricted to discrete distributions over a finite set of support. We naturally lift this restriction to consider a richer class of distributions in this paper including Gaussian, Poisson, Uniform or Exponential random variables. Our setup can use any distributions whose expectations (and some higher moments) exist, and are available. Furthermore, our technique synthesizes invariants that are polynomial expressions involving the program variables. In particular, *indicator functions* over program assertions are not considered in this paper [13,17]. Indicator functions complicate the computation of the pre-expectation when a richer class of distributions are allowed. Finally, McIver & Morgan treat demonic non-deterministic as well as stochastic inputs. Our approach, currently, does not support (demonic) non-determinism; but is potentially extensible when demonic non-determinism is present. Our previous work [3] first considered the relationship between quantitative invariants and the well-known concept of martingales and super-martingales from probability theory [24]. In particular, it demonstrates the use of concentration of measure inequalities to prove probability bounds on assertions at various points in the program [10]. The notion of inductive expectation invariants is a strict generalization of that considered in our previous work. While martingales and super-martingales are analogous to a single inductive linear inequality, we consider the analog of multiple *mutually inductive* linear invariants. The use of abstract interpretation framework is an additional contribution. The generation of quantitative invariants was first studied by Katoen et al. [13], using a constraint-based approach [6,23], implemented in the tool PRINSYS [11]. An experimental comparison is provided in Section 5.

```
real x := rand(-5,3)
real y := rand(-3,5)
int count := 0
while (x+y <= 10)
    if flip(3/4)
        x := x + rand(0,2)
        y := y + 2
    count++
```

```
real x := rand(-5,3)
real y := rand(-3,5)
int count := 0
while (forever)
    if (x + y <= 10)
        if flip(3/4)
            x := x + rand(0,2)
            y := y + 2
        count++
    else
        // Preserve x,y,count
```

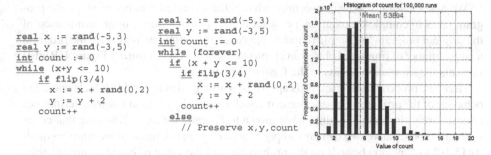

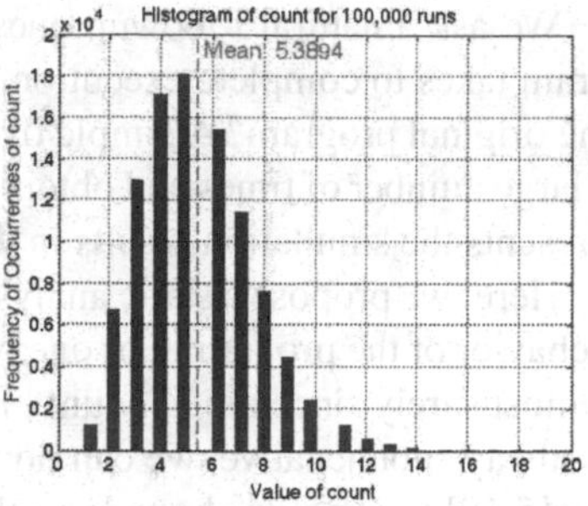

Fig. 1. (**Left**) Simple example of a probabilistic program loop, (**Middle**) Modified loop with *stuttering* semantics, and (**Right**) histogram of the value of count after executing the stuttering loop for at most 25 steps.

Abstract domains for probabilistic programs were first considered by Monniaux [18], by enriching standard abstract domains with bounds on the measure. Refinements of this idea appear in the work of Mardziel et al [15] and Bouissou et al. [2]. Instead of the explicit representations of distributions found in these works, we characterize sets of distributions by means of bounds on moments of expressions. Alternatively, Monniaux presents a backward abstract interpretation scheme to compute the probability of an observable assertion at the program output, and characterize the output distribution [19]. The backwards approach treats the program as a measurable function, and the backward abstract interpretation follows the natural definition of the output distribution through the inverse mapping [5]. However, the approach seemingly requires a user generated query or a systematic gridding of the output states to define the distribution. Cousot and Monerau [9] present a systematic and general abstract semantics for probabilistic programs that views the abstract probabilistic semantics obtained by separately considering abstractions of the program semantics, the probability (event) space, and a "law abstraction" that is a function mapping abstract states to the distribution over the set of possible abstract next states obtained from a single step of program execution. Their approach conveniently captures existing techniques as instances of their framework, while providing new ways of abstracting probabilistic program semantics. Based on our current understanding, the approach in this paper fits into their framework by viewing expectation invariants as representing sets of distributions, and the proposed transfer functions as *law abstractions* that characterize next state distributions.

Example 1. Figure 1 shows a simple probabilistic program written in an imperative language. Each execution of the loop updates variables x,y with probability $\frac{3}{4}$ or chooses to leave them unchanged with probability $\frac{1}{4}$. The variable count acts as a loop counter. Our approach first rewrites the program to yield a *stuttering loop* (see Fig. 1(**Middle**)). Analyzing the stuttering loop yields *expectation invariants* such as

$$(\forall\, n \in \mathbb{N})\ \mathbb{E}(\text{count} \mid n) \leq \frac{56}{9}\,.$$

Here, n refers to the number of iterations of the stuttered loop and $\mathbb{E}(\text{count} \mid n)$ is the expected value of count over the distribution of reachable states after $n \in \mathbb{N}$ iterations.

We ask a natural followup question: what is the expected number of steps the program takes to complete execution, i.e. what is the value $\mathbb{E}(count)$ upon termination of the original program? A simple dynamic approach is to simulate (execute) the program a large number of times and obtain an empirical estimate for $\mathbb{E}(count)$. Figure 1(**Right**) presents the simulation results in the form of a histogram.

Here, we propose a static analysis approach whose goal is to establish facts about the behavior of the program. For one, we can conclude that the original program terminates almost surely since the $\mathbb{E}(\text{count} \mid n)$ is shown to be finite for all n. Knowing that count is always nonnegative, we can now apply Markov's *concentration of measure* inequality [5,10] to conclude bounds on the probabilities of the value of count at any program step: $\mathbb{P}(\text{count} \geq 25 \mid n) \leq \frac{\mathbb{E}(\text{count} \mid n)}{25} \leq \frac{56}{175} \approx 0.32$. Often, we can use much stronger inequalities, should the necessary conditions for these be met. In addition, our analysis yields many other interesting results, for instance: $\forall\, n \in \mathbb{N},\ \mathbb{E}(3\text{count} - 2\text{y} + 2 \mid n) = 0$ and $\mathbb{E}(4\text{x} + 4\text{y} - 9\text{count} \mid n) = 0$.

Outline. The remainder of this paper is organized as follows: Section 2 introduces the preliminaries of probabilistic programs before we extend the discussion to expectation invariants and cones in Section 3. Section 4 presents an abstract interpretation based iterative approach to compute fixed points under the pre-expectation operator. Section 5 is a summary of the experiments we conducted using our prototype version of the tool and a comparison with the PRINSYS tool. Proofs of our main results and details of our probabilistic benchmarks have been provided in an extended version [4].

2 Preliminaries

Probabilistic Programs. Let $\mathcal{P}$ be a probabilistic program in an imperative language with random number generators including `unifInt(lb, ub)`, `unifReal(lb, ub)`, and `gaussian(mean, var)`. These constructs draw values from standard distributions with well-defined, finite expected values. Let $X = \{x_1, \ldots, x_m\}$ be a set of real-valued *program variables* and $R = \{r_1, \ldots, r_l\}$ be a set of real-valued *random variables*. Vectors $\boldsymbol{x}$ and $\boldsymbol{r}$ denote valuations of all program, respectively random, variables. The random variables have a joint distribution $\mathcal{D}_R$. Formally, the distribution is defined over an underlying σ-algebra $(\Omega, \mathcal{F})$ with an appropriate measure μ_r.

A linear inequality over X is an expression of the form $\boldsymbol{a}^T\, \boldsymbol{x} \leq b$ for a vector $\boldsymbol{a} \in \mathbb{R}^m, b \in \mathbb{R}$. A linear assertion $\varphi[X]$ involving X is a conjunction of linear inequalities $\varphi :\ \bigwedge_{i=1}^{n} \boldsymbol{a}_i^T \boldsymbol{x} \leq b_i$ and can be succinctly expressed in matrix notation as $\varphi : A\boldsymbol{x} \leq \boldsymbol{b}$.

Definition 1 (Probabilistic Loops). *A* probabilistic loop *is a tuple* $\langle \mathcal{T}, \mathcal{D}_0, n\rangle$*, wherein* $\mathcal{T} : \{\tau_1, \ldots, \tau_k\}$ *is a set of probabilistic transitions (from the loop head to itself),* $\mathcal{D}_0$ *is the* initial probability distribution *and* n *is a formal* loop counter variable.

Each probabilistic transition $\tau_i : \langle \mathrm{g}_i, \mathcal{F}_i\rangle$ *consists of (a)* guard *assertion* $\mathrm{g}_i[X]$ *over* X*; and (b)* update function $\mathcal{F}_i(\boldsymbol{x}, \boldsymbol{r})$ *that yields the next state* $\boldsymbol{x}' := \mathcal{F}_i(\boldsymbol{x}, \boldsymbol{r})$.

In this paper, we restrict ourselves to *piecewise linear* (PWL) probabilistic programs, wherein each transition τ_i has linear assertion guards and piecewise linear updates. Further, we also restrict ourselves to studying expectation invariants over simple loops.

An extension of these ideas to programs with arbitrary control flow structure including nested loops will be discussed in our extended version [4].

Definition 2 (PWL Transitions). *A* piecewise linear *transition* $\tau : \langle \mathsf{g}, \mathcal{F}(\boldsymbol{x}, \boldsymbol{r})\rangle$ *has the following special structure:*

- g *is a* linear *guard assertion over* X*;*
- $\mathcal{F}(\boldsymbol{x}, \boldsymbol{r})$ *is a (continuous)* piecewise linear *update function for* X*, where, for ease of presentation,* $\boldsymbol{r}$ *is decomposed into a vector of* continuous (random) choices $\boldsymbol{r}_c$ *and a vector of* discrete Bernoulli choices (coin flips) $\boldsymbol{r}_b$. *As a result, the update function may be written as*

$$F(\boldsymbol{x}, \boldsymbol{r}) = \begin{cases} \mathsf{f}_1 : A_1\boldsymbol{x} + B_1\boldsymbol{r}_c + d_1, & \textit{with probability } p_1, \\ \qquad \vdots & \\ \mathsf{f}_k : A_k\boldsymbol{x} + B_k\boldsymbol{r}_c + d_k, & \textit{with probability } p_k, \end{cases}$$

Options $\mathsf{f}_1, \ldots, \mathsf{f}_k$*, abstract the effect of the Bernoulli choices in* $\boldsymbol{r}_b$*, and are called* forks*, while* $p_1, \ldots, p_k$ *are* fork probabilities *satisfying* $0 < p_i \leq 1$*, and* $\sum_{i=1}^{k} p_i = 1$. $A_1, \ldots, A_k \in \mathbb{R}^{m\times m}$*,* $B_1, \ldots, B_k \in \mathbb{R}^{m\times l}$*, and* $d_1, \ldots, d_k \in \mathbb{R}$.

No Nondeterminism. For a probabilistic loop $\langle \mathcal{T}, \mathcal{D}_0, n\rangle$, we preclude demonic nondeterminism using two restrictions:

Mutual Exclusion: For all pairs $\tau_1 : \langle \mathsf{g}_1, \mathcal{F}_1\rangle$ and $\tau_2 : \langle \mathsf{g}_2, \mathcal{F}_2\rangle$ in $\mathcal{T}$, $\mathsf{g}_1 \wedge \mathsf{g}_2 \equiv false$.
Exhaustiveness: For all transitions τ_i, $\bigvee_{\tau_i \in \mathcal{T}} \mathsf{g}_i \equiv true$.

Mutual exclusion and mutual exhaustiveness together guarantee that precisely one transition can be taken at a time step n and the choice is a function of the state $\boldsymbol{x}$.

Execution Model. A *state* of the probabilistic loop is a tuple $\langle \boldsymbol{x}, n\rangle$ that provides values for the program variables X and the loop counter n. The state $\langle \boldsymbol{x}_0, 0\rangle$ is called an *initial state* if $\boldsymbol{x}_0$ is a sample drawn from the initial distribution $\mathcal{D}_0$ and $n = 0$.

Definition 3 (Sample Path). *A* sample path *(or an execution) of the loop is an infinite sequence* $(\boldsymbol{x}_0, 0) \xrightarrow{\tau^{(0)}, \boldsymbol{r}_0} (\boldsymbol{x}_1, 1) \xrightarrow{\tau^{(1)}, \boldsymbol{r}_1} (\boldsymbol{x}_2, 2) \rightarrow \cdots \xrightarrow{\tau^{(n-1)}, \boldsymbol{r}_{n-1}} (\boldsymbol{x}_n, n) \rightarrow \cdots,$ *wherein,* **(a)** $(\boldsymbol{x}_0, 0)$ *is a sample from* $\mathcal{D}_0$ *and* **(b)** *for each* $i \geq 0$*,* $(\boldsymbol{x}_{i+1}, i+1)$ *is obtained by executing the unique transition* $\tau^{(i)} : (\mathsf{g}_i, \mathcal{F}_i)$ *that is enabled on the state* $(\boldsymbol{x}_i, i)$*. This execution involves a sample from the Bernoulli (discrete) random variables to choose a fork of the transition* $\tau^{(i)}$ *and a choice of the continuous random variables* $\boldsymbol{r}_c$ *to obtain* $\boldsymbol{x}_{i+1} = \mathcal{F}_i(\boldsymbol{x}_i, \boldsymbol{r}_i)$.

We demonstrate the definitions above on a simple example.

Example 2. In Figure 1 (**Middle**) we present the *stuttering version* of a simple probabilistic program with a loop, where the initial values of the program variables reaching the loop head come from the joint distribution $\mathcal{D}_0 : \langle \mathsf{x}, \mathsf{y}, \mathsf{count}\rangle \sim U[-5, 3]\times U[-3, 5]\times \{0\}$. This modification adds a new program path that preserves the values of program variables once the loop guard $\mathsf{x} + \mathsf{y} \leq 10$ is violated. The program has two transitions $\mathcal{T} : \{\tau_1, \tau_2\}$, where τ_1 represents the loop body:

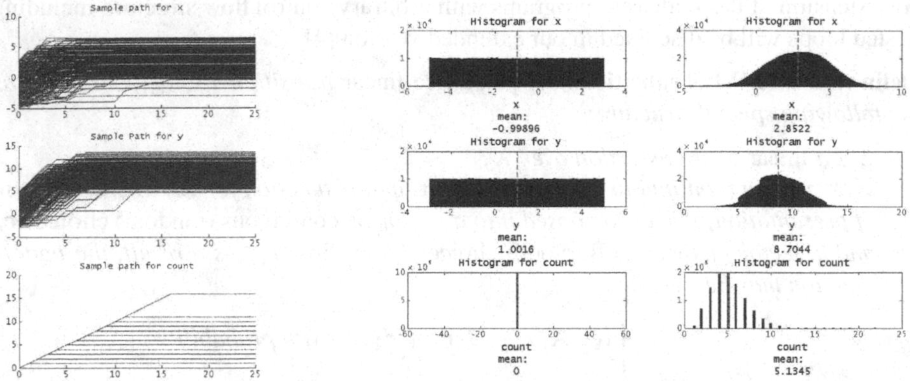

Fig. 2. **(Left)** Some sample paths for the program in Figure 1. **(Right)** Frequency histograms for the distributions $\mathcal{D}_n$ for n = 0, 25.

τ_1 (loop body)	τ_2 (stuttering)
$\mathsf{g}_1 : (x + y \leq 10)$ $\mathcal{F}_{\tau_1} : \begin{cases} f_1 : \begin{bmatrix} \text{x'} \mapsto \text{x} + r_1, \\ \text{y'} \mapsto \text{y} + 2, \\ \text{count'} \mapsto \text{count} + 1, \end{bmatrix} & \text{w.p. } \frac{3}{4} \\ f_2 : \begin{bmatrix} \text{x'} \mapsto \text{x}, \\ \text{y'} \mapsto \text{y}, \\ \text{count'} \mapsto \text{count} + 1, \end{bmatrix} & \text{w.p. } \frac{1}{4} \end{cases}$	$\mathsf{g}_2 : (x + y > 10)$ $\mathcal{F}_{\tau_2} : \begin{cases} \text{x'} \mapsto \text{x}, \\ \text{y'} \mapsto \text{y}, \\ \text{count'} \mapsto \text{count}, \end{cases}$

Here r_1 represents the uniform random variable over $[0, 2]$. Transition τ_2 represents the *stuttering* after $x + y > 10$. It is added to satisfy the mutual exclusiveness and exhaustiveness requirements. It has a single fork that preserves the values of x, y, count. Figure 2 depicts 200 sample paths obtained by simulating the program (for 25 steps) and distributions $\mathcal{D}_n$ for $n = 0$ and $n = 25$ obtained by running the program 10^6 times.

Operator Semantics: Probabilistic program semantics can be thought of as continuous linear operators over over the state distributions, starting from the initial distribution $\mathcal{D}_0$: $\mathcal{D}_0 \xrightarrow{[\![\mathcal{P}]\!]} \mathcal{D}_1 \xrightarrow{[\![\mathcal{P}]\!]} \cdots \xrightarrow{[\![\mathcal{P}]\!]} \mathcal{D}_n \xrightarrow{[\![\mathcal{P}]\!]} \cdots$. Here $[\![\mathcal{P}]\!]$ models the effect of a single loop iteration and $\mathcal{D}_n$ is the distribution of the states after n iterations of the loop. This matches the standard probabilistic program semantics [14,19]. The definition of $\mathcal{D}_n$ and $[\![\mathcal{P}]\!]$ are described in the extended version [4].

Pre-Expectations. We now define the useful concept of pre-expectation of an expression e over the program variables across a transition τ following earlier work by McIver and Morgan [17]. Let $\tau : \langle \mathsf{g}, \mathcal{F} \rangle$ be a transition and $\mathsf{e}[\boldsymbol{x}]$ be an expression involving the state variables $\boldsymbol{x}$ of the program.

The pre-expectation operator $\mathtt{pre}\mathbb{E}_\tau$ is an *expression transformer* that associates each expression e with the next-step *expectation* expression $\mathtt{pre}\mathbb{E}_\tau(\mathsf{e}[\boldsymbol{x}'])$ across τ, in terms of the *current state variables of the program.* Formally,

$$\mathtt{pre}\mathbb{E}_\tau(\mathsf{e}[\boldsymbol{x}']) : \mathbb{E}_{\mathcal{R}}(\mathsf{e}[\boldsymbol{x}' \mapsto \mathcal{F}(\boldsymbol{x}, \boldsymbol{r})] \mid \boldsymbol{x})$$

The expectation $\mathbb{E}_{\mathcal{R}}$ is taken over the distribution of $\boldsymbol{r}$ in the transition τ.

Consider a PWL transition τ with $k > 0$ forks, $\mathsf{f}_1, \ldots, \mathsf{f}_\mathsf{k}$, each of the form f_j : $A_j\boldsymbol{x} + B_j\boldsymbol{r} + d_j$ with fork probability p_j. The pre-expectation operator is defined as

$$\mathtt{pre}\mathbb{E}_\tau(\mathsf{e}') = \sum_{j=1}^{k} p_j \mathbb{E}_{\mathcal{R}}(\text{PRE}(\mathsf{e}', f_j) \mid \boldsymbol{x})$$

where $\text{PRE}(\mathsf{e}', f_j)$ is the substitution of post variables $\boldsymbol{x}'$ for their update values $f_j(\boldsymbol{x}, \boldsymbol{r})$ in expression e. The expectation $\mathbb{E}_{\mathcal{R}}(g)$ denotes the expectation of g over the joint distribution $\mathcal{R}$ of the random variables.

Example 3. We illustrate the notion of a pre-expectation of a program expression by considering the expression $3 + 2\mathsf{x} - \mathsf{y}$ across transition τ_1 in the Figure 1.

$$\mathtt{pre}\mathbb{E}_{\tau_1}(3 + 2\mathsf{x}' - \mathsf{y}') : \begin{pmatrix} \frac{3}{4}[3 + 2\mathbb{E}_{r_1}(x + r_1) - (y+2)] + & // \text{ from fork } f_1 \\ \frac{1}{4}[3 + 2x - y] & // \text{ from fork } f_2 \end{pmatrix}.$$

Simplifying, we obtain $\mathtt{pre}\mathbb{E}_{\tau_1}(3 + 2\mathsf{x}' - \mathsf{y}') = 3 + 2x - y + \frac{3}{2}\mathbb{E}_{r_1}(r_1) - \frac{3}{2}$. Noting that $\mathbb{E}_{r_1}(r_1) = 1$, we obtain $\mathtt{pre}\mathbb{E}_{\tau_1}(3 + 2\mathsf{x}' - \mathsf{y}') = 3 + 2\mathsf{x} - \mathsf{y}$.

Likewise, we define $\mathtt{pre}\mathbb{E}(\mathsf{e}')$ (without a transition as a subscript) as

$$\mathbb{1}_{g_{\tau_1}} \times \mathtt{pre}\mathbb{E}_{\tau_1}(\mathsf{e}') + \cdots + \mathbb{1}_{g_{\tau_k}} \times \mathtt{pre}\mathbb{E}_{\tau_k}(\mathsf{e}'),$$

wherein $\mathbb{1}_g(\boldsymbol{x})$ is the *indicator* function: $\mathbb{1}_g(\boldsymbol{x}) = 1$ if $\boldsymbol{x} \models g(\boldsymbol{x})$, and 0, otherwise.

We now state a key result involving pre-expectations. Consider a prefix σ of a sample execution $(\boldsymbol{x}_0, 0) \to (\boldsymbol{x}_1, 1) \to \cdots \to (\boldsymbol{x}_n, n)$. Given that the current state is $(\boldsymbol{x}_n, n)$, we wish to find out the expectation of an expression e over the distribution of *all possible* next states $(\boldsymbol{x}_{n+1}, n+1)$. Let $\hat{\mathsf{e}} : \mathtt{pre}\mathbb{E}(\mathsf{e}')$.

Lemma 1. *The expected value of* e *over the post-state distribution starting from state* $(\boldsymbol{x}_n, n)$ *is the value of the pre-expectation* $\hat{\mathsf{e}}$ *evaluated over the current state* $\boldsymbol{x}_n$*:*

$$\mathbb{E}(\mathsf{e}(\boldsymbol{x}_{n+1}) | \boldsymbol{x}_n, n) = \hat{\mathsf{e}}(\boldsymbol{x}_n) = \sum_{\tau_i \in \mathcal{T}} \mathbb{1}_{g_i}(\boldsymbol{x}_n) \mathtt{pre}\mathbb{E}_{\tau_i}(\mathsf{e}').$$

Finally, we extend Lemma 1 to the full *distribution* $\mathcal{D}_n$ from which $\boldsymbol{x}_n$ is drawn.

Lemma 2. *The expected value of* e *over the post-state distribution* $\mathcal{D}_{n+1}$ *given a distribution* $\mathcal{D}_n$ *for the current state valuations* $\boldsymbol{x}_n$ *satisfies:*

$$\mathbb{E}_{\mathcal{D}_{n+1}}(\mathsf{e}(\boldsymbol{x}_{n+1})) = \mathbb{E}_{\mathcal{D}_n}(\mathtt{pre}\mathbb{E}(\mathsf{e})(\boldsymbol{x}_n)) = \mathbb{E}_{\mathcal{D}_n}[\hat{\mathsf{e}}] = \mathbb{E}_{\mathcal{D}_n}\left[\sum_{\tau_i \in \mathcal{T}} \mathbb{1}_{g_i}(\boldsymbol{x}_n) \mathtt{pre}\mathbb{E}_{\tau_i}(\mathsf{e}')\right].$$

3 Expectation Invariants

Expectation invariants are invariant inequalities on the expected value of program expressions. Therefore, one could view the set of possible state distributions $\mathcal{D}_i$ at step i as the concrete domain over which our analysis operates to produce the abstract facts in the form of *expectation invariants* over these distributions. We formalize expectation invariants and derive a fixed point characterization of expectation invariants.

3.1 Definitions and Examples

Let $\mathcal{P} : \langle \mathcal{T}, \mathcal{D}_0, n \rangle$ be a probabilistic loop and let $\langle \boldsymbol{x}_0, 0 \rangle$ be the initial state of the system. From Section 2 we know that $\boldsymbol{x}_0$ is drawn from an initial distribution $\mathcal{D}_0$ and that any n-step sample execution of $\mathcal{P}$ defines a sample trajectory through the distributions of reachable states $\mathcal{D}_0, \ldots, \mathcal{D}_n$ at step i for any $0 \leq i \leq n$. We then define the *expectation* of a program expression e *at time step* n as $\mathbb{E}(\mathsf{e}(\boldsymbol{x}_n) \mid n) = \mathbb{E}_{\mathcal{D}_n}(\mathsf{e}(\boldsymbol{x}_n))$.

Definition 4 (Expectation Invariants). *An* e *over the program variables* X *is called an* expectation invariant *(EI) iff for all* $n \geq 0, \mathbb{E}(\mathsf{e} \mid n) \geq 0$.

Thus, expectation invariants are program expressions whose expectations over the initial distribution are non-negative, and under *any* number of iterations of the probabilistic loop remain non-negative.

Example 4. Consider the program from Example 1, and the expression $\mathsf{y} - \mathsf{x}$. Initially, $\mathbb{E}(\mathsf{y} - \mathsf{x} \mid 0) = \mathbb{E}_{\mathcal{D}_0}(\mathsf{y} - \mathsf{x}) = 1 - (-1) = 2 \geq 0$. We can show that $\mathbb{E}(\mathsf{y} - \mathsf{x} \mid i) = \mathbb{E}(\mathsf{y} \mid i) - \mathbb{E}(\mathsf{x} \mid i) \geq 0$ at any step i. Therefore, $\mathsf{y} - \mathsf{x}$ is an expectation invariant.

The concept of expectation invariant defined here is closely related to that of martingales studied in our earlier work [3]. The importance of expectation invariants is that a set of "inductive" EI is a set of mutually inductive constraints over state distributions. This allows the analysis to track and transfer sufficient amount of information about the distributions across loop iterations without ever having to explicitly construct these.

Proving EI. We now focus on the question of proving that a given expression e over the program variables is an expectation invariant. This requires constructing (approximations) to the distribution $\mathcal{D}_n$ for each n, or alternatively, an argument based on mathematical induction. We first observe an important property of each $\mathcal{D}_n$.

Definition 5 (Admissible Distribution). *We say that a distribution* $\mathcal{D}$ *over the state-space* $\mathcal{X}$ *is* admissible *if all moments exist.*[1] *In other words, for any polynomial* $p(\boldsymbol{x})$ *over the program variables,* $\mathbb{E}_{\mathcal{D}}(p(\boldsymbol{x}))$ *exists, and is finite.*

Let us assume that any program $\mathcal{P}$ which we attempt to analyze is such that

[1] While the existence of only the first moment suffices, our experiments demonstrate that our current synthesis approach can be extended to polynomial expectation invariants.

1. $\mathcal{D}_0$, the initial state distribution, is admissible;
2. For each transition τ, the distribution of the random variables $\mathcal{D}_R$ is admissible.

Under these assumptions and following the linearity of the statements and the guards in the program, we can show the following fact.

Lemma 3. *For all $n \in \mathbb{N}$, the distribution $\mathcal{D}_n$ is admissible.*

Rather than construct $\mathcal{D}_n$ explicitly for each n (which quickly becomes impractical), we formulate the principle of inductive expectation invariants. Consider expressions $E = \{\mathtt{e}_1, \ldots, \mathtt{e}_m\}$ wherein each $\mathtt{e}_i$ is a linear (or polynomial) expression involving the program variables.

Definition 6 (Inductive Expectation Invariants). *The set E of expressions forms an inductive expectation invariant of the program $\mathcal{P}$ iff for each $\mathtt{e}_j$, $j \in [1, m]$,*

1. *$\mathbb{E}_{\mathcal{D}_0}(\mathtt{e}_j) \geq 0$, i.e., the expectation at the initial step is non-negative.*
2. *For every admissible distribution $\mathcal{D}$ over the state-space $\mathcal{X}$,*

$$(\mathbb{E}_{\mathcal{D}}(\mathtt{e}_1) \geq 0 \wedge \cdots \wedge \mathbb{E}_{\mathcal{D}}(\mathtt{e}_m) \geq 0) \models \mathbb{E}_{\mathcal{D}}(\mathtt{pre}\mathbb{E}(\mathtt{e}_j)) \geq 0 . \quad (1)$$

The inductive expectation invariant principle stated above follows the standard Floyd-Hoare approach of "abstracting away" the distribution at the nth step by the inductive invariant itself, and using these to show that the invariant continues to hold for one more step. Furthermore, it abstracts away from a specific $\mathcal{D}_n$ to any admissible distribution $\mathcal{D}$. However, Def. 6 is quite unwieldy, in practice, since the quantification over *all possible admissible distributions* $\mathcal{D}$ over the state space $\mathcal{X}$ is a higher order quantifier (over probability spaces and measurable functions). Rather than reason with this quantifier, we will use the following facts about expectations to formulate a new principle:

Theorem 1 (Facts About Expectations over Admissible Distributions). *The following hold over all possible admissible distributions $\mathcal{D}$ over a σ-algebra $\mathcal{X}$, linear assertion φ, and linear (or polynomial expressions) $\mathtt{e}, \mathtt{e}_1, \ldots, \mathtt{e}_k$:*

1. *Linearity of expectation: $\mathbb{E}_{\mathcal{D}}(\lambda_1 \mathtt{e}_1 + \ldots + \lambda_k \mathtt{e}_k) = \lambda_1 \mathbb{E}_{\mathcal{D}}(\mathtt{e}_1) + \cdots + \lambda_k \mathbb{E}_{\mathcal{D}}(\mathtt{e}_k)$, for $\lambda_i \in \mathbb{R}$.*
2. *Indicator Functions: $\mathbb{E}_{\mathcal{D}}(\mathbb{1}_{\mathtt{e} \geq 0} \times \mathtt{e}) \geq 0$, and in general, if $\varphi \models \mathtt{e} \geq 0$ then $\mathbb{E}_{\mathcal{D}}(\mathbb{1}_{\varphi} \times \mathtt{e}) \geq 0$, provided $[\![\varphi]\!]$ is measurable.*
3. *$\mathbb{E}_{\mathcal{D}}(\mathbb{1}_{\varphi}\mathtt{e} + \mathbb{1}_{\neg\varphi}\mathtt{e}) = \mathbb{E}_{\mathcal{D}}(\mathtt{e})$, provided $[\![\varphi]\!]$ is measurable.*

Using these facts as "axioms", we attempt to reformulate the key step 2 of Def. 6 as a simple quantified statement in (first-order) linear arithmetic. Consider, once again, the key statement of the principle (1). The central idea of our approach is to express the pre-expectation $\mathtt{pre}\mathbb{E}(\mathtt{e}_j)$ for each $\mathtt{e}_j \in E$ as

$$\mathtt{pre}\mathbb{E}(\mathtt{e}_j) = \sum_{i=1}^{m} \lambda_{j,i} \mathtt{e}_i + \sum_{p} \mu_{j,p} \left(\mathbb{1}_{\varphi_p} \times g_p\right), \quad (2)$$

wherein $\lambda_{j,i} \geq 0$ and $\mu_{j,p} \geq 0$ are real-valued multipliers, g_p are linear expressions over the program variables and φ_p are assertions such that $\varphi_p \models g_p \geq 0$. The origin of the expressions g_p and assertions φ_p will be made clear, shortly. Let us fix a finite set of expressions $E = \{\mathtt{e}_1, \ldots, \mathtt{e}_m\}$.

Lemma 4. *If E satisfies the relaxed induction principle* (2) *then E satisfies the original induction principle* (1).

3.2 Conic Inductive Expectation Invariants

We now formalize this intuition using the concept of *conic inductive expectation invariants*. Let $\mathcal{P}$ be a program with transitions $\mathcal{T}$. Let g_i be a linear assertion representing the guard of the transition τ_i. We express g_i as $\bigwedge_{j=1}^{n_i} g_{i,j} \geq 0$, wherein $g_{i,j}$ are affine program expressions. Let $\boldsymbol{g_i} : (g_{i,1} \ \cdots \ g_{i,n_i})^T$ be a vector representing g_i. Likewise, let $E = \{\mathsf{e}_1, \ldots, \mathsf{e}_m\}$ be a finite set of expressions, we denote the vector of expressions as $\boldsymbol{e} : (\mathsf{e}_1, \ldots, \mathsf{e}_m)^T$.

Definition 7 (Conic Inductive Expectation Invariants). *The finite set E is a* conic inductive invariant *of the program $\mathcal{P}$ iff for each $\mathsf{e}_j \in E$,*

1. *Initial Condition:* $\mathbb{E}_{\mathcal{D}_0}(\mathsf{e}_j) \geq 0$
2. *Induction Step: There exists a vector of multipliers $\boldsymbol{\lambda}_j \geq 0$, such that for each transition $\tau_l : (\mathsf{g}_l, \mathcal{F}_l)$, $\mathtt{pre}\mathbb{E}_{\tau_l}(\mathsf{e}_j)$ can be expressed as a conic combination of expressions in E and the expressions in g_l:*

$$(\exists\, \boldsymbol{\lambda}_j \geq 0)\ (\forall\, \tau_l \in \mathcal{T})\ (\exists\, \boldsymbol{\mu}_l \geq 0)\ \mathtt{pre}\mathbb{E}_{\tau_l}(\mathsf{e}_j) = \boldsymbol{\lambda}_j^T\, \boldsymbol{e} + \boldsymbol{\mu}_l{}^T \boldsymbol{g}_l\,. \qquad (3)$$

In particular, we note that the order of quantification in Eq. (3) is quite important. We note for a given expression e_j the multipliers $\boldsymbol{\lambda}_j$ must stay the same across all the transitions $\tau_l \in \mathcal{T}$. This will ensure the applicability of the linearity of expectation. Changing the order of quantification makes the rule unsound, as discussed in the extended version of the paper[4].

Example 5. The set $E = \{e_1 : \mathsf{y} - 2\mathsf{x},\ e_2 : 2\mathsf{x} - \mathsf{y} + 3,\ e_3 : 4\mathsf{x} - 3\mathsf{count} + 4,\ e_4 : -2\mathsf{x} + \mathsf{y} - 3,\ e_5 : -4\mathsf{x} + 3\mathsf{count} - 4\}$ is a conic inductive invariant for the program in Example 1. Consider $\mathsf{e}_1 : \mathsf{y} - 2\mathsf{x}$. We have

$$\mathtt{pre}\mathbb{E}_{\tau_1}(\mathsf{e}_1) : \mathbb{E}_{r_1}\left(\frac{3}{4}(\mathsf{y} + 2 - 2\mathsf{x} - 2r_1) + \frac{1}{4}(\mathsf{y} - 2\mathsf{x})\right) = \mathsf{y} - 2\mathsf{x}.$$

Likewise, $\mathtt{pre}\mathbb{E}_{\tau_2}(\mathsf{e}_1) : \mathsf{e}_1$, since τ_2 is a stuttering transition.

Therefore, setting $\boldsymbol{\lambda} : (1\,0\,0\,0\,0)^T$, we obtain $\mathtt{pre}\mathbb{E}(\mathsf{e}_1) : \boldsymbol{\lambda}^T \boldsymbol{e} + \mathbf{0} \times \mathbb{1}_{x+y\leq 10}$. For a non-trivial example, see the extended version of the paper [4].

Theorem 2. *Let E be a conic inductive invariant for a program $\mathcal{P}$ as given by Definition 7. It follows that each $\mathsf{e}_j \in E$ is an expectation invariant of the program.*

Thus far, we have presented inductive expectation invariants as a finite set of expressions $E = \{\mathsf{e}_1, \ldots, \mathsf{e}_m\}$, satisfying the conditions in Definitions 6 or 7. We transfer our notion from a finite set of expressions to a finitely generated cone of these in preparation for our fixed point characterization given in the next section.

Definition 8 (Cones). *Let $E = \{\mathsf{e}_1, \ldots, \mathsf{e}_k\}$ be a finite set of program expressions over the program variables $\boldsymbol{x}$. The set of* conic combinations (the cone) *of E is defined as*

$$\mathsf{Cone}(E) = \left\{ \lambda_0 + \sum_{i=1}^{k} \lambda_i \mathsf{e}_i \mid 0 \leq \lambda_i, 0 \leq i \leq k \right\}.$$

Expressions e_i are called the generators *of the cone.*

Given a non-empty linear assertion assertion $\varphi : \bigwedge_{i=1}^{k} \mathsf{e}_i \geq 0$, it is well-known that $\varphi \models \mathsf{e} \geq 0$ iff $\mathsf{e} \in \mathsf{Cone}(\mathsf{e}_1, \ldots, \mathsf{e}_k)$. Likewise, let E be an inductive expectation invariant. It follows that any $\mathsf{e} \in \mathsf{Cone}(E)$ is an expectation invariant of the program $\mathcal{P}$.

Example 6. Revisiting Example 5, we consider the conic combination:

$$4(-2\mathrm{x} + \mathrm{y} - 3) + 3(4\mathrm{x} - 3\mathrm{count} + 4) = 4\mathrm{x} + 4\mathrm{y} - 9\mathrm{count}$$

As a result, we conclude that $\mathbb{E}_{\mathcal{D}_n}(4\mathrm{x} + 4\mathrm{y} - 9\mathrm{count}) \geq 0$ at each step $n \geq 0$.

Analyzing the program by replacing the probabilistic statements with non-deterministic choice, and performing polyhedral abstract interpretation yields the invariant $\mathrm{x} + \mathrm{y} \leq 14$ [8]. This allows us to bound the set of support for $\mathcal{D}_n$, and also allows us to conclude that $\mathbb{E}_{\mathcal{D}_n}(14 - \mathrm{x} - \mathrm{y}) \geq 0$. Combining these facts, we obtain,

$$\mathbb{E}_{\mathcal{D}_n}(56 - 9\mathrm{count}) \geq 0, \text{ or equivalently, } \mathbb{E}_{\mathcal{D}_n}(\mathrm{count}) \leq \frac{56}{9}.$$

4 Expectation Invariants as Fixed Points

In this section, we show that the notion of conic invariants as presented in Definition 7 can be expressed as a (pre-) fixed point of a monotone operator over finitely generated cones representing sets of expressions. This naturally allows us to use abstract interpretation starting from the cone representing all expressions ($\top$) and performing a downward Kleene iteration until convergence. We use a (dualized) widening operator to ensure fast convergence to fixed point in finitely many iterations.

Let $\mathcal{P}$ be a program over variables $\boldsymbol{x}$ with transitions $\mathcal{T} : \{\tau_1, \ldots, \tau_k\}$ and initial distribution $\mathcal{D}_0$. For simplicity, we describe our approach to generate affine expressions of the form $c_0 + \boldsymbol{c}^T \boldsymbol{x}$ for $c_0 \in \mathbb{R}, \boldsymbol{c} \in \mathbb{R}^n$. Let $\mathbb{A}(\boldsymbol{x})$ represent the set of all affine expressions over $\boldsymbol{x}$.

Polyhedral Cones of Expectation Invariant Candidates: Our approach uses finitely generated cones $I : \mathsf{Cone}(E)$ where $E = \{\mathsf{e}_1, \ldots, \mathsf{e}_m\}$ is a finite set of affine expressions over $\boldsymbol{x}$. Each element $\mathsf{e} \in I$ represents a *candidate expectation invariant.* Once a (pre-) fixed point is found by our technique, we obtain a cone $I^* : \mathsf{Cone}(E^*)$, wherein E^* will be shown to be a conic inductive invariant according to Definition 7.

A finitely generated cone of affine expressions $I : \mathsf{Cone}(E)$ is represented by a polyhedral cone of its coefficients $C(I) : \{(c_0, \boldsymbol{c}) \mid c_0 + \boldsymbol{c}^T \boldsymbol{x} \in I\}$. The generators of $C(I)$ are coefficient vectors $(c_{0,i}, \boldsymbol{c}_i)$ representing the expression $\mathsf{e}_i : c_{0,i} + \boldsymbol{c}_i^T \boldsymbol{x}$.

Our analysis operates on the lattice of polyhedral cone representations, CONES, ordered by the set theoretic inclusion operator $\subseteq$. This is, in fact, dual to the polyhedral domain, originally proposed by Cousot & Halbwachs [8].

Initial Cone: For simplicity, we will assume that $\mathcal{D}_0$ is specified to us, and we are able to compute $E_{\mathcal{D}_0}(x)$ precisely for each program variable. The initial cone I_0 is given by

$$I_0 : \mathsf{Cone}\left(\{x_1 - \mathbb{E}_{\mathcal{D}_0}(x_1), \mathbb{E}_{\mathcal{D}_0}(x_1) - x_1, \cdots, \mathbb{E}_{\mathcal{D}_0}(x_n) - x_n, x_n - \mathbb{E}_{\mathcal{D}_0}(x_n)\}\right).$$

Such a cone represents the invariant candidates $x_i = \mathbb{E}_{\mathcal{D}_0}(x_i)$.

Pre-Expectation Operators: We now describe the parts of the monotone operator over finitely generated cones. Let $E = \{\mathsf{e}_1, \ldots, \mathsf{e}_m\}$ be a set of expressions. Let $\tau : \langle \mathsf{g}, \mathcal{F}\rangle$ be a transition, wherein $\mathsf{g} : \bigwedge_{l=1}^{p} g_l \geq 0$. We first present a pre-expectation operator over cones, lifting the notation $\mathtt{pre}\mathbb{E}_\tau$ from expressions to cones of such:

Definition 9 (Pre-Expectation Operator). *The* pre-expectation *of a cone* $I : \mathsf{Cone}(E)$ w.r.t a transition τ *is defined as:*

$$\mathtt{pre}\mathbb{E}_\tau(I) = \{(\mathsf{e}, \boldsymbol{\lambda}) \in \mathbb{A}(x) \times \mathbb{R}^m \mid \boldsymbol{\lambda} \geq 0 \wedge \exists\, \boldsymbol{\mu} \geq 0\, (\mathtt{pre}\mathbb{E}_\tau(\mathsf{e}) \equiv \sum_{j=1}^{m} \boldsymbol{\lambda}_j \mathsf{e}_j + \sum_{i=1}^{p} \boldsymbol{\mu}_i g_i)\,\}.$$

The refinement $\mathtt{pre}\mathbb{E}_\tau(I)$ of a cone contains all affine program expressions whose pre-expectation belongs to the conic hull of I and the cone generated by the guard assertion. For technical reasons, we attach to each expression a certificate $\boldsymbol{\lambda}$ that shows its membership back in the cone. This can be seen as a way to ensure the proper order of quantification in Definition 7.

Given a polyhedron $C(I)$ representing I, we can show that $C(\mathtt{pre}\mathbb{E}_\tau(I))$ is a polyhedral cone over the variables $(c_0, \boldsymbol{c})$ representing the expression coefficients and $\boldsymbol{\lambda}$ for the multipliers. Our extended version [4] presents in detail the steps for computing the pre-expectation of a cone as well as the fixpoint computation across multiple transitions.

Next, we define a pre-expectation operator across all transitions:

$$\mathtt{pre}\mathbb{E}(I) = \{\mathsf{e} \in \mathbb{A}(x) \mid (\exists\, \boldsymbol{\lambda} \geq 0)\ (\mathsf{e}, \boldsymbol{\lambda}) \in \bigcap_{j=1}^{k} \mathtt{pre}\mathbb{E}_{\tau_j}(I)\}$$

An expression e belongs to $\mathtt{pre}\mathbb{E}(I)$ if for some $\boldsymbol{\lambda} \geq 0$, $(e, \boldsymbol{\lambda}) \in \mathtt{pre}\mathbb{E}_{\tau_j}(I)$ for each transition $\tau_j \in \mathcal{T}$.

Given a cone $C(I)$, we first compute the cones $C(\hat{I}_1), \ldots, C(\hat{I}_k)$ representing the pre-expectations across transitions $\tau_1, \ldots, \tau_k$, respectively. Next, we compute $C(I') : (\exists\, \boldsymbol{\lambda}) \bigcap_{j=1}^{k} C(\hat{I}_j)$, representing $I' : \mathtt{pre}\mathbb{E}(I)$, by intersecting the cones $C(\hat{I}_j)$ and projecting the dimensions corresponding to $\boldsymbol{\lambda}$.

We define the operator $\mathcal{G}$ over cones as $\mathcal{G}(I) : I_0 \cap \mathtt{pre}\mathbb{E}(I)$, where I_0 is the initial cone.

Theorem 3. *The operator $\mathcal{G}$ satisfies the following properties:*

1. *$\mathcal{G}$ is a monotone operator over the lattice* CONES *ordered by set-theoretic inclusion.*
2. *A finite set of affine expressions E is a conic inductive invariant (Def. 7) if and only if I :* $\mathsf{Cone}(E)$ *is a pre-fixed point of $\mathcal{G}$, i.e, $I \subseteq \mathcal{G}(I)$.*

Iteration over Polyhedral Cones: Our goal is to compute the greatest fixed point of $\mathcal{G}$ representing the largest cone of expressions whose generators satisfy Definition 7. We implement this by a downward Kleene iteration until we obtain a pre-fixed point, which in the ideal case is also the greatest fixed point of $\mathcal{G}$.

$$(J_0 : \mathbb{A}(x)) \supseteq (J_1 : \mathcal{G}(J_0)) \supseteq \cdots (J_{k+1} : \mathcal{G}(J_k)) \cdots \text{ until convergence: } J_i \subseteq J_{i+1} .$$

However, the domain CONES has infinite descending chains and is not a complete lattice. Therefore, the greatest fixed point cannot necessarily be found in finitely many steps by the Kleene iteration. We resort to a *dual widening* operator $\widetilde{\nabla}$ to force convergence of the downward iteration.

Definition 10 (Dual Widening). *Let I_1, I_2 be two successive cone iterates, satisfying $I_1 \supseteq I_2$. The operator $\widetilde{\nabla}(I_1, I_2)$ is a* dual widening operator *if:*

- $\widetilde{\nabla}(I_1, I_2) \subseteq I_1$, $\widetilde{\nabla}(I_1, I_2) \subseteq I_2$;
- *For every infinite descending sequence $J_0 \supseteq \mathcal{G}(J_0) \supseteq \mathcal{G}^2(J_0) \supseteq \cdots$, the* widened sequence $J'_0 = J_0$, $J'_n = J'_{n-1} \widetilde{\nabla} J_n$ *converges in finitely many steps.*

A common strategy to compute an approximation of the greatest fixed point when using dual widening is to delay widening for a fixed number K of iterations.

Example 7. Consider a simulation of a peg performing an unbounded random walk in two dimensions (x, y). Starting at the origin, at every step the peg chooses uniformly at random a direction {N, E, S, W} and a random step size $r_1 \sim U[0, 2]$. The program 2D-WALK tracks the steps (count) and the Manhattan distance (dist) to the origin.

The following table summarizes the result of the expectation invariant analysis:

Cone	Generators	Constraints	Cone	Generators	Constraints
I_0	1, −**count**, count, x, −x, y, −y, dist, −dist,	$c_0 \geq 0$	I_4	1, **4** − **count**, count, x, −x, y, −y, dist, −dist	$c_0 + 4c_4 \geq 0$, $c_0 \geq 0$
I_1	1, **1** − **count**, count, x, −x, y, −y, dist, −dist	$c_0 + c_4 \geq 0$, $c_0 \geq 0$	I_5	1, **5** − **count**, count, x, −x, y, −y, dist, −dist	$c_0 + 4c_4 \geq 0$, $c_0 \geq 0$
I_2	1, **2** − **count**, count, x, −x, y, −y, dist, −dist	$c_0 + 2c_4 \geq 0$, $c_0 \geq 0$	⋮	⋮	⋮
I_3	1, **3** − **count**, count, x, −x, y, −y, dist, −dist	$c_0 + 3c_4 \geq 0$, $c_0 \geq 0$	I_∞	1, count, x, −x, y, −y, dist, −dist	$c_4 \geq 0$, $c_0 \geq 0$

The table shows the value of expression count is unbounded from above. To force convergence, we employ dual widening after a predefined number ($K = 5$) of iterations.

Definition 11 (Standard Dual Widening). *Let $I_1 = Cone(g_1, \ldots, g_k)$ and $I_2 = Cone(h_1, \ldots, h_l)$ be two finitely generated cones such that $I_1 \supseteq I_2$. The dual widening operator $I_1 \widetilde{\nabla} I_2$ is defined as $I = Cone(g_i \mid g_i \in I_2)$. Cone I is the cone generated by the generators of I_1 that are* subsumed *by I_2.*

Example 8. Returning to Example 7, we consider cone iterates I_4, I_5. In this case generator subsumption reduces to a simple containment check. Since generator 4 − **count** is not subsumed in I_5, we arrive at $I'_5 \equiv I_4 \widetilde{\nabla} I_5 = \widetilde{I^*} = I_\infty$.

Note 1. Alternatively, one can define dual widening as a widening operator [12,1] over the dual polyhedron that the generators of I_1, I_2 give rise to. On the set of PWL loop benchmarks our dual widening approach and those based on [12] and [1] produce identical fixed points where the difference in timings is not statistically significant.

Table 1. Summary of results: $|X|$ is the number of program variables; $|\mathcal{T}|$ - transitions; # - iterations to convergence; $\widetilde{\nabla}$ - use of dual widening. Lines (Rays) is the number of resultant inductive expectation equalities (inequalities). Time is taken on a MacBook Pro (2.4 GHz) laptop with 8 GB RAM, running MacOS X 10.9.1 (where $\varepsilon = 0.05$ sec).

Name	Description	$\|X\|$	$\|\mathcal{T}\|$	Iters		Fixpoint-gen		Time
				#	$\widetilde{\nabla}$	Lines	Rays	
MOT-EXAMPLE	Motivating Example of Figure 1	3	2	2	No	2	1	$\leq \varepsilon$
MOT-EX-LOOP-INV	Example 1 with added loop invariants	3	2	2	No	2	2	0.10
MOT-EX-POLY	Ex. 1 generate poly constr (deg $\leq$ 2)	9	2	2	No	5	2	0.18
2D-WALK	Random walk in 2 dimensions	4	4	7	Yes	3	1	$\leq \varepsilon$
AGGREGATE-RV	Accumulate RVs	3	2	2	No	2	0	$\leq \varepsilon$
HARE-TURTLE	Stochastic Hare-Turtle race	3	2	2	No	1	1	$\leq \varepsilon$
COUPON5	Coupon Collector's Problem (n = 5)	2	5	2	No	1	2	$\leq \varepsilon$
FAIR-COIN-BIASED	Simulating biased coin with fair coin	3	2	3	No	1	1	$\leq \varepsilon$
HAWK-DOVE-FAIR	Stochastic 2-player game (collaborate)	6	2	2	No	4	1	$\leq \varepsilon$
HAWK-DOVE-BIAS	Stochastic 2-player game (exploit)	6	2	2	No	3	1	$\leq \varepsilon$
FAULTY-INCR	Faulty incrementor	2	2	7	Yes	1	1	$\leq \varepsilon$

5 Experimental Results and Future Work

We present the experimental results of our prototype implementation that relies on PPL [1] for manipulating the polyhedral representations of cones. Table 1 presents the summary of the experiments we conducted on a set of probabilistic benchmarks. In [4], we present a description of these models and the expectation invariants obtained.

In all experiments we emphasize precision over computational effort. All examples except MOT-EX-LOOP-INV and MOT-EX-POLY run in under $\varepsilon = 0.05$ seconds, so we choose not to report these timing. Accordingly, dual widening $\widetilde{\nabla}$ delay was set sufficiently large at $K = 5$ to only force finite convergence but not to speed up computation. Nevertheless, the iterations converge quite fast and in many cases without the use of widening. Programs 2D-WALK and FAULTY-INCR require the widening ($\widetilde{\nabla}$) operator to ensure convergence. In all cases, *line* generators of the final pre-fixed point yield expectation invariants like $\mathbb{E}(\mathsf{e}) = 0$ and *rays* yield the invariants $\mathbb{E}(\mathsf{e}) \geq 0$.

Comparison with PRINSYS[11]. PRINSYS[11] implements the constraint-based quantitative invariant synthesis approach developed by Katoen et al. [13]. The tool uses a manually supplied template with unknown coefficients. The REDUCE computer algebra system is used to perform quantifier elimination and simplify the constraints. We applied PRINSYS with a linear template expression $\sum_j c_j x_j$ for state variables x_j in the program. Our comparison was carried out over 6 benchmark examples that are distributed with the tool. The comparison checked whether PRINSYS could discover quantitative invariants discovered by our approach. From a total set of 28 inductive expectation invariants our tool generates, PRINSYS could generate 3 of them. This shows that mutual inductive expectation invariants investigated in this paper are significant for probabilistic loops. Next, we attempted to check whether PRINSYS can discover additional linear quantitative invariants not discovered by our approach due to the incompleteness of widening. Unfortunately, this check turned out inconclusive at the time of the experiment. The existing PRINSYS implementation automatically generates and simplifies nonlinear constraints on the template coefficients. However, the process of deriving an actual quantitative invariant requires manually extracting solutions from a set of nonlinear inequalities. Our manual efforts failed to find new invariants unique to the PRINSYS tool, but the overall comparison remains incomplete since we could not arguably find all solutions manually. However, it is important to observe that PRINSYS can generate invariants for templates that include indicator functions, while our technique does not. Similarly, PRINSYS handles nondeterminism in the programs, while we do not. The full details of the comparison can be found in the extended version [4].

Ongoing/Future Work. In many of the benchmark examples presented, invariants found using standard abstract interpretation by treating the stochastic choices as demonic nondeterminism help improve the quality of our expectation invariants. Going further, we would like to combine classical abstract interpretation with the techniques presented here to handle programs that mix non-deterministic and stochastic choices. Finally, we demonstrate polynomial invariant synthesis in Example MOT-EX-POLY by instrumenting monomials of fixed degree (deg ≤ 2) as fresh variables. Our analysis is thus able to generate *polynomial* expectation invariants such as $\mathbb{E}(4x^2-4xy+y^2 \mid n) \geq 0$, and $\mathbb{E}(4x^2-4xy+y^2-y+6 \mid n) = 0$. A sound formalization of polynomial invariant generation under relaxed independence conditions, and generalization of this approach to higher-order moments are also part of our future work.

Acknowledgments. The authors thank the anonymous reviewers for their insightful comments and Friedrich Gretz for helping us compare our work with PRINSYS. This work was supported by US National Science Foundation (NSF) under award number 1320069. All opinions are those of the authors and not necessarily of the NSF.

References

1. Antonopoulos, T., Gorogiannis, N., Haase, C., Kanovich, M., Ouaknine, J.: Foundations for decision problems in separation logic with general inductive predicates. In: Muscholl, A. (ed.) FOSSACS 2014. LNCS, vol. 8412, pp. 411–425. Springer, Heidelberg (2014)
2. Bouissou, O., Goubault, E., Goubault-Larrecq, J., Putot, S.: A generalization of p-boxes to affine arithmetic. Computing 94(2-4), 189–201 (2012)
3. Chakarov, A., Sankaranarayanan, S.: Probabilistic program analysis with martingales. In: Sharygina, N., Veith, H. (eds.) CAV 2013. LNCS, vol. 8044, pp. 511–526. Springer, Heidelberg (2013)
4. Chakarov, A., Sankaranarayanan, S.: Expectation invaraiants for probabilistic program loops as fixed points (2014) (extended version) (Draft, Available upon request)
5. Chung, K.L.: A course in probability theory, vol. 3. Academic Press, New York (1974)
6. Colón, M.A., Sankaranarayanan, S., Sipma, H.B.: Linear invariant generation using nonlinear constraint solving. In: Hunt Jr., W.A., Somenzi, F. (eds.) CAV 2003. LNCS, vol. 2725, pp. 420–432. Springer, Heidelberg (2003)

7. Cousot, P., Cousot, R.: Abstract Interpretation: A unified lattice model for static analysis of programs by construction or approximation of fixpoints. In: ACM Principles of Programming Languages, pp. 238–252 (1977)
8. Cousot, P., Halbwachs, N.: Automatic discovery of linear restraints among the variables of a program. In: POPL 1978, pp. 84–97 (January 1978)
9. Cousot, P., Monerau, M.: Probabilistic abstract interpretation. In: Seidl, H. (ed.) ESOP 2012. LNCS, vol. 7211, pp. 169–193. Springer, Heidelberg (2012)
10. Dubhashi, D., Panconesi, A.: Concentration of Measure for the Analysis of Randomized Algorithms. Cambridge University Press (2009)
11. Gretz, F., Katoen, J.-P., McIver, A.: Prinsys - on a quest for probabilistic loop invariants. In: Joshi, K., Siegle, M., Stoelinga, M., D'Argenio, P.R. (eds.) QEST 2013. LNCS, vol. 8054, pp. 193–208. Springer, Heidelberg (2013)
12. Halbwachs, N.: Détermination automatique de relations linéaires vérifiées par les variables d'un programme. PhD thesis, Institut National Polytechnique de Grenoble-INPG (1979)
13. Katoen, J.-P., McIver, A.K., Meinicke, L.A., Morgan, C.C.: Linear-invariant generation for probabilistic programs. In: Cousot, R., Martel, M. (eds.) SAS 2010. LNCS, vol. 6337, pp. 390–406. Springer, Heidelberg (2010)
14. Kozen, D.: Semantics of probabilistic programs. J. Comput. Syst. Sci. 22(3), 328–350 (1981)
15. Mardziel, P., Magill, S., Hicks, M., Srivatsa, M.: Dynamic enforcement of knowledge-based security policies. In: 2011 IEEE 24th Computer Security Foundations Symposium (CSF), pp. 114–128. IEEE (2011)
16. McAdams, H., Arkin, A.: It's a noisy business! genetic regulation at the nanomolar scale. Trends Genetics 15(2), 65–69 (1999)
17. McIver, A., Morgan, C.: Abstraction, Refinement and Proof for Probabilistic Systems. Monographs in Computer Science. Springer (2004)
18. Monniaux, D.: Abstract interpretation of probabilistic semantics. In: SAS 2000. LNCS, vol. 1824, pp. 322–340. Springer, Heidelberg (2000)
19. Monniaux, D.: Backwards abstract interpretation of probabilistic programs. In: Sands, D. (ed.) ESOP 2001. LNCS, vol. 2028, pp. 367–382. Springer, Heidelberg (2001)
20. Monniaux, D.: Abstract interpretation of programs as markov decision processes. Science of Computer Programming 58(1), 179–205 (2005)
21. Motwani, R., Raghavan, P.: Randomized Algorithms. Cambridge University Press (1995)
22. Sankaranarayanan, S., Chakarov, A., Gulwani, S.: Static analysis for probabilistic programs: inferring whole program properties from finitely many paths. In: PLDI, pp. 447–458. ACM (2013)
23. Sankaranarayanan, S., Sipma, H.B., Manna, Z.: Constraint-based linear-relations analysis. In: Giacobazzi, R. (ed.) SAS 2004. LNCS, vol. 3148, pp. 53–68. Springer, Heidelberg (2004)
24. Williams, D.: Probability with Martingales. Cambridge University Press (1991)

An Abstract Domain to Infer Octagonal Constraints with Absolute Value*

Liqian Chen[1], Jiangchao Liu[2], Antoine Miné[2,3], Deepak Kapur[4], and Ji Wang[1]

[1] National Laboratory for Parallel and Distributed Processing,
National University of Defense Technology, Changsha, P.R.China
{lqchen,wj}@nudt.edu.cn
[2] École Normale Supérieure, Paris, France
{jliu,mine}@di.ens.fr
[3] CNRS, France
[4] University of New Mexico, NM, USA
kapur@cs.unm.edu

Abstract. The octagon abstract domain, devoted to discovering octagonal constraints (also called Unit Two Variable Per Inequality or UTVPI constraints) of a program, is one of the most commonly used numerical abstractions in practice, due to its quadratic memory complexity and cubic time complexity. However, the octagon domain itself is restricted to express convex sets and has limitations in handling non-convex properties which are sometimes required for proving some numerical properties in a program. In this paper, we intend to extend the octagon abstract domain with absolute value, to infer certain non-convex properties by exploiting the absolute value function. More precisely, the new domain can infer relations of the form $\{\pm X \pm Y \leq c, \pm X \pm |Y| \leq d, \pm|X| \pm |Y| \leq e\}$. We provide algorithms for domain operations such that the new domain still enjoys the same asymptotic complexity as the octagon domain. Moreover, we present an approach to support strict inequalities over rational or real-valued variables in this domain, which also fits for the octagon domain. Experimental results of our prototype are encouraging; The new domain is scalable and able to find non-convex invariants of interest in practice but without too much overhead (compared with that using octagons).

1 Introduction

The precision and efficiency of program analysis based on abstract interpretation [9,10] rely a lot on the chosen abstract domains. Most existing numerical abstract domains (such as intervals [8], octagons [24], polyhedra [11], etc.) can only express convex sets, due to the fact that they usually utilize a conjunction of convex constraints to represent abstract elements. At control-flow joins in programs, an abstract domain often exploits a join operation to abstract the disjunction (union) of the convex constraint sets from the incoming edges into a conjunction of new convex constraints. The convexity limitations of abstract domains may lead to imprecision in the analysis and thus may cause many

* This work is supported by the 973 Program under Grant No. 2014CB340703, the NSFC under Grant Nos. 61120106006, 61202120, 91118007.

M. Müller-Olm and H. Seidl (Eds.): SAS 2014, LNCS 8723, pp. 101–117, 2014.

false alarms. E.g., to remove a division-by-zero false alarm, the analysis needs to find a range excluding 0 for the divisor, which is in general a non-convex property and may be out of the reasoning power of convex abstract domains.

The *Absolute Value* (AV) function is one of the most used functions in mathematics and widely used in numerical computations. The AV function is supported by many modern program languages. E.g., the C99 standard for the C programming language provides the `abs()` and `fabs()` functions to compute the absolute value of an integer number and a floating-point number respectively. However, due to non-convexity, the AV function in the program code is rarely well handled during program analysis. Moreover, the AV function has natural ability to encode disjunctions of linear constraints in a program that account for a large class of non-convex constraints in practice. E.g., $x \leq -1 \vee x \geq 1$ can be encoded as $|x| \geq 1$, while $(x \neq 1 \vee y \neq 2)$ can be encoded as $|x-1| + |y-2| > 0$. Hence, we could exploit the non-convex expressiveness of the AV function to design non-convex abstract domains. Based on this insight, in [7], Chen et al. proposed an abstract domain of linear AV inequalities but which is exponential in complexity and thus has scalability limitations in practice.

In this paper, we propose a new abstract domain, namely the abstract domain of octagonal constraints with absolute value (AVO), to infer relations of the form $\{\pm X \pm Y \leq c, \pm X \pm |Y| \leq d, \pm|X| \pm |Y| \leq e\}$ over each pair of variables X, Y in the program where constants $c, d, e \in \mathbb{R}$ are automatically inferred by the analysis. AVO is more expressive than the classic octagon abstract domain and allows expressing certain non-convex (even unconnected) sets, thanks to the non-convex expressiveness of the AV function. We propose several closure algorithms over AV octagons to offer different time-precision tradeoffs. On this basis, we provide algorithms for domain operations such that the new domain still enjoys the same asymptotic complexity as the octagon domain. In addition, we show how to extend AVO to support strict inequalities over rational or real-valued variables. In other words, after the extension, AVO can additionally infer relations that are of the form $\{\pm X \pm Y < c, \pm X \pm |Y| < d, \pm|X| \pm |Y| < e\}$. Experimental results of our prototype are encouraging on benchmark programs and large embedded C programs; AVO is scalable to large-scale programs and able to find non-convex invariants of interest in practice.

Motivating Example. In Fig. 1, we show a small instructive example adapted from [14] (by replacing the **`double`** type by **`real`** type), which is originally extracted from the XTIDE[1] package that provides tide and current predictions in various formats. It shows a frequently used pattern in implementing a Digital Differential Analyzer algorithm in computer graphics. This example is challenging to analyze as it involves complicated non-convex constraints (due to disjunctions, the usage of the AV function) as well as strict inequalities, and precise reasoning over these constraints is required to prove the absence of the potential risk of division-by-zero errors.

At location ① in Fig. 1, it holds that $(dx \neq 0 \vee dy \neq 0)$ which describes a non-convex set of points that includes all points in $\mathbb{R}^2$ except the origin $(0, 0)$. Using octagonal constraints with absolute value, it can be encoded as $-|dx| - |dy| < 0$. At location ②, it holds that $-|dx| - |dy| < 0 \wedge |dx| - |dy| < 0$ which implies that $-|dy| < 0$ and thus the division by dy in the `then` branch will not cause division-by zero error. At location ③,

[1] `http://www.flaterco.com/xtide/`

it holds that $-|dx| - |dy| < 0 \wedge -|dx| + |dy| \leq 0$ which implies that $-|dx| < 0$ and thus the division by dx in the `else` branch will not cause division-by zero error. However, if using convex abstract domains such as octagons and polyhedra, ⊤ (no information) will be obtained at ① and thus the division-by-zero false alarms will be issued in both the `then` and `else` branches. Moreover, since the program involves strict inequality tests, we need an abstract domain supporting strict inequalities to do precise reasoning.

```
static void p_line16_primary (...) {
    real dx, dy, x, y, slope;
    ...
    if (dx == 0.0 && dy == 0.0)
        return;
 ① if (fabs(dy) > fabs(dx)) {
     ② slope = dx / dy;
       ...
    } else {
     ③ slope = dy / dx;
       ...
    } }
```

Loc	AV octagons
①	$-\lvert dx\rvert - \lvert dy\rvert < 0$
②	$-\lvert dx\rvert - \lvert dy\rvert < 0 \wedge$ $\lvert dx\rvert - \lvert dy\rvert < 0 \wedge$ $-\lvert dy\rvert < 0$
③	$-\lvert dx\rvert - \lvert dy\rvert < 0 \wedge$ $-\lvert dx\rvert + \lvert dy\rvert \leq 0 \wedge$ $-\lvert dx\rvert < 0$

Fig. 1. Motivating example from [14] which is originally extracted from the XTIDE package

The rest of the paper is organized as follows. Section 2 reviews the octagon abstract domain. Section 3 presents a new abstract domain of octagonal constraints with absolute value. Section 4 presents our prototype implementation together with experimental results. Section 5 discusses some related work before Section 6 concludes.

2 The Octagon Abstract Domain

In this section, we give a brief review of the background of the octagon abstract domain and we refer the reader to [24] for details.

2.1 Octagon Representation

Let $\mathcal{V} = \{V_1, \ldots, V_n\}$ be a finite set of program variables in a numerical set $\mathbb{I}$ (which can be $\mathbb{Q}$, or $\mathbb{R}$). The octagon abstract domain manipulates a set of so-called *octagonal constraints* (also called Unit Two Variable Per Inequality or UTVPI constraints) that are of the form $\pm V_i \pm V_j \leq c$ where $\pm \in \{-1, 0, +1\}$ and $c \in \mathbb{I}$. From the geometric point of view, the set of points satisfying a conjunction of octagonal constraints forms an *octagon* (the projection of which on a 2D plane parallel to the axes is a 8-sided polygon).

Potential Constraints. An octagonal constraint over $\mathcal{V} = \{V_1, \ldots, V_n\}$ can be reformulated as a so-called potential constraint that is of the form $V'_i - V'_j \leq c$ over

$\mathcal{V}' = \{V'_1, \ldots, V'_{2n}\}$ where V'_{2k-1} represents $+V_k$ and V'_{2k} represents $-V_k$. E.g., the octagonal constraint $V_i + V_j \leq c$ can be encoded as either $V'_{2i-1} - V'_{2j} \leq c$ or $V'_{2j-1} - V'_{2i} \leq c$. Moreover, a unary octagonal constraint such as $V_i \leq c$ (and $-V_i \leq c$) can be encoded as $V'_{2i-1} - V'_{2i} \leq 2c$ (and $V'_{2i} - V'_{2i-1} \leq 2c$). A conjunction of potential constraints can be represented as a directed weighted graph $\mathcal{G}$ with nodes $\mathcal{V}'$ and edges labeled with weights in $\mathbb{I}$. For each constraint $V'_j - V'_i \leq c$ in the constraint conjunction, there will be an edge from V'_i to V'_j labelled with weight c in $\mathcal{G}$.

Difference Bound Matrices. An equivalent but more practical representation for the conjunction of potential constraints C over n variables is to use a *Difference Bound Matrix* (DBM) [12]. A DBM representing C is a $n \times n$ matrix M defined by

$$M_{ij} \stackrel{\text{def}}{=} \inf\{\, c \mid (V_j - V_i \leq c) \in C\}$$

where $\inf(\emptyset) = +\infty$ and n is the number of variables involved in C. For a set of potential constraints described by a DBM M of dimension n, we define the following concretization function $\gamma^{Pot} : \mathsf{DBM} \to \mathcal{P}(\mathcal{V} \to \mathbb{I})$:

$$\gamma^{Pot}(M) \stackrel{\text{def}}{=} \{\, (V_1, \ldots, V_n) \in \mathbb{I}^n \mid \forall i, j, V_j - V_i \leq M_{ij} \,\}.$$

Similarly, for a set of octagonal constraints described by a DBM M of dimension $2n$, we define the following concretization function $\gamma^{Oct} : \mathsf{DBM} \to \mathcal{P}(\mathcal{V} \to \mathbb{I})$:

$$\gamma^{Oct}(M) \stackrel{\text{def}}{=} \{\, (V_1, \ldots, V_n) \in \mathbb{I}^n \mid (V_1, -V_1, \ldots, V_n, -V_n) \in \gamma^{Pot}(M) \,\}.$$

Some octagonal constraints over $\mathcal{V}$ have two different encodings as potential constraints over $\mathcal{V}'$, and thus can be represented by two elements in the DBM. E.g., $V_i + V_j \leq c$ can be described by either $V'_{2i-1} - V'_{2j} \leq c$ (i.e., $M_{(2j)(2i-1)} = c$) or $V'_{2j-1} - V'_{2i} \leq c$ (i.e., $M_{(2i)(2j-1)} = c$). To ensure that elements of such pairs encode equivalent constraints, we define the coherence of a DBM as

$$M \text{ is coherent} \iff \forall i, j,\ M_{ij} = M_{\bar{j}\bar{\imath}}$$

where the $\bar{\cdot}$ operator on indices is defined as:

$$\bar{\imath} \stackrel{\text{def}}{=} \begin{cases} i+1 & \text{if } i \text{ is odd} \\ i-1 & \text{if } i \text{ is even} \end{cases}$$

Let DBM denote the set of all DBMs. We enrich DBM with a new smallest element, denoted by $\bot^{\mathsf{DBM}}$. Then we get a lattice $(\mathsf{DBM}, \sqsubseteq^{\mathsf{DBM}}, \sqcup^{\mathsf{DBM}}, \sqcap^{\mathsf{DBM}}, \bot^{\mathsf{DBM}}, \top^{\mathsf{DBM}})$ where

$$\begin{array}{llll} M \sqsubseteq^{\mathsf{DBM}} N \stackrel{\text{def}}{\iff} \forall i, j, M_{ij} \leq N_{ij} & & (M \sqcup^{\mathsf{DBM}} N)_{ij} \stackrel{\text{def}}{=} \max(M_{ij}, N_{ij}) \\ (\top^{\mathsf{DBM}})_{ij} \stackrel{\text{def}}{=} +\infty & & (M \sqcap^{\mathsf{DBM}} N)_{ij} \stackrel{\text{def}}{=} \min(M_{ij}, N_{ij}) \end{array}$$

2.2 Closure

An octagon can still have several distinct representations using coherent DBMs. To compare octagons, we thus construct a normal form on DBMs to represent octagons.

The octagon abstract domain utilizes a so-called *strong closure* of the DBM, as the normal form for a non-empty DBM representing octagons. The strong closure (denoted as $M^\bullet$) of a DBM M encoding octagonal constraints is defined as:

$$M^\bullet \stackrel{\text{def}}{=} \inf_{\sqsubseteq^{\mathsf{DBM}}} \{X^\sharp \in \mathsf{DBM} \mid \gamma^{Oct}(M) = \gamma^{Oct}(X^\sharp)\}$$

The octagon domain uses a modified version of the Floyd-Warshall algorithm to compute $M^\bullet$ (which is firstly proposed by Miné [23] and later improved by Bagnara et al. [3]), which is of cubic-time complexity. Strong closure is a basic operator in the octagon domain. Most abstract operators over octagons can be obtained based on the strong closure of DBMs. We refer the reader to [24] for details.

3 An Abstract Domain of Octagonal Constraints with Absolute Value

In this section, we show how to extend the octagon abstract domain with absolute value.

3.1 Octagonal Constraints with Absolute Value

A constraint is said to be an *AV octagonal constraint* if it is of the following forms:

- octagonal constraints: $\pm V_i \pm V_j \leq a$
- constraints with absolute value of one variable per inequality: $\pm V_i \pm |V_j| \leq b$
- constraints with absolute value of two variables per inequality: $\pm|V_i| \pm |V_j| \leq c$

where $\pm \in \{-1, 0, +1\}$ and $a, b, c \in \mathbb{I} \cup \{+\infty\}$. From the geometric point of view, we call *AV octagon* the geometric shape of the set of points satisfying a conjunction of AV octagonal constraints. Now, we will design a new abstract domain, namely AVO, to infer AV octagonal constraints among program variables $\mathcal{V} = \{V_1, \ldots, V_n\}$.

According to Theorem 1 in [7], it is easy to derive the following theorem.

Theorem 1. *Let e be an arbitrary expression that does not involve variable X. Then*

$$|X| + e \leq c \iff \begin{cases} X + e \leq c \\ -X + e \leq c \end{cases}$$

A direct consequence of Theorem 1 is that those constraints with positive coefficients on the AV term are redundant with other AV octagonal constraints and do not bring additional expressiveness. Hence, in the domain representation of AVO, we only need to encode AV octagonal constraints of the following forms:

- $\pm V_i \pm V_j \leq a$
- $\pm V_i - |V_j| \leq b$
- $-|V_i| - |V_j| \leq c$

For example, to describe a planar AV octagon over program variables x, y, we only need to consider at most 15 AV octagonal constraints, which are listed in Fig. 4(a).

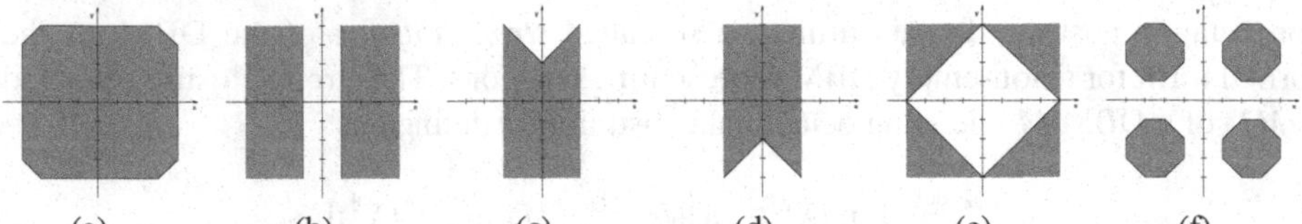

Fig. 2. The geometric shape of AV octagonal constraints. (a) depicts an octagon with constraint set $C = \{x \leq 4, -x \leq 4, y \leq 4, -y \leq 4, x + y \leq 7, x - y \leq 7, -x + y \leq 7, -x - y \leq 7\}$; (b) depicts $-|x| \leq -1$; (c) depicts $-|x| + y \leq 2$; (d) depicts $-|x| - y \leq 2$; (e) depicts $-|x| - |y| \leq -4$; (f) depicts an AV octagon with constraint set $C' = C \cup \{-|x| \leq -1, -|y| \leq -1, -|x| + y \leq 2, -|x| - y \leq 2, x - |y| \leq 2, -x - |y| \leq 2, -|x| - |y| \leq -4\}$.

Due to the non-convexity expressiveness of the AV function, an AV octagon is *non-convex* in general, but its intersection with each orthant in $\mathbb{R}^n$ gives a (possibly empty) octagon. Fig. 2 shows typical geometric shape of AV octagonal constraints. In particular, Fig. 2(a) shows a typical shape of octagons, while Fig. 2(f) shows an example of an AV octagon that is non-convex and even unconnected.

Expressiveness Lifting. Note that in the AVO domain representation, the AV function $|\cdot|$ applies to only (single) variables rather than expressions. E.g., consider the relation $y = ||x| - 1| + 2$ which encodes a piecewise linear function with more than two pieces, whose plot is shown in Fig. 3. The AVO domain cannot express directly this piecewise linear function (in the space of x, y), since $|\cdot|$ applies to an expression $|x| - 1$. Indeed, in Fig. 3 the region in the orthant where both x and y are positive is not an octagon.

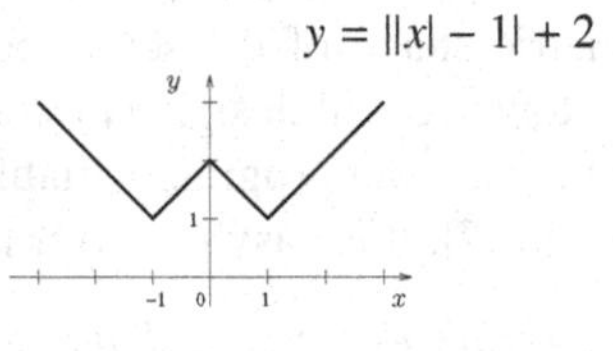

Fig. 3. A piecewise linear function with nested AV functions

In order to express such complicated relations, we follow the same strategy as in [7]. We introduce new auxiliary variables to denote those expressions that appear inside the AV function. E.g., we could introduce an auxiliary variable v to denote the value of the expression $|x| - 1$. Then using AVO domain elements in the space with higher dimension (involving 3 variables: x, y, v), such as $\{y = |v| + 2, v = |x| - 1\}$, we could express complicated relations in the space over lower dimension (involving 2 variables: x, y), such as $y = ||x| - 1| + 2$. Note that due to the octagonal shape, the expression inside the AV function can only be

$$e ::= \ \pm X \pm c \ \mid \ \pm|e| \pm c$$

where c is a constant and X is a variable.

3.2 Extending Difference-Bound Matrices

Now, we show how to encode AV octagonal constraints using DBMs. Similarly to octagonal constraints, an AV octagonal constraint over $\{V_1, \ldots, V_n\}$ can be reformulated as a potential constraint of the form $V_i'' - V_j'' \leq c$ over $\{V_1'', \ldots, V_{4n}''\}$ where

- V_{4k-3}'' represents $+V_k$,
- V_{4k-2}'' represents $-V_k$,
- V_{4k-1}'' represents $|V_k|$,
- V_{4k}'' represents $-|V_k|$.

As an example, in Fig. 4, we show a general set of constraints for a planar AV octagon (left) and its DBM representation (right).

x		$\leq a_1$
$-x$		$\leq a_2$
	y	$\leq a_3$
	$-y$	$\leq a_4$
x	$+y$	$\leq a_5$
x	$-y$	$\leq a_6$
$-x$	$+y$	$\leq a_7$
$-x$	$-y$	$\leq a_8$

	$-\lvert x\rvert$			$\leq b_1$
			$-\lvert y\rvert$	$\leq b_2$
	$-\lvert x\rvert$	$+y$		$\leq b_3$
	$-\lvert x\rvert$	$-y$		$\leq b_4$
x			$-\lvert y\rvert$	$\leq b_5$
$-x$			$-\lvert y\rvert$	$\leq b_6$
	$-\lvert x\rvert$		$-\lvert y\rvert$	$\leq c_1$

(a)

	x	$-x$	$\lvert x\rvert$	$-\lvert x\rvert$	y	$-y$	$\lvert y\rvert$	$-\lvert y\rvert$
x	0	$2a_2$						
$-x$	$2a_1$	0						
$\lvert x\rvert$			0	$2b_1$				
$-\lvert x\rvert$				0				
y	a_6	a_8		b_4	0	$2a_4$		
$-y$	a_5	a_7		b_3	$2a_3$	0		
$\lvert y\rvert$	b_5	b_6		c_1			0	$2b_2$
$-\lvert y\rvert$								0

(b)

Fig. 4. DBMs for AV octagons. (a) shows a constraint set for a planar AV octagon; (b) shows a DBM to encode the constraints.

For a set of AV octagonal constraints described by a DBM M of dimension $4n$, we define the following concretization function $\gamma^{AVO} : \mathsf{DBM} \to \mathcal{P}(\mathcal{V} \to \mathbb{I})$:

$$\gamma^{AVO}(M) \stackrel{\text{def}}{=} \left\{ (V_1, \ldots, V_n) \in \mathbb{I}^n \mid (V_1, -V_1, |V_1|, -|V_1|, \ldots, V_n, -V_n, |V_n|, -|V_n|) \in \gamma^{Pot}(M) \right\}.$$

Some AV octagonal constraints have two different encodings as potential constraints in $\mathcal{V}''$, and can be represented by two elements in the DBM. E.g., $-|V_i| - |V_j| \leq c$ can be described by either $V_{4j}'' - V_{4i-1}'' \leq c$ (i.e., $M_{(4i-1)(4j)} = c$) or $V_{4i}'' - V_{4j-1}'' \leq c$ (i.e., $M_{(4j-1)(4i)} = c$). In addition, according to the specific property over AV constraints shown in Theorem 1, DBMs encoding AV octagons have another restriction, i.e.,

$$e + V_i \leq c_1 \wedge e - V_i \leq c_2 \implies e + |V_i| \leq \max(c_1, c_2) \tag{1}$$

where $e \in \{\pm V_j, \pm |V_j|\}$. To this end, we define the AV coherence of a DBM as

M is *AV coherent* $\iff$

$$\begin{cases} \forall i, j, \; M_{ij} = M_{\bar{j}\bar{\imath}} \\ \forall j, k, \; M_{(4k)j} = \max(M_{(4k-3)j}, M_{(4k-2)j}) & \text{if } j \neq 4k \\ \forall i, k, \; M_{i(4k-1)} = \max(M_{i(4k-2)}, M_{i(4k-3)}) & \text{if } i \neq 4k-1 \end{cases}$$

The first condition is similar to the coherence condition for DBMs that encode octagons. The second condition is due to the restriction (1) over the $-|V_k|$ row, while the third condition is due to the restriction (1) over the $|V_k|$ column.

3.3 Conversions between Octagons and AV Octagons

The intersection of an AV octagon with each orthant gives an octagon. Based on this insight, we now present operators for conversions between octagons and AV octagons. Let $u = (1, \ldots, 1)^T$ be the unit vector, and $S^n = \{s \in \mathbb{R}^n \mid |s| = u\}$. We define an operator $C = \mathsf{S2Cons}(s)$ to derive a conjunction C of sign constraints from $s \in S^n$, such that

$$C_i \stackrel{\text{def}}{=} \begin{cases} x_i \geq 0 & \text{if } s_i = 1 \\ x_i \leq 0 & \text{if } s_i = -1 \end{cases}$$

First, we define an operator $\mathsf{AVO2Oct}(M, s)$ to convert an AV octagon (described by M that is a DBM of dimension $4n$) into an octagon (described by N that is a DBM of dimension $2n$) with respect to a given orthant (described by $s \in S^n$), as:

$$N \stackrel{\text{def}}{=} \mathsf{AVO2Oct}(M, s)$$

such that $\gamma^{Oct}(N)$ equals to the solution set of the conjunction of $\mathsf{S2Cons}(s)$ with the constraint set corresponding to M. From the algorithmic view, N can be easily obtained from M, by considering the sign of each variable defined in s. E.g.,

$$N_{(2k-1)(2k)} = \begin{cases} M_{(4k-3)(4k-2)} & \text{if } s_k = -1 \\ \min(M_{(4k-3)(4k-2)}, M_{(4k-1)(4k)}) & \text{if } s_k = 1 \end{cases}$$

where $M_{(4k-3)(4k-2)}$ and $M_{(4k-1)(4k)}$ denote the upper bounds for $(-V_k) - V_k$ and $(-|V_k|) - |V_k|$ respectively. If $V_k \geq 0$, we know the upper bound for $(-V_k) - V_k$ (denoted by $N_{(2k-1)(2k)}$ in the DBM representation of octagons) will be $\min(M_{(4k-3)(4k-2)}, M_{(4k-1)(4k)})$.

Note that an octagon itself is an AV octagon. However, if we know the orthant that an octagon lies in, we could deduct additionally upper bounds for AV expressions (such as $-|X| - |Y|$), to saturate the DBM. To this end, we define an operator $\mathsf{Oct2AVO}(N, s)$ to convert an octagon (N) in a given orthant ($s \in S^n$) into an AV octagon (M), as:

$$M \stackrel{\text{def}}{=} \mathsf{Oct2AVO}(N, s)$$

such that the solution set of the conjunction of the constraint set corresponding to M with $\mathsf{S2Cons}(s)$ is equivalent to $\gamma^{Oct}(N)$.

3.4 Closure Algorithms

To obtain a unique representation for a non-empty AV octagon, we define the so-called *AV strong closure* $M^{|\bullet|}$ for a DBM encoding a non-empty AV octagon, as

$$M^{|\bullet|} \stackrel{\text{def}}{=} \inf_{\sqsubseteq^{\mathsf{DBM}}} \{X^\sharp \in \mathsf{DBM} \mid \gamma^{AVO}(M) = \gamma^{AVO}(X^\sharp)\}$$

Strong Closure by Enumerating the Signs of all n Variables. We provide an approach to compute the AV strong closure $M^{|\bullet|}$ by enumerating the signs of all n variables:

$$\mathsf{AVOStrClo}(M) \stackrel{\text{def}}{=} \sqcup^{\mathsf{DBM}}_{s \in S^n} \{M' \in \mathsf{DBM} \mid M' = \mathsf{Oct2AVO}(N^\bullet, s), N = \mathsf{AVO2Oct}(M, s)\}$$

The intuition is as follows. The intersection of an AV octagon M with each orthant s gives an octagon N. Hence, we could enumerate all orthants and in each orthant we compute the AV strong closure via the regular strong closure of the octagon domain.

```
DBM^{4n×4n} WeakCloVia3Sign(M : DBM^{4n×4n}){
    M', M'', M'^{|•|} : DBM^{12×12};
    N : DBM^{6×6};
    for k ← 1 to n
        for i ← 1 to n
            for j ← 1 to n
                M' ← M/{V_k, V_i, V_j};
                M'^{|•|} ← ⊔^{DBM}_{s∈S^3} {M'' ∈ DBM | M'' = Oct2AVO(N•, s), N = AVO2Oct(M', s)};
                M/{V_k, V_i, V_j} ← M'^{|•|};
    for i ← 1 to 4n
        if (M_ii < 0) return ⊥^{DBM}; else M_ii ← 0;
    return M; }
```

Fig. 5. The weak closure algorithm by enumerating the signs of 3 variables in each step. $M/\{V_k, V_i, V_j\}$ denotes the sub-matrix of M consisting of the rows and columns corresponding to variables in $\{V_k, V_i, V_j\}$.

It is not hard to see that $\mathsf{AVOStrClo}(M) = M^{|\bullet|}$. However, the time complexity of this approach is $O(2^n \times n^3)$. At the moment, we do not know whether the problem of computing the AV strong closure for AV octagons is NP-hard or not.

To offer different time-precision tradeoffs, we now propose two approaches that are of cubic time complexity to compute weak closures M° (such that $M^\bullet \sqsubseteq^{\mathsf{DBM}} M^\circ$) for AV octagons. Note that the key behind the closure algorithm is to combine the constraints over (V_i, V_k) and those over (V_k, V_j) to tighten the constraints over (V_i, V_j), by constraint propagation through the intermediate variable V_k. Based on this insight, we first propose a weak closure algorithm WeakCloVia3Sign() by enumerating the signs of 3 variables $\{V_i, V_k, V_j\}$ each time to perform constraint propagation. Then we propose a cheaper weak closure algorithm WeakCloVia1Sign() by enumerating only the sign of the intermediate variable V_k each time to perform constraint propagation.

Weak Closure by Enumerating the Signs of 3 Variables Each Time. In Fig 5, we show the WeakCloVia3Sign() algorithm. In the loop body, we compute the AV strong closure among three variables V_i, V_k, V_j (by enumerating 8 orthants due to the signs of 3 variables), and then update the tightened constraints over V_i, V_k, V_j in the original DBM. Note that WeakCloVia3Sign() gives AV strong closure for AV octagons involving only 3 variables. However, in general, WeakCloVia3Sign() does not guarantee to result in the AV strong closure for more than 3 variables.

Weak Closure by Enumerating the Sign of One Variable Each Time. In Fig 7, we show the WeakCloVia1Sign() algorithm. Rather than enumerating the signs of 3 variables, in the loop body of WeakCloVia1Sign() we enumerate only the sign of the intermediate variable V_k. For each case of the sign of V_k, we call TightenIJviaK() which is shown in Fig. 6 to tighten the constraints over $\{\pm V_i, \pm|V_i|, \pm V_j, \pm|V_j|\}$ by combining the constraints over $\{\pm V_i, \pm|V_i|, \pm V_k\}$ and those over $\{\pm V_k, \pm|V_j|, \pm V_j\}$. We now explain how TightenIJviaK() works by considering the case where $V_k \geq 0$. When $V_k \geq 0$, we have $|V_k| = V_k$. Hence, it holds that $V'' - |V_k| \leq c \implies V'' - V_k \leq c$ where $V'' \in \{0, \pm V_i, \pm|V_i|, \pm V_j, \pm|V_j|\}$. Then, we use $V'' - |V_k| \leq c$ to tighten the upper bound for $V'' -$

```
1  DBM^{12×12} TightenIJviaK(M : DBM^{12×12}, Kpositive : bool){
2    M′, M′^{|•|} : DBM^{12×12};
3    M′ ← M;  k ← 1; i ← 2; j ← 3;  //Let 𝒱″ = {0, ±V_i, ±|V_i|, ±V_j, ±|V_j|}
4    if (Kpositive == true){  //V″ − |V_k| ≤ c ⟹ V″ − V_k ≤ c where V″ ∈ 𝒱″
5        M′_{(4k−3)(4k−2)} ← min(0, M′_{(4k−3)(4k−2)}, M′_{(4k−1)(4k)});
6        for n ← 0 to 3 {
7            M′_{(4k−3)(4i−n)} ← min(M′_{(4k−3)(4i−n)}, M′_{(4k−1)(4i−n)});
8            M′_{(4j−n)(4k−2)} ← min(M′_{(4j−n)(4k−2)}, M′_{(4j−n)(4k)}); } }
9    else{  //V″ − |V_k| ≤ c ⟹ V″ + V_k ≤ c where V″ ∈ 𝒱″
10       M′_{(4k−2)(4k−3)} ← min(0, M′_{(4k−2)(4k−3)}, M′_{(4k−1)(4k)});
11       for n ← 0 to 3 {
12           M′_{(4k−2)(4i−n)} ← min(M′_{(4k−2)(4i−n)}, M′_{(4k−1)(4i−n)});
13           M′_{(4j−n)(4k−3)} ← min(M′_{(4j−n)(4k−3)}, M′_{(4j−n)(4k)}); } }
14   for n ← (4 ∗ i − 3) to 4 ∗ j
15       for m ← (4 ∗ i − 3) to 4 ∗ j
16           M′_{nm} ← min(M′_{nm}, M′_{n(4k−3)} + M′_{(4k−3)m}, M′_{n(4k−2)} + M′_{(4k−2)m});
17             //V_k − V″_n ≤ c ∧ V″_m − V_k ≤ d ⟹ V″_m − V″_n ≤ c + d where V″_n, V″_m ∈ 𝒱″ \ {0}
18   return M′; }
```

Fig. 6. A algorithm to tighten AV constraints between V_i and V_j through V_k

V_k. E.g., if we have $-V_k \leq c_1$ and $-|V_k| \leq c_2$ in the input DBM, we can derive a upper bound for $-V_k$ as $-V_k \leq \min(0, c_1, c_2)$, which corresponds to line 5 in TightenIJviaK(). After line 14, the information over the rows and columns corresponding to $\pm|V_k|$ in the DBM becomes redundant. Hence, from line 14 to line 16, we only need to consider the propagation through $\pm V_k$ (without need through $\pm|V_k|$). Overall, WeakCloVia1Sign() is less precise but cheaper than WeakCloVia3Sign().

```
DBM^{4n×4n} WeakCloVia1Sign(M : DBM^{4n×4n}){
    M′, M′^{|•|}, N, N′ : DBM^{12×12};
    for k ← 1 to n
        for i ← 1 to n
            for j ← 1 to n {
                M′ ← M/{V_k, V_i, V_j};
                N ← TightenIJviaK(M′, true);  //when V_k ≥ 0
                N′ ← TightenIJviaK(M′, false);  //when V_k ≤ 0
                M′^{|•|} ← N ⊔^{DBM} N′;
                M/{V_i, V_j} ← M′^{|•|}/{V_i, V_j};  }
    for i ← 1 to 4n
        for j ← 1 to 4n
            M_{ij} ← min(M_{ij}, (M_{iī} + M_{j̄j})/2);
    for i ← 1 to 4n
        if (M_{ii} < 0) then return ⊥^{DBM}; else M_{ii} ← 0;
    return M; }
```

Fig. 7. The weak closure algorithm by enumerating the sign of one variable in each step

The initial constraint set

$y \leq 24$	$-\lvert y\rvert + x \leq 10$	$-s - \lvert x\rvert \leq 36$
$-\lvert s\rvert - z \leq 8$	$-z - y \leq 84$	$s + y \leq 80$

Common constraints found by 3 closure algorithms

$s - z \leq 164$	$y + x \leq 58$	$y - z \leq 132$
$-z \leq 108$	$x - \lvert z\rvert \leq 94$	

AV strong closure	WeakCloVia3Sign	WeakCloVia1Sign
$-\lvert x\rvert - z \leq 86$	$-\lvert x\rvert - z \leq 86$	$-\lvert x\rvert - z \leq 108$
$x - z \leq 112$	$x - z \leq 142$	$x - z \leq 142$

Fig. 8. An example of applying 3 closure algorithms on the same initial constraint set

Example 1. In Fig 8, we apply the above 3 closure algorithms on the same initial set of constraints. The AV strong closure finds $x - z \leq 112$ while WeakCloVia3Sign() and WeakCloVia1Sign() are less precise and can only find $x - z \leq 142$. Moreover, WeakCloVia1Sign() gives less precise result $-|x| - z \leq 108$ than WeakCloVia3Sign() which can find $-|x| - z \leq 86$.

3.5 Other Domain Operations

Closure is a basic operator in the AVO domain. Most abstract operators over AV octagons can be obtained following similar ideas as those over octagons by replacing strong closure with AV strong closure (if necessary). In practice, since our AV strong closure is of exponential-time complexity, we use weak closure instead. When we use weak closure, all the AVO domain operations can be $O(n^3)$ in the worst case. However, we do not have a normal form for AV octagons when using weak closure, and most domain operations are not guaranteed to be the best abstraction. E.g., for the inclusion test, we have $\gamma^{AVO}(M) \subseteq \gamma^{AVO}(N) \iff M^{|\bullet|} \sqsubseteq^{\mathsf{DBM}} N$ when using AV strong closure. If we use any of our weak closures, denoted as $M^{|\circ|}$, it holds that $M^{|\circ|} \sqsubseteq^{\mathsf{DBM}} N \Longrightarrow \gamma^{AVO}(M) \subseteq \gamma^{AVO}(N)$ but it may not hold that $\gamma^{AVO}(M) \subseteq \gamma^{AVO}(N) \Longrightarrow M^{|\circ|} \sqsubseteq^{\mathsf{DBM}} N$.

For test transfer functions, first, constraints in the tests are abstracted into AV octagonal constraints, following similar ideas as abstracting arbitrary constraints into octagonal constraints [24]. Moreover, we employ AVO join operation to try to encode disjunctive constraints in tests as conjunctive AV octagonal constraints. E.g., consider the condition that holds at ① in Fig. 1, i.e., $|dx| \neq 0 \vee |dy| \neq 0$. The disequality $|dx| \neq 0$ which itself can be rewritten as a disjunction $dx < 0 \vee -dx < 0$, can be encoded as $-|dx| < 0$ by the AVO join operation. Then, $-|dx| < 0 \vee -|dy| < 0$ can be further encoded as $-|dx| - |dy| < 0$ by the AVO join operation. Hence, even when the original condition test does not involve AV, AV may be introduced during constraint abstraction. After the process of constraint abstraction, the AV octagonal constraints derived from the tests are then used to tighten the current AVO abstract element.

For assignment transfer functions, we allow the right-hand side expression to involve AV, such as $x := \pm|y| \pm c$. However, we can simply transform assignments with AV into conditional branches with assignments that do not involve AV. E.g., the assignment $x := a*|e|+c$ where a, e, c are expressions, can be transformed into: `if` $(e \geq 0)$ `then` $x := a * e + c$; `else` $x := -a * e + c$; `fi`.

3.6 Supporting Strict Inequalities

In practice, strict inequalities (such as $|x| + |y| > 0$) may appear in branch conditions of a program. To this end, we extend the AVO domain to support strict inequalities. In the domain representation, we maintain a boolean matrix S of the same size as the DBM M that encodes an AV octagon, such that

$$S_{ij} \stackrel{\text{def}}{=} \begin{cases} 0 & \text{if } V''_j - V''_i < M_{ij} \\ 1 & \text{if } V''_j - V''_i \leq M_{ij} \end{cases}$$

We define the order over pairs (m, s)'s where $m \in \mathbb{I}$ and $s \in \{0, 1\}$, as

$$(m, s) \sqsubseteq (m', s') \stackrel{\text{def}}{\Longleftrightarrow} (m < m') \vee (m = m' \wedge s \leq s'))$$

Note that $\sqsubseteq$ is a total order on $(\mathbb{I}, \mathsf{bool})$, i.e., at least one of $(m, s) \sqsubseteq (m', s')$ and $(m', s') \sqsubseteq (m, s)$ holds. Let DBMS denote the set of all pairs of DBMs and boolean matrices. A lattice over DBMS can be obtained by "lifting" the operations from DBM and the boolean matrices element-wise. In addition, we define the addition over DBMS as:

$$(M_{ik}, S_{ik}) + (M_{kj}, S_{kj}) \stackrel{\text{def}}{=} (M_{ik} + M_{kj}, S_{ik} \& S_{kj})$$

Then in the abstract domain supporting strict inequalities, all domain operations can be adapted from the domain that supports only non-strict inequalities by replacing operations over DBM with operations over DBMS. E.g., in the AVO domain supporting strict inequalities, the emptiness test is to check whether it holds that $\exists i, M_{ii} < 0 \vee (S_{ii} = 0 \wedge M_{ii} = 0)$. Whereas, in the regular AVO domain, we only need to check whether it holds that $\exists i, M_{ii} < 0$.

4 Implementation and Experimental Results

We have implemented the AVO domain in the APRON abstract domain library [19].

4.1 Experimental Comparison of Three Closure Algorithms

We first compare in precision and efficiency the three closure algorithms proposed in Sect.3.4 for AV octagons. We conduct our experiments on randomly generated DBMs (of dimension $4n$ but partially initialized) over different numbers of variables (n). The experimental result is shown in Fig 9. "♯cases" gives the number of test cases for each such number n. "str" denotes the AV strong closure algorithm, "wk3s" denotes WeakCloVia3Sign(), and "wk1s" denotes WeakCloVia1Sign(). "%same_results" shows the percentage of test cases where the two compared algorithms give the same resulting DBMs. The column "%different_elements" presents the average percentage of the number of different elements in the resulting DBMs to the size of the DBMs, when the two compared algorithms produce different resulting DBMs.

From the result, we can see that WeakCloVia1Sign() is much more efficient than the other two closure algorithms. For those test cases where the two compared algorithms produce different resulting DBMs, the percentage of the number of different elements

♯vars	♯cases	average time			%same_results			%different_elements		
		str	wk3s	wk1s	str= wk3s	str= wk1s	wk3s= wk1s	str≠ wk3s	str≠ wk1s	wk3s ≠ wk1s
4	10000	2.4ms	7ms	0.19ms	94%	94%	99%	0.94%	0.79%	0.78%
8	1000	380ms	160ms	20ms	36%	28%	74%	0.83%	1.5%	0.26%
10	1000	5.7s	410ms	53ms	10%	5.3%	51%	1.1%	2.1%	0.18%

Fig. 9. An experimental comparison of 3 closure algorithms on randomly generated DBMs

in the resulting DBMs is very low. In other words, the two different resulting DBMs are mostly the same except for very few elements. During our experiments, at the moment, we found no test case for which weak closures give $+\infty$ for an element where the strong closure gives a finite constant in the resulting DBMs.

4.2 Experiments on NECLA Division-by-Zero Benchmarks

We have conducted experiments using the INTERPROC [20] static analyzer on the NECLA Benchmarks: Division-by-zero False Alarms [14]. The benchmark set is extracted from source code of several open-source projects. These programs illustrate commonly used techniques that programmers use to protect a division-by-zero (e.g., by using the AV function), and are challenging for analysis since they involve non-convex constraints (e.g., disjunctions, constraints involving the AV function) and strict inequalities.

Fig. 10 shows the comparison of invariants inferred by AVO (using the weak closure algorithm WeakCloVia1Sign) with those by the octagon domain [24] and by the donut domain [14] (the main idea of which is to represent concrete object by the so-called hole that is the set minus of two convex sets). The `motiv` program corresponds to the motivating example (shown in Fig. 1) with its two branches. The column "WCfS" gives the weakest condition to prove the absence of the division-by-zero error in the program. The results given in the column "donut domain" are taken from [14] (using boxes to encode holes). From Fig. 10, we can see that the octagon domain fails to prove the absence of division-by-zero error for all programs since it cannot express non-convex properties nor strict inequalities. Our AVO domain succeeds to prove the absence of the division-by-zero errors for all programs including *xcor* on which the donut domain fails (due to its default heuristic for choosing holes).

program	WCfS	donut domain		octagons		AV octagons	
		invariants	♯false alarms	invariants	♯false alarms	invariants	♯false alarms
motiv(if)	$dy \neq 0$	$dy \neq 0$	0	$dy \in [-\infty, +\infty]$	1	$\|dy\| > 0$	0
motiv(else)	$dx \neq 0$	$dx \neq 0$	0	$dx \in [-\infty, +\infty]$	1	$\|dx\| > 0$	0
gpc	$den \neq 0$	$den \notin [-0.1, 0.1]$	0	$den \in [-\infty, +\infty]$	1	$\|den\| \geq 0.1$	0
goc	$d \neq 0$	$d \notin [-0.09, 0.09]$	0	$d \in [-\infty, +\infty]$	1	$\|d\| \geq 0.1$	0
x2	$Dx \neq 0$	$Dx \neq 0$	0	$Dx \in [-\infty, +\infty]$	1	$\|Dx\| > 0$	0
xcor	$usemax \neq 0$	$usemax \notin [1, 10]$	1	$usemax \geq 0$	1	$usemax > 0$	0

Fig. 10. Experimental results on NECLA division-by-zero benchmarks

code id	size (KLOC)	octagons			AV octagons			result comparison		
		time (s)	♯alarm	♯iter.	time (s)	♯alarm	♯iter.	♯ alarm reduction	time increase	♯ iter. reduction
*P*1	154	6216	881	110	7687	881	110	0	23.66%	0
*P*2	186	6460	1114	116	7854	1114	115	0	21.58%	1
*P*3	103	1112	403	25	2123	403	25	0	90.92%	0
*P*4	493	17195	4912	158	38180	4912	158	0	122.04%	0
*P*5	661	18949	7075	105	43660	7070	104	5	130.41%	1
*P*6	616	34639	8192	118	70541	8180	108	12	103.65%	10
*P*7	2428	99853	10980	317	217506	10959	317	21	117.83%	0
*P*8	3	517	0	19	581	0	19	0	12.38%	0
*P*9	18	534	16	27	670	16	27	0	25.47%	0
*P*10	26	1065	102	42	1133	102	42	0	6.38%	0

Fig. 11. Experimental results using ASTRÉE on large embedded C codes

4.3 Experiments on ASTRÉE

We have also evaluated the scalability of AVO when analyzing large realistic programs, by integrating it into the ASTRÉE analyzer [4] and analyzing its dedicated benchmarks: a set of large embedded industrial C codes performing much integer and float computation. ASTRÉE contains many abstract domains, including octagons and disjunctive domains (such as trace partitioning and decision diagrams) and domains specialized for the analyzed benchmarks; It is carefully tuned to give few alarms and remain efficient. Hence, we did not expect the AVO domain to bring a notable increase in precision (by simply replacing octagons with AVO, a single program featured a reduction of 4 alarms). For a more fair comparison, we evaluated how AVO could replace, by its natural ability to represent disjunctions, the dedicated disjunctive domains in ASTRÉE. We disabled these disjunctive domains and ran analyses with the regular octagon domain and with AVO. Following the experiments from Fig. 9, we chose to use the more scalable weak closure WeakCloVia1Sign for these large analyses. The results are shown in Fig. 11. The last columns give the number of alarms removed by using AVO and the increase in analysis time. We observe three instances of alarm reductions and an increase of up to +130% of analysis time at worst. Additionally, the majority of codes are composed of a single large synchronous loop running 10^6 iterations, and we provide for those the number of abstract iterations needed to reach a fixpoint. Our experiments show that using the more precise AVO domain can slightly increase the convergence rate and never decrease it. Overall, our results show that, although it cannot compete with domains specifically tailored to analyze a code family, AVO nevertheless brings modest improvements in precision, and keeps the analysis time in the same order of magnitude.

5 Related Work

In abstract interpretation, most existing numerical abstract domains can only express convex sets, such as the classical convex polyhedra domain [11] together with all its subdomains (including octagons [24], two variables per inequality (TVPI) [27], template polyhedra [26], subpolyhedra [21], etc.)

Until now, only a few numerical abstract domains natively allow representing non-convex sets, e.g., congruences [15], max-plus polyhedra [2], interval linear abstract domains [5,6] and quadratic templates [1]. To enhance numerical abstract domain with non-convex expressiveness, some work makes use of BDDs [17,18] while some makes use of mathematical functions that could express non-convex properties such as max [16] and the absolute value function [7]. The donut domain [14] utilizes the set difference of two convex sets to express non-convex properties. Recently, [13] studies the impact of using non-lattice abstract domains (including non-convex numerical abstract domains) and proposes general remedies for precision and termination.

The AVO domain that we introduce in this paper is closest to the abstract domain of linear AV inequalities [7] which can infer general linear AV constraints but is of exponential complexity. The AVO domain enjoys abstract operators in cubic time complexity and quadratic memory complexity. Moreover, the AVO domain supports strict inequalities. [25] presents an abstract domain extending DBMs (encoding potential constraints) with disequality constraints of the form "$x \neq y$" or "$x \neq 0$", rather than extending the octagon domain. Moreover, disequalities are different from strict inequalities in that a disequality is a disjunction of two strict inequalities, while in this paper we consider the conjunction of strict inequalities. The pentagon domain [22] also chooses on purpose to perform the closure in an incomplete (but sound) way, to improve the efficiency in practice at the cost of precision. Our purpose to have weak closure in this paper is similar, but to low down the complexity due to absolute value.

6 Conclusion

In this paper, we present an analysis to discover octagonal (or UTVPI) relations among the values and the absolute values of variables of a program ($\pm X \pm Y \leq c, \pm X \pm |Y| \leq d, \pm|X| \pm |Y| \leq e$) , which generalizes the octagon abstract domain ($\pm X \pm Y \leq c$) [24]. The analysis explores the absolute value function as a mean to describe non-convex behaviors in the program. First, we present a representation to encode AV octagons via DBMs. Then we propose 3 closure algorithms for AV octagons to offer different time precision tradeoffs. On this basis, we provide algorithms for domain operations such that the new domain still enjoys the cubic time complexity, as octagons. In addition, we present an approach to extend AVO to support strict inequalities over rational or real-valued variables, which also fits for octagons. Experimental results are encouraging on benchmark programs and large embedded C programs: AVO is scalable and able to find useful non-convex invariants, without too much overhead compared with octagons.

It remains for future work to consider the domain of AV integer octagonal constraints (i.e., AV octagonal constraints with integers as constant terms), wherein the key is to have a tight closure algorithm for AV integer octagonal constraints.

References

1. Adjé, A., Gaubert, S., Goubault, E.: Coupling policy iteration with semi-definite relaxation to compute accurate numerical invariants in static analysis. In: Gordon, A.D. (ed.) ESOP 2010. LNCS, vol. 6012, pp. 23–42. Springer, Heidelberg (2010)

2. Allamigeon, X., Gaubert, S., Goubault, É.: Inferring min and max invariants using max-plus polyhedra. In: Alpuente, M., Vidal, G. (eds.) SAS 2008. LNCS, vol. 5079, pp. 189–204. Springer, Heidelberg (2008)
3. Bagnara, R., Hill, P.M., Mazzi, E., Zaffanella, E.: Widening operators for weakly-relational numeric abstractions. In: Hankin, C., Siveroni, I. (eds.) SAS 2005. LNCS, vol. 3672, pp. 3–18. Springer, Heidelberg (2005)
4. Blanchet, B., Cousot, P., Cousot, R., Feret, J., Mauborgne, L., Miné, A., Monniaux, D., Rival, X.: A static analyzer for large safety-critical software. In: PLDI, pp. 196–207. ACM Press (2003)
5. Chen, L., Miné, A., Wang, J., Cousot, P.: Interval polyhedra: An abstract domain to infer interval linear relationships. In: Palsberg, J., Su, Z. (eds.) SAS 2009. LNCS, vol. 5673, pp. 309–325. Springer, Heidelberg (2009)
6. Chen, L., Miné, A., Wang, J., Cousot, P.: An abstract domain to discover interval linear equalities. In: Barthe, G., Hermenegildo, M. (eds.) VMCAI 2010. LNCS, vol. 5944, pp. 112–128. Springer, Heidelberg (2010)
7. Chen, L., Miné, A., Wang, J., Cousot, P.: Linear absolute value relation analysis. In: Barthe, G. (ed.) ESOP 2011. LNCS, vol. 6602, pp. 156–175. Springer, Heidelberg (2011)
8. Cousot, P., Cousot, R.: Static determination of dynamic properties of programs. In: Proc. of the 2nd International Symposium on Programming, pp. 106–130. Dunod, Paris (1976)
9. Cousot, P., Cousot, R.: Abstract interpretation: a unified lattice model for static analysis of programs by construction or approximation of fixpoints. In: POPL, pp. 238–252. ACM Press (1977)
10. Cousot, P., Cousot, R.: Systematic design of program analysis frameworks. In: POPL, pp. 269–282. ACM Press (1979)
11. Cousot, P., Halbwachs, N.: Automatic discovery of linear restraints among variables of a program. In: POPL, pp. 84–96. ACM Press (1978)
12. Dill, D.L.: Timing assumptions and verification of finite-state concurrent systems. In: Sifakis, J. (ed.) Automatic Verification Methods for Finite State Systems. LNCS, vol. 407, pp. 197–212. Springer, Heidelberg (1990)
13. Gange, G., Navas, J.A., Schachte, P., Søndergaard, H., Stuckey, P.J.: Abstract interpretation over non-lattice abstract domains. In: Logozzo, F., Fähndrich, M. (eds.) SAS 2013. LNCS, vol. 7935, pp. 6–24. Springer, Heidelberg (2013)
14. Ghorbal, K., Ivančić, F., Balakrishnan, G., Maeda, N., Gupta, A.: Donut domains: Efficient non-convex domains for abstract interpretation. In: Kuncak, V., Rybalchenko, A. (eds.) VMCAI 2012. LNCS, vol. 7148, pp. 235–250. Springer, Heidelberg (2012)
15. Granger, P.: Static analysis of arithmetical congruences. International Journal of Computer Mathematics, 165–199 (1989)
16. Gulavani, B.S., Gulwani, S.: A numerical abstract domain based on expression abstraction and max operator with application in timing analysis. In: Gupta, A., Malik, S. (eds.) CAV 2008. LNCS, vol. 5123, pp. 370–384. Springer, Heidelberg (2008)
17. Gurfinkel, A., Chaki, S.: Boxes: A symbolic abstract domain of boxes. In: Cousot, R., Martel, M. (eds.) SAS 2010. LNCS, vol. 6337, pp. 287–303. Springer, Heidelberg (2010)
18. Howe, J.M., King, A., Lawrence-Jones, C.: Quadtrees as an abstract domain. Electr. Notes Theor. Comput. Sci. 267(1), 89–100 (2010)
19. Jeannet, B., Miné, A.: Apron: A library of numerical abstract domains for static analysis. In: Bouajjani, A., Maler, O. (eds.) CAV 2009. LNCS, vol. 5643, pp. 661–667. Springer, Heidelberg (2009)
20. Lalire, G., Argoud, M., Jeannet, B.: Interproc., `http://pop-art.inrialpes.fr/people/bjeannet/bjeannet-forge/interproc/`

21. Laviron, V., Logozzo, F.: Subpolyhedra: A (more) scalable approach to infer linear inequalities. In: Jones, N.D., Müller-Olm, M. (eds.) VMCAI 2009. LNCS, vol. 5403, pp. 229–244. Springer, Heidelberg (2009)
22. Logozzo, F., Fähndrich, M.: Pentagons: A weakly relational abstract domain for the efficient validation of array accesses. Sci. Comput. Program. 75(9), 796–807 (2010)
23. Miné, A.: The octagon abstract domain. In: Proc. of the Workshop on Analysis, Slicing, and Transformation, AST 2001, pp. 310–319. IEEE CS Press (2001)
24. Miné, A.: The octagon abstract domain. Higher-Order and Symbolic Computation 19(1), 31–100 (2006)
25. Péron, M., Halbwachs, N.: An abstract domain extending difference-bound matrices with disequality constraints. In: Cook, B., Podelski, A. (eds.) VMCAI 2007. LNCS, vol. 4349, pp. 268–282. Springer, Heidelberg (2007)
26. Sankaranarayanan, S., Sipma, H.B., Manna, Z.: Scalable analysis of linear systems using mathematical programming. In: Cousot, R. (ed.) VMCAI 2005. LNCS, vol. 3385, pp. 25–41. Springer, Heidelberg (2005)
27. Simon, A., King, A., Howe, J.M.: Two Variables per Linear Inequality as an Abstract Domain. In: Leuschel, M. (ed.) LOPSTR 2002. LNCS, vol. 2664, pp. 71–89. Springer, Heidelberg (2003)

Verifying Recursive Programs Using Intraprocedural Analyzers

Yu-Fang Chen[1], Chiao Hsieh[1,2], Ming-Hsien Tsai[1],
Bow-Yaw Wang[1], and Farn Wang[2]

[1] Institute of Information Science, Academia Sinica, Taiwan
[2] Graduate Institute of Electrical Engineering, National Taiwan University, Taiwan

Abstract. Recursion can complicate program analysis significantly. Some program analyzers simply ignore recursion or even refuse to check recursive programs. In this paper, we propose an algorithm that uses a recursion-free program analyzer as a black box to check recursive programs. With extended program constructs for assumptions, assertions, and nondeterministic values, our algorithm computes function summaries from inductive invariants computed by the underlying program analyzer. Such function summaries enable our algorithm to check recursive programs. We implement a prototype using the recursion-free program analyzer CPAChecker and compare it with other program analyzers on the benchmarks in the 2014 Competition on Software Verification.

1 Introduction

Program verification is a grand challenge with significant impact in computer science. Its main difficulty is in great part due to complicated program features such as concurrent execution, pointers, recursive function calls, and unbounded basic data types [7]. Subsequently, it is extremely tedious to develop a verification algorithm that handles all features. Researches on program verification typically address some of these features and simplify others. Verification tools however are required to support as many features as possible. Since implementation becomes increasingly unmanageable with additional features, incorporating algorithms for all features in verification tools can be a nightmare for developers.

One way to address the implementation problem is by reduction. If verifying a new feature can be transformed to existing features, development efforts can be significantly reduced. In this paper, we propose an algorithm to extend intraprocedure (recursion-free) program analyzers to verify recursive programs. Such analyzers supply an *inductive invariant* when a program is verified to be correct and support program constructs such as assumptions, assertions, and nondeterministic values. Our algorithm transforms any recursive program into non-recursive ones and invokes an intraprocedure program analyzer to verify properties about the generated non-recursive programs. The verification results allow us to infer properties on the given recursive program.

Our algorithm proceeds by iterations. In each iteration, it transforms the recursive program into a non-recursive program that *under-approximates* the

M. Müller-Olm and H. Seidl (Eds.): SAS 2014, LNCS 8723, pp. 118–133, 2014.

behaviors of the original and sends the under-approximation to an intraprocedure program analyzer. If the analyzer verifies the under-approximation, purported *function summaries* for recursive functions are computed. Our algorithm then transforms the original recursive program into more non-recursive programs with purported function summaries. It finally checks if purported function summaries are correct by sending these non-recursive programs to the analyzer.

Compared with other analysis algorithms for recursive programs, ours is very lightweight. It only performs syntactic transformation and requires standard functionalities from underlying intraprocedure program analyzers. Moreover, our technique is very modular. Any intraprocedural analyzer providing proofs of inductive invariants can be employed in our algorithm. With the interface between our algorithm and program analyzers described here, incorporating recursive analysis with existing program analyzers thus only requires minimal implementation efforts. Recursive analysis hence benefits from future advanced intraprocedural analysis with little cost through our lightweight and modular technique.

We implement a prototype using CPACHECKER (over 140 thousand lines of JAVA code) as the underlying program analyzer [6]. In our prototype, 1256 lines of OCAML code are for syntactic transformation and 705 lines of PYTHON code for the rest of the algorithm. 270 lines among them are for extracting function summaries. Since syntactic transformation is independent of underlying program analyzers, only about 14% of code need to be rewritten should another analyzer be employed. We compare it with program analyzers specialized for recursion in experiments. Although CPACHECKER does not support recursion, our prototype scores slightly better than the second-place tool ULTIMATE AUTOMIZER on the benchmarks in the 2014 Competition on Software Verification [9].

Organization: Preliminaries are given in Section 2. We give an overview of our technique in Section 3. Technical contributions are presented in Section 4. Section 5 reports experimental results. Section 6 describes related works. Finally, some insights and improvements are discussed in Section 7.

2 Preliminaries

We consider a variant of the WHILE language [17]:

$\texttt{Expression} \ni p ::=$	$\texttt{x}$	$\texttt{x} \in \texttt{Vars}$
	$\mid$ $\texttt{false} \mid \texttt{true} \mid \texttt{0} \mid \texttt{1} \mid \ldots$	constant
	$\mid$ $\texttt{nondet}$	nondeterministic value
	$\mid$ $\texttt{f}(\overline{p})$	function invocation
	$\mid$ $p \odot p$	$\odot \in \{+, -, =, >, \texttt{and}, \texttt{or}\}$
	$\mid$ $\texttt{not}\ p$	
$\texttt{Command} \ni c ::=$	$\overline{\texttt{x}} := \overline{p}$	assignment
	$\mid$ $c; c$	sequential composition
	$\mid$ $\texttt{return}\ \overline{p}$	function return
	$\mid$ $\texttt{assume}\ p$	assumption
	$\mid$ $\texttt{assert}\ p$	assertion

Vars denotes the set of *program variables*, and $\texttt{Vars}' = \{\texttt{x}' : \texttt{x} \in \texttt{Vars}\}$ where $\texttt{x}'$ represents the new value of x after execution of a command. The nondet expression evaluates to a type-safe nondeterministic value. Simultaneous assignments are allowed in our language. To execute a simultaneous assignment, all expressions on the right hand side are first evaluated and then assigned to respective variables. We assume that simultaneous assignments are type-safe in the sense that the number of variables on the left-hand-side always matches that of the right-hand-side. The return command accepts several expressions as arguments. Together with simultaneous assignments, functions can have several return values.

A function f is represented as a *control flow graph (CFG)* $G^{\texttt{f}} = \langle V, E, \text{cmd}^{\texttt{f}}, \overline{\texttt{u}}^{\texttt{f}}, \overline{\texttt{r}}^{\texttt{f}}, s, e\rangle$ where the nodes in V are *program locations*, $E \subseteq V \times V$ are *edges*, each edge $(\ell, \ell') \in E$ is labeled by the command $\text{cmd}^{\texttt{f}}(\ell, \ell')$, $\overline{\texttt{u}}^{\texttt{f}}$ and $\overline{\texttt{r}}^{\texttt{f}}$ are *formal parameters* and *return variables* of f, and $s, e \in V$ are the *entry* and *exit* locations of f. The superscript in $G^{\texttt{f}}$ denotes the CFG corresponds to the function f. The special main function specifies where a program starts. To simplify presentation, we assume the functions in a program use disjoint sets of variables and the values of formal parameters never change in a function. Notice that this will not affect the expressiveness of a CFG because one can still make copies of formal parameters by assignments and change the values of the copied versions. Also we assume that there are no global variables because they can be simulated by allowing simultaneous assignment to return variables [3].

Figure 1 shows control flow graphs for the McCarthy 91 program from [16]. The main function assumes the variable n is non-negative. It then checks if the result of mc91(n) is no less than 90 (Figure 1a). The mc91 function branches on whether the variable m is greater than 100. If so, it returns $\texttt{m} - 10$. Otherwise, mc91(m) stores the result of $\texttt{mc91}(\texttt{m} + 11)$ in s, and returns the result of mc91(s) (Figure 1b). Observe that a conditional branch is modeled with the assume command in the figure. Loops can be modeled similarly.

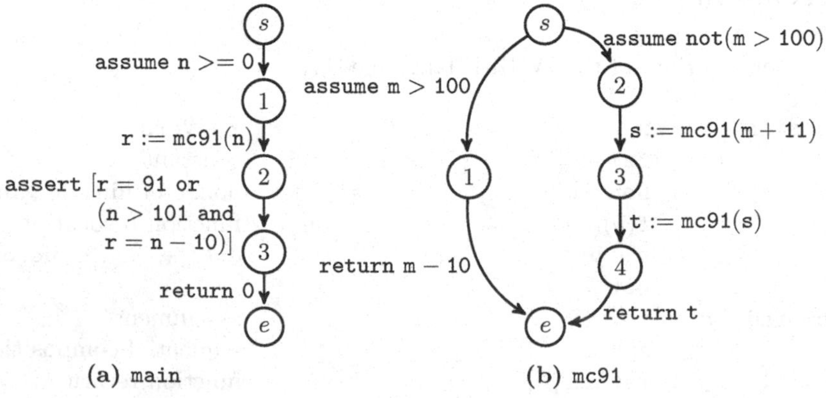

Fig. 1. McCarthy 91

Let $G^{\mathtt{f}} = \langle V, E, \mathrm{cmd}^{\mathtt{f}}, \overline{\mathtt{u}}^{\mathtt{f}}, \overline{\mathtt{r}}^{\mathtt{f}}, s, e\rangle$ be a CFG. An *inductive invariant* $\Pi(G^{\mathtt{f}}, I_0) = \{I_\ell : \ell \in V\}$ for $G^{\mathtt{f}}$ from I_0 is a set of first-order logic formulae such that $I_s = I_0$, and for every $(\ell, \ell') \in E$

$$I_\ell \wedge \tau_{\mathrm{cmd}^{\mathtt{f}}(\ell,\ell')} \implies I'_{\ell'}$$

where I' is obtained by replacing every $\mathtt{x} \in \mathtt{Vars}$ in I with $\mathtt{x}' \in \mathtt{Vars}'$, and $\tau_{\mathrm{cmd}^{\mathtt{f}}(\ell,\ell')}$ specifies the semantics of the command $\mathrm{cmd}^{\mathtt{f}}(\ell, \ell')$. An inductive invariant $\Pi(G^{\mathtt{f}}, I_0)$ is an over-approximation to the computation of $G^{\mathtt{f}}$ from I_0. More precisely, assume that the function f starts from a state satisfying I_0. For every $\ell \in V$, $G^{\mathtt{f}}$ must arrive in a state satisfying I_ℓ when the computation reaches ℓ.

Let T be a program fragment (it can be either a function represented as a CFG or a sequence of program commands). P and Q are logic formulae. A *Hoare triple* $(\!|P|\!)T(\!|Q|\!)$ specifies that the program fragment T will reach a program state satisfying Q provided that T starts with a program state satisfying P and terminates. The formula P is called the *precondition* and Q is the *postcondition* of the Hoare triple. We use the standard proof rules for partial correctness with two additional rules for the assumption and assertion commands:

$$\text{Assume}\ \frac{}{(\!|P|\!)\ \mathtt{assume}\ q\ (\!|P \wedge q|\!)} \qquad \text{Assert}\ \frac{P \implies q}{(\!|P|\!)\ \mathtt{assert}\ q\ (\!|P|\!)}$$

The assume command excludes all computation not satisfying the given expression. The assert command aborts the computation if the given expression is not implied by the precondition. No postcondition can be guaranteed in such a case. Observe that an inductive invariant $\Pi(G^{\mathtt{f}}, I_0)$ establishes $(\!|I_0|\!)G^{\mathtt{f}}(\!|I_e|\!)$. A *program analyzer* accepts programs as inputs and checks if all assertions (specified by the assert command) are satisfied. One way to implement program analyzers is to compute inductive invariants.

Proposition 1. *Let* $G^{\mathtt{f}} = \langle V, E, cmd^{\mathtt{f}}, \overline{\mathtt{u}}^{\mathtt{f}}, \overline{\mathtt{r}}^{\mathtt{f}}, s, e\rangle$ *be a CFG and* $\Pi(G^{\mathtt{f}}, \mathtt{true})$ *be an inductive invariant for* $G^{\mathtt{f}}$ *from* true. *If* $\models I_\ell \implies B_\ell$ *for every edge* $(\ell, \ell') \in E$ *with* $cmd(\ell, \ell') = \mathtt{assert}(B_\ell)$, *then all assertions in* $G^{\mathtt{f}}$ *are satisfied.*

A program analyzer checks assertions by computing inductive invariants is called an *inductive* program analyzer. Note that an inductive program analyzer need not give any information when an assertion fails. Indeed, most inductive program analyzers simply report false positives when inductive invariants are too coarse. A *recursion-free inductive program analyzer* is a program analyzer that checks recursion-free programs by computing inductive invariants. Several recursion-free inductive program analyzers are available, such as CPACHECKER [6], BLAST [5], UFO [2], ASTRÉE [10], etc. Our goal is to check recursive programs by using a recursion-free inductive program analyzer as a black box.

3 Overview

Let BASICANALYZER denote a recursion-free inductive program analyzer, and let a program $P = \{G^{\mathtt{main}}\} \cup \{G^{\mathtt{f}} : \mathtt{f}$ is a function$\}$ consist of the CFGs of the `main` function and functions that may be invoked (transitively) from `main`. Since non-recursive functions can be replaced by their control flow graphs after proper variable renaming, we assume that P only contains the `main` and recursive functions. If P does not contain recursive functions, BasicAnalyzer is able to check P by computing inductive invariants.

When P contains recursive functions, we transform $G^{\mathtt{main}}$ into a recursion-free program $\underline{G}^{\mathtt{main}}$. The program $\underline{G}^{\mathtt{main}}$ under-approximates the computation of $G^{\mathtt{main}}$. That is, every computation of $\underline{G}^{\mathtt{main}}$ is also a computation of $G^{\mathtt{main}}$. If BasicAnalyzer finds an error in $\underline{G}^{\mathtt{main}}$, our algorithm terminates and reports it. Otherwise, BasicAnalyzer has computed an inductive invariant for the recursion-free under-approximation $\underline{G}^{\mathtt{main}}$. Our algorithm computes function summaries of functions in P from the inductive invariant of $\underline{G}^{\mathtt{main}}$. It then checks if every function summary over-approximates the computation of the corresponding function. If so, the algorithm terminates and reports that all assertions in P are satisfied. If a function summary does not over-approximate the computation, our algorithm unwinds the recursive function and reiterates (Algorithm 1).

Input: A program $P = \{G^{\mathtt{main}}\} \cup \{G^{\mathtt{f}} : \mathtt{f} \text{ is a function}\}$
$k \leftarrow 0$;
$P_0 \leftarrow P$;
repeat
  $k \leftarrow k + 1$;
  $P_k \leftarrow$ unwind every CFG in P_{k-1};
  switch BasicAnalyzer $(\underline{G}_k^{\mathtt{main}})$ **do**
    case $Pass(\Pi(\underline{G}_k^{\mathtt{main}}, \mathtt{true}))$:
      S := ComputeSummary(P_k, $\Pi(\underline{G}_k^{\mathtt{main}}, \mathtt{true})$)
    case *Error*: **return** *Error*
  complete? $\leftarrow$ CheckSummary(P_k, S);
until *complete?*;
return $Pass(\Pi(\underline{G}_k^{\mathtt{main}}, \mathtt{true}))$, S;

Algorithm 1. Overview

To see how to under-approximate computation, consider a control flow graph $G_k^{\mathtt{main}}$. The under-approximation $\underline{G}_k^{\mathtt{main}}$ is obtained by substituting the command `assume false` for every command with recursive function calls (Figure 2). The substitution effectively blocks all recursive invocations. Any computation of $\underline{G}_k^{\mathtt{main}}$ hence is also a computation of $G_k^{\mathtt{main}}$. Note that $\underline{G}_k^{\mathtt{main}}$ is recursion-free. BasicAnalyzer is able to check the under-approximation $\underline{G}_k^{\mathtt{main}}$.

When BasicAnalyzer does not find any error in the under-approximation $\underline{G}_k^{\mathtt{main}}$, it computes an inductive invariant $\Pi(\underline{G}_k^{\mathtt{main}}, \mathtt{true})$. Our algorithm then computes summaries of functions in P. For each function `f` with formal parameters $\overline{\mathtt{u}}^{\mathtt{f}}$ and return variables $\overline{\mathtt{r}}^{\mathtt{f}}$, a *function summary* for `f` is a first-order conjunctive formula which specifies the relation between its formal parameters and return variables. The algorithm ComputeSummary(P_k, $\Pi(\underline{G}_k^{\mathtt{main}}, \mathtt{true})$) computes summaries S by inspecting the inductive invariant $\Pi(\underline{G}_k^{\mathtt{main}}, \mathtt{true})$ (Section 4.3).

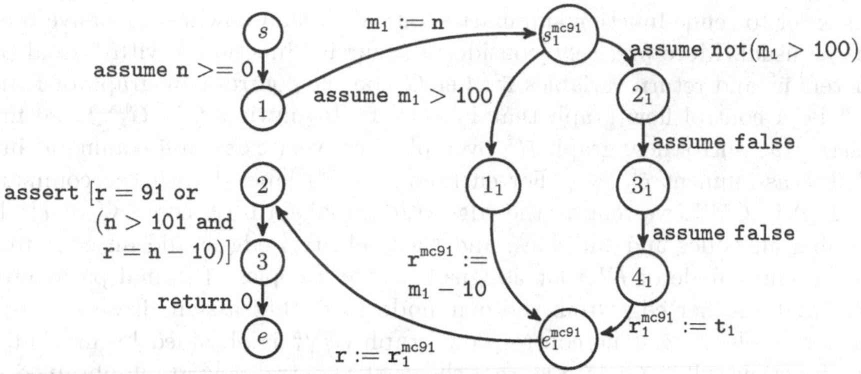

Fig. 2. Under-approximation of McCarthy 91

After function summaries are computed, Algorithm 1 verifies whether function summaries correctly specify computations of functions by invoking CheckSummary(P_k, S). The algorithm CheckSummary(P_k, S) checks this by constructing a recursion-free control flow graph $\tilde{G}^{\mathtt{f}}$ with additional assertions for each function f and verifying $\tilde{G}^{\mathtt{f}}$ with BasicAnalyzer. The control flow graph $\tilde{G}^{\mathtt{f}}$ is obtained by substituting function summaries for function calls. It is transformed from $G^{\mathtt{f}}$ by the following three steps:

1. Replace every function call by instantiating the summary for the callee;
2. Replace every return command by assignments to return variables;
3. Add an assertion to validate the summary at the end.

Figure 3 shows the control flow graph $\tilde{G}^{\mathtt{mc91}}$ with the function summary $S[\mathtt{mc91}] = \mathtt{not}(\mathtt{m} \geq 0)$. Observe that $\tilde{G}^{\mathtt{mc91}}$ is recursion-free. BasicAnalyzer is able to check $\tilde{G}^{\mathtt{mc91}}$ and invalidates this function summary.

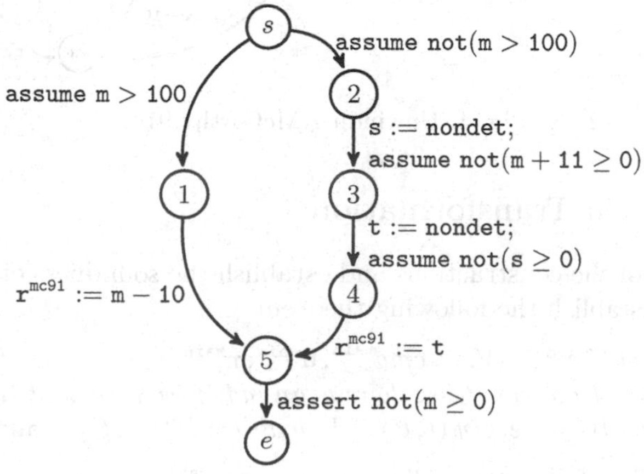

Fig. 3. Check Summary in McCarthy 91

In order to refine function summaries, our algorithm unwinds recursive functions as usual. More precisely, consider a recursive function f with formal parameters $\overline{\mathtt{u}}^{\mathtt{f}}$ and return variables $\overline{\mathtt{r}}^{\mathtt{f}}$. Let $G^{\mathtt{f}}$ be the control flow graph of f and $G_k^{\mathtt{main}}$ be a control flow graph that invokes f. To unwind f in $G_k^{\mathtt{main}}$, we first construct a control flow graph $H^{\mathtt{f}}$ by replacing every `return` $\overline{q}$ command in f with the assignment $\overline{\mathtt{r}}^{\mathtt{f}} := \overline{q}$. For each edge (ℓ, ℓ') labeled with the command $\overline{\mathtt{x}} := \mathtt{f}(\overline{p})$ in $G_k^{\mathtt{main}}$, we remove the edge (ℓ, ℓ'), make a fresh copy $K^{\mathtt{f}}$ of $H^{\mathtt{f}}$ by renaming all nodes and variables, and then add two edges: add an edge from ℓ to the entry node of $K^{\mathtt{f}}$ that assigns $\overline{p}$ to fresh copies of formal parameters in $K^{\mathtt{f}}$ and another edge from the exit node to ℓ' that assigns fresh copies of return variables to $\overline{\mathtt{x}}$. The control flow graph $G_{k+1}^{\mathtt{main}}$ is obtained by unwinding every function call in $G_k^{\mathtt{main}}$. Figure 4 shows the control flow graph obtained by unwinding `main` twice. Note that the unwinding graph $G_{k+1}^{\mathtt{main}}$ still has recursive function calls. Its under-approximation $\underline{G}_{k+1}^{\mathtt{main}}$ is more accurate than $\underline{G}_k^{\mathtt{main}}$.

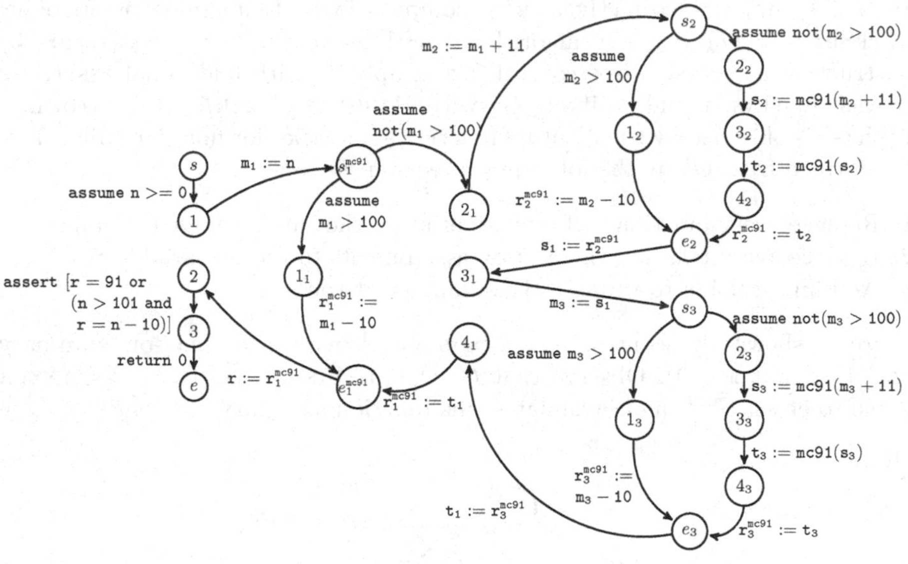

Fig. 4. Unwinding McCarthy 91

4 Proving via Transformation

We give details of the constructions and establish the soundness of Algorithm 1. Our goal is to establish the following theorem:

Theorem 1. *Let* $G^{\mathtt{main}} = \langle V, E, cmd^{\mathtt{main}}, \overline{\mathtt{u}}^{\mathtt{main}}, \overline{\mathtt{r}}^{\mathtt{main}}, s, e\rangle$ *be a control flow graph in* P*. If Algorithm 1 returns Pass, there is an inductive invariant* $\Pi(G^{\mathtt{main}}, \mathtt{true})$ *such that* $I_\ell \implies B_\ell$ *for every* $(\ell, \ell') \in E$ *with* $cmd^{\mathtt{main}}(\ell, \ell') = \mathtt{assert}\ B_\ell$.

By Proposition 1, it follows that all assertions in $G^{\mathtt{main}}$ are satisfied. Moreover, by the semantics of the `assert` command, all assertions in the program are satisfied.

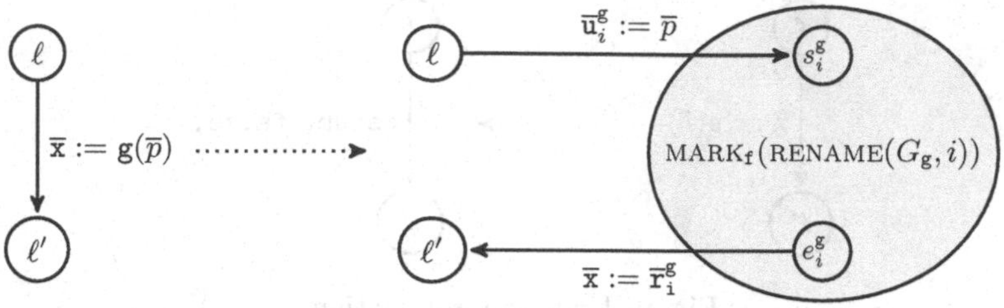

Fig. 5. Unwinding Function Calls

4.1 Unwinding

We first define the rename function $\text{RENAME}(G^{\mathtt{f}}, i)$. It returns a CFG $\langle V_i, E_i, \text{cmd}_i^{\mathtt{f}}, \overline{\mathtt{u}}_i^{\mathtt{f}}, \overline{\mathtt{r}}_i^{\mathtt{f}}, s_i, e_i \rangle$ obtained by first replacing every return command $\mathtt{return}\ \overline{q}$ by assignments to return variables $\overline{\mathtt{r}}^{\mathtt{f}} := \overline{q}$ and then renaming all variables and locations in $G^{\mathtt{f}}$ with the index value i. The function $\text{UNWIND}(G^{\mathtt{f}})$ returns a CFG $K^{\mathtt{f}}$ obtained by replacing all function call edges in $G^{\mathtt{f}}$ with the CFG of the called function after renaming. In order to help extracting summaries from the $K^{\mathtt{f}}$, $\text{UNWIND}(G^{\mathtt{f}})$ annotates in $K^{\mathtt{f}}$ the outermost pair of the entry and exit locations s_i and e_i of each unwound function g with an additional superscript g, i.e., $s_i^{\mathtt{g}}$ and $e_i^{\mathtt{g}}$ (Figure 5). The formal definition is given below.

Given a CFG $G^{\mathtt{f}} = \langle V, E, \text{cmd}^{\mathtt{f}}, \overline{\mathtt{u}}^{\mathtt{f}}, \overline{\mathtt{r}}^{\mathtt{f}}, s, e \rangle$, we use $\hat{E} = \{e \in E : \text{cmd}^{\mathtt{f}}(e) = (\overline{\mathtt{x}} := \mathtt{g}(\overline{\mathtt{p}}))\}$ to denote the set of function call edges in E and define a function $\text{IDX}(e)$ that maps a call edge e to a unique index value. The function $\text{MARK}_{\mathtt{f}}(G^{\mathtt{g}})$ returns a CFG that is identical to $G^{\mathtt{g}}$, except that, for the case that no location with superscript g appears in V (the locations of $G^{\mathtt{f}}$), it annotates the entry and exit locations, s_k and e_k, of the returned CFG with superscript g, i.e., $s_k^{\mathtt{g}}$ and $e_k^{\mathtt{g}}$. Note that, for each unwinding of function call, we mark only the outermost pair of its entry and exit locations. Formally, $\text{UNWIND}(G^{\mathtt{f}}) = \langle V_u, E_u, \text{cmd}_u^{\mathtt{f}}, \overline{\mathtt{u}}^{\mathtt{f}}, \overline{\mathtt{r}}^{\mathtt{f}}, s, e \rangle$ such that (1) $V_u = V \cup \bigcup \{V_i : (\ell, \ell') \in \hat{E} \wedge \text{cmd}^{\mathtt{f}}(\ell, \ell') = (\overline{\mathtt{x}} := \mathtt{g}(\overline{\mathtt{p}})) \wedge \text{IDX}(\ell, \ell') = i \wedge \text{MARK}_{\mathtt{f}}(\text{RENAME}(G^{\mathtt{g}}, i)) = \langle V_i, E_i, \text{cmd}_i^{\mathtt{g}}, \overline{\mathtt{u}}_i^{\mathtt{g}}, \overline{\mathtt{r}}_i^{\mathtt{g}}, s', e' \rangle\}$ (2) $E_u = E \setminus \hat{E} \cup \bigcup \{E_i \cup \{(\ell, s'), (e', \ell')\} : (\ell, \ell') \in \hat{E} \wedge \text{cmd}^{\mathtt{f}}(\ell, \ell') = (\overline{\mathtt{x}} := \mathtt{g}(\overline{\mathtt{p}})) \wedge \text{IDX}(\ell, \ell') = i \wedge \text{MARK}_{\mathtt{f}}(\text{RENAME}(G^{\mathtt{g}}, i)) = \langle V_i, E_i, \text{cmd}_i^{\mathtt{g}}, \overline{\mathtt{u}}_i^{\mathtt{g}}, \overline{\mathtt{r}}_i^{\mathtt{g}}, s', e' \rangle\}$ with $\text{cmd}_u^{\mathtt{f}}(\ell, s') = (\overline{\mathtt{u}}_i^{\mathtt{g}} := \overline{\mathtt{p}})$ and $\text{cmd}_u^{\mathtt{f}}(e', \ell') = (\overline{\mathtt{x}} := \overline{\mathtt{r}}_i^{\mathtt{g}})$.

Proposition 2. *Let $G^{\mathtt{f}}$ be a control flow graph. P and Q are logic formulae with free variables over program variables of $G^{\mathtt{f}}$. $(\!|P|\!)\ G^{\mathtt{f}}\ (\!|Q|\!)$ if and only if $(\!|P|\!)\ \text{UNWIND}(G^{\mathtt{f}})\ (\!|Q|\!)$.*

Essentially, $G^{\mathtt{f}}$ and $\text{UNWIND}(G^{\mathtt{f}})$ represent the same function f. The only difference is that the latter has more program variables after unwinding, but this does not affect the states over program variables of $G^{\mathtt{f}}$ before and after the function.

4.2 Under-Approximation

Let $G^{\mathtt{f}} = \langle V, E, \text{cmd}^{\mathtt{f}}, \overline{\mathtt{u}}^{\mathtt{f}}, \overline{\mathtt{r}}^{\mathtt{f}}, s, e \rangle$ be a control flow graph. The control flow graph $\underline{G^{\mathtt{f}}} = \langle V, E, \underline{\text{cmd}}^{\mathtt{f}}, \overline{\mathtt{u}}^{\mathtt{f}}, \overline{\mathtt{r}}^{\mathtt{f}}, s, e \rangle$ is obtained by replacing every function call in G with `assume false` (Figure 6). That is,

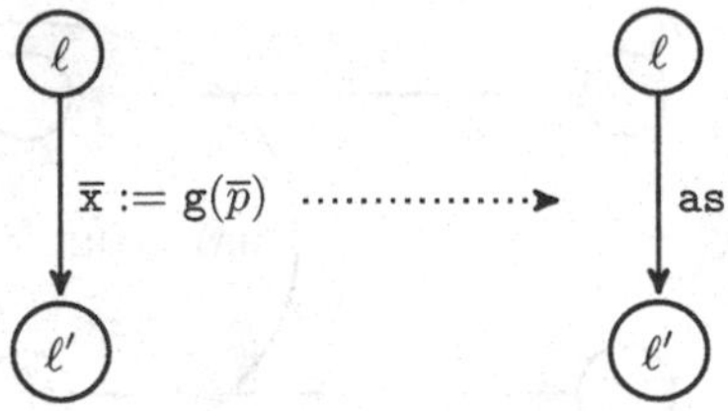

Fig. 6. Under-approximation

$$\underline{\mathrm{cmd}}^{\mathtt{f}}(\ell,\ell') = \begin{cases} \mathrm{cmd}^{\mathtt{f}}(\ell,\ell') & \text{if } \mathrm{cmd}^{\mathtt{f}}(\ell,\ell') \text{ does not contain function calls} \\ \mathtt{assume\ false} & \text{otherwise} \end{cases}$$

Proposition 3. *Let $G^{\mathtt{f}}$ be a control flow graph. P and Q are logic formulae with free variables over program variables of $G^{\mathtt{f}}$. If $(\!|P|\!)G^{\mathtt{f}}(\!|Q|\!)$, then $(\!|P|\!)\underline{G}^{\mathtt{f}}(\!|Q|\!)$.*

The above holds because the computation of $\underline{G}^{\mathtt{f}}$ under-approximates the computation of $G^{\mathtt{f}}$. If all computation of $G^{\mathtt{f}}$ from a state satisfying P always ends with a state satisfying Q, the same should also hold for the computation of $\underline{G}^{\mathtt{f}}$.

4.3 Computing Summaries

Let the CFG for the `main` function $\underline{G}_k^{\mathtt{main}} = \langle V, E, \underline{\mathrm{cmd}}^{\mathtt{main}}, \overline{\mathtt{u}}^{\mathtt{main}}, \overline{\mathtt{r}}^{\mathtt{main}}, s, e\rangle$. Function ComputeSummary(P_k, $\Pi(\underline{G}_k^{\mathtt{main}}, \mathtt{true})$) extracts summaries from the inductive invariant $\Pi(\underline{G}_k^{\mathtt{main}}, \mathtt{true}) = \{I_\ell : \ell \in V\}$ (Algorithm 2).

Input: P_k: a program; $\{I_\ell : \ell \in V\}$: an inductive invariant of $\underline{G}_k^{\mathtt{main}}$
Output: $S[\bullet]$: function summaries
foreach *function* `f` *in the program* P_k **do**
  $S[\mathtt{f}] := \mathtt{true}$;
  foreach *pair of locations* $(s_i^{\mathtt{f}}, e_i^{\mathtt{f}}) \in V \times V$ **do**
    if $I_{s_i^{\mathtt{f}}}$ *contains return variables of* `f` **then** $S[\mathtt{f}] := S[\mathtt{f}] \wedge \forall X_{\mathtt{f}}.I_{e_i^{\mathtt{f}}}$
  else $S[\mathtt{f}] := S[\mathtt{f}] \wedge \forall X_{\mathtt{f}}.(I_{s_i^{\mathtt{f}}} \implies I_{e_i^{\mathtt{f}}})$
return $S[\bullet]$;

Algorithm 2. ComputeSummary(P_k, $\Pi(\underline{G}_k^{\mathtt{main}}, \mathtt{true})$)

For each function `f` in the program P_k, we first initialize its summary $S[\mathtt{f}]$ to `true`. The set $X_{\mathtt{f}}$ contains all variables appearing in $\underline{G}_k^{\mathtt{main}}$ except the set of formal parameters and return variables of `f`. For each pair of locations $(s_i^{\mathtt{f}}, e_i^{\mathtt{f}}) \in V \times V$ in $\underline{G}_k^{\mathtt{main}}$, if the invariant of location $s_i^{\mathtt{f}}$ contains return variables of `f`, we update $S[\mathtt{f}]$ to the formula $S[\mathtt{f}] \wedge \forall X_{\mathtt{f}}.I_{e_i^{\mathtt{f}}}$. Otherwise, we update it to a less restricted version $S[\mathtt{f}] \wedge \forall X_{\mathtt{f}}.(I_{s_i^{\mathtt{f}}} \implies I_{e_i^{\mathtt{f}}})$ (Figure 7).

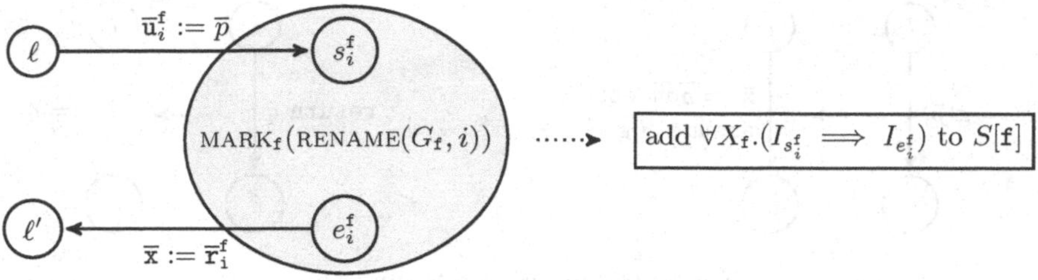

Fig. 7. Updating a Summary

Proposition 4. *Let Q be a formula over all variables in $\underline{G_k^{\mathtt{main}}}$ except $\overline{\mathtt{r}}^{\mathtt{f}}$. We have $(\!|Q|\!)\ \overline{\mathtt{r}}^{\mathtt{f}} := \mathtt{f}(\overline{\mathtt{u}}^{\mathtt{f}})\ (\!|Q|\!)$.*

The proposition holds because the only possible overlap of variables in Q and in $\overline{\mathtt{r}}^{\mathtt{f}} := \mathtt{f}(\overline{\mathtt{u}}^{\mathtt{f}})$ are the formal parameters $\overline{\mathtt{u}}^{\mathtt{f}}$. However, we assume that values of formal parameters do not change in a function (see Section 2); hence the values of all variables in Q stay the same after the execution of the function call $\overline{\mathtt{r}}^{\mathtt{f}} := \mathtt{f}(\overline{\mathtt{u}}^{\mathtt{f}})$.

Proposition 5. *Given the CFG $\underline{G_k^{\mathtt{main}}} = \langle V, E, \underline{cmd}^{\mathtt{main}}, \overline{\mathtt{u}}^{\mathtt{main}}, \overline{\mathtt{r}}^{\mathtt{main}}, s, e\rangle$. If $(\!|\mathtt{true}|\!)\ \overline{\mathtt{r}}^{\mathtt{f}} := \mathtt{f}(\overline{\mathtt{u}}^{\mathtt{f}})\ (\!|S[\mathtt{f}]|\!)$ holds, then $(\!|I_{s_i^{\mathtt{f}}}|\!)\ \overline{\mathtt{r}}^{\mathtt{f}} := \mathtt{f}(\overline{\mathtt{u}}^{\mathtt{f}})\ (\!|I_{e_i^{\mathtt{f}}}|\!)$ for all $(s_i^{\mathtt{f}}, e_i^{\mathtt{f}}) \in V \times V$.*

For each pair $(s_i^{\mathtt{f}}, e_i^{\mathtt{f}}) \in V \times V$, we consider two cases:

1. $I_{s_i^{\mathtt{f}}}$ contains some return variables of $\mathtt{f}$:
   In this case, the conjunct $\forall X_{\mathtt{f}}.I_{e_i^{\mathtt{f}}}$ is a part of $S[\mathtt{f}]$, we then have

$$\cfrac{\cfrac{\cfrac{(\!|\mathtt{true}|\!)\ \overline{\mathtt{r}}^{\mathtt{f}} := \mathtt{f}(\overline{\mathtt{u}}^{\mathtt{f}})\ (\!|S[\mathtt{f}]|\!)}{(\!|\mathtt{true}|\!)\ \overline{\mathtt{r}}^{\mathtt{f}} := \mathtt{f}(\overline{\mathtt{u}}^{\mathtt{f}})\ (\!|\forall X_{\mathtt{f}}.I_{e_i^{\mathtt{f}}}|\!)}\ \text{Postcondition Weakening}}{(\!|\mathtt{true}|\!)\ \overline{\mathtt{r}}^{\mathtt{f}} := \mathtt{f}(\overline{\mathtt{u}}^{\mathtt{f}})\ (\!|I_{e_i^{\mathtt{f}}}|\!)}\ \text{Postcondition Weakening}}{(\!|I_{s_i^{\mathtt{f}}}|\!)\ \overline{\mathtt{r}}^{\mathtt{f}} := \mathtt{f}(\overline{\mathtt{u}}^{\mathtt{f}})\ (\!|I_{e_i^{\mathtt{f}}}|\!)}\ \text{Precondition Strengthening}$$

2. $I_{s_i^{\mathtt{f}}}$ does not contain any return variables of $\mathtt{f}$:
   In this case, the conjunct $\forall X_{\mathtt{f}}.(I_{s_i^{\mathtt{f}}} \implies I_{e_i^{\mathtt{f}}})$ is a part of $S[\mathtt{f}]$, we then have

$$\cfrac{\text{Prop. 4}\ \cfrac{}{(\!|I_{s_k^{\mathtt{f}}}|\!)\ \overline{\mathtt{r}}^{\mathtt{f}} := \mathtt{f}(\overline{\mathtt{u}}^{\mathtt{f}})\ (\!|I_{s_k^{\mathtt{f}}}|\!)} \qquad \cfrac{\cfrac{\cfrac{(\!|\mathtt{true}|\!)\ \overline{\mathtt{r}}^{\mathtt{f}} := \mathtt{f}(\overline{\mathtt{u}}^{\mathtt{f}})\ (\!|S[\mathtt{f}]|\!)}{(\!|\mathtt{true}|\!)\ \overline{\mathtt{r}}^{\mathtt{f}} := \mathtt{f}(\overline{\mathtt{u}}^{\mathtt{f}})\ (\!|\forall X_{\mathtt{f}}.(I_{s_k^{\mathtt{f}}} \implies I_{e_k^{\mathtt{f}}})|\!)}}{(\!|\mathtt{true}|\!)\ \overline{\mathtt{r}}^{\mathtt{f}} := \mathtt{f}(\overline{\mathtt{u}}^{\mathtt{f}})\ (\!|I_{s_k^{\mathtt{f}}} \implies I_{e_k^{\mathtt{f}}}|\!)}}{(\!|I_{s_k^{\mathtt{f}}}|\!)\ \overline{\mathtt{r}}^{\mathtt{f}} := \mathtt{f}(\overline{\mathtt{u}}^{\mathtt{f}})\ (\!|I_{s_k^{\mathtt{f}}} \implies I_{e_k^{\mathtt{f}}}|\!)}}{(\!|I_{s_k^{\mathtt{f}}}|\!)\ \overline{\mathtt{r}}^{\mathtt{f}} := \mathtt{f}(\overline{\mathtt{u}}^{\mathtt{f}})\ (\!|I_{e_k^{\mathtt{f}}}|\!)}$$

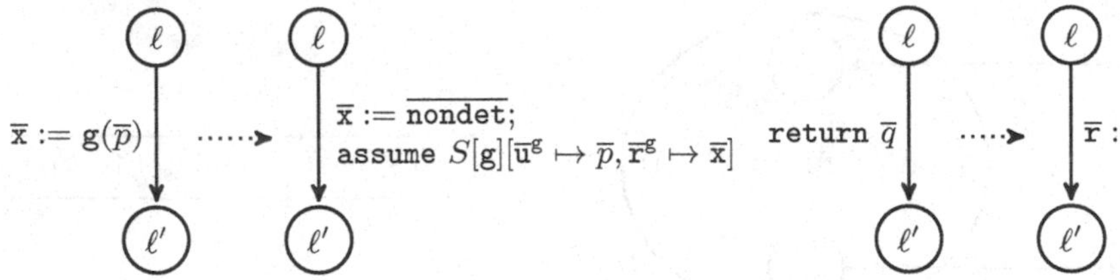

Fig. 8. Instantiating a Summary

4.4 Checking Summaries

Here we explain how to handle the function CheckSummary($P_k, S[\bullet]$), where P_k is an unwound program and $S[\bullet]$ is an array of function summaries. Let $G_k^f = \langle V, E, \text{cmd}^f, \overline{u}^f, \overline{r}^f, s, e\rangle$ be a control flow graph for the function f in P_k. In order to check whether the function summary $S[f]$ for f specifies the relation between the formal parameters and return values of f, we define another control flow graph $\hat{G}_{k,S}^f = \langle V, E, \hat{\text{cmd}}^f, \overline{u}^f, \overline{r}^f, s, e\rangle$ where

$$\hat{\text{cmd}}^f(\ell,\ell') = \begin{cases} \overline{x} := \overline{\texttt{nondet}}; \texttt{assume } S[g][\overline{u}^g \mapsto \overline{p}, \overline{r}^g \mapsto \overline{x}] & \text{if } \text{cmd}^f(\ell,\ell') = \overline{x} := g(\overline{p}) \\ \overline{r}^f := \overline{q} & \text{if } \text{cmd}^f(\ell,\ell') = \texttt{return } \overline{q} \\ \text{cmd}^f(\ell,\ell') & \text{otherwise} \end{cases}$$

The control flow graph $\hat{G}_{k,S}^f$ replaces every function call in G_k^f by instantiating a function summary (Figure 8). Using the Hoare Logic proof rule for recursive functions [22], we have the following proposition:

Proposition 6. *Let $G_k^f = \langle V, E, cmd^f, \overline{u}^f, \overline{r}^f, s, e\rangle$ be the control flow graph for the function* f *and $S[\bullet]$ be an array of logic formulae over the formal parameters and return variables of each function. If $(\!|\texttt{true}|\!)\ \hat{G}_{k,S}^g\ (\!|S[g]|\!)$ for every function* g *in P, then $(\!|\texttt{true}|\!)\ \overline{r}^f := f(\overline{u}^f)\ (\!|S[f]|\!)$.*

It is easy to check $(\!|\texttt{true}|\!)\ \hat{G}_{k,S}^g\ (\!|S[g]|\!)$ by program analysis. Let G_k^f be the control flow graph for the function f and $\hat{G}_{k,S}^g = \langle V, E, \hat{\text{cmd}}^f, \overline{u}^f, \overline{r}^f, s, e\rangle$ as above. Consider another control flow graph $\tilde{G}_{k,S}^f = \langle \tilde{V}, \tilde{E}, \tilde{\text{cmd}}^f, \overline{u}^f, \overline{r}^f, s, e\rangle$ where

$$\begin{aligned} \tilde{V} &= V \cup \{\tilde{e}\} \\ \tilde{E} &= E \cup \{(e, \tilde{e})\} \\ \tilde{\text{cmd}}^f(\ell,\ell') &= \begin{cases} \hat{\text{cmd}}^f(\ell,\ell') & \text{if } (\ell,\ell') \in E \\ \texttt{assert } S[f] & \text{if } (\ell,\ell') = (e,\tilde{e}) \end{cases} \end{aligned}$$

Corollary 1. *Let $G_k^f = \langle V, E, cmd^f, \overline{u}^f, \overline{r}^f, s, e\rangle$ be the control flow graph for the function* f *and $S[\bullet]$ be an array of logic formulae over the formal parameters and return variables of each function. If* BasicChecker($\tilde{G}_{k,S}^g$) *returns Pass for every function* g *in P, then $(\!|\texttt{true}|\!)\ \overline{r}^f := f(\overline{u}^f)\ (\!|S[f]|\!)$.*

Input: P_k : an unwound program; $S[\bullet]$: an array of function summaries
Output: `true` if all function summaries are valid; `false` otherwise
foreach *function* $G^{\mathtt{g}}_k \in P_k$ **do**
  if BasicChecker($\tilde{G}^{\mathtt{g}}_{k,S}$) $\neq$ *Pass* **then return false**
return true;

Algorithm 3. CheckSummary(P_k, S)

4.5 Correctness

We are ready to sketch the proof of Theorem 1. Assume Algorithm 1 returns $Pass(\Pi(\underline{G}^{\mathtt{main}}_k, \mathtt{true}))$ and $S[\bullet]$ on the input control flow graph $G^{\mathtt{main}} = \langle V, E, \mathrm{cmd}^{\mathtt{main}}, \overline{\mathtt{u}}^{\mathtt{main}}, \overline{\mathtt{r}}^{\mathtt{main}}, s, e\rangle$. Let $\underline{G}^{\mathtt{main}}_k = \langle \underline{V}_k, \underline{E}_k, \underline{\mathrm{cmd}}^{\mathtt{main}}_k, \overline{\mathtt{u}}^{\mathtt{main}}, \overline{\mathtt{r}}^{\mathtt{main}}, s, e\rangle$ and $\Pi(\underline{G}^{\mathtt{main}}_k, \mathtt{true}) = \{\underline{I}_\ell : \ell \in \underline{V}_k\}$. By the definition of inductive invariants, we have $(\!|\underline{I}_\ell|\!)\ \underline{\mathrm{cmd}}^{\mathtt{main}}_k(\ell,\ell')\ (\!|\underline{I}_{\ell'}|\!)$ for every $(\ell,\ell') \in \underline{E}_k$. Moreover, $V \subseteq \underline{V}_k$ since $\underline{G}^{\mathtt{main}}_k$ is obtained by unwinding $G^{\mathtt{main}}$. Define $\Gamma(G^{\mathtt{main}}, \mathtt{true}) = \{\underline{I}_\ell \in \Pi(\underline{G}^{\mathtt{main}}_k, \mathtt{true}) : \ell \in V\}$. We claim $\Gamma(G^{\mathtt{main}}, \mathtt{true})$ is in fact an inductive invariant for $G^{\mathtt{main}}$.

Let $\hat{E} = \{(\ell,\ell') \in E : \mathrm{cmd}^{\mathtt{main}}(\ell,\ell') = \overline{\mathtt{x}} := \mathtt{f}(\overline{p})\}$. We have $\mathrm{cmd}^{\mathtt{main}}(\ell,\ell') = \underline{\mathrm{cmd}}^{\mathtt{main}}_k(\ell,\ell')$ for every $(\ell,\ell') \in E \setminus \hat{E}$. Thus $(\!|\underline{I}_\ell|\!)\ \mathrm{cmd}^{\mathtt{main}}(\ell,\ell')\ (\!|\underline{I}_{\ell'}|\!)$ for every $(\ell,\ell') \in E \setminus \hat{E}$ by the definition of $\Gamma(G, \mathtt{true})$ and the inductiveness of $\Pi(\underline{G}^{\mathtt{main}}_k, \mathtt{true})$. It suffices to show that

$$(\!|\underline{I}_\ell|\!)\ \overline{\mathtt{x}} := \mathtt{f}(\overline{p})\ (\!|\underline{I}_{\ell'}|\!) \text{ or, equivalently, } (\!|\underline{I}_\ell|\!)\ \overline{\mathtt{u}}^{\mathtt{f}} := \overline{p};\ \overline{\mathtt{r}}^{\mathtt{f}} := \mathtt{f}(\overline{\mathtt{u}}^{\mathtt{f}});\ \overline{\mathtt{x}} := \overline{\mathtt{r}}^{\mathtt{f}}\ (\!|\underline{I}_{\ell'}|\!)$$

for every $(\ell,\ell') \in \hat{E}$. By the inductiveness of $\Pi(\underline{G}^{\mathtt{main}}_k, \mathtt{true})$, we have $(\!|\underline{I}_\ell|\!)\ \overline{\mathtt{u}}^{\mathtt{f}} := \overline{p}\ (\!|\underline{I}_{s^{\mathtt{f}}_k}|\!)$ and $(\!|\underline{I}_{e^{\mathtt{f}}_k}|\!)\ \overline{\mathtt{x}} := \overline{\mathtt{r}}^{\mathtt{f}}\ (\!|\underline{I}_{\ell'}|\!)$. Moreover, $(\!|\underline{I}_{s^{\mathtt{f}}_k}|\!)\ \overline{\mathtt{r}}^{\mathtt{f}} := \mathtt{f}(\overline{\mathtt{u}}^{\mathtt{f}})\ (\!|\underline{I}_{e^{\mathtt{f}}_k}|\!)$ by Proposition 5 and 6. Therefore

$$\dfrac{\dfrac{(\!|\underline{I}_\ell|\!)\ \overline{\mathtt{u}}^{\mathtt{f}} := \overline{p}\ (\!|\underline{I}_{s^{\mathtt{f}}_k}|\!) \qquad (\!|\underline{I}_{s^{\mathtt{f}}_k}|\!)\ \overline{\mathtt{r}}^{\mathtt{f}} := \mathtt{f}(\overline{\mathtt{u}}^{\mathtt{f}})\ (\!|\underline{I}_{e^{\mathtt{f}}_k}|\!) \qquad (\!|\underline{I}_{e^{\mathtt{f}}_k}|\!)\ \overline{\mathtt{x}} := \overline{\mathtt{r}}^{\mathtt{f}}\ (\!|\underline{I}_{\ell'}|\!)}{(\!|\underline{I}_\ell|\!)\ \overline{\mathtt{u}}^{\mathtt{f}} := \overline{p};\ \overline{\mathtt{r}}^{\mathtt{f}} := \mathtt{f}(\overline{\mathtt{u}}^{\mathtt{f}});\ \overline{\mathtt{x}} := \overline{\mathtt{r}}^{\mathtt{f}}\ (\!|\underline{I}_{\ell'}|\!)}}{(\!|\underline{I}_\ell|\!)\ \overline{\mathtt{x}} := \mathtt{f}(\overline{p})\ (\!|\underline{I}_{\ell'}|\!)}$$

5 Experiments

A prototype tool of our approach has been implemented with CPAChecker 1.2.11-svcomp14b[1] as the underlying intraprocedural analyzer. In addition, because CPAChecker does not support universal quantifiers in the expression of an `assume` command, we used Redlog [19] for quantifier elimination. To evaluate our tool, we performed experiments with all the benchmarks from the **recursive**

---

[1] We use script/cpa.sh to invoke CPAChecker and use the configuration file available at `https://github.com/fmlab-iis/transformer/blob/master/tool/verifier-conf/myCPA-PredAbstract-LIA.properties`.

category in the 2014 Competition on Software Verification (SV-COMP 2014) [9] and followed the rules and the score schema (shown in Table 1) of the competition. The experimental results show that our tool is quite competitive even compared with the winners of the competition. It is solid evidence that our approach not only extends program analyzers to handle recursion but also provides comparable effectiveness.

Our tool was compared with four participants of SV-COMP 2014, namely BLAST 2.7.2[2] [5], CBMC 4.5-sv-comp-2014 [8] with a wrapper cbmc-wrapper.sh[3], ULTIMATE AUTOMIZER [13], and ULTIMATE KOJAK [21]. The latter three tools are the top three winners of the **recursive** category in SV-COMP 2014. The recursive programs from the benchmarks of the **recursive** category comprise 16 bug-free and 7 buggy C programs. The experiments were performed on a virtual machine with 4 GB of memory running 64-bit Ubuntu 12.04 LTS. The virtual machine ran on a host with an Intel Core i7-870 Quad-Core CPU running 64-bit Windows 7. The timeout of a verification task is 900 seconds.

The results are summarized in Table 2 where k is the number of unwindings of recursive functions in Algorithm 1, Time is measured in seconds, the superscript ! or ? indicates that the returned result is respectively incorrect or unknown, E indicates exceptions, and T.O. indicates timeouts. The parenthesized numbers of CBMC are obtained by excluding certain cases, which will be explained later.

The results show that CBMC outperforms all the other tools. However, CBMC reports safe if no bug is found in a program within a given time bound[4], which is set to 850 seconds in cbmc-wrapper.sh. In this case, the behaviors of the program within certain length bounds are proven to be safe, but the absence of bugs is not guaranteed (see Addition03_false.c in Table 2 for a counterexample). If we ignore such cases in the experiments, CBMC will obtain a score of 14, and the gap between the scores of CBMC and our tool becomes much smaller. Moreover, this gap may be narrowed if we turn on some important optimizations such as adjustment of block encoding provided in CPACHECKER. We chose to disable the optimizations in order to simplify the implementation of our prototype tool.

Compared to ULTIMATE AUTOMIZER, ULTIMATE KOJAK, and BLAST, our tool can verify more programs and obtain a higher score. The scores of our tool and ULTIMATE AUTOMIZER are very close mainly because of a false positive produced by our tool. The false positive in fact came from a spurious error trace reported by CPACHECKER because modulo operation is approximated in CPACHECKER. If this case is excluded, our tool can obtain a score of 16.

6 Related Works

In [14,15], a program transformation technique for checking context-bounded concurrent programs to sequential analysis is developed. Numerous intraprocedural

---

[2] We use the arguments **-alias empty -enable-recursion -noprofile -cref -sv-comp -lattice -include-lattice symb -nosserr** with BLAST.

[3] The wrapper cbmc-wrapper.sh is provided by CBMC 4.5-sv-comp-2014, which is a special version for SV-COMP 2014.

[4] This was confirmed in a private communication with the developers of CBMC.

Table 1. Score schema in SV-COMP 2014

Points	Program Correctness	Reported Result
0	TRUE or FALSE	UNKNOWN (due to timeout or exceptions)
+1	FALSE	FALSE
-4	TRUE	FALSE
+2	TRUE	TRUE
-8	FALSE	TRUE

Table 2. Experimental results of verifying programs in the **recursive** category of the 2014 Competition on Software Verification. (Time in sec.).

Program	Our Tool		ULTIMATE AUTOMIZER	ULTIMATE KOJAK	CBMC 4.5	BLAST 2.7.2
	k	Time	Time	Time	Time	Time
Ackermann01_true.c	1	6.5	T.O.	T.O.	850.0	E
Ackermann02_false.c	4	57.3	4.2	T.O.	1.0	E
Ackermann03_true.c		T.O.	T.O.	T.O.	850.0	E
Ackermann04_true.c		T.O.	T.O.	T.O.	850.0	E
Addition01_true.c	2	14.1	T.O.	T.O.	850.0	E
Addition02_false.c	2	9.9	3.7	3.5	0.3	4.0
Addition03_false.c		T.O.	T.O.	T.O.	850.0$^!$	E
EvenOdd01_true.c	1	2.9$^!$	T.O.	T.O.	1.3	0.1$^!$
EvenOdd03_false.c	1	2.9	3.2	3.2	0.1	0.1
Fibonacci01_true.c	6	348.4	T.O.	T.O.	850.0	E
Fibonacci02_true.c		T.O.	60.7	72.1$^?$	0.8	E
Fibonacci03_true.c		T.O.	T.O.	T.O.	850.0	E
Fibonacci04_false.c	5	107.3	7.4	8.2	0.4	E
Fibonacci05_false.c		T.O.	128.9	23.2	557.2	E
gcd01_true.c	1	6.6	5.4	7.3	850.0	16.1$^!$
gcd02_true.c		T.O.	T.O.	T.O.	850.0	E
McCarthy91_false.c	1	2.8	3.2	3.1	0.3	0.1
McCarthy91_true.c	2	12.5	81.3	6.8	850.0	16.2$^!$
MultCommutative_true.c		T.O.	T.O.	T.O.	850.0	E
Primes_true.c		T.O.	T.O.	T.O.	850.0	E
recHanoi01_true.c		T.O.	T.O.	T.O.	850.0	E
recHanoi02_true.c	1	5.6	T.O.	T.O.	0.7	1.9$^!$
recHanoi03_true.c		T.O.	T.O.	T.O.	0.7	E
correct results		11	9	7	22 (10)	3
false negative		0	0	0	1 (0)	0
false positive		1	0	0	0 (0)	4
score		13	12	9	30 (14)	-13

analysis techniques have been developed over the years. Many tools are in fact freely available (see, for instance, BLAST [5], CPACHECKER [6], and UFO [2]). Interprocedural analysis techniques are also available (see [20,4,10,12,11,18] for a partial list). Recently, recursive analysis attracts new attention. The Competition on Software Verification adds a new category for recursive programs in 2014 [9]. Among the participants, CBMC [8], ULTIMATE AUTOMIZER [13], and ULTIMIATE KOJAK [21] are the top three tools for the **recursive** category.

Inspired by WHALE [1], we use inductive invariants obtained from verifying under-approximation as candidates of summaries. Also, similar to WHALE, we apply a Hoare logic proof rule for recursive calls from [22]. However, our technique works on control flow graphs and builds on an intraprocedural analysis tool. It is hence very lightweight and modular. Better intraprocedural analysis tools easily give better recursive analysis through our technique. WHALE, on the other hand, analyzes by exploring abstract reachability graphs. Since WHALE extends summary computation and covering relations for recursion, its implementation is more involved.

7 Discussion

The number of unwindings is perhaps the most important factor in our recursive analysis technique (Table 2). We find that CPACHECKER performs poorly when many unwindings are needed. We however do not enable the more efficient block encoding in CPACHECKER for the ease of implementation. One can improve the performance of our algorithm with the efficient but complicated block encoding. A bounded analyzer may also speed up the verification of bounded properties.

Our algorithm extracts function summaries from inductive invariants. There are certainly many heuristics to optimize the computation of function summaries. For instance, some program analyzers return error traces when properties fail. In particular, a valuation of formal parameters is obtained when CheckSummary (Algorithm 3) returns `false`. If the valuation is not possible in the `main` function, one can use its inductive invariant to refine function summaries. We in fact exploit error traces computed by CPACHECKER in the implementation.

Acknowledgment. This work was partially supported by Ministry of Science and Technology under grant numbers 100-2221-E-002 -122 -, 102-2221-E-001 -017 -, 102-2221-E-001 -018 -, and the postdoctoral fellow program of Academia Sinica, Taiwan.

References

1. Albarghouthi, A., Gurfinkel, A., Chechik, M.: Whale: An interpolation-based algorithm for inter-procedural verification. In: Kuncak, V., Rybalchenko, A. (eds.) VMCAI 2012. LNCS, vol. 7148, pp. 39–55. Springer, Heidelberg (2012)

2. Albarghouthi, A., Li, Y., Gurfinkel, A., Chechik, M.: UFO: A framework for abstraction- and interpolation-based software verification. In: Madhusudan, P., Seshia, S.A. (eds.) CAV 2012. LNCS, vol. 7358, pp. 672–678. Springer, Heidelberg (2012)
3. Ball, T., Rajamani, S.K.: Bebop: A symbolic model checker for boolean programs. In: Havelund, K., Penix, J., Visser, W. (eds.) SPIN 2000. LNCS, vol. 1885, pp. 113–130. Springer, Heidelberg (2000)
4. Ball, T., Rajamani, S.K.: The SLAM toolkit. In: Berry, G., Comon, H., Finkel, A. (eds.) CAV 2001. LNCS, vol. 2102, pp. 260–264. Springer, Heidelberg (2001)
5. Beyer, D., Henzinger, T.A., Jhala, R., Majumdar, R.: The software model checker Blast. STTT 9(5-6), 505–525 (2007)
6. Beyer, D., Keremoglu, M.E.: CPAchecker: A tool for configurable software verification. In: Gopalakrishnan, G., Qadeer, S. (eds.) CAV 2011. LNCS, vol. 6806, pp. 184–190. Springer, Heidelberg (2011)
7. Clarke, E.M., Jain, H., Sinha, N.: Grand challenge: Model check software. In: VISSAS, pp. 55–68 (2005)
8. Clarke, E., Kroning, D., Lerda, F.: A tool for checking ANSI-C programs. In: Jensen, K., Podelski, A. (eds.) TACAS 2004. LNCS, vol. 2988, pp. 168–176. Springer, Heidelberg (2004)
9. Competition on software verification, `http://sv-comp.sosy-lab.org/2014`
10. Cousot, P., Cousot, R., Feret, J., Mauborgne, L., Miné, A., Monniaux, D., Rival, X.: The ASTREÉ analyzer. In: Sagiv, M. (ed.) ESOP 2005. LNCS, vol. 3444, pp. 21–30. Springer, Heidelberg (2005)
11. Coverity, `http://www.coverity.com/`
12. Cuoq, P., Kirchner, F., Kosmatov, N., Prevosto, V., Signoles, J., Yakobowski, B.: Frama-C - a software analysis perspective. In: Eleftherakis, G., Hinchey, M., Holcombe, M. (eds.) SEFM 2012. LNCS, vol. 7504, pp. 233–247. Springer, Heidelberg (2012)
13. Heizmann, M., et al.: Ultimate Automizer with SMTInterpol - (competition contribution). In: Piterman, N., Smolka, S.A. (eds.) TACAS 2013. LNCS, vol. 7795, pp. 641–643. Springer, Heidelberg (2013)
14. Lal, A., Reps, T.: Reducing concurrent analysis under a context bound to sequential analysis. In: Gupta, A., Malik, S. (eds.) CAV 2008. LNCS, vol. 5123, pp. 37–51. Springer, Heidelberg (2008)
15. Lal, A., Reps, T.: Reducing concurrent analysis under a context bound to sequential analysis. Formal Methods in System Design 35(1), 73–97 (2009)
16. Manna, Z., Pnueli, A.: Formalization of properties of functional programs. J. ACM 17(3), 555–569 (1970)
17. Nielson, F., Nielson, H.R., Hankin, C.: Principles of Program Analysis. Springer (1999) ISBN 978-3-540-65410-0
18. Polyspace, `http://www.mathworks.com/products/polyspace/`
19. Redlog, `http://www.redlog.eu/`
20. Reps, T.W., Horwitz, S., Sagiv, S.: Precise interprocedural dataflow analysis via graph reachability. In: POPL, pp. 49–61 (1995)
21. Ultimate Kojak, `http://ultimate.informatik.uni-freiburg.de/kojak/`
22. von Oheimb, D.: Hoare logic for mutual recursion and local variables. In: Pandu Rangan, C., Raman, V., Sarukkai, S. (eds.) FST TCS 1999. LNCS, vol. 1738, pp. 168–180. Springer, Heidelberg (1999)

Automatic Analysis of Open Objects in Dynamic Language Programs

Arlen Cox[1], Bor-Yuh Evan Chang[1], and Xavier Rival[2]

[1] University of Colorado Boulder, Boulder, Colorado, USA
{arlen.cox,evan.chang}@colorado.edu
[2] INRIA, CNRS, ENS Paris, Paris, France
xavier.rival@ens.fr

Abstract. In dynamic languages, objects are *open*—they support iteration over and dynamic addition/deletion of their attributes. Open objects, because they have an unbounded number of attributes, are difficult to abstract without a priori knowledge of all or nearly all of the attributes and thus pose a significant challenge for precise static analysis. To address this challenge, we present the HOO (Heap with Open Objects) abstraction that can precisely represent and infer properties about open-object-manipulating programs without any knowledge of specific attributes. It achieves this by building upon a relational abstract domain for sets that is used to reason about partitions of object attributes. An implementation of the resulting static analysis is used to verify specifications for dynamic language framework code that makes extensive use of open objects, thus demonstrating the effectiveness of this approach.

1 Introduction

```
for(var p in s)
  if(p in c) r[p] = "conflict";
  else       r[p] = s[p];
```

Fig. 1. The essence of open object-manipulating

Static analysis of dynamic languages is challenging because objects in these languages are open. *Open objects* have mutable and iterable attributes (also called fields, properties, instance variables, etc.); developers can programmatically add, remove, and modify attributes of existing objects. Because of their flexibility, open objects enable dynamic language developers to create frameworks with object-manipulating routines [30] that decrease code size, increase code reuse, and improve program flexibility and extensibility. In Fig. 1, we show JavaScript code that conditionally adds attributes to the object `r` with attributes from object `s`—code similar to this snippet is repeated in various forms in, for instance, frameworks that implement class and trait systems. Because specific attributes of the objects `r`, `s`, and `c` are unknown, we cannot conclude exactly what the structure of the object `r` is at the end of this code. However, it can be derived from the structure of the original `r`, `s`, and `c` that each attribute (written $\hat{f}$) in the set of all attributes of `r` (written attr(`r`)) can fall into one of three parts. First, if $\hat{f}$ is in both attr(`s`) and attr(`c`), the corresponding value is 'conflict'. Second, if $\hat{f}$ is in attr(`s`) but not in attr(`c`), the corresponding value is from `s`. Lastly, if $\hat{f}$ is not in attr(`s`), the value of attribute $\hat{f}$ of object `r` is unchanged. In this paper, we argue that inferring these partitions is a solution to what we call the open object abstraction problem.

M. Müller-Olm and H. Seidl (Eds.): SAS 2014, LNCS 8723, pp. 134–150, 2014.

The *open object abstraction problem* occurs when the attributes of objects cannot be known statically. Unfortunately, the open object abstraction problem significantly increases the difficulty of static analysis. Objects no longer have a fixed set of attributes but instead an unbounded number of attributes. Thus, abstractions of objects must not only abstract the values to which the attributes point but also the attributes themselves. Such abstractions must potentially conflate many attributes into a single abstract attribute. As we demonstrate in this paper, the open object abstraction problem precludes simple adaptations of abstractions for closed-object languages like Java to dynamic languages.

This paper develops the HOO (Heap with Open Objects) abstract domain [7] that does not require knowledge of specific attributes to be precise. It partitions attributes of objects into sets of attributes. Then it relates those sets of attributes with sets of attributes from other objects. Thus, it can represent complex relationships like those that form in the aforementioned example through a relational abstraction for sets. For example, it can automatically infer the three partitions in the attributes of object `r` in the previous example.

Unlike existing analyses that adapt closed-object abstractions [21, 31], the HOO abstract domain is particularly suited for analyzing programs where significant pieces of the program are unknown and thus many attributes of objects are unknown. Because HOO partitions attributes on the fly and relates partitions to one another, it maintains useful information even when unknown attributes are accessed and manipulated. Such information is necessarily lost in closed-object adaptations and thus a domain like HOO is a fundamental building block towards modular analysis of dynamic language programs.

In this paper we make the following contributions:

- We introduce HOO, an abstraction for objects that relates partitions of attributes between multiple objects by building on a relational abstract domain for sets. Using these relations, we directly abstract open objects instead of adapting existing object abstractions that require knowledge of specific attributes. (Section 3).
- We introduce attribute materialization, an operation that extracts individual symbolic attributes from attribute summaries, allowing strong updates of open objects. Using attribute materialization, we derive transfer functions that use strong updates for precisely reading from objects and writing to objects (Section 4).
- We develop algorithms for widening and inclusion checking that are used to automatically infer loop invariants in open-object-manipulating programs. These algorithms use iteration-progress sets to allow strong updates across loop iterations, thus inferring partitions of object attributes (Section 5).
- We evaluate HOO by using inferred post-conditions for object-transforming functions like those commonly found in JavaScript libraries to prove properties about the structure of objects (Section 6).

2 Overview

In this section we demonstrate the features of the abstraction by analyzing the example loop from the introduction. Fig. 2 shows key analysis states in the final iteration of abstract interpretation after starting from an annotated pre-condition shown at ①. In this iteration, the analysis proves that the loop invariant is inductive.

Before executing the loop, ① is the abstract state, where we show three separate abstract objects at addresses $\hat{a}_1$, $\hat{a}_3$, and $\hat{a}_5$ (where $\hat{a}_n$ represents a singleton set of addresses and $\hat{A}_n$ represents a summary of addresses) that are pointed to by variables `r`, `s`, and `c` (shown in dotted circles) respectively. The attributes of `r`, attr(`r`) are $\hat{F}_{\mathtt{r}}$ (where $\hat{f}_n$ represents a singleton set of attributes; $\hat{F}_n$ represents any summary of attributes). Similarly, attr(`s`) is $\hat{F}_{\mathsf{in}} \uplus \hat{F}_{\mathsf{out}}$. Each attribute in attr(`r`) contains an object address from the summary $\hat{A}_2$ (shown with a double circle). Since many dynamic languages permit reading attributes that do not exist, the partition noti maps to the value of all attributes *not in* the object. If this partition does not exist, the object is *incomplete* and behaves similarly to a C# or a Java object (Section 3). Boxed on the right are constraints on attribute partitions. These constraints are represented by a relational abstraction for sets, such as QUIC graphs [10].

Appropriate partitioning of objects is vital for performing strong updates. To take advantage of strong updates across loop iterations, ① shows a special partitioning of `s`. The partition $\hat{F}_{\mathsf{in}}$ is the set of all attributes that have not yet been visited by the loop, whereas the partition $\hat{F}_{\mathsf{out}}$ is the set of all attributes that have already been visited by the loop and thus is initially empty. On each iteration an element is removed from $\hat{F}_{\mathsf{in}}$ and placed into $\hat{F}_{\mathsf{out}}$, allowing relationships to represent not just the initial iteration of the loop, but any iteration. We see these relationships in the loop invariant ⓘ.

The loop invariant ⓘ shows the three partitions of attr(`r`) mentioned in the introduction. The partitions are constrained by $\hat{F}_{\mathsf{out}}$, because the overwritten portion of attr(`r`) can only be from the elements that have already been visited by the loop. Additionally the $\hat{F}''_{\mathsf{out}}$ partition is restricted to have no elements in common with $\hat{F}_{\mathtt{c}}$. This corresponds to the branch within the loop that determines whether 'conflict' or `s[p]` is written. This invariant was inferred using abstract interpretation [7] by the HOO abstract domain.

Once in the body of the loop, the variable `p` is bound to a singleton set $\hat{f}$ that is split from $\hat{F}_{\mathsf{in}}$. Depending on the value of $\hat{f}$, one of two cases occurs. In ② we highlight the changes using blue and dashed points-to arrows, showing that $\hat{f}$ is contained in the properties of $\hat{a}_5$ $\hat{F}_{\mathtt{c}}$. Storing 'conflict' into `r[p]` gives ③ by first removing $\hat{f}$ from all partitions that make up attr(`r`) and then adding a new partition $\hat{f}$ and thus performing *attribute materialization* of $\hat{f}$ from the object summary. Because $\hat{f}$ is now materialized, subsequent updates to $\hat{f}$ will update the same $\hat{f}$, rather than weakening the value abstraction that corresponds to one of the larger partitions. Here, the abstract value that corresponds to $\hat{f}$ is set to 'conflict'.

The second case writes `s[p]` to `r[p]` when $\hat{f}$ is not contained in $\hat{F}_{\mathtt{c}}$. The starting state ④ is like ② except that $\hat{f} \not\subseteq \hat{F}_{\mathtt{c}}$. The result similarly materializes $\hat{f}$ in $\hat{a}_1$ before pointing that partition to the abstract value $\hat{A}_4$. Thus in both branches of the **`if`**, we perform strong updates in the abstraction. Transfer functions and strong updates are detailed in Section 4.

After the **`if`**, we join the two abstract states ③ and ⑤. In essence, the join process (Section 5) merges partitions that have common properties. Here, $\hat{f}$ is summarized into $\hat{F}'_{\mathsf{out}}$ in ③ and $\hat{F}''_{\mathsf{out}}$ in ⑤. The three partitions of attr(`r`) thus arise from the part of attr(`r`) that was left after materializing $\hat{f}$, and the two branches of the **`if`**, which is represented in the set domain with a partial path condition. Once $\hat{f}$ is summarized into $\hat{F}'_{\mathsf{out}}$ or $\hat{F}''_{\mathsf{out}}$, the graphs match and thus the joined graph also matches as is shown in ⑥. However, because of the folding and the branch condition, the side constraints do not match and thus a join is computed in the abstract domain for sets. Because the domain is sufficiently precise, the set constraints shown in ⑥ are derived. Thus join is implemented by graph matching intertwined with queries and join operations in the abstract domain for sets.

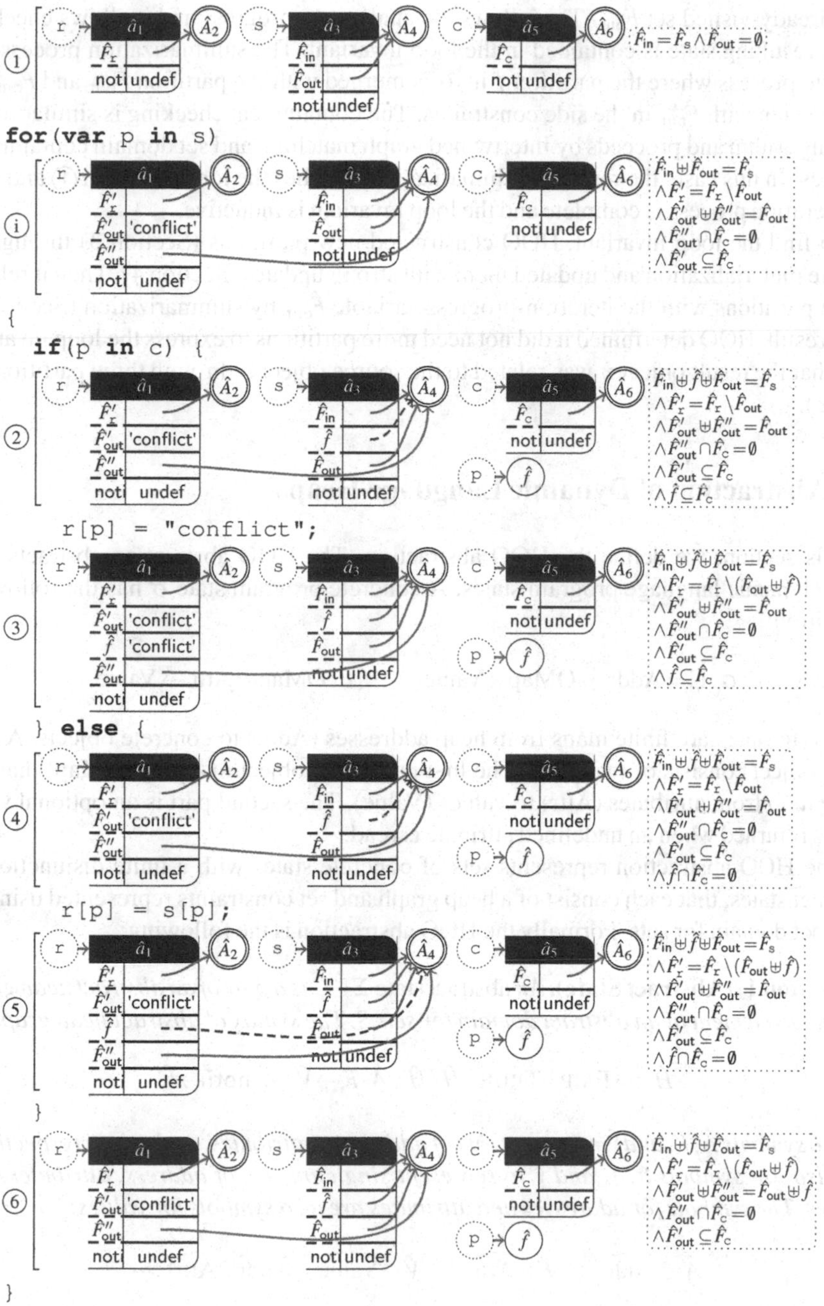

Fig. 2. Final iteration of analysis of the example loop from the Introduction. The loop invariant (i) shows the three inferred partitions of attr(r), and the set constraints (on the right) relate those three partitions to the partitions originally found in the three objects.

At the end of the loop body, it is necessary to summarize the iteration element $\hat{f}$ into the already-visited set $\hat{F}_{\text{out}}$. This allows the analysis to progress and it allows checking if the resulting state is contained in the loop invariant. The summarization process is a rewrite process where the partition $\hat{f}$ in $\hat{a}_3$ is merged with the partition $\hat{F}_{\text{out}}$ and $\hat{F}_{\text{out}} \uplus \hat{f}$ is rewritten with $\hat{F}_{\text{out}}$ in the side constraints. The containment checking is similar to the join algorithm and proceeds by intertwined graph matching and set domain containment queries. In this case, the result of summarization matches the loop invariant ⓘ and thus the iteration process is complete and the loop invariant is inductive.

To find the loop invariant, HOO constructed new partitions (Section 3) through attribute materialization and updated them with strong updates (Section 4). Then it related those partitions with the iteration-progress variable $\hat{F}_{\text{out}}$ by summarization (Section 5). As a result, HOO determined it did not need more partitions to express the loop invariant and that the result object `r` was related to the source object `s` through three partitions of attr(`r`).

3 Abstraction of Dynamic Language Heaps

In this section, we define the HOO abstraction. The HOO abstraction abstracts concrete dynamic language program states. A concrete program state σ has the following definition:

$$\sigma : \mathrm{C} = \mathrm{Addr} \xrightarrow{\text{fin}} \mathrm{OMap} \times \mathrm{Value}_{\perp} \qquad o : \mathrm{OMap} = \mathrm{Attr} \xrightarrow{\text{fin}} \mathrm{Value}$$

Concrete states are finite maps from heap addresses (Addr) to concrete objects. A concrete object consists of two parts. The first part is the object mapping (OMap) that is a finite map from attributes (Attr) to values (Value). The second part is an optional value that is returned when an undefined attribute is read.

The HOO abstraction represents sets of concrete states with a finite disjunction of abstract states, that each consist of a heap graph and set constraints represented using an abstract domain for sets. Formally the HOO abstraction is the following:

Definition 1 (Abstract State). *An* abstract state $\Sigma \in \widehat{C}$ *is a pair of an abstract heap graph* $\hat{H}$ *and an element of an abstract domain for sets* $\hat{S}$. *The syntax of abstract heap graphs is*

$$\hat{H} ::= \mathrm{EMP} \mid \mathrm{TRUE} \mid \hat{H} * \hat{H} \mid \hat{A} \cdot \hat{F} \mapsto \hat{V} \mid \hat{A} \cdot \mathsf{noti} \mapsto \hat{V}$$

where symbols $\hat{A}$, $\hat{F}$, *and* $\hat{V}$ *represent sets of addresses, attributes, and values respectively. We also use symbols* $\hat{a}$, $\hat{f}$, *and* $\hat{v}$ *to represent singleton sets of address, attributes, and values. The symbols for addresses and attributes are also symbols for values:*

$$\hat{A} \in \widehat{\mathrm{Addr}} \qquad \hat{F} \in \widehat{\mathrm{Attr}} \qquad \hat{V} \in \widehat{\mathrm{Value}} = \widehat{\mathrm{Addr}} \cup \widehat{\mathrm{Attr}} \cup \cdots$$

The resulting abstract domain is a reduced product [8] between a heap abstract domain element $\hat{H}$ and a set abstract domain element $\hat{S}$. The set domain is used to represent relationships between sets of attributes of objects. The information from the set domain affects points-to facts $\hat{A} \cdot \hat{F} \mapsto \hat{V}$ by constraining the sets of addresses $\hat{A}$, attributes $\hat{F}$, and values $\hat{V}$. Therefore the meaning of a HOO abstract state is closely tied to the meaning of set constraints. Since HOO is parametric with respect to the abstract domain for sets, its concretization is given in terms of a concretization for the set domain $\gamma(\hat{S})$:

$$\gamma(\hat{H},\hat{S}) \stackrel{\text{def}}{=} \{(\eta,\sigma) \mid (\eta,\sigma) \in \gamma(\hat{H}) \wedge \eta \in \gamma(\hat{S})\}$$
$$\text{where} \quad \eta : \mathrm{E} = \widehat{\mathrm{Value}} \rightharpoonup \wp(\mathrm{Value})$$

The η is a valuation function that maps value symbols (including address and attribute symbols) to sets of concrete values. The set domain restricts the η function, which in turn restricts the concrete state σ through the concretization of the heap. If _ is a placeholder for unused existentially quantified variables, the concretization of the heap is defined as follows:

$$\begin{array}{ll}
\gamma(\textsc{Emp}) & \stackrel{\text{def}}{=} \{\eta,\sigma \mid \mathrm{Dom}(\sigma) = \emptyset\} \\
\gamma(\textsc{True}) & \stackrel{\text{def}}{=} \mathrm{E} \times \mathrm{C} \\
\gamma(\hat{A} \cdot \hat{F} \mapsto \hat{V}) & \stackrel{\text{def}}{=} \{\eta,\sigma \mid \forall a \in \eta(\hat{A}), f \in \eta(\hat{F}). \exists v \in \eta(\hat{V}), o. (o,_) = \sigma(a) \wedge v = o(f)\} \\
\gamma(\hat{A} \cdot \mathsf{noti} \mapsto \hat{V}) & \stackrel{\text{def}}{=} \{\eta,\sigma \mid \forall a \in \eta(\hat{A}). \exists v \in \eta(\hat{V}). (_,v) = \sigma(a)\} \\
\gamma(\hat{H}_1 * \hat{H}_2) & \stackrel{\text{def}}{=} \{\eta,\sigma \mid \exists \sigma_1,\sigma_2. (\eta,\sigma_1) \in \gamma(\hat{H}_1) \wedge (\eta,\sigma_2) \in \gamma(\hat{H}_2) \wedge \sigma = \sigma_1 \otimes \sigma_2\}
\end{array}$$

The concretization of a points-to fact can represent part of many objects. The base addresses of the objects are retrieved from the valuation $\eta(\hat{A})$, but only the attributes retrieved from the valuation $\eta(\hat{F})$ are considered by this points-to fact. HOO uses an *attribute splitting* model similar to JStar [27] or Xisa [4], thus not every attribute of every object in $\eta(\hat{A})$ is represented in $\eta(\hat{F})$. Because each of the symbols $\hat{A}$ is a set, each abstract address may be a summary, but if the set domain can represent singletons [10, 28], these need not always be summaries.

The points-to fact for the default value $\hat{A} \cdot \mathsf{noti} \mapsto \hat{V}$ restricts the default value for each object in $\eta(\hat{A})$. These default value points-to facts serve a dual purpose, however. Because of the field splitting model, not all objects must have all of their attributes in a formula. The presence of a default points-to fact indicates that all of the objects of $\eta(\hat{A})$ are *complete*; they have all of their attributes represented in the formula. *Incomplete* objects may not have all of their attributes represented in the formula and thus abstract transfer functions may only access attributes that must be in the known parts of the object (see Section 4).

The separating conjunction has mostly the standard semantics [29]. Because objects can be split and the attributes are not fixed, we must define the composition $\otimes$ of two separate concrete states differently:

$$\sigma_1 \otimes \sigma_2 = \lambda a. \begin{cases} \sigma_1(a) & a \in \mathrm{Dom}(\sigma_1) \setminus \mathrm{Dom}(\sigma_2) \\ \sigma_2(a) & a \in \mathrm{Dom}(\sigma_2) \setminus \mathrm{Dom}(\sigma_1) \\ \begin{pmatrix} o_1 \oplus o_2, \\ d_1 \boxplus d_2 \end{pmatrix} & \begin{array}{l} (o_1,d_1) = \sigma_1(a) \\ (o_2,d_2) = \sigma_2(a) \\ a \in \mathrm{Dom}(\sigma_1) \cap \mathrm{Dom}(\sigma_2) \end{array} \end{cases}$$

$$o_1 \oplus o_2 = \lambda s. \begin{cases} o_1(f) & f \in \mathrm{Dom}(o_1) \setminus \mathrm{Dom}(o_2) \\ o_2(f) & f \in \mathrm{Dom}(o_2) \setminus \mathrm{Dom}(o_1) \end{cases}$$

Separate objects are composed trivially, but objects that have been split have their object maps composed using object map composition $\oplus$. This is only defined if there are disjoint attributes in each partial object map. Additionally, default values are composed with $\boxplus$ which yields the non-bottom value if possible and is undefined for two non-bottom values.

Graphical Notation. In most of this paper, we use a graphical notation to help ease understanding. This notation can be translated to the formalization given in this section. In the graphical notation, a single circle represents an object address. If that circle is labeled with a $\hat{a}_n$, $\hat{f}_n$, or $\hat{v}_n$ the object is a singleton address, attribute or value respectively and thus corresponds to a single concrete value. If that circle is labeled with a $\hat{A}_n$, $\hat{F}_n$, or $\hat{V}_n$ and has a double border, the object is a summary. If that circle is labeled with a program variable, it represents a singleton stack location. Objects with fields are represented using the table notation, where each row corresponds to a points-to fact starting from a base address from the set $\hat{A}_n$.

Example 1 (Graphical Notation Equivalence). The following graphical notation and logical notation are equivalent. We use the unit attribute () to represent the points-to relationship from the stack variable `r` to the singleton object $\hat{a}_1$.

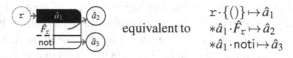

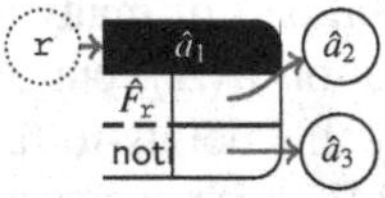

equivalent to

$$\mathtt{r}\cdot\{()\}\mapsto\hat{a}_1$$
$$*\hat{a}_1\cdot\hat{F}_{\mathtt{r}}\mapsto\hat{a}_2$$
$$*\hat{a}_1\cdot\mathsf{noti}\mapsto\hat{a}_3$$

4 Materialization and Transfer Functions

To precisely analyze programs that manipulate values in summaries, it is necessary to materialize individual elements from the summaries. Materialization occurs in execution of transfer functions in the language of commands c that represents the core behaviors for open-object manipulation in dynamic languages:

$$\begin{array}{rll} c ::= & \textbf{let}\, x = \mathrm{attr}(x_1) \mid \textbf{let}\, x = \mathrm{choose}(x_1) & \multirow{2}{*}{\}\text{set operations}} \\ & \mid \textbf{let}\, x = x_1 \cup x_2 \mid \textbf{let}\, x = x_1 \setminus x_2 & \\ & \mid \textbf{let}\, x = x_1[x_2] \mid x_1[x_2] := x_3 \mid \textbf{for}\, x_1\, \textbf{in}\, x_2\, \textbf{do}\, c & \}\text{object operations} \\ & \mid \textbf{let}\, x = \textbf{new}\{\} \mid c_1 ; c_2 \mid \textbf{while}\, e\, \textbf{do}\, c \mid \textbf{let}\, x = e & \}\text{standard operations} \end{array}$$

This section is concerned with load and store object operations because these operations require attribute materialization, which is mandatory for inferring precise relationships between objects with unknown attributes. Aside from **`for-in`**, which is defined in the next section, other operations, including choose(x_1), which selects a singleton set from a set and attr(x_1), which gets the union of all attributes of an object, are straightforward and given in the technical report [11].

The concrete semantics of load $\textbf{let}\, x = x_1[x_2]$ and store $x_1[x_2] := x_3$ are straightforward. They look up the object x_1, then try to find the given attribute x_2. Load binds to x the value that corresponds to the attribute if it is found, otherwise it binds the default value for the object. Store removes the given attribute if it is found and adds a new attribute that corresponds to the right-hand side x_3.

To perform loads and stores on abstract objects the abstract transformers for load and store must determine how to manipulate and utilize the partitions on the accessed object. The process of transforming an object so that it has precisely the partitions necessary for performing a particular load or store is attribute materialization.

Concrete and abstract transfer functions are defined over the command language c. Concrete transformers $[\![c]\!] : \mathrm{C} \to \mathrm{C}$ transition a single concrete state to a single concrete state. Abstract transformers $\widehat{[\![c]\!]} : \widehat{\mathrm{C}} \to \wp(\widehat{\mathrm{C}})$ (shown as Hoare triples [20] with the graphical notation), however, transition a single abstract state to a set of abstract states representing a disjunction. This disjunction capability is used in transfer functions that perform case splits, such as the load transfer function. In the implementation of HOO, we use a disjunctive domain combinator to manage these sets.

It is possible to implement transfer functions that manipulate complete, incomplete, summary, and singleton objects. Here we define the store and load transfer functions for complete singleton objects. For incomplete objects, there are separate transfer functions: before a materialization can occur, it must be proven that the attribute already exists in the object. This ensures that attributes that are defined in the missing part of the object cannot be read or overwritten by any operations. When operating on a summary object, a singleton must first be materialized. This materialization is trivially defined through case splits that result in finite disjunctions.

Attribute Materialization for Store: Attribute materialization for store operations is simple. Since the value of the particular attribute is about to be overwritten, there is no need to preserve the original value. The implementation of store is the following:

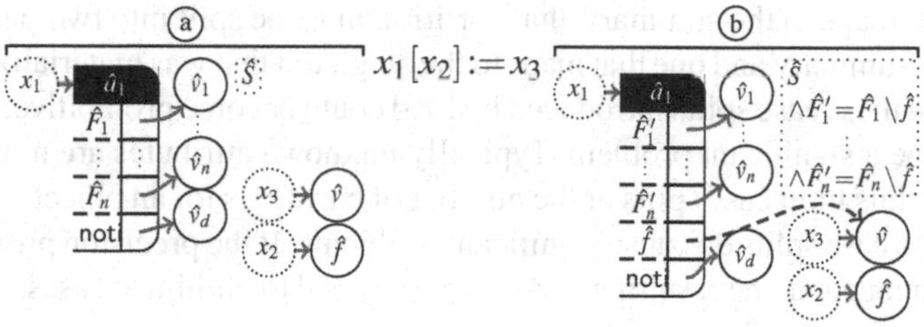

Store looks up the corresponding objects to x_1, x_2, and x_3 in ⓐ, which in this case are $\hat{a}_1$, $\hat{f}$, and $\hat{v}$ respectively. Attribute materialization then iterates through each partition in $\hat{a}_1$ and reconstructs the partition by removing $\hat{f}$ from the partition. If $\hat{f}$ was not already present in the partition, this represents no change, otherwise it explicitly removes $\hat{f}$. Finally, after all of the existing partitions have been reconstructed, a new partition for $\hat{f}$ is created and it is pointed to the stored value $\hat{v}$ giving ⓑ. By performing this attribute materialization, we have guaranteed that subsequent reads of the same property $\hat{f}$, even if we do not know its concrete value, will be directed to $\hat{f}$, and thus store performs strong updates.

Attribute Materialization for Load: Attribute materialization for load is similar to store. The key difference is that there is a possible result for each partition of the read object. The HOO abstract domain uses a finite disjunction to represent the result of this case split:

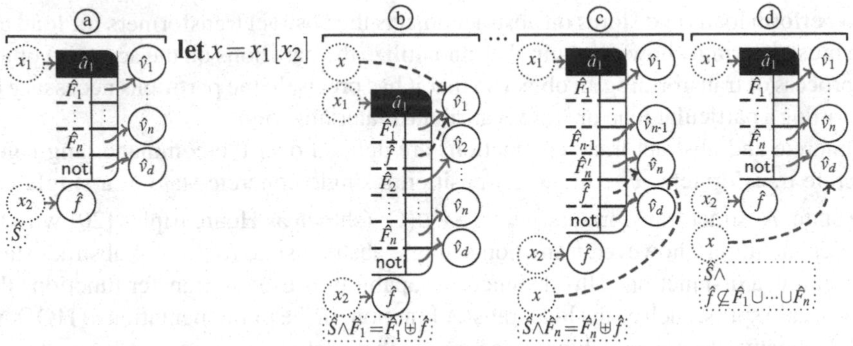

A load operation must determine which, if any, of the partitions the attribute $\hat{f}$ is in. In the worst case, it could be in any of the partitions and therefore a result must be considered for each case. In each non-noti case, $\hat{f}$ is constrained to be in that particular partition and therefore in no other partition. If this is inconsistent under the current analysis state, the abstract state will become bottom for that case and it can be dropped. The noti partition, which implicitly represents all attributes not currently in the object, must be considered as a possible source for materialization if there is a chance the attribute does not already exist in the object. Such a materialization does not explicitly cause any repartitioning because noti still represents all of the not present attributes (which now does not include $\hat{f}$).

If the values that are being loaded (in this case $\hat{v}_1, \cdots, \hat{v}_n, \hat{v}_d$) are not singleton values, the load operation must also materialize one value from that summary. When materializing from a summary object, additional partitions can be generated. For each object that has a partition that maps to the summary, that partition must be split into two parts: one that maps to a new summary and one that maps to the singleton that was materialized. While it is possible that these case splits introduced by load could become prohibitive, we have not found this to be a significant problem. Typically unknown attributes are not completely unknown and thus limit case splits or the number of partitions for an object is sufficiently small that these case splits do cause significant problems. If the precision provided by the case splits is unneeded, the resulting states can be joined to eliminate cases.

Example 2 (Store with summary values). When loading from an attribute $\hat{f}$ that is contained in a partition $\hat{F}$ of an object $\hat{a}$ that maps to a summary $\hat{V}$, additional partitions are produced. The result contains three partitions instead of two. Some attributes from $\hat{F}$ map to $\hat{V}'$ and some map to $\hat{v}$. Therefore, while the analysis knows that $\hat{f}$ maps to $\hat{v}$ because that is why it chose to materialize $\hat{v}$, it does not know that other attributes of $\hat{F}$ do not also map to $\hat{v}$. Therefore, it splits the remainder of $\hat{F}$ into two partitions: one $\hat{F}'$ that maps to the remainder of the values $\hat{V}'$ and another $\hat{F}''$ that maps to the materialized value $\hat{v}$.

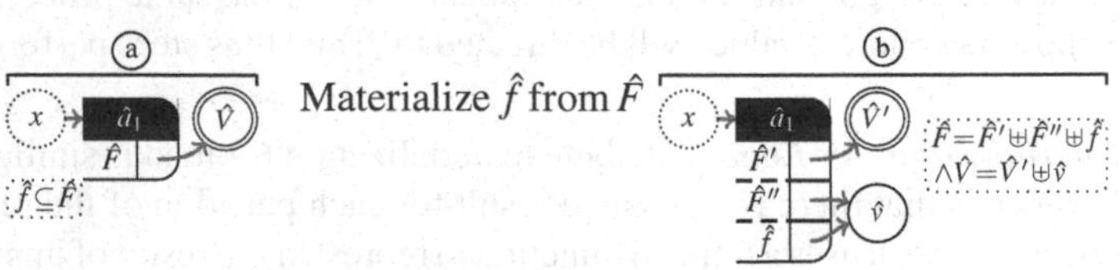

Theorem 1 (Soundness of transfer functions). *Transfer functions are sound because for any command c, the following property holds:*

$$\forall(\hat{H},\hat{S})\in\widehat{C},\sigma\in\gamma(\hat{H},\hat{S}),\bar{\Sigma}\subseteq\widehat{C}.$$
$$\bar{\Sigma}=\widehat{[\![c]\!]}(\hat{H},\hat{S})\Rightarrow\exists(\hat{H}',\hat{S}')\in\bar{\Sigma}.\,[\![c]\!]\sigma\in\gamma(\hat{H}',\hat{S}')$$

5 Automatic Invariant Inference

In this section we give the join, widening, and inclusion check algorithms that are required for automatically and soundly generating program invariants. Here the focus is inferring loop invariants for **for-in** loops — the primary kind of loop for object-manipulation. The analysis of **for-in** loops first translates these loops into **while** loops. This allows HOO to follow the standard abstract interpretation procedure for loops, while introducing iteration-progress variables to aid the analysis in inferring precise loop invariants.

$$\begin{aligned}&\textbf{for}\ x_1\ \textbf{in}\ x_2\ \textbf{do}\ c\stackrel{\text{def}}{=}\\&\quad\textbf{let}\ s=\textbf{new}\{\};\\&\quad s[\text{'in'}]:=\text{attr}(x_2);\\&\quad s[\text{'out'}]:=\emptyset;\\&\quad\textbf{while}\ s[\text{'in'}]\neq\emptyset\ \textbf{do}\\&\qquad\textbf{let}\ x_1=\text{choose}(s[\text{'in'}]);\\&\qquad s[\text{'in'}]:=s[\text{'in'}]\setminus\{x_1\}\\&\qquad c;\\&\qquad s[\text{'out'}]=s[\text{'out'}]\cup\{x_1\}\end{aligned}$$

These iteration-progress variables are introduced in the translation process shown in the inset figure. For the object being iterated over x_2, the $s[\text{'in'}]$ variable keeps track of attributes that have not yet been visited by the loop, while $s[\text{'out'}]$ keeps track of attributes that have already been visited by the loop. To keep these variables up to date, the translation employs the set manipulating commands introduced in Section 4.

Once translated, HOO takes advantage of $s[\text{'in'}]$ and $s[\text{'out'}]$ to represent relations between partitions of attributes. Adding these ghost variables, allows partitions to be equal to a function of the already visited portion $\text{attr}(x_2)$. On the exit of the loop, $s[\text{'in'}]$ is the empty set and $s[\text{'out'}]$ is $\text{attr}(x_2)$, so partitions related to $s[\text{'out'}]$ are now related to $\text{attr}(x_2)$.

These iteration-progress variables are essential for performing strong updates. When analyzing an iteration of a loop, partitions that arise from attribute materialization arise simultaneously with partitions that arise in iteration-progress variables. Thus these partitions become related and even when partitions from attribute materialization must be summarized, the relationship with the iteration progress variable is maintained. The summarization process occurs as part of join and widening.

Join Algorithm: The join algorithm takes two abstract states $\hat{H}_1,\hat{S}_1$ and $\hat{H}_2,\hat{S}_2$ and computes an overapproximation of all program states described by each of these abstract states. When joining abstractions of memory, the algorithm must match objects in $\hat{H}_1$ and objects in $\hat{H}_2$ to objects in a resulting abstract memory $\hat{H}_3$. This matching of objects can be described by two mapping functions M_1 and M_2, where $M_1:\widehat{\text{Addr}_1}\stackrel{\text{fin}}{\to}\widehat{\text{Addr}_3}$ maps symbols from $\hat{H}_1$ to symbols from $\hat{H}_3$ and $M_2:\widehat{\text{Addr}_2}\stackrel{\text{fin}}{\to}\widehat{\text{Addr}_3}$ maps symbols from $\hat{H}_2$ to symbols from $\hat{H}_3$. However, because HOO abstracts open objects, the join algorithm must match partitions of objects as well. This matching is represented with a relation $P_J\subseteq\wp(\widehat{\text{Attr}_1})\times\wp(\widehat{\text{Attr}_2})\times\widehat{\text{Attr}_3}$ that relates sets of partitions from objects in $\hat{H}_1$ and $\hat{H}_2$ to partitions in $\hat{H}_3$. Because partitions can be split and because new, empty partitions can be created, join can produce an unbounded number of partitions.

Table 1. Join templates match objects in two abstract heaps, producing a third heap that overapproximates both. Matchings M_1, M_2, P_J are generated on the fly and used in joining the set domain after the heaps are joined.

Prerequisites	$\hat{H}_1, \hat{S}_1 \sqcup \hat{H}_2, \hat{S}_2 \rightsquigarrow$	Result
$M_1(\hat{A}_1)=\hat{A}_3$ $M_2(\hat{A}_2)=\hat{A}_3$	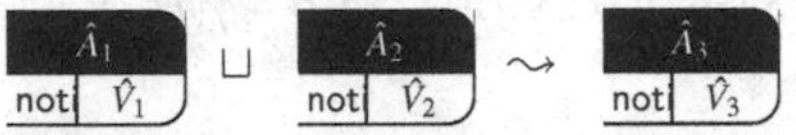	$M_1(\hat{V}_1)=\hat{V}_3$ $M_2(\hat{V}_2)=\hat{V}_3$
$M_1(\hat{A}_1)=\hat{A}_3$ $M_2(\hat{A}_2)=\hat{A}_3$	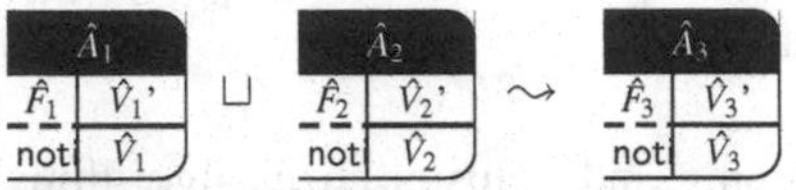	$M_1(\hat{V}_1)=\hat{V}_3$, $M_2(\hat{V}_2)=\hat{V}_3$ $M_1(\hat{V}_1')=\hat{V}_3'$, $M_2(\hat{V}_2')=\hat{V}_3'$ $(\{\hat{F}_1\},\{\hat{F}_2\},\hat{F}_3)\in P_J$
$M_1(\hat{A}_1)=\hat{A}_3$ $M_2(\hat{A}_2)=\hat{A}_3$ remainder of object matches	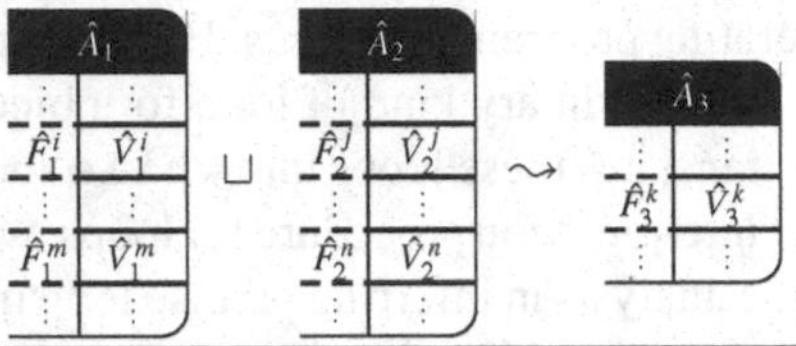	$(\{\hat{F}_1^i,\cdots,\hat{F}_1^m\},\{\hat{F}_2^j,\cdots\hat{F}_2^n\},\hat{F}_3^k)\in P_J$ $M_1(\hat{V}_1^i)=\hat{V}_3^k$, $M_2(\hat{V}_2^j)=\hat{V}_3^k$ $\vdots$ $M_1(\hat{V}_1^m)=\hat{V}_3^k$, $M_2(\hat{V}_2^n)=\hat{V}_3^k$

The fundamental challenge for the HOO abstraction's join algorithm is computing these symbol matchings M_1, M_2, and P_J. To construct the matchings, the join algorithm begins at the symbolic addresses of stack allocated variables. It adds equivalent variables from the three graphs to M_1 and M_2, then it begins an iterative process. Starting from a matching that already exists in M_1 and M_2, it derives additional matchings that are potential consequences. To derive these additional matchings, a template system is used. The templates are shown in Table 1. These templates consume corresponding parts of a memory abstraction, producing a resultant memory abstraction that holds under the matchings. This iterative process is applied until no more templates can be applied. Any remaining heap at this point results in TRUE being added to the result. The result of join is complete matchings M_1, M_2, and P_J, as well as, a memory abstraction $\hat{H}_3$. To get the resulting set abstraction $\hat{S}_3$, the sets are joined under the same matchings, where multiple matchings are interpreted as a union.

There are three templates described in Table 1. The first trivially joins any two empty objects into an empty object. The default values are subsequently matched. The second template joins any two objects that have only one partition. The values from that partition are added to the mapping as well as the default values. The last template is parametric. If some number of partitions can be matched with some number of partitions then those can all be merged into a single partition in the result. This template requires applying other rules to complete the joining of the objects. If it is unknown how to match partitions for all of an object, this template allows matching part of the object. If the result is that remaining partitions are single partitions, even if there is no natural way to match them, they will be matched by applying template two.

Example 3 (Joining objects). Here we join $\hat{a}_1$ objects from the overview example at program points ③ and ⑤ to get the result shown at ⑥. To compute the join we construct matchings M_1, M_2, and P_J. Initially $M_1 = [\hat{a}_1 \mapsto \hat{a}_1]$, $M_2 = [\hat{a}_1 \mapsto \hat{a}_1]$, and $P_J = \emptyset$. If we were to match $\hat{F}'_{\text{out}}$ with $\hat{F}'_{\text{out}}$ or $\hat{F}''_{\text{out}}$ with $\hat{F}''_{\text{out}}$, we would get an imprecise join because we would be forced to match $\hat{f}$ with itself even though it has two values that should not be joined. Instead, we apply the third template to merge partitions with like values, thus merging $\hat{f}$ with $\hat{F}''_{\text{out}}$ in ③ and with $\hat{F}''_{\text{out}}$ in ⑤. Since the only remaining partition is $\hat{F}'_{\mathtt{r}}$, we match $\hat{F}'_{\mathtt{r}}$ and $\hat{F}'_{\mathtt{r}}$ giving the following matchings and join result:

$$M_1 = [\hat{a}_1 \mapsto \hat{a}_1, \hat{a}_2 \mapsto \hat{a}_2, \hat{a}_4 \mapsto \hat{a}_4]$$
$$M_2 = [\hat{a}_1 \mapsto \hat{a}_1, \hat{a}_2 \mapsto \hat{a}_2, \hat{a}_4 \mapsto \hat{a}_4]$$
$$P_J = \{(\{\hat{F}'_{\mathtt{r}}\}, \{\hat{F}'_{\mathtt{r}}\}, \hat{F}'_{\mathtt{r}}), (\{\hat{F}'_{\text{out}}, \hat{f}\}, \{\hat{F}'_{\text{out}}\}, \hat{F}'_{\text{out}}), (\{\hat{F}''_{\text{out}}\}, \{\hat{F}''_{\text{out}}, \hat{f}\}, \hat{F}''_{\text{out}})\}$$

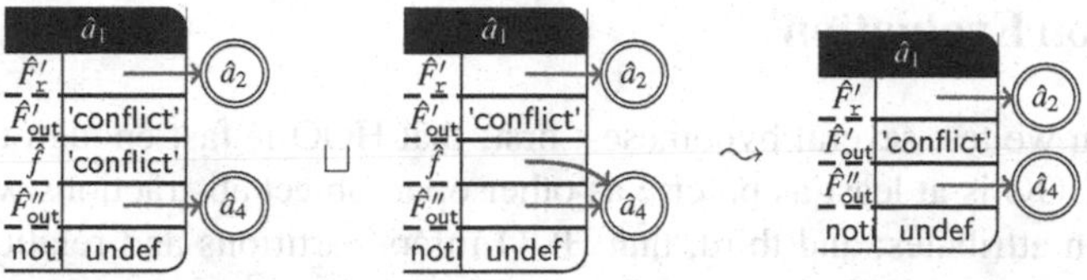

Widening algorithm: In HOO, the join and widening algorithms are nearly identical. However, unlike join, widening must select matchings that ensure convergence of the analysis, by guaranteeing that the number of partitions does not grow unboundedly and that the arrangement of the partitions is fixed (i.e. there is no oscillation in which partitions are matched during widening). While there are many possible approaches that meet these criteria, we utilize allocation site information to resolve decisions during the matching process. Only objects from the same allocation site may be matched, which causes only attribute sets whose corresponding values are from the same allocation site to be matched. To ensure convergence, after some number of iterations, all objects from the same allocation site can be forced to be matched. This bounds the partitions per abstract object to one per allocation site and bounds the number of abstract objects to one per allocation site, so as long as the underlying set domain converges on an abstraction for each partition, the analysis will converge.

Inclusion Check Algorithm: Inclusion checking determines if an abstract state is already described by another abstract state. The process for deciding if an inclusion holds is similar to the join processes. If $M, P_I \vdash \hat{H}_a, \hat{S}_a \sqsubseteq \hat{H}_b, \hat{S}_b$, all concrete states described by $\hat{H}_a, \hat{S}_a$ must be contained in the set of all concrete states described by $\hat{H}_b, \hat{S}_b$. It works in a fashion similar to join by constructing matchings M and P_I from symbols in $\hat{H}_a, \hat{S}_a$ to symbols in $\hat{H}_b, \hat{S}_b$. It employs the same methodology as join. Objects are matched, one-by-one, until no more matches can be made. This matching builds up the mapping M that is then used for an inclusion check in the set domain. If the mapping was successfully constructed and the inclusion check holds in the set domain, the inclusion check holds on the HOO domain. The templates for augmenting the mapping are essentially the same as those for join shown in Table 1, except with only M_1 and with P_I only using the first and third components and where $\hat{H}_2, \hat{S}_2$ is ignored with $\hat{H}_1, \hat{S}_1$ corresponding to $\hat{H}_a, \hat{S}_a$ and the result corresponding to $\hat{H}_b, \hat{S}_b$.

Theorem 2 (Join Soundness). *Join is sound under matchings M_1, M_2, P_J because*

If $M_1, M_2, P_J \vdash \hat{H}_1, \hat{S}_1 \sqcup \hat{H}_2, \hat{S}_2 \rightsquigarrow \hat{H}_3, \hat{S}_3$ *then*

$$\forall \sigma, \eta. (\eta, \sigma) \in \gamma(\hat{H}_1, \hat{S}_1) \wedge (\eta, \sigma) \in \gamma(\hat{H}_2, \hat{S}_2) \Rightarrow \exists \eta_3. (\eta_3, \sigma) \in \gamma(\hat{H}_3, \hat{S}_3)$$

We do not state properties other than soundness due to the dependence of HOO's behavior on its instantiation. Because of the non-trivial interaction between the set domain and HOO, properties of HOO are affected by properties of the set domain. More precise set domain operations typically yield more precision in HOO. Additionally, the choice of heuristics for template application can affect the results of join, widening, and inclusion check, thus leading to a complex dependency between precision and heuristics. While this dependence can affect many properties, it does not affect soundness.

6 Precision Evaluation

In this section we test several hypotheses: first, that HOO is fast enough to be useful; second, that HOO is at least as precise as other open-object abstractions when objects have unknown attributes; and third, that HOO infers partitions and relations between partitions of unknown attributes precisely enough to verify properties of intricate object-manipulating programs. To investigate these hypotheses, we created a prototype implementation in OCaml and ran it on a number of small diagnostic benchmarks, each of which consists of one or more loops that manipulate open objects. These benchmarks are drawn from real JavaScript frameworks such as JQuery, Prototype.js, and Traits.js[1]. We chose them to test commonly occurring idioms that manipulate open objects in dynamic languages. To have properties to verify, we developed partial correctness specifications for each of the benchmarks. We then split the post-conditions of the specifications into a number of properties to verify that belong in one of two categories: memory properties assert facts about pointers (e.g., `r` $\neq$ `s`), and object properties assert facts about the structure of objects (e.g., if the object at $\hat{a}_1$ has attribute $\hat{f}$, then object at $\hat{a}_2$ also has attribute $\hat{f}$).

We use these benchmarks to compare HOO with TAJS [21], which is currently the most precise (for open objects) JavaScript analyzer. Because TAJS is a whole-program analysis, it is not intended to verify partial correctness specifications and consequently, it adapts a traditional field-sensitive object representation for open objects. However, it employs several features to improve precision when unknown attribute are encountered during analysis: it implements a recency abstraction [1] to allow strong updates on straight-line code, and it implements correlation tracking [31] to allow statically known attributes to be iteratively copied using **`for-in`** loops.

In the results in Table 2, we find that TAJS and HOO are able to prove the same memory properties. The diagnostic benchmarks are not designed to exercise intricate memory structures, so all properties are provable with an allocation site abstraction. Because both TAJS and HOO use allocation site information, both prove all memory properties.

For object properties, HOO is always at least as precise as TAJS, and significantly more so when unknown attributes are involved. The `static` benchmark is designed to simulate the "best-case scenario" for whole program analyses: it supplies all attributes to objects before iterating over them. Here, TAJS relies on correlation tracking to prove all properties. HOO can also prove all of these properties. It infers a separate partition for each statically known attribute, effectively making it equivalent to TAJS's object abstraction.

---

[1] `http://jquery.com`, `http://prototypejs.org`, and `http://traitsjs.org`

Table 2. Analysis results of diagnostic benchmarks. Time compare analysis time excluding JVM startup time. Memory properties compares TAJS and HOO in verifying pointer properties. Object properties compares TAJS and HOO in verifying object structure properties. The # Props columns are the total number of properties of that kind.

	Time (s)		Memory Properties			Object Properties		
Program	TAJS	HOO	TAJS	HOO	# Props	TAJS	HOO	# Props
`static`	0.06	0.09	1	1	1	3	3	3
`copy`	0.13	0.02	1	1	1	0	3	3
`filter`	0.40	0.10	0	0	0	0	6	6
`compose`	0.71	0.54	0	0	0	0	7	7
`merge`	0.19	0.06	2	2	2	0	5	5

Our other benchmarks iterate over objects where the attributes are unknown. Here, HOO proves all properties, while TAJS fails to prove any. TAJS's imprecision is unsurprising because correlation tracking does not work with unknown attributes and recency abstraction does not enable strong updates in loops. HOO, on the other hand, succeeds because it infers partitions of object attributes and relates those partitions to other partitions. In the `copy` benchmark, attributes and values are copied one attribute at a time to a new object. HOO infers that after the iteration is complete, the attributes of both objects are equal. HOO can also verify the `filter` benchmark, which is the example presented throughout this paper that requires conditional and partial overwriting of objects. Additionally, HOO continues to be precise even when complex compositions are involved, as in the `compose` and `merge` benchmarks, which perform parallel and serial composition of objects. For these benchmarks HOO infers relationships between multiple objects and sequentially updates objects through multiple **`for-in`** loops.

On these benchmarks, HOO is often faster than TAJS, but this is likely due to TAJS's full support for JavaScript and the DOM and thus performance is really incomparable. Actually, HOO's performance is highly dependent on the efficiency of the underlying set domain due to the large number of set domain operations that HOO uses. However, despite not having a heavily optimized set domain, HOO analyzes these benchmarks quickly.

This evaluation demonstrates that HOO is effective at representing and verifying properties of open objects, both with statically known attributes and with entirely unknown attributes. Additionally it shows that HOO provides significant precision improvement over existing open-object abstractions when attributes are unknown and that HOO does not take a significant amount of time to verify complex properties.

7 Related Work

Analyses for dynamic languages: Because one of the main features of dynamic languages is open objects, all analyses for dynamic languages must handle open objects to a degree. As opposed to directly abstracting open objects, TAJS [21, 22], WALA [31], and JSAI [19, 24] extend standard field-sensitive analyses to JavaScript by adding a summary field for all unknown attributes. They employ clever interprocedural analysis tricks to propagate statically known object attributes through loops and across function call boundaries. Consequently, with the whole program, they can often precisely verify properties of open-object manipulating programs. Without the whole program, these techniques lose precision because they conflate all unknown object attributes into a single summary field and weakly update it through loops.

Analyses for containers: Because objects in dynamic languages behave similarly to containers, it is possible that a container analysis could be adapted to this task. Powerful container analyses such as [14] and [17] can represent and infer arbitrary partitions of containers. This is similar to HOO except that they do not use set abstractions to represent the partitions, but instead use SMT formulas and quantifier templates. For some applications these are excellent choices, but for dynamic languages where the key type of the containers is nearly always strings, this suffers. HOO can use abstract domains for sets [10, 28] and thus if these domains are parametric over their value types, HOO can support nearly any key-type abstraction.

Arrays and lists are restricted forms of containers on which there has been a significant amount of work [2, 9, 13, 16, 18, 23, 25]. The primary difference between arrays and more general containers and open objects is that arrays typically contain related values next to one another. Partitions of arrays are implicitly ordered and because array keys typically do not have gaps, partitions are defined using expressions that identify partition boundaries. Because open objects have gaps and are unordered, array analyses are not applicable. Regardless, array abstraction inspires the partitioning of open objects that we use.

Decision procedures: In addition there are analyses that do not handle loops without annotations for both dynamic languages and containers. DJS [5, 6] is a flow-sensitive dependent type system for JavaScript. It can infer intermediate states in straight-line code, but it requires annotations for loops and functions. Similarly JuS [15] supports straight-line code for JavaScript. Jahob and its brethren [26] use a battery of different decision procedures to analyze containers and the heap together for Java programs. Finally, array decision procedures [3, 12] can be adapted to containers, but all of these approaches require significant annotation of non-trivial loop invariants to be effective on open-object-manipulating programs.

8 Conclusion and Future Work

In an effort to verify properties of incomplete, open-object-manipulating programs, we created the HOO abstract domain. It is capable of verifying complex object manipulations even when object attributes are completely unknown. While it is effective today, we want to extend it to allow inferring relationships between attributes and their corresponding values. Such relationships enable determining precisely which value in a summary is being materialized and proving properties about specific values, even when they are included in a summary. We plan to pursue such an extension as we believe that it could enable verification of programs that use open objects not only as objects, but also as containers.

Acknowledgements. Thank you to our anonymous reviewers and members of CUPLV and Antique for the helpful reviews and feedback. This material is based upon work supported in part by the National Science Foundation under Grant Numbers CCF-1055066 and CCF-1218208. The research leading to these results has also received funding from the European Research Council under the FP7 grant agreement 278673, Project MemCAD.

References

1. Balakrishnan, G., Reps, T.: Recency-abstraction for heap-allocated storage. In: Yi, K. (ed.) SAS 2006. LNCS, vol. 4134, pp. 221–239. Springer, Heidelberg (2006)
2. Bouajjani, A., Drăgoi, C., Enea, C., Sighireanu, M.: Abstract domains for automated reasoning about list-manipulating programs with infinite data. In: Kuncak, V., Rybalchenko, A. (eds.) VMCAI 2012. LNCS, vol. 7148, pp. 1–22. Springer, Heidelberg (2012)
3. Bradley, A.R., Manna, Z., Sipma, H.B.: What's decidable about arrays? In: Emerson, E.A., Namjoshi, K.S. (eds.) VMCAI 2006. LNCS, vol. 3855, pp. 427–442. Springer, Heidelberg (2006)
4. Chang, B.-Y.E., Rival, X.: Relational inductive shape analysis. In: POPL, pp. 247–260 (2008)
5. Chugh, R., Herman, D., Jhala, R.: Dependent types for JavaScript. In: OOPSLA, pp. 587–606 (2012)
6. Chugh, R., Rondon, P.M., Jhala, R.: Nested refinements: A logic for duck typing. In: POPL, pp. 231–244 (2012)
7. Cousot, P., Cousot, R.: Abstract interpretation: A unified lattice model for static analysis of programs by construction or approximation of fixpoints. In: POPL, pp. 238–252 (1977)
8. Cousot, P., Cousot, R.: Systematic design of program analysis frameworks. In: POPL, pp. 269–282 (1979)
9. Cousot, P., Cousot, R., Logozzo, F.: A parametric segmentation functor for fully automatic and scalable array content analysis. In: POPL, pp. 105–118 (2011)
10. Cox, A., Chang, B.-Y.E., Sankaranarayanan, S.: QUIC graphs: Relational invariant generation for containers. In: Castagna, G. (ed.) ECOOP 2013. LNCS, vol. 7920, pp. 401–425. Springer, Heidelberg (2013)
11. Cox, A., Chang, B.-Y.E., Rival, X.: Automatic analysis of open objects in dynamic language programs (extended). Technical report, University of Colorado Boulder (2014)
12. de Moura, L.M., Bjørner, N.: Generalized, efficient array decision procedures. In: FMCAD, pp. 45–52 (2009)
13. Dillig, I., Dillig, T., Aiken, A.: Fluid updates: Beyond strong vs. weak updates. In: Gordon, A.D. (ed.) ESOP 2010. LNCS, vol. 6012, pp. 246–266. Springer, Heidelberg (2010)
14. Dillig, I., Dillig, T., Aiken, A.: Precise reasoning for programs using containers. In: POPL, pp. 187–200 (2011)
15. Gardner, P., Maffeis, S., Smith, G.D.: Towards a program logic for JavaScript. In: POPL, pp. 31–44 (2012)
16. Gopan, D., Reps, T.W., Sagiv, S.: A framework for numeric analysis of array operations. In: POPL, pp. 338–350 (2005)
17. Gulwani, S., McCloskey, B., Tiwari, A.: Lifting abstract interpreters to quantified logical domains. In: POPL, pp. 235–246 (2008)
18. Halbwachs, N., Péron, M.: Discovering properties about arrays in simple programs. In: PLDI, pp. 339–348 (2008)
19. Hardekopf, B., Wiedermann, B., Churchill, B., Kashyap, V.: Widening for control-flow. In: McMillan, K.L., Rival, X. (eds.) VMCAI 2014. LNCS, vol. 8318, pp. 472–491. Springer, Heidelberg (2014)

20. Hoare, C.A.R.: An axiomatic basis for computer programming. Commun. ACM 12(10), 576–580 (1969)
21. Jensen, S.H., Møller, A., Thiemann, P.: Type analysis for JavaScript. In: Palsberg, J., Su, Z. (eds.) SAS 2009. LNCS, vol. 5673, pp. 238–255. Springer, Heidelberg (2009)
22. Jensen, S.H., Møller, A., Thiemann, P.: Interprocedural analysis with lazy propagation. In: Cousot, R., Martel, M. (eds.) SAS 2010. LNCS, vol. 6337, pp. 320–339. Springer, Heidelberg (2010)
23. Jhala, R., McMillan, K.L.: Array abstractions from proofs. In: Damm, W., Hermanns, H. (eds.) CAV 2007. LNCS, vol. 4590, pp. 193–206. Springer, Heidelberg (2007)
24. Kashyap, V., Sarracino, J., Wagner, J., Wiedermann, B., Hardekopf, B.: Type refinement for static analysis of JavaScript. In: DLS, pp. 17–26 (2013)
25. Kovács, L., Voronkov, A.: Finding loop invariants for programs over arrays using a theorem prover. In: Chechik, M., Wirsing, M. (eds.) FASE 2009. LNCS, vol. 5503, pp. 470–485. Springer, Heidelberg (2009)
26. Kuncak, V.: Modular Data Structure Verification. PhD thesis, EECS Department, Massachusetts Institute of Technology (February 2007)
27. Parkinson, M.J.: Local reasoning for Java. PhD thesis, University of Cambridge (2005)
28. Pham, T.-H., Trinh, M.-T., Truong, A.-H., Chin, W.-N.: Fixbag: A fixpoint calculator for quantified bag constraints. In: Gopalakrishnan, G., Qadeer, S. (eds.) CAV 2011. LNCS, vol. 6806, pp. 656–662. Springer, Heidelberg (2011)
29. Reynolds, J.C.: Separation logic: A logic for shared mutable data structures. In: LICS, pp. 55–74 (2002)
30. Richards, G., Lebresne, S., Burg, B., Vitek, J.: An analysis of the dynamic behavior of JavaScript programs. In: PLDI, pp. 1–12 (2010)
31. Sridharan, M., Dolby, J., Chandra, S., Schäfer, M., Tip, F.: Correlation tracking for points-to analysis of JavaScript. In: Noble, J. (ed.) ECOOP 2012. LNCS, vol. 7313, pp. 435–458. Springer, Heidelberg (2012)

Invariance of Conjunctions of Polynomial Equalities for Algebraic Differential Equations*

Khalil Ghorbal[1], Andrew Sogokon[2], and André Platzer[1]

[1] Carnegie Mellon University, Computer Science Department, Pittsburgh, PA, USA
{kghorbal,aplatzer}@cs.cmu.edu

[2] University of Edinburgh, LFCS, School of Informatics, Edinburgh, Scotland, UK
a.sogokon@sms.ed.ac.uk

Abstract In this paper we seek to provide greater automation for formal deductive verification tools working with continuous and hybrid dynamical systems. We present an efficient procedure to check invariance of conjunctions of polynomial equalities under the flow of polynomial ordinary differential equations. The procedure is based on a necessary and sufficient condition that characterizes invariant conjunctions of polynomial equalities. We contrast this approach to an alternative one which combines fast and sufficient (but not necessary) conditions using differential cuts for soundly restricting the system evolution domain.

1 Introduction

The problem of reasoning about invariant sets of dynamical systems is of fundamental importance to verification and modern control design [3,22,28,26]. A set is an invariant of a dynamical system if no trajectory can escape from it. Of particular interest are safety assertions that describe states of the system which are deemed safe; it is clearly important to ensure that these sets are indeed invariant.

Hybrid systems combine discrete and continuous behavior and have found application in modelling a vast quantity of industrially relevant designs, many of which are safety-critical. In order to verify safety properties in hybrid models, one often requires the means of reasoning about safety in continuous systems. This paper focuses on developing and improving the automation of reasoning principles for a particular class of invariant assertions for continuous systems – conjunctions of polynomial equalities; these can be used, e.g. to assert the property that certain values (temperature, pressure, water level, etc.) in the system are maintained at a constant level as the system evolves.

In practice, it is highly desirable to have the means of deciding whether a given set is invariant in a particular dynamical system. It is equally important that such methods be efficient enough to be of practical utility. This paper seeks to address both of these issues. The contributions of this paper are twofold:

- It extends differential radical invariants [11] to obtain a characterization of invariance for algebraic sets under the flow of algebraic differential equations. It also introduces an optimized decision procedure to decide the invariance of algebraic sets.

* This material is based upon work supported by the National Science Foundation by NSF CAREER Award CNS-1054246, NSF EXPEDITION CNS-0926181, CNS-0931985, DARPA FA8750-12-2-0291 and EPSRC EP/I010335/1.

M. Müller-Olm and H. Seidl (Eds.): SAS 2014, LNCS 8723, pp. 151–167, 2014.

- It explores an approach combining deductively less powerful rules [15,27,17,25] using differential cuts [23] to exploit the structure of the system to yield efficient proofs even for non-polynomial systems. Furthermore, differential cuts [23] are shown to fundamentally improve the deductive power of Lie's criterion [15].

The two approaches to proving invariance of conjunctive equational assertions explored in this paper are complementary and aim at improving proof automation—deductive power and efficiency—in deductive formal verification tools. The detailed proofs of all presented results are available in [12].

Content. In Section 2, we recall some basic definitions and concepts. Section 3 introduces a new proof rule to check the invariance of a conjunction of polynomial equations along with an optimized implementation. Section 4 presents another novel approach to check invariance of a conjunction; it leverages efficient existing proof rules together with *differential cuts* and *differential weakening*. An automated proof strategy that builds on top of this idea is given in Section 5. The average performance of these different approaches is assessed using a set of 32 benchmarks (Section 6).

2 Preliminaries

Let $\boldsymbol{x} = (x_1, \dots, x_n) : \mathbb{R}^n$, and $\boldsymbol{x}(t) = (x_1(t), \dots, x_n(t))$, where $x_i : \mathbb{R} \to \mathbb{R}$, $t \mapsto x_i(t)$. The ring of polynomials over the reals will be denoted by $\mathbb{R}[x_1, \dots, x_n]$. We consider autonomous[1] differential equations described by polynomial vector fields.

Definition 1 (Polynomial Vector Field). *Let p_i, $1 \le i \le n$, be multivariate polynomials in the polynomial ring $\mathbb{R}[\boldsymbol{x}]$. A* polynomial vector field, $\boldsymbol{p}$, *is an explicit system of ordinary differential equations with polynomial right-hand side:*

$$\frac{dx_i}{dt} = \dot{x}_i = p_i(\boldsymbol{x}), \quad 1 \le i \le n \ . \tag{1}$$

One important problem is that of checking the invariance of a *variety* (or algebraic set), with evolution domain constraints H; that is, we ask whether a polynomial conjunction $h_1 = 0 \land \cdots \land h_r = 0$, initially true, holds true in all reachable states that satisfy the evolution domain constraints. The problem is equivalent to the validity of the following formula in differential dynamic logic [22]:

$$(h_1 = 0 \land \cdots \land h_r = 0) \to [\dot{\boldsymbol{x}} = \boldsymbol{p} \,\&\, H](h_1 = 0 \land \cdots \land h_r = 0) \tag{2}$$

where $[\dot{\boldsymbol{x}} = \boldsymbol{p} \,\&\, H]\psi$ is true in a state $\boldsymbol{x}_\iota$ if the postcondition ψ is true in all states reachable from $\boldsymbol{x}_\iota$—satisfying H—by following the differential equation $\dot{\boldsymbol{x}} = \boldsymbol{p}$ for any amount of time as long as H is not violated. For simplicity, for a polynomial h in $\boldsymbol{x}$, we write $h = 0$ for $h(\boldsymbol{x}) = 0$.

[1] Autonomous means that the rate of change of the system over time depends only on the system's state, not on time. Non-autonomous systems with time dependence can be made autonomous by adding a new state variable to account for the progress of time.

Geometrically, the dL formula in Eq. (2) is true if and only if the solution $\boldsymbol{x}(t)$ of the initial value problem ($\dot{\boldsymbol{x}} = \boldsymbol{p}$, $\boldsymbol{x}(0) = \boldsymbol{x}_\iota$), with $h_i(\boldsymbol{x}_\iota) = 0$ for $i = 1, \dots, r$, is a real root of the system $h_1 = 0, \dots, h_r = 0$ as long as it satisfies the constraints H.

The algebraic counterpart of varieties are ideals. Ideals are sets of polynomials that are closed under addition and external multiplication. That is, if I is an ideal, then for all $h_1, h_2 \in I$, the sum $h_1 + h_2 \in I$; and if $h \in I$, then, $qh \in I$, for all $q \in \mathbb{R}[x_1 \dots, x_n]$.

We will use ∇h to denote the gradient of a polynomial h, that is the vector of its partial derivatives $\left(\frac{\partial h}{\partial x_1}, \dots, \frac{\partial h}{\partial x_n}\right)$. The *Lie derivative* of a polynomial h along a vector field $\boldsymbol{p}$ is defined as follows (the symbol "$\cdot$" denotes the scalar product):

$$\mathfrak{L}_{\boldsymbol{p}}(h) \stackrel{\text{def}}{=} \nabla h \cdot \boldsymbol{p} = \sum_{i=1}^{n} \frac{\partial h}{\partial x_i} p_i \ . \tag{3}$$

Higher-order Lie derivatives are: $\mathfrak{L}_{\boldsymbol{p}}^{(k+1)}(h) = \mathfrak{L}_{\boldsymbol{p}}(\mathfrak{L}_{\boldsymbol{p}}^{(k)}(h))$, where $\mathfrak{L}_{\boldsymbol{p}}^{(0)}(h) = h$.

3 Characterizing Invariance of Conjunctive Equations

In this section we give an exact characterization of invariance for conjunctions of polynomial equalities under the flow of algebraic differential equations. The characterization, as well as the proof rule, generalize our previous work which handles purely equational invariants of the form $h = 0$ without considering evolution domains.

The differential radical invariants proof rule DRI [11, Theorem 2] has been shown to be a necessary and sufficient criterion for the invariance of equations of the form $h = 0$:

$$(\text{DRI})\frac{h = 0 \to \bigwedge_{i=0}^{N-1} \mathfrak{L}_{\boldsymbol{p}}^{(i)}(h) = 0}{h = 0 \to [\dot{\boldsymbol{x}} = \boldsymbol{p}]\, h = 0} \ . \tag{4}$$

The *order* $N \geq 1$ denotes the length of the chain of ideals $\langle h \rangle \subseteq \langle h, \mathfrak{L}_{\boldsymbol{p}}(h) \rangle \subseteq \cdots$ which reaches a fixed point after finitely many steps by the ascending chain property of Noetherian rings. Thus, the order N is always finite and computable—using Göbner Bases [4]—for polynomials with rational coefficients. The premise of the proof rule DRI is a real quantifier elimination problem and can be solved algorithmically [5].

A naïve approach to prove invariance of a conjunction $h_1 = 0 \wedge \cdots \wedge h_r = 0$, without evolution domain constraints, is to use the proof rule DRI together with the following sum-of-squares equivalence from real arithmetic:

$$h_1 = 0 \wedge \cdots \wedge h_r = 0 \equiv_{\mathbb{R}} \sum_{i=1}^{r} h_i^2 = 0 \ . \tag{5}$$

Sums-of-squares come at the price of doubling the polynomial degree, thereby increasing the complexity of checking the premise (Section 3.2 discusses the link between polynomial degree and the complexity of DRI-based proof rules). Instead, we present an extension of the proof rule DRI that exploits the underlying logical structure of conjunctions. For a conjunction of equations $h_1 = 0 \wedge \cdots \wedge h_r = 0$, the order N is generalized to the length of the chain of ideals formed by *all* the polynomials $h_1, \dots, h_r$ and their successive Lie derivatives:

$$I = \langle h_1, \dots, h_r \rangle \subseteq \langle h_1, \dots, h_r, \mathfrak{L}_{\boldsymbol{p}}(h_1), \dots, \mathfrak{L}_{\boldsymbol{p}}(h_r) \rangle \subseteq \langle h_1, \dots, \mathfrak{L}_{\boldsymbol{p}}^{(2)}(h_r) \rangle \cdots \tag{6}$$

Theorem 2 (Conjunctive Differential Radical Characterization). *Let $h_1, \ldots, h_r \in \mathbb{R}[\boldsymbol{x}]$ and let H denote some evolution domain constraint. Then, the conjunction $h_1 = 0 \wedge \cdots \wedge h_r = 0$, is invariant under the flow of the vector field $\boldsymbol{p}$, subject to the evolution constraint H, if and only if*

$$H \vdash \bigwedge_{j=1}^{r} h_j = 0 \rightarrow \bigwedge_{j=1}^{r} \bigwedge_{i=1}^{N-1} \mathfrak{L}_{\boldsymbol{p}}^{(i)}(h_j) = 0 \ . \tag{7}$$

where N denotes the order of the conjunction.

Here $\vdash$ is used, as in sequent calculus, to assert that whenever the constraint H (antecedent) is satisfied, then at least one (in this case, the only) formula to the right of $\vdash$ is also true. The proof is in the companion report [12]. When the evolution domain constraints are dropped ($H =$ True) and $r = 1$ (one equation), one recovers exactly the statement of [11, Theorem 2] which characterizes invariance of atomic equations. Intuitively, Theorem 2 says that on the invariant algebraic set, all higher-order Lie derivatives of each polynomial h_i must vanish. It adds however a crucial detail: checking finitely many—exactly N—higher-order Lie derivatives is both necessary and sufficient. The theorem does not check for invariance of each conjunct taken separately, rather it handles the conjunction simultaneously. The order N is a property of the ideal chain formed by *all* the polynomials and their Lie derivatives. If N_i denotes the order of each atom h_i taken separately, then one can readily see that

$$N \leq \max_i N_i \ . \tag{8}$$

The equality does not hold in general: consider for instance $h_1 = x_1$, $h_2 = x_2$ and $\boldsymbol{p} = (x_2, x_1)$. Since $\mathfrak{L}_{\boldsymbol{p}}^{(2)}(h_i) = h_i$, for $i = 1, 2$, we have $N_1 = N_2 = 2$. However,

$$\langle x_1, x_2 \rangle = \langle h_1, h_2 \rangle \subseteq \langle h_1, h_2, \mathfrak{L}_{\boldsymbol{p}}(h_1), \mathfrak{L}_{\boldsymbol{p}}(h_2) \rangle = \langle x_1, x_2, x_2, x_1 \rangle = \langle x_1, x_2 \rangle,$$

which means that $N = 1$. This example highlights one of the main differences between this work and the characterization given in [16, Theorem 24], where the criterion is given by

$$H \vdash \bigwedge_{j=1}^{r} h_j = 0 \rightarrow \bigwedge_{j=1}^{r} \bigwedge_{i=1}^{N_j-1} \mathfrak{L}_{\boldsymbol{p}}^{(i)}(h_j) = 0 \ . \tag{9}$$

The computation of *each* order N_j requires solving N_j ideal membership problems. One can appreciate the difference with the criterion of Theorem 2 which only requires N ideal membership checks for the entire conjunction. In the worst case, when $N = N_k = \max_i N_i$, Theorem 2 performs $\sum_{j=1, j\neq k}^{r} N_j$ fewer ideal membership checks compared to the criterion of Eq. (9). A smaller order N confers an additional benefit of reducing the cost of quantifier elimination—discussed in Section 3.2—by bringing down both the total number of polynomials and their maximum degree.

Remark 3. The order N in Theorem 2 can be reduced further at the prohibitive cost[2] of computing the real radicals of the ideals in Eq. (6). Ideally, one should also account for H when computing N. When H is an algebraic set, its generators should be appended to the ideal $\langle h_1, \dots, h_r \rangle$. We leave the semi-algebraic case for future work.

Using Theorem 2, the differential radical invariant proof rule DRI [11] generalizes to conjunctions of equations with evolution domain constraints as follows:

$$(\mathrm{DRI}_\wedge)\frac{H \vdash \left(\bigwedge_{j=1}^{r} h_j = 0\right) \rightarrow \bigwedge_{j=1}^{r} \bigwedge_{i=1}^{N-1} \mathfrak{L}_{\boldsymbol{p}}^{(i)}(h_j) = 0}{\left(\bigwedge_{j=1}^{r} h_j = 0\right) \rightarrow [\dot{\boldsymbol{x}} = \boldsymbol{p} \,\&\, H] \left(\bigwedge_{j=1}^{r} h_j = 0\right)} \,. \tag{10}$$

Next, we implement the proof rule $\mathrm{DRI}_\wedge$ and discuss its theoretical complexity.

3.1 Decision Procedure

To check the validity of the premise in the proof rule $\mathrm{DRI}_\wedge$, one needs to compute the order N and to decide a purely universally quantified sentence in the theory of real arithmetic. These two tasks do not have to be performed in that precise order. We present an algorithm that computes N on the fly while breaking down the quantifier elimination problem into simpler sub-problems.

Algorithm 1 implements the proof rule $\mathrm{DRI}_\wedge$. The algorithm returns True if and only if the candidate is an invariant. The variable $\check{N}$ strictly increases and converges, from below, toward the finite unknown order N. It is therefore a decision procedure for the invariance problem with conjunctive equational candidates.

At each iteration of the **while** loop it checks whether a fixed point of the chain of ideals has been reached, implying $\check{N} = N$. To this end, it computes a Gröbner basis (`GB`) of the ideal `I` (line 2), containing the polynomials h_i as well as their respective higher-order Lie derivatives up to the derivation order $\check{N} - 1$. Then it enters a **foreach** loop (line 8), where it computes the $\check{N}$th order Lie derivatives and their respective reductions (or remainders) (`LieD`) by the Gröbner basis `GB`. All Lie derivatives with non-zero remainders are stored in the list `LD` (line 12). If the list is empty, then all $\check{N}$th Lie derivatives are in the ideal `I`: the fixed point of the chain of ideals is reached, and $\check{N} = N$. This also means that True can be returned since all prior quantifier elimination calls returned True. Otherwise, the outermost **while** loop (line 5) needs to be executed one more time after increasing $\check{N}$ (line 20). Before re-executing the **while** loop, however, we make sure that the premise of the proof rule $\mathrm{DRI}_\wedge$ holds up to $\check{N}$. Since in this case, we know that $\check{N} < N$, if the quantifier elimination fails to discharge the premise of the proof rule $\mathrm{DRI}_\wedge$ at $\check{N}$, then we do not need to go any further as the invariance property is already falsified.

The **while** loop decomposes the right hand side of the implication in Eq. (10) along the conjunction $\bigwedge_{i=1}^{N-1}$: the ith iteration checks whether the conjunction $\bigwedge_{j=1}^{r} \mathfrak{L}_{\boldsymbol{p}}^{(i)} h_j$ vanishes. The main purpose of the **foreach** loop in line 16 is to decompose further the

[2] The upper bound on the degrees of the generators of the real radical of an ideal I is $d^{2^{O(n^2)}}$ [20], where d is the maximum degree of the generators of I.

Algorithm 1. Checking invariance of a conjunction of polynomial equations.

Data: H (evolution domain constraints), $\boldsymbol{p}$ (vector field), $\boldsymbol{x}$ (state variables)
Data: $h_1, \ldots, h_r$ (conjunction candidate)
Result: True if and only if $h_1 = 0 \wedge \ldots \wedge h_r = 0$ is an invariant of $[\dot{\boldsymbol{x}} = \boldsymbol{p} \,\&\, H]$

1 $\check{N} \leftarrow 1$
2 `I` $\leftarrow \{h_1, \ldots, h_r\}$ `// Elements of the chain of ideals`
3 `L` $\leftarrow \{h_1, \ldots, h_r\}$ `// Work list of polynomial to derive`
4 `symbs` $\leftarrow$ Variables[$\boldsymbol{p}, h_1, \ldots, h_r$]
5 **while** True **do**
6   `GB` $\leftarrow$ GröbnerBasis[`I`, $\boldsymbol{x}$]
7   `LD` $\leftarrow \{\}$ `// Work list of Lie derivatives not in I`
8   **foreach** ℓ in `L` **do**
9   `LieD` $\leftarrow$ LieDerivative[$\ell, \boldsymbol{p}, \boldsymbol{x}$]
10   `Rem` $\leftarrow$ PolynomialRemainder[`LieD`, `GB`, $\boldsymbol{x}$]
11   **if** `Rem` $\neq 0$ **then**
12   `LD` $\leftarrow$ `LD` $\cup$ `LieD`
13   **if** `LD` $= \{\}$ **then**
14   **return** True
15   **else**
16   **foreach** ℓ in `LD` **do**
17   **if** QE[$\forall$ `symbs` $(H \wedge h_1 = 0 \wedge \cdots \wedge h_r = 0 \rightarrow \ell = 0)$] $\neq$ True **then**
18   **return** False
19   `I` $\leftarrow$ `GB` $\cup$ `LD`
20         $\check{N} \leftarrow \check{N} + 1$
21   `L` $\leftarrow$ `LD`

conjunction $\bigwedge_{j=1}^{r}$ using the logical equivalence $a \rightarrow (b \wedge c) \equiv (a \rightarrow b) \wedge (a \rightarrow c)$ for any boolean variables a, b, and c. This leads to more tractable problems of the form:

$$H \vdash \bigwedge_{j=1}^{r} h_j = 0 \rightarrow \mathfrak{L}_{\boldsymbol{p}}^{(i)}(h_j) = 0 \ . \tag{11}$$

Observe that the quantifier elimination problem in line 17 performs a universal closure for all involved symbols—state variables and parameters— denoted by `symbs` and determined once at the beginning of the algorithm using the procedure `Variables` (line 4). Besides, the quantifier elimination problem in line 17 can be readily adapted to explicitly return extra conditions on the parameters to ensure invariance of the given conjunction. When the algorithm returns False, any counterexample to the quantifier elimination problem of line 17 can be used as an initial condition for a concrete counterexample that falsifies the invariant.

3.2 Complexity

Algorithm 1 relies on two expensive procedures: deciding purely universally quantified sentences in the theory of real arithmetic (line 17) and ideal membership of multivariate polynomials using Gröbner bases (line 6). We discuss their respective complexity.

Quantifier elimination over the reals is decidable [29]. The purely existential fragment of the theory of real arithmetic has been shown to exhibit singly exponential time complexity in the number of variables [1]. Theoretically, the best bound on the complexity of deciding a sentence in the existential theory of $\mathbb{R}$ is given by $(sd)^{O(n)}$, where s is the number of polynomials in the formula, d their maximum degree and n the number of variables [1]. However, in practice this has not yet led to an efficient decision procedure, so typically it is much more efficient to use partial cylindrical algebraic decomposition (PCAD) due to Collins & Hong [5], which has running time complexity doubly-exponential in the number of variables.

Ideal membership of multivariate polynomials with rational coefficients is complete for `EXPSPACE` [18]. Gröbner bases [4] allow membership checks in ideals generated by multivariate polynomials. Significant advances have been made for computing Gröbner bases [9,10] which in practice can be expected to perform very well. The degree of the polynomials involved in a Gröbner basis computation can be very large. Theoretically, a Gröbner basis may contain polynomials with degree 2^{2^d} [19]. The degrees of all the polynomials involved are bounded by $O(d^{2^n})$ [8]. Gröbner bases are also highly sensitive to the monomial order arranging the different monomials of a multivariate polynomial (see, e.g., [6, Chapter 2] for formal definitions). The Degree Reverse Lexicographic (`degrevlex`) order gives (on average) Gröbner bases with the smallest total degree [2], although there exist known examples (cf. Mora's example in [14]) for which, even for the `degrevlex` monomial ordering, the (reduced) Gröbner basis contains a polynomial of total degree $O(d^2)$. Finally, the rational coefficients of the generators of Gröbner bases may become involved (compared to the rational coefficients of the original generators of the ideal), which can have a negative impact on the running time and memory requirements.

3.3 Optimization

The theoretical complexity of both the quantifier elimination and Gröbner bases algorithms suggests several opportunities for optimization for Algorithm 1. The maximal degree of the polynomials appearing in H is assumed to be fixed. We can reduce the polynomial degrees in the right-hand side of the implication in Eq. (11) as follows: by choosing a total degree monomial ordering (e.g. `degrevlex`), the remainder `Rem` has at most the same total degree as `LieD`; replacing `LieD` by `Rem` serves to reduce (on average) the cost of calling a quantifier elimination procedure. Lem. 4 proves that substituting `LieD` by its remainder `Rem` in line 17 does not compromise correctness.

Lemma 4. *Let q be the remainder of the reduction of the polynomial s by the Gröbner basis of the ideal generated by the polynomials $h_1, \ldots, h_r$. Then,*

$$h_1 = 0 \wedge \cdots \wedge h_r = 0 \rightarrow s = 0 \textit{ if and only if } h_1 = 0 \wedge \cdots \wedge h_r = 0 \rightarrow q = 0 \, .$$

The same substitution reduces the Gröbner basis computation cost since it attempts to keep a low maximal degree in all the polynomials appearing in the generators of the ideal `I`. Lem. 5 shows that it is safe to perform this substitution: the ideal `I` remains unchanged regardless of whether we choose to construct the list `LD` using `LieD` or `Rem`.

Lemma 5. *Let q be the remainder of the reduction of the polynomial s by the Gröbner basis of the ideal generated by the polynomials $h_1, \ldots, h_r$. Then,*

$$\langle h_1, \ldots, h_r, s \rangle = \langle h_1, \ldots, h_r, q \rangle \ .$$

Although this optimization reduces the total degree of the polynomials involved, the coefficients of the remainder q may get more involved than the coefficients of the original polynomial s. In [12], we give an example featuring the Motzkin polynomial where such problem occurs. In Section 6 we give an empirical comparison of the optimized—as detailed in this section—versus the unoptimized version of Algorithm 1.

4 Sufficient Conditions for Invariance of Equations

The previous section dealt with a method for proving invariance which is both necessary and sufficient for conjunctions of polynomial equalities. Given the proof rule $\text{DRI}_\wedge$, it is natural to ask whether previously proposed *sufficient* proof rules are still relevant. After all, theoretically, $\text{DRI}_\wedge$ is all that is required for producing proofs of invariance in this class of problems. This is a perfectly legitimate question; however, given the complexity of the underlying decision procedures needed for $\text{DRI}_\wedge$ it is perhaps not surprising that one will eventually face scalability issues. This, in turn, motivates a different question - can one use proof rules (which are perhaps deductively weaker than $\text{DRI}_\wedge$) in such a way as to attain more computationally efficient proofs of invariance?

Before addressing this question, this section will review existing sufficient proof rules which allow reasoning about invariance of atomic equational assertions. In Fig. 1, $\text{DI}_=$ shows the equational differential invariant [23] proof rule. The condition is sufficient (but not necessary) and characterizes polynomial invariant functions [23,25]. The premise of the Polynomial-consecution rule [27,17], P-c in Fig. 1, requires $\mathfrak{L}_{\boldsymbol{p}}(h)$ to be in the ideal generated by h. This condition is also only sufficient and was mentioned as early as 1878 [7]. The Lie proof rule gives Lie's criterion [15,21,25] for invariance of $h = 0$ and characterizes *smooth* invariant manifolds. The rule DW is called *differential weakening* [24] and covers the trivial case when the evolution constraint implies the invariant candidate; in contrast to all other rules in the table, DW can work with arbitrary invariant assertions.

Unlike the necessary and sufficient condition provided by the rule DRI (see Eq. (4)), all the other proof rules in Figure 1 only impose sufficient conditions and may thus fail at a proof even in cases when the candidate is indeed an invariant.

The purpose of all the rules shown in Figure 1, save perhaps DW, is to show invariance of atomic equations. However, in general, one faces the problem $F \to [\dot{\boldsymbol{x}} = \boldsymbol{p} \ \& \ H]C$, where F is a formula defining a set of states where the system is initialized, and C is the post-condition where the system always enters after following the differential equation $\dot{\boldsymbol{x}} = \boldsymbol{p}$ as long as the domain constraint H is satisfied.

$$(\mathrm{DI}_=)\,\frac{H \vdash \mathfrak{L}_{\boldsymbol{p}}(h) = 0}{(h = 0) \to [\dot{\boldsymbol{x}} = \boldsymbol{p}\,\&\, H](h = 0)} \qquad (\text{P-c})\,\frac{H \vdash \mathfrak{L}_{\boldsymbol{p}}(h) \in \langle h \rangle}{(h = 0) \to [\dot{\boldsymbol{x}} = \boldsymbol{p}\,\&\, H](h = 0)}$$

$$(\text{Lie})\,\frac{H \vdash h = 0 \to (\mathfrak{L}_{\boldsymbol{p}}(h) = 0 \land \nabla h \neq \mathbf{0})}{(h = 0) \to [\dot{\boldsymbol{x}} = \boldsymbol{p}\,\&\, H](h = 0)} \qquad (\text{DW})\,\frac{H \vdash F}{F \to [\dot{\boldsymbol{x}} = \boldsymbol{p}\,\&H\,]F}$$

Fig. 1. Proof rules for checking the invariance of $h = 0$ w.r.t. the vector field $\boldsymbol{p}$: $\mathrm{DI}_=$ [25, Theorem 3], P-c [27, Lemma 2], Lie [21, Theorem 2.8], DW [24, Lemma 3.6]

One way to prove such a statement is to find an invariant I which is true initially (i.e. $F \to I$), is indeed an invariant for the system ($I \to [\dot{\boldsymbol{x}} = \boldsymbol{p}\,\&\, H]I$), and implies the post-condition ($I \to C$). These conditions can be formalized in the proof rule [26]

$$(\text{Inv})\,\frac{F \to I \qquad I \to [\dot{\boldsymbol{x}} = \boldsymbol{p}\,\&H\,]I \qquad I \to C}{F \to [\dot{\boldsymbol{x}} = \boldsymbol{p}\,\&H\,]C}.$$

In this paper we consider the special case when the invariant is the same as the post-condition, so we can drop the last clause and the rule becomes

$$(\text{Inv})\,\frac{F \to C \qquad C \to [\dot{\boldsymbol{x}} = \boldsymbol{p}\,\&H\,]C}{F \to [\dot{\boldsymbol{x}} = \boldsymbol{p}\,\&H\,]C}.$$

In the following sections, we will be working in a proof calculus, rather than considering a single proof rule, and will call upon this definition in the proofs we construct.

5 Differential Cuts and Lie's Rule

When considering a conjunctive invariant candidate $h_1 = 0 \land h_2 = 0 \land \cdots \land h_r = 0$, it may be the case that each conjunct considered separately is an invariant for the system. Then, one could simply invoke the following basic result about invariant sets to prove invariance of each atomic formula individually.

Proposition 6. *Let $S_1, S_2 \subseteq \mathbb{R}^n$ be invariant sets for the differential equation $\dot{\boldsymbol{x}} = \boldsymbol{p}$, then the set $S_1 \cap S_2$ is also an invariant.*

Corollary 7. *The proof rule*

$$(\land_{\text{Inv}})\,\frac{h_1 = 0 \to [\dot{\boldsymbol{x}} = \boldsymbol{p}\,\&H\,]h_1 = 0 \qquad h_2 = 0 \to [\dot{\boldsymbol{x}} = \boldsymbol{p}\,\&H\,]h_2 = 0}{h_1 = 0 \land h_2 = 0 \to [\dot{\boldsymbol{x}} = \boldsymbol{p}\,\&H\,](h_1 = 0 \land h_2 = 0)} \quad (12)$$

is sound and may be generalized to accommodate arbitrarily many conjuncts.

Of course, one still needs to choose an appropriate proof rule from Figure 1 (or DRI) in order to prove invariance of atomic equational formulas. For purely polynomial problems it would be natural to attempt a proof using DRI first, but in the presence of transcendental functions, one may need to resort to other rules. In general however, even if the conjunction defines an invariant set, the individual conjuncts need *not* themselves be

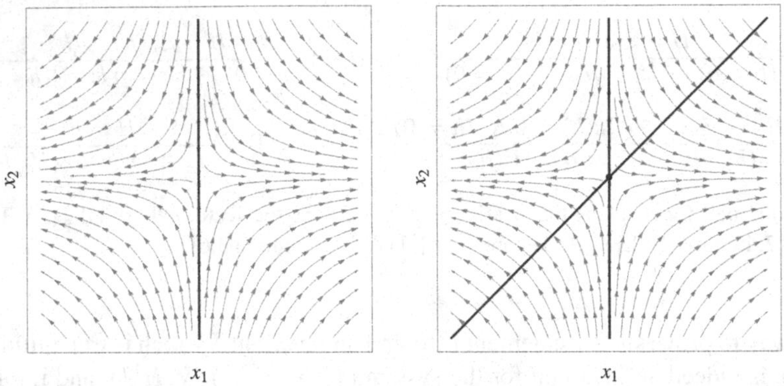

Fig. 2. System invariant $x_1 = 0$ (**left**) used in a differential cut to show that the intersection at the origin (**right**) is an invariant

invariants. If such is the case, one cannot simply break down the conjunctive assertion using the rule $\wedge_{\text{Inv}}$ and prove invariance of each conjunct individually. In this section, we explore using a proof rule called *differential cut* (DC) to address this issue.

Differential cuts were introduced as a fundamental proof principle for differential equations [23] and can be used to (soundly) strengthen assumptions about the system evolution.

Proposition 8 (Differential Cut [23]). *The proof rule*

$$\text{(DC)}\frac{F \to [\dot{\boldsymbol{x}} = \boldsymbol{p}]C \qquad\qquad F \to [\dot{\boldsymbol{x}} = \boldsymbol{p} \,\&\, C]F}{F \to [\dot{\boldsymbol{x}} = \boldsymbol{p}]F},$$

where C and F denote quantifier-free first-order formulas, is sound.

Remark 9. The rule $\wedge_{\text{Inv}}$ may in fact be derived from DW, Inv, and DC.

One may appreciate the geometric intuition behind the rule DC if one realizes that the left branch requires one to show that the set of states satisfying C is an invariant for the system initialized in any state satisfying F. Thus, the system does not admit any trajectories starting in F that leave C and hence by adding C to the evolution constraint, one does not restrict the behavior of the original system.

Differential cuts may be applied repeatedly to the effect of refining the evolution constraint with more invariant sets. It may be profitable to think of successive differential cuts as showing an *embedding of invariants* in a system.

There is an interesting connection between differential cuts and embeddings of invariant sub-manifolds, when used with the proof rule Lie. To develop this idea, let us remark that if one succeeds at proving invariance of some $h_1 = 0$ using the rule Lie in a system with no evolution constraint, one shows that $h_1 = 0$ is a smooth invariant sub-manifold of $\mathbb{R}^n$. If one now considers the system evolving inside that invariant manifold and finds some $h_2 = 0$ which can be proved to be invariant using Lie with $h_1 = 0$ acting as an evolution constraint, then inside the manifold $h_1 = 0$, $h_2 = 0$ defines an invariant sub-manifold (even in cases when $h_2 = 0$ might not define a sub-manifold of the ambient space $\mathbb{R}^n$). One can proceed using Lie in this way to look for further embedded invariant sub-manifolds. We will illustrate this idea using a basic example.

Example 10 (Differential cut with Lie*).* Let the system dynamics be $\boldsymbol{p} = (x_1, -x_2)$. This system has an equilibrium at the origin, i.e. $\boldsymbol{p}(\boldsymbol{0}) = \boldsymbol{0}$. Consider an invariant candidate $x_1 = 0 \land x_1 - x_2 = 0$. One cannot use Lie directly to prove the goal

$$x_1 = 0 \land x_1 - x_2 = 0 \rightarrow [\dot{\boldsymbol{x}} = \boldsymbol{p}]\ (x_1 = 0 \land x_1 - x_2 = 0).$$

Instead, DC can be used to cut by $x_1 = 0$, which is an invariant for this system provable using Lie. The left branch of DC is proved as follows:

$$\dfrac{(\mathbb{R})\dfrac{*}{x_1 = 0 \land x_1 - x_2 = 0 \rightarrow x_1 = 0} \qquad (\text{Lie})\dfrac{(\mathbb{R})\dfrac{*}{x_1 = 0 \rightarrow x_1 = 0 \land (1 \neq 0)}}{x_1 = 0 \rightarrow [\dot{\boldsymbol{x}} = \boldsymbol{p}]\ x_1 = 0}}{x_1 = 0 \land x_1 - x_2 = 0 \rightarrow [\dot{\boldsymbol{x}} = \boldsymbol{p}\ \&\ x_1 = 0]\ x_1 = 0}\ (\text{Inv})$$

One can also prove that $x_1 = x_2$ is a invariant under the evolution constraint $x_1 = 0$:

$$\dfrac{(\text{DW})\dfrac{*}{x_1 = 0 \rightarrow [\dot{\boldsymbol{x}} = \boldsymbol{p}\ \&\ x_1 = 0]\ x_1 = 0} \qquad (\text{Lie})\dfrac{(\mathbb{R})\dfrac{*}{x_1 = 0 \vdash x_1 - x_2 = 0 \rightarrow x_1 + x_2 = 0 \land (1 \neq 0 \lor -1 \neq 0)}}{x_1 - x_2 = 0 \rightarrow [\dot{\boldsymbol{x}} = \boldsymbol{p}\ \&\ x_1 = 0]\ x_1 - x_2 = 0}}{x_1 = 0 \land x_1 - x_2 = 0 \rightarrow [\dot{\boldsymbol{x}} = \boldsymbol{p}\ \&\ x_1 = 0]\ (x_1 = 0 \land x_1 - x_2 = 0)}\ (\land_{\text{Inv}})$$

Using these two sub-proofs to close the appropriate branches, the rule DC proves

$$x_1 = 0 \land x_1 - x_2 = 0 \rightarrow [\dot{\boldsymbol{x}} = \boldsymbol{p}]\ (x_1 = 0 \land x_1 - x_2 = 0).$$

While this example is very simplistic, it provides a good illustration of the method behind differential cuts. We used DC to restrict system evolution to an invariant manifold $x_1 = 0$ using Lie and then used Lie again to show that $x_1 - x_2 = 0$ defines an invariant sub-manifold inside $x_1 = 0$. This is illustrated in Fig. 2.

It is also worth noting that the choice of conjunct for use in the differential cut was crucial. Had we initially picked $x_1 - x_2 = 0$ to act as C in DC, the proof attempt would have failed, since this does not define an invariant sub-manifold of $\mathbb{R}^2$ (see Fig. 2).

Let us now remark that by employing DC, we proved invariance of a conjunction which could not be described by an atomic equational assertion which is provable using the rule Lie, or by using Lie to prove invariance of each conjunct after breaking down the conjunction with the rule $\land_{\text{Inv}}$. It has previously been shown that differential cuts increase the deductive power of the system when used in concert with differential invariants [23,26,25]. We prove that the same is true for differential cuts with Lie. Indeed, differential cuts serve to address some of the limitations inherent in both $\text{DI}_=$ and Lie.

Theorem 11. *The deductive power of* Lie *together with* DC *is strictly greater than that of* Lie *considered separately. We write this as* $\text{DC} + \text{Lie} \succ \text{Lie}$.

Proof. In Example 10 we demonstrate the use of Lie together with DC to prove invariance of a conjunction of polynomial equalities which is *not* provable using Lie alone. To see this, suppose that for the system in Example 10 there exists some real-valued differentiable function $g(\boldsymbol{x})$ whose zero level set is precisely the origin, i.e. $(g(\boldsymbol{x}) = 0) \equiv (\boldsymbol{x} = \boldsymbol{0})$. Then, for all $\boldsymbol{x} \in \mathbb{R}^2 \setminus \{\boldsymbol{0}\}$ this function evaluates to $g(\boldsymbol{x}) > 0$ or $g(\boldsymbol{x}) < 0$ (by continuity of $g(\boldsymbol{x})$) and $\boldsymbol{0}$ is thus the global minimum or global maximum, respectively. In either case, $g(\boldsymbol{x}) = 0 \implies \nabla g(\boldsymbol{x}) = \boldsymbol{0}$ is valid, which cannot satisfy the premise of Lie. □

Similar to the embedding of invariants observed when combining differential cuts with Lie proof rule, we briefly explore an intriguing connection between the use of differential cuts together with DI$_=$ and *higher integrals* of dynamical systems.

The premise of the rule DI$_=$ establishes that $h(\boldsymbol{x})$ is a *first integral* (i.e. a constant of motion) for the system in order to conclude that $h = 0$ is an invariant. More general notions of invariance have been introduced to study integrability of dynamical systems. For instance, $h(\boldsymbol{x})$ is a *second integral* if $\mathfrak{L}_{\boldsymbol{p}}(h) = \alpha h$, where α is some function; this is also sufficient to conclude that $h = 0$ is an invariant. Let us remark that in a purely polynomial setting, such an $h \in \mathbb{R}[\boldsymbol{x}]$ is known as a *Darboux polynomial* [13,7] and the condition corresponds to ideal membership in the premise of P-c. Going further, a *third integral* is a function $h(\boldsymbol{x})$ that remains constant on some level set of a first integral $g(\boldsymbol{x})$ [13, Section 2.6], i.e. $\mathfrak{L}_{\boldsymbol{p}}(h) = \alpha g$ where g is a first integral and α is some function. These ideas generalize to higher integrals (see [13, Section 2.7]).

Example 12 (Deconstructed aircraft [25] - differential cut with DI$_=$*).* Consider the system $\dot{\boldsymbol{x}} = \boldsymbol{p} = (-x_2, x_3, -x_2)$ and consider the invariant candidate $x_1^2 + x_2^2 = 1 \land x_3 = x_1$. One cannot use DI$_=$ directly to prove the goal

$$x_1^2 + x_2^2 = 1 \land x_3 = x_1 \to [\dot{\boldsymbol{x}} = \boldsymbol{p}]\,(x_1^2 + x_2^2 = 1 \land x_3 = x_1)\,.$$

We can apply DC to cut by $x_1 = x_3$, which is a first integral for the system and is thus provable using DI$_=$. The left branch of DC is proved as follows:

$$(\text{Inv})\,\dfrac{(\mathbb{R})\,\dfrac{*}{x_1^2 + x_2^2 = 1 \land x_3 = x_1 \to x_3 = x_1} \qquad (\text{DI}_=)\,\dfrac{(\mathbb{R})\,\dfrac{*}{-x_2 = -x_2}}{x_3 = x_1 \to [\dot{\boldsymbol{x}} = \boldsymbol{p}]x_3 = x_1}}{x_1^2 + x_2^2 = 1 \land x_3 = x_1 \to [\dot{\boldsymbol{x}} = \boldsymbol{p}]x_3 = x_1}$$

For the right branch of DC we need to show that $x_1^2 + x_2^2 = 1$ is an invariant under the evolution constraint $x_3 = x_1$. This is again provable using DI$_=$:

$$(\land\text{Inv})\,\dfrac{(\text{DW})\,\dfrac{*}{x_3 = x_1 \to [\dot{\boldsymbol{x}} = \boldsymbol{p} \,\&\, x_3 = x_1]\,x_3 = x_1} \qquad (\text{DI}_=)\,\dfrac{(\mathbb{R})\,\dfrac{*}{x_3 = x_1 \vdash -2x_1x_2 + 2x_2x_3 = 0}}{x_1^2 + x_2^2 = 1 \to [\dot{\boldsymbol{x}} = \boldsymbol{p} \,\&\, x_3 = x_1]\,x_1^2 + x_2^2 = 1}}{x_1^2 + x_2^2 = 1 \land x_3 = x_1 \to [\dot{\boldsymbol{x}} = \boldsymbol{p} \,\&\, x_3 = x_1]\,(x_1^2 + x_2^2 = 1 \land x_3 = x_1)}$$

We can now construct a proof of invariance for the conjunction using DC.

Note that in this example, we have only ever had to resort to the rule DI$_=$ for showing invariance of an equational candidate. We first showed that $x_3 - x_1$ is an invariant function (first integral) for the system. After restricting the evolution domain to the zero set of the first integral, $x_3 - x_1 = 0$, we proved that the polynomial $x_1^2 + x_2^2 - 1$ is conserved in the constrained system. In this example we have $\mathfrak{L}_{\boldsymbol{p}}(x_1^2 + x_2^2 - 1) =$

$-2x_1x_2 + 2x_2x_3 = 2x_2(x_3 - x_1)$, where $(x_3 - x_1)$ is a first integral of the system. Thus, $x_1^2 + x_2^2 - 1$ is in fact a (polynomial) third integral.

5.1 Proof Strategies using Differential Cuts

Differential cuts can be used to search for a proof of invariance of conjunctive equational assertions. This involves selecting some conjunct $h_i = 0$ to cut by (that is use it as C in DC). If the conjunct is indeed an invariant, it will be possible to strengthen the evolution domain constraint and proceed in a similar fashion by selecting a new C from the remaining conjuncts until a proof is attained. A formal proof of invariance using differential cuts can be quite long and will repeatedly resort to proof rules such as $(\wedge_{\text{Inv}})$ (Eq. (12)) and DW (Fig. 1), which is used to prune away conjuncts that have already been added to the evolution domain constraint.

Our proof strategy iteratively selects a conjunct with which to attempt a differential cut as a recursive function (DCSearch, elaborated in [12]). Before calling this function, the conjuncts are put into ascending order with respect to the number of variables appearing in the conjunct. For purely polynomial problems, the ordering is also ascending with respect to the total degree of the polynomials. The aim of this pre-processing step is to ensure that conjuncts which are potentially less expensive to check for invariance are processed first (see Section 3.2). There is in general no easy way of selecting the "right" proof rule for showing invariance of atomic equations; a possible, albeit not very efficient, solution would be to iterate through all the available proof rules. This would combine their deductive power, but could also lead do diminished performance. In practice, selecting a good proof rule for atomic invariants is very much a problem-specific matter. We have implemented DCSearch to use the proof rule $\text{DI}_=$ before trying Lie.

5.2 Performance and Limitations

Unlike with purely automated methods, such as $\text{DRI}_\wedge$, knowledge about the system is often crucial for differential cuts to be effective; however, this knowledge can sometimes be used to construct proofs that are more computationally efficient. We have identified an example—detailed in [12]—with 13 state variables which defeats the current implementation of $\text{DRI}_\wedge$ and which is easily provable using differential cuts together with both $\text{DI}_=$ and Lie (solved quickly by running DCSearch). Though very much an artificial problem, it demonstrates that structure in the problem can sometimes be exploited to yield efficient proofs using DC. This is especially useful for large systems with many variables where the structure of the problem is well-understood. Additionally, we see that a combination of proof rules ($\text{DI}_=$, Lie, DC) can be both helpful and efficient.

While differential cuts can serve to increase the deductive power of sufficient proof rules, there are invariant conjunctions of equalities for which applying DC on the conjuncts given in the problem will altogether fail to be fruitful. This is due to DCSearch relying on the fact that at least some of the conjuncts considered individually are invariants for the system, which may not be the case even if the conjunction is invariant.

6 Experiments

In this section, we empirically compare the performance of three families of proof rules for checking the invariance of conjunctions: (1) DRI-related proof rules including SoSDRI (DRI plus sum-of-squares rewriting), $\text{DRI}_\wedge$ as well as their optimized versions as detailed in Section 3.3, (2) DCSearch: the differential cut proof search presented in Section 5.1, and (3) the Liu et al. procedure [16] applied to a conjunction of equalities.

We do not consider domain constraints, i.e. $H = \text{True}$. The running time for each proof rule as well as the dimension, the different degrees of the candidates and the vector fields, of the used set of benchmarks can be found in the companion report [12]. In Fig. 3, the pair (k, t) in the plot of a proof rule P reads: the proof rule P solved k problems each in less than t seconds. The set of benchmarks contains 32 entries composed of equilibria (16), singularities (8), higher integrals (4) and abstract examples (4). The examples we used in our benchmarks originate from a number of sources - many of them come from textbooks on Dynamical Systems; others have been hand-crafted to exploit sweetspots of certain proof rules. For instance, we constructed Hamiltonian systems, systems with equilibria and systems with smooth invariants of various polynomial degrees. The most involved example has 13 state variables, a vector field with a maximum total degree of 291 and an invariant candidate with total degree of 146. It should be noted that these benchmarks are not necessarily representative, but nevertheless, an important first step towards a more comprehensive empirical analysis we hope to pursue.

One can clearly see that for the considered set of examples, the proof rule $\text{DRI}_\wedge$ is much more efficient on average compared to SoSDRI as it solves 31—out of 32—in less than 0.1s each. The optimization discussed in Section 3.3 yields a slight improvement in the performance of both SoSDRI and $\text{DRI}_\wedge$. Notice that its benefit is clearer in SoSDRI as the involved polynomials have large degrees. In most examples, both $\text{DRI}_\wedge$

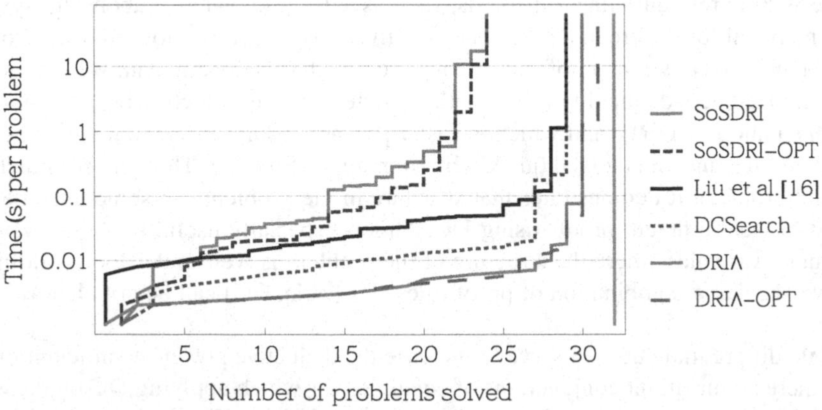

Fig. 3. Empirical performance comparison of different proof rules and strategies. The total number of problems solved each in at most ts (log scale) is given in the x-axis for each method.

and $\mathrm{DRI}_\wedge$-OPT are very efficient. However, the optimized version was able to falsify, in 1.2s, an invariant whereas the unoptimized version, as well as all the other proof rules, timed out after 60s. We also noticed for another example—featuring the Motzkin polynomial—that SoSDRI-OPT timed out whereas SoSDRI was able to check the invariance in 15s. When we investigated this example, it turned out that the rational coefficients of the remainder gets complicated compared to the original polynomial before reduction. For this particular example, the optimized version was able to prove the invariance in 300s which is 20 times slower than the unoptimized version. For a third example, all DRI-related proof rules timed out after 60s in one example which was discharged by DCSearch in less than 6s. (cf. [12] for more details about those different examples).

7 Related Work

In this paper we focus on *checking* invariance of algebraic sets under the flow of polynomial vector fields. For similar techniques used to automatically *generate* invariant algebraic sets we refer the reader to the discussion in [11].

Nagumo's Theorem [3], proved by Mitio Nagumo in 1942, characterizes invariant closed sets—a superset of algebraic sets—of locally Lipschitz-continuous vector fields—a superset of polynomial vector fields. The geometric criterion of the theorem is however intractable. The analyticity of solutions of analytic vector fields—a superset of polynomial vector fields—also gives a powerful, yet intractable, criterion to reason about invariant sets. In [28], the authors attempted to define several special cases exploiting either Nagumo's theorem or the analyticity of solutions, to give proof rules for checking invariance of (closed) semi-algebraic sets under the flow of polynomial vector fields. Liu et al. in [16] also used analyticity of solutions to polynomial ordinary differential equations and extended [28] using the ascending chain condition in Noetherian rings to ensure termination of their procedure; they gave a necessary and sufficient condition for invariance of arbitrary semi-algebraic sets under the flow of polynomial vector fields and proved the resulting conditions to be decidable.

We develop a purely algebraic approach where the ascending chain condition is also used but without resorting to local Taylor series expansions. As in [16], we require finitely many higher-order Lie derivatives to vanish; what is different, however, is the definition of the finite number each characterization requires: in [16], one is required to compute orders N_i of *each* atom h_i and to prove that all higher-order Lie derivatives of h_i, up to order $N_i - 1$, vanish. We state a weaker condition as we only require that all higher-order Lie derivatives of h_i up to order $(N-1)$, for all i, vanish. A straightforward benefit of our characterization is the immediate reduction of the computational complexity as discussed in Section 3 and shown empirically in Section 6.

Zerz and Walcher [30] have previously considered the problem of deciding invariance of algebraic sets in polynomial vector fields; they gave a sufficient condition for checking invariance of algebraic sets which can be seen as one iteration of Algorithm 1. Therefore, Section 3 generalizes their work by providing a complete characterization of invariant algebraic sets in polynomial vector fields.

8 Conclusion

We have introduced an efficient decision procedure ($\text{DRI}_\wedge$) for deciding invariance of conjunctive equational assertions for polynomial dynamical systems. We have explored the use of the differential cut rule both as a means of increasing the deductive power of existing sufficient proof rules and also as a way of constructing more computationally efficient proofs of invariance.

The empirical performance we observe in the optimized implementations of DRI and $\text{DRI}_\wedge$ is very encouraging and we are confident that a proof strategy in a deductive formal verification system should give precedence to these methods. However, certain problems fall out of scope of these rules. For instance, when the problems involve transcendental functions, or still take unreasonably long time to prove. We leave these interesting questions for future work.

References

1. Basu, S., Pollack, R., Roy, M.F.: On the combinatorial and algebraic complexity of quantifier elimination. J. ACM 43(6), 1002–1045 (1996)
2. Bayer, D., Stillman, M.E.: A criterion for detecting m-regularity. Inventiones Mathematicae 87, 1 (1987)
3. Blanchini, F.: Set invariance in control. Automatica 35(11), 1747–1767 (1999)
4. Buchberger, B.: Gröbner-Bases: An Algorithmic Method in Polynomial Ideal Theory, ch. 6, pp. 184–232. Reidel Publishing Company, Dodrecht (1985)
5. Collins, G.E., Hong, H.: Partial cylindrical algebraic decomposition for quantifier elimination. J. Symb. Comput. 12(3), 299–328 (1991)
6. Cox, D.A., Little, J., O'Shea, D.: Ideals, Varieties, and Algorithms - an introduction to computational algebraic geometry and commutative algebra, 2nd edn. Springer (1997)
7. Darboux, J.G.: Mémoire sur les équations différentielles algébriques du premier ordre et du premier degré. Bulletin des Sciences Mathématiques et Astronomiques 2(1), 151–200 (1878)
8. Dubé, T.: The structure of polynomial ideals and Gröbner bases. SIAM J. Comput. 19(4), 750–773 (1990)
9. Faugère, J.C.: A new efficient algorithm for computing Gröbner bases (F4). Journal of Pure and Applied Algebra 139(1-3), 61–88 (1999)
10. Faugère, J.C.: A new efficient algorithm for computing Gröbner bases without reduction to zero (F5). In: Proceedings of the 2002 International Symposium on Symbolic and Algebraic Computation, ISSAC 2002, pp. 75–83. ACM, New York (2002)
11. Ghorbal, K., Platzer, A.: Characterizing algebraic invariants by differential radical invariants. In: Ábrahám, E., Havelund, K. (eds.) TACAS 2014. LNCS, vol. 8413, pp. 279–294. Springer, Heidelberg (2014)
12. Ghorbal, K., Sogokon, A., Platzer, A.: Invariance of conjunctions of polynomial equalities for algebraic differential equations. Tech. Rep. CMU-CS-14-122, School of Computer Science, CMU, Pittsburgh, PA (June 2014), `http://reports-archive.adm.cs.cmu.edu/anon/2014/abstracts/14-122.html`
13. Goriely, A.: Integrability and Nonintegrability of Dynamical Systems. Advanced series in nonlinear dynamics. World Scientific (2001)
14. Lazard, D.: Gröbner-bases, Gaussian elimination and resolution of systems of algebraic equations. In: van Hulzen, J.A. (ed.) EUROCAL 1983. LNCS, vol. 162, pp. 146–156. Springer, Heidelberg (1983)

15. Lie, S.: Vorlesungen über continuierliche Gruppen mit Geometrischen und anderen Anwendungen, Teubner, Leipzig (1893)
16. Liu, J., Zhan, N., Zhao, H.: Computing semi-algebraic invariants for polynomial dynamical systems. In: Chakraborty, S., Jerraya, A., Baruah, S.K., Fischmeister, S. (eds.) EMSOFT, pp. 97–106. ACM (2011)
17. Matringe, N., Moura, A.V., Rebiha, R.: Generating invariants for non-linear hybrid systems by linear algebraic methods. In: Cousot, R., Martel, M. (eds.) SAS 2010. LNCS, vol. 6337, pp. 373–389. Springer, Heidelberg (2010)
18. Mayr, E.W.: Membership in polynomial ideals over Q is exponential space complete. In: Cori, R., Monien, B. (eds.) STACS 1989. LNCS, vol. 349, pp. 400–406. Springer, Heidelberg (1989)
19. Mayr, E.W., Meyer, A.R.: The complexity of the word problems for commutative semigroups and polynomial ideals. Advances in Mathematics 46(3), 305–329 (1982)
20. Neuhaus, R.: Computation of real radicals of polynomial ideals II. Journal of Pure and Applied Algebra 124(1-3), 261–280 (1998)
21. Olver, P.J.: Applications of Lie Groups to Differential Equations. Springer (2000)
22. Platzer, A.: Differential dynamic logic for hybrid systems. J. Autom. Reasoning 41(2), 143–189 (2008)
23. Platzer, A.: Differential-algebraic dynamic logic for differential-algebraic programs. J. Log. Comput. 20(1), 309–352 (2010)
24. Platzer, A.: Logical Analysis of Hybrid Systems - Proving Theorems for Complex Dynamics. Springer (2010)
25. Platzer, A.: A differential operator approach to equational differential invariants. In: Beringer, L., Felty, A. (eds.) ITP 2012. LNCS, vol. 7406, pp. 28–48. Springer, Heidelberg (2012)
26. Platzer, A.: The structure of differential invariants and differential cut elimination. Logical Methods in Computer Science 8(4), 1–38 (2012)
27. Sankaranarayanan, S., Sipma, H.B., Manna, Z.: Constructing invariants for hybrid systems. Formal Methods in System Design 32(1), 25–55 (2008)
28. Taly, A., Tiwari, A.: Deductive verification of continuous dynamical systems. In: Kannan, R., Kumar, K.N. (eds.) FSTTCS. LIPIcs, vol. 4, pp. 383–394. Schloss Dagstuhl - Leibniz-Zentrum fuer Informatik (2009)
29. Tarski, A.: A decision method for elementary algebra and geometry. Bulletin of the American Mathematical Society 59 (1951)
30. Zerz, E., Walcher, S.: Controlled invariant hypersurfaces of polynomial control systems. Qualitative Theory of Dynamical Systems 11(1), 145–158 (2012)

On Program Equivalence with Reductions

Guillaume Iooss[1,2], Christophe Alias[2], and Sanjay Rajopadhye[1]

[1] Colorado State University
[2] ENS-Lyon, CNRS UMR 5668, INRIA, UCB-Lyon

Abstract. Program equivalence is a well-known problem with a wide range of applications, such as algorithm recognition, program verification and program optimization. This problem is also known to be undecidable if the class of programs is rich enough, in which case semi-algorithms are commonly used. We focus on programs represented as Systems of Affine Recurrence Equations (SARE), defined over parametric polyhedral domains, a well known formalism for the *polyhedral model*. SAREs include as a proper subset, the class of affine control loop programs. Several program equivalence semi-algorithms were already proposed for this class. Some take into account algebraic properties such as associativity and commutativity. To the best of our knowledge, none of them manage reductions, i.e., accumulations of a *parametric* number of sub-expressions using an associative and commutative operator. Our main contribution is a new semi-algorithm to manage reductions. In particular, we outline the ties between this problem and the perfect matching problem in a parametric bipartite graph.

1 Introduction

Program equivalence is an old and well-known problem in computer science with many applications, such as program comprehension, algorithm recognition [1], program verification [2,3], semi-automated debugging, compiler verification [4], translation validation [5,6,7,8] to name just a few. However, the program equivalence problem is known to be undecidable as soon as the considered program class is rich enough to be interesting. Moreover, if we account for the semantic properties of objects manipulated in the program and relax the considered equivalence, the problem becomes harder.

Considerable prior work on program equivalence exists, in particular in the context of translation validation (in which we seek to prove the equivalence between a source and a target program). Necula [5] builds a correlation relation between the control flow graphs of the source and the target programs, and relies on a solver to check whether this relation is a *bisimulation* [9,10]. Such an approach is restricted to *structure preserving* optimizations, and cannot deal with advanced transformations like loop reordering which can arbitrarily change the control structure of the program. Zuck et al. [7] override these limits and introduce "permutation rules" to validate a reordering transformation. They also derive a *runtime test* for advanced loop optimizations. When a problem is detected, the code escapes to an unoptimized version. Kundu et al. [8] combine the benefits of these approaches to check statically that an optimizing transformation is sound.

In this paper, we focus on *Systems of Affine Recurrence Equations* (SARE) with reductions. SAREs are a formalism for reasoning about many compute- and data-intensive

M. Müller-Olm and H. Seidl (Eds.): SAS 2014, LNCS 8723, pp. 168–183, 2014.

programs in the *polyhedral model* and used in automatic parallelization. A *reduction* is the application of an associative and commutative operator to a set of (sub) expressions.[1] Thus, in order to decide equivalence between two reductions, we need to take care of the associativity and commutativity properties over a potentially parametric number of elements.

A well known semi-algorithm for SAREs was proposed by Barthou et al [11]. The idea is to encode the problem of equivalence of two programs into a *Memory State Automaton*, i.e., an automaton whose states are associated with vectors and whose edges are associated with conditions on these vectors. The equivalence problem on SARE can be reduced to a reachability problem on this automaton, which is also undecidable, but for which, several heuristics are applicable (based on the transitive closure operation). However, no semantic properties are considered (the equivalence is purely structural). Shashidhar et al. [12] proposed another equivalence algorithm based on *Array Data Dependence Graph* (ADDG). Their algorithm manages associativity and commutativity over a finite number of elements. However, because complicated recurrences are managed by unfolding loops, it cannot manage parametrized programs. Verdoolaege et al [13] proposed an improved formalism based on a *dependence graph*, that allows them to manage parametrized program. They also present an alternative way to deal with recurrences, based on the widening operation. In the two previous papers, commutativity is managed by testing every permutation of the arguments of operators until we find a good one. This approach is no longer possible if the number of arguments is parametrized. Karfa et al. [14] also proposed an algorithm to decide equivalence based on ADDG. The idea behind their equivalence checking is to build an arithmetic expression corresponding to the computation done by the considered program. By normalizing this expression, they are able to manage the semantic properties of binary operators. However, because they need to have a finite arithmetic expression, they are not able to manage recursion and reductions.

In this paper, we propose a semi-algorithm that decides the equivalence of two programs containing *reductions*. More precisely, our contributions are as follows.

- Building on the Barthou et al. formalization, we propose a rule to manage the equivalence between two reductions (Section 3). This rule can be extended to cover equivalence with a finite number of reductions combined with the same operator.
- The previous rule maps corresponding sub-terms of both reductions through a bijection. We propose a semi-algorithm to infer such bijection (Section 4) that
  - first extracts the set of constraints our bijection needs to satisfy,
  - transforms them into a finite list of *partial bijection* (i.e., bijections defined over subsets of the actual space), and finally
  - simply combines these partial bijections together to form our bijection.

  We show the relation between our problem of partial bijection combination, and the *perfect matching* problem on a parametric bipartite graph.
- We propose heuristics to solve the perfect matching problem for graphs of parametric size. One in particular, is based on a novel extension of the well-known *augmenting path* algorithm (that addresses only the non-parametric case).

[1] Some authors do not require commutativity, in which case a reduction must be applied to an *ordered* set of sub-expressions. In this paper we would like to allow many general reordering transformations, and therefore insist on commutativity.

2 Preliminaries

We first describe the class of programs we consider. Then, we define the notion of equivalence modulo associativity and commutativity, and detail Barthou's semi-algorithm, since it serves as our starting point.

2.1 System of Affine Recurrence Equations with Reductions

A *reduction* is the application of an associative and commutative binary operator $\oplus$ on a parametric set of (sub) expressions. For example $\bigoplus_{0\le i<N} A[i]$ is a reduction of N sub-expressions $A[i]$, N being a parameter. We study the equivalence of programs in the language Alpha, as defined by Mauras [15] and extended by Le Verge [16]. Any Alpha program represents a *System of Affine Recurrence Equations* (SARE) with reductions, defined as follows.

Definition 2.1. A SARE with reductions *is a set of equations of the form:*

$$X[\boldsymbol{i}] = \begin{cases} \vdots \\ Expr(\ldots Y[u_{Y,k}(\boldsymbol{i})]\ldots) & \text{if } \boldsymbol{i} \in \mathcal{D}_k^X \\ \vdots \end{cases}$$

where X is defined over $\mathcal{D}_X = \biguplus_k \mathcal{D}_k^X \subseteq \mathbb{Z}^d$, *the* $\mathcal{D}_k^X$ *being disjoint.*

- $X, Y, \ldots$ *are called* variables. *They are defined over a polyhedral domain* $\mathcal{D}_X$ *and associate a value to each point of their domain.*
- *Some variables are marked as* input *(or* output*) variables. An input variable cannot be defined by an equation of the SARE and any other variable X has exactly one equation which computes its value, for each point of* $\mathcal{D}_X$.
- $Expr[\boldsymbol{i}]$ *is an expression and may be one of*
  - *A* variable $Y[u_{Y,k}(\boldsymbol{i})]$ *where* $u_{Y,k}$ *is an affine function.*
  - *An* operation $f(Expr_1[\boldsymbol{i}], \ldots Expr_n[\boldsymbol{i}])$ *where f is a n-ary operator.*
  - *A* reduction $\bigoplus_{\pi(\boldsymbol{i}')=\boldsymbol{i}} Expr'[\boldsymbol{i}']$ *where* π *is called the* projection function. *Because* $\boldsymbol{i}' \in \mathcal{D}_{Expr'}$, *we can control the set of expressions summed together through the definition domain of* `Expr'`.

Example 2.1. The standard matrix multiplication algorithm for $N \times N$ matrices is described by following SARE with inputs `A` and `B`, and output `C`, each defined over $\mathcal{D}_A = \mathcal{D}_B = \mathcal{D}_C = [|0; N-1|]^2$.

$$\texttt{C[i,j]} = \sum_{k=0}^{N-1} \texttt{A[i,k] * B[k,j]}$$

Our equivalence semi-algorithm accepts as inputs, a pair of SAREs with reductions. We currently do not treat "recursive" reductions, i.e., those in which a variable being defined by a reduction appears inside the reduction. For example, the following SARE for a "recursive prefix sum," which combines a parametric number of elements of `A` to define the ith element `A[i]`, is not accepted:

$$\texttt{O = A[N]}$$

$$\texttt{A[i]} = \begin{cases} \sum_{0 \le k < i} \texttt{A[k]} & \text{if } 0 < i \le N \\ 1 & \text{if i=0} \end{cases}$$

2.2 Equivalence Modulo Associativity and Commutativity

There are several notions of equivalence of programs. The simplest one is called *Herbrand equivalence* and corresponds to the structural equivalence (the computation performed by both programs is identical). We also need to give a *mapping between the inputs* of the two programs, to say which inputs are equivalent. For example, the SARE `O[i] = f(A[i]) + B[i]` is equivalent to the SARE `O'[i] = Temp'[i] + B'[i]`, `Temp'[i] = f(A'[i])` assuming that the input pairs `A/A'` and `B/B'` are equivalent. It will be also equivalent to any SARE obtained by applying any data-dependence preserving transformation (i.e., a transformation which does not modify the computation). However, if we permute the arguments of the addition (commutativity) in one of them, it will no longer be equivalent to the other. The problem of Herbrand equivalence of general SAREs is undecidable [11].

We consider Herbrand equivalence modulo associativity and commutativity: a SARE is equivalent to any other SARE obtained by applying any data-dependence preserving transformation plus associativity and commutativity of the corresponding binary operators. For example, the SARE `O[i] = (A[i] + 2) + B[i]` is equivalent to `O'[i] = Temp'[i] + 2`, `Temp'[i] = A'[i] + B'[i]`. Moreover, because reductions implicitly use associativity and commutativity, we need this extended notion of equivalence to compare SAREs with reductions. For example, under such equivalence, the SARE $\texttt{O[i]} = \sum_{i} \texttt{A[i]}$ is equivalent to $\texttt{O'[i']} = \sum_{i'} \texttt{A'[N-i']}$

2.3 Deciding Herbrand Equivalence of Two SAREs

Barthou et al. [11] proposed a semi-algorithm to decide Herbrand equivalence of SAREs. It first builds an *equivalence memory state automaton* encodeing the equivalence problem and then studies the *accessibility set* of particular states of this automaton.

Definition 2.2. *A* Memory State Automaton *(MSA) [11] is a finite automaton where:*

- *Every state p is associated with an integer vector v_p of some dimension n_p.*
- *Every transition from p to q is associated with a firing relation $F_{p,q} \in \mathbb{Z}^{n_p} \times \mathbb{Z}^{n_q}$.*
- *A transition from $\langle p, v_p \rangle$ to $\langle q, v_q \rangle$ can only happen if $(v_p, v_q) \in F_{p,q}$.*

We say that a state p is *accessible* iff there exists a finite path from the initial state p_0 to p for some associated vector. The *accessibility relation* of a state p is:

$$\mathcal{R}_p = \{(v_0, v_p) \mid \langle p_0, v_0 \rangle \to^* \langle p, v_p \rangle\}$$

Step 1: Building the equivalence MSA: Consider two SAREs. We use the convention that expressions, operators and indices of the second SARE are "primed" (e.g., X', E'_1). The equivalence MSA is defined (and built) as follows:

- **States:** A state is labeled by an equation $e(\mathbf{i}) = e'(\mathbf{i}')$ and is associated with the vector $(\mathbf{i}, \mathbf{i}')$.
- **Initial state:** The initial state of the automaton is $O[\mathbf{i_0}] = O'[\mathbf{i}'_0]$
- **Final state:** There are two kinds of final states: the *success states* and the *failure states*. The *failure states* are:
  - $f(\ldots) = f'(\ldots)$ where f and f' are different operators,
  - $I_k[\mathbf{i}] = f'(\ldots)$ or $f(\ldots) = I'_k[\mathbf{i}']$,
  - $I_k[\mathbf{i}] = I'_{k'}[\mathbf{i}]$ where I_k and $I'_{k'}$ are not corresponding inputs.

  In contrast, the *accept states* are:
  - $f() = f'()$ (i.e., two identical constants)
  - $I_k = I'_{k'}$ where I_k and $I'_{k'}$ are corresponding inputs.
- **Transitions:** We have 3 types of transitions (*rules*) in the equivalence MSA: *Decompose*, *Compute* and *Generalize*, as described in Fig 1. The *Decompose* rule deals with operators and simply says that two expressions using the same operator are equivalent iff their arguments are equivalent. The *Compute* rule allows us to "unroll" a definition and creates a state per case. Note that for each value $(\mathbf{i}, \mathbf{i}')$ associated with the source state, there is only one accessible state among the created states. The *Generalize* rule is useful to deal with recursions. It replaces an affine expression by a fresh index, allowing us to go into a state we may have already encountered, but with different index values.

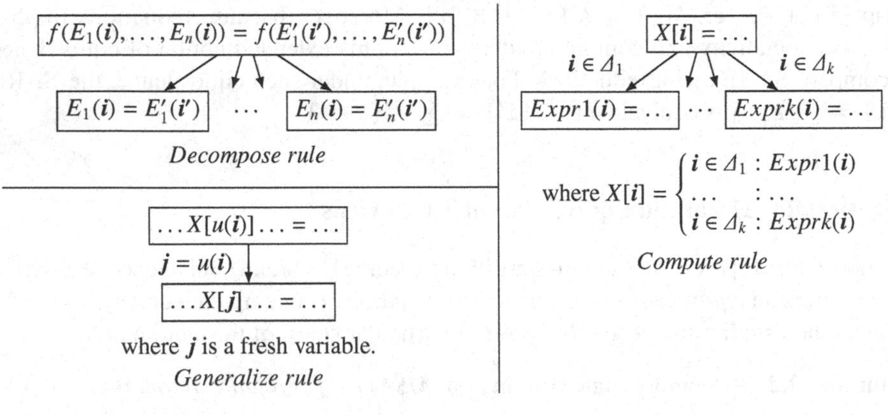

Fig. 1. Construction rules for the equivalence automaton

Step 2: Equivalence and reachability problem in the equivalence automaton: Intuitively, if a state $Expr[i] = Expr[i']$ can be reached for a given $(\mathbf{i}, \mathbf{i}')$, then these two expressions must be equivalent in order for the two SAREs to be equivalent. Thus, the equivalence problem between the two considered SAREs can be decided by studying the accessibility sets of the success and failure states.

Theorem 2.1 (from [11]). *Two SAREs are equivalent iff, in their equivalence MSA:*

- *All failure states are not accessible from the start state.*
- *The accessibility relation of each success state is included in the identity relation.*

Indeed, a failure state corresponds to the comparison of two expressions which are obviously not equivalent. The success condition states that, if we start from the initial states with an equality of the indices of the outputs, the indices of any reachable success state must be the same (i.e., `I[i]` cannot be identical to `I[j]` for $i \neq j$).

Example: As an example, let us compare the following SARE with itself:

$$O = A[N]$$
$$A[i] = \begin{cases} 1 \leq i \leq N : f(I[i], A[i-1]) \\ i = 0 \quad\quad\;\; : I[0] \end{cases}$$

where O is the output of the SARE and I the input. The equivalence automaton is the following (success states are in blue and failure states in red):

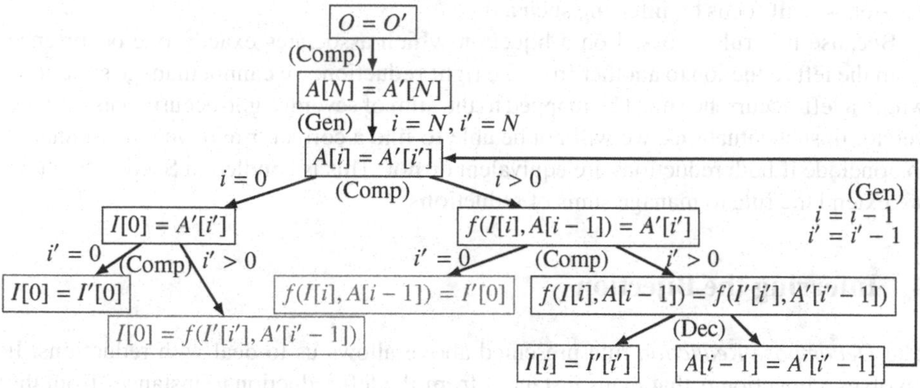

Notice how the automaton has a cycle: it corresponds to the comparison between the recursions of both SARE. We can notice that, for every state of the automaton, we have $i = i'$ (indeed, for each transition we are modifying i, we are also modifying i' in the same way). Thus, because the reachability set of the failure states are respectively $\{i, i' \mid i = 0 \wedge i' > 0\}$ and $\{i, i' \mid i > 0 \wedge i' = 0\}$, then they are both empty. Moreover, the equalities that need to be satisfied when reaching a success state are respectively $0 = 0$ (trivially satisfied) and $i = i'$ (satisfied). Thus, according to Thm 2.1 these two SARE are equivalent.

Limitation of the equivalence algorithm: This algorithm only checks Herbrand equivalence, semantic properties like associativity/commutativity of operators are not taken into account. For instance, if we try to compare the SAREs $O = I_1 + I_2$ and $O' = I'_2 + I'_1$, the equivalent automaton will have a *decompose* rule which will generate two failure states with respective labels $(I_1 = I'_2)$ and $(I_2 = I'_1)$.

3 Decompose Reduce Rule

In the previous section, we presented Barthou's equivalence algorithm, based on the construction of an equivalence automaton. This algorithm can be extended to manage reductions, by adding a new construction rule (called *Decompose Reduce*):

$$\bigoplus_{\pi(\boldsymbol{k})=i} E[\boldsymbol{k}] = \bigoplus_{\pi'(\boldsymbol{k}')=i'} E'[\boldsymbol{k}']$$

$$\downarrow \ \sigma(\boldsymbol{k}) = \boldsymbol{k}'$$

$$E[\boldsymbol{k}] = E'[\boldsymbol{k}']$$

The idea of this rule is to map every occurrence of the left reduction $E[\boldsymbol{k}]$ to an equivalent occurrence $E'[\boldsymbol{k}']$ on the right reduction, such that these two occurrences are equivalent. In other words, if we manage to find a bijection σ between the occurrences $\boldsymbol{k}$ of the left reduction and the occurrences $\boldsymbol{k}'$ of the right reduction such that $E[\boldsymbol{k}]$ is equivalent to $E'[\boldsymbol{k}']$, then both reductions are equivalent. During the equivalence automaton construction step, we leave σ as a symbolic function (it does not impact the construction of the rest of the automaton), and the rest of the algorithm (described in Section 4) will focus on inferring such a σ.

Because this rule is based on a bijection which associates exactly one occurrence from the left reduction to another from the right reduction, we cannot manage situations where a left-occurrence must be mapped to the sum of several right-occurrences (or vice versa). In such situations, we will not be able to find a correct σ and we will be unable to conclude if both reductions are equivalent or not. This is handled in Section 5 where we extend the rule to manage sums of reductions.

4 Inferring the Bijection

The *Decompose Reduction* rule presented above allows us to deal with reductions. It involves a bijection σ that maps instances from the left reduction to instances from the right reduction. However, we still need to find the actual value of σ (or, at least, prove its existence), such that the conditions of Thm 2.1 are still valid, and we now tackle this problem.

4.1 Illustrative Example

To give the intuition of the algorithm, let us first consider the following SAREs:

$$O = \sum_i A[i] \qquad\qquad O' = \sum_{i'} A'[i']$$

$$A[i] = \begin{cases} 0 < i \leq N : I[i] \\ i = 0 \qquad\ : I[i+1] \end{cases} \qquad A'[i'] = \begin{cases} i' = N \qquad\ : I'[1] \\ 0 \leq i' < N : I'[i'+1] \end{cases}$$

These two SAREs sum up all the $I[i]$, except for $I[0]$, but with $I[1]$ being counted twice (for index points $i = 0, 1$ in the first SARE, and for $i' = 0, N$ in the second one).

Thus, when we compare the terms of the two bijections, we should map $A[0]$ to either $A'[0]$ or $A'[N]$ and $A[1]$ to the other one, and each remaining $A[i]$ to $A'[i']$. Let us derive these bijections from the equivalence automaton, which is shown below, where $\sigma : [|0; N|] \mapsto [|0; N|]$:

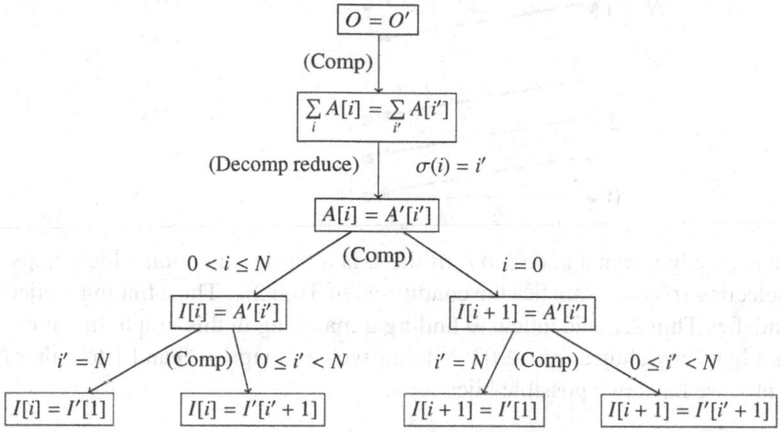

Extraction of the constraints: We want to find a bijection σ such that the conditions of Thm 2.1 are satisfied, i.e., one that makes all failure state unreachable, and the indices of all success states equal. For example, let us consider the second success state $I[i] = I'[i' + 1]$: we need $i = i' + 1$ at this state, thus because we have to go through two conditions $0 < i$ and $i' < N$. Thus, if σ maps a non-negative i to a i' below N, then i' must be equal to $i - 1$. By studying the accessibility set of each final state, we obtain the following constraints:

$$\begin{array}{lllll} [\ \sigma(i) = i' \wedge (1 \leq i \leq N) \wedge & (i' = N) & \wedge & i = 1 &] \\ \vee[\ \sigma(i) = i' \wedge (1 \leq i \leq N) \wedge & (0 \leq i' < N) & \wedge & i = i' + 1 &] \\ \vee[\ \sigma(i) = i' \wedge \quad (i = 0) \quad \wedge & (i' = N) & \wedge & i + 1 = 1 &] \\ \vee[\ \sigma(i) = i' \wedge \quad (i = 0) \quad \wedge & (0 \leq i' < N) & \wedge & i + 1 = i' + 1 &] \end{array}$$

Obtaining the partial bijections: Notice that our constraints admit a kind of structure: the constraints on i and i' are separated, except for the equalities coming from the success state itself. In our example, each Diophantine equation admits a unique solution, and we can express i' as a function of i. We end up with an injective affine function whose definition and image domain is given by the constraints on i and i'. We can refine these domains to make this function a partial bijection $\tilde{\sigma}$ (i.e., a bijection defined over a subset of the whole space). At this point, if σ is equal to $\tilde{\sigma}$ for each $i \in \mathcal{D}$, then σ will satisfy the constraints for every $(\boldsymbol{i}, \tilde{\sigma}(\boldsymbol{i}))$, therefore we will satisfy the conditions of Thm 2.1 for these values of $\boldsymbol{i}$.

In our example, let us consider the first constraint. The Diophantine equations are $i = 1$, $i' = N$. Thus, the corresponding partial bijection will be defined on the domain $\{1\}$ and will have $\{N\}$ as an image domain. By doing the same for all constraints, we obtain the following set of partial bijections:

$$\tilde{\sigma}_1 : \begin{cases} \{1\} \mapsto \{N\} \\ 1 \ \mapsto \ N \end{cases} \quad \tilde{\sigma}_2 : \begin{cases} [|1; N|] \mapsto [|0; N-1|] \\ \quad i \quad \mapsto \quad i - 1 \end{cases} \quad \tilde{\sigma}_3 : \begin{cases} \{0\} \mapsto \{N\} \\ 0 \ \mapsto \ N \end{cases} \quad \tilde{\sigma}_4 : \begin{cases} \{0\} \mapsto \{0\} \\ 0 \ \mapsto \ 0 \end{cases}$$

Sticking the partial bijections: We can represent the definition and image domain of σ as the nodes of a bipartite graph and the partial bijections as the edges of this graph:

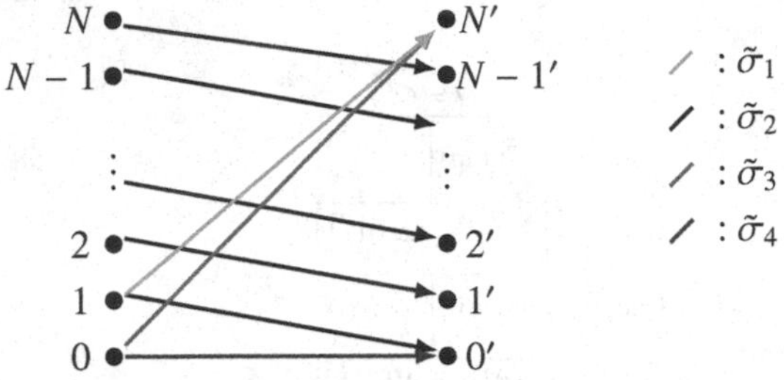

There is an edge from a node i to i' iff there is a partial bijection which maps i to i', i.e., iff selecting $\sigma(i) = i'$ satisfies the conditions of Thm 2.1. Thus, finding a bijection σ which satisfies Thm 2.1 is identical to finding a matching in this graph. In our example, we do not have any choice for $i \in [|2; N|]$, but we can map $i = 0$ and 1 to either $i' = 0'$ or N'. Thus, we have two possible bijections:

$$\sigma : \begin{cases} 1 \mapsto N & (\tilde{\sigma}_1) \\ i \mapsto i-1 \text{ when } i \geq 2 & (\tilde{\sigma}_2) \\ 0 \mapsto 0 & (\tilde{\sigma}_4) \end{cases} \quad \text{or } \sigma : \begin{cases} i \mapsto i-1 \text{ when } i \geq 1 & (\tilde{\sigma}_2) \\ 0 \mapsto N & (\tilde{\sigma}_3) \end{cases}$$

We managed to build a bijection, thus we can conclude that the two reductions are equivalent. Therefore, the two considered SAREs are equivalent. In summary, our semi-algorithm proceeds in the three steps below, each of which is explained in the following subsections.

1. Extract the constraints on σ from the equivalence automaton,
2. Transform these constraints into partial bijections $\tilde{\sigma}$, which are portions of σ where the equivalence constraints are satisfied,
3. Combine these partial bijections to obtain σ.

4.2 Extraction of the Constraints

To prove the equivalence, we need to find a valid σ satisfying the constraints of Thm 2.1. However, these constraints are obtained on the final states, whose indices might be different from the ones used to define σ. Thus, we need to "pull up" the constraints from the final state to the state just below the *Decompose Reduce* rule. To do this, we introduce the notion of *accept domain*:

Definition 4.1. *An* accept domain C_{accept} *of a state s is the set of values* $(\mathbf{i}, \mathbf{i'})$ *such that all paths starting from s with vector* $(\mathbf{i}, \mathbf{i'})$ *will never end up in a failure state, and will end up with equal values of* $\mathbf{i}$ *and* $\mathbf{i'}$ *on a success state.*

Intuitively, the accept domain consists of all index points for which the conditions of Thm 2.1 will be satisfied. Thus, to obtain the conditions on σ, we need to compute the accept domain of the *topmost state*, i.e., the one below the *Decompose Reduce* rule.

The accept domain C_{accept} of a state can be computed by a bottom-up recurrence:

- **Success state** $I[u(i)] = I'[v(i')]$: $C_{accept} = \{i, i' \mid u(i) = v(i')\}$.
- **Failure state:** $C_{accept} = \emptyset$
- **Compute rule:** The accept domain is the *union* of the accept domains of its children, each intersected with the corresponding conditionals from its definition.
- **Decompose rule:** The accept domain is the *intersection* of the accept domains of its children.
- **Generalize rule:** The accept domain is the *preimage* by the generalization function of the accept domain of its child.

If the sub-automaton below the *Decompose Reduce* rule is *acyclic*, we can easily compute the accept domain of the top-most state. We end up with the constraints that σ must satisfy for equivalence. If the sub-automaton below the *Decompose Reduce* rule is *cyclic*, we cannot do a bottom-up recurrence directly.

In general, the sub-automaton below the *Decompose Reduce* rule can be cyclic. These loops can be handled by using a *transitive closure* operation. However, the transitive closure operation might give us an over-approximation. Thus, to remain sound, we consider the complementary set of *accept domain*, called *reject domain* (i.e., the set of values (i, i') such that there exists a path ending in a failure state or on a success state with different index values). Moreover, the way we apply our transitive closure (based on Finite State Automaton) forces us to use reject domains for the cyclic case.

4.3 Obtaining the Partial Bijections

First of all, let us prove that the constraints obtained in the previous step of the algorithm have a particular form:

Proposition 4.1 *The constraints on σ can be represented as a disjunction of constraints in which the constraints involving indices from both SAREs must be equalities.*

Proof. The constraints on σ come from two places in the equivalence automaton: the transitions and the accept states. Because of the transition rules, there are no guards (or actions) that simultaneously use both sets of indices ($\boldsymbol{i}$ and $\boldsymbol{i}'$). Thus, these constraints will end up in $\mathcal{D}$ and $\mathcal{D}'$. As for accept states, the only constraints we have are equalities between an affine function of $\boldsymbol{i}$ and another affine function of $\boldsymbol{i}'$. Thus, when we perform the bottom-up recursion, we will still have an equality between two affine functions.

We have a system of parametric linear Diophantine equations $[u(\boldsymbol{i}) = v(\boldsymbol{i}')]$ where $\boldsymbol{i}' \in \mathcal{D}'$ are the unknowns. By solving this system, we obtain 3 cases:

- **No solution:** the constraint is unsatisfiable, thus we can remove it.
- **A single solution:** $\boldsymbol{i}' = A_i.\boldsymbol{i} + A_p.\boldsymbol{p} + \boldsymbol{b}$ where A_i is full-column rank. We have a single partial bijection $\tilde{\sigma}(\boldsymbol{i}) = A_i.\boldsymbol{i} + A_p.\boldsymbol{p} + \boldsymbol{b}$. Its antecedent and image domains can be computed by using the constraints from $\mathcal{D}$ and $\mathcal{D}'$.
- **Multiple solutions:** $\boldsymbol{i}' = A_t.\boldsymbol{t} + A_i.\boldsymbol{i} + A_p.\boldsymbol{p} + \boldsymbol{b}$ where $\boldsymbol{t}$ parametrizes the set of solutions. Likewise, we can compute the antecedent and image domains of the partial bijection.

Our illustrative example in Sec. 4.1 was in the second case. To illustrate the third case, let us consider the following set of constraints: $0 \leq i, j < N \wedge 0 \leq i', j' < N \wedge i + j = i' + j'$. We have the following solutions: $i' = i + t$ and $j' = j - t$ where $t \in \mathbb{Z}$. Thus, we have a family of partial bijections, parametrized by t.

If we manage to combine these partial bijections together into a full bijection σ, then this full bijection will satisfy the constraints we derived in the previous subsection. Thus, this full bijection σ will satisfy the conditions of Thm 2.1 and the two reductions will be equivalent. Therefore, we need to combine these partial bijections into a full bijection to finish the derivation of σ.

4.4 Parametric Perfect Matching Problem

Now that we have a list of partial bijections derived from the constraints that σ need to satisfy, we need to combine them together to form a full bijection. This can be done by using a greedy heuristic which builds a total bijection σ made of pieces of partial bijections. The idea is to iterate over the partial bijections in an arbitrary order, and add them to the construction of σ if it can be used to extend it while making sure that we still have a bijection.

However, because the antecedent or the image domain between two partial bijections may overlap, picking one to build σ might discard other choices of mapping. This might lead us to something similar to a "local optimum:" a situation where we arrive at a partial bijection which cannot be improved by extending it with a partial bijection.

Note that finding such σ is exactly finding a perfect matching of a bipartite graph of parametric size. Indeed, if we consider a bipartite graph whose classes of nodes are respectively the antecedent domain $\mathcal{D}_{ant}$ (i.e., the set of points on which σ is defined) and the image domain $\mathcal{D}_{im}$ of the bijection σ, and whose edges $(\boldsymbol{i}, \boldsymbol{i}')$ are all the couples such that we have a partial bijection $\tilde{\sigma}$ such that $\boldsymbol{i}' = \tilde{\sigma}(\boldsymbol{i})$. Thus, finding a perfect matching in this bipartite graph corresponds to picking a single image $\boldsymbol{i}'$ for every element $\boldsymbol{i}$ of the antecedent domain, while covering the whole image domain $\mathcal{D}_{im}$ uniquely.

In the non-parametric case, a perfect matching to a bipartite graph $G = ((U, V), E)$ can be found by applying the *augmenting path algorithm* [17]. This polynomial algorithm determines if a given matching is a maximal matching (which can be used to check for the existence of a perfect matching), and if not, how to extend it (which can be used to incrementally build this perfect matching). The idea of this algorithm is to search for an *augmenting path*, i.e., a path starting at a point of $x \in U$ and ending on a point $y \in V$ which is not saturated by the current matching σ, and alternating between edges belonging to σ and edges not belonging to σ. If an augmenting path is found, it is possible to improve the current matching σ by removing from σ, all the edges of the augmenting path, and by adding all the edges of the path not belonging to σ.

For example, in the following non-parametric bipartite graph, the current matching admits an augmenting path, which is $[3, 2', 2, 1', 0, 0']$ (with $x = 3$ and $y = 0'$).

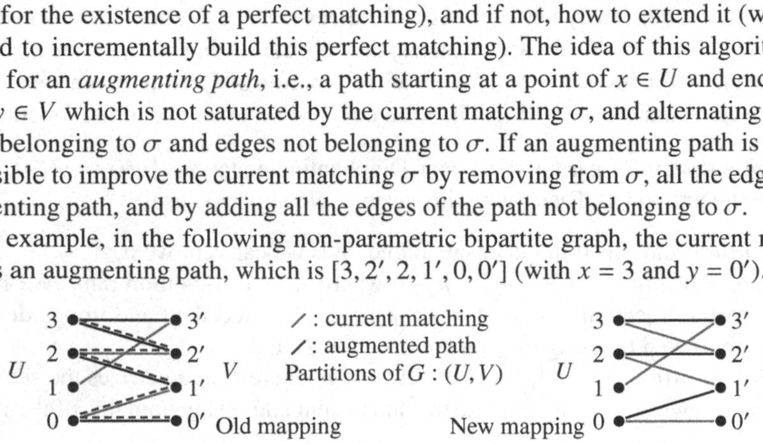

For a parametric bipartite graph, the perfect matching problem is much harder, because we cannot afford to iterate over all the points (and edges) of the graph. However, in our case, because we have a finite compact representation of the edges (the partial bijections), we are able to do operations in constant time (such as computing the neighborhood of a point). Thus, it is possible to extend the augmenting path algorithm to manage partially the augmenting paths of these graphs. This extended augmenting path algorithm is shown in Algorithm 1.

Input : Bipartite graph $G = (\mathcal{D}_{ant}, \mathcal{D}_{im})$ whose edges are described by a family of $\tilde{\sigma}$
Current matching $\sigma_{cur} : \mathcal{D}_{cur} \mapsto \mathcal{D}'_{cur}$
Output: Either a proof that σ is a maximum matching, or an augmenting-path

$U = \mathcal{D}_{ant} - \mathcal{D}_{cur}$; `// Unsaturated points of the antecedent domain`
$V = \mathcal{D}_{im} - \mathcal{D}'_{cur}$; `// Unsaturated points of the image domain`
$AP = [\ (U, [])\ ]$; `// List of augmenting paths beginnings`
$U_{explored} = U$; `// Points toward which an augmenting path has been found`
N_U = neighborhood of U ; `// Union of the images of` U `by all the` $\tilde{\sigma}$
while *($N_U \cap V = \emptyset$)* **do**
  foreach *[U_{AP}, path] in AP and $\tilde{\sigma}$ partial bijection* **do**
    $U_{\tilde{\sigma}} = \sigma_{cur}^{-1}(\tilde{\sigma}(U_{AP})) - U_{explored}$; `// Path to new points discovered`
    if *($U_{\tilde{\sigma}} \neq \emptyset$)* **then** `// New augmenting path portion discovered`
      Add ($U_{\tilde{\sigma}}$, *path* :: $\tilde{\sigma}$) to AP ; `// Updating the augmenting path list`
      $U_{explored} = U_{explored} \cup U_{\tilde{\sigma}}$
    end
  end
  if $U_{explored}$ *did not change during this iteration* **then**
    σ_{cur} is a maximum matching
  end
  N_U = neighborhood of $U_{explored}$
end
Find one set (U_{AP}, *path*) in AP whose neighborhood intersect V
Find the partial bijection $\tilde{\sigma}$ which send the previously found set partially into V
Return the augmenting path (*path* :: $\tilde{\sigma}$)

Algorithm 1. Parametric augmenting path algorithm

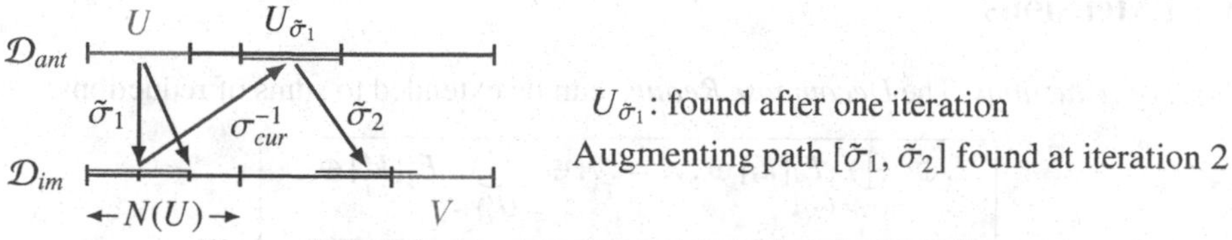

Illustration of the parametric augmented path algorithm

The algorithm builds an augmenting path by exploring the augmenting path tree of the bipartite graph in a breadth-first fashion. To improve the current mapping σ, we need to get the actual augmenting path. The algorithm keeps track of the "potential starts" of augmenting paths in the list AP. If a pair ($U_{AP} \subset \mathcal{D}_{ant}$, *path*) is added to AP (line 10), then we have found a set of paths starting from U, finishing at U_{AP}, that are the starts of augmenting paths, and that use the partial bijections listed in *path* to go from $\mathcal{D}_{ant}$ to $\mathcal{D}_{im}$.

When we find an augmenting path, we actually find a (potentially parametric) set of augmenting paths, each of them non-mutually interfering (because σ and all the $\tilde{\sigma}$ are bijections), which can all be used together to improve σ. Also, keeping track of the partial bijections used in an augmenting path is enough information to characterize them: indeed, all the edges of an augmenting path going from $\mathcal{D}_{im}$ to $\mathcal{D}_{ant}$ use σ.

We also note that iterating on all the partial bijection can be done in constant non-parametric time: indeed, if we get a family of partial bijections $\tilde{\sigma}_t$ in the previous step, we can still compute the image of a set through any $\tilde{\sigma}_t$ directly, instead of iterating over all the values of t.

This algorithm is only able to find augmenting paths of non-parametric length. For example, we need N iterations of the algorithm to find the augmenting path in the following graph:

$\nearrow$: current σ

$\nearrow$: $\tilde{\sigma}_1$

$U = \{0\}$

$U_{explored}(\text{iteration } i) = [|0; i|]$

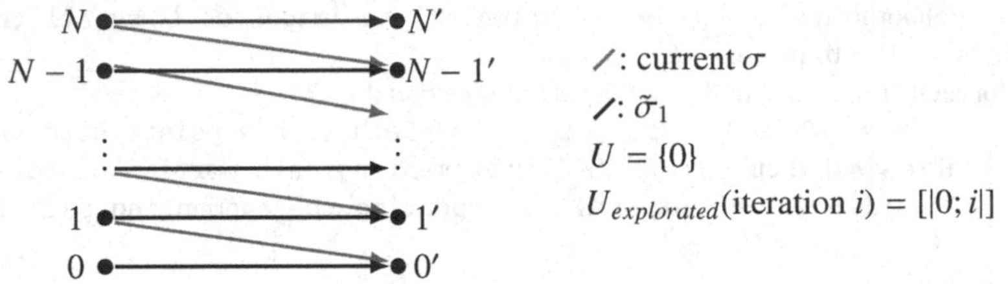

In summary, to combine the partial bijections into σ, we proceed as follows: first we use a greedy heuristic to quickly build a bijection. If the bijection is not total, then we try to improve it by using the augmenting path algorithm. There are three possible results to this algorithm: (i) a set of non-interfering augmenting paths is found, and we can improve our current bijection, (ii) our current σ is a maximum matching (thus, it is not possible to combine the partial bijections into a total bijection) or (iii) the algorithm does not terminate after an arbitrary number of iterations (there might be an augmenting path of parametric length, but we are not able to deal with this situation). While σ is not total, we keep applying the augmenting path algorithm.

5 Extensions

Sums of reductions The *Decompose Reduce* can be extended to sums of reductions:

$$\ldots \oplus \bigoplus_{\pi_i(k_i)=i} E_i[k_i] \oplus \ldots = \ldots \oplus \bigoplus_{\pi'_i(k'_i)=i'} E'_i[k'_i] \oplus \ldots$$

$$\sigma(1, k_1) = (1, k'_1) \qquad\qquad \sigma(n, k_n) = (m, k'_m)$$

$$\boxed{E_1[k_1] = F_1[k'_1]} \quad \cdots \quad \cdots \quad \boxed{E_n[k_n] = F_m[k'_m]}$$

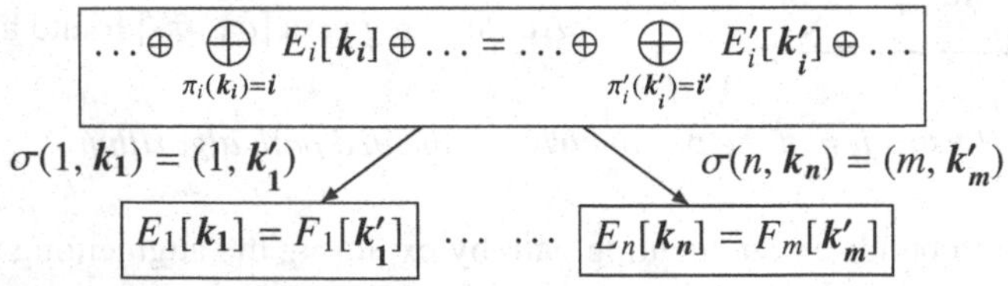

Because an occurrence of a given left reduction can be mapped to an occurrence to *any* right reduction, this rule is creating $n \times m$ sub-states, each one corresponding

Table 1. Execution time (in milliseconds) that the algorithm spends in each phase for a few simple examples. Experiments were done on an Intel core i5-3210M running Linux.

Example	Nstates	Automaton	Partial Bijections	Gathering	Total
Example 4.1	15	74	206	133	414
Loop reverse	5	48	56	21	126
Distributed summation	15	75	788	297	1161
Non equivalence	4	45	48	84	179
Tiling	7	71	245	83	400

to all possible pairwise comparisons between the expressions. Moreover, we add one scalar dimension to the antecedent and image domains of σ: the value of this dimension corresponds to the reduction number in which the occurrence occurs. Thus, because each occurrence $(\alpha, \boldsymbol{k}_\alpha)$ from the α-th left reduction will be mapped through σ to a single occurrence of the β-th right reduction, all the other sub-states $E_\alpha = E'_\gamma$ (where $\gamma \neq \beta$) will become inaccessible for the index $\boldsymbol{k}_\alpha$. That way, the bijection extraction will naturally end up with a correct correspondence between the reductions.

This rule can be adapted to manage the associativity and commutativity of a finite sum of non reduce expressions: indeed, we can use the following identity: $E[i] = \bigoplus_{Id(k)=i} E[k]$. This ends up checking all possible equivalences between a left and a right expression, which is the idea to manage associativity and commutativity in Verdoolaege's equivalence algorithm [13].

Reduction behind another reduction If we encounter a *Decompose Reduce* behind another *Decompose Reduce*, then the second bijection σ_2 might depend on the first bijection σ_1. Thus, the derivation of both σ is related, and must not be separated. Instead of deriving independently the constraints for each bijection, we can introduce $\sigma = (\sigma_1, \sigma_2)$ the bijection whose first dimensions correspond to σ_1 and last dimensions correspond to σ_2. The extracted constraints will deal with σ and the rest of the derivation algorithm will apply. This result can be extended to any number of *reduction*, as soon as there is a finite non-parametric number of instances of σ_k (to be able to define σ).

6 Implementation

We have implemented a prototype of the equivalence algorithm[2] in Java, based on our polyhedral compilation/transformation framework, *AlphaZ*. The implementation is still in progress: currently we do not support loops behind a *Decompose Reduction* rule in the equivalence automaton, and we do not support our second extension (combination of reduction expressions using the same operator). We have run our implementation on several examples, and we report their corresponding execution time in Figure 1. Every example manages parametric reductions, thus their equivalence cannot be decided by the previous work.

[2] Available at: `http://cs.colostate.edu/AlphaZ/equivalence/index.html`

The *Loop reverse* example compares two 1D summation, one summing in increasing order and the other one in decreasing order. The *Distributed summation* example compares two sums of reductions, summing the terms $I[i]$ for $0 \leq i < 2N$ differently. In the first sum, the terms are split across the two reductions according to the parity of i. In the second sum, the terms are split between $0 \leq i < N$ and $N \leq i < 2N$. The *Non Equivalence* example compares two reductions which are not equivalent (the second reduction has one extra term). The *Tiling* example compares a 1D summation ($\sum_i I[i]$) with its tiled counterpart ($\sum_{ib} \sum_{il} I[16ib + il]$ where $0 \leq il < 16$).

7 Conclusion

We have presented an extension to Barthou's program equivalence semi-algorithm for SAREs to support the associativity and commutativity properties of reductions applied to parametric number of sub-terms. The key idea was to find a bijection σ that correctly maps each sub-expression of one reduction expression to a corresponding sub-expression of another reduction. We developed an algorithm to infer σ, and showed its relationship with the perfect matching problem in a parametric bipartite graph.

The idea of using and deriving a bijection can probably be used in other existing equivalence algorithms, such as the one by Verdoolaege et al. [13]. Some of these algorithms might take other program representation as input, such as *affine control loop programs*. It is possible to translate such program by extracting the true dependences using techniques such as *Array Dataflow Analysis* [18]. Moreover, if the reductions are not provided, we need to use reduction detection techniques [19,20,21]. Also, there are probably links between the notions introduced in both algorithms, such as our *accept domain* and their relation R^{want} corresponding to the ("desired correspondence between the iterations of both computations").

About the parametric augmenting path algorithm, it might be possible to detect augmenting paths of parametric sizes if they present some regularity (such as periodicity of partial bijections). It would also be interesting to determine the maximum length of all the non-parametric augmenting paths: this number will be useful to determine the needed number of iterations of the while loop in our algorithm.

Our future plans involve the use of this algorithm to recognize instances of linear algebra algorithms (which often include reductions), with a goal to subsequently do "semantic tiling," a program optimization technique that improves performance by exploiting semantic properties. Finally, we would like to thank Alain Darte for helpful discussions.

Acknowledgement. This work was supported in part by the AFOSR under grant FA9550-13-1-0064, and by the NSF under grants 0917319 and 1240991.

References

1. Alias, C.: Program Optimization by Template Recognition and Replacement. PhD thesis, Université de Versailles (2005)
2. Godlin, B., Strichman, O.: Regression Verification. In: Proceedings of the 46th Annual Design Automation Conference, pp. 466–471 (2009)

3. Feng, X., Hu, A.J.: Cutpoints for Formal Equivalence Verification of Embedded Software. In: Proceedings of the 5th ACM International Conference on Embedded Software, pp. 307–316 (2005)
4. Hoare, T.: The Verifying Compiler: A Grand Challenge for Computing Research. In: Proceedings of the 2003 Joint Modular Languages Conference, pp. 25–35 (2003)
5. Necula, G.C.: Translation Validation for an Optimizing Compiler. In: Proceedings of the 21st ACM SIGPLAN Conference on Programming Language Design and Implementation, pp. 83–95 (2000)
6. Pnueli, A., Siegel, M.D., Singerman, E.: Translation Validation. In: Steffen, B. (ed.) TACAS 1998. LNCS, vol. 1384, pp. 151–166. Springer, Heidelberg (1998)
7. Zuck, L., Pnueli, A., Goldberg, B., Barrett, C., Fang, Y., Hu, Y.: Translation and Run-Time Validation of Loop Transformations. Formal Methods in System Design 27(3), 335–360 (2005)
8. Kundu, S., Tatlock, Z., Lerner, S.: Proving Optimizations Correct using Parameterized Program Equivalence. In: Proceedings of the 30th ACM SIGPLAN Conference on Programming Language Design and Implementation, pp. 327–337 (2009)
9. Sangiorgi, D.: Introduction to Bisimulation and Coinduction. Cambridge University Press (2011)
10. Jančar, P.: Decidability of Bisimilarity for One-Counter Processes. Information and Computation 158, 1–17 (2000)
11. Barthou, D., Feautrier, P., Redon, X.: On the Equivalence of Two Systems of Affine Recurrence Equations (Research Note). In: Monien, B., Feldmann, R.L. (eds.) Euro-Par 2002. LNCS, vol. 2400, pp. 309–313. Springer, Heidelberg (2002)
12. Shashidhar, K.C., Bruynooghe, M., Catthoor, F., Janssens, G.: Verification of Source Code Transformations by Program Equivalence Checking. In: Bodik, R. (ed.) CC 2005. LNCS, vol. 3443, pp. 221–236. Springer, Heidelberg (2005)
13. Verdoolaege, S., Janssens, G., Bruynooghe, M.: Equivalence Checking of Static Affine Programs Using Widening to Handle Recurrences. ACM Transactions on Programming Languages and Systems 34(3), 11:1–11:35 (2012)
14. Karfa, C., Banerjee, K., Sarkar, D., Mandal, C.: Verification of Loop and Arithmetic Transformations of Array-Intensive Behaviors. IEEE Transactions on Computer-Aided Design of Integrated Circuits and Systems 32(11), 1787–1800 (2013)
15. Mauras, C.: ALPHA: un Langage Équationnel pour la Conception et la Programmation d'Architectures Parallèles Synchrones. PhD thesis, L'Université de Rennes I, IRISA, Campus de Beaulieu, Rennes, France (December 1989)
16. Le Verge, H.: Un Environnement de Transformations de Programmmes pour la Synthèse d'Architectures Régulières. PhD thesis, L'Université de Rennes I, IRISA, Campus de Beaulieu, Rennes, France (October 1992)
17. West, D.B.: Introduction to Graph Theory. Prentice Hall (1999)
18. Feautrier, P.: Dataflow Analysis of Array and Scalar References. International Journal of Parallel Programming 20, 23–53 (1991)
19. Redon, X., Feautrier, P.: Detection of Scans. Parallel Algorithms and Applications 15, 229–263 (2000)
20. Sato, S., Iwasaki, H.: Automatic Parallelization via Matrix Multiplication. In: Proceedings of the 32nd ACM SIGPLAN Conference on Programming Language Design and Implementation, pp. 470–479 (2011)
21. Zou, Y., Rajopadhye, S.: Scan Detection and Parallelization in "Inherently Sequential" Nested Loop Programs. In: Proceedings of the 10th International Symposium on Code Generation and Optimization, pp. 74–83 (2012)

A Progress Bar for Static Analyzers*

Woosuk Lee, Hakjoo Oh, and Kwangkeun Yi

Seoul National University, Seoul, Korea

Abstract. We present a technique for devising a progress indicator of static analyzers. Progress indicator is a useful user interface that shows how close a static analysis has progressed so far to its completion. Because static analysis' progress depends on the semantic complexity, not on the code size, of the target software, devising an accurate progress-indicator is not obvious. Our technique first combines a semantic-based pre-analysis and a statistical method to approximate how a main analysis progresses in terms of lattice height of the abstract domain. Then, we use this information during the main analysis and estimate the analysis' current progress. We apply the technique to three existing analyses (interval, octagon, and pointer analyses) for C and show the technique estimates the actual analysis progress for various benchmarks.

1 Introduction

We aim to develop a progress bar for static analyzers. Realistic semantic-based static analyzers usually take a long time to analyze real-world software. For instance, SPARROW [1], our static analyzer for full C, takes more than 4 hours to analyze one million lines of C code [14]. Astrée [2] has also been reported to take over 20 hours to analyze programs of size over 500KLOC [5]. Nonetheless, such static analyzers are silent during their operation and users cannot but wait several hours without any progress information.

Estimating static analysis progress at real-time is challenging in general. Static analyzers take most of their time in fixpoint computation, but estimating the progress of fixpoint algorithms has been unknown. One challenge is that the analysis time is generally not proportional to the size of the program to analyze. For instance, SPARROW [14] takes 4 hours in analyzing one million lines but require 10 hours to analyze programs of sizes around 400KLOC. Similar observations have been made for Astrée as well: Astrée takes 1.5 hours for 70KLOC but takes 40 minutes for 120KLOC [5].

In this paper, we present an idea for estimating static analysis progress. Our basic approach is to measure the progress by calculating lattice heights of intermediate analysis results and comparing them with the height of the final analysis result. To this end, we employ a semantic-based pre-analysis and a statistical regression technique. First, we use the pre-analysis to approximate the

* This work was supported by the Engineering Research Center of Excellence Program of Korea Ministry of Science, ICT & Future Planning(MSIP) / National Research Foundation of Korea(NRF) (Grant NRF-2008-0062609).

M. Müller-Olm and H. Seidl (Eds.): SAS 2014, LNCS 8723, pp. 184–200, 2014.

height of the fixpoint. This estimated height is then fine-tuned with the statistical method. Second, because this height progress usually does not indicate the actual progress (speed), we normalize the progress using the pre-analysis.

We show that our technique effectively estimates static analysis progress in a realistic setting. We have implemented our idea on top of SPARROW [1]. In our experiments with various open-source benchmarks, the proposed technique is found to be useful to estimate the progress of interval, octagon, and pointer analyses. The pre-analysis overheads are 3.8%, 7.3%, and 36.6% on average in interval, pointer, and octagon analysis, respectively.

Contributions. This paper makes the following contributions:

- We present a technique for estimating static analysis progress. To our knowledge, our work is the first attempt to estimate static analysis progress.
- We show its applicability for numerical analyses (with intervals and octagons) and a pointer analysis on a suite of real C benchmarks.

Related Work. Though progress estimation techniques have been extensively studied in other fields [12,7,4,8,10,11], there have been no research for static analyzers. For instance, a varaiety of progress estimation techniques have been proposed for long-running software systems such as databases [7,4,8] and parallel data processing systems [11,10]. Static analyzers are also a long-running software system but there are no progress estimation techniques for them. Furthermore, our method is different from existing techniques. Existing progress estimators [10,8,11,4] and algorithm runtime prediction [6] are based solely on statistics or machine learning. By contrast, we propose a technique that combines a semantics-based pre-analysis with machine learning.

Outline. Section 2 describes the overall approach to our progress estimation and the remaining sections fill the details. Section 3 defines a class of non-relational static analyses and Section 4 gives the details on how we develop a progress bar for these analyses. Section 5 experimentally evaluates the proposed technique. Section 6 discusses the application to relational analyses. Section 7 concludes.

2 Overall Approach to Progress Estimation

In this section, we describe the high-level idea of our progress estimation technique. In Section 4, we give details that we used in our experiments.

2.1 Static Analysis

We consider a static analysis designed by abstract interpretation. In abstract interpretation, a static analysis is specified with an abstract domain $\mathbb{D}$ and semantic function $F : \mathbb{D} \to \mathbb{D}$, where $\mathbb{D}$ is a cpo (complete partial order).The analysis' job is to compute the following sequence until stabilized:

$$\bigsqcup_{i \in \mathbb{N}} F^i(\bot) = F^0(\bot) \sqcup F^1(\bot) \sqcup F^2(\bot) \sqcup \cdots \quad (1)$$

where $F^0(\bot) = \bot$ and $F^{i+1}(\bot) = F(F^i(\bot))$. When the chain is infinitely long, we can use a widening operator $\nabla : \mathbb{D} \times \mathbb{D} \to \mathbb{D}$ to accelerate the sequence.

2.2 Progress Estimation

We aim to develop a progress bar that proceeds at a linear rate. That is, the estimated progress directly indicates the amount of work that has been completed so far. Suppose that the sequence in (1) requires n iterations to stabilize, and assume that computing the abstract semantics $F(X)$ at each iteration takes a constant time regardless of the input X. Then, the *actual progress* of the analysis at ith iteration is defined by $\frac{i}{n}$. We aim at estimating this progress.

Basically, our method estimates the progress by calculating the lattice heights of intermediate analysis results. Suppose that we have a function $\mathsf{H} : \mathbb{D} \to \mathbb{N}$ that takes an abstract domain element $X \in \mathbb{D}$ and computes its height. The heights of domain elements need not be precisely defined, but we assume that H satisfies two conditions: 1) the height is initially zero. 2) H is monotone. The second condition is for building a progress bar that monotonically increases as the analysis makes progress.

The first job in our progress estimation is to approximate the height of the final analysis result. Let H_{final} be the height of the final analysis result, i.e., $H_{\mathit{final}} = \mathsf{H}(\bigsqcup_{i \in \mathbb{N}} F^i(\bot))$. In Section 4.3, we describe a method for precisely estimating H_{final} with the aid of statistical regression. This height estimation method is orthogonal to the rest part of our progress estimation technique. In this overview, let $H^\sharp_{\mathit{final}}$ be the estimated final height and assume, for simplicity, that $H^\sharp_{\mathit{final}} = H_{\mathit{final}}$.

A Naive Approach. Given H and $H^\sharp_{\mathit{final}}$, a simple progress bar could be developed as follows. At each iteration i, we first compute the height of the current analysis result:

$$H_i = \mathsf{H}(F^i(\bot)).$$

Then, we show to the users the following *height progress* of the analysis :

$$P_i = \frac{H_i}{H^\sharp_{\mathit{final}}}$$

Note that we can use P_i as a progress estimation: P_i is initially 0, monotonically increases as the analysis makes progress, and has 1 when the analysis is completed.

Problem of the Naive Approach. We noticed that this simple method for progress estimation is, however, unsatisfactory in practice. The main problem is that the height progress does not necessarily indicate the amount of computation that has been completed. For instance, the solid line in Figure 1(a) depicts how the height progress increases during our interval analysis of program `sendmail-8.14.6` (The dotted diagonal line represents the ideal progress bar). As the figure shows,

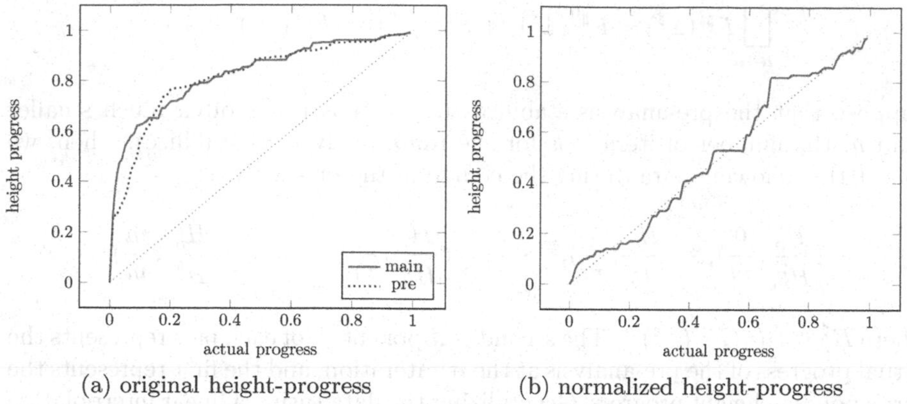

Fig. 1. The height progress of a main analysis can be normalized using a pre-analysis. In this program (`sendmail-8.14.6`), the pre-analysis takes only 6.6% of the main analysis time.

the height progress rapidly increases during the early stage of the analysis and after that slowly converges. We found that this progress bar is not much useful to infer the actual progress nor to predict the remaining time of the analysis.

Our Approach. We overcome this problem by normalizing the height progress using the relationship between the actual progress and the height progress. Suppose at the moment that we are given a function $\mathsf{normalize} : [0, 1] \to [0, 1]$ that maps the height progress into the corresponding actual progress. Indeed, $\mathsf{normalize}$ represents the inverse of the graph (the solid line) shown in Figure 1(a). Given such $\mathsf{normalize}$, the normalized height progress is defined as follows:

$$\bar{P}_i = \mathsf{normalize}(P_i) = \mathsf{normalize}(\frac{H_i}{H^\sharp_{final}}) \quad (2)$$

Note that, unlike the original height progress P_i, the normalized progress $\bar{P}_i$ would represent the actual progress, increasing at a linear rate. However, note also that we cannot compute $\mathsf{normalize}$ unless we run the main analysis.

The key insight of our method is that we can predict the $\mathsf{normalize}$ function by using a less precise, but cheaper pre-analysis than the main analysis. Our hypothesis is that if the pre-analysis is semantically related with the main analysis, it is likely that the pre-analysis' height-progress behavior is similar to that of the main analysis. In this article, we show that this hypothesis is experimentally true and allows to estimate sufficiently precise normalization functions.

We first design a pre-analysis as a further abstraction of the main analysis. Let $\mathbb{D}^\sharp$ and $F^\sharp : \mathbb{D}^\sharp \to \mathbb{D}^\sharp$ be such abstract domain and semantic function of the pre-analysis, respectively. In Section 4.2, we give the exact definition of the pre-analysis design we used. Next, we run this pre-analysis, computing the following sequence until stabilized:

$$\bigsqcup_{i \in \mathbb{N}} F^{\sharp^i}(\bot^\sharp) = F^{\sharp^0}(\bot^\sharp) \sqcup F^{\sharp^1}(\bot^\sharp) \sqcup F^{\sharp^2}(\bot^\sharp) \sqcup \cdots$$

Suppose that the pre-analysis stabilizes in m steps (m is often much smaller than n, the number of iterations for the main analysis to stabilize). Then, we collect the following data during the course of the pre-analysis:

$$(\frac{H_0^\sharp}{H_m^\sharp}, \frac{0}{m}), \quad (\frac{H_1^\sharp}{H_m^\sharp}, \frac{1}{m}), \quad \cdots, \quad (\frac{H_i^\sharp}{H_m^\sharp}, \frac{i}{m}), \quad \cdots, \quad (\frac{H_m^\sharp}{H_m^\sharp}, \frac{m}{m})$$

where $H_i^\sharp = \mathsf{H}(\gamma(F^{\sharp^i}(\bot^\sharp)))$. The second component $\frac{i}{m}$ of each pair represents the actual progress of the pre-analysis at the ith iteration, and the first represents the corresponding height progress. Generalizing the data (using a linear interpolation method), we obtain a normalization function $\mathsf{normalize}^\sharp : [0,1] \to [0,1]$ for the pre-analysis.

The normalization function $\mathsf{normalize}^\sharp$ of such a pre-analysis can be a good estimation of the normalization function $\mathsf{normalize}$ of the main analysis. For instance, the dotted curve in Figure 1(a) shows the height progress of our pre-analysis (defined in Section 4.2), which has a clear resemblance with the height progress (the solid line) of the main analysis. Thanks to this similarity, it is acceptable in practice to use the normalization function $\mathsf{normalize}^\sharp$ for the pre-analysis instead of $\mathsf{normalize}$ in our progress estimation. Thus, we revise (2) as follows:

$$\bar{P}_i^\sharp = \mathsf{normalize}^\sharp(\frac{H_i}{H_{\mathit{final}}}) \tag{3}$$

That is, at each iteration i of the main analysis, we show the estimated normalized progress $\bar{P}_i^\sharp$ to the users. Figure 1(b) depicts $\bar{P}_i^\sharp$ for `sendmail-8.14.6` (on the assumption that $H_{\mathit{final}}^\sharp = H_{\mathit{final}}$). Note that, unlike the original progress bar (the solid line in Figure 1(a)), the normalized progress bar progresses at an almost linear rate.

3 Setting

In this section, we define a class of static analyses on top of which we develop our progress estimation technique. For presentation brevity, we consider non-relational analyses. However, our overall approach to progress estimation is also applicable to relational analyses. In Section 6, we discuss the application to a relational analysis with the octagon domain.

Static Analysis. A program is a tuple $\langle \mathbb{C}, \hookrightarrow \rangle$ where $\mathbb{C}$ is a set of program points, $(\hookrightarrow) \subseteq \mathbb{C} \times \mathbb{C}$ is a relation that denotes control flows: $c \hookrightarrow c'$ indicates that c' is a next program point of c. Each program point is associated with a command: $\mathsf{cmd}(c)$ denotes the command associated with program point c.

We consider a class of static analyses whose abstract domain maps program points to abstract states:

$$\mathbb{D} = \mathbb{C} \to \mathbb{S}$$

where the abstract state is a map from abstract locations to abstract values:

$$\mathbb{S} = \mathbb{L} \to \mathbb{V}$$

We assume that the set of abstract locations is finite and $\mathbb{V}$ is a complete lattice. The abstract semantics of the program is characterized by the least fixpoint of abstract semantic function $F \in (\mathbb{C} \to \mathbb{S}) \to (\mathbb{C} \to \mathbb{S})$ defined as,

$$F(X) = \lambda c \in \mathbb{C}. f_c(\bigsqcup_{c' \hookrightarrow c} X(c')) \tag{4}$$

where $f_c \in \mathbb{S} \to \mathbb{S}$ is the transfer function for control point c.

Example 1 (Interval Analysis). Consider the following imperative language.:

$$x := e \mid \mathsf{assume}(x < n) \quad \text{where} \quad e \to n \mid x \mid e + e$$

All basic commands are assignments or assume commands. An expression may be a constant integer (n), a binary operation ($e + e$), a variable expression (x). Let *Var* be the set of all program variables. We define the abstract state as a map from program variables to the lattice of intervals:

$$\mathbb{L} = \mathit{Var} \qquad \mathbb{V} = \{[l, u] \mid l, u \in \mathbb{Z} \cup \{-\infty, +\infty\} \ \wedge \ l \leq u\} \cup \{\bot\} \tag{5}$$

The transfer function $f_c : \mathbb{S} \to \mathbb{S}$ is defines as follows:

$$f_c(s) = \begin{cases} s[x \mapsto \mathcal{V}(e)(s)] & \mathsf{cmd}(c) = x := e \\ s[x \mapsto s(x) \sqcap [-\infty, n-1])] & \mathsf{cmd}(c) = \mathsf{assume}(x < n) \end{cases}$$

where auxiliary function $\mathcal{V}(e) \in \mathbb{S} \to \mathbb{V}$ computes the abstract value for e under s:

$$\mathcal{V}(n)(s) = [n, n], \quad \mathcal{V}(e_1 + e_2)(s) = \mathcal{V}(e_1)(s) \oplus \mathcal{V}(e_2)(s), \quad \mathcal{V}(x)(s) = s(x)$$

where $\oplus$ denotes the abstract binary operator for the interval domain.

Example 2 (Pointer Analysis). Consider the following imperative language:

$$x := e \mid *x := e \quad \text{where} \quad e \to x \mid \&x \mid *x$$

We design a (flow-sensitive) pointer analysis as follows. The abstract state is a map from program variables to its points-to set, i.e.,

$$\mathbb{L} = \mathit{Var} \qquad \mathbb{V} = \mathcal{P}(\mathit{Var}) \tag{6}$$

The transfer function $f_c : \mathbb{S} \to \mathbb{S}$ is defines as follows:

$$f_c(s) = \begin{cases} s[x \mapsto \mathcal{V}(e)(s)] & \mathsf{cmd}(c) = x := e \\ s[l_1 \mapsto s(l_1) \cup \mathcal{V}(e)(s)] \cdots [l_n \mapsto s(l_n) \cup \mathcal{V}(e)(s)] & \mathsf{cmd}(c) = *x := e \end{cases}$$

where $s(x) = \{l_1, \ldots, l_n\}$. For simplicity, we do not consider strong updates. In this case, $\mathcal{V}(e)(s)$ is defined as follows:

$$\mathcal{V}(x)(s) = s(x), \quad \mathcal{V}(\&x)(s) = \{x\}, \quad \mathcal{V}(*x)(s) = \bigcup_{l \in s(x)} s(l)$$

Fixpoint Computation with Widening. When the domain of abstract values ($\mathbb{V}$) has infinite height, we need a widening operator $\nabla : \mathbb{V} \times \mathbb{V} \to \mathbb{V}$ to approximate the least fixpoint of F. In practice, the widening operator is applied at only headers of flow cycles [3]. Let $\mathbb{W} \subseteq \mathbb{C}$ be the set of widening points (all loop headers in the program) in the program.

Example 3. We use the following widening operator in our interval analysis:

$$[l, u] \nabla [l', u'] = [\textit{if } (l' < l) \textit{ then } -\infty \textit{ else } l, \textit{if } (u' > u) \textit{ then } +\infty \textit{ else } u].$$

4 Details on Our Progress Estimation

As described in Section 2, our progress estimation is done in two steps: (1) we first run a pre-analysis to obtain an estimated normalization function $\mathsf{normalize}^\sharp$ and an estimated final height $H^\sharp_{final}$; (2) using them, at each iteration of the main analysis, we measure the height progress, convert it to the estimated actual progress, and show it to users. However, Section 2 has left out a number of details. In this section, we give the details that we tried:

- In Section 4.1, we define our height function H.
- In Section 4.2, we describe our pre-analysis design.
- In Section 4.3, we present techniques for precise estimation of the final height.

4.1 The Height Function

We first define height function $\mathsf{H} : (\mathbb{C} \to \mathbb{S}) \to \mathbb{N}$ that takes an abstract domain element and computes its height. Since our analysis is non-relational, we assume that the height of an abstract domain element is computed point-wise as follows:

$$\mathsf{H}(X) = \sum_{c \in \mathbb{C}} \sum_{l \in \mathbb{L}} \mathsf{h}(X(c)(l)) \tag{7}$$

where $\mathsf{h} : \mathbb{V} \to \mathbb{N}$ is the height function for the abstract value domain ($\mathbb{V}$).

Example 4. For the interval domain $\mathbb{V}$ in (5), we use the following height function:

$$\mathsf{h}(\bot) = 0$$

$$\mathsf{h}([a, b]) = \begin{cases} 1 & a = b \ \land \ a, b \in \mathbb{Z} \\ 2 & a < b \ \land \ a, b \in \mathbb{Z} \\ 3 & a \in \mathbb{Z} \ \land \ b = +\infty \\ 3 & a = -\infty \ \land \ b \in \mathbb{Z} \\ 4 & a = -\infty \ \land \ b = +\infty \end{cases}$$

We defined this height function based on the actual workings of our interval analysis. Constant intervals (the first case) have height 1 since they are usually immediately generated from program texts. The finite intervals (the second case) are often introduced by joining two constant intervals. Intervals with one infinite bound (the third and fourth cases) are due to the widening operator. Note that our widening operator (Example 3) immediately assigns $\pm\infty$ to unstable bounds. $[-\infty, +\infty]$ is generated with the widening is applied to both bounds.

Example 5. For the pointer domain $\mathbb{V}$ in (6), we use the following height function:

$$\mathsf{h}(S) = \begin{cases} 4 & \parallel S \parallel \geq 4 \\ \parallel S \parallel & \text{otherwise} \end{cases}$$

This definition is based on our observation that, in flow-sensitive pointer analysis of C programs, most of the points-to sets have sizes less than 4.

4.2 Pre-analysis via Partial Flow-Sensitivity

A key component of our method is the pre-analysis that is used to estimate both the height-progress behavior and the maximum height of the main analysis. One natural method for further abstracting static analyses in Section 3 is to approximate the level of flow-sensitivity. In this subsection, we design a pre-analysis that was found to be useful in progress estimation.

We consider a class of pre-analyses that is partially flow-sensitive version of the main analysis. While the main analysis is fully flow-sensitive (i.e., the orders of program statements are fully respected), our pre-analysis only respects the orders of some selected program points and regards other program points flow-insensitively.

In particular, we are interested in a pre-analysis that only distinguishes program points around headers of flow cycles. In static analysis, the most interesting things usually happen in flow cycles. For instance, because of widening and join, significant changes in abstract states occur at flow cycle headers. Thus, it is reasonable to pay particular attention to height increases occurred at widening points ($\mathbb{W}$). To control the level of flow-sensitivity, we also distinguish some preceding points of widening points.

Formally, the set of distinguished program points is defined as follows. Suppose that a parameter *depth* is given, which indicates how many preceding points of flow cycle headers are separated in our pre-analysis. Then, we decide to distinguish the following set $\Phi \subseteq \mathbb{C}$ of program points:

$$\Phi = \{c \in \mathbb{C} \mid w \in \mathbb{W} \wedge c \hookrightarrow^{depth} w\}$$

where $c \hookrightarrow^{i} c'$ means that c' is reachable from c within i steps of $\hookrightarrow$.

We define the pre-analysis that is flow-sensitive only for Φ as a special instance of the trace partitioning [16]. The set of partitioning indicies Δ is defined by $\Delta = \Phi \cup \{\bullet\}$, where $\bullet$ represents all the other program points not included in Φ. That is, we use the following partitioning function $\delta : \mathbb{C} \to \Delta$:

$$\delta(c) = \begin{cases} c & c \in \Phi \\ \bullet & c \notin \Phi \end{cases}$$

With δ, we define the abstract domain ($\mathbb{D}^\sharp$) and semantic function ($F^\sharp$) of the pre-analysis as follows:

$$\mathbb{C} \to \mathbb{S} \underset{\alpha}{\overset{\gamma}{\leftrightarrows}} \Delta \to \mathbb{S}$$

where

$$\gamma(X) = \lambda c.\ X(\delta(c)).$$

The semantic function $F^\sharp : (\Delta \to \mathbb{S}) \to (\Delta \to \mathbb{S})$ is defined as,

$$F^\sharp(X) = \lambda i \in \Delta.\ (\bigsqcup_{c \in \delta^{-1}(i)} f_c(\bigsqcup_{c' \hookrightarrow c} X(\delta(c')))) \tag{8}$$

where $\delta^{-1}(i) = \{c \in \mathbb{C} \mid \delta(c) = i\}$.

Note that, in our pre-analysis, we can control the granularity of flow-sensitivity by adjusting the parameter *depth* $\in [0, \infty]$. A larger *depth* value yields a more precise pre-analysis. In our experiments (Section 5), we use 1 for the default value of *depth* and show that how the progress estimation quality improves with higher *depth* values. It is easy to check that our pre-analysis is sound with respect to the main analysis regardless of parameter *depth*.

4.3 Precise Estimation of the Final Height

The last component in our approach is to estimate H_{final}, the height value of the final analysis result. Note that H_{final} cannot be computed unless we actually run the main analysis. Instead, we compute $H^\sharp_{final}$, an estimation of H_{final}. We replace the H_{final} in (3) by $H^\sharp_{final}$ as follows:

$$\bar{P}^\sharp_i = \mathsf{normalize}^\sharp(\frac{H_i}{H^\sharp_{final}}) \tag{9}$$

Our goal is to compute $H^\sharp_{final}$ such that $|H^\sharp_{final} - H_{final}|$ is as smaller as possible, for which we use the pre-analysis and a statistical method. First, we compute H_{pre}, the final height of the pre-analysis result, i.e.,

$$H_{pre} = \mathsf{H}(\gamma(\mathbf{lfp}F^\sharp))$$

Next, we statistically refine H_{pre} into $H^\sharp_{final}$ such that $|H^\sharp_{final} - H_{final}|$ is likely smaller than $|H_{pre} - H_{final}|$. The job of the statistical method is to predict $\alpha = \frac{H_{final}}{H_{pre}}$ $(0 \le \alpha \le 1)$ for a given program. With α, $H^\sharp_{final}$ is defined as follows:

$$H^\sharp_{final} = \alpha \cdot H_{pre}$$

We assume that α is defined as a linear combination of a set of program features in Table 1. We used eight syntactic features and six semantic features.

The features are selected among over 30 features by feature selection for the purpose of removing redundant or irrelevant ones for better accuracy. We used L1 based recursive feature elimination to find optimal subset of features using 254 benchmark programs.

The feature values are normalized to real numbers between 0 and 1. The Post-fixpoint features are about the post-fixpoint property. Since the pre-analysis result is a post fixpoint of the semantic function F, i.e., $\gamma(\mathbf{lfp}F^\sharp) \in \{x \in \mathbb{D} \mid x \sqsupseteq F(x)\}$, we can refine the result by iteratively applying F to the pre-analysis result. Instead of doing refinement, we designed simple indicators that show possibility of the refinement to avoid extra cost. For every traning example, a feature vector is created with a negligible overhead.

We used the ridge linear regression as the learning algorithm. The ridge linear regression algorithm is known as a quick and effective technique for numerical prediction.

Table 1. The feature vector used by linear regression to construct prediction models

Category	Feature
Inter-procedural (syntactic)	# function calls in the program
	# functions in recursive call cycles
	# undefined library function calls
Loop-related (syntactic)	the maximum loop size
	the average loop sizes
	the standard deviation of loop sizes
	the standard deviation of depths of loops
	# loopheads
Numerical analysis (semantic)	# bounded intervals in the pre-analysis result
	# unbounded intervals in the pre-analysis result
Pointer analysis (semantic)	# points-to sets of cardinality over 4 in the pre-analysis result
	# points-to sets of cardinality under 4 in the pre-analysis result
Post-fixpoint (semantic)	# program points where applying the transfer function once improves the precision
	height decrease when transfer function is applied once

In a way orthogonal to the statistical method, we further reduce $|H^\sharp_{\mathit{final}} - H_{\mathit{final}}|$ by tuning the height function. We reduce $|H^\sharp_{\mathit{final}} - H_{\mathit{final}}|$ by considering only subsets of program points and abstract locations. However, it is not the best way to choose the smallest subsets of them when computing heights. For example, we may simply set both of them to be an empty set. Then, $|H^\sharp_{\mathit{final}} - H_{\mathit{final}}|$ will be zero, but both H_{final} and $H^\sharp_{\mathit{final}}$ will be also zero. Undoubtedly, that results in a useless progress bar as estimated progress is always zero in that case.

Our goal is to choose program points and abstract locations as small as possible, while maintaining the progress estimation quality. To this end, we used the following two heuristics:

- We focus only on abstract locations that contribute to increases of heights during the main analysis. Let $\mathsf{D}(c)$ an over-approximation of the set of such abstract locations at program point c:

$$\mathsf{D}(c) \supseteq \{l \in \mathbb{L} \mid \exists i \in \{1 \ldots n\}.\mathsf{h}(X_i(c)(l)) - \mathsf{h}(X_{i-1}(c)(l)) > 0\}$$

  Note that since we cannot obtain the set a priori, we use an over-approximation.
- We consider only on flow cycle headers in the height calculation. This is because cycle headers are places where significant operations (join and widening) happen.

Thus, we revise the height function $\mathsf{H} : \mathbb{D} \to \mathbb{N}$ in (7) as follows:

$$\mathsf{H}(X) = \sum_{c \in \mathbb{W}} \sum_{l \in \mathsf{D}(c)} \mathsf{h}(X(c)(l)) \tag{10}$$

Because $\mathbb{W} \subseteq \mathbb{C}$ and $\forall c.\ \mathsf{D}(c) \subseteq \mathbb{L}$, the height approximation error for the new H is smaller than that of the original H in (7).

We performed 3-fold cross validation using 254 benchmarks including GNU softwares and linux packages. For interval analysis, we obtained 0.06 as a mean absolute error of α, and 0.05 for pointer analysis.

5 Experiments

In this section, we evaluate our progress estimation technique described so far. We show that our technique effectively estimates the progress of an interval domain–based static analyzer, and a pointer analyzer for C programs.

5.1 Setting

We evaluate our progress estimation technique with SPARROW [1], a realistic C static analyzer that detects memory errors such as buffer-overruns and null dereferences. SPARROW basically performs a flow-sensitive and context-insensitive analysis with the interval abstract domain. The abstract state is a map from abstract locations (including program variables, allocation-sites, and structure fields) to abstract values (including intervals, points-to sets, array and structure blocks). Details on SPARROW's abstract semantics is available at [13]. SPARROW performs a sparse analysis [14] and the analysis has two phases: data dependency generation and fixpoint computation. Our technique aims to estimate the progress of the fixpoint computation step and, in this paper, we mean by analysis time the fixpoint computation time.

We have implemented our technique as described in Section 2 and 4. We used the height function defined in Example 4 and 5. To estimate numerical, and pointer analysis progresses, we split the SPARROW into two analyzers so that each of them may analyze only numeric or pointer-related property respectively. The pre-analysis is based on the partial flow-sensitivity defined in Section 4.2, where we set the parameter *depth* as 1 by default. That is, the pre-analysis is flow-sensitive only for flow cycle headers and their immediate preceding points.

All our experiments were performed on a machine with a 3.07 GHz Intel Core i7 processor and 24 GB of memory. For statistical estimation of the final height, we used the `scikit-learn` machine learning library [15].

5.2 Results

We tested our progress estimation techniques on 8 GNU software packages for each of analyses. Table 2 and 3 show our results.

Table 2. Progress estimation results (interval analysis). **LOC** shows the lines of code before pre-processing. **Main** reports the main analysis time. **Pre** reports the time spent by our pre-analysis. **Linearity** indicates the quality of progress estimation (best : 1). **Height-Approx.** denotes the precision of our height approximation (best : 1). **Err** denotes mean of absolute difference between **Height-Approx.** and 1 (best : 0).

Program	LOC	Time(s)		Linearity	Overhead	Height-Approx.
		Main	Pre			
bison-1.875	38841	3.66	0.91	0.73	24.86%	1.03
screen-4.0.2	44745	40.04	2.37	0.86	5.92%	0.96
lighttpd-1.4.25	56518	27.30	1.21	0.89	4.43%	0.92
a2ps-4.14	64590	32.05	11.26	0.51	35.13%	1.06
gnu-cobol-1.1	67404	413.54	99.33	0.54	24.02%	0.91
gnugo	87575	1541.35	7.35	0.89	0.48%	1.12
bash-2.05	102406	16.55	2.26	0.80	13.66%	0.93
sendmail-8.14.6	136146	1348.97	5.81	0.69	0.43%	0.93
TOTAL	686380	3423.46	130.5	**0.74**	**3.81%**	**Err : 0.07**

Table 3. Progress estimation results (pointer analysis).

Program	LOC	Time(s)		Linearity	Overhead	Height-Approx.
		Main	Pre			
screen-4.0.2	44745	15.89	1.56	0.90	9.82%	0.98
lighttpd	56518	11.54	0.87	0.76	7.54%	1.03
a2ps-4.14	64590	10.06	3.48	0.65	34.59%	1.04
gnu-cobol-1.1	67404	32.27	12.22	0.91	37.87%	1.03
gnugo	87575	217.77	3.88	0.64	1.78%	0.97
bash-2.05	102406	3.68	0.78	0.56	21.20%	1.04
proftpd-1.3.2	126996	74.64	11.14	0.82	14.92%	1.03
sendmail-8.14.6	136146	145.62	3.15	0.58	2.16%	0.98
TOTAL	686380	511.47	37.08	**0.73**	**7.25%**	**Err : 0.03**

The **Linearity** column in Table 2, and 3 quantifies the "linearity", which we define as follows:

$$1 - \frac{\sum_{1 \leq i \leq n}(\frac{i}{n} - \bar{P}^{\sharp}_{i})^2}{\sum_{1 \leq i \leq n}(\frac{i}{n} - \frac{n+1}{2n})^2}$$

where n is the number of iterations required for the analysis to stabilize and $\bar{P}_i^\sharp$ is the estimated progress at ith iteration of the analysis. This metric is just a simple application of the coefficient of determination in statistics, i.e., R^2, which presents how well $\bar{P}^\sharp$ fits the actual progress rate $\frac{i}{n}$. The closer to 1 linearity is, the more similar to the ideal progress bar $\bar{P}_i^\sharp$ is. Figure 3 presents the resulting progress bars for each of benchmark programs providing graphical descriptions of the linearity. In particular, the progress bar proceeds almost linearly for programs of the linearity close to 0.9 (`lighttpd-1.4.25`, `gnugo-3.8` in interval analysis, `gnu-cobol-1.1`, `bash-2.05` in pointer analysis). For some programs of relatively low linearity (`gnu-cobol-1.1`, `bash-2.05` in interval analysis, `gnugo-3.8`, `proftpd-1.3.2` in pointer analysis), the progress estimation is comparatively rough but still useful.

The **Height-Approx.** column stands for the accuracy of final height approximation $\frac{H_{final}}{H_{final}^\sharp}$ where $H_{final}^\sharp$ is estimated final height via the statistical technique described in section 4.3. **Err** denotes an average of absolute errors |**Height-Approx.** -1|. To prove our statistical method avoids overfitting problem, we performed 3-fold cross validation using 254 benchmarks including GNU softwares and linux packages. For interval analysis, we obtained 0.063 **Err** with 0.007 standard deviation. For pointer analysis, 0.053 **Err** with 0.001 standard deviation. These results show our method avoids overfitting, evenly yielding precise estimations at the same time.

The **Overhead** column shows the total overhead of our method, which includes the pre-analysis running time (Section 4.2). The average performance overheads of our method are 3.8% in interval analysis, and 7.3% in pointer analysis respectively.

5.3 Discussion

Linearity vs. Overhead. In our progress estimation method, we can make tradeoffs between the linearity and overhead. Table 2, 3 show our progress estimations when we use the default parameter value ($depth = 1$) in the pre-analysis. By using a higher *depth* value, we can improve the precision of the pre-analysis and hence the quality of the resulting progress estimation at the cost of extra overhead. For two programs, the following table shows the changes in linearity and overhead when we change *depth* from 1 to 3:

Program	Linearity change	Overhead change
bash-2.05 (pointer)	0.56 → 0.70	21.2% → 37.5%
sendmail-8.14.6 (interval)	0.69 → 0.95	0.4% → 18.4%

Height Approximation Error. In our experiments, we noticed that our progress estimation method is sensitive to the height approximation error ($H_{final}^\sharp - H_{final}$). Although we precisely estimate heights of the fixpoints, there are cases where even small error sometimes leads to unsatisfactory results. For instance,

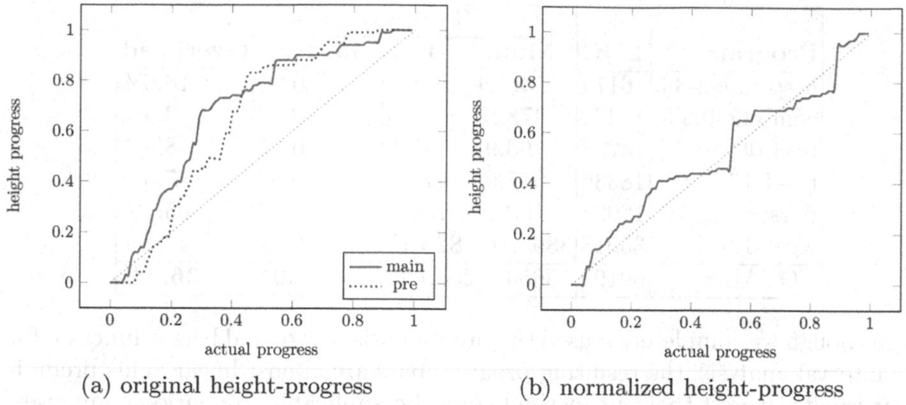

Fig. 2. Our method is also applicable to octagon domain–based static analyses

the reason why the progress for `gnu-cobol-1.1` is under-estimated is the height approximation error(0.09).

We believe enhancing the precision will be achieved by increasing training examples and relevant features.

6 Application to Relational Analyses

The overall approach of our progress estimation technique may adapt easily to relational analyses as well. In this section, we check the possibility of applying our technique to the octagon domain–based static analysis [9].

We have implemented a prototype progress estimator for the octagon analysis as follows. For pre-analysis, we used the same partial flow-sensitive abstraction described in Section 4.2 with *depth* $= 1$. Regarding the height function H, we also used that of the interval analysis. Note that, since an octagon domain element is a collection of intervals denoting ranges of program variables such as x and y, their sum $x + y$, and their difference $x - y$, we can use the same height function in Example 4. In this prototype implementation, we assumed that we are given heights of the final analysis results.

Figure 2 shows that our technique effectively normalizes the height progress of the octagon analysis. The solid lines in Figure 2(a) depicts the height progress of the main octagon analysis of program `wget-1.9` and the dotted line shows that of the pre-analysis. By normalizing the main analysis' progress behavior, we obtain the progress bar depicted in Figure 2(b), which is almost linear.

Figure 3 depicts the resulting progress bar for other benchmark programs, and the following table reports detailed experimental results.

		Time(s)			
Program	**LOC**	**Main**	**Pre**	**Linearity**	**Overhead**
httptunnel-3.3	6174	49.5	8.2	0.91	16.6%
combine-0.3.3	11472	478.2	16	0.89	3.4%
bc-1.06	14288	63.9	43.8	0.96	68.6%
tar-1.17	18336	977.0	73.1	0.82	7.5%
parser	18923	190.1	104.8	0.97	55.1%
wget-1.9	35018	3895.36	1823.15	0.92	46.8%
TOTAL	69193	5654.0	2069.49	**0.91**	**36.6%**

Even though we completely reused the pre-analysis design and height function for the interval analysis, the resulting progress bars are almost linear. This preliminary results suggest that our method could be applicable to relational analyses.

7 Conclusion

We have proposed a technique for estimating static analysis progress. Our technique is based on the observation that semantically related analyses would have similar progress behaviors, so that the progress of the main analysis can be estimated by a pre-analysis. We implemented our technique on top of a realistic C static analyzer and show our technique effectively estimates its progress.

Acknowledgment. The authors would like to thank the anonymous referees for their comments in improving this work.

References

1. Sparrow, `http://ropas.snu.ac.kr/sparrow`
2. Blanchet, B., Cousot, P., Cousot, R., Feret, J., Mauborgne, L., Miné, A., Monniaux, D., Rival, X.: A static analyzer for large safety-critical software. In: Proceedings of the ACM SIGPLAN-SIGACT Conference on Programming Language Design and Implementation, pp. 196–207 (2003)
3. Bourdoncle, F.: Efficient chaotic iteration strategies with widenings. In: Pottosin, I.V., Bjorner, D., Broy, M. (eds.) FMP&TA 1993. LNCS, vol. 735, pp. 128–141. Springer, Heidelberg (1993)
4. Chaudhuri, S., Narasayya, V., Ramamurthy, R.: Estimating progress of execution for sql queries. In: Proceedings of the 2004 ACM SIGMOD International Conference on Management of Data, SIGMOD 2004, pp. 803–814. ACM, New York (2004)
5. Cousot, P., Cousot, R., Feret, J., Mauborgne, L., Miné, A., Rival, X.: Why does astrée scale up? Formal Methods in System Design 35(3), 229–264 (2009)
6. Hutter, F., Xu, L., Hoos, H.H., Leyton-Brown, K.: Algorithm runtime prediction: The state of the art. CoRR, abs/1211.0906 (2012)
7. König, A.C., Ding, B., Chaudhuri, S., Narasayya, V.: A statistical approach towards robust progress estimation. Proc. VLDB Endow. 5(4), 382–393 (2011)

8. Luo, G., Naughton, J.F., Ellmann, C.J., Watzke, M.W.: Toward a progress indicator for database queries. In: Proceedings of the 2004 ACM SIGMOD International Conference on Management of Data, SIGMOD 2004, pp. 791–802. ACM, New York (2004)
9. Miné, A.: The Octagon Abstract Domain. Higher-Order and Symbolic Computation 19(1), 31–100 (2006)
10. Morton, K., Friesen, A., Balazinska, M., Grossman, D.: Estimating the progress of MapReduce pipelines. In: Proc. of ICDE, pp. 681–684. IEEE (2010)
11. Morton, K., Balazinska, M., Grossman, D.: Paratimer: a progress indicator for mapreduce dags. In: Proceedings of the 2010 ACM SIGMOD International Conference on Management of Data, SIGMOD 2010, pp. 507–518. ACM, New York (2010)
12. Myers, B.A.: The importance of percent-done progress indicators for computer-human interfaces. In: Proceedings of the SIGCHI Conference on Human Factors in Computing Systems, CHI 1985, pp. 11–17. ACM, New York (1985)
13. Oh, H., Brutschy, L., Yi, K.: Access analysis-based tight localization of abstract memories. In: Jhala, R., Schmidt, D. (eds.) VMCAI 2011. LNCS, vol. 6538, pp. 356–370. Springer, Heidelberg (2011)
14. Oh, H., Heo, K., Lee, W., Lee, W., Yi, K.: Design and implementation of sparse global analyses for C-like languages. In: Proceedings of the ACM SIGPLAN Conference on Programming Language Design and Implementation (2012)
15. Pedregosa, F., Varoquaux, G., Gramfort, A., Michel, V., Thirion, B., Grisel, O., Blondel, M., Prettenhofer, P., Weiss, R., Dubourg, V., Vanderplas, J., Passos, A., Cournapeau, D., Brucher, M., Perrot, M., Duchesnay, E.: Scikit-learn: Machine learning in Python. Journal of Machine Learning Research 12, 2825–2830 (2011)
16. Rival, X., Mauborgne, L.: The trace partitioning abstract domain. ACM Trans. on Programming Languages and System 29(5), 26–51 (2007)

A Progress Graphs

In this appendix, progress graphs are presented. Figure 3 presents the resulting interval, pointer, and octagon analysis progress bars respectively. Dotted diagonal line denotes the ideal progress bar.

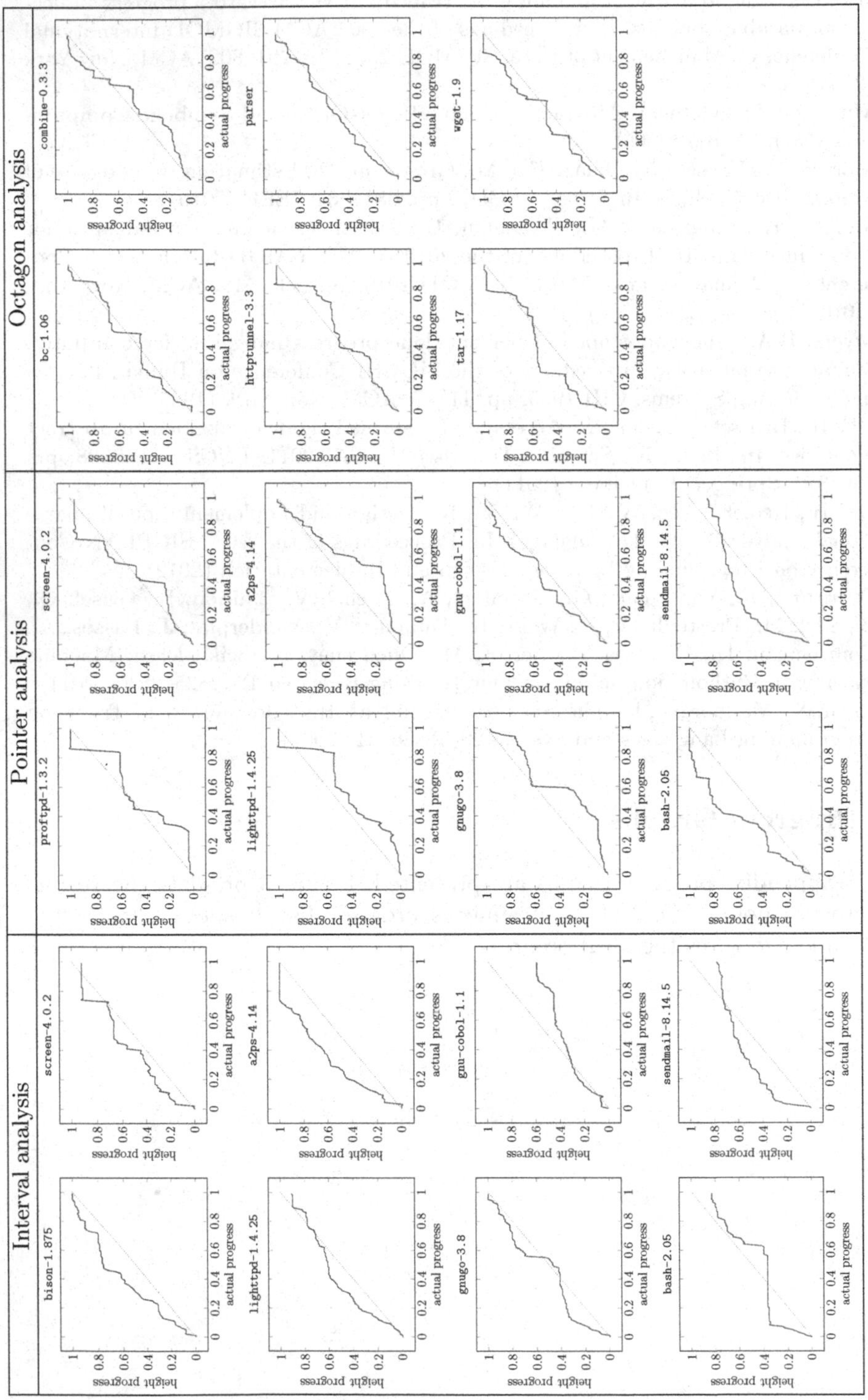

Fig. 3. Our progress estimation when $depth = 1$.

Sparse Dataflow Analysis with Pointers and Reachability

Magnus Madsen and Anders Møller

Aarhus University, Denmark
{magnusm,amoeller}@cs.au.dk

Abstract. Many static analyzers exploit sparseness techniques to reduce the amount of information being propagated and stored during analysis. Although several variations are described in the literature, no existing technique is suitable for analyzing JavaScript code. In this paper, we point out the need for a sparse analysis framework that supports pointers and reachability. We present such a framework, which uses static single assignment form for heap addresses and computes def-use information on-the-fly. We also show that essential information about dominating definitions can be maintained efficiently using quadtrees. The framework is presented as a systematic modification of a traditional dataflow analysis algorithm.

Our experimental results demonstrate the effectiveness of the technique for a suite of JavaScript programs. By also comparing the performance with an idealized staged approach that computes pointer information with a pre-analysis, we show that the cost of computing def-use information on-the-fly is remarkably small.

1 Introduction

Previous work on dataflow analysis has demonstrated that sparse analysis is a powerful technique for improving performance of many kinds of static analysis without sacrificing precision [7,8,14,15,20,21], compared to more basic dataflow analysis frameworks [12,13]. The key idea in sparse analysis is that dataflow should be propagated directly from definitions to uses in the program code, unlike "dense" analysis that propagates dataflow along the control-flow. A potential advantage of sparse analysis is that it propagates and stores only relevant information, not entire abstract states. Another advantage is that transfer functions need only be recomputed when their dependencies change.

While developing analysis tools for JavaScript we have found that the existing approaches described in the literature for building sparse analyses do not apply to the language features and common programming patterns that appear in JavaScript code. Specifically, context-sensitive branch pruning (a variant of unreachable code elimination by Wegman and Zadeck [21]) is an important analysis technique, as explained below, for handling the use of function overloading, which in JavaScript is programmed using reflection. Moreover, the common wisdom from analysis of e.g. Java code that context-insensitive analysis is usually faster

M. Müller-Olm and H. Seidl (Eds.): SAS 2014, LNCS 8723, pp. 201–218, 2014.

than context-sensitive analysis [18] apparently does not apply to JavaScript code, which, as discussed below, makes it difficult to design practically useful staged sparse analyses for this language.

```
function f(b, x, y) {
  var r;
  if (b.p) {
    r = x.a;
  } else {
    r = y.a;
  }
  return r;
}
```

As a motivating example, consider the JavaScript function on the right that exhibits a simple form of overloading. Here, the branch condition `b.p` decides whether the `f` function should have one behavior or another (in real-world JavaScript code, complex function overloading is mimicked using various kinds of reflection in branch conditions, but the pattern is the same). It is often the case that the branch condition is *determinate* relative to the call context [17]. That is, in one call context, `b.p` is known to be true, and in another call context, it is known to be false. In a context-sensitive dense analysis, this is no problem for the precision: `f` is simply analyzed in two contexts, corresponding to the two cases, such that the analysis logically clones `f` and analyzes it twice. When dataflow reaches the `if` statement, the analysis can then discover that one branch is dead and only propagate dataflow along the live branch.

To reason precisely about such program code, for example, with the purpose of computing call graphs or information about types of expressions, a static analysis must account for *reachability*, i.e. whether branches are live or dead in the individual contexts. At the same time it must handle heap allocated storage, as objects are pervasive in JavaScript. Moreover, even apparently simple operations in JavaScript, such as reading an object property, are complex procedures that involve e.g. type coercion and traversal of dynamically constructed prototype chains. This makes it beneficial to design analysis techniques that support complex transfer functions, for example, all computable monotone functions [12]. It is well known how to accomplish all this using dense analysis (see e.g. the TAJS analysis [9]). Our goal is to take the step to sparse analysis, without sacrificing precision compared to the original dense version.

One way to build sparse analyses for programs with pointers is to use a staged approach where a pre-analysis computes a sound approximation of the memory addresses that are defined or used at each operation in the code, and then establish def-use edges that the main analysis can use for sparse flow-sensitive dataflow propagation [8, 14]. Unfortunately, this does not work in our setting, unless the pre-analysis is as precise as the main analysis (and in that case, there would be no need for the main analysis, obviously): If the pre-analysis is flow-insensitive, for example, it would establish def-use edges from both `x.a` and `y.a` to `r` in our example, which would destroy the precision of the main analysis. Note that one of the main results of Oh et al. [14] is that, in their setting, approximations in the pre-analysis may lead to less sparseness but it will never affect the precision of the main analysis (due to their use of data dependence instead of def-use chains). However, for a language like JavaScript where most operations may throw exceptions, their algorithm largely degrades to a dense analysis if reachability is involved. In another line of work, Tok et al. [20] and Chase et al. [2] compute def-use edges on-the-fly rather than using a pre-analysis, but also without taking reachability into account. Conversely, the sparse conditional constant analysis by Wegman and Zadeck [21] handles reachability, but not pointers. In summary, no existing technique satisfies the needs for making sparse analysis for languages like JavaScript.

Our contributions are as follows:

- We present the first algorithm for sparse dataflow analyses that supports pointers, reachability, and arbitrary monotone transfer functions, while preserving the precision of the corresponding dense analysis, and without requiring a pre-analysis to compute def-use information.
- We describe experimental results, based on a dataflow analysis for JavaScript, that show a considerable performance improvement when using sparse analysis compared to a traditional dense approach, which demonstrates that it is possible to perform efficient sparse analysis in a setting that involves pointers and reachability.
- We show experimentally that the overhead of computing dominating definitions on-the-fly is small, which makes our approach preferable to staged approaches that compute that information with a pre-analysis.
- We demonstrate that quadtrees are a suitable data structure for maintaining essential information about dominating definitions in sparse analysis.

We explain the technique as a framework where we can switch from dense to sparse analysis, without affecting the abstract domains or the transfer functions.

2 A Basic Analysis Framework

Our starting point is a variant of the classical monotone framework for flow-sensitive dataflow analysis [12] where programs are represented as control-flow graphs with abstract states associated with the entry and exit program points of each node. For simplicity this presentation focuses on intraprocedural analysis, although our implementation supports interprocedural analysis as discussed in Section 4.

We assume that we are given a control-flow graph where each node represents a statement $s \in S$, together with a set of abstract memory addresses $a \in A$, a lattice of abstract values $v \in V$, and a transfer function T_s for each statement s. The transfer functions are assumed to be expressed using the following three primitive operations:

- $\text{READ}(s \in S, a \in A) : V$. Returns the value v at the address a at the program point immediately before the statement s.
- $\text{WRITE}(v \in V, s \in S, a \in A)$. Writes the value v to the address a at the program point immediately after the statement s. Note that an invocation $\text{WRITE}(v, s, a)$ models a strong update [2]; if a weak update is desired, the transfer function should invoke $\text{WRITE}(v \sqcup \text{READ}(s, a), s, a)$.

- CONTINUE($s_{src} \in S, s_{dst} \in S$). Indicates that the transfer function $T_{s_{src}}$ has completed and that s_{dst} is a possible successor, in other words that s_{dst} is reachable from s_{src}. (For example, this allows the transfer function for an `if` statement to selectively propagate dataflow to one of its branches.)

As conventional, the framework applies the transfer functions using an iterative worklist algorithm, starting from a designated program entry statement, until the global fixpoint is reached. The ordering of the worklist W is left unspecified, so the analysis implementor may freely choose any. We assume the lattice V has finite height; for simplicity we ignore widening.

In the case of JavaScript, most transfer functions are complex operations that involve multiple READ and WRITE operations. For example, the transfer function for a simple assignment `x = y.p` in general requires traversal of scope chains and prototype chains. This can be accomplished as shown in previous work on the TAJS analysis [9]. Although that analysis uses more elaborate abstract domains, it can in principle all be expressed within the present framework.

A traditional dense propagation strategy [12] maintains an entire abstract state at each program point as a map from addresses to values:

$I : S \times A \to V$ is the map of *incoming states*
$O : S \times A \to V$ is the map of *outgoing states*

Reading from an address is then simply a matter of looking up its value in the abstract state in I, and writing similarly updates O. (In practice, analysis implementations often maintain only O, since the information in I can be inferred when needed; we include both maps explicitly to simplify the presentation in Section 3.) Continuing from s_{src} to s_{dst} is handled by joining the entire outgoing state at s_{src} into the incoming state at s_{dst}. To initiate the analysis, I and O return the bottom element $\bot$ of V for every statement and address, except that we assume an entry statement s_{entry} with a no-op transfer function (that just calls CONTINUE) and where $I(s_{entry}, a)$ and $O(s_{entry}, a)$ both describe the initial abstract state for every address a. The initial worklist is then $W = \{s_{entry}\}$.

More formally, reading the value of an address $a \in A$ at statement $s \in S$ is implemented simply by looking up the value in the incoming state:

READ($s \in S, a \in A$) : V
return $I(s, a)$

Similarly, writing a value $v \in V$ to the address $a \in A$ at statement $s \in S$ is implemented by writing to the outgoing state:

WRITE($v \in V, s \in S, a \in A$)
$O(s, a) := v$

Propagation of dataflow from statement $s_{src} \in S$ to $s_{dst} \in S$ is implemented by joining all the values from the outgoing state of s_{src} into the incoming state of s_{dst}. If a value is changed then s_{dst} is added to the worklist. Reachability is implicitly supported since an unreachable statement has every value set to the bottom element $\bot$, whereas we assume that every reachable statement will have at least one value set to non-bottom, and so propagation from a reachable statement to an unreachable statement will always cause the unreachable statement to be added to the worklist:

CONTINUE($s_{src} \in S, s_{dst} \in S$)

for each $a \in A$
  let $v = O(s_{src}, a)$
  let $v' = I(s_{dst}, a)$
  if $v \not\sqsubseteq v'$
    $I(s_{dst}, a) := v \sqcup v'$
    $W := W \cup \{s_{dst}\}$

The main fixpoint computation is implemented by the SOLVE procedure. It maintains a global worklist W of pending statements and iteratively extracts a statement and evaluates its transfer function, which may cause new statements to be added to the worklist. The fixpoint is found when the worklist is empty:

SOLVE($E : A \rightarrow V$), where E is the entry state

$I(s, a) := O(s, a) := \bot$ for all $s \in S$, $a \in A$
$I(s_{entry}, a) := O(s_{entry}, a) := E(a)$ for all $a \in A$
$W := \{s_{entry}\}$
while $W \neq \emptyset$
  let $s =$ DEQUEUE(W)
  $O(s, a) := I(s, a)$ for all $a \in A$
  apply the transfer function T_s

3 Sparse Analysis

We now show how the basic analysis framework from the preceding section can be changed into our sparse analysis technique. As a first step, we modify the definitions of the incoming and outgoing states to become partial maps, $I : S \times A \hookrightarrow V$ and $O : S \times A \hookrightarrow V$, since we now want to maintain values only for the statements and addresses that are involved in READ or WRITE operations, respectively. Next, we add four new components that are all built incrementally during the fixpoint computation:

- $R \subseteq S \times S$ is the set of *reachable edges*
- $P : S \times A \hookrightarrow V$ specifies the placement and values of *ϕ-nodes*
- $DU \subseteq S \times A \times S$ is the set of *def-use edges*
- $F : S \times S \rightarrow \mathcal{P}(A)$ is the map of *frontier addresses*

The R component now explicitly tracks the set of reachable edges in the control-flow graph: if CONTINUE(s_{src}, s_{dst}) has been invoked, then $(s_{src}, s_{dst}) \in R$. As in previous sparse analysis techniques, we use SSA (static single assignment form) to ensure that each use site has a unique associated definition site [4,7,21]. When $P(s, a)$ is defined with some value v, the statement s plays the role of a ϕ-node for address a, where v is then the merged value from the incoming dataflow. As effect we obtain SSA for all addresses, not only for local variables. Each triple $(s_1, a, s_2) \in DU$ represents a def-use edge, where s_1 is a definition site or a ϕ-node and s_2 is a use site or a ϕ-node for a.

Since the analysis discovers definition sites and use sites incrementally, the set of def-use edges changes during the analysis. The F map supports this construction of def-use edges whenever frontier edge becomes reachable, as explained later in this section.

The SOLVE procedure is unmodified, except that line 6 is omitted in the sparse analysis version. The remainder of this section explains the modifications of the READ, WRITE, and CONTINUE procedures.

Notation and terminology We view maps as mutable dictionaries. For example, if $f : A \to B$ is a map, then $f(x) := v$ denotes the update of f such that subsequently $f(x) = v$. If $f : X \hookrightarrow Y$ is a partial map, then $f_\star$ denotes the domain of f, i.e. the subset of X where f is defined. We assume the reader is familiar with the concepts of *SSA*, *dominance frontiers*, and *dominator trees* from e.g. Cytron et al. [4]. Specifically, a statement s_2 is in the *dominance frontier* of a statement s_0 if s_0 dominates some predecessor s_1 of s_2 in the control-flow graph, but s_0 does not dominate s_2. The edge (s_1, s_2) is then called a *frontier edge* of s_0. We say that a statement s is a *ϕ-node* (resp. *definition site* or *use site*) for an address a if $(s, a) \in P_\star$ (resp. $(s, a) \in O_\star$ or $(s, a) \in I_\star$). Only merge points in the control-flow graph can be used as ϕ-nodes. For simplicity, we assume that the statements at merge points are no-ops, such that they cannot be definition sites or use sites (thus, $P_\star$ and $I_\star \cup O_\star$ are disjoint).

The following key invariants are maintained by the READ, WRITE, and CONTINUE operations in the sparse analysis framework:

[*flow*] If $(s_1, a, s_2) \in DU$ for some statements s_1, s_2 and some address a, then

- either $O(s_1, a)$ or $P(s_1, a)$ is defined with some value v,
- either $I(s_2, a)$ or $P(s_2, a)$ is defined with some value v', and
- the value of a at s_1 has been propagated to s_2, i.e. $v \sqsubseteq v'$.

[*def-use*] If (and only if) a statement s_1 is a definition site or ϕ-node for some address a, i.e. $(s_1, a) \in O_\star \cup P_\star$, s_k is a use site or ϕ-node for a, i.e. $(s_k, a) \in I_\star \cup P_\star$, such that s_1 dominates s_k and there is a path $s_1, s_2, \ldots, s_k$ where each step is reachable, i.e. $(s_i, s_{i+1}) \in R$ for all i, and moreover, there is no definition site or ϕ-node for a between s_1 and s_k, i.e. $(s_i, a) \notin I_\star \cup P_\star$ for all $i = 2, 3, \ldots, k-1$, then there exists a def-use edge $(s_1, a, s_k) \in DU$.

[*phi-use*] If s is a ϕ-node for a, i.e. $(s, a) \in P_\star$, then for every reachable incoming control-flow graph edge $(s_1, s) \in R$ there is a def-use edge $(s_2, a, s) \in DU$ where s_2 is the nearest dominator of s_1 and s_2 is a definition site or ϕ-node for a.

[*phi*] If a statement s_0 is a definition site or ϕ-node for some address a, i.e. $(s_0, a) \in O_\star \cup P_\star$, then for every frontier edge (s_1, s_2) of s_0 that is reachable, i.e. $(s_1, s_2) \in R$, the statement s_2 is a ϕ-node for a, i.e. $(s_2, a) \in P_\star$.

[*frontier*] If $a \in F(s_1, s_2)$ for some statements s_1, s_2 and some address a, then (s_1, s_2) is a frontier edge of a dominator s_0 of s_1 that defines a, i.e. $(s_0, a) \in O_\star \cup P_\star$.

Intuitively, the [*flow*] invariant ensures that dataflow has always been propagated along the existing def-use edges; [*def-use*] expresses the main requirements for construction of def-use edges, in particular that def-use edges respect reachability and dominance of definitions; [*phi-use*] ensures that def-use edges to ϕ-nodes also exist for all reachable incoming edges; [*phi*] ensures that ϕ-nodes are created along reachable dominance frontiers; and [*frontier*] expresses that F records which addresses are relevant for contructing def-use edges whenever a frontier edge becomes reachable.

3.1 Reading Values

The READ(s, a) operation retrieves the requested value from the incoming state if s is already known to be a use site for a. If a new use is discovered, the appropriate def-use edge must be introduced and the value propagated to s:

READ$(s \in S, a \in A) : V$

```
if (s, a) ∉ I⋆
    I(s, a) := ⊥
    let s1 = FINDDEF(s′, a) where s′ is the immediate dominator of s
    DU := DU ∪ {(s1, a, s)}
    PROPAGATE(s1, a, s)
return I(s, a)
```

The FINDDEF procedure searches up the dominator tree to find the nearest definition site or ϕ-node for a:

FINDDEF$(s \in S, a \in A) : S$

```
if (s, a) ∈ O⋆ ∪ P⋆
    return s
else
    return FINDDEF(s′, a) where s′ is the immediate dominator of s
```

We show in Section 3.4 how FINDDEF can be implemented more efficiently than this pseudo-code suggests. Also note that by initializing $I(s_{entry}, a)$ and $O(s_{entry}, a)$ for every address a according to the initial abstract state when the analysis starts, READ and FINDDEF are well-defined because s_{entry} is the root of the dominator tree.

The PROPAGATE procedure, which is also used by the WRITE operation later, propagates a single value from a definition site or ϕ-node to a use site or ϕ-node, in order to satisfy the [*flow*] invariant. If the destination is a use site and its incoming state changes, then that statement is added to the worklist W. If the destination is a ϕ-node then propagation is invoked recursively for all its outgoing def-use edges:

PROPAGATE($s_{src} \in S, a \in A, s_{dst} \in S$)
1 **if** $(s_{src}, a) \in O_\star$
2   **let** $v = O(s_{src}, a)$
3 **else** // must have $(s_{src}, a) \in P_\star$
4   **let** $v = P(s_{src}, a)$
5 **if** $(s_{dst}, a) \in I_\star$
6   **let** $v_{old} = I(s_{dst}, a)$
7   **if** $v \not\sqsubseteq v_{old}$
8          $I(s_{dst}, a) := v \sqcup v_{old}$
9          $W := W \cup \{s_{dst}\}$
10 **else** // must have $(s_{dst}, a) \in P_\star$
11   **let** $v_{old} = P(s_{dst}, a)$
12   **if** $v \not\sqsubseteq v_{old}$
13         $P(s_{dst}, a) := v \sqcup v_{old}$
14   **for each** s **where** $(s_{dst}, a, s) \in DU$
15   PROPAGATE(s_{dst}, a, s)

Notice that recursive calls to PROPAGATE can only happen along chains of def-use edges between ϕ-nodes, which are placed only at merge points, so the recursion is bounded by the block nesting depth of the program being analyzed.

3.2   Writing Values

The WRITE operation writes the given value to the outgoing state. If a new definition site is discovered, the set of def-use edges must be updated. Moreover, the written value is propagated along the outgoing def-use edges:

WRITE($v \in V, s \in S, a \in A$)
1 **if** $(s, a) \notin O_\star$
2   UPDATE(s, a)
3      $O(s, a) := v$
4   FORWARD(s, a)
5 **else**
6      $O(s, a) := v$
7 **for each** s_{dst} **where** $(s, a, s_{dst}) \in DU$
8   PROPAGATE(s, a, s_{dst})

Whenever a new definition site is discovered in WRITE (line 1), def-use edges that bypass the new definition site and have the same address must be updated (line 2) and ϕ-nodes must be introduced at the iterated dominance frontiers along with associated def-use edges (line 4).

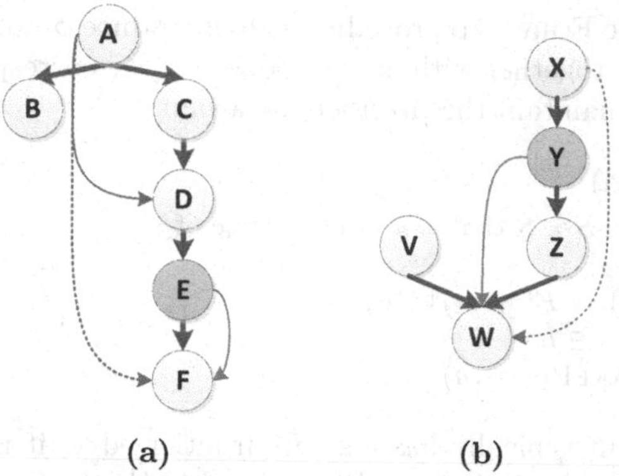

Fig. 1. Two control-flow graph fragments (with thick edges representing control-flow) that illustrate the UPDATE procedure. **(a)** The statement A defines some address that is used at both statements D and F (corresponding to the def-use edges A → D and A → F). At some point a definition is discovered at E. The dominating definition at E is A. Its use at D is *not* dominated by E and thus not affected by the new definition at E. The use at F, however, is dominated by E, so the def-use edge A → F is replaced by E → F. **(b)** The statement X defines some address that is used by the ϕ-node at W (corresponding to the def-use edge X → W). If a new definition is discovered at Y then X → W must be replaced by Y → W since X dominates Y.

```
UPDATE(s ∈ S, a ∈ A)
1  let s1 = FINDDEF(s, a)
2  for each s2 where (s1, a, s2) ∈ DU
3      if s strictly dominates s2
4          DU := (DU \ {(s1, a, s2)}) ∪ {(s, a, s2)}
5  for each (s3, s4) ∈ S × S that is a frontier edge of s
6      let s0 = FINDDEF(s3, a)
7      if s0 strictly dominates s
8          if (s0, a, s4) ∈ DU
9              DU := (DU \ {(s0, a, s4)}) ∪ {(s, a, s4)}
```

The UPDATE procedure updates the def-use edges that bypass the new definition. The first part (lines 1–4) handles the def-use edges that end at a statement dominated by the new definition, to restore the [*def-use*] invariant as illustrated in Figure 1(a); the second part (lines 5–9) handles the def-use edges that end at a dominance frontier node of the new definition, corresponding to [*phi-use*] as illustrated in Figure 1(b).

Note that DU does not always grow monotonically, since UPDATE both adds and removes edges. Termination is still ensured: a def-use edge (s_1, a, s_2) is only removed if a new definition site s_d is discovered such that s_d dominates s_2. Definitions are never removed, so the edge (s_1, a, s_2) can never be re-added, and only a finite number of def-use edges can be created. All other components in the sparse framework are monotonically increasing during the fixpoint computation.

The purpose of the FORWARD procedure is to introduce ϕ-nodes at the iterated dominance frontiers, together with def-use edges for the corresponding reachable frontier edges, and maintain the [*frontier*] invariant:

```
FORWARD(s ∈ S, a ∈ A)
1  for each (s1, s2) ∈ S × S that is a frontier edge of s
2      if a ∉ F(s1, s2)
3          F(s1, s2) := F(s1, s2) ∪ {a}
4          if (s1, s2) ∈ R
5              MAKEPHI(s2, a)
```

Although a statement typically has a single frontier edge, it is possible to have multiple, for example, in connection to statements that may throw exceptions. Line 3 in FORWARD adds a to the frontier addresses of the frontier edge (s_1, s_2), which indicates that a has been defined by a statement that dominates s_1. If that edge is already known to be reachable, we may need to add a new ϕ-node at the frontier, which is handled by MAKEPHI as explained next.

```
MAKEPHI(s ∈ S, a ∈ A)
1  if (s, a) ∉ P⋆
2      UPDATE(s, a)
3      P(s, a) := ⊥
4  for each s1 ∈ S where s1 is an immediate predecessor of s in the control-flow graph
5      if (s1, s) ∈ R
6          let s2 = FINDDEF(s1, a)
7          DU := DU ∪ {(s2, a, s)}
8          PROPAGATE(s2, a, s)
9  FORWARD(s, a)
```

The MAKEPHI procedure is only invoked with s being a dominance frontier node. If s is not already a ϕ-node for a (line 1), we mark it as one (line 3). However, since a ϕ-node has a similar effect as a definition site, UPDATE is called first to update the def-use edges, c.f. line 2 in WRITE. A ϕ-node also has a similar effect as a use site, although generally with multiple incoming def-use edges. For this reason, we make sure a def-use edge exists for every reachable income edge (lines 4–8), c.f. lines 3–5 in READ. Finally, the process is continued recursively for the iterated dominance frontiers (line 9).

3.3 Propagating Reachability

As the propagation of dataflow values is performed along def-use edges by PROPAGATE, the primary role of CONTINUE is to propagate reachability:

```
CONTINUE(s_src ∈ S, s_dst ∈ S)
1  if (s_src, s_dst) ∉ R
2      R := R ∪ {(s_src, s_dst)}
3      W := W ∪ {s_dst}
4      for each a ∈ A where a ∈ F(s_src, s_dst) ∨ (s_dst, a) ∈ P⋆
5          MAKEPHI(s_dst, a)
```

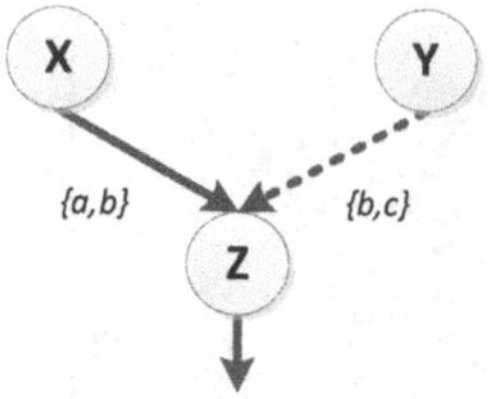

Fig. 2. A control-flow graph fragment, where the frontier edges X $\rightarrow$ Z and Y $\rightarrow$ Z hold the addresses $\{a, b\}$ and $\{b, c\}$, respectively. The edge X $\rightarrow$ Z is already reachable, and ϕ-nodes for $\{a, b\}$ at Z have already been introduced. Now CONTINUE is invoked for the edge Y $\rightarrow$ Z. CONTINUE ensures that appropriate def-uses edge to Z are introduced for all the addresses a, b, and c, and for all the incoming edges to Z.

If the given control-flow graph edge (s_{src}, s_{dst}) is not already reachable, we mark it as reachable (line 2) and add s_{dst} to the worklist. However, this may trigger calls to MAKEPHI in two situations, corresponding to the two cases in line 4: The condition $a \in F(s_{src}, s_{dst})$ signals that (s_{src}, s_{dst}) is a frontier edge of a statement that defines a, so we must ensure that s_{dst} is a ϕ-node for a and therefore call MAKEPHI. The condition $(s_{dst}, a) \in P_\star$ captures the case where s_{dst} is already a ϕ-node for a, but now there is a new reachable incoming edge, which is handled by lines 4–8 in MAKEPHI as illustrated in Figure 2. Notice that we carefully ensure in FORWARD, MAKEPHI, and CONTINUE that no dataflow is propagated across control-flow edges, in particular frontier edges, until they are known to be reachable.

Proposition. *The sparse framework has same analysis precision as the basic framework. Specifically, if $O(s, a) = v$ for some $s \in S$, $a \in A$, and $v \in V$ after analyzing a given program with the sparse framework, then we also have $O(s, a) = v$ when analyzing the program with the basic framework.*

3.4 A Data Structure for Finding Dominating Definitions

During the fixpoint computation new definition sites and use sites are discovered incrementally by the READ and WRITE operations. A key challenge is how to ensure that the FINDDEF operation is able to quickly find the nearest dominating definition for any statement in the control-flow graph.

The naive version of FINDDEF from Section 3.1 is easy to implement, as also suggested by Chase et al. [2]. It is, however, impractical because each invocation requires a traversal along a spine of the dominator tree, in the worst case from the given statement all the way to the root. As an example, consider a straight-line program consisting of k statements in sequence. Invoking FINDDEF at the last statement may then require traversal of all k statements to find the nearest dominating definition.

A better approach is to maintain dominator information separately for each address and only for the nodes that are known to be definition sites or ϕ-nodes. The idea is to equip each statement in the control-flow graph with two numbers,

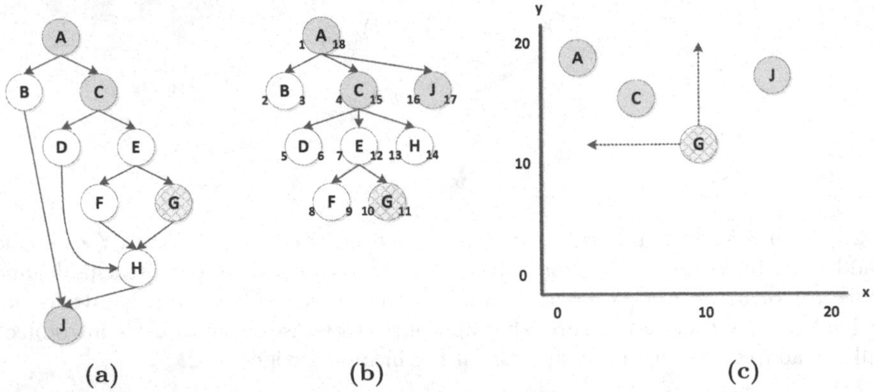

Fig. 3. **(a)** A control-flow graph fragment where the statements A, C and J are definition sites for some address. The statement G is a use site of the same address. **(b)** The dominator tree for the control-flow graph with the definition sites and use site marked. **(c)** The 2d points associated with the timestamps of the dominator tree.

x and y, as shown in Figure 3. The numbers are obtained through a depth-first traversal of the dominator tree, such that the first number x is the discovery time and the second number y is the exit time. Using these numbers we can determine dominance between nodes: if p dominates q, then p must have been discovered before q, i.e. $x_p < x_q$, and all children of q must have been visited before exiting p, i.e. $y_q < y_p$. As an example, in Figure 3, statement E dominates F since $x_\mathsf{E} < x_\mathsf{F}$ and $y_\mathsf{F} < y_\mathsf{E}$.

A key observation is that to find the *nearest* dominating definition of a node q we need to find a node p where $x_p < x_q$ and $y_q < y_p$. Of all nodes that satisfy these conditions we wish to find the one with maximum x value. For example, in Figure 3 the nearest dominating definition at G is C, which satisfies these properties.

One approach is to store the definitions in a resizable array and perform a linear scan to find the nearest dominating definition, as in Staiger-Stöhr [19]. Unfortunately, this requires $\mathcal{O}(d)$ time, where d is the number of definitions. Another approach is to define an ordering such that finding all dominating definitions takes $\mathcal{O}(\log d)$ time and then scan through these to find the nearest dominating definition, as in Tok et al. [20]. However, the scanning may still require $\mathcal{O}(d)$ time.

Our solution works as follows. If we interpret the number pair (x_q, y_q) of a node q as a point in a two dimensional space, then finding the nearest dominating definition p is equivalent to finding the point (x_p, y_p) in the rectangle $[0, x_q] \times [y_q, \infty]$ with the maximum x_p. This is a well-known problem in the computational geometry literature; one data structure solving this problem is the quadtree [5]. Finding the nearest dominating definition then takes $\mathcal{O}(\sqrt{n})$ time where n is the number of control-flow graph nodes, and a new node can be inserted in $\mathcal{O}(\log n)$ time. Quadtrees are simple to implement and have a low constant-factor overhead.

Our experimental comparison (see Section 4) confirms that quadtrees lead to a faster implementation than the naive version of FINDDEF and Staiger-Stöhr's approach. In principle one could combine the techniques and get $\mathcal{O}(\min(\sqrt{n}, d))$, but in practice using the quadtrees alone seems to work well.

To summarize, we pre-compute the two numbers for every statement in the control-flow graph and then maintain a quadtree y_a for each $a \in A$ containing every statement $s \in S$ where $(s, a) \in O_\star \cup P_\star$. The FINDDEF procedure from Section 3.1 is then replaced by a search in y_a.

4 Implementation and Evaluation

We have implemented a dataflow analysis for JavaScript, configurable for both the traditional dense propagation (Section 2) and the sparse analysis with on-the-fly SSA construction (Section 3). The dataflow lattices and transfer functions are designed in the style of the TAJS analysis by Jensen et al. [9], structured such that all transfer functions are expressed using the READ, WRITE and CONTINUE operations. For the quadtrees, we use a variant called *compressed quadtrees* [6]. Interprocedural dataflow is handled by straightforward generalizations of the algorithms from the preceding sections. Call graphs are built on-the-fly, similar to TAJS. For the interprocedural sparse analysis, ϕ-nodes are made at function entries and at no-op statements that are placed after call sites where dataflow may merge from different functions. Searching for dominating definitions may then span multiple functions backward via the call edges, and similarly, definitions inside a function are propagated forward along dominance frontiers of the call sites. The full implementation is approximately 20,000 lines of Scala code, whereof the core that corresponds to Section 2 and 3 constitutes less than 1,000 lines.

Our experiments are based on the collection of JavaScript programs shown in Table 1. (Our current implementation does not contains models of the browser API and HTML DOM, so we settle for stand-alone JavaScript programs.) The collection contains programs from the Mozilla SunSpider and Google Octane benchmark suites, plus a few additional programs found on the web. All experiments are performed on an Intel Core 2 Duo 2.5 GHz PC. The analysis implementation and all benchmarks are available online.[1]

We consider the following three research questions:

Q1: Is our sparse analysis technique more efficient than the basic analysis framework? The literature shows that sparse analysis is usually highly effective, but since none of the existing techniques are applicable to our setting, which involves both pointers and reachability, we cannot know *a priori* whether our sparse analysis has similar advantages.

Q2: How does the performance of our sparse analysis algorithm compare to staged analysis techniques? As argued in Section 1, performing sparse analysis on the basis of imprecise reachability information would affect not only

[1] `http://www.brics.dk/sparse/`

Table 1. Experimental results. *Lines* shows the number of source code lines and *Nodes* shows the number of control-flow graph statements for each program, to indicate their sizes. *Basic* and *Sparse* are the total analysis time for the basic and sparse frameworks, respectively. *SSA overhead* shows the time spent on SSA construction during the sparse analysis, using three different implementations for maintaining dominating definitions. All times are shown in milliseconds, with *timeout* representing a timeout of 90 seconds.

Program			*Total time*		*SSA overhead*			
Name	*Lines*	*Nodes*	*Basic*	*Sparse*	%	*Quadtree*	*Naive*	*Array*
`deltablue.js`	885	3303	*timeout*	35780	43%	15223	23347	21927
`richards.js`	541	1655	*timeout*	703	31%	216	391	405
`splay.js`	398	1058	79844	705	28%	198	268	273
`3d-cube.js`	343	2875	*timeout*	1974	24%	482	991	899
`3d-raytrace.js`	443	3000	*timeout*	2723	30%	812	1686	2954
`access-nbody.js`	170	847	63864	488	39%	189	262	218
`crypto-aes.js`	426	2581	*timeout*	713	25%	177	451	486
`crypto-md5.js`	295	1508	30561	2091	3%	53	111	117
`garbochess.js`	2812	16146	*timeout*	5764	26%	1501	3138	4362
`simplex.js`	450	2121	*timeout*	465	28%	128	282	235
`jpg.js`	889	5146	*timeout*	2621	21%	538	1035	992
`javap.js`	1430	5561	*timeout*	1693	33%	559	1479	3037

the degree of sparseness but also the precision of the main analysis, and we want our sparse analysis to be as precise as with the basic framework. On the other hand, our algorithm could potentially be simplified without affecting analysis precision by using a pre-analysis to compute definition sites and use sites for SSA construction, instead of performing it all on-the-fly. For this reason, it is interesting to measure the overhead of computing that information in our on-the-fly sparse analysis framework.

Q3: Are quadtrees a suitable choice in practice, compared to other techniques for maintaining information about reaching definitions? In Section 3.4 we argued that quadtrees have a good theoretical complexity, however, this needs to be supported empirically.

To answer Q1 we instantiate the analysis with both configurations (using quadtrees for the sparse analysis). The columns *Basic* and *Sparse* in Table 1 show the corresponding analysis times. The numbers show that our sparse analysis is in most cases more than an order of magnitude faster than the basic framework. As result, we have demonstrated that it is possible to perform efficient sparse analysis in a setting that involves pointers and reachability.

We address Q2 by assuming an *ideal* pre-analysis that computes the definition sites and use sites and from this constructs the SSA form, with the full precision of the on-the-fly sparse analysis. Designing a realistic pre-analysis involves a trade-off: it has to be fast (at least, faster than the original dense analysis), and it has to be reasonably precise (since imprecision can lead to less sparseness in the main analysis). With such a pre-analysis, we can perform sparse analysis and still account for reachability – reminiscent of the sparse conditional constant analysis by Wegman and Zadeck [21]. The *SSA overhead* columns (% and *Quadtree*) in Table 1 show how much time is spent by our sparse analysis inside the operations FindDef, Update, Forward, and MakePhi (excluding Propagate), relative to the entire sparse analysis and in milliseconds, when using the quadtree implementation of FindDef. This constitutes work that in principle could be omitted if using a pre-analysis. We observe that between 3% and 43% of the analysis time is spent in these parts. In other words, the best imaginable pre-analysis will only be able to achieve a speedup of less than 1.7x (for `deltablue.js`) and on average less than 1.4x. Moreover, by using our on-the-fly approach, the analysis developer is relieved of the burden of designing and implementing a fast and precise pre-analysis.

Regarding Q3, the columns *Quadtree*, *Naive*, and *Array* show the time for SSA construction with different implementations of the data structure used for finding dominating definitions. The *Quadtree* column corresponds to our quadtree-based implementation described in Section 3.4, *Naive* corresponds to FindDef from Section 3.1, and *Array* follows the approach of Staiger-Stöhr [19], as discussed in Section 3.4. In all cases the quadtree implementation is the fastest and typically outperforms the alternatives by a factor of 1.4x to 5.4x.

5 Related Work

The basic ideas in sparse analysis originate from Reif and Lewis [15] who suggested the use of *global value graphs*, for example for efficient constant propagation analysis. The concept of SSA form is attributed to Rosen et al. [16]. Cytron et al. [4] introduced the concept of dominance frontiers as an effective mechanism for placing ϕ-nodes. As mentioned in the introduction, the *sparse conditional constant* analysis by Wegman and Zadeck [21] builds on top of this work and takes reachability into account during the analysis by tracking which def-use edges represent executable flow. The notion of *dependence flow graphs* by Johnson et al. [11] is a variant of SSA that incorporates branch conditions and thereby supports subsequent dataflow analysis with reachability. Common to this line of work is that heap objects and pointers are not supported.

For programming languages with pointers, most work on sparse analysis has focused on pointer analysis, not dataflow analysis in general. The *semi-sparse* pointer analysis by Hardekopf and Lin [7] uses SSA and sparse analysis for top-level variables that are not accessed via pointers, whereas address-taken variables and heap allocated data are treated using standard flow-sensitive analysis without sparseness.

Other techniques handle pointers typically by staging the analysis using a pre-analysis to approximate possible definition sites and use sites [3,8,14]. However, as discussed previously, that approach cannot support reachability without sacrificing analysis precision or sparseness. By computing definition sites and use sites on-the-fly, we avoid that problem.

The analysis by Chase et al. [2] handles pointers and performs sparse analysis on the basis of ϕ-nodes that are computed on-the-fly, however, it does not account for reachability. The analysis framework by Tok et al. [20] is based on similar ideas. The algorithms used in those analyses for finding dominating definitions are discussed in Section 3.4. A related analysis framework has been presented by Staiger-Stöhr [19].

Numerous other program analysis techniques have been designed to prevent various kinds of redundancy in the dataflow propagation. Of particular relevance is the *lazy propagation* technique by Jensen et al. [10] that restricts dataflow at call sites that is not needed by the function being called. When use sites are incrementally discovered, the relevant values are recovered by a backward traversal of the call graph, which is reminiscent of the search for nearest dominating definitions in our sparse analysis. We conjecture that our sparse analysis may be more efficient than lazy propagation; however, lazy propagation is known to work smoothly together with recency abstraction [1,9], which is a useful technique for boosting analysis precision, and it is an open problem whether sparse analysis and recency abstraction can also be combined effectively.

In summary, the present work can be understood as a generalization and combination of ideas from on-the-fly SSA construction [2, 19, 20] while taking reachability into account [11,21]. Furthermore, we propose a more efficient data structure, based on insights from computational geometry [5], for managing dominating definitions, compared to the existing techniques [19,20].

6 Conclusion

We conclude that it is possible to perform efficient sparse dataflow analysis in a setting that requires reasoning about pointers and reachability. Our experimental evaluation shows not only that the sparse analysis is significantly faster than the dense counterpart, but also that the overhead of on-the-fly SSA construction is small, which makes the approach a promising alternative to staged analyses. Moreover, we have demonstrated that quadtrees are suitable for maintaining information about dominating definitions.

Our next step is to integrate the analysis algorithm into the TAJS tool to become able to explore the performance on a larger class of JavaScript application. It may also be interesting to apply the algorithm to other programming languages and other abstract domains.

Acknowledgments. The authors thank Casper Kejlberg-Rasmussen, Jesper Sindal Nielsen, and Ondřej Lhoták for inspiring discussions about data structures and dataflow analysis. The work presented in this paper was supported by the Danish Research Council for Technology and Production.

References

1. Balakrishnan, G., Reps, T.: Recency-abstraction for heap-allocated storage. In: Yi, K. (ed.) SAS 2006. LNCS, vol. 4134, pp. 221–239. Springer, Heidelberg (2006)
2. Chase, D.R., Wegman, M., Kenneth Zadeck, F.: Analysis of pointers and structures. In: Proc. ACM SIGPLAN Conference on Programming Language Design and Implementation (June 1990)
3. Chow, F., Chan, S., Liu, S.-M., Lo, R., Streich, M.: Effective representation of aliases and indirect memory operations in SSA form. In: Gyimóthy, T. (ed.) CC 1996. LNCS, vol. 1060, pp. 253–267. Springer, Heidelberg (1996)
4. Cytron, R., Ferrante, J., Rosen, B.K., Wegman, M.N., Kenneth Zadeck, F.: Efficiently computing static single assignment form and the control dependence graph. ACM Transactions on Programming Languages and Systems 13(4), 451–490 (1991)
5. de Berg, M., Cheong, O., van Kreveld, M., Overmars, M.: Computational Geometry: Algorithms and Applications. Springer (1997)
6. Har-Peled, S.: Geometric Approximation Algorithms. American Mathematical Society, Boston (2011)
7. Hardekopf, B., Lin, C.: Semi-sparse flow-sensitive pointer analysis. In: Proc. 36th ACM SIGPLAN-SIGACT Symposium on Principles of Programming Languages (January 2009)
8. Hardekopf, B., Lin, C.: Flow-sensitive pointer analysis for millions of lines of code. In: Proc. 9th International Symposium on Code Generation and Optimization (April 2011)
9. Jensen, S.H., Møller, A., Thiemann, P.: Type analysis for JavaScript. In: Palsberg, J., Su, Z. (eds.) SAS 2009. LNCS, vol. 5673, pp. 238–255. Springer, Heidelberg (2009)
10. Jensen, S.H., Møller, A., Thiemann, P.: Interprocedural analysis with lazy propagation. In: Cousot, R., Martel, M. (eds.) SAS 2010. LNCS, vol. 6337, pp. 320–339. Springer, Heidelberg (2010)
11. Johnson, R., Pingali, K.: Dependence-based program analysis. In: Proc. ACM SIGPLAN Conference on Programming Language Design and Implementation (June 1993)
12. Kam, J.B., Ullman, J.D.: Monotone data flow analysis frameworks. Acta Informatica 7, 305–317 (1977)
13. Kildall, G.A.: A unified approach to global program optimization. In: Proc. ACM Symposium on Principles of Programming Languages (October 1973)
14. Oh, H., Heo, K., Lee, W., Lee, W., Yi, K.: Design and implementation of sparse global analyses for C-like languages. In: Proc. ACM SIGPLAN Conference on Programming Language Design and Implementation (June 2012)
15. Reif, J.H., Lewis, H.R.: Symbolic evaluation and the global value graph. In: Proc. 4th ACM Symposium on Principles of Programming Languages (January 1977)
16. Rosen, B.K., Wegman, M.N., Kenneth Zadeck, F.: Global value numbers and redundant computations. In: Proc. 15th ACM Symposium on Principles of Programming Languages (January 1988)
17. Schäfer, M., Sridharan, M., Dolby, J., Tip, F.: Dynamic determinacy analysis. In: Proc. ACM SIGPLAN Conference on Programming Language Design and Implementation (June 2013)
18. Smaragdakis, Y., Bravenboer, M., Lhoták, O.: Pick your contexts well: understanding object-sensitivity. In: Proc. 38th ACM Symposium on Principles of Programming Languages (January 2011)

19. Staiger-Stöhr, S.: Practical integrated analysis of pointers, dataflow and control flow. ACM Transactions on Programming Languages and Systems 35(1), 5:1–5:48 (2013)
20. Tok, T.B., Guyer, S.Z., Lin, C.: Efficient flow-sensitive interprocedural data-flow analysis in the presence of pointers. In: Mycroft, A., Zeller, A. (eds.) CC 2006. LNCS, vol. 3923, pp. 17–31. Springer, Heidelberg (2006)
21. Wegman, M.N., Kenneth Zadeck, F.: Constant propagation with conditional branches. ACM Transactions on Programming Languages and Systems 13(2), 181–210 (1991)

Reactivity of Cooperative Systems
Application to ReactiveML

Louis Mandel[1,3] and Cédric Pasteur[2,3]

[1] Collège de France
[2] DI École normale supérieure (now at ANSYS-Esterel Technologies)
[3] INRIA Paris-Rocquencourt

Abstract. Cooperative scheduling enables efficient sequential implementations of concurrency. It is widely used to provide lightweight threads facilities as libraries or programming constructs in many programming languages. However, it is up to programmers to actually cooperate to ensure the reactivity of their programs.

We present a static analysis that checks the reactivity of programs by abstracting them into so-called *behaviors* using a type-and-effect system. Our objective is to find a good compromise between the complexity of the analysis and its precision for typical reactive programs. The simplicity of the analysis is mandatory for the programmer to be able to understand error messages and how to fix reactivity problems.

Our work is applied and implemented in the functional synchronous language ReactiveML. It handles recursion, higher-order processes and first-class signals. We prove the soundness of our analysis with respect to the big-step semantics of the language: a well-typed program with reactive effects is reactive. The analysis is easy to implement and generic enough to be applicable to other models of concurrency such as coroutines.

1 Introduction

Most programming languages offer lightweight thread facilities, either integrated in the language like the asynchronous computations [30] of F#, or available as a library like GNU Pth [12] for C, Concurrent Haskell [15] or Lwt [34] for OCaml. These libraries are based on cooperative scheduling: each thread of execution cooperates with the scheduler to let other threads execute. This enables an efficient and sequential implementation of concurrency, allowing to create up to millions of separate threads, which is impossible with operating system threads. Synchronization also comes almost for free, without requiring synchronization primitives like locks.

The downside of cooperative scheduling is that it is necessary to make sure that threads actually cooperate:

- Control must regularly be returned to the scheduler. This is particularly true for infinite loops, which are very often present in *reactive* and *interactive* systems.
- Blocking functions, like operating system primitives for I/O, cannot be called.

M. Müller-Olm and H. Seidl (Eds.): SAS 2014, LNCS 8723, pp. 219–236, 2014.

The solution to the latter is simple: never use blocking functions inside cooperative threads. All the facilities mentioned earlier provide either I/O libraries compatible with cooperative scheduling or a means to safely call blocking functions. See Marlow et al. [22] for an overview on how to implement such libraries.

Dealing with the first issue is usually the responsibility of the programmer. For instance, in the Lwt manual [11], one can find:

> [...] do not write function that may take time to complete without using Lwt [...]

The goal of this paper is to design a static analysis, called *reactivity analysis*, to statically remedy this problem of absence of cooperation points. The analysis checks that the programmer does not forget to cooperate with the scheduler. Our work is applied to the ReactiveML language [19], which is an extension of ML with a synchronous model of concurrency [6] (Section 2). However, we believe that our approach is generic enough to be applied to other models of concurrency (Section 6). The contributions of this paper are the following:

- A reactivity analysis based on a type-and-effect system [18] in Section 4. The computed effects are called *behaviors* [3] and are introduced in Section 3. They represent the temporal behaviors of processes by abstracting away values but keeping part of the structure of the program and are used to check if processes cooperate or not.
- A novel approach to *subeffecting* [23], that is, subtyping on effects, based on row polymorphism [26] in Section 4.4. It allows to build a conservative extension of the existing type system with little overhead.
- A proof of the soundness of the analysis (Section 4.5): *a well-typed program with reactive effects is reactive.*

The paper ends with some examples (Section 5), discussion (Section 6) and related work (Section 7). The work presented here is implemented in the ReactiveML compiler[1] and it has already helped detecting many reactivity bugs. An extended version of the paper, the implementation, the source code of the examples and an online toplevel are available at `http://reactiveml.org/sas14`.

2 Overview of the Approach

ReactiveML extends ML with programming constructs inspired from synchronous languages [6]. It introduces a built-in notion of parallelism where time is defined as a succession of logical instants. Each parallel process must cooperate to let time elapse. It is a deterministic model of concurrency that is compatible with the dynamic creation of processes [9]. Synchrony gives us a simple definition for reactivity: a reactive ReactiveML program is one where each logical instant terminates.

Let us first introduce ReactiveML syntax and informal semantics using a simple program that highlights the problem of non-reactivity. Then we will discuss the design choices and limitations of our reactivity analysis using a few other examples.

[1] `http://www.reactiveml.org`

2.1 A First Example

We start by creating a *process* that emits a signal every `timer` seconds:[2]

```
1 let process clock timer s =
2   let time = ref (Unix.gettimeofday ()) in
3   loop
4     let time' = Unix.gettimeofday () in
5     if time' -. !time >= timer then (emit s (); time := time')
6   end
```

In ReactiveML, there is a distinction between regular ML functions and *processes*, that is, functions whose execution can span several logical instants. Processes are defined using the `process` keyword. The `clock` process is parametrized by a float `timer` and a signal `s`. Signals are communication channels between processes, with instantaneous broadcast. The process starts by initializing a local reference `time` with the current time (line 2), read using the `gettimeofday` function of the `Unix` module from the standard library. Then it enters an infinite loop (line 3 to 6). At each iteration, it reads the new current time and emits the unit value on the signal `s` if enough time has elapsed (line 5). The compiler prints the following warning when compiling this process:

```
W: Line 3, characters 2-115, this expression may be an instantaneous loop
```

The problem is that the body of the loop is instantaneous. It means that this process never cooperates, so that logical instants do not progress. In ReactiveML, cooperating is done by waiting for the next instant using the `pause` operator. We solve our problem by calling it at the end of the loop (line 6):

```
5     if time' -. !time >= timer then (emit s (); time := time');
6     pause
7   end
```

The second part of the program is a process that prints `top` every time a signal `s` is emitted. The `do/when` construct executes its body only when the signal `s` is present (i.e. it is emitted). It terminates by returning the value of its body instantaneously after the termination of the body. Processes have a consistent view of a signal's status during an instant. It is either present or absent and cannot change during the instant.

```
10 let process print_clock s =
11   loop
12     do
13       print_string "top"; print_newline ()
14     when s done
15   end
```

```
W: Line 11, characters 2-78, this expression may be an instantaneous loop
```

Once again, this loop can be instantaneous, but this time it depends on the presence of the signal. While the signal s is absent, the process cooperates. When it is present, the body of the `do/when` executes and terminates instantaneously. So the body of the loop also terminates instantaneously, and a new iteration of the loop is started in the same logical instant. Since the signal is still present,

[2] The vocabulary is the one of synchronous languages, not the one of FRP.

the body of the **do/when** executes one more time, and so on. This process can also be fixed by adding a **pause** statement in the loop.

We can then declare a local signal s and put these two processes in parallel. The result is a program that prints top every second:

```
let process main =
  signal s default () gather (fun x y -> ()) in
  run (print_clock s) || run (clock 1. s)
```

The declaration of a signal takes as arguments the default value of the signal and a combination function that is used to compute the value of the signal when there are multiple emissions in a single instant. Here, the default value is () and the signal keeps this value in case of multi-emission. The || operator represents synchronous parallel composition. Both branches are executed at each instant and communicate through the local signal s.

2.2 Intuitions and Limitations

In the previous example, we have seen the first cause of non-reactivity: instantaneous loops. The second one is instantaneous recursive processes:

```
let rec process instantaneous s =
  emit s (); run (instantaneous s)
W: This expression may produce an instantaneous recursion
```

The execution of **emit** is instantaneous, therefore the recursive call creates a loop that never cooperates. A sufficient condition to ensure that a recursive process is reactive is to have *at least one instant between the instantiation of the process and any recursive call.* The idea of our analysis is to statically check this condition.

This condition is very strong and is not always satisfied by interesting reactive programs. For instance, it does not hold for a parallel map (the **let/and** construct executes its two branches in parallel, matching is instantaneous):

```
let rec process par_map p l =
  match l with
  | [] -> []
  | x :: l -> let x' = run (p x)
              and l' = run (par_map p l) in x' :: l'
W: This expression may produce an instantaneous recursion
```

This process has instantaneous recursive calls, but it is reactive because the recursion is finite if the list l is finite. As the language allows to create mutable and recursive data structures, it is hard to prove the termination of such processes. For instance, the following expression never cooperates:

```
let rec l = 0 :: l in run (par_map p l)
```

Consequently, our analysis only prints warnings and does not reject programs.

ML functions are always considered instantaneous. So they are reactive if and only if they terminate. Since we do not want to prove their termination, our analysis has to distinguish recursions through functions and processes. This allows us to assume that ML functions always terminate and to issue warnings only for processes.

Furthermore, we do not deal with blocking functions, such as I/O primitives, that can also make programs non-reactive. Indeed, such functions should *never* be used in the context of cooperative scheduling. There are standard solutions for this problem [22].

This analysis does not either consider the presence status of signals. It over-approximates the possible behaviors, as in the following example:

```
let rec process imprecise =
  signal s default () gather (fun x y -> ()) in
  present s then () else (* implicit pause *) ();
  run imprecise
W: This expression may produce an instantaneous recursion
```

The `present/then/else` construct executes its first branch instantaneously if the signal is present or executes the second branch with a delay of one instant if the signal is absent. This delayed reaction to absence, first introduced by Boussinot [9], avoids inconsistencies in the status of signals. In the example, the signal is absent so the `else` branch is executed. It means that the recursion is not instantaneous and the process is reactive. Our analysis still prints a warning, because if the signal `s` could be present, the recursion would be instantaneous.

Finally, we only guarantee that the duration of each instant is finite, not that the program is real-time, that is, that there exists a bound on this duration for all instants, as shown in this example:

```
let rec process server add =
  await add(p, ack) in
  run (server add) || let v = run p in emit ack v
```

The `server` process listens on a signal `add` to receive both a process `p` and a signal `ack` on which to send back results. As it creates one new process each time the `add` signal is emitted, this program can execute an arbitrary number of processes at the same time. It is thus not real-time, but it is indeed reactive, as waiting for the value of a signal takes one instant (one has to collect and combine all the values emitted during the instant).

3 The Algebra of Behaviors

The idea of our analysis is to abstract processes into a simpler language called *behaviors*, following Amtoft et al. [3] and to check reactivity on these behaviors. The main design choice is to completely abstract values and the presence of signals. It is however necessary to keep an abstraction of the structure of the program in order to have a reasonable precision.

3.1 The Behaviors

The algebra of behaviors is given by:[3]

$$\kappa ::= \bullet \mid 0 \mid \phi \mid \kappa \,||\, \kappa \mid \kappa + \kappa \mid \kappa ; \kappa \mid \mu\phi.\, \kappa \mid \mathbf{run}\ \kappa$$

[3] Precedence of operators is the following (from highest to lowest): **run**, ;, +, || and finally μ. For instance: $\mu\phi.\, \kappa_1 \,||\, \mathbf{run}\ \kappa_2 + \bullet; \kappa_3$ means $\mu\phi.\, (\kappa_1 \,||\, ((\mathbf{run}\ \kappa_2) + (\bullet; \kappa_3)))$.

Actions that take at least one instant to execute, i.e. surely non-instantaneous actions, such as `pause`, are denoted $\bullet$. Potentially instantaneous ones, like calling a pure ML function or emitting a signal, are denoted 0. The language also includes behavior variables ϕ to represent the behaviors of processes taken as arguments, since ReactiveML has higher-order processes.

Behaviors must reflect the structure of the program, starting with parallel composition. This is illustrated by the following example, which defines a combinator `par_comb` that takes as inputs two processes `q1` and `q2` and runs them in parallel in a loop:

```
let process par_comb q1 q2 = loop (run q1 || run q2) end
```

The synchronous parallel composition terminates when both branches have terminated. It means that the loop is non-instantaneous if either `q1` or `q2` is non-instantaneous. To represent such processes, behaviors include the parallel composition, simply denoted $||$. Similarly, we can define another combinator that runs one of its two inputs depending on a condition `c`:

```
let process if_comb c q1 q2 = loop (if c then run q1 else run q2) end
```

In the case of `if_comb`, both processes must be non-instantaneous. As we want to abstract values, we represent the different alternatives using a non-determinstic choice operator $+$ and forget about the conditions.

It is also necessary to have a notion of sequence, denoted ; in the language of behaviors, as illustrated by the two following processes:

```
let rec process good_rec = pause; run good_rec
let rec process bad_rec = run bad_rec; pause
W: This expression may produce an instantaneous recursion
```

The order between the recursive call and the `pause` statement is crucial as the `good_rec` process is reactive while `bad_rec` loops instantaneously. As it is defined recursively, the behavior κ associated with the `good_rec` process must verify that $\kappa = \bullet; \mathbf{run}\ \kappa$. The `run` operator is associated with running a process. This equation can be solved by introducing an explicit recursion operator μ so that $\kappa = \mu\phi.\ \bullet; \mathbf{run}\ \phi$. Recursive behaviors are defined as usual:

$$\mu\phi.\ \kappa = \kappa[\phi \leftarrow \mu\phi.\ \kappa] \qquad\qquad \mu\phi.\ \kappa = \kappa \text{ if } \phi \notin \mathit{fbv}(\kappa)$$

We denote $\mathit{fbv}(\kappa)$ the set of free behavior variables in κ. There is no operator for representing the behavior of a loop. Indeed, a loop is just a special case of recursion. The behavior of a loop, denoted κ^∞ (where κ is the behavior of the body of the loop), is thus defined as a recursive behavior by $\kappa^\infty \triangleq \mu\phi.\ (\kappa; \mathbf{run}\ \phi)$.

3.2 Reactive Behaviors

Using the language of behaviors, we can now characterize the behaviors that we want to reject, that is instantaneous loops and recursions. To formally define which behaviors are reactive, we first have to define the notion of a *non-instantaneous* behavior, i.e. processes that take at least one instant to execute:

Definition 1 (Non-instantaneous Behavior). *A behavior is* non-instantaneous, *denoted* $\kappa\downarrow$, *if:*

$$\frac{}{\bullet\downarrow} \qquad \frac{}{\phi\downarrow} \qquad \frac{\kappa_1\downarrow}{\kappa_1;\kappa_2\downarrow} \qquad \frac{\kappa_2\downarrow}{\kappa_1;\kappa_2\downarrow} \qquad \frac{\kappa_1\downarrow}{\kappa_1 \mid\mid \kappa_2\downarrow} \qquad \frac{\kappa_2\downarrow}{\kappa_1 \mid\mid \kappa_2\downarrow} \qquad \frac{\kappa_1\downarrow \quad \kappa_2\downarrow}{\kappa_1+\kappa_2\downarrow}$$

$$\frac{\kappa\downarrow}{\mu\phi.\,\kappa\downarrow} \qquad \frac{\kappa\downarrow}{\mathbf{run}\ \kappa\downarrow}$$

Note that function calls are not non-instantaneous. The fact that variables are considered non-instantaneous means that any process taken as argument is supposed to be non-instantaneous. The reactivity is then checked when this variable is instantiated with the actual behavior of the process.

A behavior is said to be *reactive* if for each recursive behavior $\mu\phi.\,\kappa$, the recursion variable ϕ does not appear in the first instant of the body κ. This enforces that there must be at least one instant between the instantiation of a process and each recursive call and is formalized in the following definition.

Definition 2 (Reactive Behavior). *A behavior* κ *is* reactive *if* $\emptyset \vdash \kappa$, *where the relation* $R \vdash \kappa$ *is defined by:*

$$\frac{}{R\vdash 0} \qquad \frac{}{R\vdash \bullet} \qquad \frac{\phi\notin R}{R\vdash\phi} \qquad \frac{R\vdash\kappa_1 \quad \mathit{not}(\kappa_1\downarrow) \quad R\vdash\kappa_2}{R\vdash\kappa_1;\kappa_2}$$

$$\frac{R\vdash\kappa_1 \quad \kappa_1\downarrow \quad \emptyset\vdash\kappa_2}{R\vdash\kappa_1;\kappa_2} \qquad \frac{R\vdash\kappa_1 \quad R\vdash\kappa_2}{R\vdash\kappa_1 \mid\mid \kappa_2} \qquad \frac{R\vdash\kappa_1 \quad R\vdash\kappa_2}{R\vdash\kappa_1+\kappa_2}$$

$$\frac{R\cup\{\phi\}\vdash\kappa}{R\vdash\mu\phi.\,\kappa} \qquad \frac{R\vdash\kappa}{R\vdash\mathbf{run}\ \kappa}$$

The predicate $R \vdash \kappa$ means that the behavior κ is reactive with respect to the set of variables R, that is, these variables do not appear in the first instant of κ and all the recursions inside κ are not instantaneous. The rule for a variable ϕ checks that ϕ is not a recursion variable introduced in the current instant. The recursion variables are added to the set R when checking the reactivity of a recursive behavior $\mu\phi.\,\kappa$. In the case of the sequence $\kappa_1;\kappa_2$, we can remove variables from R if κ_1 is non-instantaneous. One can also check from the definition of κ^∞ as a recursive behavior that this definition also implies that the body of a loop is non-instantaneous.

3.3 Equivalence on Behaviors

We can define an equivalence relation $\equiv$ on behaviors that will be used to simplify the behaviors. The relation is reflexive, symmetric and transitive closure of the following rules. The operators ; and || and + are idempotent and associative. || and + are commutative (but not ;). The 0 behavior (resp. $\bullet$) is the neutral element of ; and || (resp. +). The relation also satisfies the following rules (where *op* is ; or || or +):

$$\frac{\kappa_1 \equiv \kappa_2}{\mu\phi.\,\kappa_1 \equiv \mu\phi.\,\kappa_2} \qquad \frac{\kappa_1 \equiv \kappa_2}{\texttt{run}\ \kappa_1 \equiv \texttt{run}\ \kappa_2} \qquad \bullet^\infty \equiv \bullet \qquad \frac{\kappa_1 \equiv \kappa_1' \quad \kappa_2 \equiv \kappa_2'}{\kappa_1\, op\, \kappa_2 \equiv \kappa_1'\, op\, \kappa_2'}$$

It is easy to show, for example, that: $\mu\phi.\,((\bullet \parallel 0); (\texttt{run}\ \phi + \texttt{run}\ \phi)) \equiv \mu\phi.\,(\bullet; \texttt{run}\ \phi)$. An important property of this relation is that it preserves reactivity. It is expressed as follows:

Property 1. if $\kappa_1 \equiv \kappa_2$ and $R \vdash \kappa_1$ then $R \vdash \kappa_2$.

Proof. By induction on the proof of $\kappa_1 \equiv \kappa_2$. □

4 The Type-and-Effect System

The link between processes and behaviors is done by a type-and-effect system [18], following the work of Amtoft et al. [3]. The behavior of a process is its effect computed using the type system. After type-checking, the compiler checks the inferred behaviors and prints a warning if one of them is not reactive.

The type system is a conservative extension of the original one of ReactiveML, that is, it is able to assign a behavior to any ReactiveML program that was accepted previously. It is an important feature as we only want to show warnings and not reject programs.

4.1 Abstract Syntax

We consider here a kernel of ReactiveML:

$$\begin{aligned} v ::=\ & c \mid (v, v) \mid n \mid \lambda x.e \mid \texttt{process}\ e \\ e ::=\ & x \mid c \mid (e, e) \mid \lambda x.e \mid e\ e \mid \texttt{rec}\ x = v \mid \texttt{process}\ e \mid \texttt{run}\ e \mid \texttt{pause} \\ & \mid \texttt{let}\ x = e\ \texttt{and}\ x = e\ \texttt{in}\ e \mid \texttt{signal}\ x\ \texttt{default}\ e\ \texttt{gather}\ e\ \texttt{in}\ e \mid \texttt{emit}\ e\ e \\ & \mid \texttt{present}\ e\ \texttt{then}\ e\ \texttt{else}\ e \mid \texttt{loop}\ e \mid \texttt{do}\ e\ \texttt{until}\ e(x) \to e \mid \texttt{do}\ e\ \texttt{when}\ e \end{aligned}$$

Values are constants c (integers, unit value `()`, etc.), pairs of values, signal names n, functions and processes. The language is a call-by-value lambda-calculus, extended with constructs for creating (`process`) and running (`run`) processes, waiting for the next instant (`pause`), parallel definitions (`let`/`and`), declaring signals (`signal`), emitting a signal (`emit`) and several control structures: the test of presence of a signal (`present`), the unconditional loop (`loop`), weak preemption (`do`/`until`) and suspension (`do`/`when`). The expression `do` e_1 `until` $s(x) \to e_2$ executes its body e_1 and interrupts it if s is present. In case of preemption, the continuation e_2 is executed on the next instant, binding x to the value of s. We denote _ variables that do not appear free in the body of a `let` and `()` the unique value of type `unit`. From this kernel, we can encode most constructs of the language:

$$\begin{aligned} e_1 \parallel e_2 &\triangleq \texttt{let}\ \_ = e_1\ \texttt{and}\ \_ = e_2\ \texttt{in}\ () \\ e_1; e_2 &\triangleq \texttt{let}\ \_ = ()\ \texttt{and}\ \_ = e_1\ \texttt{in}\ e_2 \\ \texttt{await}\ e_1(x)\ \texttt{in}\ e_2 &\triangleq \texttt{do}\ (\texttt{loop pause})\ \texttt{until}\ e_1(x) \to e_2 \\ \texttt{let rec process}\ f\ x_1 \ldots x_p = e_1\ \texttt{in}\ e_2 & \\ &\triangleq \texttt{let}\ f = (\texttt{rec}\ f = \lambda x_1. \ldots \lambda x_p.\texttt{process}\ e_1)\ \texttt{in}\ e_2 \end{aligned}$$

4.2 Types

Types are defined by:

$$\tau ::= \alpha \mid T \mid \tau \times \tau \mid \tau \rightarrow \tau \mid \tau\,\texttt{process}[\kappa] \mid (\tau, \tau)\,\texttt{event} \qquad \text{(types)}$$
$$\sigma ::= \tau \mid \forall \phi.\, \sigma \mid \forall \alpha.\, \sigma \qquad \text{(type schemes)}$$
$$\Gamma ::= \emptyset \mid \Gamma, x : \sigma \qquad \text{(environments)}$$

A type is either a type variable α, a base type T (like `bool` or `unit`), a product, a function, a process or a signal. The type of a process is parametrized by its return type and its behavior. The type $(\tau_1, \tau_2)\,\texttt{event}$ of a signal is parametrized by the type τ_1 of emitted values and the type τ_2 of the received value (since a gathering function of type $\tau_1 \rightarrow \tau_2 \rightarrow \tau_2$ is applied).

Types schemes quantify universally over type variables α and behavior variables ϕ. We denote $ftv(\tau)$ (resp. $fbv(\tau)$) the set of type (resp. behavior) variables free in τ and $fv(\tau) = ftv(\tau), fbv(\tau)$. Instantiation and generalization are defined in a classic way: $\sigma[\alpha \leftarrow \tau] \leq \forall \alpha.\, \sigma \quad \sigma[\phi \leftarrow \kappa] \leq \forall \phi.\, \sigma$

$$gen(\tau, e, \Gamma) = \tau \qquad \text{if } e \text{ is expansive}$$
$$gen(\tau, e, \Gamma) = \forall \bar{\alpha}.\forall \bar{\phi}.\ \tau \text{ where } \bar{\alpha}, \bar{\phi} = fv(\tau) \setminus fv(\Gamma) \qquad \text{otherwise}$$

Analogously to the treatment of references in ML, we must be careful not to generalize expressions that allocate signals. We use the syntactic criterion of expansive and non-expansive expressions [33]. An expression is expansive if it can allocate a signal or a reference, in which case its type should not be generalized.

The notions of reactivity and equivalence are lifted from behaviors to types. A type is reactive if it contains only reactive behaviors. Two types are equivalent, also denoted $\tau_1 \equiv \tau_2$, if they have the same structure and their behaviors are equivalent.

4.3 Typing Rules

Typing judgments are given by $\Gamma \vdash e : \tau \mid \kappa$ meaning that, in the type environment Γ, the expression e has type τ and behavior κ. We write $\Gamma \vdash e : \tau \mid \_ \equiv 0$ when the behavior of the expression e is equivalent to 0. The initial typing environment Γ_0 gives the types of primitives:

$$\Gamma_0 \triangleq [\texttt{true} : \texttt{bool}; \texttt{fst} : \forall \alpha_1, \alpha_2.\, \alpha_1 \times \alpha_2 \rightarrow \alpha_1; \ldots]$$

The rules defining the type system are given in Figure 1. If all the behaviors are erased, it is exactly the same type system as the one presented in [19], which is itself an extension of the ML type system. We discuss here the novelties of the rules related to behaviors:

- The Process rule stores the behavior of the body in the type of the process, as usual in type-and-effect systems. The presence of the κ' behavior and the Mask rule are related to subeffecting and will be discussed in Section 4.4.

$$\frac{\tau \leq \Gamma(x)}{\Gamma \vdash x : \tau \mid 0} \qquad \frac{\tau \leq \Gamma_0(c)}{\Gamma \vdash c : \tau \mid 0} \qquad \frac{\Gamma \vdash e_1 : \tau_1 \mid \_ \equiv 0 \qquad \Gamma \vdash e_2 : \tau_2 \mid \_ \equiv 0}{\Gamma \vdash (e_1, e_2) : \tau_1 \times \tau_2 \mid 0}$$

$$\frac{\Gamma, x : \tau_1 \vdash e : \tau_2 \mid \_ \equiv 0}{\Gamma \vdash \lambda x.e : \tau_1 \to \tau_2 \mid 0} \qquad (\textsc{App})\ \frac{\Gamma \vdash e_1 : \tau_2 \to \tau_1 \mid \_ \equiv 0 \qquad \Gamma \vdash e_2 : \tau_2 \mid \_ \equiv 0}{\Gamma \vdash e_1\ e_2 : \tau_1 \mid 0}$$

$$\frac{\Gamma, x : \tau \vdash v : \tau \mid \_ \equiv 0}{\Gamma \vdash \texttt{rec}\ x = v : \tau \mid 0} \qquad (\textsc{Process})\ \frac{\Gamma \vdash e : \tau \mid \kappa}{\Gamma \vdash \texttt{process}\ e : \tau\, \texttt{process}[\kappa + \kappa'] \mid 0}$$

$$\frac{\Gamma \vdash e : \tau\, \texttt{process}[\kappa] \mid \_ \equiv 0}{\Gamma \vdash \texttt{run}\ e : \tau \mid \texttt{run}\ \kappa} \qquad \Gamma \vdash \texttt{pause} : \texttt{unit} \mid \bullet$$

$$\frac{\Gamma \vdash e_1 : \tau_1 \mid \kappa_1 \quad \Gamma \vdash e_2 : \tau_2 \mid \kappa_2 \quad \Gamma, x_1 : gen(\tau_1, e_1, \Gamma), x_2 : gen(\tau_2, e_2, \Gamma) \vdash e_3 : \tau \mid \kappa_3}{\Gamma \vdash \texttt{let}\ x_1 = e_1\ \texttt{and}\ x_2 = e_2\ \texttt{in}\ e_3 : \tau \mid (\kappa_1 \parallel \kappa_2); \kappa_3}$$

$$\frac{\Gamma \vdash e_1 : \tau_2 \mid \_ \equiv 0 \qquad \Gamma \vdash e_2 : \tau_1 \to \tau_2 \to \tau_2 \mid \_ \equiv 0 \qquad \Gamma, x : (\tau_1, \tau_2)\, \texttt{event} \vdash e : \tau \mid \kappa}{\Gamma \vdash \texttt{signal}\ x\ \texttt{default}\ e_1\ \texttt{gather}\ e_2\ \texttt{in}\ e : \tau \mid 0; \kappa}$$

$$\frac{\Gamma \vdash e : (\tau_1, \tau_2)\, \texttt{event} \mid \_ \equiv 0 \qquad \Gamma \vdash e_1 : \tau \mid \kappa_1 \qquad \Gamma \vdash e_2 : \tau \mid \kappa_2}{\Gamma \vdash \texttt{present}\ e\ \texttt{then}\ e_1\ \texttt{else}\ e_2 : \tau \mid \kappa_1 + (\bullet; \kappa_2)}$$

$$\frac{\Gamma \vdash e_1 : (\tau_1, \tau_2)\, \texttt{event} \mid \_ \equiv 0 \qquad \Gamma \vdash e_2 : \tau_1 \mid \_ \equiv 0}{\Gamma \vdash \texttt{emit}\ e_1\ e_2 : \texttt{unit} \mid 0} \qquad \frac{\Gamma \vdash e : \tau \mid \kappa}{\Gamma \vdash \texttt{loop}\ e : \texttt{unit} \mid (0; \kappa)^\infty}$$

$$\frac{\Gamma \vdash e_1 : \tau \mid \kappa_1 \qquad \Gamma \vdash e : (\tau_1, \tau_2)\, \texttt{event} \mid \_ \equiv 0 \qquad \Gamma, x : \tau_2 \vdash e_2 : \tau \mid \kappa_2}{\Gamma \vdash \texttt{do}\ e_1\ \texttt{until}\ e(x) \to e_2 : \tau \mid \kappa_1 + (\bullet; \kappa_2)}$$

$$\frac{\Gamma \vdash e_1 : \tau \mid \kappa \qquad \Gamma \vdash e : (\tau_1, \tau_2)\, \texttt{event} \mid \_ \equiv 0}{\Gamma \vdash \texttt{do}\ e_1\ \texttt{when}\ e : \tau \mid \kappa + \bullet^\infty} \qquad (\textsc{Mask})\ \frac{\Gamma \vdash e : \tau \mid \kappa \qquad \phi \notin fbv(\Gamma, \tau)}{\Gamma \vdash e : \tau \mid \kappa[\phi \leftarrow \bullet]}$$

Fig. 1. Type-and-effect rules

- A design choice made in ReactiveML is to separate pure ML expressions, that are surely instantaneous, from processes. For instance, it is impossible to call `pause` within the body of a function, that must be instantaneous. A static analysis (used for efficient code generation) performed before typing checks this well-formation of expressions, denoted $k \vdash e$ in [19] and recalled in Appendix A [20]. Requiring the behavior of some expressions, like the arguments of an application or the body of a function, to be equivalent to 0 does not add any new constraint with respect to this existing analysis.
- We do not try to prove the termination of pure ML functions without any reactive behavior. The App rule shows that we assume that function calls always terminate instantaneously.
- In the case of **present** e **then** e_1 **else** e_2, the first branch e_1 is executed immediately if the signal e is present and the second branch e_2 is executed

at the next instant if it is absent. This is reflected in the behavior associated with the expression. Similarly, for `do` e_1 `until` $e(x) \rightarrow e_2$, the expression e_2 is executed at the instant following the presence of e.
- The reason why the behavior associated with `loop` is equal to $(0; \kappa)^\infty$ and not simply κ^∞ will be explained in Section 4.5. Intuitively, the soundness proof will use an induction on the size of the behaviours and thus requires the behavior of a sub-expression to always be smaller. This also applies for `signal` and `do/when`.
- Finally, note that there is no special treatment for recursive processes. We will see in the next section that recursive behaviors are introduced during unification.

4.4 Subeffecting with Row Polymorphism

The typing rule (PROCESS) for the creation of processes intuitively mean that a process has *at least* the behavior of its body. The idea is to add a free behavior variable to represent other potential behaviors of the process. This subtyping restricted to effects is often referred to as *subeffecting* [23]: we can always replace an effect with a bigger, i.e. less precise, one. It allows to assign a behavior to any correct ReactiveML program. For instance, it is possible to build a list of two processes with different behaviors (the • behavior is printed `'*'` and behavior variables ϕ are denoted `'r`):

```
let process p1 = ()
val p1: unit process[0 + 'r1]
let process p2 = pause
val p2: unit process[* + 'r2]
let l = [p1; p2]
val l: unit process[0 + * + 'r] list
```

If the behavior of a process had been exactly equal to the behavior of its body, this expression would have been rejected by the type system.

The consequence of the typing rule for processes is that the principal type of an expression `process` e is always of the form $\kappa + \phi$ where κ is the behavior of e and ϕ a free variable. The idea to use a free type variable to represent other possible types is reminiscent of Remy's row types [26]. It makes it possible to implement subeffecting using only unification, without manipulating constraint sets as in traditional approaches [31,3]. It thus becomes easier to integrate it into any existing ML type inference implementation. For instance, OCaml type inference is also based on row polymorphism [27], so it would be easy to implement our type system on top of the full language.

We can reuse any existing inference algorithm, like algorithm $\mathcal{W}$ or $\mathcal{M}$ [16] and add only the following algorithm $\mathcal{U}_\kappa$ for unification of behaviors. It takes as input two behaviors and returns a substitution that maps behavior variables to behaviors, that we denote $[\phi_1 \mapsto \kappa_1; \phi_2 \mapsto \kappa_2; \ldots]$. During unification, the behavior of a process is always either a behavior variable ϕ, a row $\kappa + \phi$ or a recursive row $\mu\phi.\,(\kappa + \phi')$. Therefore, the unification algorithm only has to consider these cases:

$$\begin{aligned}
\mathcal{U}_\kappa(\kappa, \kappa) &= [] \\
\mathcal{U}_\kappa(\phi, \kappa) = \mathcal{U}_\kappa(\kappa, \phi) &= \begin{cases} [\phi \mapsto \mu\phi.\,\kappa] & \text{if } \mathtt{occur_check}(\phi, \kappa) \\ [\phi \mapsto \kappa] & \text{otherwise} \end{cases} \\
\mathcal{U}_\kappa(\kappa_1 + \phi_1, \kappa_2 + \phi_2) &= [\phi_1 \mapsto \kappa_2 + \phi; \phi_1 \mapsto \kappa_1 + \phi],\ \phi \text{ fresh} \\
\mathcal{U}_\kappa(\mu\phi_1'.\,(\kappa_1 + \phi_1), \kappa_2) &= \mathcal{U}_\kappa(\kappa_2, \mu\phi_1'.\,(\kappa_1 + \phi_1)) \\
&= \mathtt{let}\ K_1 = \mu\phi_1'.\,(\kappa_1 + \phi_1)\ \mathtt{in}\ \mathcal{U}_\kappa(\kappa_1[\phi_1' \leftarrow K_1] + \phi_1, \kappa_2)
\end{aligned}$$

It should be noted that unification never fails, so that we obtain a conservative extension of ReactiveML type system. This unification algorithm reuses traditional techniques for handling recursive types [13]. The last case unfolds a recursive row to reveal the row variable, so that it can be unified with other rows.

A downside of our approach is that it introduces one behavior variable for each process, so that the computed behaviors may become very big and unreadable. The purpose of the MASK rule is to remedy this, by using *effect masking* [18]. The idea is that if a behavior variable appearing in the behavior is free in the environment, it is not constrained so we can give it any value. In particular, we choose to replace it with $\bullet$, which is the neutral element of $+$, so that it can be simplified away.

4.5 Proof of Soundness

We now present the proof sketch of the soundness of our analysis, that is, that at each instant, the program admits a finite derivation in the big-step semantics of the language and rewrites to a well-typed program with reactive effects.

The big-step semantics of ReactiveML, also called the behavioral semantics in reference to the semantics of Esterel [25], describes the reaction of an expression during an instant i by the smallest signal environment S_i (the set of present signals) such that:

$$e_i \xrightarrow[S_i]{E_i, b_i} e_{i+1}$$

which means that during the instant i, in the signal environment S_i, the expression e_i rewrites to e_{i+1} and emits the signals in E_i. The boolean b_i indicates if e_{i+1} has terminated. Additional conditions express, for instance, the fact that the emitted values in E_i must agree with the signal environment S_i. An execution of a program comprises a succession of a (potentially infinite) number of reactions and terminates when the status b_i is equal to true. The definition of the semantics was introduced in [19] and is recalled in Appendix B [20].

A program is reactive if at each instant, the semantics derivation of e_i is finite. To prove that, we first isolate the first instant of the behavior of e_i, noted $\mathtt{fst}(\kappa_i)$. This function is formally defined by:

$$\texttt{fst}(0) = \texttt{fst}(\bullet) = 0 \qquad \texttt{fst}(\kappa_1 + \kappa_2) = \texttt{fst}(\kappa_1) + \texttt{fst}(\kappa_2)$$

$$\texttt{fst}(\phi) = \phi \qquad \texttt{fst}(\kappa_1; \kappa_2) = \begin{cases} \texttt{fst}(\kappa_1) & \text{if } \kappa_1 \downarrow \\ \texttt{fst}(\kappa_1); \texttt{fst}(\kappa_2) & \text{otherwise} \end{cases}$$

$$\texttt{fst}(\texttt{run}\ \kappa) = \texttt{run}\ (\texttt{fst}(\kappa))$$

$$\texttt{fst}(\kappa_1 \mid\mid \kappa_2) = \texttt{fst}(\kappa_1) \mid\mid \texttt{fst}(\kappa_2) \qquad \texttt{fst}(\mu\phi.\, \kappa) = \texttt{fst}(\kappa[\phi \leftarrow \mu\phi.\, \kappa])$$

The important property of this function is that if a behavior κ_i of e_i is reactive (as defined in Section 3.2), then $\texttt{fst}(\kappa_i)$ is finite. Hence we can prove by induction on the size of $\texttt{fst}(\kappa_i)$ that the semantics derivation is finite. The soundness theorem is stated as follows:

Theorem 1 (Soundness). *If $\Gamma \vdash e : \tau \mid \kappa$ and τ and κ are reactive and we suppose that function calls terminate, then there exists e' such that $e \xrightarrow[S]{E,b} e'$ and $\Gamma \vdash e' : \tau \mid \kappa'$ with κ' reactive.*

Proof. The proof has two parts. The first part is the proof that the result is well-typed. We use classic syntactic techniques for type soundness [24] on the small-step semantics described in [19]. The proof of equivalence of the two semantics is also given in the same paper. The second part is the proof that the semantics derivation of one instant is finite by induction on the size of the first-instant behavior of well-typed expressions. We only consider one instant because thanks to type preservation, if the theorem is true for one instant, it is true for the following ones. The details of the proof are given in Appendix C [20]. □

5 Examples

We present here the result of the analysis on some examples. These examples can be downloaded and tried at **http://reactiveml.org/sas14**.

Using a type-based analysis makes it easy to deal with cases of aliasing, as in the following example:[4]

```
let rec process p =
  let q = (fun x -> x) p in run q
val p: 'a process[rec 'r. (run 'r + ..)]
W: This expression may produce an instantaneous recursion
```

The process `q` has the same type as `p`, and thus the same behavior, so the instantaneous recursion is easily detected. As for objects in OCaml [27], row variables that appear only once are printed '`..`'.

The analysis can also handle combinators like the `par_comb` and `if_comb` examples of Section 3.1. Here is another more complex example using higher-order functions and processes. We define a function `h_o` that takes as input a combinator `f`. It then creates a recursive process that applies `f` to itself and runs the result:

[4] Some behaviors are simplified using the extension described in Appendix D [20].

```
let h_o f =
  let rec process p = let q = f p in run q
  in p
val h_o: ('a process[run 'r1 + 'r2] -> 'a process['r1])
               -> 'a process[run 'r1 + 'r2]
```

If we instantiate this function with a process that waits an instant before calling its argument, we obtain a reactive process:

```
let process good = run (h_o (fun x -> process (pause; run x)))
val good: 'a process[run (run (rec 'r1. *; run (run 'r1))) + ..]
```

This is no longer the case if the process calls its argument instantaneously. The instantaneous recursion is again detected by our static analysis:

```
let process pb = run (h_o (fun x -> process (run x)))
val pb: 'a process[run (run (rec 'r1. run run 'r1)) + ..]
W: This expression may produce an instantaneous recursion
```

Another process that can be analyzed is a fix-point operator. It takes as input a function expecting a continuation, and applies it with itself as the continuation. This fix-point operator can be used to create a recursive process:

```
let rec fix f x = f (fix f) x
val fix: (('a -> 'b) -> 'a -> 'b) -> 'a -> 'b

let process main =
  let process p k v = print_int v; run (k (v+1)) in run (fix p 0)
val main: 'a process[(run (rec 'r. run 'r)) + ..]
W: This expression may produce an instantaneous recursion
```

In the example, the analysis detects the problem of reactivity although there is no explicit recursive process.

6 Discussion

Implementation. The type inference algorithm of ReactiveML has been extended to compute the behaviors of processes, with minimal impact on its structure and complexity thanks to the use of row polymorphism for subeffecting (see Section 4.4). The rules given in Section 3.2 are easily translated into an algorithm for checking the reactivity of behaviors that is polynomial in the size of behaviors.

In practice, the analysis has an impact on the type-checking time but it is negligible compared to the global compilation time. For example on a 1.7GHz Intel Core i5 with 4Go RAM, the compilation of the examples of the ReactiveML distribution (about 5000 lines of code) takes about 0.15s where 0.02s are spent in the type checker (0.005s without the reactivity analysis). Then it takes 3.5s to compile the generated OCaml code.

Evaluation. The analysis is very useful to detect early small reactivity bugs such as the one presented Section 2.1. We have also used the analysis on bigger applications: a mobile ad-hoc network simulator (1800 Source Lines Of Code), a sensor network simulator (1700 SLOC), and a mixed music sequencer (3400 SLOC).

There is no warning for both simulators. For the mixed music sequencer, there are warnings on eleven processes. Eight warnings are due to structural recursions (similar to the example `par_map`). Most of them come from the fact that the program is a language interpreter defined as a set of mutually recursive processes on the abstract syntax tree. Another warning comes from a record containing a process that is not annotated with a non-instantaneous behavior. The last two warnings are due to loops around the execution of a musical score. In this case, the analysis does not use the fact that the score is a non-empty list.

In all these cases, it was easy for the programmer to check that these warnings were false positives. The last three warnings can be removed by adding a **pause** in parallel to the potentially instantaneous expressions.

Other Models of Concurrency. We have already extended our analysis to take into account time refinement [21]. We believe this work could be applied to other models of concurrency. One just needs to give the behavior • to operations that cooperate with the scheduler, like `yield`. We are considering an extension to the X10 language,[5] where cooperation points could be clocks.

In a synchronous world, the fact that each process cooperates at each instant implies the reactivity of the whole program, as processes are executed in lock-step. In another model, assumptions on the fairness of the scheduler may be required. This should not be a major obstacle, as these hypotheses are already made in most systems, e.g. in Concurrent Haskell [15]. The distinction between processes and functions is important to avoid showing a warning for all recursive functions.

7 Related Work

The analysis of instantaneous loops is an old topic on which much has already been written, even recently [1,14,4]. It is related to the analysis of productivity and deadlocks in list programs [29] or guard conditions in proof assistants [5], etc. Our purpose was to define an analysis that can be used in the context of a general purpose language (mutable values, recursion, etc.). We tried to find a good compromise between the complexity of the analysis and its precision for typical reactive programs written in ReactiveML. The programmer must not be surprised by the analysis and the error messages. We focus here only on directly related work.

Our language of behaviors and type system are inspired by the work of Amtoft et al. [3]. Their analysis is defined on the ConcurrentML [28] language, which extends ML with message passing primitives. The behavior of a process records emissions and receptions on communication channels. The authors use the type system to prove properties on particular examples, not for a general analysis. For instance, they prove that emission on a given channel always precedes the emission on a second channel in a given program. The idea of using a type-and-effect system for checking reactivity or termination is not new. For instance, Boudol [8]

[5] `http://x10-lang.org/`

uses a type-and-effect system to prove termination of functional programs using references, by stratifying memory to avoid recursion through references.

Reactivity analysis is a classic topic in synchronous languages, that can also be related to causality. In Esterel [25], the first imperative synchronous language, it is possible to react immediately to the presence *and* the absence of a signal. The consequence is that a program can be non-reactive because there is no consistent status for a given signal: the program supposes that a signal is both present and absent during the same instant. This problem is solved by checking that programs are *constructively correct* [25]. Our concurrency model, inherited from the work of Boussinot [9], avoids these problems by making sure that processes are causal by construction. We then only have to check that loops are not instantaneous, which is called *loop-safe* by Berry [25]. It is easy to check that an Esterel program is loop-safe as the language is first order without recursion [32].

Closer to ReactiveML, the reactivity analysis of FunLoft [2] not only checks that instants terminate, but also gives a bound on the duration of the instants through a value analysis. The analysis is also restricted to the first-order setting. In ULM [7], each recursive call induces an implicit pause. Hence, it is impossible to have instantaneous recursions, at the expense of expressivity. For instance, in the `server` example of Section 2.2, a message could be lost between receiving a message on `add` and awaiting a new message.

The causality analysis of Lucid Synchrone [10] is a type-and-effect system using row types. It is based on the exception analysis defined by Leroy et al. [17]. Both are a more direct application of row types [26], whereas our system differs in the absence of labels in rows.

8 Conclusion

We have presented a reactivity analysis for the ReactiveML language. The idea of the analysis is to abstract processes into a simpler language called behaviors using a type-and-effect system. Checking reactivity of behaviors is then straightforward. We have proven the soundness of our analysis, that is, that a well-typed program with reactive effects is reactive. Thanks in particular to the syntactic separation between functions and processes, the analysis does not detect too many false positives in practice. It is implemented in the ReactiveML compiler and it has been proven very useful for avoiding reactivity bugs. We believe that this work can be applied to other models of cooperative scheduling.

Acknowledgments. This work would not have been possible without previous experiments made with Florence Plateau and Marc Pouzet. Timothy Bourke helped us a lot in the preparation of this article. We are grateful for the proofreading and discussions with Guillaume Baudart and Adrien Guatto. Finally, we also thank the reviewers for there numerous comments and suggestions.

References

1. Abel, A., Pientka, B.: Well-founded recursion with copatterns. In: International Conference on Functional Programming (2013)
2. Amadio, R., Dabrowski, F.: Feasible reactivity in a synchronous π-calculus. In: Principles and Practice of Declarative Programming, pp. 221–230 (2007)
3. Amtoft, T., Nielson, F., Nielson, H.: Type and Effect Systems: Behaviours for Concurrency. Imperial College Press (1999)
4. Atkey, R., McBride, C.: Productive coprogramming with guarded recursion. In: International Conference on Functional Programming (2013)
5. Barthe, G., Frade, M.J., Giménez, E., Pinto, L., Uustalu, T.: Type-based termination of recursive definitions. Mathematical Structures in Computer Science 14(01), 97–141 (2004)
6. Benveniste, A., Caspi, P., Edwards, S.A., Halbwachs, N., Guernic, P.L., De Simone, R.: The synchronous languages twelve years later. In: Proc. of the IEEE (2003)
7. Boudol, G.: ULM: A core programming model for global computing. In: Schmidt, D. (ed.) ESOP 2004. LNCS, vol. 2986, pp. 234–248. Springer, Heidelberg (2004)
8. Boudol, G.: Typing termination in a higher-order concurrent imperative language. Information and Computation 208(6), 716–736 (2010)
9. Boussinot, F.: Reactive C: an extension of C to program reactive systems. Software: Practice and Experience 21(4), 401–428 (1991)
10. Cuoq, P., Pouzet, M.: Modular Causality in a Synchronous Stream Language. In: Sands, D. (ed.) ESOP 2001. LNCS, vol. 2028, pp. 237–251. Springer, Heidelberg (2001)
11. Dimino, J.: Lwt User Manual (2014), `http://ocsigen.org/lwt/`
12. Engelschall, R.: Portable multithreading: The signal stack trick for user-space thread creation. In: USENIX Annual Technical Conference (2000)
13. Huet, G.: A unification algorithm for typed λ-calculus. Theoretical Computer Science 1(1), 27–57 (1975)
14. Jeffrey, A.: Functional reactive programming with liveness guarantees. In: International Conference on Functional Programming (2013)
15. Jones, S., Gordon, A., Finne, S.: Concurrent Haskell. In: Principles of Programming Languages, pp. 295–308 (1996)
16. Lee, O., Yi, K.: Proofs about a folklore let-polymorphic type inference algorithm. Transactions on Programming Languages and Systems 20(4), 707–723 (1998)
17. Leroy, X., Pessaux, F.: Type-based analysis of uncaught exceptions. Transactions on Programming Languages and Systems 22(2), 340–377 (2000)
18. Lucassen, J.M., Gifford, D.K.: Polymorphic effect systems. In: Principles of Programming Languages (1988)
19. Mandel, L., Pouzet, M.: ReactiveML: A reactive extension to ML. In: Principles and Practice of Declarative Programming (2005)
20. Mandel, L., Pasteur, C.: Reactivity of cooperative systems – extended version. Research Report 8549, INRIA (2014), `http://reactiveml.org/sas14`
21. Mandel, L., Pasteur, C., Pouzet, M.: Time refinement in a functional synchronous language. In: Principles and Practice of Declarative Programming. (2013)
22. Marlow, S., Jones, S., Thaller, W.: Extending the Haskell foreign function interface with concurrency. In: Haskell 2004, pp. 22–32. ACM (2004)
23. Nielson, F., Nielson, H.: Type and effect systems. Correct System Design (1999)
24. Pierce, B.: Types and programming languages. The MIT Press (2002)
25. Potop-Butucaru, D., Edwards, S.A., Berry, G.: Compiling Esterel. Springer (2007)

26. Rémy, D.: Type inference for records in a natural extension of ML. Theoretical Aspects of Object-Oriented Programming. MIT Press (1993)
27. Rémy, D.: Using, understanding, and unraveling the OCaml language from practice to theory and vice versa. In: Barthe, G., Dybjer, P., Pinto, L., Saraiva, J. (eds.) Applied Semantics. LNCS, vol. 2395, pp. 413–536. Springer, Heidelberg (2002)
28. Reppy, J.: Concurrent programming in ML. Cambridge University Press (2007)
29. Sijtsma, B.A.: On the productivity of recursive list definitions. Transactions on Programming Languages and Systems 11(4), 633–649 (1989)
30. Syme, D., Petricek, T., Lomov, D.: The F# asynchronous programming model. Practical Aspects of Declarative Languages, 175–189 (2011)
31. Talpin, J.P., Jouvelot, P.: The type and effect discipline. In: Logic in Computer Science (1992)
32. Tardieu, O., de Simone, R.: Loops in Esterel. Transaction on Embedded Computing 4(4), 708–750 (2005)
33. Tofte, M.: Type inference for polymorphic references. Information and computation 89(1), 1–34 (1990)
34. Vouillon, J.: Lwt: A cooperative thread library. In: ACM workshop on ML (2008)

Synthesis of Memory Fences via Refinement Propagation

Yuri Meshman[2], Andrei Dan[1], Martin Vechev[1], and Eran Yahav[2]

[1] ETH Zurich
{andrei.dan,martin.vechev}@inf.ethz.ch
[2] Technion
{yurime,yahave}@cs.technion.ac.il

Abstract. We address the problem of fence inference in infinite-state concurrent programs running on relaxed memory models such as TSO and PSO. We present a novel algorithm that can automatically synthesize the necessary fences for infinite-state programs.

Our technique is based on two main ideas: (i) *verification with numerical domains*: we reduce verification under relaxed models to verification under sequential consistency using integer and boolean variables. This enables us to combine abstraction refinement over booleans with powerful numerical abstractions over the integers. (ii) *synthesis with refinement propagation*: to synthesize fences for a program P, we combine abstraction refinements used for successful synthesis of programs coarser than P into a new candidate abstraction for P. This "proof reuse" approach dramatically reduces the time required to discover a proof for P.

We implemented our technique and successfully applied it to several challenging concurrent algorithms, including state of the art concurrent work-stealing queues.

1 Introduction

Modern architectures use relaxed memory models in which memory operations may be reordered and executed non-atomically [2]. To allow programmer control over those orderings, processors provide special *memory fence* instructions. Unfortunately, manually reasoning where to place fences in a concurrent program running on a relaxed architecture is a challenging task. Using too many fences hinders performance, while missing necessary fences leads to incorrect programs.

Placing Memory Fences. Finding a correct and efficient fence assignment is important for expert designers of concurrent algorithms as well as for developers wishing to implement a concurrent algorithm from the literature (these algorithms are regularly published without any mention of fences). Yet, manually finding the right fence assignment is difficult as these algorithms often rely on subtle ordering of events, which may be violated under relaxed memory models [11, Ch.7]. Further, the process of placing fences has to be repeated whenever the algorithm changes or is ported to another architecture.

Our Approach. In this work we propose a novel automatic framework for synthesis of memory fences that can handle infinite-state programs. Given a program P, a safety

M. Müller-Olm and H. Seidl (Eds.): SAS 2014, LNCS 8723, pp. 237–252, 2014.

specification S, an abstraction α and a memory model M, our system automatically synthesizes a memory fence assignment f such that the program P with fence assignment f (denoted by $P\langle f\rangle$) can be shown to satisfy the specification S under M using α, that is $[\![P\langle f\rangle]\!]^{\alpha}_{M} \models S$. This is a particularly challenging task as even automatic verification is a difficult problem: currently there is very little work on automatic verification of infinite-state concurrent programs [8,1] running on relaxed architectures, yet most concurrent algorithms are infinite-state (e.g. [23,6]). Our system is based on two key ideas.

Synthesis via Abstraction Refinement Across Programs. First, we introduce a synthesis algorithm which explores the abstraction refinements needed to verify a program P by *combining* abstraction refinements used for successful verification of programs *coarser* than P (programs that use a superset of fences). This is important as finding an abstraction refinement that is precise enough to verify a concurrent program is known to be a difficult problem. Our "proof reuse" approach reduces the time required to prove P. To the best of our knowledge, this is the first work which performs abstraction refinement by learning information *across multiple programs*, as opposed to the traditional abstraction refinement typically performed within a single program.

Verification via Reduction with Numerical Abstract Domains. Second, we verify a program under relaxed memory models by reduction to a program under sequential consistency. This reduction approach, also advocated by other works [3,8], is powerful as it enables one to leverage advances in the analysis of concurrent programs under sequential consistency. Based on this general idea, we reduce the verification problem under relaxed models to a problem of verification under sequential consistency *using integer and boolean variables*.

This reduction enables us to use powerful numerical abstract domains such as Polyhedra [7] and allows us for the first time to verify properties of infinite state concurrent algorithms such as the Chase-Lev [6] and THE [9] work stealing queues. However, numerical domains are insufficient by themselves as they can only represent convex information and the non-determinism introduced by relaxed memory models often requires capturing *disjunctions*. To track such information precisely, we leverage the expressive power of an abstract domain that *combines numerical information with finite boolean information (predicates)*. We track the non-deterministic aspects of the relaxed memory model using disjunctions in the finite part of the domain.

Main Contributions. The novel contributions of our system are:

- A verification procedure based on transforming a program under relaxed semantics into a program under sequential consistency, enabling application of powerful numerical abstract domains. To refine the abstraction, we show how to track the non-deterministic aspects (which induce non-convex information) inherent in relaxed memory models via disjunctions encoded in the finite part of the domain.
- An efficient synthesis procedure which searches for minimal fence assignments by combining abstraction refinements used in successful proofs of coarser programs.
- An implementation and evaluation of our system for the x86-TSO and PSO memory models instantiated with classical numerical domains such as Polyhedra. We performed an extensive experimental study on a set of 15 concurrent algorithms. We believe this is the first time classic abstract interpretation has been used to prove properties of infinite-state work-stealing queues [6,9].

2 Overview

In this section, we provide an informal overview of our approach using Peterson's mutual exclusion algorithm (shown in Fig. 1). More elaborate examples are considered in Section 5.

2.1 Motivating Example

In Fig. 1, each of the two threads attempts to reach their critical section (CS) at Line 7. To enter the critical section, a thread first checks whether the other thread intends to enter the critical section (by checking the value of `flag0` or `flag1`), as well as its turn (value of `turn`).

Our goal is to guarantee that both threads do not enter the critical section simultaneously. This property holds when the two threads run on a sequentially consistent machine, but no longer holds when they run on a relaxed memory model such as PSO or TSO. Under relaxed memory models, the writes to `flag0`, `flag1`, and `turn` performed by one thread may be buffered and not yet visible to the other thread when it reaches the condition at Line 5. As a result, both processes may enter the critical section simultaneously. For example, if thread 1 enters the critical section, and its write to `flag0=1` has not yet been flushed to main memory, thread 2 will pass its check at Line 5 and also enter the critical section. To guarantee that the mutual exclusion holds under relaxed memory models, the programmer has to explicitly add *memory fences* to the program. However, because fences are expensive, the programmer faces the challenge of inserting the minimal set of sufficient fences that makes mutual exclusion hold.

2.2 Searching for Fence Assignment and Refinement Placement

Our goal is to synthesize a minimal *fence assignment* for a given program, specification, and memory model. Finding such a minimal fence assignment involves a search over the space of possible fences and automatically checking the correctness of each program in the space. To automatically verify a program, we employ *abstraction refinement*. In our setting, abstraction refinement is described as a set of program locations (discussed in detail later) which we refer to as a *refinement placement*.This leads to the following two-dimensional synthesis challenge:

Find a refinement placement and a minimal fence assignment which verify the program

Thread 1:

```
1 flag0 = 1;
2 turn = 1;
3 f1 = flag1;
4 lt1 = turn;
5 if ((lt1 != 0) & (f1 != 0))
6   goto 3;
7 nop; // CS
8 flag0 = 0;
9 goto 1;
```

Thread 2:

```
1 flag1 = 1;
2 turn = 0;
3 f2 = flag0;
4 lt2 = turn;
5 if ((f2 != 0) & (lt2 = 0))
6   goto 3;
7 nop; // CS
8 flag1 = 0;
9 goto 1;
```

assert always $((pc1 \neq 7) \vee (pc2 \neq 7))$

Fig. 1. Peterson mutual exclusion algorithm

Naive Approach. A naive approach where we perform an exhaustive search of the fence/refinement space is almost always non-feasible. For example, even for Peterson's algorithm, there are 2^6 potential fence assignments and 2^{23} potential refinement placements (we explain these in Section 2.3), leading to a total number of 2^{29} points in the fence/refinement space!

Our approach: semantic program and proof propagation. Our approach works by pruning large parts of the search space, based on the following two observations (here we use the notation $P\langle f, r\rangle$ to mean program P with fence assignment f and refinement placement r):

- *implied correctness:* if the program $P\langle f, r\rangle$ is verified successfully, then it *implies the correctness* of any other point in space which uses a superset of the fences in f or a superset of the refinement locations in r.
- *implied incorrectness:* if the program $P\langle f, r\rangle$ fails to verify, then it *implies the incorrectness* of any other point in space which uses a subset of the fences in f or a subset of the refinement locations in r.

Fig. 2 shows an example of one of our propagation techniques (discussed in Section 3.1) and is meant to give an intuition. Here, successful verification of $P\langle f_1, r_1\rangle$ and $P\langle f_2, r_2\rangle$ implies the correctness of all programs in the search space "below" these two (all programs with a subset of the fences). Further exploration of the space can first attempt to verify the point $P\langle f_3, r_3\rangle$ which employs a smaller set of fences ($f_3 = f_1 \cap f_2$) yet uses a refinement placement which *combines successful refinement placements from different programs* (i.e. r_1 and r_2). The intuition behind this combination is that slight relaxation of the program via fewer fences should only require slight adjustment of the abstraction refinement. Our experimental evaluation (Section 5) shows that propagation is effective for finding a minimal fence assignment for many of our benchmarks.

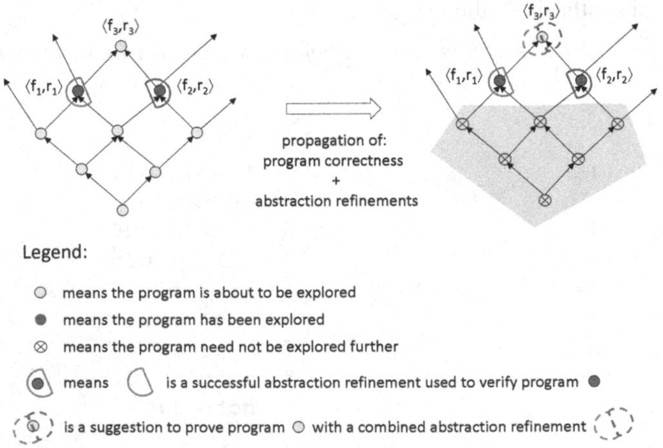

Fig. 2. Propagation of program correctness and abstraction refinements

2.3 Refinement Placement - Reduction and Abstraction

We next describe several ingredients of our approach to verification of infinite-state programs running on relaxed memory models.

As described in the motivating example, on a relaxed memory model, writes to shared memory are not immediately visible to all processes: writes are first placed into a local buffer and then (non-deterministically), a flush instruction pops values from that buffer and writes them to shared memory. In our setting, this mechanism is encoded in source code via a translation phase.

```
/* begin store */
if flag0_cnt_0 > 0 {
   overflow = true;
   halt;
}
flag0_cnt_0 = flag0_cnt_0 + 1;
if flag0_cnt_0 < 2
   flag0_1_0 = 1;
/* end store */
/* begin flush */
yield;
while * do {
   if flag0_cnt_0 > 0 {
      flag0 = flag0_1_0;
      flag0_cnt_0 = flag0_cnt_0 - 1;
      yield;
   }
}
/* end flush */
yield;
```

Fig. 3. Translation of `flag0=1` under PSO

Non-determinism due to flushes. Fig. 3 shows the translation of the statement `flag0=1` for the PSO memory model (in this model, each thread maintains a FIFO buffer for each shared variable). Intuitively, `flag0=1` is translated into two parts: i) the write to the FIFO buffer and a non-deterministic `flush`. Details of this translation are discussed in Section 4. Here, we only discuss the translation of the `flush`. A `flush` from a store buffer works by writing back to shared memory an arbitrary number of items from the buffer. This is captured by the `while (*)` loop that has a non-deterministic termination condition (denoted by $*$).

The non-deterministic loop introduces a significant challenge when reasoning with numerical domains (which capture state via relations between variables). The reason is that two program states appearing right after the while loop has completed differ significantly depending on whether the `flush` was performed or not. Both states can be captured with disjunctions, but standard (convex) numerical domains often dramatically lose precision exactly in such (disjunctive) cases.

Local abstraction refinement. To address this loss of precision, we use an abstract domain that combines numerical information with a finite boolean domain. By carefully introducing boolean predicates, we can refine the abstraction (by splitting the numerical state) in a *local* manner. While local refinement may restore sufficient precision for successful verification, it unfortunately comes at an exponential cost. The addition of new predicates can lead to an exponential blowup of the program analysis, as each predicate may double the state space. Further, such a refinement is not required for all locations of a `flush`. For example, if we can prove that a `flush` is always reached with an empty buffer, the `flush` will have no effect, and thus there is no need to refine the abstraction at such locations (we elaborate on this point in Section 4.4).

This introduces the challenge of finding a suitable *refinement placement* (a subset of the `flush` program locations) that is precise enough to enable verification yet is scalable enough for the analysis to terminate in reasonable time.

3 Abstraction-Guided Fence Synthesis

In this section, we present a new synthesis algorithm which propagates both fence assignments and refinement placements. Our algorithm leverages implied correctness/incorrectness to reduce the search space. The algorithm treats the two dimensions of the problem as having the same importance, and looks for a minimal fence assignment and a minimal refinement. In addition, the algorithm strives to minimize the number of fences based on a new concept where an abstraction refinement is obtained by combining successful refinements *across programs*.

3.1 Abstraction-Guided Fence Synthesis

Algorithm 1 provides a declarative description of our approach. The algorithm takes as input a program P, a specification S, a memory model M and an abstraction α, and produces a (possibly modified) program P' that satisfies the specification under M with a minimal verifiable fence assignment. The algorithm leverages information *from several points in the space* in the verification effort of a given point.

Fence assignment and refinement placement. A *fence assignment* f for a program P with program labels Lab_p is simply a subset of program labels $f \subseteq Lab_p$. A *refinement placement* r for a program P is also a subset of program labels, but it is restricted only to program labels of flush operations. The details of the refinement are elaborated in Section 4 and are not important for understanding the central concept of the synthesis algorithm presented in this section. For a given fence assignment $\mathtt{f}$ and a refinement placement $\mathtt{r}$, $P\langle\mathtt{f},\mathtt{r}\rangle$ denotes the program P with fences placed according to $\mathtt{f}$ and an abstraction refinement selected according to $\mathtt{r}$.

Searching for satisfying placements. The algorithm begins by initializing a `worklist` with (i) the program under a full fence assignment (Line 3) together with (ii) a refinement placement of program locations that are reasonable (Line 4) as determined by our Empty Buffer Analysis (EBA) (see Section 4.4).

For each element of the `worklist`, the algorithm tries to improve the fence assignment and refinement placement (Lines 8 and 9). The operation of these two functions is discussed later in this section. Our algorithm then invokes the underlying verifier to check if $[\![P\langle\mathtt{f},\mathtt{r}\rangle]\!]^{\alpha}_{M} \models [\![S]\!]^{\alpha}_{M}$ (Line 10).

Optimized Semantic Search. Our algorithm maintains the two sets `verified` and `falsified` for storing points $\langle\mathtt{f},\mathtt{r}\rangle$ that have been verified or where verification failed, respectively. Initially, both of these sets are empty. In the case of successful verification, the algorithm adds $\langle\mathtt{f},\mathtt{r}\rangle$ to the set of verified points in space. However, the algorithm does more than that: it also adds to `verified` all points which consist of a superset of fences as well as a superset of refinements. Successful verification of $P\langle\mathtt{f},\mathtt{r}\rangle$ means that the search can proceed to explore *more relaxed* versions of the program. The helper function `relax(f,r,K)` is used to compute a set of $\langle$`f',r'`$\rangle$ pairs that admit more behaviors (via a subset of fences) as well as coarser abstractions:

$$\texttt{relax(f,r,K)} = \{\langle \texttt{f',r'} \rangle \mid \texttt{f'} \subset \texttt{f} \text{ and } \texttt{r'} \subseteq \texttt{r} \text{ and } \langle \texttt{f',r'} \rangle \notin \texttt{K}\}$$

Input: P - program, S - Spec, M - memory model, α - abstraction, s.t. $[\![P]\!]^{\alpha}_{SC} \models [\![S]\!]^{\alpha}$
Output: P' - program such that $[\![P']\!]^{\alpha}_{M} \models [\![S]\!]^{\alpha}_{M}$ with minimal a number of fences

```
1  verified = ∅
2  falsified = ∅
3  f = fullFenceAssignment(P)
4  worklist = {⟨f,EBA(P,f)⟩}
5  while worklist ≠ ∅ do
6      ⟨f,r⟩ = select some pair from worklist
7      known = verified ∪ falsified
8      f = improveF(f,known)
9      r = improveR(f,r,known)
10     if ⟦P⟨f,r⟩⟧^α_M ⊨ ⟦S⟧^α_M then
11         verified ∪= {⟨f̂,r̂⟩ | f ⊆ f̂,r ⊆ r̂}
12         alternatives = relax(f,r,known)
13     else
14         falsified ∪= {⟨f',r'⟩ | f' ⊆ f, r' ⊆ r}
15         alternatives = restrict(f,r,known)
16     end
17     worklist = (worklist ∪ alternatives) \ known
18 end
19 ⟨f,r⟩ = min(verified)
20 return P⟨f,r⟩
```

Algorithm 1. Semantic search for finding minimal verifiable fence assignments

In the case of failed verification, the algorithms can add $\langle$`f,r`$\rangle$ to the set of falsified points in space, but once again, it can do more than that. That is, the algorithm adds to the set `falsified` all points in the space which consist of a subset of fences and a subset of abstraction refinements. Failed verification $\langle$`f,r`$\rangle$ means that the search should explore *more restricted* versions of the program. The helper function `restrict(f,r,K)` computes a set of $\langle$`f',r'`$\rangle$ pairs that admit fewer behaviors (via a superset of fences) as well as more refined abstractions:

$$\texttt{restrict(f,r,K)} = \{\langle \texttt{f',r'} \rangle \mid \texttt{f} \subseteq \texttt{f'} \text{ and } \texttt{r} \subset \texttt{r'} \text{ and } \langle \texttt{f',r'} \rangle \notin \texttt{K}\}$$

The algorithm terminates when there are no more alternatives to explore, and returns a program with a minimal fence assignment (in our implementation, we return all non-comparable minimal fence assignments).

Parametric choices. Our algorithm is parameterized on three dimensions:

- the choice for the next pair $\langle$`f,r`$\rangle$ to select at Line 6. The method of choosing the next element determines if our search will be similar to a depth-first search, to a breadth-first search or to a search that explores random elements of the space.

- the function `ImproveF`. This function leverages the knowledge of previous verification attempts (i.e., from the set `known`). For example, if `f` already verified for a different refinement `r'` and `f'` is a configuration in `known` which verified, then we can inspect `f ∩ f'` instead of `f`.
- the function `ImproveR`. With this function we improve the refinement `r` based on available knowledge (i.e., from the set `known`). For a fence assignment `f` and a refinement `r`, if ⟨`f'`,`r`⟩ and ⟨`f"`,`r'`⟩ both previously successfully verified and if `f'` and `f"` are stronger than `f` (that is, a superset of fences), then `ImproveR` will return `r ∪ r'`. Intuitively, this makes the abstraction refinement more precise, increasing the chances of success.

4 Automatic Verification

In this section we discuss the three steps of our automatic verification procedure: the reduction procedure, the underlying program analysis and the mechanism of abstraction refinement. We also discuss a static *empty buffer analysis* that is used by our algorithm to compute a set of possible abstraction placements to chose from (as discussed earlier).

4.1 Reduction

Similarly to [3,8], we reduce a program P running on a relaxed model M to a program P_M running on sequential consistency. This enables us to directly leverage advances in program analysis for sequential consistency. We adopt a similar translation procedure to [8] where the key idea in constructing P_M is representing the abstraction of the store buffers of M as variables in P_M. We illustrate the process for when M is the PSO memory model. The process for x86-TSO is similar. For PSO, it is sufficient to consider a program P_{PSO} where every shared variable X in the program P is also associated with: (i) additional k *local* variables for each thread t: $x_{1\_t}, \ldots, x_{k\_t}$, representing the content of a local store buffer for this variable in each thread t, (ii) a buffer counter variable x_{cnt_t} that records the current position in the store buffer of X in thread t.

The translation uses the function $[\![]\!]$ which takes as input a statement S, a thread t, and a bound k on the maximum buffer size and produces a new statement as output $[\![S]\!]_k^t$ (Fig. 4). The translation procedure is described in detail in [8]. Let us take a closer look at the most challenging method, the `flush`.

A `flush` is translated into a non-deterministic loop. If the buffer counter for the variable is positive, then it non-deterministically decides whether to update the shared variable X. If it has decided to update X, the earliest write (i.e. x_{1_t}) is stored in X. The contents of the local variables are then updated by shifting: the content of each x_{i_t} is taken from the content of the successor $x_{(i+1)\_t}$ where $1 \leq i < k$. Finally, the buffer count is decremented.

In our encoding of concurrent programs, context switches between threads are explicitly specified with `yield` statements (we place `yield` statements after every instruction). Because under the relaxed memory model a `flush` can be executed non-deterministically by the memory subsystem at any moment during program execution, our reduction places a (translated) `flush` after every `yield`.

$[\![X = r]\!]^t_k$
  if $x_{cnt\_t} = k$ **then**
  abort("overflow");
  $x_{cnt\_t} = x_{cnt\_t} + 1$;
  if $x_{cnt\_t} = 1$ **then** $x_{1\_t} = r$; ...
  if $x_{cnt\_t} = k$ **then** $x_{k\_t} = r$;

$[\![r = X]\!]^t_k$
  if $x_{cnt\_t} = 0$ **then** $r = X$; ...
  if $x_{cnt\_t} = k$ **then** $r = x_{k\_t}$;

$[\![\text{fence}]\!]^t_k$
  ▷ for each shared variable X
  generate:
  assume $(x_{cnt\_t} = 0)$;
  ▷ end of generation

$[\![\text{flush}]\!]^t_k$
while * **do**
  ▷ for each shared variable X
  generate:
  if $x_{cnt\_t} > 0$ **then**
    if * **then**
      $X = x_{1\_t}$;
      if $x_{cnt\_t} > 1$ **then**
        $x_{1\_t} = x_{2\_t}$;
        ...
        if $x_{cnt\_t} = k$
        then
        $x_{(k-1)\_t} =$
        x_{k_t}
      end
      $x_{cnt\_t} = x_{cnt\_t} - 1$;
    end
  end
  ▷ end of generation
end

Fig. 4. PSO Translation Rules: each sequence is atomic

4.2 Analysis with Numerical Abstract Domains

Once we have obtained the reduced program P_M, we use abstract interpretation with advanced numerical domains to verify its properties under sequential consistency. In particular, if the property we are interested in verifying relates only to shared numerical variables G appearing in program P (for example, the property of no array access out of bounds), then when translating accesses to variables of G by P, the reduction to program P_M will only introduce additional numerical variables over the variables in G: these are the local variables and counters. This enables us to directly use powerful numerical domains such as the Polyhedra abstract domain over the resulting program P_M. There are three possible outcomes of the automatic verification step:

- The program P_M verifies in which case the verification is successful.
- The program P_M does not verify because an overflow occurred during the analysis. There could be two reasons why overflow occurs:
  - there exists a concrete execution in the program which indeed does lead to an overflow (e.g. multiple stores to a shared variable without a fence in between).
  - the abstraction is imprecise enough to establish that there is no overflow.

  We cannot distinguish between these two cases and hence, when overflow occurs, we increase k to a small bound (at most the number of removed fences) or refine the abstraction (detailed below). Our experience is that small values of k combined with an abstraction refinement of the numerical analysis work well in practice.
- The program P_M does not verify because the property being checked fails to verify under the current abstraction. In this case, we typically apply abstraction refinement to the numerical analysis.

4.3 Abstraction Refinement of Numerical Analysis

As discussed above, abstraction refinement is often a vital step to enable successful verification of the program P_M. A key question then is which parts of the program P_M require a more refined treatment in the abstract? To find these statements in P_M, we employ a two-step approach, where we always first verify the program P under sequential consistency, before trying to verify the translated program P_M. This allows us to focus the search for abstraction refinement on the statements in P_M that are the root cause for the new behaviors. In our setting, these are the `flush` instructions appearing in P_M as it is via these statements that relaxed memory effects eventually become visible.

Abstraction refinement of the numerical analysis is accomplished in our system by directly encoding the suggested refinement into the program P_M by automatically introducing boolean auxiliary variables at places where the memory model relaxation takes effect. In particular, the number of boolean variables is proportional to k and these boolean variables are initialized appropriately inside the branches of the translated `flush` statement (to $true$ or $false$ respectively, depending at which branch the boolean variable is assigned). E.g. for peterson's algorithm (Fig. 1), under minimal verifiable fence placement for TSO, our analysis found that a boolean variable was needed at the flush after Thread 1 assignment to `turn` but not after that assignment for Thread 0.

This is yet another advantage of the reduction approach: it enables us to quickly experiment with and provide the abstraction refinements over the base numerical domains by modifying the program P_M instead of trying to somehow change the internals of an existing program analyzer (or build a new analysis). In particular, our system integrates with CIP [13] (which supports logico-numerical domains) enabling us to match the auxiliary boolean variables with the logical part of the combined domain.

Overall, we believe that we have found a good match between the particular type of abstraction refinement required in our context, the fact that this refinement can be encoded in the program and the ability of an existing analyzer to consume this encoding directly into its abstract domain.

4.4 Empty-Buffer Analysis

The additional predicates from refinement placement track the non-determinism due to flushes. However, such non-determinism is only relevant when the store buffers are not empty. When the store buffers are empty, a `flush` operation has no effect, and thus there is no need for a refinement at that program point. The challenge of course is to statically identify program locations in which the store buffers are guaranteed to be empty in any possible execution of the program. Towards that end, we use a simple static analysis that identifies program points where buffers are guaranteed to be empty. The analysis is sound, when it reports that a store buffer is empty, it guarantees that it will be empty in any possible execution. In Section 5, we show that the empty buffer analysis is effective and produces an upper bound on refinements that is significantly lower than the total number of possible locations.

5 Evaluation

We implemented our approach as described in previous sections and evaluated it on a range of challenging concurrent algorithms. To the best of our knowledge, this is the first extensive analysis study in the context of relaxed memory models involving infinite-state reasoning and abstract interpretation. All of our experiments were performed on an Intel(R) Xeon(R) 2.13GHz machine with 250 GB RAM.

For the automatic verification step, we used ConcurInterProc [14] which uses the APRON numerical abstract domain library [15]. To check that the inferred invariants imply the specification, we used the Z3 SMT solver.

5.1 Concurrent Algorithms

In our experiments we used 15 concurrent algorithms (7 finite-state and 8 infinite-state). Among these, there are 3 (infinite-state) array-based work-stealing queues and 7 mutual exclusion algorithms. We are not aware of any previous attempts to automatically verify properties of concurrent data structures such as the work stealing queues (WSQs) under relaxed models. For all of the algorithms we verified safety properties (e.g. a pair of labels is unreachable). For the WSQs, we verified consistency properties such as: the head index of the queue is always less than the tail index.

While our technique never reports incorrect fence assignments, due to non-monotonic analysis, the final result might lose the minimality guarantee. We note that in our benchmarks, this situation was never encountered. To cope with non-monotonicity, the tool has to spend more time searching when intermediate points fail to verify. In specific situations (certain outputs from ConcurInterProc), the search continues or even retries to verify a program when the verification tool ConcurInterProc returns "unknown".

5.2 Results

Our experimental results for both PSO and TSO memory models are summarized in Tables 1, 2, 3, and 4. Not all of the algorithms are shown due to space restriction. Graphs for the remaining results can be found in [22]. The first column of each table contains a tuple, under each benchmark name – the first element is the maximal number of fences for the algorithm, and the second element is the total number of locations for abstraction placements. For each benchmark, we bounded the search time to an hour, two hours and four hours. Each time bound result has two parts: the minimal number of fences achieved (columns labeled f) and the minimal relaxation under that fence assignment that the algorithm was able to find (columns labeled r). We compared three versions of our search:(i) breadth-first search (lines labeled bfs), (ii) depth-first search (lines labeled dfs) both without propagation and (iii) search with propagation (`prop`). At each point, the algorithm explores the next element from the worklist which is highest in the lattice for bfs, or lowest for dfs. After successful or failed verification and updating the set `known`, we update the worklist with the immediate successors of the attempted configuration (above or below the explored element - depending on whether it was verified or not). The third search configuration (labeled `prop`) is a bfs search *with propagation*.

The graphs depict the time it took to discover the minimal fence assignment. The x-axis is the time in a "hour:minute:seconds" format and the y-axis is the number of fences discovered. For some cases, such as PC1, it can be seen that the initial behavior of the `prop` approach is similar to that of dfs. This is due to a "streak" of successful verifications where a successful verification from a previous stage (say fence assignments "remove #9" and "remove #8" verified) affects the next element attempted by the `prop` approach (for the example given "remove #8 and #9" will be attempted). This behavior is similar to dfs. For algorithms such as KESSEL and PGSQL, it can be seen that the dfs approach finds early in the search a non-optimal fence assignment (the prop approach finds a better assignment later) and no new points appear in the graph. In those cases the dfs approach proceeds to explore lower elements in the lattice and fails repeatedly.

For several algorithms only the full assignment of fences was verified. Those algorithms are described in Table 2. Here (unlike Table 1), the graph's y-axis is the abstraction refinement placement that verified. Those graphs have more points and describe more clearly the difference between the three approaches (dfs, bfs and prop). In many cases, bfs explores "too many" elements high in the lattice, dfs converges fast to the lowest element it can verify but then it needs to backtrack. For WSQ-THE, dfs didn't find a placement smaller than the full one. Perhaps given more time it would "backtrack" and find a placement equivalent to the one the prop approach found.

Summary. It can be seen that the search with propagation (prop) finds smaller fence assignments quicker than bfs and fewer or equal fence assignments than dfs.

6 Related Work

Next, we discuss some of the work that is most closely related to ours. These works include automatic verification (most closely related) techniques, dynamic analysis and bounded model checking approaches, search propagation in synthesis as well as robust-

Table 1. PSO results. The graphs show discovered fence assignments over time.

algorithm		1h		2h		4h	
max(f, r)		f	r	f	r	f	r
abp	prop	0	0	0	0	0	0
(2,17)	bfs	0	0	0	0	0	0
	dfs	0	0	0	0	0	0
concloop	prop	2	4	2	4	2	4
(4,14)	bfs	2	8	2	4	2	4
	dfs	2	4	2	4	2	4
kessel	prop	3	0	3	0	3	0
(6,12)	bfs	5	2	4	7	4	1
	dfs	4	7	4	7	4	7
loop2-TLM	prop	4	5	4	5	4	5
(6,21)	bfs	5	2	4	4	4	3
	dfs	5	6	4	10	4	10
pc1	prop	2	0	2	0	1	3
(9,27)	bfs	9	2	9	2	8	6
	dfs	1	0	1	0	1	0
pgsql	prop	4	0	4	0	4	0
(8,23)	bfs	8	2	8	1	7	1
	dfs	7	8	7	8	7	8

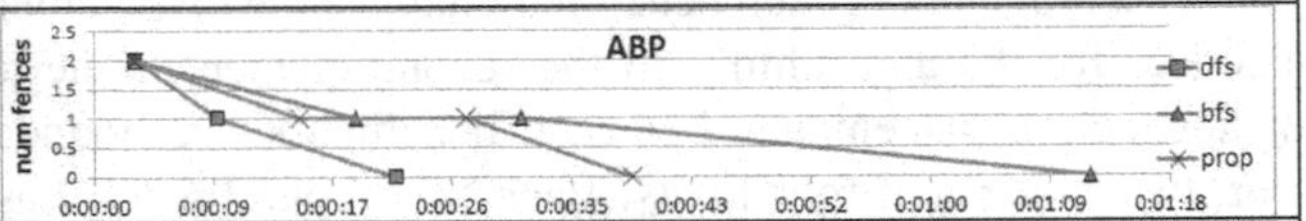

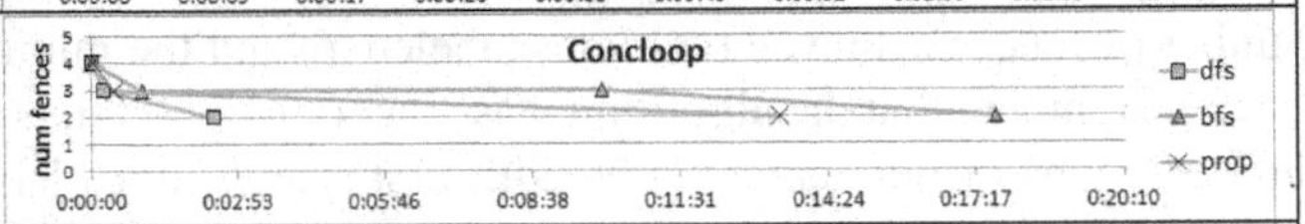

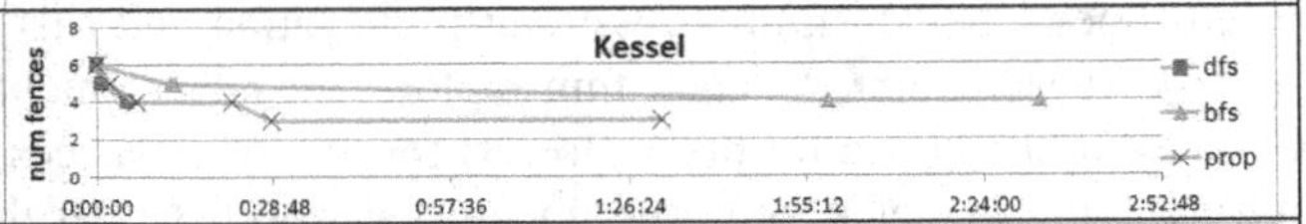

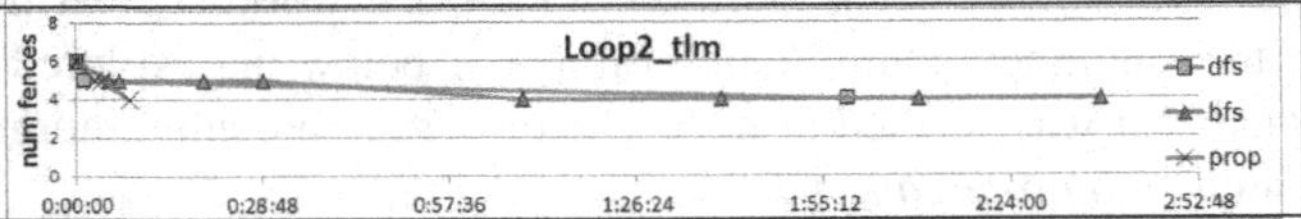

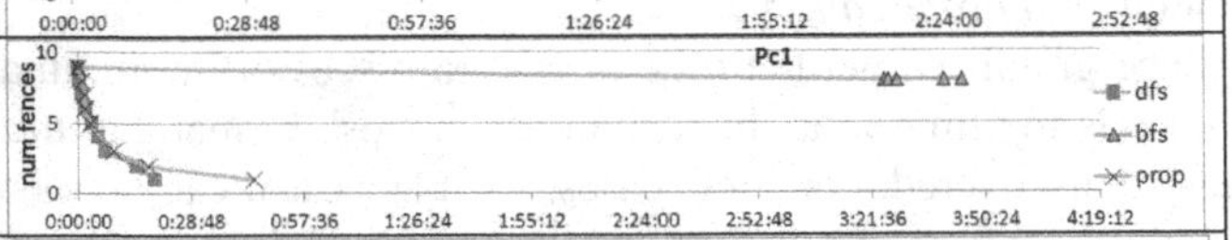

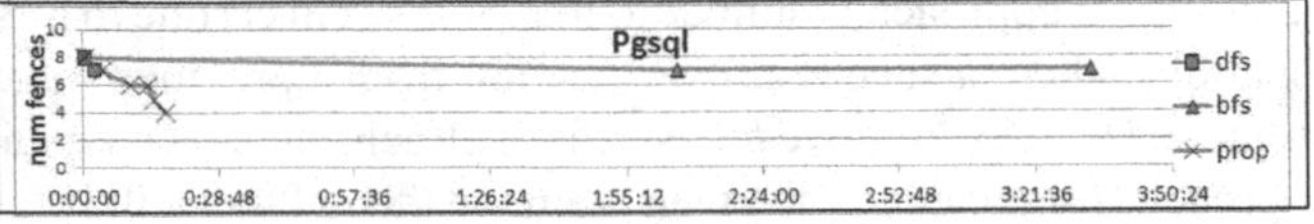

Table 2. PSO results. The graphs show discovered refinement placements over time.

algorithm		1h		2h		4h	
max (f, r)		f	r	f	r	f	r
wsq-chase (4,19)	prop	4	0	4	0	4	0
	bfs	4	0	4	0	4	0
	dfs	4	0	4	0	4	0
wsq-fifo (2,13)	prop	2	0	2	0	2	0
	bfs	2	6	2	5	2	4
	dfs	2	6	2	0	2	0
wsq-the (7,33)	prop	7	5	7	4	7	0
	bfs	7	5	7	4	7	3
	dfs	7	7	7	7	7	7

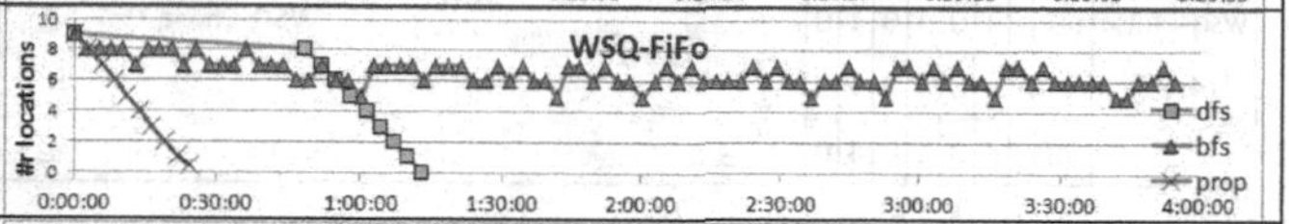

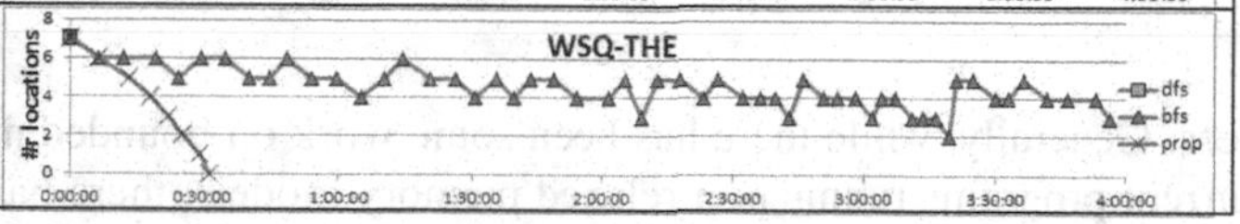

Table 3. TSO results. The graphs show discovered fence assignments over time

algorithm		1h		2h		4h	
(f, r)		f	r	f	r	f	r
abp (2,17)	prop	0	0	0	0	0	0
	bfs	0	0	0	0	0	0
	dfs	0	0	0	0	0	0
concloop (4,14)	prop	2	4	2	4	2	4
	bfs	2	8	2	4	2	4
	dfs	2	4	2	4	2	4
kessel (6,12)	prop	5	3	4	0	4	0
	bfs	5	3	5	1	5	1
	dfs	5	6	5	6	5	6
loop2-TLM (6,21)	prop	6	2	5	8	4	14
	bfs	5	8	5	8	5	7
	dfs	5	10	5	10	5	10
pc1 (9,27)	prop	3	3	3	3	1	14
	bfs	9	3	9	2	8	6
	dfs	5	9	5	9	5	9
peterson (6,23)	prop	5	2	4	3	4	3
	bfs	6	0	5	5	5	2
	dfs	4	7	4	7	4	7
pgsql (8,23)	prop	5	7	5	7	5	7
	bfs	8	4	8	3	8	1
	dfs	8	8	8	8	8	8

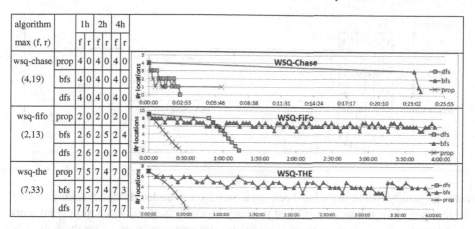

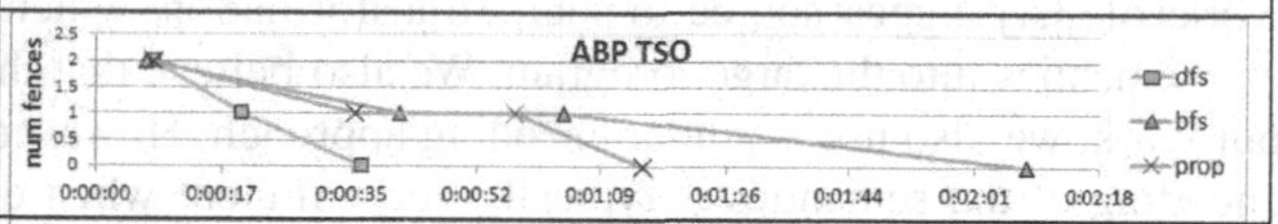

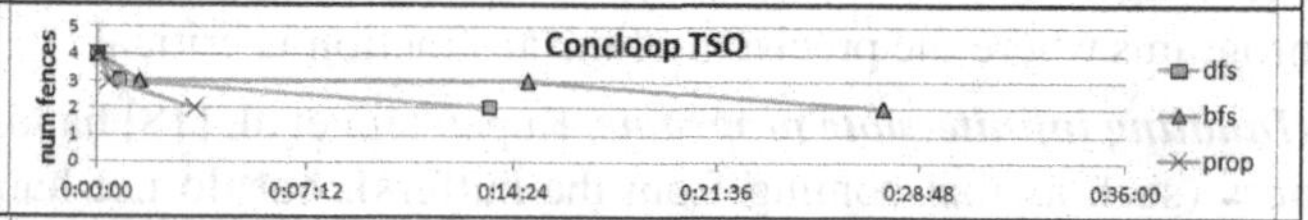

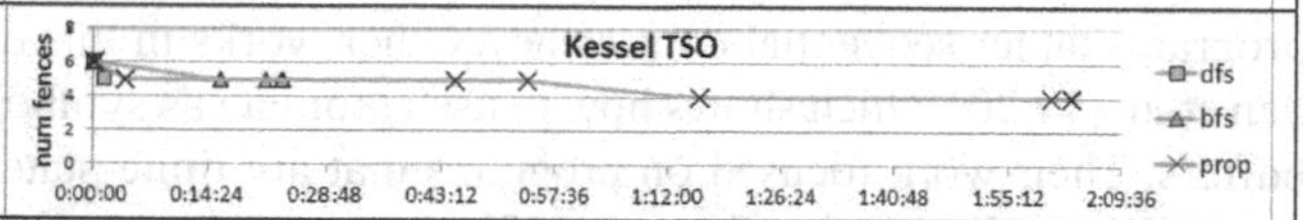

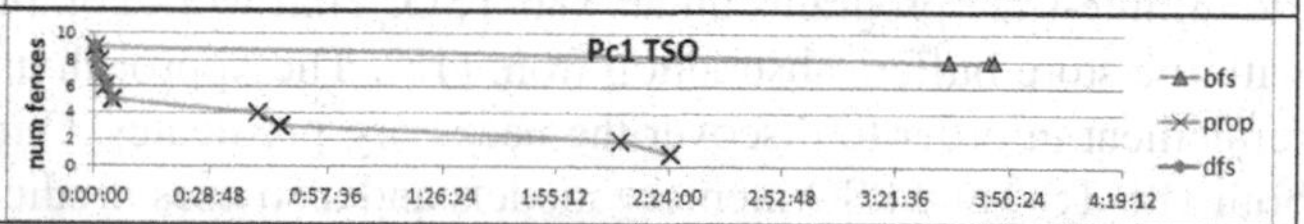

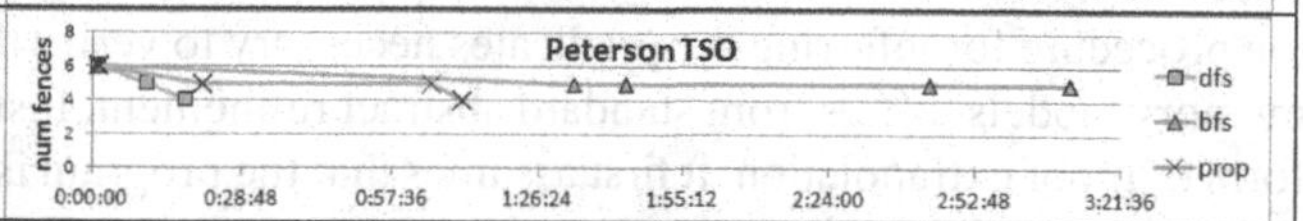

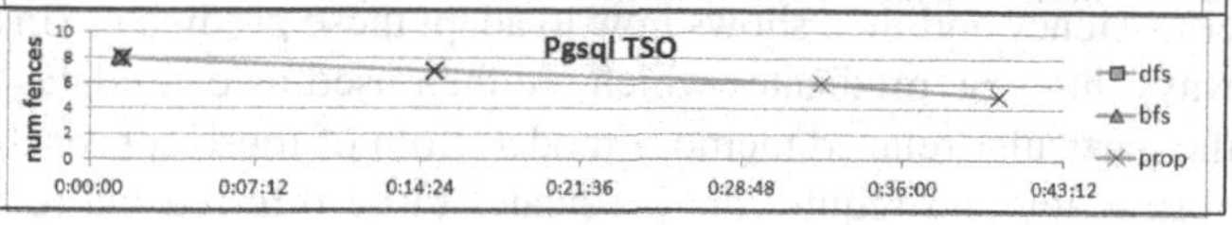

Table 4. TSO results - The graphs show discovered refinement placements over time

algorithm		1h		2h		4h		
(f, r)		f	r	f	r	f	r	
queue	prop	1	0	1	0	1	0	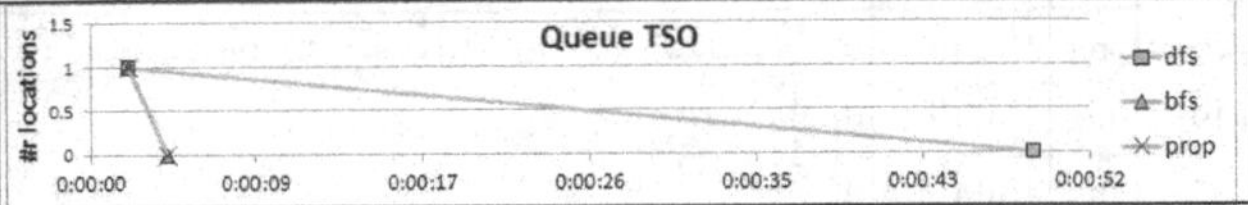
(1,13)	bfs	1	0	1	0	1	0	
	dfs	1	0	1	0	1	0	
wsq-chase	prop	4	0	4	0	4	0	
(4,19)	bfs	4	0	4	0	4	0	
	dfs	4	0	4	0	4	0	

ness. Generally, while there has been some work on bounded model checking of concurrent programs running on relaxed memory models, there has been almost no work on automatically verifying *infinite-state* concurrent programs running on these models.

Program Transformation. One general direction for handling relaxed memory model programs is to encode their effects into a program and then analyze the resulting program using standard tools geared towards sequential consistency. Towards that, the works of [3,4] suggest source-to-source transformations which encode the relaxed memory semantics into the target program. We also believe that this is a viable path and in our work, we also use a similar encoding approach. However, as we have seen, direct encoding of the semantics is typically not sufficient when dealing with infinite-state programs where the precision of the abstraction is critical.

Handling infinite-state programs. Kuperstein et al. [18] handle some forms of infiniteness (such as that coming from the buffers), but do not handle general infinite-state programs under sequential consistency. Other works in this direction are those of Linden et al. [19,20] which shows how to use automata as symbolic representation of store buffers. Their work focused on programs that are finite-state under sequential consistency. The work of Vafeiadis et al. [25] presents an approach for eliminating fences under x86-TSO. Their approach is based on compiler transformations and assumes that the input program is correct. The work of Abdulla et al. [1] builds on [18] and is able to handle infinite-state programs under x86-TSO. That work combines predicate abstraction with the store buffers abstraction from [18]. The approach uses traditional abstraction refinement in order to discover the necessary predicates. Our recent work [8] handles both x86-TSO and PSO memory models and also uses predicate abstraction. However, the procedure for inferring the predicates necessary to verify the program under relaxed memory models differs from standard abstract refinement. Instead, the paper proposes a form of proof extrapolation: it first assumes that the program is verified under sequential consistency and then shows how to adapt these predicates (in a memory-model specific way) into new predicates which are then used as candidates for the verification under the particular relaxed memory model. Both of these approaches are based on predicate abstraction and require the predicates to be inferred via refinement or adaptation. In contrast, the techniques presented in this work are based on iterative numerical abstract interpretation which promises to scale better (but is focused on numerical domains). In addition, our search algorithm combines propagation of abstraction refinements *across* programs with program restriction via fence inference. Our work also has relevance to the well known technique of lazy abstraction [10] which introduces the concept of adjusting the level of abstraction for different sections of the verified program's state space. In our approach, the search can be seen as selectively introducing refinements which guide the analyzer. However, unlike previous work, we learn new refinements by combining existing successful refinements from *several* programs.

Explicit Model Checking for Relaxed Memory Models. There have been several works (e.g., [18,16,17,12]) focusing on explicit-state model checking under relaxed memory models. Among those, [17] focuses on fence inference and [12] also describes an explicit-state model checking and inference technique for the .NET memory model. These approaches are sound only for finite-state programs, and cannot handle infinite-state programs. CheckFence [5] takes a different approach, instead of working with operational memory models and explicit model-checking, they convert a program into a form that can be checked against an axiomatic model specification. This technique unrolls loops at a preprocessing stage and cannot handle infinite-state programs.

In addition, there has recently been interest in exploring dynamic techniques for testing programs running on various relaxed memory models. The work of Liu et al. [21] dynamically analyzes (via a demonic scheduler) concurrent algorithms under the TSO and PSO memory models and whenever it finds a violating trace proposes a repair which inserts memory fences into the program. Recently, there has also been work on leveraging various partial order reduction techniques for bounded model checking of concurrent C++ programs [24]. Both of these works attempt to handle larger programs by sacrificing soundness.

7 Conclusion

In this work, we presented a system that can automatically synthesize fences in infinite-state concurrent algorithms running on relaxed memory models such as TSO and PSO. Our system is based on two core ideas.

First, in addition to propagating correctness between different fence assignments, the synthesizer explores the space of programs by using a form of "proof propagation": computing a candidate abstraction refinement of a given program by combining successful abstraction refinements of coarser programs. Second, we reduce the problem of automatic verification under a relaxed memory model into one of verification under sequential consistency using only integer and boolean variables. This enables us to leverage powerful numerical abstractions over the integers and to refine these abstractions by directly encoding the boolean refinement in the reduced program.

Finally, we evaluated our system on 15 challenging concurrent algorithms, including concurrent work-stealing queues. We believe that this is the first extensive study of using abstract interpretation techniques in the context of relaxed memory models and the first time properties of some of these algorithms have been verified.

References

1. Abdulla, P.A., Atig, M.F., Chen, Y.-F., Leonardsson, C., Rezine, A.: Automatic fence insertion in integer programs via predicate abstraction. In: Miné, A., Schmidt, D. (eds.) SAS 2012. LNCS, vol. 7460, pp. 164–180. Springer, Heidelberg (2012)

2. Adve, S.V., Gharachorloo, K.: Shared memory consistency models: A tutorial. IEEE Computer 29, 66–76 (1995)
3. Alglave, J., Kroening, D., Nimal, V., Tautschnig, M.: Software verification for weak memory via program transformation. In: Felleisen, M., Gardner, P. (eds.) ESOP 2013. LNCS, vol. 7792, pp. 512–532. Springer, Heidelberg (2013)
4. Atig, M.F., Bouajjani, A., Parlato, G.: Getting rid of store-buffers in TSO analysis. In: Gopalakrishnan, G., Qadeer, S. (eds.) CAV 2011. LNCS, vol. 6806, pp. 99–115. Springer, Heidelberg (2011)
5. Burckhardt, S., Alur, R., Martin, M. M.K.: CheckFence: checking consistency of concurrent data types on relaxed memory models. In: PLDI 2007 (2007)
6. Chase, D., Lev, Y.: Dynamic circular work-stealing deque. In: SPAA (2005)
7. Cousot, P., Halbwachs, N.: Automatic discovery of linear restraints among variables of a program. In: POPL 1978 (1978)
8. Dan, A.M., Meshman, Y., Vechev, M., Yahav, E.: Predicate abstraction for relaxed memory models. In: Logozzo, F., Fähndrich, M. (eds.) Static Analysis. LNCS, vol. 7935, pp. 84–104. Springer, Heidelberg (2013)
9. Frigo, M., Leiserson, C.E., Randall, K.H.: The implementation of the cilk-5 multithreaded language. In: PLDI 1998 (1998)
10. Henzinger, T.A., Jhala, R., Majumdar, R., Sutre, G.: Lazy abstraction. In: POPL 2002 (2002)
11. Herlihy, M., Shavit, N.: The Art of Multiprocessor Programming. Morgan Kaufmann (April 2008)
12. Huynh, T.Q., Roychoudhury, A.: Memory model sensitive bytecode verification. Form. Methods Syst. Des. 31(3) (December 2007)
13. Jeannet, B.: The CONCURINTERPROC interprocedural analyzer for concurrent programs, `http://pop-art.inrialpes.fr/interproc/concurinterprocweb.cgi`
14. Jeannet, B.: Relational interprocedural verification of concurrent programs. Software and System Modeling 12(2), 285–306 (2013)
15. Jeannet, B., Miné, A.: APRON: A library of numerical abstract domains for static analysis. In: Bouajjani, A., Maler, O. (eds.) CAV 2009. LNCS, vol. 5643, pp. 661–667. Springer, Heidelberg (2009)
16. Jonsson, B.: State-space exploration for concurrent algorithms under weak memory orderings (preliminary version). SIGARCH Comput. Archit. News 36(5), 65–71 (2009)
17. Kuperstein, M., Vechev, M., Yahav, E.: Automatic inference of memory fences. In: FMCAD 2010 (2010)
18. Kuperstein, M., Vechev, M., Yahav, E.: Partial-coherence abstractions for relaxed memory models. In: PLDI 2011 (2011)
19. Linden, A., Wolper, P.: An automata-based symbolic approach for verifying programs on relaxed memory models. In: van de Pol, J., Weber, M. (eds.) Model Checking Software. LNCS, vol. 6349, pp. 212–226. Springer, Heidelberg (2010)
20. Linden, A., Wolper, P.: A verification-based approach to memory fence insertion in PSO memory systems. In: Piterman, N., Smolka, S.A. (eds.) TACAS 2013 (ETAPS 2013). LNCS, vol. 7795, pp. 339–353. Springer, Heidelberg (2013)
21. Liu, F., Nedev, N., Prisadnikov, N., Vechev, M., Yahav, E.: Dynamic synthesis for relaxed memory models. In: PLDI 2012 (2012)
22. Meshman, Y., Dan, A., Vechev, M., Yahav, E.: Synthesis of memory fences via refinement propagation. Tech. rep.
23. Michael, M.M., Vechev, M.T., Saraswat, V.A.: Idempotent work stealing. In: PPoPP 2009 (2009)
24. Norris, B., Demsky, B.: CDSchecker: checking concurrent data structures written with c/c++ atomics. In: OOPSLA 2013 (2013)
25. Vafeiadis, V., Zappa Nardelli, F.: Verifying fence elimination optimisations. In: Yahav, E. (ed.) Static Analysis. LNCS, vol. 6887, pp. 146–162. Springer, Heidelberg (2011)

Speeding Up Logico-Numerical Strategy Iteration*

David Monniaux[1] and Peter Schrammel[2]

[1] CNRS / VERIMAG
[2] University of Oxford

Abstract. We introduce an efficient combination of polyhedral analysis and predicate partitioning. Template polyhedral analysis abstracts numerical variables inside a program by one polyhedron per control location, with *a priori* fixed directions for the faces. The strongest inductive invariant in such an abstract domain may be computed by a combination of strategy iteration and SMT solving. Unfortunately, the above approaches lead to unacceptable space and time costs if applied to a program whose control states have been partitioned according to predicates. We therefore propose a modification of the strategy iteration algorithm where the strategies are stored succinctly, and the linear programs to be solved at each iteration step are simplified according to an equivalence relation. We have implemented the technique in a prototype tool and we demonstrate on a series of examples that the approach performs significantly better than previous strategy iteration techniques.

1 Introduction

Program verification for unbounded execution times generally relies on finding inductive loop (or procedure) invariants. In the *abstract interpretation* approach, loop invariants are automatically searched within a class known as an *abstract domain.* When dealing with numerical variables, it is common to search for invariants shaped as products of intervals (constraints $l \leq x \leq u$ with the program variable x and bounds l, u), convex polyhedra (constraint system $\boldsymbol{Ax} \leq \boldsymbol{c}$ with the matrix $\boldsymbol{A}$, the vector of program variables $\boldsymbol{x}$, and the vector of bounds $\boldsymbol{c}$), or restricted classes of convex polyhedra such as *octagons* ($\pm x_i \pm x_j \leq c$). Intervals and octagons are instances of *template polyhedra*: polyhedra where $\boldsymbol{A}$ is fixed *a priori*, whereas in the general polyhedral approach, $\boldsymbol{A}$ is discovered. The restriction to fixed $\boldsymbol{A}$ reduces the problem to finding suitable values for a fixed number of bounds $\boldsymbol{c}$, and even, for certain classes of transitions, minimizing these bounds using *strategy iteration* [1] (also known as *policy iteration*) or other techniques, thereby producing the least (or *strongest*) inductive invariant in the abstract

* The research leading to these results has received funding from the European Research Council under the European Unions Seventh Framework Programme (FP7/20072013) / ERC grant agreement 306595 "STATOR" and the ARTEMIS Joint Undertaking under grant agreement number 295311 "VeTeSS"

M. Müller-Olm and H. Seidl (Eds.): SAS 2014, LNCS 8723, pp. 253–267, 2014.

domain. In contrast, for unknown $\boldsymbol{A}$ the number of constraints (rows in the $\boldsymbol{A}$ matrix) may grow quickly and is most often limited by *widening* heuristics [2].

In order to handle programs that contain constructs other than linear arithmetic, for example, pointers, dynamic data stuctures, non-linear arithmetic, etc, one can split control nodes according to n predicates, as in *predicate abstraction*. The number of control nodes may thus grow exponentially in n. A similar situation arises in *reactive programs* for control applications, where a main loop updates global variables at each iteration, including Booleans encoding "modes" of operation. Such a system has a single distinguished control point (the head of the main loop), yet, one wants to distinguish invariants according to the mode of operation of the system. Assuming modes are defined by the values of the n Boolean variables, this can be achieved by splitting the loop head into 2^n distinct control nodes and computing one invariant for each of them.

Should we apply a max-strategy iteration modulo SMT algorithm [1] to these 2^n control nodes, its running time would be in the worst case proportional to 2^{d2^n} where d is the number of disjuncts in the formula defining the semantics of the program. Worse, it would construct linear programming problems with $2^n \ell$ unknowns, where ℓ is the number of rows in the $\boldsymbol{A}$ matrix. While high worst case complexity is not necessarily an objection (many algorithms behave in practice better than their worst case), constructing exponentially-*sized* linear programs at every iteration of the algorithm is certainly too costly. We thus previously left this partitioning variant as an open problem [1, §9] [3, §3.5].

Contributions. The main contribution of this paper is an algorithm that computes the *same* result as these prohibitively expensive methods, but limits the costs by computing on-the-fly equivalence between constraint bounds (of which there are exponentially many) and constructing problems whose size depends on the number of these equivalence classes. These equivalence classes, in intuitive terms, distinguish Boolean variables *with respect to the abstraction chosen* (the $\boldsymbol{A}$ matrix). This is a novel aspect that distinguishes our approach from quotienting techniques (*e.g.* [4]). Finally, we show the results of an experimental evaluation conducted with our prototype implementation that demonstrate the largely improved performance in comparison to previous strategy iteration techniques.

2 Strategy Iteration Basics

Let us now recall the framework of strategy iteration over template linear constraint domains [5], reformulating it to the setting of programs with linear arithmetic and Boolean variables. As explained above, Boolean variables may be introduced by predicate abstraction or by the encoding of the control flow as in reactive systems. Similar to [1], this allows us to represent an exponential number of paths as a single compact transition formula. We then explain why previous algorithms [1, 5] are unacceptably inefficient on exponentially many control nodes.

Notation. We distinguish values by denoting them $\hat{x}, \hat{y} \ldots$ as opposed to variables $x, y, \ldots$. Variables $x_1, \ldots, x_n$ are denoted collectively as a vector $\boldsymbol{x}$. $(\boldsymbol{x}, \boldsymbol{y}) \models F$ means that $\boldsymbol{x}, \boldsymbol{y}$ are free variables of formula F that should satisfy F.

2.1 Program Model and Abstract Domain

We model a program as a transition system with m rational variables $\boldsymbol{x} \in \mathbb{Q}^m$ (the *numeric state*) and n Boolean variables $\boldsymbol{b} \in \mathbb{B}^n$ (the *Boolean state*), where $\mathbb{B} = \{0, 1\}$. Let $I = (\boldsymbol{b}^0, \boldsymbol{x}^0)$ be the initial state. The transition relation τ is of the form $\exists y_1, \ldots, y_E \in \mathbb{Q}, \exists p_1, \ldots, p_d \in \mathbb{B}.\ T$ where T is a quantifier-free formula in negation normal form, whose atoms are either propositional (b_i, $\neg b_i$, p_i, $\neg p_i$), linear (in)equalities ($\sum \alpha_i x_i + \sum \alpha'_i x'_i + \sum \beta_i y_i \bowtie c$, where the α_i, α'_i, β_i and c are rational constants) with $\bowtie\ \in \{\leq, <, =\}$, and y_i variables to encode nondeterminism, e.g. reactive inputs or linearization of non-linear arithmetic; the free variables of τ are $\boldsymbol{x}, \boldsymbol{x}', \boldsymbol{b}$ where primed (respectively, unprimed) variables denote the state after (respectively, before) the transition. Furthermore, we add p_i variables to each disjunction with non-propositional literals, *i.e.*, $x \leq 3 \vee x \geq 6$ becomes $(p_i \wedge x \leq 3) \vee (\neg p_i \wedge x \geq 6)$. This encoding is necessary to uniquely identify each disjunct by a Boolean proposition and extract it from a SAT model. The free variables of T are thus grouped into $\boldsymbol{b}, \boldsymbol{b}', \boldsymbol{x}, \boldsymbol{x}', \boldsymbol{p}, \boldsymbol{y}$ where $(\boldsymbol{b}, \boldsymbol{x})$ and $(\boldsymbol{b}', \boldsymbol{x}')$ define respectively the departure and arrival states and $\boldsymbol{p}, \boldsymbol{y}$ stand for intermediate values and choices.

Example. We consider the following running example (a variant of the classical thermostat model):

```
bool error = 0, heat_on = 1;
bool fan_on = read_button();
real t = 16;
while(1) {
  real te = read_external_temp();
  assume(14<=te && te<=19);
  fan_on = read_button() ? !fan_on : fan_on;
  if(!error && (t<15 || t>30)) error = 1;
  else if(!error && heat_on && t>22) heat_on = 0;
  else if(!error && heat_on && t<=22) t = (15*t + te)/16 + 1;
  else if(!heat_on && t<18) heat_on = 1;
  else if(!heat_on && t>=18) t = (15*t + te)/16;
}
```

This program has the following transition relation T with $n = 3$ Boolean variables $\boldsymbol{b} = (e, h, f)$ (short for (error,heat_on,fan_on)), $m = 1$ numerical variables $\boldsymbol{x} = (t)$, $d = 3$ path choice variables $\boldsymbol{p} = (p_0, p_1, p_2)$), $\boldsymbol{y} = (te)$, and initial states $\neg e \wedge h \wedge t = 16$:

$$
\begin{array}{lr}
\neg p_0 \wedge p_1 \wedge p_2 \wedge \neg e \wedge e' \wedge (h = h') \wedge & t > 30 \wedge t' = t \vee \\
\neg p_0 \wedge p_1 \wedge \neg p_2 \wedge \neg e \wedge e' \wedge (h = h') \wedge & t < 15 \wedge t' = t \vee \\
p_0 \wedge p_1 \wedge p_2 \wedge \neg e \wedge h \wedge \neg e' \wedge \neg h' \wedge & 22 < t \leq 30 \wedge t' = t \vee \\
p_0 \wedge p_1 \wedge \neg p_2 \wedge \neg e \wedge h \wedge \neg e' \wedge h' & \wedge t \leq 22 \wedge 14 \leq te \leq 19 \wedge t' = \frac{15t+te}{16} + 1 \vee \\
p_0 \wedge \neg p_1 \wedge p_2 \wedge \neg h \wedge h' \wedge (e = e') \wedge & 15 \leq t < 18 \wedge t' = t \vee \\
p_0 \wedge \neg p_1 \wedge \neg p_2 \wedge \neg h \wedge \neg h' \wedge (e = e') \wedge & t \geq 18 \wedge 14 \leq te \leq 19 \wedge t' = \frac{15t+te}{16}
\end{array}
$$

The disjuncts stem from lines 9 –13; line 9 produces two path choices.

Abstract Domain. Let $\boldsymbol{A}$ be a $\ell \times m$ rational matrix, with rows $\boldsymbol{A}_1, \ldots, \boldsymbol{A}_\ell$. An element ρ of the abstract domain $D^\sharp$ is a function $\mathbb{B}^n \to \overline{\mathbb{Q}}^\ell$ with $\overline{\mathbb{Q}} = \mathbb{Q} \cup \{-\infty, +\infty\}$. $\rho(\boldsymbol{b}) = \boldsymbol{c}$ means that at a Boolean state $\boldsymbol{b}$ the vector of numerical variables $\boldsymbol{x}$ is such that $\boldsymbol{Ax} \leq \boldsymbol{c}$ coordinate-wise. Moreover, we write $\rho(\boldsymbol{b}) = -\infty$ if any coordinate $c_i = -\infty$, meaning that the Boolean state $\boldsymbol{b}$ is unreachable (because $\boldsymbol{Ax} \leq \boldsymbol{c}$ is *false*). We note $\gamma(\rho)$ the set of states $(\boldsymbol{b}, \boldsymbol{x})$ verifying these conditions. $\mathbb{Q}^\ell$ is ordered by coordinate-wise $\leq$, inducing a point-wise ordering $\sqsubseteq$ on $D^\sharp$. γ is thus monotone w.r.t. $\sqsubseteq$ and the inclusion ordering on sets of states. We denote by $\rho(i, \boldsymbol{b})$ the i-th coordinate of $\rho(\boldsymbol{b})$. ρ is said to be an *inductive invariant* if it contains the initial state ($\boldsymbol{Ax}^0 \leq \rho(\boldsymbol{b}^0)$) and it is stable by transitions:

$$\forall \boldsymbol{b}, \boldsymbol{x}, \boldsymbol{b}', \boldsymbol{x}'.\ (\boldsymbol{b}, \boldsymbol{x}) \in \gamma(\rho) \wedge (\boldsymbol{b}, \boldsymbol{x}, \boldsymbol{b}', \boldsymbol{x}') \models \tau \implies (\boldsymbol{b}', \boldsymbol{x}') \in \gamma(\rho'),$$

The main contribution of this paper is an effective way to compute the least inductive invariant ρ in this abstract domain w.r.t. $\sqsubseteq$.

2.2 Strategy Iteration

Recall that the original strategy iteration algorithm [5] applies to disjunctive systems of linear inequalities (of exponential size in d) induced by the collecting semantics of the program over template polyhedra (see Equ. (1) below). Previous work [1] improves the algorithm by keeping the system implicit, only extracting a linear size system at any given time using SMT solving. Note that τ, after replacing each free Boolean variable by a Boolean constant, is equivalent to a disjunction of (at most) 2^d formulas of the form $\exists \boldsymbol{y}.C$ where C is a conjunction of non-strict linear inequalities, and d is the number of Boolean existential quantifiers in τ. In both algorithms, a *strategy* selects one disjunct in C for each template row i'. Hence, we can use these algorithms in our setting by selecting a disjunct for each template row *and* each Boolean valuation for $(\boldsymbol{b}', \boldsymbol{p})$. This motivates the following definition:

A *strategy* associates with each Boolean state $\boldsymbol{b}'$ and each constraint index $1 \leq i' \leq \ell$ either the special value $\bot$, meaning that $\boldsymbol{b}'$ is unreachable and denoted by $\sigma(i', \boldsymbol{b}') = \pi(i', \boldsymbol{b}') = \bot$, or a pair $\big(\sigma(i', \boldsymbol{b}'), \pi(i', \boldsymbol{b}')\big)$ where $\sigma(i', \boldsymbol{b}') \in \mathbb{B}^n$ is a Boolean state and $\pi(i', \boldsymbol{b}') \in \mathbb{B}^d$ gives "path choices". Once $\pi \in \mathbb{B}^d$ is chosen, the result of substituting $T[\pi/\boldsymbol{p}]$ is a conjunction of linear inequalities and a propositional formula (in the variables $\boldsymbol{b}, \boldsymbol{b}'$); let T_π denote the conjunction of these linear inequalities.

Algorithm. Let us now see how the algorithm iterates until the least inductive invariant is reached. The algorithm maintains, at iteration number k, a current strategy (σ_k, π_k). Initially, the abstract value ρ_0 is $\bot$ everywhere save at the initial Boolean state $\boldsymbol{b}^0$, where $\rho(\boldsymbol{b}^0) = \boldsymbol{Ax}^0$; σ_0 and π_0 are $\bot$ everywhere. For $k \geq 0$, the strategy yields ρ_{k+1} as the least fixed point $\mu_{\geq \rho_k} \Psi_\pi$ greater than ρ_k, Ψ_π being an order-continuous operator on the lattice $(\mathbb{B}^n \times \{1, \ldots, \ell\}) \to \overline{\mathbb{Q}}$ defined as:

$$\Psi_\pi(\rho) \triangleq (i', \boldsymbol{b}') \mapsto \sup\left\{ \boldsymbol{A}_i\boldsymbol{x}' \mid \exists \boldsymbol{x}, \boldsymbol{y}.\ T_{\pi(i',\boldsymbol{b}')} \wedge (\boldsymbol{A}\boldsymbol{x} \le \rho(\sigma(i', \boldsymbol{b}')))\right\} \quad (1)$$

We explain in §2.3 how to compute this fixed point; let us now see how σ_{k+1} and π_{k+1} are obtained from σ_k and π_k, and how termination is decided [1, §6.5]. Each iteration goes as follows: for all Boolean states $\hat{\boldsymbol{b}}' \in \mathbb{B}^n$ and all $\hat{\boldsymbol{b}}$ with $\rho_k(\hat{\boldsymbol{b}}) \neq -\infty$:

1. construct formula $T[\hat{\boldsymbol{b}}/\boldsymbol{b}, \hat{\boldsymbol{b}}'/\boldsymbol{b}']$, that is, T where variables $\boldsymbol{b}$ and $\boldsymbol{b}'$ have been replaced by Boolean values $\hat{\boldsymbol{b}}$ and $\hat{\boldsymbol{b}}'$;
2. conjoin it with constraints $\boldsymbol{A}\boldsymbol{x} \le \rho_k(\boldsymbol{b})$ and $\boldsymbol{A}_i\boldsymbol{x} > \rho_k(i, \boldsymbol{b}')$, thus obtaining
$$T[\hat{\boldsymbol{b}}/\boldsymbol{b}, \hat{\boldsymbol{b}}'/\boldsymbol{b}'] \wedge \boldsymbol{A}\boldsymbol{x} \le \rho_k(\hat{B}) \wedge \boldsymbol{A}_i\boldsymbol{x}' > \rho_k(i, \hat{\boldsymbol{b}}') \quad (2)$$
3. check whether this formula (in free variables $x_1, \ldots, x_m, x_1', \ldots, x_m', y_1, \ldots, y_E$, $p_1, \ldots, p_d$) is satisfiable;
4. if this formula is satisfiable, ρ_k does not describe an inductive invariant: the satisfying instance describes a transition from a state $(\boldsymbol{b}, \boldsymbol{x})$ to a state $(\boldsymbol{b}', \boldsymbol{x}')$ such that $(\boldsymbol{b}, \boldsymbol{x})$ lies within the invariant but $(\boldsymbol{b}', \boldsymbol{x}')$ does not; this solution yields a new strategy $\pi_{k+1}(i, \hat{\boldsymbol{b}}') = \hat{\boldsymbol{p}}$ and $\sigma_{k+1}(i, \hat{\boldsymbol{b}}') = \hat{\boldsymbol{b}}$, which *improves* on the preceding one [1, §6.3];
5. if $\pi_{k+1}(i, \hat{\boldsymbol{b}}')$ and $\sigma_{k+1}(i, \hat{\boldsymbol{b}}')$ are not set by the preceding step, leave them to the their previous values $\pi_k(i, \hat{\boldsymbol{b}}')$ and $\sigma_k(i, \hat{\boldsymbol{b}}')$; if none have been updated, this means ρ_k is the least inductive invariant, thus **exit**;
6. otherwise, compute $\rho_{k+1} = \mu_{\ge \rho_k} \Psi_{\pi_{k+1}}$ and continue iterating.

The main loop of this algorithm enumerates each of the $2^{(n+d)m2^n}$ strategies at most once. Remark the important improvement condition: at every iteration but the last, $\Psi_\pi(\rho) > \rho$. Since there is a finite number of strategies that may deem ρ non-inductive and each of them is chosen at most once, we are guaranteed to terminate with the least fixed point (without using any widening) within a finite number of steps.

Example. Let us analyze our running example using the box template $(t, -t)^T$. Assume the current abstract value[1] $\rho_k(i, \bar{e}hf) = 16$ for $i \in \{1, 2\}$. To compute an improved strategy σ_{k+1}, π_{k+1}, we have to check all values of $(\hat{\boldsymbol{b}}, \hat{\boldsymbol{b}}')$, *e.g.*, $(\bar{e}hf, \bar{e}'h'f')$: instantiating Equ. 2 with these values (with T from our running example and $i = 1$) gives

$$(p_0 \wedge p_1 \wedge \neg p_2 \wedge t \le 22 \wedge 14 \le te \le 19 \wedge (t' = \tfrac{15t+te}{16} + 1)) \wedge (t = 16) \wedge (t' > 16)$$

which is satisfied, for instance, by the model $(\hat{\boldsymbol{x}}, \hat{\boldsymbol{x}}', \hat{\boldsymbol{p}}) = (16, 17, (1, 1, 0))$. Hence, we update the strategy by setting $\sigma_{k+1}(1, \bar{e}hf) = \bar{e}hf$ and $\pi_{k+1}(1, \bar{e}hf) = (1, 1, 0)$, which induces

$$T_{\pi_{k+1}(1,\bar{e}hf)} = (t \le 22 \wedge 14 \le te \le 19 \wedge (t' = \tfrac{15t+te}{16} + 1)).$$

[1] For better readability, we write, for example, $\bar{e}hf$ for the value $(0, 1, 1)$ of (e, h, f).

After having checked all $(\hat{\boldsymbol{b}}, \hat{\boldsymbol{b}}')$, we can compute the strategy value, *i.e.*, the fixed point of $\Psi_{\pi_{k+1}}$, which updates $\rho_{k+1}(1, \bar{e}hf)$ to $\frac{365}{16}$ in this case.[2] The way this is computed is explained in the next section.

2.3 Computing the Strategy Value

We recall now how to compute the strategy fixed point $\mu_{\geq\rho}\Psi_\pi$ [1, §6.4], under the condition that $\Psi_\pi(\rho) \geq \rho$ (which is always the case, because of the way π is chosen).

The first step is to identify the Boolean states $\boldsymbol{b}$ "abstractly unreachable": such $\boldsymbol{b}$ form the least set Z containing all $\boldsymbol{b} \neq \boldsymbol{b}^0$ such that $\pi(i, \boldsymbol{b}) = \bot$ and stable by: if $\boldsymbol{b}' \neq \boldsymbol{b}^0$ is such that $\sigma(i, \boldsymbol{b}') \in Z$ then $\boldsymbol{b}' \in Z$; for all $\boldsymbol{b} \in Z$, set $\rho(\boldsymbol{b}) := -\infty$.

Construct a system of linear inequalities in the unknowns $v_{i,\boldsymbol{b}}$ for $\boldsymbol{b} \in \mathbb{B}^n$ and $1 \leq i \leq m$, plus fresh variables: for all $\boldsymbol{b}' \notin Z$, for all $1 \leq i' \leq m$ such that $\rho(i', \boldsymbol{b}') < +\infty$, add the inequalities

- $\boldsymbol{A}_j\boldsymbol{x} \leq v_{j,\sigma(i',\boldsymbol{b}')}$ for all $1 \leq j \leq m$ ("in departure state invariant")
- $\boldsymbol{A}_{i'}\boldsymbol{x}' \geq v_{i',\boldsymbol{b}'}$ ("in arrival state invariant")
- those from the conjunction $T_{\pi(i',\boldsymbol{b}')}$ ("obeys the transition relation")

where variables $\boldsymbol{x}$ and $\boldsymbol{y}$ have been replaced by fresh variables (each different $i, \boldsymbol{b}'$ has its own set of fresh replacements). $\rho(i, \boldsymbol{b}')$ is obtained by linear programming as the maximum of $v_{i',\boldsymbol{b}'}$ satisfying this system. This linear program has solutions, otherwise the strategy σ, π would not have been chosen; if it has no *optimal* solution it means that $\rho(i', \boldsymbol{b}') = +\infty$.

Note that these $O(2^n m)$ linear programs have $O(2^n m)$ variables and a system of inequalities of size $O(2^n|T|)$ where $|T|$ is the size of formula T. It is in fact possible to replace these $O(2^n m)$ linear programs by two linear programs of size $O(2^n m)$: first, one using the ∞-abstraction (see [6, §8,9]) to obtain which of the $v_{i',\boldsymbol{b}'}$ go to $+\infty$, then another for maximizing $\sum v_{i',\boldsymbol{b}'}$ restricted to the $v_{i',\boldsymbol{b}'}$ found not to be $+\infty$ by the ∞-abstraction.

3 Our Algorithm

Notice three difficulties in the preceding algorithm: there are, *a priori*, 2^{2n} SMT-solving tests to be performed at each iteration; the linear programs have exponential size; and there are at most $2^{(n+d)2^n}$ strategies, thus a doubly exponential bound on the number of iterations. In intuitive terms, the first two difficulties stem from the explicit expansion of the exponential set of Boolean states, despite the implicit representation of the exponential set of execution paths between any two control (Boolean) states $\boldsymbol{b}$ and $\boldsymbol{b}'$, a weakness that we shall now remedy.

3.1 Strategy Improvement Step

The first difficulty is the easiest to solve: the 2^{2n} SMT-tests, one for each pair $(\boldsymbol{b}, \boldsymbol{b}')$ of control states, can be folded into one single test where the $\boldsymbol{b}$ and $\boldsymbol{b}'$ also are unknowns to be solved for.

[2] By maximizing t for any te, we get $\frac{15 \cdot 22+19}{16} + 1 = \frac{365}{16}$.

Note that the structure of ρ, $\mathbb{B}^n \rightarrow \overline{\mathbb{Q}}^\ell$, can be viewed as $\{1, \ldots, \ell\} \rightarrow (\mathbb{B}^n \rightarrow \overline{\mathbb{Q}})$. Hence, we need not store a $2^n \times \ell$ array of rationals (or infinities), but we can implement it efficiently as an array (of size ℓ) of MTBDDs [7] with the bounds $c_{i,j}$ in the leaves. Assume for a given template row i, we have s_i different bounds $c_{i,j}$, and denote $\phi_{i,j}$ the propositional formula describing the set of Boolean states that map to bound $c_{i,j}$. Then, observe that $\phi_{i,j}$ for $1 \leq j \leq s_i$ form a partition of $\mathbb{B}^n$. We use the notation $\rho(i) = \{\phi_{i,1} \rightarrow c_{i,1}, \ldots, \phi_{i,s_i} \rightarrow c_{i,s_i}\}$ to represent an MTBDD, and $\rho(i, \boldsymbol{b}) = c_{i,j}$ to obtain the bound $c_{i,j}$ for state $\boldsymbol{b}$ for template row i.

Strategy improvement condition. In Equ. 2, one may replace $\boldsymbol{Ax} \leq \rho(\boldsymbol{b})$ and $\boldsymbol{A}_i\boldsymbol{x} > \rho(i', \boldsymbol{b}')$ respectively by ψ_1 and ψ_2:

$$\psi_1 \triangleq \bigwedge_i \bigvee_{j=1}^{s_i} \phi_{i,j}(\boldsymbol{b}) \wedge \boldsymbol{A}_i\boldsymbol{x} \leq c_{i,j} \tag{3}$$

$$\psi_2 \triangleq \bigvee_{j=1}^{s_i} \phi_{i',j}(\boldsymbol{b}') \wedge \boldsymbol{A}_i\boldsymbol{x}' = c_{i',j} + \Delta \wedge \Delta > 0 \tag{4}$$

Remark that $\psi =_{def} \psi_1 \wedge T \wedge \psi_2$ is satisfiable iff there is a transition from $(\boldsymbol{b}, \boldsymbol{x})$ inside the invariant defined by ρ to $(\boldsymbol{b}', \boldsymbol{x}')$ outside of it. The strategy iteration algorithm progresses regardless of Δ as long as $\Delta > 0$.

Obtaining a solution $\boldsymbol{b}, \boldsymbol{x}, \boldsymbol{b}', \boldsymbol{x}', \boldsymbol{y}, \boldsymbol{p} \models \psi$ enables us to improve the strategy by setting $\sigma(i, \boldsymbol{b}') := \boldsymbol{b}$ and $\pi(i, \boldsymbol{b}') := \boldsymbol{p}$, as in §2.2.

Example. Let us assume the following current abstract value in the analysis of our running example:

$$\begin{aligned} \rho(1) &= \{\neg e \wedge h \rightarrow 16, \quad e \vee \neg h \rightarrow -\infty\} \\ \rho(2) &= \{\neg e \wedge h \rightarrow -16, e \vee \neg h \rightarrow -\infty\} \end{aligned}$$

We build Equ. 2 using Equs. 3 and 4:

$$\psi = T \wedge \left(\begin{array}{ll} (\neg e \wedge h \wedge t \leq 16 & \vee\ (e \vee \neg h) \wedge t \leq -\infty) \wedge \\ (\neg e \wedge h \wedge -t \leq -16 & \vee\ (e \vee \neg h) \wedge -t \leq -\infty) \wedge \\ (\neg e' \wedge h' \wedge (t' = 16 + \Delta) & \vee\ (e' \vee \neg h') \wedge (-t' = -\infty + \Delta)) \end{array} \right) \wedge \Delta > 0$$

This formula is satisfied, *e.g.*, by the model $(\hat{\boldsymbol{b}}, \hat{\boldsymbol{b}}', \hat{\boldsymbol{x}}, \hat{\boldsymbol{x}}', \hat{\boldsymbol{p}}) = (\bar{e}hf, \bar{e}hf, 16, 17, (1, 1, 0))$. Hence, we update $\sigma(1, \bar{e}hf) := \bar{e}hf$ and $\pi(1, \bar{e}hf) := (1, 1, 0)$. We have to repeat this check excluding the above solution to find other models, *e.g.*, $(\bar{e}h\bar{f}, \bar{e}hf, 16, 17, (1, 1, 0))$.

Improving the strategy this way would however be costly, since we would have to do it one $\hat{\boldsymbol{b}}'$ at a time (by naive model enumeration).

Model generalization. There is however a better way by *generalizing* from an obtained model to a set of $\hat{\boldsymbol{b}}'$ that can be updated at once: Notice now that, fixing $\hat{\boldsymbol{x}}$ and $\hat{\boldsymbol{y}}$ arising from a solution, $\psi[\hat{\boldsymbol{x}}/\boldsymbol{x}, \hat{\boldsymbol{y}}/\boldsymbol{y}]$ becomes a purely propositional formula, whose models also yield suitable solutions for $\boldsymbol{b}, \boldsymbol{b}', \boldsymbol{p}$. Fix $\hat{\boldsymbol{b}}$ and $\hat{\boldsymbol{p}}$ from a solution, then the free variables are now only the $\boldsymbol{b}'$; then for any solution $\hat{\boldsymbol{b}}'$ of $\psi[\hat{\boldsymbol{x}}/\boldsymbol{x}, \hat{\boldsymbol{y}}/\boldsymbol{y}, \hat{\boldsymbol{b}}/\boldsymbol{b}, \hat{\boldsymbol{p}}/\boldsymbol{p}]$, we can set $\pi(\hat{\boldsymbol{b}}', i) := \hat{\boldsymbol{p}}$ and $\sigma(\hat{\boldsymbol{b}}', i) := \hat{\boldsymbol{b}}$. We can thus improve strategies for whole sets of $\hat{\boldsymbol{b}}'$ at once in nondeterministic systems.

Algorithm 1. IMPROVE: Selecting the strategy improvement

$\mathit{stable} := \mathit{true}$
for $i' \in \{1,\dots,\ell\}$ **do**
  $U := \mathit{false}$ // U defines the set of $\boldsymbol{b}'$ such that $\pi(i',\boldsymbol{b}')$ has been updated.
  while $\neg U \wedge \left(\bigwedge_i \bigvee_{j=1}^{s_i} \phi_{i,j}(\boldsymbol{b}) \wedge \boldsymbol{A}_i\boldsymbol{x} \le c_{i,j}\right) \wedge T_{i'} \wedge$ $\left(\bigvee_{j=1}^{s_i} \phi_{i,j}(\boldsymbol{b}') \wedge \boldsymbol{A}_i\boldsymbol{x}' = c_{i,j} + \Delta\right) \wedge \Delta > 0$ is satisfiable **do**
    $\langle \hat{\boldsymbol{b}}, \hat{\boldsymbol{x}}, \hat{\boldsymbol{b}'}, \hat{\boldsymbol{x}}', \hat{\boldsymbol{p}}, \hat{\boldsymbol{y}} \rangle :=$ a model of the above formula
    $F := T_i[\hat{\boldsymbol{x}}/\boldsymbol{x}, \hat{\boldsymbol{y}}/\boldsymbol{y}] \wedge \neg U$
    $\mathit{stable} := \mathit{false}$
    while F is satisfiable **do**
      $\langle \hat{\boldsymbol{b}_1}, \hat{\boldsymbol{b}_1'}, \hat{\boldsymbol{p}_1} \rangle :=$ a model of F
      $G := F[\hat{\boldsymbol{b}}_1/\boldsymbol{b}, \hat{\boldsymbol{p}}_1/\boldsymbol{p}]$
      $F := F \wedge \neg G$
      $\pi[i', G] := \hat{\boldsymbol{p}}$ // $\pi[i', G] := \hat{\boldsymbol{p}}$ means "in the mapping $\boldsymbol{b}' \mapsto \pi(i', \boldsymbol{b}')$,
      $\sigma[i', G] := \hat{\boldsymbol{b}}$ // replace all images of $\boldsymbol{b}'$ satisfying formula G
      $U := U \vee G$ // by $\hat{\boldsymbol{p}}$" (respectively for σ).
    end while
  end while
end for

Algorithm 2. ITERATE: Main strategy iteration algorithm

for $i \in \{1,\dots,\ell\}$ **do**
  $\phi_{1,i} := (\boldsymbol{b} = \boldsymbol{b}^0)$; $c_{1,i} := \boldsymbol{A}_i\boldsymbol{x}^0$; $\phi_{2,i} := (\boldsymbol{b} \ne \boldsymbol{b}^0)$; $c_{2,i} := -\infty$
end for
$\mathit{stable} := \mathit{false}$
while $\neg\mathit{stable}$ **do**
  IMPROVE
  if $\neg\mathit{stable}$ **then**
    COMPUTE-STRATEGY-VALUE   (see §3.2)
  end if
end while

Our strategy improvement algorithm (procedure IMPROVE, Alg. 1) thus proceeds as follows: it maintains a set U of "already improved" values of $\boldsymbol{b}'$, and requests $(\boldsymbol{b}, \boldsymbol{b}', \boldsymbol{p})$ by SMT-solving as described above, with the additional constraint that $\boldsymbol{b}' \notin U$; if no such solution is found, it terminates, having done all improvements, otherwise it generalizes $\boldsymbol{b}'$ to a whole set of solutions as described above, and improves the strategy for all these $\boldsymbol{b}'$. The strategy π, σ and the set U are stored in BDDs.

Example. Let us assume we have the current abstract value

$$\rho(1) = \{\neg e \wedge h \to \tfrac{365}{16},\ e \vee \neg h \to -\infty\}$$
$$\rho(2) = \{\neg e \wedge h \to -16,\ e \vee \neg h \to -\infty\}.$$

Moreover, assume that we have obtained the model of ψ: $(\hat{\boldsymbol{b}}, \hat{\boldsymbol{b}'}, \hat{\boldsymbol{x}}, \hat{\boldsymbol{x}}', \hat{\boldsymbol{p}}) = (\bar{e}hf, \bar{e}\bar{h}f, \frac{365}{16}, \frac{365}{16}, (1,1,1))$. Substituting the values of this solution for $\boldsymbol{x}$ and $\boldsymbol{x}'$ in formula ψ, we get $F = p_0 \wedge p_1 \wedge p_2 \wedge \neg e \wedge h \wedge \neg e' \wedge \neg h'$. Now, we substitute the above values for $\boldsymbol{b}$ and $\boldsymbol{p}$ in F, which gives us $G = \neg e' \wedge \neg h'$. We update the strategy σ, π for the whole set of states satisfying G, *i.e.*, $\{\bar{e}\bar{h}f, \bar{e}\bar{h}\bar{f}\}$ at once, and we add G to U. Then we ask the SAT solver again for a model of the formula $F \wedge \neg G$, which is unsatisfiable in this example. We continue enumerating the solutions of ψ, but this time excluding U, *i.e.*, we call the SMT solver with $\psi \wedge \neg U$, which is unsatisfiable in our example. Hence, we have completed strategy improvement for the first template row. For row 2, we proceed similarly and obtain the same strategy update. The associated strategy value computation yields the abstract value ρ:

$$\rho(1) = \{\neg e \to \tfrac{365}{16}, \qquad e \to -\infty\}$$
$$\rho(2) = \{\neg e \wedge h \to -16, \neg e \wedge \neg h \to -22, e \to -\infty\}.$$

Theorem 1. ITERATE *(Alg. 2) terminates in at most* $2^{(n+d)m2^n}$ *iterations, with the final* ρ *being equal to that computed by the algorithm of* §*2.2, yielding the least inductive invariant in the domain.*[3]

3.2 Computing the Strategy Value with Fewer Unknowns

There remains the second difficulty: computing the value of a given strategy, that is, computing $\rho(\boldsymbol{b})$ for $\boldsymbol{b} \in \mathbb{B}^n$, thus solving linear programs with at least $m2^n$ variables [1, §6.4]. We solve this difficulty by remarking that $\rho(i, \boldsymbol{b})$ is the same for all $\boldsymbol{b}$ in the same equivalence class with respect to $\sim_i$: $\boldsymbol{b}_1 \sim_i \boldsymbol{b}_2 \iff \pi(i, \boldsymbol{b}_1) = \pi(i, \boldsymbol{b}_2) \wedge \sigma(i, \boldsymbol{b}_1) = \sigma(i, \boldsymbol{b}_2)$. Assuming $\boldsymbol{b} \mapsto \sigma(i, \boldsymbol{b})$ and $\boldsymbol{b} \mapsto \pi(i, \boldsymbol{b})$ are stored as MTBDDs, the equivalence classes are obtained as BDDs using the reverse images of these functions.

We then apply the algorithm from §2.3, but instead of the whole set of $\rho(i, \boldsymbol{b})$ unknowns for $\boldsymbol{b} \in \mathbb{B}^n$ and $1 \le i \le m$, we only pick one unknown $c_{i,j}$ per equivalence class; these unknowns define ρ in the form expected by the strategy improvement step of §3.1. Remark that, if the equivalence classes are computed as BDDs, it is trivial to turn them into logical formulas $\phi_{i,j}$ of linear size w.r.t. that of the BDD. Notice that also the ∞-abstraction technique [6, §8,9] applies. Let $\bar{\boldsymbol{b}}^i$ denote the equivalence class of $\boldsymbol{b}$ with respect to $\sim_i$; π directly maps from equivalence classes as $\pi(i, \bar{\boldsymbol{b}}^i) \triangleq \pi(i, \boldsymbol{b})$ (resp. for σ).

Example. Let us assume the current abstract value

$$\rho(1) = \{\neg e \to \tfrac{365}{16}, \qquad e \to -\infty\}$$
$$\rho(2) = \{\neg e \wedge h \to -16, \neg e \wedge \neg h \to -22, e \to -\infty\}.$$

Moreover, assume that we have computed the following strategy for the first template row: $\sigma(1, \bar{e}\bar{h}f) = \sigma(1, \bar{e}\bar{h}\bar{f}) \in \{\bar{e}\bar{h}f, \bar{e}\bar{h}\bar{f}\}$ and $\pi(1, \bar{e}\bar{h}f) = \pi(1, \bar{e}\bar{h}\bar{f}) = (1, 0, 0)$. Then the states $\bar{e}\bar{h}f$ and $\bar{e}\bar{h}\bar{f}$ will be in the same equivalence class, because both bounds will have the same value in the strategy fixed point. Hence, we have to generate only one set of constraints for both states when solving the LP problem that characterizes the strategy fixed point ρ.

[3] Due to space limitations, we refer to the extended version [8] for the proofs.

We finally obtain[4] $\begin{cases} \rho(1) = \{\neg e \to \frac{365}{16}, & e \to -\infty\} \\ \rho(2) = \{\neg e \wedge h \to -16, \neg e \wedge \neg h \to -\frac{71}{4}, & e \to -\infty\}. \end{cases}$ This is actually the strongest inductive abstract invariant of our program: $\neg e \wedge h \wedge 16 \leq t \leq \frac{365}{16} \vee \neg e \wedge \neg h \wedge \frac{71}{4} \leq t \leq \frac{365}{16}$.

Theorem 2. *Let $\rho^\sharp$ be the result of the modified strategy evaluation and $\rho_{k+1} = \mu_{\geq \rho_k} \Psi_{\pi_{k+1}}$ be the result of the original strategy evaluation. Then for all $i, \boldsymbol{b}$, $\rho(i, \boldsymbol{b}) = \rho^\sharp(i, \bar{\boldsymbol{b}}^i)$.*

3.3 Abstraction through Limitation of Partitioning

Even though we have taken precautions against unnecessarily large numbers of unknowns by grouping "equivalent" Boolean states together, it is still possible that the number of equivalence classes to consider grows too much as the algorithm proceeds. It is however possible to freeze them permanently to their last sufficiently small value. Only small modifications to the algorithms are necessary: The strategy value computation (§3.2) remains the same except that the equivalence classes are never recomputed. Let $\phi_{i,1}, \ldots, \phi_{i,s_i}$ denote the propositional formulas (in $\boldsymbol{b}$) defining the equivalence classes with respect to constraint number i. In the strategy improvement step (§3.1) $\sigma(i,j) \in \mathbb{B}^n$ (resp. $\pi(i,j)$) is now defined for the index $1 \leq j \leq s_i$ of an equivalence class with respect to constraint i.

4 Experiments

We have prototypically implemented the algorithm in the static analyzer ReaVer [9] (taking Lustre code as input) using the LP solver QSOpt_Ex[5], the SMT solver Yices[6] and the BDD package Cudd[7]. The implementation makes heavy use of incremental SMT solving.

Tested variants of the algorithm. We implemented the following variants of the algorithm to compare their performance:

(n) Naive model enumeration using SMT solving per template row as explained in the first part of §3.1. This corresponds to updating π and σ in Alg. 1 using the model obtained in line 5 ($G = (\boldsymbol{b}' = \hat{\boldsymbol{b}}')$) without doing lines 6 to 11 and 15.

(t) Enhancement of (n) by trying to reapply successfully improving models to other template rows.

---

[4] By maximizing $-t$ for any te in $t \geq 18 \wedge 14 \leq te \leq 19 \wedge t' = \frac{15t+te}{16}$, we get $-\frac{15 \cdot 18 + 14}{16} = -\frac{71}{4}$.

[5] version 2.5.6, `http://www.dii.uchile.cl/~daespino/ESolver_doc/main.html`

[6] version 1.0.40, `http://yices.csl.sri.com/`

[7] version 2.4.2, `http://vlsi.colorado.edu/~fabio/CUDD/`

(s) Symbolic encoding of template rows and model enumeration over the whole template at once, *i.e.*, lines 2 and 17 are omitted because the template row i' becomes part of the SMT formula to be solved for in line 4, and is then retrieved from the model returned in line 5.

(g) Alg. 1 with *generalization* as described in §3.1, but without the inner iterations (*i.e.*, without lines 7 to 9 and 15) that search for models of the purely propositional formula F. Hence, (g) obtains the models to be generalized from the SMT formula in line 4 only.

(m) Alg. 1 as given.

All these variants reduce the number of unknowns in the LP problem using equivalence classes (see §3.2). Furthermore, we used an implementation of the original max-strategy algorithm [5] (GS07), and the improvements using SMT solving proposed in [10] (GM11). Note that these latter two algorithms need to enumerate $\mathcal{O}(2^n)$ control states (where n is the number of Booleans in the recurrent state). Yet, the size of the control flow graphs (see Table 1) generated using the method described in [9, §7.3] is often far smaller than the worst case. The difference between GS07 and GM11 is essentially that, for each template row, the former tests all strategies to find an improvement, whereas the latter asks the SMT solver to find an improving strategy in the disjunction of available strategies.

It is important to note that all these variants of the algorithm return the *same* invariants, *i.e.* the strongest invariants in the domain $\mathbb{B}^n \to A$ where A is a given template abstract domain. The only difference is the way the strategy improvement is computed.

Comparisons. We performed two kinds of comparisons:[8]

1. We evaluated the scalability of various variants of the max-strategy improvement algorithm on small benchmarks (1-, 2-, and 3-dimensional array traversals, parametric in size by duplicating functionality and adding Boolean variables) that exhibit the strategy and state space explosion expected to occur in larger benchmarks. We used box and octagonal templates, giving a total of 96 benchmarks.
2. We compared the max-strategy improvement algorithm with standard forward analysis with widening and with abstract acceleration [11, 12] (both using widening after two iterations and applying two descending iterations[9]) on reactive system models (traffic lights [13], our thermostat, car window controller [14], and drug pump [15]), again deriving the more complex variants 2 and 3 by adding and duplicating functionality (e.g. branching *multiple* drug pumps to a patient and checking the concentration in the blood).

Results. The first comparison (see Fig. 1) shows that the various variants of the algorithm behave quite differently in terms of runtime: The GM11 improvement

[8] The examples and detailed experimental results can be found on `http://www.cs.ox.ac.uk/people/peter.schrammel/reaver/maxstrat/`.

[9] We did not not observe any improvement in precision beyond these values.

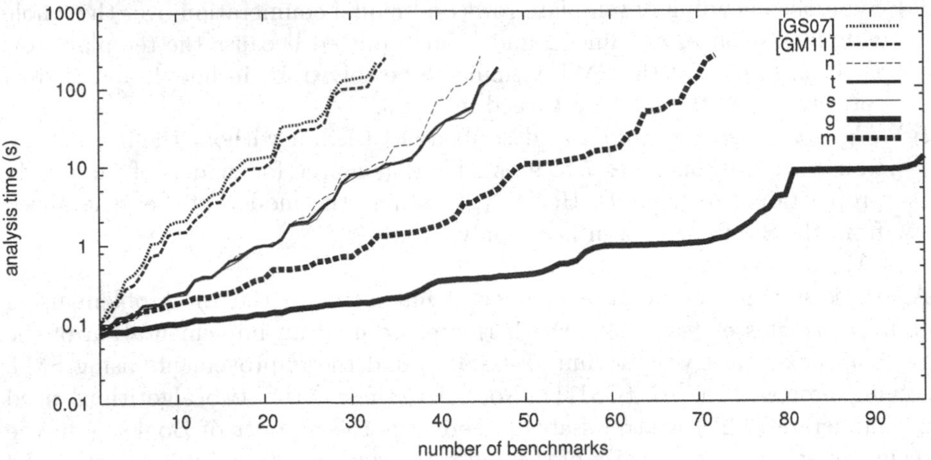

Fig. 1. Comparison of various variants of the max-strategy improvement algorithm. All these algorithms compute the *same* invariant. The timeout was 5 minutes.

Table 1. Comparison of max-strategy iteration with standard analysis approaches (dom: domain used (boxes (B), zones (Z), octagons (O)); number of variables: Boolean (b), numerical (n), Boolean and numerical inputs (bi, ni); number of locations (lc) and edges (ed) of the control flow graph (CFG); analysis time in seconds; property proved (p); fastest in bold). (* computed with octagons, because zones are not available).

		size						previous algorithms				this paper				std.		abstr.	
		vars				CFG		GS07 [5]		GM11 [10]		g		s		analysis		accel.	
	dom	b	n	bi	ni	lc	ed	time	p	time	p	time	p	time	p	time	p	time	p
Traffic 1	B	6	6	0	0	18	61	2.16	✓	2.10	✓	2.33	✓	2.16	✓	1.22	✓	**0.43**	✓
Traffic 2	Z	6	8	0	0	18	151	122	✓	114	✓	108	✓	**97.0**	✓	3.49		2.86*	
Traffic 3	Z	8	8	1	0	50	619	674	✓	640	✓	357	✓	**329**	✓	22.1		19.2*	
Thermostat 1	B	4	3	0	2	6	15	0.36	✓	0.32	✓	0.28	✓	**0.26**	✓	0.82		0.85	
Thermostat 2	B	6	5	0	4	18	145	16.8	✓	15.1	✓	3.44	✓	**3.23**	✓	26.6		30.4	
Thermostat 3	B	8	7	0	6	66	1357	720	✓	715	✓	66.5	✓	**61.9**	✓	674		908	
Window 1	O	9	5	5	0	21	120	109	✓	102	✓	**70.7**	✓	73.4	✓	4.57		4.70	
Window 2	O	11	5	6	0	45	452	394	✓	372	✓	**189**	✓	286	✓	18.57		23.5	
Window 3	O	13	5	7	0	81	1388	1412	✓	1220	✓	**242**	✓	697	✓	70.2		93.5	
DrugPump 1	B	4	10	4	1	6	231	92.6	✓	90.3	✓	6.05	✓	**4.55**	✓	210		120	
DrugPump 2	B	7	12	8	1	34	11201	timeout > 1800				149	✓	**95.5**	✓	timeout > 1800			
DrugPump 3	B	10	14	8	1	146	112561	timeout > 1800				**1019**	✓	1396	✓	timeout > 1800			

is on average 22% faster than the original algorithm. (t) and (s) scale better than (n). It is interesting to observe that (t) and (s) perform similarly although their algorithms are very different. The most important optimization of the strategy improvement algorithm proposed in this paper is the generalization step which makes it scale several orders of magnitude better than the other variants, because it avoids naive model enumeration. The results indicate that the full Alg. 1 (variant (m)) is slower than the variant (g) without the innermost iterations. A possible explanation for this is that as soon as all models have been enumerated, (m) has to confirm unsatisfiability by checking both $F \wedge \neg G$ and $\psi \wedge \neg U$.

The results of the second comparison (see Table 1) indicate that max-strategy iteration is able to compute better invariants than techniques relying on widening in the *same* $\mathbb{B}^n \to A$ abstract domain. Enhanced widening techniques, such as abstract acceleration, do occasionally improve on precision, but without guarantee to find the best invariant.

An open problem w.r.t. all template-based analysis techniques is however the generation of good templates. For our experiments, we have chosen the weakest of the standard templates (boxes, zones, octagons) that can express the required invariant. Strategy iteration is in general the more expensive technique, but due to our improvements the performance is pushing forward into a reasonable range. Variant (g) – although a bit slower than (s) in many cases – seems to scale best.

5 Related Work

It has long been recognized that it is a good idea to distinguish states according to Boolean variables or arbitrary predicates (as in *predicate abstraction*). Yet, taking all Boolean variables into account tends to be unbearably expensive. Various heuristics have therefore been proposed so as to partition $\mathbb{B}^n$ into a reasonably small number of subsets [16]. Relations between the Boolean and numerical states are only kept w.r.t. these equivalence classes [3]. Combining the latter technique with the method presented in this paper to limit partitioning would certainly improve efficiency, however, to the detriment of precision of the obtained invariant which strongly depends on the choice of a clever partitioning heuristics.

Early work in compilation and verification of reactive systems [4] advocated quotienting the Boolean state space according to some form of *concrete* bisimulation. In contrast, we compute coarser equivalences according to per-constraint *abstract* semantics. In the ASTRÉE analyzer, static heuristics determine reasonably small packs of "related" Booleans and numerical variables, such that the values of the numerical variables are analyzed separately for each Boolean valuation [17, §6.2.4]. In contrast, our equivalence classes are computed dynamically and per-constraint.

The strategy iteration we have applied proceeds "upward", by successive under-approximations of the least inductive invariant; strategies correspond to to "max" operators in a high-level vision of the problem. There also exists "downward" strategy iteration, where strategies correspond to "min" operators: iterations produce successive *over*-approximations of the least inductive invariant [18, 19], to which convergence is ensured in some cases. A bonus of such an approach is that each iteration produces an over-approximation of the least inductive invariant, which may be used to prove safety properties without having to wait for convergence. Sadly, it does not seem to be easily adapted to approaches based on SMT solving, since the SMT formulas would contain universal quantifiers.

For a more comprehensive discussion of related work, we refer to the extended version [8].

6 Conclusion

We propose a method for computing strongest invariants in linear template domains when the control states are partitioned according to n Booleans or arbitrary predicates, thereby combining predicate abstraction and template polyhedral abstraction. Our method performs strategy iteration, and dynamically partitions the states according to an equivalence relation depending on the current abstraction at each step. The final result is optimal in the sense that it is the strongest invariant in the abstract domain which a naive algorithm would obtain in at least exponential time and space. Our experimental results demonstrate the significant performance impact of various optimizations and the ability to compute more precise invariants in comparison to widening-based techniques.

In preceding work without partitioning [1, 10], the single-exponential upper bound was shown to be reached by a contrived example program, and the decision problem associated with the least invariant computation ("given a template, a transition relation, an initial state and a bad state, is there an inductive invariant that excludes the bad state") was shown to be Σ_2^p-complete. In contrast, although we have an NEXPTIME upper bound and proved EXPTIME-hardness (see [8] for a proof) for the problem with partitioning, we have not yet been able to prove NEXPTIME-completeness—thus the worst-case complexity could possibly be better.

References

1. Gawlitza, T.M., Monniaux, D.: Invariant generation through strategy iteration in succinctly represented control flow graphs. Logical Methods in Computer Science (2012) Journal version of an article in ESOP 2011
2. Halbwachs, N., Proy, Y.E., Roumanoff, P.: Verification of real-time systems using linear relation analysis. Formal Methods in System Design 11, 157–185 (1997)
3. Schrammel, P., Subotic, P.: Logico-numerical max-strategy iteration. In: Giacobazzi, R., Berdine, J., Mastroeni, I. (eds.) VMCAI 2013. LNCS, vol. 7737, pp. 414–433. Springer, Heidelberg (2013)
4. Bouajjani, A., Fernandez, J.C., Halbwachs, N., Raymond, P.: Minimal state graph generation. Sci. Comput. Program. 18, 247–269 (1992)
5. Gawlitza, T., Seidl, H.: Precise relational invariants through strategy iteration. In: Duparc, J., Henzinger, T.A. (eds.) CSL 2007. LNCS, vol. 4646, pp. 23–40. Springer, Heidelberg (2007)
6. Gawlitza, T.M., Seidl, H.: Solving systems of rational equations through strategy iteration. ACM Trans. Program. Lang. Syst. 33, 11:1–11:48 (2011)
7. Bryant, R.E.: Graph-based algorithms for boolean function manipulation. IEEE Trans. Computers 35, 677–691 (1986)
8. Monniaux, D., Schrammel, P.: Scaling up logico-numerical strategy iteration (extended version) (2014), `http://arxiv.org/abs/1403.2319`
9. Schrammel, P.: Logico-Numerical Verification Methods for Discrete and Hybrid Systems. PhD thesis, Université de Grenoble (2012)
10. Gawlitza, T.M., Monniaux, D.: Improving strategies via SMT solving. In: Barthe, G. (ed.) ESOP 2011. LNCS, vol. 6602, pp. 236–255. Springer, Heidelberg (2011)
11. Gonnord, L., Halbwachs, N.: Combining widening and acceleration in linear relation analysis. In: Yi, K. (ed.) SAS 2006. LNCS, vol. 4134, pp. 144–160. Springer, Heidelberg (2006)
12. Schrammel, P., Jeannet, B.: Applying abstract acceleration to (co-)reachability analysis of reactive programs. J. of Symb. Comp. 47, 1512–1532 (2012)

13. Bonakdarpour, B., Kulkarni, S.S., Arora, A.: Disassembling real-time fault-tolerant programs. In: EMSOFT, pp. 169–178. ACM (2008)
14. Schrammel, P., Melham, T., Kroening, D.: Chaining test cases for reactive system testing. In: Yenigün, H., Yilmaz, C., Ulrich, A. (eds.) ICTSS 2013. LNCS, vol. 8254, pp. 133–148. Springer, Heidelberg (2013)
15. Sankaranarayanan, S., Homaei, H., Lewis, C.: Model-based dependability analysis of programmable drug infusion pumps. In: Fahrenberg, U., Tripakis, S. (eds.) FORMATS 2011. LNCS, vol. 6919, pp. 317–334. Springer, Heidelberg (2011)
16. Schrammel, P., Jeannet, B.: Logico-numerical abstract acceleration and application to the verification of data-flow programs. In: Yahav, E. (ed.) SAS 2011. LNCS, vol. 6887, pp. 233–248. Springer, Heidelberg (2011)
17. Blanchet, B., Cousot, P., Cousot, R., Feret, J., Mauborgne, L., Miné, A., Monniaux, D., Rival, X.: A static analyzer for large safety-critical software. In: PLDI, pp. 196–207. ACM (2003)
18. Gaubert, S., Goubault, É., Taly, A., Zennou, S.: Static analysis by policy iteration on relational domains. In: De Nicola, R. (ed.) ESOP 2007. LNCS, vol. 4421, pp. 237–252. Springer, Heidelberg (2007)
19. Sotin, P., Jeannet, B., Védrine, F., Goubault, E.: Policy iteration within logico-numerical abstract domains. In: Bultan, T., Hsiung, P.-A. (eds.) ATVA 2011. LNCS, vol. 6996, pp. 290–305. Springer, Heidelberg (2011)

Cost-Aware Automatic Program Repair

Roopsha Samanta[1,*], Oswaldo Olivo[2], and E. Allen Emerson[2]

[1] The University of Texas at Austin and IST Austria
rsamanta@ist.ac.at
[2] The University of Texas at Austin
{olivo,emerson}@cs.utexas.edu

Abstract. We present a formal framework for repairing infinite-state, imperative, sequential programs, with (possibly recursive) procedures and multiple assertions; the framework can generate repaired programs by modifying the original erroneous program in multiple program locations, and can ensure the readability of the repaired program using user-defined expression templates; the framework also generates a set of inductive assertions that serve as a proof of correctness of the repaired program. As a step toward integrating programmer intent and intuition in automated program repair, we present a *cost-aware* formulation — given a cost function associated with permissible statement modifications, the goal is to ensure that the total program modification cost does not exceed a given repair budget. As part of our predicate abstraction-based solution framework, we present a sound and complete algorithm for repair of Boolean programs. We have developed a prototype tool based on SMT solving and used it successfully to repair diverse errors in benchmark C programs.

1 Introduction

Program debugging — the process of fault localization and error elimination — is an integral part of ensuring correctness in existing or evolving software. Being essentially manual, program debugging is often a lengthy, expensive part of a program's development cycle. There is an evident need for improved formalization and mechanization of this process. However, program debugging is hard to formalize — there are multiple types of programming mistakes with diverse manifestations, and multiple ways of eliminating a detected error. Moreover, it is particularly challenging to assimilate and mechanize the expert human intuition involved in the choices made in manual program debugging.

In this paper, we present a *cost-aware* formulation of the automated program debugging problem that addresses the above concerns. Our formulation obviates the need for a separate fault localization phase by directly focusing on error elimination, i.e., program repair. We fix a set $\mathcal{U}$ of *update schemas* that may be applied to program statements for modifying them. An update schema is a

* This author was supported in part by the European Research Council (ERC) under grant agreement 267989 (QUAREM) and by the Austrian Science Fund (FWF) NFN project S11402-N23 (RiSE)

M. Müller-Olm and H. Seidl (Eds.): SAS 2014, LNCS 8723, pp. 268–284, 2014.

compact description of a class of updates that may be applied to a program statement in order to repair it. For instance, the update schema `assign` $\mapsto$ `assign` permits replacement of the assignment statement $x := y$ with other assignment statements such as $x := x + y$ or $y := x + 1$, `assign` $\mapsto$ `skip` permits deletion of an assignment statement, etc. In this paper, $\mathcal{U}$ includes deletion of statements, replacement of assignment statements with other assignment statements, and replacement of the guards of conditional and loop statements with other guards. We assume we are given a *cost function* that assigns some user-defined cost to each application of an update schema to a program statement. Given an erroneous program $\mathcal{P}$, a cost function c and a repair budget δ, the goal of *cost-aware automatic program repair* is to compute a program $\widehat{\mathcal{P}}$ such that: $\widehat{\mathcal{P}}$ is correct, $\widehat{\mathcal{P}}$ is obtained by modifying $\mathcal{P}$ using a set of update schemas from $\mathcal{U}$ and the total modification cost does not exceed δ. We postulate that this *quantitative* formulation [6] is a flexible and convenient way of incorporating user intent and intuition in automatic program debugging. For instance, the user can define appropriate cost functions to search for $\widehat{\mathcal{P}}$ that differs from $\mathcal{P}$ in at most δ statements, or to penalize any modification within some *trusted* program fragment, or to favor the application of a particular update schema over another, and so on.

Our approach to cost-aware repair of imperative, sequential programs is based on predicate abstraction [13], which is routinely used by verification tools such as SLAM [5], SLAM2 [2], SATABS [8], etc. for analyzing infinite-state programs. These tools generate Boolean programs which are equivalent in expressive power to pushdown systems and enjoy desirable computational properties such as decidability of reachability [4]. Inevitably, Boolean programs have also been explored for use in automatic repair of sequential programs for partial correctness [14] and total correctness [22]. These papers, however, do not accommodate a quantitative formulation of the repair problem and can only compute repaired programs that differ from the original erroneous program in exactly one expression. Moreover, these papers do not attempt to improve the *readability* of the concrete program $\widehat{\mathcal{P}}$, obtained by concretizing a repaired Boolean program.

Our predicate abstraction-based approach to automatic program repair relaxes the above limitations. Besides erroneous $\mathcal{P}$, c, and δ, our framework requires a Boolean program $\mathcal{B}$, obtained from $\mathcal{P}$ through iterative predicate abstraction-refinement, such that $\mathcal{B}$ exhibits a non-spurious path to an error. We present an algorithm which casts the question of *repairability of* $\mathcal{B}$, given U, c, and δ, as an SMT query; if the query is satisfiable, the algorithm extracts a correct Boolean program $\widehat{\mathcal{B}}$ from the witness to its satisfiability. Along with $\widehat{\mathcal{B}}$, we also extract a set of inductive assertions from the witness, that constitute a proof of correctness of $\widehat{\mathcal{B}}$. This algorithm for Boolean program repair is sound and complete, relative to $\mathcal{U}$, c, and δ. A repaired Boolean program $\widehat{\mathcal{B}}$, along with its proof, is concretized to obtain a repaired concrete program $\widehat{\mathcal{P}}$, along with a proof of correctness. However, the concretized repairs may not be succinct or readable. Hence, our framework can also accept user-supplied templates specifying the desired syntax of the modified expressions in $\widehat{\mathcal{P}}$ to constrain the concretization.

Alternate approaches to automatic repair and synthesis of sequential programs [17,26–28] that do not rely on abstract interpretations of concrete programs, also often encode the repair/synthesis problem as a constraint-solving problem whose solution can be extracted using SAT or SMT solvers. Except for [28], these approaches, due to their bounded semantics, are imprecise and cannot handle total correctness[1]. The authors in [17] use SMT reasoning to search for repairs satisfying user-defined templates; the templates are needed not only for ensuring readability of the generated repairs, but also for ensuring tractability of their inherently undecidable repair generation query. They also include a notion of minimal diagnoses, which is subsumed by our more general cost-aware formulation. Given user-defined constraints specifying the space of desired programs and associated proof objects, the scaffold-based program synthesis approach of [28] attempts to synthesizes a program, along with a proof of total correctness consisting of program invariants and ranking functions for loops. In contrast to [28], our framework only interacts with a user for improving the readability of the generated repairs and for the cost function; all predicates involved in the generation of the repaired Boolean program and its proof are discovered automatically. Besides the above, there have been proposals for program repair based on computing repairs as winning strategies in games [15], abstraction interpretation [18], mutations [10], genetic algorithms [1,12], using contracts [29], and focusing on data structure manipulations [25,30]. There are also customized program repair engines for grading and feedback generation for programming assignments, cf. [24]. Finally, a multitude of algorithms [3,7,16,31] have been proposed for fault localization, based on analyzing error traces. Some of these techniques can be used as a preprocessing step to improve the efficiency of our algorithm, at the cost of giving up on the completeness of the Boolean program repair module.

Summary of contributions: We define a new cost-aware formulation of automatic program repair that can incorporate programmer intuition and intent (Sec. 3). We present a formal solution framework (Sec. 4 and Sec. 5) that can repair infinite-state, imperative, sequential programs with (possibly recursive) procedures and multiple assertions. Our method can modify the original erroneous program in multiple program locations and can ensure the readability of the repaired program using user-defined expression templates. If our method succeeds in generating a repaired program $\widehat{\mathcal{P}}$, it generates a proof of $\widehat{\mathcal{P}}$'s correctness, consisting of inductive assertions, that guarantees satisfaction of *all* the assertions in the original program $\mathcal{P}$. As part of our predicate abstraction-based solution, we present a sound and complete algorithm for repair of Boolean programs. Finally, we present experimental results for repairing diverse errors in benchmark C programs using a prototype implementation (Sec. 6).

2 Background

Predicate abstraction [4, 13] is an effective technique for model checking infinite-state programs with respect to safety properties. It uses iterative

[1] Our framework can be extended to handle total correctness by synthesizing ranking functions along with inductive assertions.

counterexample-guided abstraction refinement to compute a finite-state, *conservative* abstraction of a concrete program $\mathcal{P}$ based on a finite set $\{\phi_1, \ldots, \phi_r\}$ of predicates. The resulting abstract program is termed a *Boolean program* $\mathcal{B}$ (see Fig. 1a and Fig. 1b): the control-flow of $\mathcal{B}$ is the same as that of $\mathcal{P}$ and the set $\{b_1, \ldots, b_r\}$ of variables of $\mathcal{B}$ are Boolean variables, with each b_i representing the predicate ϕ_i for $i \in [1, r]$. If $\mathcal{B}$ is found to be correct, the method concludes that $\mathcal{P}$ is correct. In our work, the interesting case is when the method terminates reporting an error. This happens when the method computes a Boolean program containing an abstract counterexample path which is found to be feasible in $\mathcal{P}$. Henceforth, we fix a concrete program $\mathcal{P}$, and a corresponding Boolean program $\mathcal{B}$ that exhibits such a non-spurious counterexample path. Let γ denote the mapping of the Boolean variables in $\mathcal{B}$ to their respective predicates: for each $i \in [1, r]$, $\gamma(b_i) = \phi_i$. The mapping γ can be extended in a standard way to expressions over the Boolean variables.

Program Syntax. For our technical presentation, we fix a common, simplified syntax for concrete and abstract programs (see [23] for a precise definition) — a program consists of a declaration of global variables, followed by a list of procedure definitions; a procedure definition consists of a declaration of local variables, followed by a sequence of (labeled) statements; a statement is a `skip`, (parallel) assignment, `assume`, `assert`, `goto`, (call-by-value) procedure `call` or `return` statement[2]. A Boolean expression is either a deterministic Boolean expression or the expression $*$, which nondeterministically evaluates to `true` or `false`.

We make the following assumptions: (a) there is a distinguished initial procedure `main`, (b) all variable and formal parameter names are globally unique, and (c) `goto` statements are used only to simulate the flow of control in structured programs. In addition, for Boolean programs, we assume: (a) all variables and formal parameters are Boolean, (b) all expressions are Boolean expressions and (c) the Boolean expressions in `assume` and `assert` statements are deterministic.

Notation. For program $\mathcal{P}$, let $\{F_0, \ldots, F_t\}$ be its set of procedures with F_0 being the `main` procedure, and let $GV(\mathcal{P})$ denote the set of global variables. For procedure F_i, let $\mathcal{L}_i$ denote the set of locations. Let $V(\mathcal{P})$ denote the set of all variables of $\mathcal{P}$, and $\mathcal{L}(\mathcal{P}) = \bigcup_{i=1}^{t} \mathcal{L}_i$ denote the set of locations of $\mathcal{P}$. For a location ℓ within a procedure F_i, let *inscope*(ℓ) denote the set of all variables in $\mathcal{P}$ whose scope includes l. We denote by *stmt*(ℓ), *formal*(ℓ) and *local*(ℓ) the statement at ℓ and the sets of formal parameters and local variables of the procedure containing ℓ, respectively. We denote by $entry_i \in \mathcal{L}_i$ the location of the first statement in F_i. For Boolean program $\mathcal{B}$, we use the same notation, replacing $\mathcal{P}$ with $\mathcal{B}$ as needed. When the context is clear, we simply use V, $\mathcal{L}$ instead of $V(\mathcal{P})$, $\mathcal{L}(\mathcal{B})$ etc.

Transition Graphs. In addition to a textual representation, we will often find it convenient to use a transition graph representation of programs (see Fig. 1c). The transition graph representation of $\mathcal{P}$, denoted $\mathcal{G}(\mathcal{P})$, comprises a set of labeled, rooted, directed graphs $\mathcal{G}_0, \ldots, \mathcal{G}_t$, with exactly one node, *err*, in common.

[2] We take the liberty of using `if` and `while` statements for our examples.

```
main() {
    int x;
    ℓ1 : if (x ≤ 0)
    ℓ2 :     while (x < 0){
    ℓ3 :        x := x + 2;
    ℓ4 :        skip;
             }
          else
    ℓ5 :      if (x == 1)
    ℓ6 :         x := x − 1;
    ℓ7 : assert (x > 1);
}
```

(a) $\mathcal{P}$

```
main() {
    /* γ(b0) = x ≤ 1, γ(b1) = x == 1, γ(b2) = x ≤ 0 */
    Bool b0, b1, b2 := *, *, *;
    ℓ1 : if (¬b2) then goto ℓ5;
    ℓ2 : if (*) then goto ℓ0;
    ℓ3 : b0, b1, b2 := *, *, *;
    ℓ4 : goto ℓ2;
    ℓ0 : goto ℓ7;
    ℓ5 : if (¬b1) then goto ℓ7;
    ℓ6 : b0, b1, b2 := *, *, *;
    ℓ7 : assert (¬b0);
}
```

(b) $\mathcal{B}$

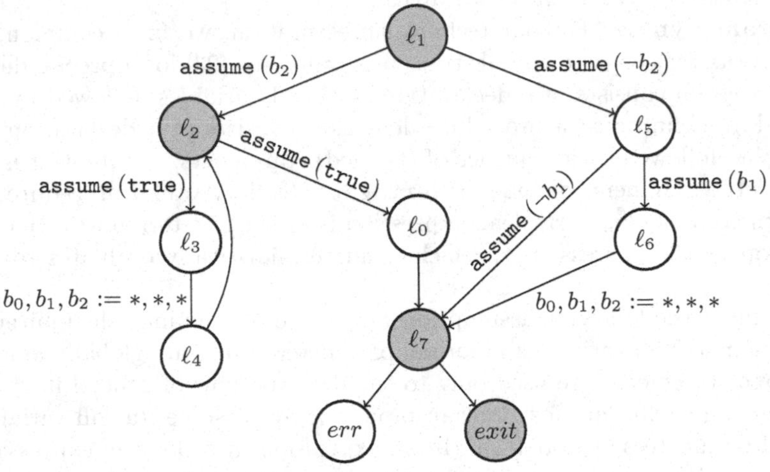

(c) $\mathcal{G}(\mathcal{B})$

Fig. 1. An example concrete program $\mathcal{P}$, a corresponding Boolean program $\mathcal{B}$ and $\mathcal{B}$'s transition graph

Informally, the ith graph $\mathcal{G}_i$ captures the flow of control in procedure F_i with its nodes and edges labeled by locations and corresponding statements of F_i, respectively (see [23] for a formal definition). The set N_i of nodes of $\mathcal{G}_i$, given by $\mathcal{L}_i \cup exit_i \cup err$, includes a unique entry node $entry_i$, a unique exit node $exit_i$ and the error node err (every node ℓ with $stmt(\ell)$ being an `assert` statement has two successors, one of which is err). A path π in $\mathcal{G}_i$ is a sequence of labeled connected edges; we denote the sequence of statements labeling the edges in π as $stmt(\pi)$.

Program Semantics and Correctness. An operational semantics can be defined for our programs in an obvious way, by formalizing the effect of each type of program statement on a program *configuration*. A configuration η of a program $\mathcal{P}$ is a tuple of the form (ℓ, Ω, ζ), where $\ell \in \mathcal{L}(\mathcal{P})$, Ω is a valuation of the variables in $inscope(\ell)$ and ζ is a stack of elements. Each element of ζ is of the form $(\widetilde{\ell}, \widetilde{\Omega})$, where $\widetilde{\ell}$ is a location and $\widetilde{\Omega}$ is a valuation of the variables in $local(\widetilde{\ell})$. A configuration (ℓ, Ω, ζ) of $\mathcal{P}$ is called an initial configuration if $\ell = entry_0$ and ζ is the empty stack. We use $\eta \rightsquigarrow \eta'$ to denote that $\mathcal{P}$ can transition from configuration η to η'; the transitions rules for each type of program statement at ℓ are standard (see [23] for details).

An *execution path* of program $\mathcal{P}$ is a sequence of configurations, $\eta \rightsquigarrow \eta' \rightsquigarrow \eta'' \rightsquigarrow \ldots$, obtained by repeated application of transition rules, starting from an initial configuration η. An execution path may be finite or infinite. The last configuration (ℓ, Ω, ζ) of a finite execution path may either be a *terminating configuration* with $\ell = exit_0$, or an *error configuration* with $\ell = err$ or a *stuck configuration*. An execution path ends in a stuck configuration η if no transition rule is applicable to η.

An assertion in program $\mathcal{P}$, is a statement of the form ℓ : `assert` (g), and represents the expected valuation of the program variables at location ℓ. We will use the term assertion to denote both the statement ℓ : `assert` (g) as well as the quantifier-free, first order expression g. We say a program configuration (ℓ, Ω, ζ) satisfies an assertion g, if the embedded variable valuation Ω satisfies g.

Given a program $\mathcal{P}$ (or, $\mathcal{B}$) annotated with a set of assertions, $\mathcal{P}$ (or, $\mathcal{B}$) is *partially correct* iff every *finite* execution path of $\mathcal{P}$ (or $\mathcal{B}$) ends in a terminating configuration (for all nondeterministic choices that $\mathcal{B}$ might make). $\mathcal{P}$ (or, $\mathcal{B}$) is *totally correct* iff every execution path is finite and ends in a terminating configuration (for all nondeterministic choices that $\mathcal{B}$ might make). Unless otherwise specified, an *incorrect* program is one that is not partially correct.

3 Cost-Aware Program Repair

3.1 The Problem

Let $\Sigma = \{\texttt{skip}, \texttt{assign}, \texttt{assume}, \texttt{assert}, \texttt{call}, \texttt{return}, \texttt{goto}\}$ denote the set of *statement types* in program $\mathcal{P}$. Given a statement s, let $\tau(s)$ be an element of Σ denoting the statement type of s. Let $\mathcal{U} = \{u_0, u_1, \ldots, u_d\}$ be a set of permissible, statement-level *update schemas*: $u_0 = id$ is the *identity* update schema that maps every statement to itself, and u_i, $i \in [1, d]$, is a function $\sigma \mapsto \widehat{\sigma}$, $\sigma, \widehat{\sigma} \in \Sigma \setminus \{\texttt{assert}\}$, that maps a statement type to a statement type. For each update schema u, given by $\sigma \mapsto \widehat{\sigma}$, we say u can be *applied* to statement s to get statement $\widehat{s}$ if $\tau(s) = \sigma$; we then have $\tau(\widehat{s}) = \widehat{\sigma}$. For example, u, given by `assign` $\mapsto$ `assign`, can be applied to the assignment statement $\ell : x := y$ to get an assignment statement $\ell : y := x + 1$. Notice that update schemas in $\mathcal{U}$ do not affect the label of a statement, and that we do not permit modifying an `assert` statement. In this paper, we fix the following set of update schemas:

$$\begin{aligned}\mathcal{U} = \{&id, \texttt{assign} \mapsto \texttt{assign}, \texttt{assign} \mapsto \texttt{skip}, \texttt{assume} \mapsto \texttt{assume},\\ &\texttt{call} \mapsto \texttt{call}, \texttt{call} \mapsto \texttt{skip}\}.\end{aligned} \tag{1}$$

We extend the notion of a statement-level update to a program-level update as follows. For programs $\mathcal{P}$, $\widehat{\mathcal{P}}$, let the respective sets of locations be $\mathcal{L}$, $\widehat{\mathcal{L}}$ and let

$stmt(\ell)$, $\widehat{stmt}(\ell)$ denote the respective statements at location ℓ. Let $\mathbb{R}_{\mathcal{U},\mathcal{L}} : \mathcal{L} \mapsto \mathcal{U}$ be an *update function* that maps each location of $\mathcal{P}$ to an update schema in $\mathcal{U}$. We say $\widehat{\mathcal{P}}$ is an $\mathbb{R}_{\mathcal{U},\mathcal{L}}$-update of $\mathcal{P}$ iff $\mathcal{L} = \widehat{\mathcal{L}}$ and for each $\ell \in \mathcal{L}$, $\widehat{stmt}(\ell)$ is obtained by applying $\mathbb{R}_{\mathcal{U},\mathcal{L}}(\ell)$ on $stmt(\ell)$.

Let $c_{\mathcal{U},\mathcal{L}} : \mathcal{U} \times \mathcal{L} \rightarrow \mathbb{N}$ be a cost function that maps a tuple, consisting of a statement-level update schema u and a location ℓ of $\mathcal{P}$, to a certain cost. Thus, $c_{\mathcal{U},\mathcal{L}}(u, \ell)$ is the cost of applying update schema u to the $stmt(\ell)$. We impose an obvious restriction on $c_{\mathcal{U},\mathcal{L}}$: $\forall \ell \in \mathcal{L} : c_{\mathcal{U},\mathcal{L}}(id, \ell) = 0$. Since we have already fixed the set $\mathcal{U}$ and the program $\mathcal{P}$, we henceforth use c, $\mathbb{R}$ instead of $c_{\mathcal{U},\mathcal{L}}$, $\mathbb{R}_{\mathcal{U},\mathcal{L}}$, respectively, The total cost, $Cost_c(\mathbb{R})$, of performing an $\mathbb{R}$-update of $\mathcal{P}$ is given by $\sum_{\ell \in \mathcal{L}} c(\mathbb{R}(\ell), \ell)$.

Given an incorrect concrete program $\mathcal{P}$ annotated with assertions, a cost function c, and a repair budget δ, the goal of cost-aware program repair is to compute $\widehat{\mathcal{P}}$ such that:

1. $\widehat{\mathcal{P}}$ is partially correct, and,
2. there exists $\mathbb{R}$:
   (a) $\widehat{\mathcal{P}}$ is some $\mathbb{R}$-update of $\mathcal{P}$, and
   (b) $Cost_c(\mathbb{R}) \leq \delta$.

If there exists such a $\widehat{\mathcal{P}}$, we say $\widehat{\mathcal{P}}$ is a *$(\mathcal{U}, c, \delta)$-repair of $\mathcal{P}$*.

Notice that without $\mathcal{U}$, c and δ, there would be no restriction on the *relation* of the repaired program $\widehat{\mathcal{P}}$ to the incorrect program $\mathcal{P}$; in particular, $\widehat{\mathcal{P}}$ could be any correct program constructed from scratch, without using $\mathcal{P}$ at all. Insightful choices for these can help prune the search space for repaired programs and help generate a repaired program *similar* to what the programmer may have in mind.

3.2 Solution Overview

We present a predicate abstraction-based framework for cost-aware program repair. Thus, in addition to $\mathcal{P}$, c, δ, our framework requires (a) a Boolean program $\mathcal{B}$ such that $\mathcal{B}$ is obtained from $\mathcal{P}$ via iterative predicate abstraction-refinement and $\mathcal{B}$ exhibits a non-spurious counterexample path, and (b) the corresponding function γ that maps Boolean variables to their respective predicates. The computation of a suitable repaired program $\widehat{\mathcal{P}}$ involves two main steps:

1. Cost-aware repair of $\mathcal{B}$ to obtain $\widehat{\mathcal{B}}$, and
2. Concretization of $\widehat{\mathcal{B}}$ to obtain $\widehat{\mathcal{P}}$.

In the following sections, we describe these two steps in detail.

4 Cost-Aware Repair of Boolean Programs

Our solution to cost-aware repair of a Boolean program $\mathcal{B}$ relies on automatically computing *inductive assertions*, along with a suitable $\widehat{\mathcal{B}}$, that together certify the partial correctness of $\widehat{\mathcal{B}}$. In what follows, we explain our adaptation of the method of inductive assertions [11,19] for cost-aware program repair.

Cut-set. Let N be the set of nodes in $\mathcal{G}(\mathcal{B})$, the transition graph representation of $\mathcal{B}$. We define a cut-set $\Lambda \subseteq N$ as a set of nodes, called *cut-points*, such that for every $i \in [0, t]$: (a) $entry_i, exit_i \in \Lambda$, (b) for every edge (ℓ, ς, ℓ') in $\mathcal{G}_i$ where $stmt(\ell)$ is a procedure `call` or an `assert` statement, $\ell, \ell' \in \Lambda$, and (c) every cycle in $\mathcal{G}$ contains at least one node in Λ. A pair of cut-points ℓ, ℓ' is said to be *adjacent* if every path from ℓ to ℓ' contains no other cut-point. A *verification path* is any path from a cut-point to an adjacent cut-point.
Example: The set $\{\ell_1, \ell_2, \ell_7, exit\}$ (shaded blue) in Fig. 1c is a valid cut-set for Boolean program $\mathcal{B}$ in Fig. 1b. The verification paths in $\mathcal{G}(\mathcal{B})$ corresponding to this cut-set are: (1) $\ell_1 \xrightarrow{\texttt{assume}\,(b_2)} \ell_2$, (2) $\ell_2 \xrightarrow{\texttt{assume}\,(\texttt{T})} \ell_3 \xrightarrow{b_0, b_1, b_2 := *, *, *} \ell_4 \rightarrow \ell_2$, (3) $\ell_2 \xrightarrow{\texttt{assume}\,(\texttt{T})} \ell_0 \rightarrow \ell_7$, (4) $\ell_1 \xrightarrow{\texttt{assume}\,(\neg b_2)} \ell_5 \xrightarrow{\texttt{assume}\,(\neg b_1)} \ell_7$, (5) $\ell_1 \xrightarrow{\texttt{assume}\,(\neg b_2)} \ell_5 \xrightarrow{\texttt{assume}\,(b_1)} \ell_6 \xrightarrow{b_1, b_1, b_2 := *, *, *} \ell_7$ and (6) $\ell_7 \rightarrow exit$.

Inductive assertions. We denote an inductive assertion associated with cut-point ℓ in Λ by $\mathcal{I}_\ell$. Informally, an inductive assertion $\mathcal{I}_\ell$ has the property that whenever control reaches ℓ in any program execution, $\mathcal{I}_\ell$ must be `true` for the current values of the variables in scope. For Boolean program $\mathcal{B}$, $\mathcal{I}_\ell$ is a Boolean formula over $V_s[\ell]$, where $V_s[\ell]$ denotes an ℓth copy of the subset V_s of the program variables, with $V_s = GV \cup formal(\ell)$ if $\ell \in \{exit_1, \ldots, exit_t\}$, and $V_s = inscope(\ell)$ otherwise. Thus, except for the `main` procedure, the inductive assertions at the exit nodes of all procedures exclude the local variables declared in the procedure. Let $\mathcal{I}_\Lambda$ denote the set of inductive assertions associated with all the cut-points in Λ.

Verification Conditions. A popular approach to verification of sequential, imperative programs is to compute $\mathcal{I}_\Lambda$ such that $\mathcal{I}_\Lambda$ satisfies a set of constraints called *verification conditions*. Let π be a verification path in $\mathcal{G}_i$, from cut-point ℓ to adjacent cut-point ℓ'. The verification condition corresponding to π, denoted $VC(\pi)$, is essentially the Hoare triple $\langle \mathcal{I}_\ell \rangle\, stmt(\pi)\, \langle \mathcal{I}_{\ell'} \rangle$, where $stmt(\pi)$ is the sequence of statements labeling π. When $\mathcal{I}_\ell$, $\mathcal{I}_{\ell'}$ are *unknown*, $VC(\pi)$ can be seen as a constraint encoding all possible solutions for $\mathcal{I}_\ell$, $\mathcal{I}_{\ell'}$ such that: every program execution along path π, starting from a set of variable valuations satisfying $\mathcal{I}_\ell$, terminates in a set of variable valuations satisfying $\mathcal{I}_{\ell'}$.

Program Verification Using the Inductive Assertions Method. Given $\mathcal{B}$ annotated with assertions, and a set Λ of cut-points, $\mathcal{B}$ is partially correct if one can compute a set $\mathcal{I}_\Lambda$ of inductive assertions such that: for every verification path π between every pair ℓ, ℓ' of adjacent cut-points in $\mathcal{G}(\mathcal{B})$, $VC(\pi)$ is valid.
Example: It is not possible to compute such a set of inductive assertions for the Boolean program in Fig. 1b as the program is incorrect.

Cost-aware Repairability Conditions. Let $\mathcal{C} : N \rightarrow \mathbb{N}$ be a function mapping nodes in $\mathcal{G}$ to costs. We find it convenient to use $\mathcal{C}_\ell$ to denote the value $\mathcal{C}(\ell)$ at node/location ℓ. We set $\mathcal{I}_{entry_0} = \texttt{true}$ and $\mathcal{C}_\ell = 0$ if $\ell \in \{entry_0, \ldots, entry_t\}$.

Informally, $\mathcal{C}_\ell$ with $\ell \in N_i$ can be seen as recording the cumulative cost of applying a sequence of update schemas to the statements in procedure F_i from $entry_i$ to ℓ. Thus, for a specific update function $\mathbb{R}$ with cost function c, $\mathcal{C}_{exit_0}$ records the total cost $Cost_c(\mathbb{R})$ of performing an $\mathbb{R}$-update of the program. Given a verification path π in $\mathcal{G}_i$, from cut-point ℓ to adjacent cut-point ℓ', we extend the definition of $VC(\pi)$ to define the cost-aware repairability condition corresponding to π, denoted $CRC(\pi)$. $CRC(\pi)$ can be seen as a constraint encoding all possible solutions for inductive assertions $\mathcal{I}_\ell$, $\mathcal{I}_{\ell'}$ and update functions $\mathbb{R}$, along with associated functions $\mathcal{C}$, such that: every program execution that proceeds along path π via statements modified by applying the update schemas in $\mathbb{R}$, starting from a set of variable valuations satisfying $\mathcal{I}_\ell$, terminates in a set of variable valuations satisfying $\mathcal{I}_{\ell'}$, for all nondeterministic choices that the program might make along π.

Before we proceed, note that $\mathcal{I}_\ell$ is a Boolean formula over $V_s[\ell]$, where for all locations $\lambda \neq \ell'$ in verification path π from ℓ to ℓ', $V_s = inscope(\lambda)$. In what follows, the notation $[\![u]\!](stmt(\lambda))$ represents the class of statements that may be obtained by applying update schema u on $stmt(\lambda)$, and is defined for our permissible update schemas in Fig. 2. Here, f, f_1, f_2 etc. denote *unknown* Boolean expressions[3], over the variables in $inscope(\lambda)$. Note that the update schema `assign` $\mapsto$ `assign`, modifies *any* assignment statement, to one that assigns unknown Boolean expressions to *all* variables in V_s.

u	$[\![u]\!](stmt(\lambda))$
id	$stmt(\lambda)$
`assign` $\mapsto$ `skip`	`skip`
`assume` $\mapsto$ `skip`	`skip`
`call` $\mapsto$ `skip`	`skip`
`assign` $\mapsto$ `assign`	$b_1, \ldots, b_{\lvert V_s \rvert} := f_1, \ldots, f_{\lvert V_s \rvert}$
`assume` $\mapsto$ `assume`	`assume` f
`call` $\mapsto$ `call`	`call` $F_j(f_1, \ldots, f_k)$, where $stmt(\lambda)$: `call` $F_j(e_1, \ldots, e_k)$

Fig. 2. Definition of $[\![u]\!](stmt(\lambda))$

We now define $CRC(\pi)$. While there are three cases to consider, due to lack of space, we only define $CRC(\pi)$ when $stmt(\pi)$ does not contain a procedure `call` or `assert` statement. We refer the reader to [23] for the definitions of $CRC(\pi)$ when $stmt(\pi)$ contains a procedure `call` and when $stmt(\pi)$ contains an `assert` statement.

Let $\mathcal{A}_\lambda$ denote a Boolean formula/assertion associated with location λ in π. $CRC(\pi)$ is given by the (conjunction of the) following set of constraints:

[3] To keep our exposition simple, we assume that these unknown Boolean expressions are deterministic. However, in our prototype tool (see Sec. 6), we have the ability to compute modified statements with nondeterministic expressions such as $*$ or `choose`(f_1, f_2).

$$\mathcal{A}_\ell = \mathcal{I}_\ell$$
$$\mathcal{A}_{\ell'} \Rightarrow \mathcal{I}_{\ell'} \tag{2}$$
$$\bigwedge_{\ell \preceq \lambda \prec \ell'} \bigwedge_{u \in \mathcal{U}_{stmt(\lambda)}} \mathbb{R}(\lambda) = u \;\Rightarrow \mathcal{C}_{\lambda'} = \mathcal{C}_\lambda + c(u,\lambda) \;\wedge$$
$$\mathcal{A}_{\lambda'} = sp([\![u]\!](stmt(\lambda)), \mathcal{A}_\lambda).$$

In the above, $\prec$ denotes the natural ordering over the sequence of locations in π with λ, λ' being consecutive locations. The notation $\mathcal{U}_{stmt(\lambda)} \subseteq \mathcal{U}$ denotes the set of all update schemas in $\mathcal{U}$ which may be applied to $stmt(\lambda)$. The notation $sp([\![u]\!](stmt(\lambda)), \mathcal{A}_\lambda)$ denotes the strongest postcondition of the assertion $\mathcal{A}_\lambda$ over the class of statements $[\![u]\!](stmt(\lambda))$. We define this strongest postcondition using multiple variable copies - a copy $V_s[\lambda]$ for each location λ in π. Let us assume that $\mathcal{A}_\lambda$ is a Boolean formula of the form[4]:

$$\mathcal{A}_\lambda = \rho[\ell, \grave{\lambda}] \wedge \bigwedge_{b \in V_s} b[\lambda] = \xi[\grave{\lambda}], \tag{3}$$

where $\grave{\lambda}$, λ are consecutive locations in π, $\rho[\ell, \grave{\lambda}]$ is a Boolean expression over all copies $V_s[\mu]$, $\ell \preceq \mu \preceq \grave{\lambda}$, representing the path condition imposed by the program control-flow, and $\xi[\grave{\lambda}]$ is a Boolean expression over $V_s[\grave{\lambda}]$ representing the λth copy of each variable b in terms of the $\grave{\lambda}^{th}$ copy of the program variables. Note that $\mathcal{A}_\ell = \mathcal{I}_\ell$ is of the form $\rho[\ell]$.

$[\![u]\!](stmt(\lambda))$	$sp([\![u]\!](stmt(\lambda)), \mathcal{A}_\lambda)$
`skip` `goto`	$\rho[\ell, \grave{\lambda}] \wedge \bigwedge_{b \in V_s} b[\lambda'] = b[\lambda]$
`assume` g	$g[\lambda] \wedge \rho[\ell, \grave{\lambda}] \wedge \bigwedge_{b \in V_s} b[\lambda'] = b[\lambda]$
`assume` f	$f[\lambda] \wedge \rho[\ell, \grave{\lambda}] \wedge \bigwedge_{b \in V_s} b[\lambda'] = b[\lambda]$
$b_1, \ldots, b_m := e_1, \ldots, e_m$	$\rho[\ell, \grave{\lambda}] \wedge \bigwedge_{b_i \in V_s, i \in [1,m]} b_i[\lambda'] = e_i[\lambda] \wedge$ $\bigwedge_{b_i \in V_s, i \notin [1,m]} b_i[\lambda'] = b_i[\lambda]$
$b_1, \ldots, b_{\lvert V_s \rvert} := f_1, \ldots, f_{\lvert V_s \rvert}$	$\rho[\ell, \grave{\lambda}] \wedge \bigwedge_{b_i \in V_s} b_i[\lambda'] = f_i[\lambda]$

Fig. 3. Definition of $sp([\![u]\!](stmt(\lambda)), \mathcal{A}_\lambda)$

Given the above $\mathcal{A}_\lambda$, $sp([\![u]\!](stmt(\lambda)), \mathcal{A}_\lambda)$ is defined in Fig. 3. Observe that $sp([\![u]\!](stmt(\lambda)), \mathcal{A}_\lambda)$ is a Boolean formula of the same form as (3), over variable

[4] In general, $\mathcal{A}_\lambda$ is a disjunction over Boolean formulas of this form; $sp([\![u]\!](stmt(\lambda)), \mathcal{A}_\lambda)$ can then be obtained by computing a disjunction over the strongest postconditions obtained by propagating each such Boolean formula through $[\![u]\!](stmt(\lambda))$ using the rules in Fig. 3.

copies from $V_s[\ell]$ to $V_s[\lambda']$. For the entries $\texttt{assume}\, g$ and $b_1, \ldots, b_m := e_1, \ldots, e_m$, the expressions $g, e_1, \ldots, e_m$ are *known* beforehand (these entries correspond to $u = id$). For the entries $\texttt{assume}\, f$ and $b_1, \ldots, b_{|V_s|} := f_1, \ldots, f_{|V_s|}$, the expressions $f, f_1, \ldots, f_{|V_s|}$ are *unknown* (these entries correspond to $u = \texttt{assume} \mapsto \texttt{assume}$ and $u = \texttt{assign} \mapsto \texttt{assign}$, respectively). Notation such as $f[\lambda]$ denotes that f is an unknown Boolean expression over $V_s[\lambda]$. For nondeterministic expressions in the RHS of an assignment statement $b_1, \ldots, b_m := e_1, \ldots, e_m$, the strongest postcondition is computed as the disjunction of the strongest postconditions over all possible assignment statements obtained by substituting each $*$ expression with either $\texttt{false}$ or $\texttt{true}$.

Thus, to summarize, the set of constraints in (2) encodes all $\mathcal{I}_\ell$, $\mathcal{C}_\ell$, $\mathcal{I}_{\ell'}$, $\mathcal{C}_{\ell'}$ and $\mathbb{R}$ such that: if $\mathbb{R}$ is applied to the sequence of statements $stmt(\pi)$ to get some modified sequence of statements, say $\widehat{stmt}(\pi)$, and program execution proceeds along $\widehat{stmt}(\pi)$, then $sp(\widehat{stmt}(\pi), \mathcal{I}_\ell) \Rightarrow \mathcal{I}_{\ell'}$, and $\mathcal{C}_{\ell'}$ equals the cumulative modification cost, counting up from $\mathcal{C}_\ell$.

Cost-aware Boolean Program Repair. Given a cut-set Λ of $\mathcal{G}(\mathcal{B})$, let Π_Λ be the set of all verification paths between every pair of adjacent cut-points in Λ. Consider the following formula:

$$\exists\, Unknown\; \forall\, Var: \;\; \mathcal{C}_{exit_0} \leq \delta \;\wedge \bigwedge_{\pi \in \Pi_\Lambda} CRC(\pi) \;\wedge\; AssumeConstraints \qquad (4)$$

where *Unknown* is the set of all unknowns and *Var* is the set of all Boolean program variables and their copies used in encoding each $CRC(\pi)$. The set of unknowns includes the set $\mathcal{I}_\Lambda$ of inductive assertions, update function $\mathbb{R}$, unknown expressions f, f_1 etc. associated with applications of update schemas in $\mathbb{R}$ and valuations at each program location of the cumulative-cost-recording function $\mathcal{C}$. Finally, *AssumeConstraints* ensures that any modifications to the guards of $\texttt{assume}$ statements corresponding to the same conditional statement are consistent. Thus, for every pair of *updated* $\texttt{assume}\,(f_1)$, $\texttt{assume}\,(f_2)$ statements labeling edges starting from the same node in the transition graph, the unknown functions f_1, f_2 are constrained to satisfy $f_1 = \neg f_2$.

If the above formula is $\texttt{true}$, then we can extract models for all the unknowns from the witness to the satisfiability of the formula: $\forall\, Var : \mathcal{C}_{exit_0} \leq \delta \wedge \bigwedge_{\pi \in \Pi_\Lambda} CRC(\pi) \wedge AssumeConstraints$. In particular, we can extract an $\mathbb{R}$ and the corresponding modified statements to yield a correct Boolean program $\widehat{\mathcal{B}}$. The following theorem states the soundness and completeness of the above algorithm for repairing Boolean programs for partial correctness (see [23] for the proof).

Theorem 41. *Given the set $\mathcal{U}$ specified in (1), and given an incorrect Boolean program $\mathcal{B}$ annotated with assertions, cost function c and repair budget δ,*

1. *if there exists a $(\mathcal{U}, c, \delta)$-repair of $\mathcal{B}$, the above method finds a $(\mathcal{U}, c, \delta)$-repair of $\mathcal{B}$,*
2. *if the above method finds a $\widehat{\mathcal{B}}$, then $\widehat{\mathcal{B}}$ is a $(\mathcal{U}, c, \delta)$-repair of $\mathcal{B}$.*

Example: For the Boolean program in Fig. 1b, our tool modifies two statements: (1) the guard for $stmt(\ell_1)$ is changed from $b2$ to $b0 \vee b1 \vee \neg b2$ and (2) the guard for $stmt(\ell_2)$ is changed from $*$ to $b0 \vee b1 \vee b2$.

5 Concretization

We now present the second step in our framework for computing a concrete repaired program $\widehat{\mathcal{P}}$. In what follows, we assume that we have already extracted models for $\widehat{\mathcal{B}}$ and $\mathcal{I}_\Lambda$.

Concretization of $\widehat{\mathcal{B}}$. This involves computing a mapping, denoted Γ, from each modified statement of $\widehat{\mathcal{B}}$ into a corresponding modified statement in the concrete program. We define Γ for each type of modified statement in $\widehat{\mathcal{B}}$. Let us fix our attention on a statement at location ℓ, with $V_s(\mathcal{B})$, $V_s(\mathcal{P})$ denoting the set of abstract, concrete program variables, respectively, whose scope includes ℓ. Let $r = |V_s(\mathcal{B})|$ and $q = |V_s(\mathcal{P})|$.

1. $\Gamma(\mathtt{skip}) = \mathtt{skip}$
2. $\Gamma(\mathtt{assume}\,(g)) = \mathtt{assume}\,(\gamma(g))$
3. $\Gamma(\mathtt{call}\ F_i(e_1, \ldots, e_k)) = \mathtt{call}\ F_i(\gamma(e_1), \ldots, \gamma(e_k))$
4. The definition of Γ for an assignment statement is non-trivial. In fact, in this case, Γ may be the empty set, or may contain multiple concrete assignment statements.
   We say that an assignment statement $b_1, \ldots, b_r := e_1, \ldots, e_r$ in $\mathcal{B}$ is *concretizable* if one can compute expressions $f_1, \ldots, f_q$ over $V_s(\mathcal{P})$, of the same type as the concrete program variables $v_1, \ldots, v_q$ in $V_s(\mathcal{P})$, respectively, such that a certain constraint is valid. To be precise, $b_1, \ldots, b_r := e_1, \ldots, e_r$ in $\mathcal{B}$ is concretizable if the following formula is `true`:
   $$\exists f_1, \ldots, f_q\ \forall v_1, \ldots, v_q : \bigwedge_{j=1}^{r} \gamma(b_j)[v_1/f_1, \ldots, v_q/f_q] \ = \ \gamma(e_j) \qquad (5)$$
   Each quantifier-free constraint $\gamma(b_j)[v_1/f_1, \ldots, v_q/f_q] \ = \ \gamma(e_j)$ above essentially expresses the concretization of the abstract assignment $b_j = e_j$. The substitutions $v_1/f_1, \ldots, v_q/f_q$ reflect the *new* values of the concrete program variables after the concrete assignment $v_1, \ldots, v_q := f_1, \ldots, f_q$. If the above formula is `true`, we can extract models $expr_1, \ldots, expr_q$ for $f_1, \ldots, f_q$, respectively, from the witness to the satisfiability of the inner $\forall$-formula. We then say:
   $$v_1, \ldots, v_q := expr_1, \ldots, expr_q \ \in \ \Gamma(b_1, \ldots, b_r := e_1, \ldots, e_r).$$

Example: For our example in Fig. 1, the modified guards, $b0 \vee b1 \vee \neg b2$ and $b0 \vee b1 \vee b2$, in $stmt(\ell_1)$ and $stmt(\ell_2)$ of $\widehat{\mathcal{B}}$, respectively are concretized into `true` and $x \leq 1$, respectively using γ.

Template-based concretization of $\widehat{\mathcal{B}}$. Our framework/tool can also accept user-supplied templates, specifying the desired syntax of the expressions in concrete modified statements. The concretization of $\widehat{\mathcal{B}}$ is then guided by the given templates. This is another avenue for incorporating programmer expertise and intent into automatic program repair. Due to lack of space, we skip a detailed description and refer the interested reader to [23].

Concretization of inductive assertions. The concretization of each inductive assertion $\mathcal{I}_\ell \in \mathcal{I}_\Lambda$ is simply $\gamma(\mathcal{I}_\ell)$.

6 Experiments with a Prototype Tool

We have built a prototype tool for repairing Boolean programs. The tool accepts Boolean programs generated by the predicate abstraction tool SATABS (version 3.2) [8] from sequential C programs. In our experience, we found that for C programs with multiple procedures, SATABS generates (single procedure) Boolean programs with all procedure calls inlined within the calling procedure. Hence, we only perform intraprocedural analysis in this version of our tool. The set of update schemas handled currently is $\{id, \texttt{assign} \rightarrow \texttt{assign}, \texttt{assume} \rightarrow \texttt{assume}\}$; we do not handle statement deletions. We set the costs $c(\texttt{assign} \rightarrow \texttt{assign}, \ell)$ and $c(\texttt{assume} \rightarrow \texttt{assume}, \ell)$ to some large number for every location ℓ where we wish to disallow statement modifications, and to 1 for all other locations — we essentially search for a repaired program with at most δ modifications amongst candidate locations. We initialize the tool with $\delta = 1$. We also provide the tool with a cut-set of locations for its Boolean program input.

The tool automatically generates an SMT query corresponding to the inner $\forall$-formula in (4). When generating this repairability query, for update schemas involving expression modifications, we stipulate every deterministic Boolean expression g be modified into a (unknown) deterministic Boolean expression f (as described in Fig. 2), and every nondeterministic Boolean expression be modified into a (unknown) nondeterministic expression of the form $\texttt{choose}(f_1, f_2)$. The SMT query is then fed to the SMT-solver Z3 (version 4.3.1) [20]. The solver either declares the formula to be satisfiable, and provides models for all the unknowns, or declares the formula to be unsatisfiable. In the latter case, we can choose to increase the repair budget by 1, and repeat the process.

Once the solver provides models for all the unknowns, we can extract a repaired Boolean program automatically. Currently, the next step, concretization, is automated in part. For assignment statements, we manually formulate SMT queries corresponding to the inner $\forall$-formula in (5), and feed these queries to Z3. If the relevant queries are satisfiable, we can obtain a repaired C program. If the queries are unsatisfiable, we attempt template-based concretization using linear-arithmetic templates. In some experiments, we allowed ourselves a degree of flexibility in guiding the solver to choose the right template parameters.

In Fig. 4, we present some of the details of repairing a C program drawn from the NEC Laboratories Static Analysis Benchmarks [21]. After our tool automatically generated a repaired Boolean program for this example, we manually wrote

`int main() {`
`int` x, y;
`int` $a[10]$;
$\ell_1 : x := 1U$;
ℓ_2 : `while` $(x \leq 10U)$ {
$\ell_3 : \quad y := 11 - x$;
$\ell_4 : \quad$ `assert` $(y \geq 0 \wedge y < 10)$;
$\ell_5 : \quad a[y] := -1$;
$\ell_6 : \quad x := x + 1$;
}
}
	Boolean program vars/predicates:
	$\gamma(b_0) = y < 0, \gamma(b_1) = y < 10$
	Boolean program repair:
	Change $stmt(\ell_3)$ from
	$b_0, b_1 := *, *$ to $b_0, b_1 :=$ F, T
	Concrete program repair:
	Change $stmt(\ell_3)$ to $y := 10 - x$
	Inductive Assertions:
	They were all *true*

Fig. 4. Repairing program `necex14`

an SMT query corresponding to (5) to concretize the assignment statement at location ℓ_3, and obtained $y := 0$ as the repair for the concrete program. Unsatisfied by this repair, we formulated a template-based SMT query, restricting the RHS of $stmt(\ell_3)$ to the template $-x + c$, where c is unknown. The query was found to be satisfiable, and yielded $c = 10$. As shown in Fig. 4, all inductive assertions generated for this example were `true`.

In Table 1, we present the results of repairing some handmade examples (`handmade2` is the same example as in Fig. 1), and some benchmark programs from NEC Labs [21] and the 2014 Competition on Software Verification [9]. The complexity of the programs from [9] stems from nondeterministic assignments and function invocations within loops. All experiments were run on the same machine, an Intel Dual Core 2.13GHz Unix desktop with 4 GB of RAM.

We enumerate the time taken for each individual step involved in generating a repaired Boolean program. The columns labeled LoC($\mathcal{P}$) and LoC($\mathcal{B}$) enumerate the number of lines of code in the original C program and the Boolean program generated by SATABS, respectively. The column labeled $V(\mathcal{B})$ enumerates the number of variables in each Boolean program. The column $\mathcal{B}$-time enumerates the time taken by SATABS to generate each Boolean program, the column Que-time enumerates the time taken by our tool to generate each repairability query and the column Sol-time enumerates the time taken by Z3 to solve the query. The columns # `Asg` and # `Asm` count the number of `assign` → `assign` and `assume` → `assume` update schemas applied, respectively, to obtain the final correct program.

Notice that our implementation either produces a repaired program very quickly, or fails to do so in reasonable time whenever there is a significant increase in the number of Boolean variables, e.g. for `veris.c_NetBSD-libc__loop_true`. This is because the SMT solver might need to search over simultaneous nondeterministic assignments to all the Boolean variables for every assignment statement in $\mathcal{B}$ in order to solve the repairability query. For the last two programs, SATABS was the main bottleneck, with SATABS failing to generate a Boolean program with a non-spurious counterexample after 10 minutes; we experienced issues while using SATABS on programs with a lot of character manipulation.

We emphasize that when successful, our tool can repair a diverse set of errors in programs containing loops, multiple procedures and pointer and array variables. In our benchmarks, we were able to repair operators (e.g., an incorrect

Table 1. Experimental results

Name	LoC($\mathcal{P}$)	LoC($\mathcal{B}$)	$V(\mathcal{B})$	$\mathcal{B}$-time	Que-time	Sol-time	# Asg	# Asm
handmade1	6	58	1	0.180s	0.009s	0.012s	0	1
handmade2	16	53	3	0.304s	0.040s	0.076s	0	2
necex6	24	66	3	0.288s	0.004s	0.148s	1	0
necex14	13	60	2	0.212s	0.004s	0.032s	1	0
while_infinite_loop_1_true	5	33	1	0.196s	0.002s	0.008s	0	1
array_true	23	57	4	0.384s	0.004s	0.116s	1	1
n.c11_true	27	50	2	0.204s	0.002s	0.024s	1	0
terminator_03_true	22	38	2	0.224s	0.004s	0.036s	1	1
trex03_true	23	58	3	0.224s	0.036s	0.540s	1	1
trex04_true	29	36	1	0.200s	0.004s	0.004s	2	0
veris.c_NetBSD − libc__loop_true	30	144	23	3.856s	-	-	-	-
vogal_true	41	-	-	$> 10m$	-	-	-	-
count_up_down_true	18	-	-	$> 10m$	-	-	-	-

conditional statement $x < 0$ was repaired to $x > 0$) and array indices (e.g., an incorrect assignment $x{:=}a[0]$ was repaired to $x{:=}a[j]$), and modify constants into program variables (e.g. an incorrect assignment $x{:=}0$ was repaired to $x{:=}d$, where d was a program variable). Also, note that for many benchmarks, the repaired programs required multiple statement modifications.

7 Discussion

The framework described in this paper computes a repaired concrete program in two separate steps: computation of a repaired Boolean program $\widehat{\mathcal{B}}$, followed by its concretization. The separation of these two steps is not necessary and is potentially sub-optimal. It may not be possible to concretize a repaired Boolean program computed in the first step, while there may exist some other concretizable $\widehat{\mathcal{B}}$. The solution is to directly search for $\widehat{\mathcal{B}}$ such that all modified statements of $\widehat{\mathcal{B}}$ are concretizable. This can be done by combining the constraints presented in Sec. 5 with the one in (4). As noted in Sec. 1, we can target total correctness of the repaired programs by associating ranking functions along with inductive assertions with each cut-point in Λ, and including termination conditions as part of the constraints. Finally, we wish to explore ways to ensure that the repaired program does not unnecessarily restrict correct behaviors of the original program. We conjecture that this can be done by computing the weakest possible set of inductive assertions and a least restrictive $\widehat{\mathcal{B}}$.

Acknowledgements. The authors would like to thank Gérard Basler, Daniel Kröning and Georg Weissenbacher for their help with SATABS.

References

1. Arcuri, A.: On the Automation of Fixing Software Bugs. In: International Conference on Software Engineering (ICSE), pp. 1003–1006. ACM (2008)
2. Ball, T., Bounimova, E., Kumar, R., Levin, V.: SLAM2: Static Driver Verification with under 4% False Alarms. In: Formal Methods in Computer Aided Design (FMCAD), pp. 35–42 (2010)

3. Ball, T., Naik, M., Rajamani, S.K.: From Symptom to Cause: Localizing Errors in Counterexample Traces. In: Principles of Programming Languages (POPL), pp. 97–105. ACM (2003)
4. Ball, T., Rajamani, S.K.: Boolean Programs: A Model and Process for Software Analysis. Tech. Rep. 2000-14, MSR (2000)
5. Ball, T., Rajamani, S.K.: Automatically Validating Temporal Safety Properties of Interfaces. In: Dwyer, M.B. (ed.) SPIN 2001. LNCS, vol. 2057, pp. 103–122. Springer, Heidelberg (2001)
6. Bloem, R., Chatterjee, K., Henzinger, T.A., Jobstmann, B.: Better Quality in Synthesis through Quantitative Objectives. In: Bouajjani, A., Maler, O. (eds.) CAV 2009. LNCS, vol. 5643, pp. 140–156. Springer, Heidelberg (2009)
7. Chandra, S., Torlak, E., Barman, S., Bodik, R.: Angelic Debugging. In: International Conference on Software Engineering (ICSE), pp. 121–130. ACM (2011)
8. Clarke, E., Kroning, D., Sharygina, N., Yorav, K.: SATABS: SAT-based Predicate Abstraction for ANSI-C. In: Halbwachs, N., Zuck, L.D. (eds.) TACAS 2005. LNCS, vol. 3440, pp. 570–574. Springer, Heidelberg (2005)
9. Competition on Software Verification (SV-COMP): Loops Benchmarks (2014), `http://sv-comp.sosy-lab.org/2014/benchmarks.php`
10. Debroy, V., Wong, W.E.: Using Mutation to Automatically Suggest Fixes for Faulty Programs. In: Software Testing, Verification and Validation (ICST), pp. 65–74 (2010)
11. Floyd, R.W.: Assigning Meanings to Programs. In: Mathematical Aspects of Computer Science, pp. 19–32. American Mathematical Society (1967)
12. Goues, C.L., Dewey-Vogt, M., Forrest, S., Weimer, W.: A Systematic Study of Automated Program Repair: Fixing 55 out of 105 Bugs for $8 Each. In: International Conference on Software Engineering (ICSE), pp. 3–13. IEEE Press (2012)
13. Graf, S., Saïdi, H.: Construction of Abstract State Graphs with PVS. In: Grumberg, O. (ed.) CAV 1997. LNCS, vol. 1254, pp. 72–83. Springer, Heidelberg (1997)
14. Griesmayer, A., Bloem, R., Cook, B.: Repair of Boolean Programs with an Application to C. In: Ball, T., Jones, R.B. (eds.) CAV 2006. LNCS, vol. 4144, pp. 358–371. Springer, Heidelberg (2006)
15. Jobstmann, B., Griesmayer, A., Bloem, R.: Program Repair as a Game. In: Etessami, K., Rajamani, S.K. (eds.) CAV 2005. LNCS, vol. 3576, pp. 226–238. Springer, Heidelberg (2005)
16. Jose, M., Majumdar, R.: Cause Clue Clauses: Error Localization using Maximum Satisfiability. In: Programming Language Design and Implementation (PLDI), pp. 437–446. ACM (2011)
17. Könighofer, R., Bloem, R.: Automated Error Localization and Correction for Imperative Programs. In: Formal Methods in Computer Aided Design (FMCAD), pp. 91–100 (2011)
18. Logozzo, F., Ball, T.: Modular and Verified Automatic Program Repair. In: Object Oriented Programming Systems Languages and Applications (OOPSLA), pp. 133–146. ACM (2012)
19. Manna, Z.: Introduction to Mathematical Theory of Computation. McGraw-Hill, Inc. (1974)
20. de Moura, L., Bjørner, N.S.: Z3: An Efficient SMT Solver. In: Ramakrishnan, C.R., Rehof, J. (eds.) TACAS 2008. LNCS, vol. 4963, pp. 337–340. Springer, Heidelberg (2008)
21. NEC: NECLA Static Analysis Benchmarks, `http://www.nec-labs.com/research/system/systems_SAV-website/benchmarks.php`

22. Samanta, R., Deshmukh, J.V., Emerson, E.A.: Automatic Generation of Local Repairs for Boolean Programs. In: Formal Methods in Computer Aided Design (FMCAD), pp. 1–10 (2008)
23. Samanta, R., Olivo, O., Emerson, E.A.: Cost-Aware Automatic Program Repair. CoRR abs/1307.7281 (2013)
24. Singh, R., Gulwani, S., Solar-Lezama, A.: Automatic Feedback Generation for Introductory Programming Assignments. In: Programming Language Design and Implementation, PLDI (2013)
25. Singh, R., Solar-Lezma, A.: Synthesizing Data-Structure Manipulations from Storyboards. In: Foundations of Software Engineering (FSE), pp. 289–299 (2011)
26. Solar-Lezama, A., Rabbah, R., Bodik, R., Ebcioglu, K.: Programming by Sketching for Bit-streaming Programs. In: Programming Language Design and Implementation (PLDI), pp. 281–294. ACM (2005)
27. Solar-Lezama, A., Tancau, L., Bodik, R., Seshia, S., Saraswat, V.: Combinatorial Sketching for Finite Programs. In: Architectural Support for Programming Languages and Operating Systems (ASPLOS), pp. 404–415. ACM (2006)
28. Srivastava, S., Gulwani, S., Foster, J.S.: From Program Verification to Program Synthesis. In: Principles of Programming Languages (POPL), pp. 313–326. ACM (2010)
29. Wei, Y., Pei, Y., Furia, C.A., Silva, L.S., Buchholz, S., Meyer, B., Zeller, A.: Automated Fixing of Programs with Contracts. In: International Symposium on Software Testing and Analysis (ISSTA), pp. 61–72. ACM (2010)
30. Nokhbeh Zaeem, R., Gopinath, D., Khurshid, S., McKinley, K.S.: History-Aware Data Structure Repair using SAT. In: Flanagan, C., König, B. (eds.) TACAS 2012. LNCS, vol. 7214, pp. 2–17. Springer, Heidelberg (2012)
31. Zeller, A., Hilebrandt, R.: Simplifying and Isolating Failure-Inducing Input. IEEE Trans. Softw. Eng. 28(2), 183–200 (2002)

An Abstract Domain Combinator for Separately Conjoining Memory Abstractions*

Antoine Toubhans[1], Bor-Yuh Evan Chang[2], and Xavier Rival[1]

[1] INRIA, ENS, CNRS, Paris, France
[2] University of Colorado, Boulder, Colorado, USA
{toubhans,rival}@di.ens.fr, bec@cs.colorado.edu

Abstract. The breadth and depth of heap properties that can be inferred by the union of today's shape analyses is quite astounding. Yet, achieving scalability while supporting a wide range of complex data structures in a generic way remains a long-standing challenge. In this paper, we propose a way to side-step this issue by defining a generic abstract domain combinator for combining memory abstractions on disjoint regions. In essence, our abstract domain construction is to the separating conjunction in separation logic as the reduced product construction is to classical, non-separating conjunction. This approach eases the design of the analysis as memory abstract domains can be re-used by applying our separating conjunction domain combinator. And more importantly, this combinator enables an analysis designer to easily create a combined domain that applies computationally-expensive abstract domains only where it is required.

1 Introduction

While there exist static analyses for the most common data structures such as lists, trees, or even overlaid lists and trees [10,4,14,11], it is uncommon for static analyses to efficiently support all of these simultaneously. For instance, consider the code fragment of Fig. 1 that simultaneously manipulates linked lists and trees, iteratively picking some value from the list and searching for it in the tree. Although verification of the memory safety and data structures preservation is possible with several tools (e.g. [18,20]), this will not take into account most efficient data-structure-specific algorithms (e.g. analysis for linked lists presented in [15] achieves polynomial complexity transfer functions). On the other hand, using only a linked-list-specific efficient analysis will lead to a dramatic loss of precision, as tree features are not supported. The general problem is much broader than just lists and trees: in real-world programs, it is common to find not only lists, trees, and overlaid lists and trees, but also buffers, arrays, and other complex heap structures, and therefore static analysis is either imprecise or inefficient.

Instead of using one monolithic analysis, we propose to combine off-the-shelf data-structure-specific analyses that reason about *disjoint* regions of memory. The approach presented in this paper is in the context of abstract interpretation [6]. Therefore, combining analyses is realized by a *separating combination* of memory abstract domains

* The research leading to these results has received funding from the European Research Council under the FP7 grant agreement 278673, Project MemCAD and the United States National Science Foundation under grant CCF-1055066.

M. Müller-Olm and H. Seidl (Eds.): SAS 2014, LNCS 8723, pp. 285–301, 2014.

```
01 : int *x = NULL;   10 : while( ... ){          24 :    r = searchTree(*x, t);
02 : List *h, *e;     11 :    x = malloc(sizeof(int));   25 :    // do something on r
03 : Tree *t, *r;     12 :    *x = e -> data            ...
    ...                   ...                         30 : }
```

Fig. 1. A code fragment manipulating simultaneously several data structures

called the *sub-domains*. Combined memory abstract domains describe each disjoint memory region using one of its sub-domains. We show how *separation* (i.e. the fact that data structures do not share cell blocks) can be used to decompose a heterogeneous memory into several sub-instances that can be handled independently.

This construction increases and eases the abstract domain design capabilities. Combined abstract domains are more extensible and flexible, as a sub-domain can be individually added, removed, strengthened, or weakened in the combination. Moreover, it allows paying the cost of complex algorithms that usually come with expressive abstract domains only in the memory region that really requires it. On the other hand, simpler light-weight abstract domains can be used to represent a significant part of the memory that does not contain complex structures.

Such a combination poses several challenges. Because, even if disjoint in memory, concrete data structures can still be correlated (e.g. have shared values or pointers to each other), we need to carefully abstract the *interface* between memory regions in the combination. Maintaining a right partitioning (i.e. which memory region should be abstracted in which sub-domain) during the analysis process is also challenging. For example, when analyzing a memory allocation, the analysis decides which sub-domains should handle it. Even though any choice is sound, there are sub-domains more relevant than others in many cases. This approach has been successfully applied to numerical domains and made it possible to obtain scalable and precise analyses [3] and reusable abstract domains [13]. Our proposal brings, in a way, the same improvement to memory abstract domains. We justify this statement by the following contributions:

- we introduce (Section 2) and formalize (Section 3.2) the separating combination functor that takes two memory abstract sub-domains matching the signature given in Section 3.1 and returns a new combined memory abstract domain;
- we define an abstract domain for the interface between memory regions (Section 3.2) that carefully describes correlations between memory regions;
- we set up the abstract transfer functions (Section 4) that compose abstract transfer functions of sub-domains and extract information from an abstract interface;
- we give a heuristic for the decision of which sub-domain should handle a newly allocated block (Section 4.1);
- we evaluate the separating combination functor by an implementation in the Mem-CAD analyzer (Section 5) and empirically verify that combined analyses remain efficient and precise while offering greater flexibility.

2   Overview

In this section, we provide an informal description of our combined analysis (formal details are presented in Sections 3 and 4). We present an abstract interpretation [6] based analysis of the code fragment of Fig. 1, using a combination of memory abstract domains. The analysis goal is to prove memory safety and data structure (lists and trees) preservation. Fig. 2 shows two abstract memories computed during the analysis.

An Abstraction of the Memory Using Several Memory Abstract Domains. The program manipulates a memory that can be decomposed in three disjoint regions (i) the list region (denoted Ⓛ) containing linked-list nodes (ii) the tree region (denoted Ⓣ) containing tree nodes (iii) the region accounting for the rest of the memory that contains only *bounded* data structures (denoted Ⓑ). This naturally leads to the choice of a separating combination of three memory abstract sub-domains $\mathbb{M}_l^\sharp$, $\mathbb{M}_t^\sharp$, $\mathbb{M}_b^\sharp$ that will reason respectively about region Ⓛ, Ⓣ and Ⓑ.

Fig. 2(a) shows the combined abstract memory computed by the analysis before line 11. Each thick black bordered boxes (labeled Ⓑ, Ⓛ and Ⓣ) contains an element $m_b^\sharp \in \mathbb{M}_b^\sharp$, $m_l^\sharp \in \mathbb{M}_l^\sharp$ and $m_t^\sharp \in \mathbb{M}_t^\sharp$ called *abstract sub-memories*. Greek letters that appear in the sub-memories are called the *symbolic names* and are used by sub-domains to internally represent concrete values and heap addresses. The combined abstract memory represents a set of memories where variable `h` (resp. `e`) points to the head (resp. the last element) of a linked list, variable `t` points to the root of a tree, variable `x` is the null pointer and content of variable `r` can be any concrete value.

Describing the interface between memory regions is crucial for precision. In particular, the combined abstract memory should account for (i) pointers from region Ⓑ to regions Ⓛ and Ⓣ and (ii) sharing of values between cells of different memory regions such as value `v` in the last list node and the left tree node from the tree root. The *interface abstract domain* $\mathbb{I}^\sharp$ (Section 3.2) achieves this by maintaining a set of equalities between symbolic names of different abstract sub-memories. An equality between two symbolic names simply means that they represent the *same* concrete value. For instance, pointer `h` crossing the memory regions Ⓑ and Ⓛ is represented by (i) β_0 representing the content of cell `h` in the $m_b^\sharp$, (ii) λ_0 representing the address of the head of the list in the $m_l^\sharp$, and (iii) equality $\beta_0 = \lambda_0$ in the abstract interface. Thus, this combined abstract memory is a quadruple made of three abstract sub-memories $m_b^\sharp \in \mathbb{M}_b^\sharp$, $m_l^\sharp \in \mathbb{M}_l^\sharp$ and $m_t^\sharp \in \mathbb{M}_t^\sharp$ and an abstract interface $i^\sharp \in \mathbb{I}^\sharp$. In the two combined abstract memories shown in Fig. 2, abstract sub-memories are represented in gray inside the thick black boxes whereas dark blue edges and values depict the abstract interface.

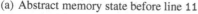

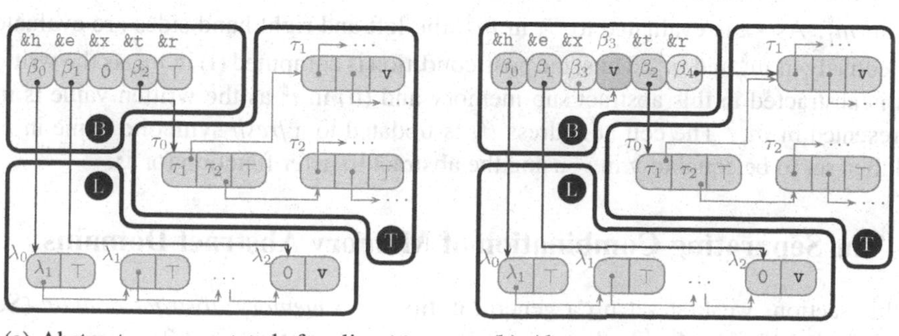

(a) Abstract memory state before line 11 (b) Abstract memory state after line 24

Fig. 2. Two combined abstract memories inferred during the analysis

Combined Analysis. The analysis automatically derives the post-condition shown in Fig. 2(b) from the pre-condition shown in Fig. 2(a) by composing abstract transfer functions for program statements between line 11 and 24. In the following, we demonstrate the key features of the combination of memory abstract domains by analyzing the two program statements at line 11 and 12. In particular, the assignment at line 11 involves a memory allocation but remains quite simple compared to the assignment at line 12 that requires post-condition computations to be distributed *across* sub-memories using the abstract interface. The first step when analyzing an assignment consists in *evaluating* its left and right hand-sides, that is, finding symbolic names representing the address of the updated cell and the written value (Section 4.2).

The right hand side of the assignment at line 11 contains a memory allocation instruction, hence the analysis should decide which sub-domain is the most relevant for handling it. Indeed, even though any choice is sound for the analysis, a bad decision could lead to a loss in precision or in efficiency. While the three sub-domains could precisely handle the memory allocation, $\mathbb{M}^\sharp_b$ is expected to be more efficient for handling *bounded* data structures. Because of the type passed to **malloc**, the new cell will likely never be *summarized* as part of a list or a tree, $m^\sharp_b$ should therefore handle the memory allocation. While not complete (C types cannot fully describe the programmer intended data structure), we find that this simple heuristic works well in practice. In Fig. 2(b), this sub-memory contains a new cell at abstract address β_3 (red background highlights created cells). The right hand side is evaluated to β_3 and evaluation of the left hand side is trivial and provides a symbolic name that is in $m^\sharp_b$ so that both are evaluated in the *same* sub-memory. Therefore and thanks to the local reasoning principle, the post-condition can be computed *only* for abstract sub-memory $m^\sharp_b$, using the sound abstract transfer function provided by $\mathbb{M}^\sharp_b$. In Fig. 2(b), the cell that correspond to x has been updated to β_3 (green background highlights updated cells).

Computing an abstract post-condition of the assignment at line 12 exhibits two main issues. First, the evaluation of its right hand side *crosses* sub-memories, requiring a mechanism for *extracting* information from the interface $i^\sharp$. Second, the left and right hand sides are not evaluated in the same sub-memories. Thus, handling the assignment requires *abstract transfer functions* for $\mathbb{I}^\sharp$. The right hand side is evaluated iteratively over its syntax: (i) the content of cell e is evaluated to β_1, which cannot be resolved as an address of a cell in $m^\sharp_b$, (ii) equality $\beta_1 = \lambda_2$ is *extracted* from $i^\sharp$ that allows the resolution to continue in $m^\sharp_l$, and (iii) the content of abstract address λ_2 at field <u>data</u> is v in $m^\sharp_l$. As *x is evaluated to β_3 in $m^\sharp_b$, the left and right hand sides are evaluated respectively in $m^\sharp_b$ and $m^\sharp_l$. Thus, the post-condition is computed (i) in $m^\sharp_b$ as the written cell is abstracted in this abstract sub-memory and (ii) in $i^\sharp$ as the written value is not represented in $m^\sharp_b$. The cell at address β_3 is updated to a *fresh* symbolic name in $m^\sharp_b$ and then set to be equal to v in $i^\sharp$ using the abstract transfer function for $\mathbb{I}^\sharp$.

3 The Separating Combination of Memory Abstract Domains

In this section, we first set up a general notion of a *memory abstract domain* (Section 3.1). before introducing the *separating combination* (Section 3.2). A memory abstract domain $\mathbb{M}^\sharp$ provides a representation for sets of concrete memories. Intuitively,

$$m_b^\sharp = \alpha_0^a \mapsto \{\underline{0} : \beta_0^c\} \ast \alpha_1^a \mapsto \{\underline{0} : \beta_1^c\} \ast \alpha_2^a \mapsto \{\underline{0} : \beta_2^c\} \ast \alpha_3^a \mapsto \{\underline{0} : \beta_3^c\} \ast \alpha_4^a \mapsto \{\underline{0} : \beta_4^c\}$$
$$\wedge\ \texttt{\&h} = \alpha_0^a \ \wedge\ \texttt{\&e} = \alpha_1^a \ \wedge\ \texttt{\&x} = \alpha_2^a \ \wedge\ \texttt{\&t} = \alpha_3^a \ \wedge\ \texttt{\&r} = \alpha_4^a \ \wedge\ \beta_2^c = \texttt{0}$$

(a) Abstract memory $m_b^\sharp$

$\texttt{\&h} = 0x\texttt{...a0}$	$0x\texttt{...b0}$
$\texttt{\&e} = 0x\texttt{...a4}$	$0x\texttt{...c0}$
$\texttt{\&x} = 0x\texttt{...a8}$	$0x\texttt{0}$
$\texttt{\&t} = 0x\texttt{...a12}$	$0x\texttt{...d0}$
$\texttt{\&r} = 0x\texttt{...a16}$	$0x\texttt{0}$

(b) Concrete memory m_b

$$\begin{array}{lll} \nu_b : & \alpha_0^a \mapsto 0x\texttt{...a0} & \beta_0^c \mapsto 0x\texttt{...b0} \\ & \alpha_1^a \mapsto 0x\texttt{...a4} & \beta_1^c \mapsto 0x\texttt{...c0} \\ & \alpha_2^a \mapsto 0x\texttt{...a8} & \beta_2^c \mapsto 0x\texttt{0} \\ & \alpha_3^a \mapsto 0x\texttt{...a12} & \beta_3^c \mapsto 0x\texttt{...d0} \\ & \alpha_4^a \mapsto 0x\texttt{...a16} & \beta_4^c \mapsto 0x\texttt{0} \end{array}$$

(c) Valuation $\nu_b : \mathcal{N}_{\mathbb{M}_b^\sharp} \to \mathbb{V}$

Fig. 3. Bounded data structure abstract domain: $(m_b, \nu_b) \in \gamma_{\mathbb{M}_b^\sharp}(m_b^\sharp)$

it consists of a set of predicates describing memory quantified on *symbolic names* (denoted $\mathcal{N}_{\mathbb{M}^\sharp}$) that represent *concrete values* (denoted $\mathbb{V}$). Thus, concretization involves *valuations* mapping symbolic names to the value they represent. Once this general notion is formalized, we formally introduce the separating combination as a binary functor that takes as input two memory abstract domains $\mathbb{M}_1^\sharp$, $\mathbb{M}_2^\sharp$ and returns a new memory abstract domain $\mathbb{M}_1^\sharp \circledast \mathbb{M}_2^\sharp$. The functor can be iteratively applied in order to cope with more than two memory abstract sub-domains. The combined abstract domain describes disjoint memory regions using either predicates of $\mathbb{M}_1^\sharp$ or $\mathbb{M}_2^\sharp$. Moreover, correlations between regions are described by the *interface abstract domain* $\mathbb{I}^\sharp$ that maintains equalities between symbolic names quantified in different sub-memories.

3.1 Memory Abstract Domain

Concrete Memories. We let $\mathbb{A}$ denote the set of concrete addresses, and we assume addresses to be concrete values (i.e. $\mathbb{A} \subseteq \mathbb{V}$). Henceforth, we adopt a standard model for concrete memories where a concrete memory m is a finite map from addresses to values. Therefore, the set of concrete memories is defined by $\mathbb{M} \stackrel{\text{def}}{=} \mathbb{A} \rightharpoonup_{\text{fin}} \mathbb{V}$. We let $\mathbb{F} = \{\underline{\mathrm{f}}, \underline{\mathrm{g}}, \ldots\}$ denote the set of valid field names, and we treat them as numerical offsets so that for $a \in \mathbb{A}$ and $\underline{\mathrm{f}} \in \mathbb{F}$, $a + \underline{\mathrm{f}}$ denotes the address at field $\underline{\mathrm{f}}$ of the block at address a. As the separating combination is reasoning about disjoint memory region, we write $m_1 \uplus m_2$ for the *union* of two *disjoint* memories (i.e. $\mathbf{dom}(m_1) \cap \mathbf{dom}(m_2) = \emptyset$, where $\mathbf{dom}(m_i)$ denotes the domain of m_i as a partial function).

A *memory abstract domain* is a lattice of abstract memories $\mathbb{M}^\sharp$, together with a fixed infinite set of symbolic names $\mathcal{N}_{\mathbb{M}^\sharp}$, a concretization function $\gamma_{\mathbb{M}^\sharp}$ and sound abstract transfer functions (detailed in Section 4). An abstract memory $m^\sharp \in \mathbb{M}^\sharp$ internally utilizes symbolic names to represent concrete values. We define the set of valuations $\mathcal{V}_{\mathbb{M}^\sharp} \stackrel{\text{def}}{=} \mathcal{N}_{\mathbb{M}^\sharp} \rightharpoonup_{\text{fin}} \mathbb{V}$. Intuitively, a valuation $\nu \in \mathcal{V}_{\mathbb{M}^\sharp}$ relates symbolic names to concrete values when concretizing. Concretization is a function $\gamma_{\mathbb{M}^\sharp} : \mathbb{M}^\sharp \to \mathcal{P}(\mathbb{M} \times \mathcal{V}_{\mathbb{M}^\sharp})$ and $\gamma_{\mathbb{M}^\sharp}(m^\sharp)$ collects a set of couples $(m, \nu) \in \mathbb{M} \times \mathcal{V}_{\mathbb{M}^\sharp}$ made of a concrete memory and a valuation that maps symbolic names quantified in $m^\sharp$ to concrete values in m.

$\nu_l : \lambda_0 \mapsto 0x...b0 \quad \lambda_2 \mapsto 0x0$
$\lambda_1 \mapsto 0x...c0 \quad \lambda_3 \mapsto 666$
(b) Valuation $\nu_l : \mathcal{N}_{\mathbb{M}_l^\sharp} \to \mathbb{V}$

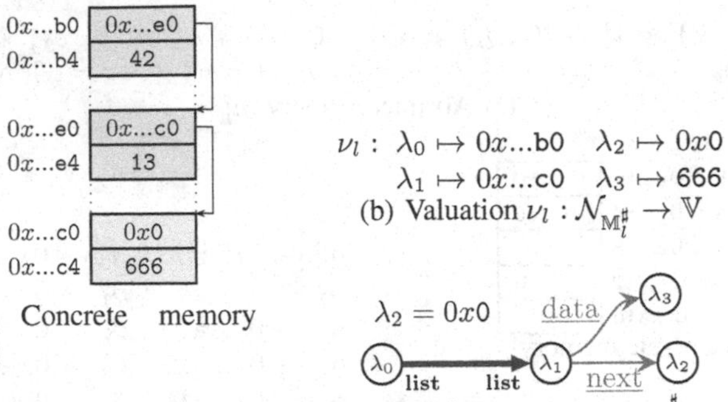

(a) Concrete memory m_l

(c) Abstract memory $m_l^\sharp$

Fig. 4. Separating shape graph abstract domain, parameterized by list inductive definition: $(m_l, \nu_l) \in \gamma_{\mathbb{M}_l^\sharp}(m_l^\sharp)$

Example 1 (Bounded structure abstract domain). As a first example, we describe a memory abstract domain that represents precisely block contents, but is unable to summarize unbounded regions such as list and tree data structures. This memory abstract domain can be considered an instantiation of $\mathbb{M}_b^\sharp$ seen in the overview (Section 2). The set of symbolic names consists of either symbols for addresses (denoted $\alpha_0^a, \alpha_1^a, \ldots$) or symbols for cell contents (denoted $\beta_0^c, \beta_1^c, \ldots$). Definitions of abstract memories and the concretization function is given by:

$m^\sharp ::=$	abstract memories	$\gamma_{\mathbb{M}_b^\sharp}(m^\sharp)$
$\mid$ **emp**	empty memory	$\{([\,], \nu) \mid \nu \in \mathcal{V}_{\mathbb{M}^\sharp}\}$
$\mid \alpha^a \mapsto \{\underline{f} : \beta^c\}$	memory cell	$\{([\nu(\alpha^a) + \underline{f} \mapsto \nu(\beta^c)], \nu) \mid \nu \in \mathcal{V}_{\mathbb{M}^\sharp}\}$
$\mid m_1^\sharp * m_2^\sharp$	disjoint memory	$\{(m_1 \uplus m_2, \nu) \mid \forall i \in \{1, 2\}. (m_i, \nu) \in \gamma_{\mathbb{M}_b^\sharp}(m_i^\sharp)\}$
$\mid m_b^\sharp \wedge n^\sharp$	with constraints	$\{(m, \nu) \mid (m, \nu) \in \gamma_{\mathbb{M}_b^\sharp}(m_b^\sharp) \wedge \nu \models n^\sharp\}$

An abstract memory $m^\sharp$ consists of a separating conjunction of atomic predicates $\alpha^a \mapsto \{\underline{f} : \beta^c\}$ abstracting a cell at address $\alpha^a + \underline{f}$ of content β^c. Fig. 3 shows the abstract submemory $m_b^\sharp$ depicted in labeled box **B** in Fig. 2(a) and a pair (m_b, ν_b) that concretizes it. Properties about values and addresses are expressed in $n^\sharp$, using a product with a numerical domain [5]. For instance, a numerical domain enabling linear equalities is used in Fig. 3(a). Besides, a product with a pointer domain may be used to capture, for example, aliasing relations. The memory abstract domain of [16] extends this basic layout (and handles unions, non-fixed cell sizes, etc.).

Example 2 (Separating shape graphs). The separating shape graph abstract domain of [4] provides a second example of a memory abstract domain. An abstract memory is a separating conjunction [17] of predicates, which could be either points-to predicates (depicted as thin edges in Fig. 4(c)) and inductive predicates (depicted as bold edges in Fig. 4(c)). Inductive predicates are annotated with inductive definitions supplied as a parameter of the domain. Thus, depending on the parameterization, this domain may provide an instantiation for $\mathbb{M}_l^\sharp$ or $\mathbb{M}_t^\sharp$ in the example of Section 2. Non-parameterizable

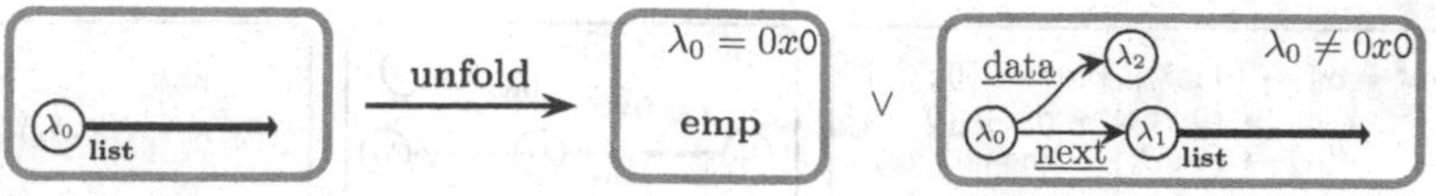

Fig. 5. List inductive definition rewriting rule

abstract domains [10] have a similar layout. A graph containing only points-to edges is concretized into the disjoint merge of the cells described by each points-to edge. The concretization of inductive predicates proceeds by unfolding. For instance the inductive definition for list leads to the unfolding rule shown in Figure 5. As in the previous example, a numerical abstract domain should be used in order to express content properties. Fig. 4(c) presents an instance $m_l^\sharp$ of the separating shape graph domain parameterized by a list definition that corresponds to the labeled box ❶ depicted in Fig. 2(a) in the overview. A pair (m_l, ν_l) that concretizes $m_l^\sharp$ is given in Fig. 4(a) and Fig. 4(b).

3.2 The Separating Combination

In this section, we assume a pair of memory abstract domains $\mathbb{M}_1^\sharp, \mathbb{M}_2^\sharp$ are fixed, with independent sets of symbolic names $\mathcal{N}_{\mathbb{M}_1^\sharp}, \mathcal{N}_{\mathbb{M}_2^\sharp}$ and concretization functions $\gamma_{\mathbb{M}_1^\sharp}, \gamma_{\mathbb{M}_2^\sharp}$. In the following, we introduce the interface abstract domain before defining the combined memory abstract domain $\mathbb{M}_1^\sharp \circledast \mathbb{M}_2^\sharp$.

Interface Abstract Domain. We let $\mathbb{I}^\sharp\langle \mathbb{M}_1^\sharp, \mathbb{M}_2^\sharp \rangle$ denote the interface abstract domain that expresses sets of equality relations between symbolic names of $\mathbb{M}_1^\sharp$ and $\mathbb{M}_2^\sharp$. Intuitively, an abstract interface is a finite set of pairs representing equalities. Thus, the interface abstract domain is defined by $\mathbb{I}^\sharp\langle \mathbb{M}_1^\sharp, \mathbb{M}_2^\sharp \rangle \stackrel{\text{def}}{=} \mathcal{P}_{\text{fin}}(\mathcal{N}_{\mathbb{M}_1^\sharp} \times \mathcal{N}_{\mathbb{M}_2^\sharp})$ and an abstract interface $i^\sharp$ is concretized into a set of pairs of valuations of $\mathbb{M}_1^\sharp$ and $\mathbb{M}_2^\sharp$ in the following way:

$$\gamma_{\mathbb{I}^\sharp}(i^\sharp) \stackrel{\text{def}}{=} \left\{ (\nu_1, \nu_2) \in \mathcal{V}_{\mathbb{M}_1^\sharp} \times \mathcal{V}_{\mathbb{M}_2^\sharp} \mid \forall (\alpha_1, \alpha_2) \in i^\sharp.\ \nu_1(\alpha_1) = \nu_2(\alpha_2) \right\}$$

We write $\mathbb{I}^\sharp$ instead of $\mathbb{I}^\sharp\langle \mathbb{M}_1^\sharp, \mathbb{M}_2^\sharp \rangle$ when there is no ambiguity about the choice of the memory abstract sub-domains. We also define a judgment $i^\sharp \vdash \alpha_1 = \alpha_2$ meaning that the pair (α_1, α_2) belongs to the transitive closure of the relation induced by $i^\sharp$. Thus, it meets the soundness condition $i^\sharp \vdash \alpha_1 = \alpha_2 \wedge (\nu_1, \nu_2) \in \gamma_{\mathbb{I}^\sharp}(i^\sharp) \Rightarrow \nu_1(\alpha_1) = \nu_2(\alpha_2)$.

The Separating Abstract Domain Combinator. Combined abstract memories consist of triples $(m_1^\sharp, m_2^\sharp, i^\sharp)$ made of two abstract sub-memories describing disjoint memory regions and an abstract interface representing correlations between the sub-memories. Thus, the combined abstract domain is defined by $\mathbb{M}_1^\sharp \circledast \mathbb{M}_2^\sharp \stackrel{\text{def}}{=} \mathbb{M}_1^\sharp \times \mathbb{M}_2^\sharp \times \mathbb{I}^\sharp\langle \mathbb{M}_1^\sharp, \mathbb{M}_2^\sharp \rangle$. We define the set of symbolic names of the combined abstract domain as the *disjoint* union of symbolic names of the abstract sub-domains. Formally:

$$\mathcal{N}_{\mathbb{M}_1^\sharp \circledast \mathbb{M}_2^\sharp} \stackrel{\text{def}}{=} \left\{ (\mathbb{M}_1^\sharp : \alpha_1) \mid \alpha_1 \in \mathcal{N}_{\mathbb{M}_1^\sharp} \right\} \uplus \left\{ (\mathbb{M}_2^\sharp : \alpha_2) \mid \alpha_2 \in \mathcal{N}_{\mathbb{M}_2^\sharp} \right\}$$

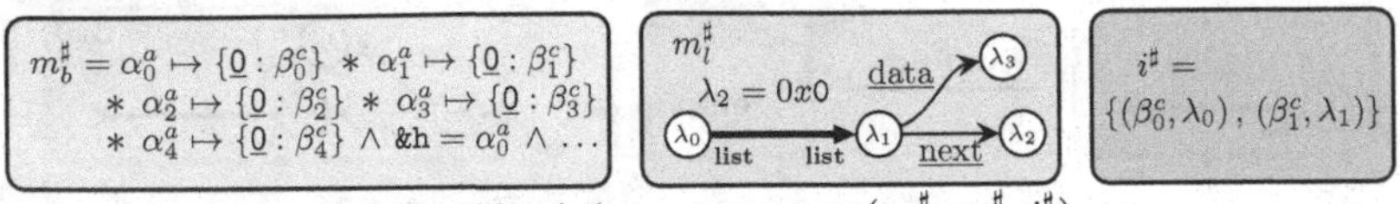

(a) Combined abstract memory $(m_b^\sharp, m_l^\sharp, i^\sharp)$

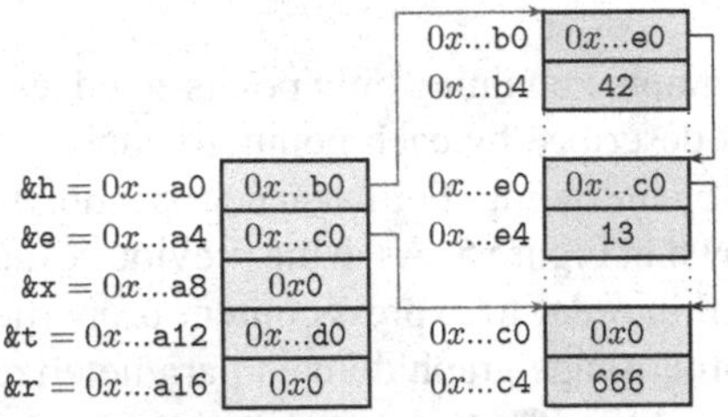

(b) Concrete memory $m_b \uplus m_l$

$$\nu_b \oplus \nu_l : \mathcal{N}_{\mathbb{M}_b^\sharp \circledast \mathbb{M}_l^\sharp} \longrightarrow \mathbb{V}$$

$(\mathbb{M}_b^\sharp : \alpha_0^a) \mapsto 0x\ldots\texttt{a0}$	$(\mathbb{M}_b^\sharp : \beta_0^c) \mapsto 0x\ldots\texttt{b0}$
$(\mathbb{M}_b^\sharp : \alpha_1^a) \mapsto 0x\ldots\texttt{a4}$	$(\mathbb{M}_b^\sharp : \beta_1^c) \mapsto 0x\ldots\texttt{c0}$
$(\mathbb{M}_b^\sharp : \alpha_2^a) \mapsto 0x\ldots\texttt{a8}$	$(\mathbb{M}_b^\sharp : \beta_2^c) \mapsto 0x0$
$(\mathbb{M}_b^\sharp : \alpha_3^a) \mapsto 0x\ldots\texttt{a12}$	$(\mathbb{M}_b^\sharp : \beta_3^c) \mapsto 0x\ldots\texttt{d0}$
$(\mathbb{M}_b^\sharp : \alpha_4^a) \mapsto 0x\ldots\texttt{a16}$	$(\mathbb{M}_b^\sharp : \beta_4^c) \mapsto 0x0$
$(\mathbb{M}_l^\sharp : \lambda_0) \mapsto 0x\ldots\texttt{b0}$	$(\mathbb{M}_l^\sharp : \lambda_2) \mapsto 0x0$
$(\mathbb{M}_l^\sharp : \lambda_1) \mapsto 0x\ldots\texttt{c0}$	$(\mathbb{M}_l^\sharp : \lambda_3) \mapsto 666$

(c) Valuation $\nu_b \oplus \nu_l \in \mathcal{V}_{\mathbb{M}_b^\sharp \circledast \mathbb{M}_l^\sharp}$

Fig. 6. Combined memory abstract domain: $(m_b \uplus m_l, \nu_b \oplus \nu_l) \in \gamma_{\mathbb{M}_b^\sharp \circledast \mathbb{M}_l^\sharp}(m_b^\sharp, m_l^\sharp, i^\sharp)$ as $(m_b, \nu_b) \in \gamma_{\mathbb{M}_b^\sharp}(m_b^\sharp)$ (Fig. 3), $(m_l, \nu_l) \in \gamma_{\mathbb{M}_l^\sharp}(m_l^\sharp)$ (Fig. 4) and $(\nu_b, \nu_l) \in \gamma_{\mathbb{I}^\sharp}(i^\sharp)$

At the combined abstract domain level, $(\mathbb{M}_i^\sharp : \alpha_i)$ denotes symbolic name α_i of the abstract sub-domain $\mathbb{M}_i^\sharp$. To define the meaning of a combined abstract memory, we give a concretization function $\gamma_{\mathbb{M}_1^\sharp \circledast \mathbb{M}_2^\sharp} : \mathbb{M}_1^\sharp \circledast \mathbb{M}_2^\sharp \to \mathcal{P}(\mathbb{M} \times \mathcal{V}_{\mathbb{M}_1^\sharp \circledast \mathbb{M}_2^\sharp})$ that derives from concretization functions $\gamma_{\mathbb{M}_i^\sharp} : \mathbb{M}_i^\sharp \to \mathcal{P}(\mathbb{M} \times \mathcal{V}_{\mathbb{M}_i^\sharp})$ of the memory abstract sub-domains. To achieve this, we define a valuation *combinator* $\oplus : \mathcal{V}_{\mathbb{M}_1^\sharp} \times \mathcal{V}_{\mathbb{M}_2^\sharp} \to \mathcal{V}_{\mathbb{M}_1^\sharp \circledast \mathbb{M}_2^\sharp}$ that puts two valuations together, that is, $(\nu_1 \oplus \nu_2)(\mathbb{M}_i^\sharp : \alpha_i) \stackrel{\text{def}}{=} \nu_i(\alpha_i)$. Then, the concretization of a combined abstract memory is given by

$$\gamma_{\mathbb{M}_1^\sharp \circledast \mathbb{M}_2^\sharp}(m_1^\sharp, m_2^\sharp, i^\sharp) \stackrel{\text{def}}{=} \left\{ (m_1 \uplus m_2, \nu_1 \oplus \nu_2) \;\middle|\; \begin{array}{c} \forall i \in \{1,2\}.\, (m_i, \nu_i) \in \gamma_{\mathbb{M}_i^\sharp}(m_i^\sharp) \\ \wedge \quad (\nu_1, \nu_2) \in \gamma_{\mathbb{I}^\sharp}(i^\sharp) \end{array} \right\}$$

Example 3 (Separating combination of $\mathbb{M}_b^\sharp$ and $\mathbb{M}_l^\sharp$). We now consider an instantiation of the separating combination functor, with the bounded data structure domain $\mathbb{M}_b^\sharp$ (presented in Example 1) and the list-parameterized separating shape graph domain $\mathbb{M}_l^\sharp$ (presented in Example 2). Fig. 6(a) presents a combined abstract memory $(m_b^\sharp, m_l^\sharp, i^\sharp)$ that combines abstract sub-memories already presented in Fig. 3(a) and Fig. 4(c) together with the abstract interface $i^\sharp = \{(\beta_0^c, \lambda_0), (\beta_1^c, \lambda_1)\}$. We provide a pair (m, ν) in Fig. 6(b) and Fig. 6(c) concretizing $(m_b^\sharp, m_l^\sharp, i^\sharp)$ obtained by combining the concrete pairs (m_b, ν_b) and (m_l, ν_l) presented in Fig. 3 and Fig. 4. Note that $(\nu_b, \nu_l) \in \gamma_{\mathbb{I}^\sharp}(i^\sharp)$ as $\nu_b(\beta_0^c) = \nu_l(\lambda_0) = 0x\ldots\texttt{b0}$ and $\nu_b(\beta_1^c) = \nu_l(\lambda_1) = 0x\ldots\texttt{c0}$.

4 Analysis Algorithms

We now discuss the inference of invariants in the combined domain. A memory abstract domain $\mathbb{M}^\sharp$ provides for each concrete memory operation $f : \mathbb{M} \to \mathcal{P}(\mathbb{M})$, a counterpart abstract transfer function $f^\sharp : \mathbb{M}^\sharp \to \mathbb{M}^\sharp$ that is *sound* (i.e. $\forall (m, \nu) \in \gamma_{\mathbb{M}^\sharp}(m^\sharp).\ \forall m' \in f(m).\ \exists \nu' \supseteq \nu.\ (m', \nu') \in (\gamma_{\mathbb{M}^\sharp} \circ f^\sharp)(m^\sharp)$). Abstract transfer functions may introduce new symbolic names but may not remove nor change the meaning of existing symbolic names. Hence, a valuation ν' in the concretization of the post-condition must extend valuation ν that concretizes the pre-condition. Abstract interpreters also require lattice operations (e.g. inclusion checking, widening) to achieve precise fixed point computations.

In a combined abstract domain, abstract transfer functions should distribute computations to the sub-memories and the abstract interface, using abstract transfer functions provided by sub-domains. In this section, we detail this mechanism for abstract transfer functions handling memory allocations (Section 4.1), assignments (Sections 4.2, and 4.3), and for inclusion checking (Section 4.4).

4.1 Creation of Memory Cells

Creation of new memory cells occurs either when a block for a new variable is created or when heap space is allocated at run time (e.g. **malloc** as at line 11 in Fig. 1). In a memory abstract domain $\mathbb{M}^\sharp$, this operation is handled by the abstract transfer function $\mathit{new}_{\mathbb{M}^\sharp}$, which is the abstract counterpart of the concrete transfer function $\mathit{new} : \mathtt{int} \times \mathbb{M} \to \mathcal{P}(\mathbb{A} \times \mathbb{M})$ (defined in a standard way). Intuitively, $\mathit{new}_{\mathbb{M}^\sharp}$ takes as input an integer size $\mathtt{s}$ and an abstract memory $m^\sharp_{\mathrm{pre}}$ and returns a pair consisting of a symbolic name α representing the address of the allocated block and an abstract memory $m^\sharp_{\mathrm{post}}$ where the cell has been created. Therefore, it ensures that, if $\mathit{new}_{\mathbb{M}^\sharp}(\mathtt{s}, m^\sharp_{\mathrm{pre}}) = (\alpha, m^\sharp_{\mathrm{post}})$ and $(m, \nu) \in \gamma_{\mathbb{M}^\sharp}(m^\sharp_{\mathrm{pre}})$, then the following holds:

$$(a, m') \in \mathit{new}(\mathtt{s}, m) \Rightarrow \exists \nu' \supseteq \nu.\ (m', \nu') \in \gamma_{\mathbb{M}^\sharp}(m^\sharp_{\mathrm{post}}) \ \wedge\ \nu'(\alpha) = a$$

Creation of Memory Cells in a Combined Domain. Because of the separation principle (Section 3.2), a cell must be represented in exactly one sub-memory in a combined abstract memory $m^\sharp = (m^\sharp_1, m^\sharp_2, i^\sharp)$. Therefore, we provide two possible definitions for $\mathit{new}_{\mathbb{M}^\sharp_1 \circledast \mathbb{M}^\sharp_2}$ deriving from two symmetric rules NEW1 and NEW2 . Intuitively, the abstract transfer function defined by rule NEW1 (resp. NEW2) always represents new cells using sub-domain $\mathbb{M}^\sharp_1$ (resp. $\mathbb{M}^\sharp_2$).

$$\textsc{New1}\quad \frac{\mathit{new}_{\mathbb{M}^\sharp_1}(\mathtt{s}, m^\sharp_1) = (\alpha_1, m^\sharp_{1,\mathrm{post}})}{\mathit{new}_{\mathbb{M}^\sharp_1 \circledast \mathbb{M}^\sharp_2}(\mathtt{s}, (m^\sharp_1, m^\sharp_2, i^\sharp)) = ((\mathbb{M}^\sharp_1 : \alpha_1), (m^\sharp_{1,\mathrm{post}}, m^\sharp_2, i^\sharp))}$$

While both choices are *sound*, some sub-domains are more suitable than others. For instance, in $\mathbb{M}^\sharp_b \circledast \mathbb{M}^\sharp_l$, it would be inappropriate to let the allocation of a cell expected to be summarized as part of a list be done in $\mathbb{M}^\sharp_b$, where summarization cannot be achieved.

$$
\begin{array}{llll}
l\ (\in \mathcal{L}_{\mathbb{M}^\sharp}) ::= \alpha & (\alpha \in \mathcal{N}_{\mathbb{M}^\sharp}) & \quad r\ (\in \mathcal{R}_{\mathbb{M}^\sharp}) ::= l & (l \in \mathcal{L}_{\mathbb{M}^\sharp}) \\
\quad\mid\ l \cdot \underline{\mathrm{f}} & (l \in \mathcal{L}_{\mathbb{M}^\sharp}; \underline{\mathrm{f}} \in \mathbb{F}) & \quad\quad \mid\ \&l & (l \in \mathcal{L}_{\mathbb{M}^\sharp}) \\
\quad\mid\ *r & (r \in \mathcal{R}_{\mathbb{M}^\sharp}) & \quad\quad \mid\ v & (v \in \mathbb{V})
\end{array}
$$

(a) Syntax of l-value and r-value expressions

$$
\frac{}{\mathcal{L}_{\mathbb{M}^\sharp}[\![\alpha]\!]\, m^\sharp = (\alpha, \underline{0})}
\qquad
\frac{\mathcal{L}_{\mathbb{M}^\sharp}[\![l]\!]\, m^\sharp = (\alpha, \underline{\mathrm{f}})}{\mathcal{L}_{\mathbb{M}^\sharp}[\![l \cdot \underline{\mathrm{g}}]\!]\, m^\sharp = (\alpha, \underline{\mathrm{f}} + \underline{\mathrm{g}})}
\qquad
\frac{\mathcal{R}_{\mathbb{M}^\sharp}[\![r]\!]\, m^\sharp = \alpha + \underline{\mathrm{f}}}{\mathcal{L}_{\mathbb{M}^\sharp}[\![*r]\!]\, m^\sharp = (\alpha, \underline{\mathrm{f}})}
$$

$$
\frac{\mathcal{L}_{\mathbb{M}^\sharp}[\![l]\!]\, m^\sharp = (\alpha, \underline{\mathrm{f}})}{\mathcal{R}_{\mathbb{M}^\sharp}[\![l]\!]\, m^\sharp = \mathit{read}_{\mathbb{M}^\sharp}(\alpha, \underline{\mathrm{f}}, m^\sharp)}
\qquad
\frac{\mathcal{L}_{\mathbb{M}^\sharp}[\![l]\!]\, m^\sharp = (\alpha, \underline{\mathrm{f}})}{\mathcal{R}_{\mathbb{M}^\sharp}[\![\&l]\!]\, m^\sharp = \alpha + \underline{\mathrm{f}}}
\qquad
\frac{}{\mathcal{R}_{\mathbb{M}^\sharp}[\![v]\!]\, m^\sharp = v}
$$

(b) Evaluation rules for l-value and r-value expressions

Fig. 7. Evaluations of l-values $\mathcal{L}_{\mathbb{M}^\sharp}[\![l]\!] : \mathbb{M}^\sharp \to \mathcal{N}_{\mathbb{M}^\sharp} \times \mathbb{F}$ and r-values $\mathcal{R}_{\mathbb{M}^\sharp}[\![r]\!] : \mathbb{M}^\sharp \to \mathcal{E}_{\mathbb{M}^\sharp}$ only rely on the reading operation $\mathit{read}_{\mathbb{M}^\sharp} : \mathcal{N}_{\mathbb{M}^\sharp} \times \mathbb{F} \times \mathbb{M}^\sharp \to \mathcal{E}_{\mathbb{M}^\sharp}$

If we consider the analysis of the memory allocation at line 11 in Fig. 1, the choice is guided by C types: the created cell has type `int` which is not recursive, and thus it will likely never require summarization. Therefore, the cell creation can be handled by any sub-memories without any loss in precision. As sub-domain $\mathbb{M}_b^\sharp$ is more lightweight than $\mathbb{M}_l^\sharp$ in terms of computational cost, it should abstract the new cell. Then, invoking $\mathit{new}_{\mathbb{M}_b^\sharp \circledast \mathbb{M}_l^\sharp}$ deriving from rule NEW1 to the combined memory of Fig. 6(a) returns symbolic name $(\mathbb{M}_b^\sharp : \alpha_5^a)$ and the following combined abstract memory:

$$
\begin{array}{l}
m_b^\sharp = \alpha_0^a \mapsto \{\underline{0} : \beta_0^c\} * \alpha_1^a \mapsto \{\underline{0} : \beta_1^c\} \\
\quad * \alpha_2^a \mapsto \{\underline{0} : \beta_2^c\} * \alpha_3^a \mapsto \{\underline{0} : \beta_3^c\} \\
\quad * \alpha_4^a \mapsto \{\underline{0} : \beta_4^c\} * \alpha_5^a \mapsto \{\underline{0} : \beta_5^c\} \\
\quad \wedge \&\mathrm{h} = \alpha_0^a \wedge \ldots
\end{array}
$$

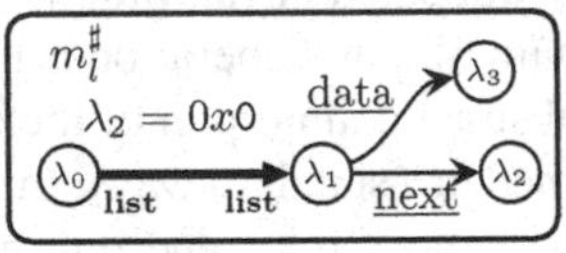

$$
i^\sharp = \{(\beta_0^c, \lambda_0), (\beta_1^c, \lambda_1)\}
$$

While not being critical for soundness, such empirical hints are important to avoid either a loss of precision or a slowdown in the analysis.

4.2 Evaluation of l-Value and r-Value Expressions

We consider the abstract transfer functions handling operations such as assignments and tests. These operations involve *l-values* $l \in \mathcal{L}_{\mathbb{M}^\sharp}$ and *r-values* $r \in \mathcal{R}_{\mathbb{M}^\sharp}$. Their syntax (shown in Fig. 7(a)) includes classical forms of expressions encountered in a C-like language (structure fields, dereferences, address of, etc.). In this section, we define a mechanism for evaluating l-value and r-value expressions. More formally, the evaluation of an l-value l in abstract memory $m^\sharp$ returns a pair $\mathcal{L}_{\mathbb{M}^\sharp}[\![l]\!]\, m^\sharp = (\alpha, \underline{\mathrm{f}})$ consisting of a symbolic name α and a field $\underline{\mathrm{f}}$ such that $\alpha + \underline{\mathrm{f}}$ denotes the address represented by l. Similarly, the evaluation of a r-value r returns an *symbolic expression* $\mathcal{R}_{\mathbb{M}^\sharp}[\![r]\!]\, m^\sharp = e$ that denotes the value represented by r. A symbolic expression $e \in \mathcal{E}_{\mathbb{M}^\sharp}$ is either of the form $\alpha + \underline{\mathrm{f}}$ (where $\alpha \in \mathcal{N}_{\mathbb{M}^\sharp}$ and $\underline{\mathrm{f}} \in \mathbb{F}$) or a concrete value $v \in \mathbb{V}$.

Evaluation Algorithm. The computation of $\mathcal{L}_{\mathbb{M}^\sharp}[\![.]\!]$ and $\mathcal{R}_{\mathbb{M}^\sharp}[\![.]\!]$ proceeds by induction over the expressions syntax as shown in Fig. 7(b), assuming a *read* operation $\mathit{read}_{\mathbb{M}^\sharp}$ is provided by memory abstract domain $\mathbb{M}^\sharp$, so as to "extract" the contents of a cell at the abstract level: partial function $\mathit{read}_{\mathbb{M}^\sharp}$ inputs a symbolic name α representing the base address of a concrete block, a field $\underline{\mathtt{f}}$ and an abstract memory state $m^\sharp$, and returns a symbolic expression representing the contents of that field. It may also fail to identify the cell and is then undefined (this may happen in a combined memory abstract domain when reading a cell in the "wrong" sub-memory). In some memory abstract domains (such as the separating shape graph domain presented in Example 2), $\mathit{read}_{\mathbb{M}^\sharp}$ may need to perform *unfolding* [4] and thus, return a finite set of disjuncts, however this issue is orthogonal to the present development, so we leave it out here. Overall, it should satisfy the following soundness condition:

$$(m,\nu) \in \gamma_{\mathbb{M}^\sharp}(m^\sharp) \wedge \mathit{read}_{\mathbb{M}^\sharp}(\alpha, \underline{\mathtt{f}}, m^\sharp) = \beta + \underline{\mathtt{g}} \Longrightarrow m(\nu(\alpha) + \underline{\mathtt{f}}) = \nu(\beta) + \underline{\mathtt{g}}$$
$$(m,\nu) \in \gamma_{\mathbb{M}^\sharp}(m^\sharp) \wedge \mathit{read}_{\mathbb{M}^\sharp}(\alpha, \underline{\mathtt{f}}, m^\sharp) = v \Longrightarrow m(\nu(\alpha) + \underline{\mathtt{f}}) = v$$

Read Operation in the Combined Domain. To read a cell at address $((\mathbb{M}_1^\sharp : \alpha_1), \underline{\mathtt{f}})$ in a combined abstract memory $(m_1^\sharp, m_2^\sharp, i^\sharp)$, the analysis first attempts to read cell at address $(\alpha_1, \underline{\mathtt{f}})$ in $m_1^\sharp$. Therefore, the read operation derives from the following rule:

READDIRECT1
$$\frac{\mathit{read}_{\mathbb{M}_1^\sharp}(\alpha_1, \underline{\mathtt{f}}, m_1^\sharp) = \beta_1 + \underline{\mathtt{g}}}{\mathit{read}_{\mathbb{M}_1^\sharp \circledast \mathbb{M}_2^\sharp}((\mathbb{M}_1^\sharp : \alpha_1), \underline{\mathtt{f}}, (m_1^\sharp, m_2^\sharp, i^\sharp)) = (\mathbb{M}_1^\sharp : \beta_1) + \underline{\mathtt{g}}}$$

It may turn out that the cell at address $(\mathbb{M}_1^\sharp : \alpha_1)$ is abstracted in sub-memory $m_2^\sharp$ in which case rule READDIRECT1 cannot be applied. In fact, by the separation principle (Section 3.2), a cell is represented in exactly one sub-memory. To cope with this issue, the reading operation can retrieve the cell by looking for a symbolic name of sub-domain $\mathbb{M}_2^\sharp$ that is bound to α_1 by the abstract interface. In such cases, the definition of $\mathit{read}_{\mathbb{M}_1^\sharp \circledast \mathbb{M}_2^\sharp}$ follows the rule:

READACROSS1
$$\frac{\mathit{read}_{\mathbb{M}_2^\sharp}(\alpha_2, \underline{\mathtt{f}}, m_2^\sharp) = \beta_2 + \underline{\mathtt{g}} \qquad i^\sharp \vdash \alpha_1 = \alpha_2}{\mathit{read}_{\mathbb{M}_1^\sharp \circledast \mathbb{M}_2^\sharp}((\mathbb{M}_1^\sharp : \alpha_1), \underline{\mathtt{f}}, (m_1^\sharp, m_2^\sharp, i^\sharp)) = (\mathbb{M}_2^\sharp : \beta_2) + \underline{\mathtt{g}}}$$

Example 4 (An evaluation across sub-memories). We consider the evaluation of the right hand side `e -> data` of assignment at line 12 in Fig. 1 on the following combined abstract memory that is computed by the analysis after assignment at line 11 (assignment is treated in Section 4.3).

$$\begin{array}{l} m_b^\sharp = \alpha_0^a \mapsto \{\underline{0} : \beta_0^c\} * \alpha_1^a \mapsto \{\underline{0} : \beta_1^c\} \\ \quad * \ \alpha_2^a \mapsto \{\underline{0} : \beta_2^c\} * \alpha_3^a \mapsto \{\underline{0} : \beta_3^c\} \\ \quad * \ \alpha_4^a \mapsto \{\underline{0} : \beta_4^c\} * \alpha_5^a \mapsto \{\underline{0} : \beta_5^c\} \\ \wedge \ \&\mathtt{e} = \alpha_1^a \wedge \&\mathtt{x} = \alpha_2^a \wedge \ldots \wedge \beta_2^c = \alpha_5^a \end{array}$$

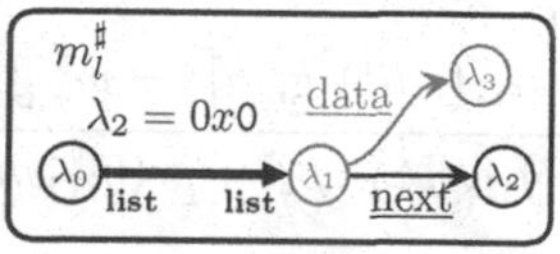

$$i^\sharp = \{(\beta_0^c, \lambda_0), (\beta_1^c, \lambda_1)\}$$

First, variable `e` is replaced by symbolic name $(\mathbb{M}_b^\sharp : \alpha_1^a)$ denoting its address and its content is evaluated to $(\mathbb{M}_b^\sharp : \beta_1^c)$. Then, reading cell at address $(\mathbb{M}_b^\sharp : \beta_1^c) + \underline{\mathtt{data}}$ fails in $\mathbb{M}_b^\sharp$ as the cell is actually abstracted in $\mathbb{M}_l^\sharp$. Therefore, the reading operation retrieves that cell at address $(\mathbb{M}_l^\sharp : \lambda_1) + \underline{\mathtt{data}}$, using the equality $(\beta_1^c, \lambda_1) \in i^\sharp$. Finally, the evaluation ends up with symbolic r-value $(\mathbb{M}_l^\sharp : \lambda_3)$.

4.3 Abstract Transfer Function for Assignment

The analysis requires a set of abstract transfer functions handling operations such as assignment and test that need to evaluate l-value and r-value expressions [5]. Among those, the assignment is arguably the most sophisticated one, thus we describe only this operation here. The classical analysis of assignment $l = r$ shown in [5] proceeds as follows: (1) the left hand side is evaluated to a pair $\mathcal{L}_{\mathbb{M}^\sharp}[\![l]\!]\, m^\sharp = (\alpha, \underline{\mathrm{f}})$ representing the address of the cell that will be updated; (2) the right hand side is evaluated to a symbolic expression $\mathcal{R}_{\mathbb{M}^\sharp}[\![r]\!]\, m^\sharp = e$ representing the written value; and (3) the cell is updated in the abstract level, using the abstract *cell write* operation $\mathit{write}_{\mathbb{M}^\sharp}$ provided by the memory abstract domain $\mathbb{M}^\sharp$. Intuitively, $\mathit{write}_{\mathbb{M}^\sharp}(\alpha, \underline{\mathrm{f}}, e, m^\sharp)$ returns an abstract memory where the cell at address $\alpha + \underline{\mathrm{f}}$ has been updated to e. To state the soundness of this operation, we extend a valuation ν to cope with symbolic expressions in a natural way by defining $\overline{\nu}(\alpha + \underline{\mathrm{f}}) \stackrel{\text{def}}{=} \nu(\alpha) + \underline{\mathrm{f}}$ and $\overline{\nu}(v) \stackrel{\text{def}}{=} v$. Therefore, $\mathit{write}_{\mathbb{M}^\sharp}$ satisfies the condition:

$$(m, \nu) \in \gamma_{\mathbb{M}^\sharp}(m^\sharp) \Rightarrow \exists \nu' \supseteq \nu.\, (m[\nu(\alpha) + \underline{\mathrm{f}} \leftarrow \overline{\nu}(e)], \nu') \in \gamma_{\mathbb{M}^\sharp}(\, \mathit{write}_{\mathbb{M}^\sharp}(\alpha, \underline{\mathrm{f}}, e, m^\sharp))$$

Cell Write Operation in a Combined Domain. A simple case occurs when left and right hand sides are both evaluated in the *same* sub-memory, in which case the cell write operation simply lifts computation to the corresponding sub-domain. However, a trickier case occurs when l-value and r-value are evaluated to *different* sub-memories, such as $((\mathbb{M}_1^\sharp : \alpha_1), \underline{\mathrm{f}})$ and $(\mathbb{M}_2^\sharp : \beta_2) + \underline{\mathrm{g}}$. In this case, the cell writing is performed in $m_1^\sharp$ as the cell requiring update is abstracted there. However, to avoid losing precision, the analysis needs a symbolic expression in $m_1^\sharp$ to relate the new content. Therefore, two cases may be encountered:

- β_2 is bound to a symbolic name $\beta_1 \in \mathcal{N}_{\mathbb{M}_1^\sharp}$ by the abstract interface, in which case $\mathit{write}_{\mathbb{M}_1^\sharp \circledast \mathbb{M}_2^\sharp}$ is defined following the rule:

WRITEACROSS1

$$\frac{\mathit{write}_{\mathbb{M}_1^\sharp}(\alpha_1, \underline{\mathrm{f}}, \beta_1 + \underline{\mathrm{g}}, m_1^\sharp) = m_{1,\mathrm{post}}^\sharp \qquad i^\sharp \vdash \beta_1 = \beta_2}{\mathit{write}_{\mathbb{M}_1^\sharp \circledast \mathbb{M}_2^\sharp}((\mathbb{M}_1^\sharp : \alpha_1), \underline{\mathrm{f}}, (\mathbb{M}_2^\sharp : \beta_2) + \underline{\mathrm{g}}, (m_1^\sharp, m_2^\sharp, i^\sharp)) = (m_{1,\mathrm{post}}^\sharp, m_2^\sharp, i^\sharp)}$$

- β_2 is not bound in the abstract interface, in which case a *fresh* variable β_1 is used to account for it in $m_1^\sharp$. Then $\mathit{write}_{\mathbb{M}_1^\sharp \circledast \mathbb{M}_2^\sharp}$ is defined following the rule:

WRITEACROSSWEAK1

$$\frac{\mathit{write}_{\mathbb{M}_1^\sharp}(\alpha_1, \underline{\mathrm{f}}, \beta_1 + \underline{\mathrm{g}}, m_1^\sharp) = m_{1,\mathrm{post}}^\sharp \qquad \beta_1 \textit{ fresh in } m_1^\sharp}{\mathit{write}_{\mathbb{M}_1^\sharp \circledast \mathbb{M}_2^\sharp}((\mathbb{M}_1^\sharp : \alpha_1), \underline{\mathrm{f}}, (\mathbb{M}_2^\sharp : \beta_2) + \underline{\mathrm{g}}, (m_1^\sharp, m_2^\sharp, i^\sharp)) = (m_{1,\mathrm{post}}^\sharp, m_2^\sharp, i^\sharp \cup \{(\beta_1, \beta_2)\})}$$

Example 5 (Assignment across sub-memories). We consider the computation of the post-condition of assignment `*x = e -> data` at line 12 in Fig. 1, from the pre-condition shown in Example 4. The left and right hand sides are respectively evaluated to $((\mathbb{M}_b^\sharp : \alpha_5^a), \underline{0})$ and $(\mathbb{M}_l^\sharp : \lambda_3)$ (as shown in Example 4). Moreover, there is no symbolic name in $m_b^\sharp$ bound to λ_3 in $m_l^\sharp$ by the abstract interface. Therefore, $\mathit{write}_{\mathbb{M}_b^\sharp \circledast \mathbb{M}_l^\sharp}$ derives from rule WRITEACROSSWEAK1, and produces the following post-condition:

$$m^\sharp_b = \alpha^a_0 \mapsto \{\underline{0} : \beta^c_0\} * \alpha^a_1 \mapsto \{\underline{0} : \beta^c_1\} * \alpha^a_2 \mapsto \{\underline{0} : \beta^c_2\} * \alpha^a_3 \mapsto \{\underline{0} : \beta^c_3\} * \alpha^a_4 \mapsto \{\underline{0} : \beta^c_4\} * \alpha^a_5 \mapsto \{\underline{0} : \gamma^c\} \wedge \&\mathrm{x} = \alpha^a_2 \wedge \ldots \wedge \beta^c_2 = \alpha^a_5$$

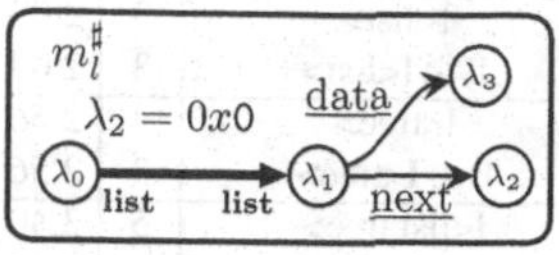

$$i^\sharp = \{(\beta^c_0, \lambda_0), (\beta^c_1, \lambda_1) (\gamma^c, \lambda_3)\}$$

4.4 Inclusion Checking

Fix-point computations [6] require widening and inclusion checking operators. In this section, we only detail the algorithm for inclusion checking as the widening algorithm is similar [5]. At a memory abstract domain $\mathbb{M}^\sharp$ level, the inclusion checking relies on the *abstract comparison* operator $\mathit{compare}_{\mathbb{M}^\sharp}$ that inputs two abstract memories $m^\sharp_\mathrm{l}$ and $m^\sharp_\mathrm{r}$ and returns a mapping Φ when it successfully establishes the abstract inclusion $m^\sharp_\mathrm{l} \sqsubseteq m^\sharp_\mathrm{r}$. Intuitively, the returned mapping relates symbolic names in $m^\sharp_r$ to symbolic names in $m^\sharp_l$ that valuations should map to the same value for the inclusion to hold. More formally, the soundness condition states the following:

$$\mathit{compare}_{\mathbb{M}^\sharp}(m^\sharp_\mathrm{l}, m^\sharp_\mathrm{r}) = \Phi \wedge (m, \nu) \in \gamma_{\mathbb{M}^\sharp}(m^\sharp_\mathrm{l}) \implies (m, \nu \circ \Phi) \in \gamma_{\mathbb{M}^\sharp}(m^\sharp_\mathrm{r})$$

Inclusion Checking in a Combined Domain. To compare the two combined abstract memories $m^\sharp_l = (m^\sharp_{1,\mathrm{l}}, m^\sharp_{2,\mathrm{l}}, i^\sharp_l)$ and $m^\sharp_r = (m^\sharp_{1,\mathrm{r}}, m^\sharp_{2,\mathrm{r}}, i^\sharp_r)$, the analysis first invokes the abstract comparisons of the sub-domains respectively on $(m^\sharp_{1,\mathrm{l}}, m^\sharp_{1,\mathrm{r}})$ and $(m^\sharp_{2,\mathrm{l}}, m^\sharp_{2,\mathrm{r}})$. When both succeed and thus return Φ_1 and Φ_2, the analysis checks the inclusion of the abstract interfaces by: $i^\sharp_l \sqsubseteq^{\Phi_2}_{\Phi_1} i^\sharp_r \iff \forall (\alpha_1, \alpha_2) \in i^\sharp_r.\ \ i^\sharp_l \vdash \Phi_1(\alpha_1) = \Phi_2(\alpha_2)$. Therefore, the abstract comparison operator is defined by the following rule:

$$\textsc{Incl}\quad \frac{\mathit{compare}_{\mathbb{M}^\sharp_1}(m^\sharp_{1,\mathrm{l}}, m^\sharp_{1,\mathrm{r}}) = \Phi_1 \quad \mathit{compare}_{\mathbb{M}^\sharp_2}(m^\sharp_{2,\mathrm{l}}, m^\sharp_{2,\mathrm{r}}) = \Phi_2 \quad i^\sharp_l \sqsubseteq^{\Phi_2}_{\Phi_1} i^\sharp_r}{\mathit{compare}_{\mathbb{M}^\sharp_1 \circledast \mathbb{M}^\sharp_2}((m^\sharp_{1,\mathrm{l}}, m^\sharp_{2,\mathrm{l}}, i^\sharp_l), (m^\sharp_{1,\mathrm{r}}, m^\sharp_{2,\mathrm{r}}, i^\sharp_r)) = \Phi_1 \oplus \Phi_2}$$

Refinement Using Initial Mappings. While *sound*, such a definition could lead to a loss of precision. For some memory abstract domains (such as the separating shape graphs domain), the abstract comparison operator internally initializes a mapping between symbolic names representing addresses of the same program variable (that valuations should clearly map to the same value). However, in a combined domain, a sub-memory with no such symbolic names is plausible (e.g. consider $m^\sharp_l$ in the combined abstract memory of Fig. 6(a)), and the sub-domain abstract comparison will therefore likely fail to establish the inclusion. To cope with that issue, the analysis provides an *initial mapping* as hint to the unsuccessful abstract comparison, that derives from the relationship inferred by the successful abstract comparison. More precisely, if $\mathit{compare}_{\mathbb{M}^\sharp_1}$ succeeds and returns Φ_1, the initial mapping defined by $\Phi^{\mathrm{init}}_2(\beta_{2,r}) = \beta_{2,l} \Leftrightarrow \exists \beta_{1,r} \in \mathcal{N}_{\mathbb{M}^\sharp_1}.\ i^\sharp_r \vdash \beta_{1,r} = \beta_{2,r} \wedge i^\sharp_l \vdash \Phi_1(\beta_{1,r}) = \beta_{2,l}$ can be passed as optional argument to $\mathit{compare}_{\mathbb{M}^\sharp_2}$.

Filename	MAD	#P	∨	t(s)	%	tCF(s)	tSD(s)	#R	#RA
insert_remove.c	I<list>	3	2.09	0.248	basis	-	0.174	230	-
(158 LOC)	B ⊛ I<list>	3	2.09	0.151	60	0.035	0.055	230	16
balancing.c	I<tree>	3	2.56	0.501	basis	-	0.376	314	-
(188 LOC)	B ⊛ I<tree>	3	2.56	0.323	64	0.068	0.125	314	72
search_list_tree.c	I<list,tree>	5	3.40	0.330	basis	-	0.286	172	-
(138 LOC)	I<list> ⊛ I<tree>	5	3.40	0.364	110	0.031	0.292	172	48
	B ⊛ I<list,tree>	5	3.40	0.194	59	0.035	0.098	172	70
	B ⊛ I<list> ⊛ I<tree>	5	3.40	0.231	70	0.071	0.113	172	70

Fig. 8. Analysis results (measured on a 2.2 Ghz Intel Core i7 with 8 GB of RAM): MAD is the memory abstract domain used (B stands for the *bounded data structure* domain, I<.> stands for the *separating shape graphs* domain instantiated with inductive definitions that are either list or tree, ⊛ stands for separating combination of domains), #P is the number of properties proven by the analysis, ∨ is average number of disjuncts at each program point, t is the total analysis time in seconds,% is the time of analysis compared to analysis using a monolithic domain, tCF (resp. tSD) is the time of analysis spent in the combination functor (resp. sub-domains), #R is the number of read operation calls and #RA is the number of read operations crossing sub-memories

5 Implementation and Empirical Evaluation

We test empirically the precision and efficiency of the combined analysis compared to a monolithic one and describe the results here. The separating combination described in this paper is implemented in the MemCAD analyzer[1]. The analysis is fully automatic. It takes as input C code and the desired structure of the memory abstract domain. The two analysis variants were applied to a set of over 15 micro-benchmarks, similar to the code fragment in Fig. 1. We verify memory safety properties, such as the absence of null pointer dereferences, as well as structural assertions (annotated in the code). In Fig. 8, we report on some representative analysis results relevant to questions in this paper. The C programs considered consist of data structure-manipulation routines (e.g. insertion, deletion, search) for lists and trees either called sequentially or interleaved. They can all be analyzed using a monolithic domain.

First, we note that importantly the combined analyses retain the same level of precision as the monolithic analyses in terms of the number of properties that can be proven (column #P). For each program, the number of properties proven on the first line (monolithic) is the same as the number proven on the subsequent lines (various combinations). The key part of the combined analysis is the interface between sub-memories. Its necessity is demonstrated by the ratio of read operations that *cross* the sub-memories in the combined analyses (column #RA over #R).

Next, we consider the relative efficiency of the various memory abstract domain combinations with respect to the monolithic version. Regardless of configuration, the MemCAD analyzer computes for each program point, a finite disjunction of abstract memories. We first observe that the use of a combined domain does not introduce an extra combinatorial factor as the number of disjuncts is the same for the monolithic and the combined analyses (column ∨). To probe into the overhead of our combination functor, we considered in search_list_tree.c decomposing the memory abstract domain into list- and tree-specific regions (I<list> ⊛ I<tree>). In this case, the list and tree

[1] `http://www.di.ens.fr/~rival/memcad.html`

domains are instantiations of the same generic, parametric separating shape graph domain. Thus, this instantiation pays for the overhead of the separating combination without the benefit of an optimized sub-domain. We observe that there is an overhead, but it seems acceptable given that the separating combination offers the possibility of replacing the sub-domains with specialized and optimized versions (a ratio of 110%-120% in the two instances shown here).

The win with our separating combination functor comes from applying it with an optimized sub-domain. In the variants with B $\circledast \cdots$, we use a *bounded data structure* domain to efficiently manage the bounded part of the memory (e.g. the top activation record in the call stack). This sub-domain is implemented efficiently knowing that it only needs to abstract bounded data structures. From Fig. 8, we see that separating out the bounded part of memory into a more efficient specialized domain is highly effective—noticeably decreasing the overall analysis times despite the overhead of combination (a ratio of around 60% in all cases).

6 Related Work

The first important abstract domain combination operation to be introduced is the reduced product [7], which has enabled constructing very expressive abstract domains from simpler ones. Intuitively, a property is decomposed into a conjunction of (possibly radically different) basic properties. This construction was applied to a wide range of analyzers, including ASTRÉE [3], where a large set of numerical abstract domains exchange information over a chain of reduced products [8]. The benefit of reduced product is even greater for libraries of abstractions with a common interface such as APRON [13]. It was also used to describe the Nelson-Oppen procedure [9].

Our contribution seeks to simplify abstract domain construction, while allowing greater expressiveness. It exploits *separation* [17], albeit in a different way than the numerous shape analyses that exploit it in the definition of their summarization predicates [10,2,4]. In these analyses, separation permits (hopefully all) updates to be handled as strong updates, which is crucial for both precision and efficiency. Our analysis exploits separation so as to combine independent memory abstract domains, so as to achieve at least the same precision and better efficiency by delegating the abstraction of particular data structures to the most appropriate sub-domains. Note that the sub-domains may (and in all the examples shown in this paper, do) also make use of separation as the aforementioned analyses. In [23], separation was used to represent distinct heap regions using heterogeneous abstractions, yet this work relies on code specifications transformed into sub-problems handled by different abstractions, and proceeds by verification, although our combinator allows inference of invariants.

Other combinations of abstractions have been proposed so as to enhance memory analyses. In particular, [14] presents an approach that uses classical conjunction together with zone variables to relate corresponding regions. Moreover, [11] combines formulae by distinguishing per-field and per-object separating conjunctions. In [15], sets of sub-graphs are used to represent properties about non-correlated data structures and to realize a gain in performance. These analyses are based on problem specific decompositions while our domain combinator is generic, in the sense that it does not make any assumptions on the way the memory properties are represented in the sub-domains.

In previous work [22], we proposed a reduced product for memory abstractions as a generic abstract domain combinator. This combinator does not rely on separation and provides a different form of separation of concerns than our separating combinator: in [22], sub-domains express a collection of properties of the same structure whereas the separating conjunction operator combines domains representing distinct structures. Moreover, we introduced a hierarchical memory abstraction to abstract structures allocated inside other structures [21]; in that work the whole memory is abstracted in the main domain, and a sub-domain describes nested structures. These combinators are implemented as ML functors in the MemCAD analyzer and can be used together (although assessing such compositions is beyond the scope of this paper).

7 Conclusion

In this paper, we introduced a combinator for separately conjoining memory abstract domains, enabling composite analyses that are precise, efficient, and flexible. Our proposal enables a separation of concerns when designing static analyses that need to deal with complex data structures, as very different domains can be combined to abstract disjoint memory regions. A natural extension of our study would be to integrate other memory abstractions, as found in 3-valued logic shape analyses [19,1,12], into our framework.

References

1. Arnold, G., Manevich, R., Sagiv, M., Shaham, R.: Combining shape analyses by intersecting abstractions. In: Emerson, E.A., Namjoshi, K.S. (eds.) VMCAI 2006. LNCS, vol. 3855, pp. 33–48. Springer, Heidelberg (2006)
2. Berdine, J., Calcagno, C., Cook, B., Distefano, D., O'Hearn, P.W., Wies, T., Yang, H.: Shape analysis for composite data structures. In: Damm, W., Hermanns, H. (eds.) CAV 2007. LNCS, vol. 4590, pp. 178–192. Springer, Heidelberg (2007)
3. Blanchet, B., Cousot, P., Cousot, R., Feret, J., Mauborgne, L., Miné, A., Monniaux, D., Rival, X.: A static analyzer for large safety-critical software. In: Programming Languages Design and Implementation, PLDI (2003)
4. Chang, B.-Y.E., Rival, X.: Relational inductive shape analysis. In: Principles of Programming Languages, POPL (2008)
5. Chang, B.-Y.E., Rival, X.: Modular construction of shape-numeric analyzers. In: SAIRP (2013)
6. Cousot, P., Cousot, R.: Abstract interpretation: A unified lattice model for static analysis of programs by construction or approximation of fixpoints. In: Principles of Programming Languages, POPL (1977)
7. Cousot, P., Cousot, R.: Systematic design of program analysis frameworks. In: Principles of Programming Languages, POPL (1979)
8. Cousot, P., Cousot, R., Feret, J., Mauborgne, L., Miné, A., Monniaux, D., Rival, X.: Combination of abstractions in the astrée static analyzer. In: Okada, M., Satoh, I. (eds.) ASIAN 2006. LNCS, vol. 4435, pp. 272–300. Springer, Heidelberg (2008)
9. Cousot, P., Cousot, R., Mauborgne, L.: The reduced product of abstract domains and the combination of decision procedures. In: Hofmann, M. (ed.) FOSSACS 2011. LNCS, vol. 6604, pp. 456–472. Springer, Heidelberg (2011)

10. Distefano, D., O'Hearn, P.W., Yang, H.: A local shape analysis based on separation logic. In: Hermanns, H., Palsberg, J. (eds.) TACAS 2006. LNCS, vol. 3920, pp. 287–302. Springer, Heidelberg (2006)
11. Drăgoi, C., Enea, C., Sighireanu, M.: Local shape analysis for overlaid data structures. In: Logozzo, F., Fähndrich, M. (eds.) Static Analysis. LNCS, vol. 7935, pp. 150–171. Springer, Heidelberg (2013)
12. Ferrara, P., Fuchs, R., Juhasz, U.: TVLA+: TVLA and value analyses together. In: Eleftherakis, G., Hinchey, M., Holcombe, M. (eds.) SEFM 2012. LNCS, vol. 7504, pp. 63–77. Springer, Heidelberg (2012)
13. Jeannet, B., Miné, A.: Apron: A library of numerical abstract domains for static analysis. In: Bouajjani, A., Maler, O. (eds.) CAV 2009. LNCS, vol. 5643, pp. 661–667. Springer, Heidelberg (2009)
14. Lee, O., Yang, H., Petersen, R.: Program analysis for overlaid data structures. In: Gopalakrishnan, G., Qadeer, S. (eds.) CAV 2011. LNCS, vol. 6806, pp. 592–608. Springer, Heidelberg (2011)
15. Manevich, R., Berdine, J., Cook, B., Ramalingam, G., Sagiv, M.: Shape analysis by graph decomposition. In: Grumberg, O., Huth, M. (eds.) TACAS 2007. LNCS, vol. 4424, pp. 3–18. Springer, Heidelberg (2007)
16. Miné, A.: Field-sensitive value analysis of embedded C programs with union types and pointer arithmetics. In: Languages, Compilers, and Tools for Embedded Systems, LCTES (2006)
17. Reynolds, J.: Separation logic: A logic for shared mutable data structures. In: Symposium on Logic in Computer Science, LICS (2002)
18. Rival, X., Chang, B.-Y.E.: Calling context abstraction with shapes. In: Principles of Programming Languages, POPL (2011)
19. Sagiv, M., Reps, T., Wilhelm, R.: Parametric shape analysis via 3-valued logic. In: Principles of Programming Languages, POPL (1999)
20. Sagiv, M., Reps, T., Wilhelm, R.: Parametric shape analysis via 3-valued logic. ACM Transactions on Programming Languages And Systems, TOPLAS (2002)
21. Sotin, P., Rival, X.: Hierarchical shape abstraction of dynamic structures in static blocks. In: Jhala, R., Igarashi, A. (eds.) APLAS 2012. LNCS, vol. 7705, pp. 131–147. Springer, Heidelberg (2012)
22. Toubhans, A., Chang, B.-Y.E., Rival, X.: Reduced product combination of abstract domains for shapes. In: Giacobazzi, R., Berdine, J., Mastroeni, I. (eds.) VMCAI 2013. LNCS, vol. 7737, pp. 375–395. Springer, Heidelberg (2013)
23. Yahav, E., Ramalingam, G.: Verifying safety properties using separation and heterogeneous asbtractions. In: Programming Languages Design and Implementation, PLDI (2004)

A Decision Tree Abstract Domain for Proving Conditional Termination*

Caterina Urban and Antoine Miné

ÉNS & CNRS & INRIA, France
{urban,mine}@di.ens.fr

Abstract. We present a new parameterized abstract domain able to refine existing numerical abstract domains with finite disjunctions. The elements of the abstract domain are decision trees where the decision nodes are labeled with linear constraints, and the leaf nodes belong to a numerical abstract domain.

The abstract domain is parametric in the choice between the expressivity and the cost of the linear constraints for the decision nodes (e.g., polyhedral or octagonal constraints), and the choice of the abstract domain for the leaf nodes. We describe an instance of this domain based on piecewise-defined ranking functions for the automatic inference of sufficient preconditions for program termination.

We have implemented a static analyzer for proving conditional termination of programs written in (a subset of) C and, using experimental evidence, we show that it performs well on a wide variety of benchmarks, it is competitive with the state of the art and is able to analyze programs that are out of the reach of existing methods.

1 Introduction

Numerical abstract domains are widely used in static program analysis and verification to maintain information about the set of possible values of the program variables along with the possible numerical relationships between them. The most common abstract domains — intervals [10], octagons [27] and convex polyhedra [14] — maintain this information using convex sets consisting of conjunctions of linear constraints. The convexity of these abstract domains makes the analysis scalable. On the other hand, it might lead to too harsh approximations and imprecisions in the analysis, ultimately yielding false alarms and a failure of the analyzer to prove the desired program property.

The key for an adequate cost versus precision trade-off is the handling of disjunctions arising during the analysis (e.g., from program tests and loops). In practice, numerical abstract domains are usually refined by adding weak forms of disjunctions to increase the expressivity while minimizing the cost of the analysis [13,18,20,29, etc.].

In this paper, we propose a novel parameterized abstract domain for the disjunctive refinement of numerical abstract domains which is particularly well-suited for proving conditional termination of imperative programs.

* The research leading to these results has received funding from the ARTEMIS Joint Undertaking under grant agreement no. 269335 (ARTEMIS project MBAT) (see Article II.9. of the JU Grant Agreement)

M. Müller-Olm and H. Seidl (Eds.): SAS 2014, LNCS 8723, pp. 302–318, 2014.

The elements of the abstract domain are inspired by the space partitioning trees [16] developed in the context of 3D computer graphics and the use of decision trees in program analysis and verification [3,23]: they are decision trees where the decision nodes are labeled with linear constraints, and the leaf nodes belong to a numerical abstract domain. These decision trees recursively partition the space of possible values of the program variables inducing disjunctions into the numerical abstract domain.

The partitioning is *dynamic*: during the analysis, partitions (respectively, decision nodes and constraints) are split (respectively, added) by tests, modified by assignments and joined (respectively, removed) when merging control flows. In order to minimize the cost of the analysis, a widening limits the height of the decision trees and the number of maintained disjunctions.

We also emphasize that the partitioning is *semantic-based* rather than syntactic-based: the linear constraints labeling the decision nodes are automatically inferred by the analysis and do not necessarily appear in the program.

The abstract domain is parametric in the choice between the expressivity and the cost of the linear constraints for the decision nodes (e.g., polyhedral or octagonal constraints), and the choice of the numerical abstract domain for the leaf nodes. As a result of its adaptability, the abstract domain is well-suited to be used for the inference of different program properties, from program invariants to ranking functions.

```
int f (int x, int y, int r) {
    while ¹( r > 0 ) {
        ²r = r + x;
        ³r = r − y;
    }⁴
    return 0;
}
```

Fig. 1. Simple C function. It terminates if $x < y$.

In the following, we describe an instance of this domain based on piecewise-defined ranking functions [30,31] for the inference of sufficient preconditions for program termination.

Through this instance we propose an approach to termination analysis of imperative programs which is *modular*, i.e., which allows reasoning on a portion of the code (e.g., a function) at a time — without any knowledge about the complete program — and reusing the analysis result whenever the same function is called.

To illustrate the potential of our approach, let us consider the simple C function in Figure 1: at each loop iteration, the value of r is increased by the value of x and decreased by the value of y. Our abstract domain, parameterized by polyhedral constraints at the decision nodes and affine ranking functions at the leaf nodes and using a widening with thresholds, is able to automatically infer that the program terminates in at most r loop iterations (i.e., in at most $3r + 1$ program steps) if $x < y$ (the constraint $x < y$ not appearing in the program).

Our Contribution. In summary, in this paper we make several contributions. First, we propose a parameterized abstract domain for the disjunctive refinement of numerical abstract domains. We show its adaptability to different abstractions, focusing in particular on piecewise-defined ranking functions for proving program conditional termination. Second, we thoroughly discuss the widening operator for ranking functions, which is non trivial and of independent interest. Finally, we evaluate our approach for termination against state-of-the-art implementations [5,19,22].

2 Termination Semantics

We consider a programming language with non-deterministic statements. The operational semantics of a program is described by a transition system $\langle \Sigma, \tau \rangle$, where Σ is the set of program states and the program transition relation $\tau \subseteq \Sigma \times \Sigma$ describes the possible transitions between states during program execution. Let $\beta_\tau \triangleq \{s \in \Sigma \mid \forall s' \in \Sigma : \langle s, s' \rangle \notin \tau\}$ denote the set of final states.

The Floyd/Turing traditional method for proving program termination [15] consists in inferring ranking functions, namely mappings from program states to elements of a well-ordered set (e.g., $\langle \mathbb{O}, < \rangle$, the well-ordered set of ordinals) whose value decreases during program execution.

Intuitively, we can define a ranking function from the states of a program to ordinal numbers in an incremental way: starting from the program final states and retracing the program backwards while counting the maximum number of performed program steps as value of the function. In [12], this intuition is formalized into a *most precise ranking function*[1] $w \in \Sigma \rightharpoonup \mathbb{O}$ that can be expressed as the least fixpoint of the operator ϕ starting from the totally undefined function $\dot{\emptyset}$:

$$w \triangleq \mathsf{lfp}^{\preccurlyeq}_{\dot{\emptyset}}\ \phi$$

$$\phi(v) \triangleq \lambda s. \begin{cases} 0 & \text{if } s \in \beta_\tau \\ \sup\{v(s') + 1 \mid \langle s, s' \rangle \in \tau\} & \text{if } s \in \widetilde{\mathsf{pre}}(\mathsf{dom}(v)) \\ \text{undefined} & \text{otherwise} \end{cases}$$

where $v_1 \preccurlyeq v_2 \triangleq \mathsf{dom}(v_1) \subseteq \mathsf{dom}(v_2) \land \forall x \in \mathsf{dom}(v_1) : v_1(x) \leq v_2(x)$ and $\widetilde{\mathsf{pre}}(X) \triangleq \{s \in \Sigma \mid \forall s' \in \Sigma : \langle s, s' \rangle \in \tau \Rightarrow s' \in X\}$. The domain $\mathsf{dom}(w)$ of w is the set of states definitely leading to program termination: any trace starting in a state $s \in \mathsf{dom}(w)$ must terminate in at most $w(s)$ execution steps, while at least one trace starting in a state $s \notin \mathsf{dom}(w)$ does not terminate.

The most precise ranking function w is sound and complete to prove program termination (see [12]). However, it is usually not computable. In [30,31], we present decidable abstractions of w by means of piecewise-defined ranking functions over natural numbers [30] and ordinals [31]. The abstractions refer to the following approximation order (see [11] for further discussion on approximation and computational orders of an abstract domain):

$$v_1 \sqsubseteq v_2 \triangleq \mathsf{dom}(v_1) \supseteq \mathsf{dom}(v_2) \land \forall x \in \mathsf{dom}(v_2) : v_1(x) \leq v_2(x).$$

They compute an *over-approximation* of the value of the function w and an *under-approximation* of its domain of definition $\mathsf{dom}(w)$. In this way, an abstraction provides sufficient preconditions for program termination: if the abstraction is defined on a program state, then all program execution traces branching from that state are terminating.

[1] $A \rightharpoonup B$ is the set of partial maps from a set A to a set B.

3 Piecewise-Defined Ranking Functions

We derive new decidable abstractions of w by introducing the abstract domain of constraint-based decision trees $\mathbb{T}$ and combining it with the piecewise-defined ranking functions abstractions from [30,31].

Let $\mathcal{X} = \{x_1, \ldots, x_n\}$ be a finite and totally ordered set of program variables with value in $\mathbb{Z}$. We split the program state space Σ into program control points $\mathcal{P}$ and environments $\mathcal{E} \triangleq \mathcal{X} \to \mathbb{Z}$, which map each program variable to its integer value at a given program control point. No approximation is made on $\mathcal{P}$. On the other hand, each program control point $p \in \mathcal{P}$ is associated with an element $t \in \mathcal{T}$ of the abstract domain $\mathbb{T}$. Specifically, t represents an abstraction of the function $v \in \mathcal{E} \rightharpoonup \mathbb{O}$ defined on the environments related to the program control point p:

$$\langle \mathcal{E} \rightharpoonup \mathbb{O}, \sqsubseteq \rangle \xleftarrow{\gamma_{\mathsf{T}}} \langle \mathcal{T}, \sqsubseteq_{\mathsf{T}} \rangle.$$

(we postpone the formal definition of γ_{T} to Section 3.2).

We assume we are given as parameter a (possibly infinite) set $\mathcal{L}$ of linear constraints over $\mathcal{X}$ (e.g., interval [10], octagonal [27] or polyhedral [14] constraints). We also assume we are given an abstraction of partial functions from environments to ordinals by means of a numerical abstract domain for functions $\mathbb{F} \triangleq \langle \mathcal{F}, \sqsubseteq_{\mathsf{F}} \rangle$ [30,31], equipped with a bottom element $\bot_{\mathsf{F}}$ representing the totally undefined function $\emptyset$.

The elements of the abstract domain $\mathbb{T}$ are disjunctive refinements of those of $\mathbb{F}$ (i.e., piecewise-defined functions) in the form of *constraint-based decision trees*, i.e., decision trees where the decision nodes are labeled by linear constraints in $\mathcal{L}$, and the leaf nodes belong to $\mathcal{F}$. As an example, in Figure 2, the constraint-based decision tree represents the piecewise-defined partial ranking function of the program in Figure 1:

$$f(x, y, r) = \begin{cases} 1 & r \leq 0 \\ 3r + 1 & r > 0 \wedge x < y \\ \text{undefined} & r > 0 \wedge x \geq y \end{cases}$$

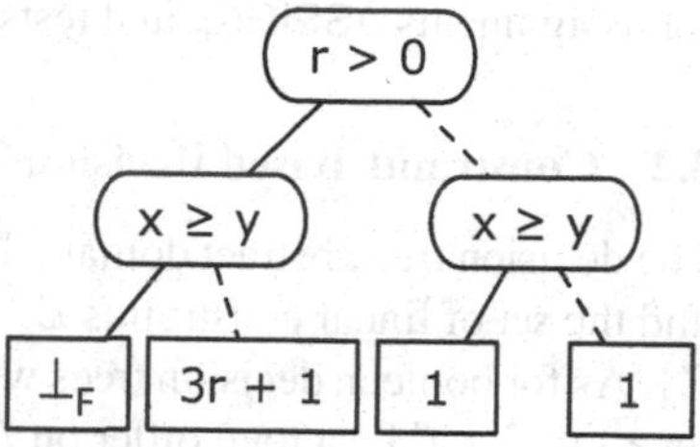

Fig. 2. Example of constraint-based decision tree abstracting a function. The leaves of the tree represent the value of the function for the satisfied constraints on the variables.

In the following, we first dive into some more details on the functions abstract domain. Then, we give a more formal presentation of our constraint-based decision trees and all abstract operators, including widening to ensure convergence.

3.1 Functions Abstract Domain

The functions abstract domain $\mathbb{F}$ abstracts a partial ranking function $v \in \mathcal{E} \rightharpoonup \mathbb{O}$ from environments to ordinals by an element $f \in \mathcal{F}$ which is a function of the program variables, or the element $\bot_{\mathsf{F}}$ representing potential non-termination, or the element $\top_{\mathsf{F}}$ representing the lack of enough information to conclude. In the following, the leaf nodes belonging to $\mathcal{F} \setminus \{\bot_\mathsf{F}, \top_\mathsf{F}\}$ and $\{\bot_\mathsf{F}, \top_\mathsf{F}\}$ will be referred to as *defined* and *undefined* leaf nodes, respectively.

In order to under-approximate the domain of definition of the most precise ranking function, the concretization function γ_F maps all undefined leaf nodes to the totally undefined function $\dot{\emptyset}$:

$$\gamma_\mathsf{F}(\bot_\mathsf{F}) = \gamma_\mathsf{F}(\top_\mathsf{F}) = \dot{\emptyset}$$

In fact, the computational and approximation ordering of the abstract domain respectively do and do not distinguish between $\bot_\mathsf{F}$ and $\top_\mathsf{F}$. In particular, the element $\top_\mathsf{F}$ is produced and used only by the widening operator discussed in the upcoming Section 3.3.

In [30], we considered instances of the abstract domain $\mathbb{F}$ based on affine functions $f(x_1, \ldots, x_n) = m_1x_1 + \cdots + m_nx_n + q$, where $m_1, \ldots, m_n, q$ are constants. In [31] we extended the abstraction to functions over ordinals.

Remark 1. In this paper, we are mainly focusing on instances of $\mathbb{T}$ for program termination. However, we emphasize that $\mathbb{T}$ is also well-suited to be instantiated with other numerical abstract domains. In fact, analogously to [20], we can have $\mathcal{F} \triangleq \{\mathbf{0}, \mathbf{1}\}$ and interpret the abstract domain $\mathbb{T}$ as the disjunctive refinement of numerical abstract domains such as intervals [10], octagons [27] and convex polyhedra [14].

We assume that the abstract domain $\mathbb{F}$ is equipped with sound binary operators for approximation ordering $\sqsubseteq_\mathsf{F}$, join $\sqcup_\mathsf{F}$ and widening $\triangledown_\mathsf{F}$, as well as sound transfer functions for assignments $\mathsf{ASSIGN}_\mathsf{F}$ and tests $\mathsf{FILTER}_\mathsf{F}$. We refer to [30,31] for examples.

3.2 Constraint-Based Decision Trees

The decision tree abstract domain $\mathbb{T}$ is parametric in the choice of the abstract domain $\mathbb{F}$ and the set of linear constraints $\mathcal{L} \subseteq \{k_1x_1 + \cdots + k_nx_n \leq k_{n+1} \mid k_1, \ldots, k_n, k_{n+1} \in \mathbb{Z}\}$. As for boolean decision trees where an ordering is imposed on all decision variables, let $<_\mathsf{L} \in \mathcal{L} \times \mathcal{L}$ be a total order on $\mathcal{L}$. As an example, we can define $<_\mathsf{L}$ to be the lexicographic order on the coefficients $k_1, \ldots, k_n$ and constant k_{n+1} of the linear constraints.

An element t of the abstract domain $\mathbb{T}$ belongs to a set $\mathcal{T}$ and is either a leaf node $\mathsf{LEAF} : f$, with f an element of $\mathcal{F}$, or a decision node $\mathsf{NODE}\{c\} : t_1; t_2$, such that c is a linear constraint in $\mathcal{L}$ (in the following denoted by $t.c$) and the left subtree t_1 and the right subtree t_2 (in the following denoted by $t.l$ and $t.r$, respectively) belong to $\mathcal{T}$. In particular, given a decision tree $\mathsf{NODE}\{c\} : t_1; t_2$, the linear constraint c is always the smallest constraint appearing in the tree, and the left and right subtrees t_1 and t_2 are either both leaf nodes or both decision nodes labeled with the same linear constraint c' (such that $c <_\mathsf{L} c'$), i.e., two decision nodes at the same height in the decision tree are always labeled with the same linear constraint. In order to ensure a canonical representation, we also avoid a constraint c and its negation $\neg c$ simultaneously appearing in a constraint-based decision tree (e.g., by keeping only the largest constraint with respect to $<_\mathsf{L}$ between c and $\neg c$).

Remark 2. The choice of maintaining the same constraints at the same height in the decision trees is important for the design of the widening operator as explained in the following Section 3.3.

Algorithm 1. Tree Unification

1: **function** UNIFICATION(t_1,t_2)
2: **if** ISLEAF(t_1) $\wedge$ ISLEAF(t_2) **then**
3: **return** $(t_1,\ t_2)$
4: **else if** ISLEAF(t_1) $\vee$ (ISNODE(t_1) $\wedge$ ISNODE(t_2) $\wedge\ t_2.c <_{\mathsf{L}} t_1.c$) **then**
5: $(l_1, l_2) \leftarrow$ UNIFICATION($t_1, t_2.l$)
6: $(r_1, r_2) \leftarrow$ UNIFICATION($t_1, t_2.r$)
7: **return** $(\mathsf{NODE}\{t_2.c\} : l_1; r_1,\ \mathsf{NODE}\{t_2.c\} : l_2; r_2)$
8: **else if** ISLEAF(t_2) $\vee$ (ISNODE(t_1) $\wedge$ ISNODE(t_2) $\wedge\ t_1.c <_{\mathsf{L}} t_2.c$) **then**
9: $(l_1, l_2) \leftarrow$ UNIFICATION($t_1.l, t_2$)
10: $(r_1, r_2) \leftarrow$ UNIFICATION($t_1.r, t_2$)
11: **return** $(\mathsf{NODE}\{t_1.c\} : l_1; r_1,\ \mathsf{NODE}\{t_1.c\} : l_2; r_2)$
12: **else**
13: $(l_1, l_2) \leftarrow$ UNIFICATION($t_1.l, t_2.l$)
14: $(r_2, r_2) \leftarrow$ UNIFICATION($t_1.r, t_2.r$)
15: **return** $(\mathsf{NODE}\{t_1.c\} : l_1; r_1,\ \mathsf{NODE}\{t_2.c\} : l_2; r_2)$

A constraint-based decision tree $t \in \mathcal{T}$, recursively partitions the space of values of the program variables inducing disjunctions into the abstract domain $\mathbb{F}$. Moreover, since two decision nodes at the same height in the decision tree are always labeled with the same linear constraint, they induce the same partition on their left and right subtrees.

Concretization Function. The concretization function γ_{T} depends on the concretization function γ_{F} of the abstract domain $\mathbb{F}$ and produces a (partial) ranking function:

$$\gamma_{\mathsf{T}}(\mathsf{LEAF} : f) = \gamma_{\mathsf{F}}(f)$$
$$\gamma_{\mathsf{T}}(\mathsf{NODE}\{c\} : t_1; t_2) = \gamma_{\mathsf{T}}(t_1)|_c \ \dot{\cup}\ \gamma_{\mathsf{T}}(t_2)|_{\neg c}$$

where $v|_c$ is the partial ranking function $v \in \mathcal{E} \rightharpoonup \mathbb{O}$ whose domain $\mathsf{dom}(v)$ is restricted to the environments satisfying the constraint c and $\dot{\cup}$ joins partial functions with disjoint domains: $(f_1 \dot{\cup} f_2)(x) \triangleq f_1(x)$, if $x \in \mathsf{dom}(f_1)$, and $(f_1 \dot{\cup} f_2)(x) \triangleq f_2(x)$, if $x \in \mathsf{dom}(f_2)$, where $\mathsf{dom}(f_1) \cap \mathsf{dom}(f_2) = \emptyset$.

Ordering, Join. The binary operators for the approximation ordering $\sqsubseteq_{\mathsf{T}}$ and join $\sqcup_{\mathsf{T}}$ of constraint-based decision trees rely on Algorithm 1 for tree unification. Given two decision trees $t_1 \in \mathcal{T}$ and $t_2 \in \mathcal{T}$, the tree unification algorithm finds a common refinement for the trees, possibly adding decision nodes (cf. Lines 5-7 and Lines 9-11). Note that the tree unification does not loose any information. Then, the binary operations are carried out "leaf-wise" on the unified constraint-based decision trees.

Ordering. Given two unified constraint-based decision trees, their approximation ordering is decided by the approximation ordering $\sqsubseteq_{\mathsf{F}}$ of the abstract domain $\mathbb{F}$:

$$(\mathsf{LEAF} : f_1) \sqsubseteq_{\mathsf{T}} (\mathsf{LEAF} : f_2) = f_1 \sqsubseteq_{\mathsf{F}} f_2$$
$$(\mathsf{NODE}\{c\} : l_1; r_1) \sqsubseteq_{\mathsf{T}} (\mathsf{NODE}\{c\} : l_2; r_2) = (l_1 \sqsubseteq_{\mathsf{T}} l_2) \wedge (r_1 \sqsubseteq_{\mathsf{T}} r_2)$$

Algorithm 2. Tree Augment

function AUGMENT(t,C)
  if ISEMPTY(C) **then return** t
  else
    $c \leftarrow \min_{<_L} C$ /* c is the smallest constraint appearing in C */
    return (NODE$\{c\}$: AUGMENT($t, C \setminus \{c\}$); AUGMENT($t, C \setminus \{c\}$))

Algorithm 3. Tree Assign

1: **function** ASSIGN(t,$x := a$)
2:   **if** ISLEAF(t) **then return** LEAF : $\mathsf{ASSIGN}_\mathsf{F}(f, x := a)$ /* $t \triangleq$ LEAF : f */
3:   **else**
4:     $C \leftarrow \mathsf{ASSIGN}_\mathsf{L}(t.c, x := a)$
5:     **if** ISEMPTY(C) **then return** ASSIGN($t.l, x := a$) $\sqcup_\mathsf{T}$ ASSIGN($t.r, x := a$)
6:     **else if** ISUNSAT(C) **then return** ASSIGN($t.r, x := a$)
7:     **else**
8:       $l \leftarrow$ AUGMENT(ASSIGN($t.l, x := a$), C)
9:       $r \leftarrow$ AUGMENT(ASSIGN($t.r, x := a$), C)
10:       **return** NODE$\{l.c\}$: $l; r$

Join. Similarly, given two unified constraint-based decision trees, their join is built using the join operator $\sqcup_\mathsf{F}$ of the abstract domain $\mathbb{F}$:

$$(\mathsf{LEAF} : f_1) \sqcup_\mathsf{T} (\mathsf{LEAF} : f_2) = \mathsf{LEAF} : (f_1 \sqcup_\mathsf{F} f_2)$$
$$(\mathsf{NODE}\{c\} : l_1; r_1) \sqcup_\mathsf{T} (\mathsf{NODE}\{c\} : l_2; r_2) = \mathsf{NODE}\{c\} : (l_1 \sqcup_\mathsf{T} l_2); (r_1 \sqcup_\mathsf{T} r_2)$$

Assignments, Tests. The transfer functions for assignments $\mathsf{ASSIGN}_\mathsf{T}$ and tests $\mathsf{FILTER}_\mathsf{T}$ add, modify or delete decision nodes of a constraint-based decision tree. In particular, both operators rely on Algorithm 2 for the extension of a constraint-based decision tree $t \in \mathcal{T}$ with decision nodes built from linear constraints in $C \subseteq \mathcal{L}$.

Assignments. We recall that the most precise ranking function w defined in Section 2 is a *backward semantics*. Consequently, we consider *backward assignments* to a constraint-based decision tree. The transfer function $\mathsf{ASSIGN}_\mathsf{T}$ is described by Algorithm 3. An assignment $x := a$ to a tree $t \in \mathcal{T}$ is carried out independently on each constraint $c \in \mathcal{L}$ appearing in t (cf. Line 4): given a constraint c, the primitive $\mathsf{ASSIGN}_\mathsf{L}$ substitutes the expression a for the variable x within the constraint c. Since the modified constraint may not be representable exactly in $\mathcal{L}$, $\mathsf{ASSIGN}_\mathsf{L}$ produces a set of constraints $C \subseteq \mathcal{L}$ approximating it. For instance, non-linear assignments can be modeled using standard linearization techniques [3]. In case C is empty, it means that the constraint c does not exist anymore and the subtrees of t should be joined (cf. Line 5). In case C is an unsatisfiable set of constraints, it means that c is no longer satisfiable and we should keep only the right subtree of t (cf. Line 6). Otherwise, C is a set of constraints that should be substituted to c in t (cf. Lines 8-10). Finally, an assignment to a leaf node is carried out by the operator $\mathsf{ASSIGN}_\mathsf{F}$ of the abstract domain $\mathbb{F}$ (cf. Line 2).

Algorithm 4. Tree Filter

1: **function** FILTER-AUX(t,c)
2:     **if** ISLEAF(t) **then return** LEAF : $\mathsf{FILTER_F}(f, c)$ $/* \; t \triangleq$ LEAF : $f \; */$
3:     **else return** NODE$\{t.c\}$: FILTER-AUX$(t.l, c)$; FILTER-AUX$(t.r, c)$

4: **function** FILTER(t,c)
5:     $C \leftarrow \mathsf{FILTER_L}(c)$
6:     **return** AUGMENT(FILTER-AUX$(t, c), C$)

Remark 3. Note that Algorithm 3 is general enough to also handle forward assignments, in case the abstract domain $\mathbb{T}$ is instantiated with other numerical abstract domains as mentioned in Remark 1. In fact, it is sufficient to modify the primitive $\mathsf{ASSIGN_L}$ accordingly in order to handle forward assignments.

Example 1. Let us consider the constraint-based decision tree NODE$\{x - y \leq 0\}$: (NODE$\{y \leq 0\}$: $\alpha; \beta$); (NODE$\{y \leq 0\}$: $\gamma; \delta$), where greek letters denote leaf nodes. The forward non-invertible assignment $y = 3$, modifies the constraint $x - y \leq 0$ to $x \leq 3$ and removes the constraint $y \leq 0$ which is no longer satisfiable: NODE$\{x \leq 3\}$: $\beta; \delta$. Instead, the backward non-deterministic assignment $y = \;?$ removes y from any constraint appearing in the tree, enforcing the join of the leaf nodes α and β and the leaf nodes γ and δ: NODE$\{x \leq 0\}$: $(\alpha \sqcup_\mathsf{T} \beta); (\gamma \sqcup_\mathsf{T} \delta)$. □

Tests. The transfer function $\mathsf{FILTER_T}$ for test statements is described by Algorithm 4. First, a test statement c is handled independently on each leaf node (cf. Line 2). The primitive $\mathsf{FILTER_L}$ approximates c producing a set of constraints $C \subseteq \mathcal{L}$ (cf. Line 5). Then, the constraint-based decision tree $t \in \mathcal{T}$ is augmented with C (cf. Line 6).

Note that, following an assignment or a test, the decision trees must be *sorted* and *normalized* in order to remove possible multiple occurrences of a constraint c and possible occurrences of both a constraint c and its negation $\neg c$ (e.g., by keeping only the largest constraint with respect to $<_\mathsf{L}$ between c and $\neg c$): for example, NODE$\{y \leq 1\}$: (NODE$\{y \leq 0\}$: $\alpha; \beta$); (NODE$\{y \leq 0\}$: $\gamma; \delta$) is sorted as NODE$\{y \leq 0\}$: (NODE$\{y \leq 1\}$: $\alpha; \gamma$); (NODE$\{y \leq 1\}$: $\beta; \delta$) and NODE$\{-y \leq -1\}$: (NODE$\{y \leq 0\}$: $\alpha; \beta$); (NODE$\{y \leq 0\}$: $\gamma; \delta$) is normalized as NODE$\{y \leq 0\}$: $\gamma; \beta$.

The soundness of all the abstract operators of $\mathbb{T}$ follows immediately from the soundness of the corresponding abstract operators of $\mathbb{F}$.

3.3 Widening

The widening operator $\triangledown_\mathsf{T}$ requires a more thorough discussion. The widening is allowed more freedom than the other operators, in the sense that it is *temporary* allowed to *under-approximate* the value of the most precise ranking function or *over-approximate* its domain of definition, or both — in contrast with the approximation order $\sqsubseteq$. This is necessary in order to extrapolate a ranking function over the program states on which

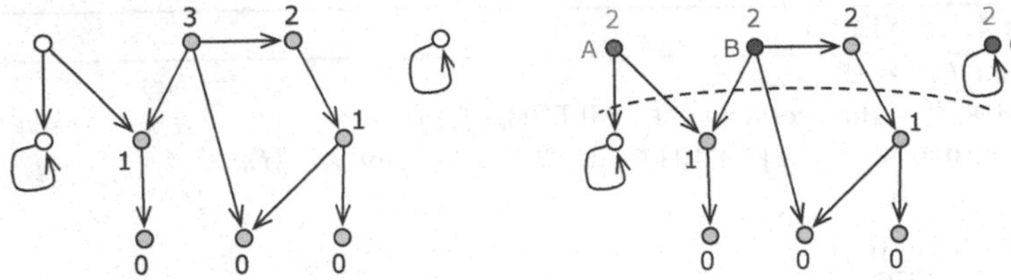

(a) Most precise ranking function. (b) Unsound abstraction.

Fig. 3. Example of unsound abstraction (b) of a most precise ranking function (a)

it is not yet defined. This is possible because the only requirement of a static analysis is that, when the iteration sequence with widening is stable for the computational order, its limit is a sound abstraction of the program semantics of interest with respect to the approximation order. For this reason, the widening ∇_T consists of many steps that need to be performed in order to guarantee the soundness of the analysis with respect to the most precise ranking function w. In the following, we will go through these steps and we will discuss them in some detail.

As running example, let us consider Figure 3. In Figure 3a we depict a transition system and the value of the most precise ranking function for the well-founded part of the transition relation. In Figure 3b we represent the concretization of a possible abstract analysis iterate. In this case the abstraction both under-approximates the value of the most precise ranking function (on the second state from the left — case B) and over-approximates its domain of definition (including the first and the last state from the left — case A and C, respectively). In case A, the loop causing non-termination is *outside* the domain of definition of the (unsound) abstract function, while in case C the loop is *inside*.

Step 1: Check for Case A. The first step that the widening operator ∇_T has to do is to check for cases like case A, where the domain of definition of the most precise ranking function has been over-approximated including a program state from which a non-terminating loop is reachable. In cases like case A, at the next iteration due to the soundness of all the other abstract operators (cf. Section 3.2) the value of the abstract function will become $\perp_F$. In order to handle such situations, the widening ∇_T has to look for leaf nodes whose value is now $\perp_F$ and that previously belonged to a defined subtree (i.e., a subtree with only defined leaf nodes). Then, it has to substitute their value with $\top_F$ in order to prevent successive iterates from mistakenly including again the same program states into the abstract function.

Step 2: Domain Widening - Tree Left Unification. At this point, the widening operator ∇_T calls Algorithm 5 for tree unification. Algorithm 5 is a slight modification of Algorithm 1: given two constraint-based decision trees[2] the left unification algorithm enforces the refinement of the first tree on the second, possibly removing decision nodes

[2] Algorithm 5 requires the constraints appearing in the first tree to be a subset of those appearing in the second, which can always be ensured by computing $t_1 \nabla_T (t_1 \sqcup_T t_2)$ instead of $t_1 \nabla_T t_2$.

Algorithm 5. Tree Left Unification

1: **function** LEFT-UNIFICATION(t_1,t_2)
2:   **if** ISLEAF(t_1) $\wedge$ ISLEAF(t_2) **then**
3:     **return** $(t_1,\ t_2)$
4:   **else**
5:     **if** ISLEAF(t_1) $\vee$ (ISNODE(t_1) $\wedge$ ISNODE(t_2) $\wedge$ $t_2.c <_{\mathsf{L}} t_1.c$) **then**
6:       **return** LEFT-UNIFICATION($t_1, t_2.l \sqcup_{\mathsf{T}} t_2.r$)
7:     **else**
8:       $(l_1, l_2) \leftarrow$ LEFT-UNIFICATION($t_1.l, t_2.l$)
9:       $(r_2, r_2) \leftarrow$ LEFT-UNIFICATION($t_1.r, t_2.r$)
10:       **return** ($\mathsf{NODE}\{t_1.c\} : l_1; r_1,\ \mathsf{NODE}\{t_2.c\} : l_2; r_2$)

(by joining subtrees, cf. Line 6) and thus *extrapolating the domain* of the abstract ranking function over program states on which it is not yet defined. In this way we might loose information but we ensure convergence limiting the size of the constraint-based decision trees.

Note that it is important to check for cases like case A before the tree left unification. Otherwise, since leaf nodes whose value is $\perp_{\mathsf{F}}$ might disappear when joining subtrees, we would not be able to detect them.

Step 3: Check for Case B and C. The third step that the widening operator ∇_{T} has to do is to check for cases like case B, where the value of the most precise ranking function has been under-approximated, and cases like case C, where its domain of definition has been over-approximated including a non-terminating loop. In cases like B and C, at the next iteration the value of the abstract function will increase. In order to handle such situations, the widening ∇_{T} has to look for leaf nodes whose value has increased between two iterates and it has to substitute their value with $\top_{\mathsf{F}}$ in order to prevent an indefinite growth. Note that the widening is not able to distinguish between an under-approximation of the value of the most precise ranking function (as in case B) and an over-approximation of its domain of definition as in case C.

The following lemma establishes that the widening operator ∇_{T} always recovers from the inclusion of non-terminating program states into the domain of an abstract ranking function at some iterate X_i (i.e., it always recovers from an over-approximation of the domain $\mathsf{dom}(w)$ of the most precise ranking function w — cases A and C):

Lemma 1. $\mathsf{dom}(\gamma_{\mathsf{T}}(X_i)) \not\subseteq \mathsf{dom}(w) \Rightarrow \mathsf{dom}(\gamma_{\mathsf{T}}(X_{i+1})) \subset \mathsf{dom}(\gamma_{\mathsf{T}}(X_i))$

It follows that the domain of the limit w_{T} of the iteration sequence with widening is a sound *under-approximation* of the domain of the most precise ranking function w:

Corollary 1. $\mathsf{dom}(\gamma_{\mathsf{T}}(w_{\mathsf{T}})) \subseteq \mathsf{dom}(w)$

In addition, the next lemma establishes that, if at some iterate X_i the value of the most precise ranking function w is under-approximated (case B), the iteration sequence with widening ∇_{T} is not stable:

Lemma 2. $\exists s \in \mathsf{dom}(\gamma_{\mathsf{T}}(X_i)) \cap \mathsf{dom}(w) : w(s) > \gamma_{\mathsf{T}}(X_i)(s) \Rightarrow s \notin \mathsf{dom}(\gamma_{\mathsf{T}}(X_{i+1}))$

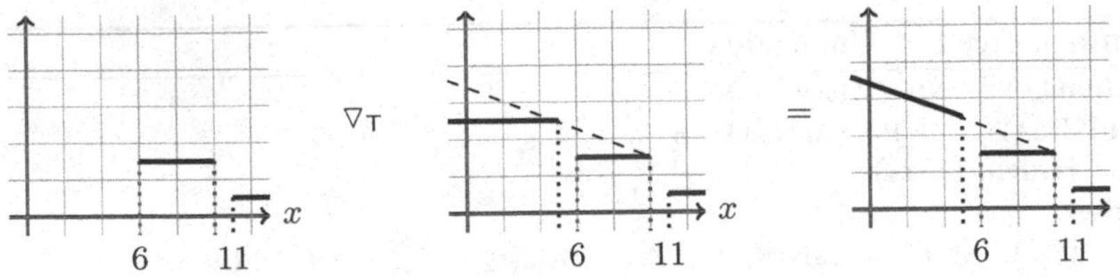

Fig. 4. Example of *Value Widening*

It follows that the value of the limit w_T of the iteration sequence with widening is a sound *over-approximation* of the value of the most precise ranking function w:

Corollary 2. $\forall s \in \mathsf{dom}(w) \cap \mathsf{dom}(\gamma_T(w_T)) : w(s) \leq \gamma_T(w_T)(s)$

Step 4: Value Widening. Once the widening operator ∇_T has checked for possible violations of the soundness and the domain of the abstract ranking function has been extrapolated, the last step is devoted to *extrapolating the value* of the ranking function over the program states on which it was not yet defined. The heuristic that we used in [30] has proved to be rather effective and justifies our choice to maintain the same linear constraint at the same height in the decision trees. We decided to widen the leaf nodes defined only in the second tree with respect to their *adjacent* leaf nodes. The rationale being that programs often loop over consecutive values of a variable, we use the information available in adjacent partitions of the domain of the ranking function to infer the shape of the ranking function for the current partitions, i.e., the leaf nodes defined only in the second tree (cf. Figure 4). Since we maintain the same linear constraint at the same height in the decisions tree, the adjacency between leaf nodes is pretty straightforward to define: two leaf nodes in a constraint-based decision tree are adjacent if their paths from the root differ for exactly one constraint satisfaction.

Remark 4. In establishing relationships only between adjacent leaf nodes, we are considering a rather naïve heuristic. Another possibility would be establishing relationships between leaf nodes based on the parity of some variable, or based on numerical relationships between variables. It is also possible to improve the widening by introducing thresholds in the left unification (in order to limit the loss of precision). We plan to investigate these possibilities as part of our future work.

Example 2. Let $\mathcal{F}$ be the set of *affine functions* of the program variables (plus $\bot_F$ and $\top_F$) [30]. We consider the widening between[3] $t_1 \triangleq \textsf{NODE}\{x \leq 0\} : (\textsf{LEAF} : 1); t'_1$ and $t_2 \triangleq \textsf{NODE}\{x \leq 0\} : (\textsf{LEAF} : 1); t'_2$ where the decision (sub)trees t'_1 and t'_2 are:

$$t'_1 \triangleq \textsf{NODE}\{x - y \leq 0\} : (\textsf{LEAF} : \bot_F); (\textsf{LEAF} : 3)$$

$$t'_2 \triangleq \textsf{NODE}\{x - y \leq 0\} : (\textsf{NODE}\{x - 2y \leq 0\} : (\textsf{LEAF} : 5); (\textsf{LEAF} : \bot_F)); (\textsf{LEAF} : 3)$$

First, the left unification modifies t'_2 into: $\textsf{NODE}\{x - y \leq 0\} : (\textsf{LEAF} : 3); (\textsf{LEAF} : 5)$. Then, the leaf node $\textsf{LEAF} : 5$, defined only in t'_2, is widened with respect to its adjacent leaf node $\textsf{LEAF} : 3$. This produces the leaf node $\textsf{LEAF} : 2x + 1$. □

[3] Redundant constraints in the decision trees are omitted for conciseness.

Since Algorithm 5 limits the height of constraint-based decision trees (cf. *Step* 2) and we prevent the indefinite growth of the value of the functions inside the leaf nodes (cf. *Step* 3), the iteration sequence with widening is eventually stable after finitely many steps. Its limit w_T is a sound abstraction of the most precise ranking function w:

Theorem 1. $w \sqsubseteq \gamma_T(w_T)$.

Proof. Follows by definition of $\sqsubseteq$ from Corollary 1 and Corollary 2. □

Remark 5. The reason for the complexity of the widening operator ∇_T is the coexistence of an approximation and a computational order in the termination semantics domain (cf. Section 2) as well as in the abstract domain. We believe that ours is the first widening in the two-order settings. In case the abstract domain $\mathbb{T}$ is instantiated with other numerical abstract domains as mentioned in Remark 1, the widening ∇_T becomes straightforward (only the tree left unification and "leaf-wise" widening ∇_F being needed).

3.4 Abstract Termination Semantics

The operators of the abstract domain are combined together to compute an abstraction of the most precise ranking function for a program, through *backward* invariance analysis. The starting point is the constant function equal to 0 at the program final control point. The ranking function is then propagated backwards towards the program initial control point taking assignments and tests into account with join and widening around loops. As a consequence of the soundness of all abstract operators and the soundness (and termination) of the iteration sequence with widening, we can establish the soundness of the analysis for proving program termination: the program states for which the analysis finds a ranking function are states from which the program indeed terminates.

Example 3. Let us consider the following simple C program:

$$\text{while}\ ^1(\ x > 0 \land y > 0\ )\ \{\ ^2x = x - y;\ \}^3$$

At each loop iteration, the value of x is decreased until it becomes less than or equal to zero. The program always terminates whatever the initial values for x and y are.

We analyze this program using our abstract domain of constraint-based decision trees, parameterized with polyhedral [14] constraints at the decision nodes and affine functions [30] at the leaf nodes. The starting point is $t_3 = \text{LEAF} : 0$ at the final control point 3. We use a widening delay of two iterations. At the first iteration, at the program control point 1 we obtain the decision tree $t_1^1 = \text{NODE}\{x \leq 0\} : (\text{LEAF} : 1); (\text{NODE}\{y \leq 0\} : (\text{LEAF} : 1); (\text{LEAF} : \bot_F))$ which, taking into account the assignment $x = x - y$, becomes $t_2^1 = \text{NODE}\{x - y \leq 0\} : (\text{NODE}\{y \leq 0\} : (\text{LEAF} : 2); (\text{LEAF} : \bot_F)); (\text{LEAF} : 2)$ at the program control point 2. At the third iteration the widening comes into action between the decision trees of Example 2 yielding a fixpoint: $t_1^3 = \text{NODE}\{x \leq 0\} : (\text{LEAF} : 1); (\text{NODE}\{x - y \leq 0\} : (\text{NODE}\{y \leq 0\} : (\text{LEAF} : 1); (\text{LEAF} : 2x + 1)); (\text{LEAF} : 3))$ (i.e., the ranking function $f_1(x, y) = 2x + 1$) which proves that the program terminates in at most $2x + 1$ program steps, whatever the initial values for x and y are. □

	Tot	FuncTion-OCT	FuncTion-POLY	FuncTion [31]	Time
FuncTion-OCT	39	–	0	18	4s
FuncTion-POLY	46	7	–	24	11s
FuncTion [31]	27	6	5	–	13s

Fig. 5. Overview of the experimental evaluation for FuncTion

4 Implementation

We have implemented our abstract domain of constraint-based decision trees $\mathbb{T}$ into our prototype static analyzer FuncTion[4] based on piecewise-defined ranking functions. A preliminary version of FuncTion [31] (without relational partitioning) participated in the *3rd International Competition on Software Verification (SV-COMP 2014)*, which featured a category for termination of C programs for the first time.

The prototype accepts programs written in a (subset of) C. It is written in OCaml and, at the time of writing, the available abstractions for handling linear constraints in decision trees are based on intervals [10], octagons [27] and convex polyhedra [14], and the available abstractions for ranking functions are based on affine functions. The operators from the intervals, octagons and convex polyhedra abstract domains are provided by the APRON library [24]. It is also possible to activate the extension to ordinal-valued ranking functions [31] and tune the precision of the analysis by adjusting the widening delay.

The analysis proceeds by structural induction on the program syntax, iterating loops until an abstract fixpoint is reached. In case of nested loops, a fixpoint on the inner loop is computed for each iteration of the outer loop.

Experiments. We have evaluated our prototype implementation against a set of 87 terminating C programs collected from the *SV-COMP 2014* termination category and from various publications in the area [1,6,9, etc.]. All the experiments were performed on a 1.30GHz Core i5 system with 4GB of RAM and running Ubuntu 12.04.

In Figure 5, we compared FuncTion to its preliminary version [31]. In particular, we evaluated the expressiveness and efficiency of two instances of our abstract domain of constraint-based decision trees: FuncTion-OCT (which uses octagonal constraints for labeling the decision nodes) and FuncTion-POLY (which uses polyhedral constraints). In the first column we report the total number of programs that each tool was able to prove termination for. In the second to the fourth column, we consider each tool and we report the number of programs that every other tool was able to prove terminating among the programs that the tool was not able to prove termination for. Finally, the last column reports the average running time in seconds for the programs where the tool proved termination. The results match the expectations: FuncTion-OCT is faster than FuncTion-POLY but less precise in seven examples; also, both FuncTion-OCT and FuncTion-POLY are more precise than FuncTion in its preliminary version. Note that, to improve precision, FuncTion [31] avoids trying to infer a ranking function for the non-reachable states while FuncTion-OCT and FuncTion-POLY do not apply yet this

[4] `http://www.di.ens.fr/~urban/FuncTion.html`

	Tot	FuncTion	AProVE [19]	T2 [5]	Ultimate [22]	Time	Timeouts
FuncTion	51	–	8	8	3	6s	5
AProVE [19]	60	17	–	7	2	35s	19
T2 [5]	73	30	20	–	3	2s	0
Ultimate [22]	79	31	21	9	–	9s	1

Fig. 6. Overview of the experimental evaluation for termination.

kind of optimizations: for this reason, FuncTion [31] was able to prove termination for respectively six and five programs that FuncTion-OCT and FuncTion-POLY were not able to prove terminating.

We also compared FuncTion (using all the available abstractions) to some of the other tools that participated to the termination category of *SV-COMP 2014*: AProVE [19], T2 [5], and Ultimate Büchi Automizer [22]. Figure 6 shows an overview of the experimental evaluation when using a time limit of 300 seconds for each example. In the first column we report the total number of programs that each tool was able to prove termination for. In the second to the fifth column, similarly to Figure 5, we consider each tool and we report the number of programs that every other tool was able to prove terminating among the programs that the tool was not able to prove termination for. Finally, the last columns report the average running time in seconds for the programs where the tool proved termination and the number of time outs (i.e., programs for which the analysis took more than 300 seconds). We observe that FuncTion proved termination of 51 of the 87 programs considered, while the other tools get better results. We noticed that the main reason for this is the value widening heuristic (cf. Section 3.3) used by FuncTion. We plan to study these issues further and improve the widening operator as part of our future work. However, we also observe that FuncTion was able to prove termination for eight programs that AProVE and T2 were not able to prove terminating, and for three programs that Ultimate Büchi Automizer was not able to prove termination for. We noticed that all these programs are characterized by the presence of multiple paths with unrelated or conflicting rankings inside loops: these programs are handled in a natural way by the inherent partitioning at the basis of our tool while the other tools must often resort to heuristics or specific workarounds [9].

5 Related Work

The use of (binary) decision trees (Binary Decision Diagrams, in particular) for verification has been devoted a large body of work, especially in the area of timed-systems and hybrid-system verification [23]. In this paper, we focus on common program analysis applications and, in this sense, our abstract domain is mostly related to the ones presented in [13,20]: both ours and these abstract domains are a disjunctive refinement of an abstract domain based on decision trees extended with linear constraints. However, the abstract domain proposed in [20] is designed specifically for the disjunctive refinement of the intervals abstract domain [10], while our abstract domain is parameterized by the (possibly relational) abstract domain we want to build the disjunctive refinement for. Moreover, while our abstract domain is based on binary decision trees where we impose the same linear constraint at the same tree level, in [13] the choices at the decision nodes may differ at each node and their number is not bounded a priori.

In general, despite all the available alternatives [3,13,18,20,21,29, etc.], it seems to us that in the literature there is no disjunctive abstract domain well-suited for program termination. A first (minor) reason is the fact that most of the existing disjunctive abstract domains are designed specifically for forward analyses while ranking functions are inferred through backward analysis (cf. Section 3.4). However, the main reason is that adapting existing widening operators to ranking functions is not obvious due to the coexistence of an approximation and computational ordering in the termination semantics domain (cf. Section 2 and Section 3.3).

As for related work on termination, we emphasize that our method is able to *directly* manipulate ranking functions which are dealt with as any other kind of invariants associated to program control points. In this sense, it differs from the majority of the literature based on the *indirect* use of invariants for synthesizing ranking functions or just proving termination [1,2,5,7,25, etc.]. Moreover, our approach is at the same time *modular* (i.e., able to reason on a portion of the code without any knowledge of the complete program) and able to deal with arbitrary control structures (i.e., it is not limited to simple loops as [28] or to non nested loops as [4]).

Finally, in the literature, we found only few works that have addressed the problem of automatically finding preconditions for program termination. In [8], the authors proposed a method based on preconditions generating ranking functions from potential rankings (i.e., mappings to elements of a well-ordered set whose value does not necessarily decrease during program execution), while our preconditions are inherently obtained from the inferred ranking functions as the set of programs state for which the ranking function is defined. Thus, our preconditions are derived by *under-approximation* of the set of terminating states as opposed to the approaches presented in [17,26] where the preconditions are derived by (complementing an) over-approximation of the non-terminating states.

6 Conclusion and Future Work

In this paper, we proposed a novel parameterized abstract domain for the disjunctive refinement of numerical abstract domains. We have shown its adaptability to different abstractions, focusing in particular on piecewise-defined ranking functions for automatically proving conditional termination. Our approach to program termination is semantic-based and approximate in a provably sound way. It is able to analyze programs that are out of the reach of state-of-the-art methods.

It remains for future work to improve the widening between ranking functions establishing cleverer relationships between leaf nodes of decision trees and introducing thresholds in order to limit the loss of precision. We also plan to design more abstract domains in order to support *non-linear* ranking functions (e.g., quadratic, cubic, exponential, . . .).

Acknowledgements. We are grateful to the developers of AProVE [19], T2 [5], and Ultimate Büchi Automizer [22] for their help with the experiments.

References

1. Alias, C., Darte, A., Feautrier, P., Gonnord, L.: Multi-Dimensional Rankings, Program Termination, and Complexity Bounds of Flowchart Programs. In: Cousot, R., Martel, M. (eds.) SAS 2010. LNCS, vol. 6337, pp. 117–133. Springer, Heidelberg (2010)
2. Berdine, J., Chawdhary, A., Cook, B., Distefano, D., O'Hearn, P.W.: Variance Analyses from Invariance Analyses. In: POPL, pp. 211–224 (2007)
3. Bertrane, J., Cousot, P., Cousot, R., Feret, J., Mauborgne, L., Miné, A., Rival, X.: Static Analysis and Verification of Aerospace Software by Abstract Interpretation. In: AIAA (2010)
4. Bradley, A.R., Manna, Z., Sipma, H.B.: Linear Ranking with Reachability. In: Etessami, K., Rajamani, S.K. (eds.) CAV 2005. LNCS, vol. 3576, pp. 491–504. Springer, Heidelberg (2005)
5. Brockschmidt, M., Cook, B., Fuhs, C.: Better Termination Proving through Cooperation. In: Sharygina, N., Veith, H. (eds.) CAV 2013. LNCS, vol. 8044, pp. 413–429. Springer, Heidelberg (2013)
6. Chen, H.Y., Flur, S., Mukhopadhyay, S.: Termination Proofs for Linear Simple Loops. In: Miné, A., Schmidt, D. (eds.) SAS 2012. LNCS, vol. 7460, pp. 422–438. Springer, Heidelberg (2012)
7. Colón, M.A., Sipma, H.B.: Practical Methods for Proving Program Termination. In: Brinksma, E., Larsen, K.G. (eds.) CAV 2002. LNCS, vol. 2404, pp. 442–454. Springer, Heidelberg (2002)
8. Cook, B., Gulwani, S., Lev-Ami, T., Rybalchenko, A., Sagiv, M.: Proving Conditional Termination. In: Gupta, A., Malik, S. (eds.) CAV 2008. LNCS, vol. 5123, pp. 328–340. Springer, Heidelberg (2008)
9. Cook, B., See, A., Zuleger, F.: Ramsey vs. Lexicographic Termination Proving. In: Piterman, N., Smolka, S.A. (eds.) TACAS 2013. LNCS, vol. 7795, pp. 47–61. Springer, Heidelberg (2013)
10. Cousot, P., Cousot, R.: Static Determination of Dynamic Properties of Programs. In: Symposium on Programming, pp. 106–130 (1976)
11. Cousot, P., Cousot, R.: Higher Order Abstract Interpretation and Application to Comportment Analysis Generalizing Strictness, Termination, Projection, and PER Analysis. In: ICCL, pp. 95–112 (1994)
12. Cousot, P., Cousot, R.: An Abstract Interpretation Framework for Termination. In: POPL, pp. 245–258 (2012)
13. Cousot, P., Cousot, R., Mauborgne, L.: A Scalable Segmented Decision Tree Abstract Domain. In: Manna, Z., Peled, D.A. (eds.) Time for Verification. LNCS, vol. 6200, pp. 72–95. Springer, Heidelberg (2010)
14. Cousot, P., Halbwachs, N.: Automatic Discovery of Linear Restraints Among Variables of a Program. In: POPL, pp. 84–96 (1978)
15. Floyd, R.W.: Assigning Meanings to Programs. Proceedings of Symposium on Applied Mathematics 19, 19–32 (1967)
16. Fuchs, H., Kedem, Z.M., Naylor, B.F.: On Visible Surface Generation by a Priori Tree Structures. SIGGRAPH Computer Graphics 14(3), 124–133 (1980)
17. Ganty, P., Genaim, S.: Proving Termination Starting from the End. In: Sharygina, N., Veith, H. (eds.) CAV 2013. LNCS, vol. 8044, pp. 397–412. Springer, Heidelberg (2013)
18. Giacobazzi, R., Ranzato, F.: Optimal Domains for Disjunctive Abstract Intepretation. Sci. Comput. Program. 32(1-3), 177–210 (1998)
19. Giesl, J., Schneider-Kamp, P., Thiemann, R.: Automatic Termination Proofs in the Dependency Pair Framework. In: IJCAR, pp. 281–286 (2006)

20. Gurfinkel, A., Chaki, S.: BOXES: A Symbolic Abstract Domain of Boxes. In: Cousot, R., Martel, M. (eds.) SAS 2010. LNCS, vol. 6337, pp. 287–303. Springer, Heidelberg (2010)
21. Gurfinkel, A., Chaki, S.: Combining Predicate and Numeric Abstraction for Software Model Checking. STTT 12(6), 409–427 (2010)
22. Heizmann, M., Hoenicke, J., Leike, J., Podelski, A.: Linear Ranking for Linear Lasso Programs. In: Van Hung, D., Ogawa, M. (eds.) ATVA 2013. LNCS, vol. 8172, pp. 365–380. Springer, Heidelberg (2013)
23. Jeannet, B.: Representing and Approximating Transfer Functions in Abstract Interpretation of Hetereogeneous Datatypes. In: Hermenegildo, M.V., Puebla, G. (eds.) SAS 2002. LNCS, vol. 2477, pp. 52–68. Springer, Heidelberg (2002)
24. Jeannet, B., Miné, A.: Apron: A Library of Numerical Abstract Domains for Static Analysis. In: Bouajjani, A., Maler, O. (eds.) CAV 2009. LNCS, vol. 5643, pp. 661–667. Springer, Heidelberg (2009)
25. Larraz, D., Oliveras, A., Rodríguez-Carbonell, E., Rubio, A.: Proving Termination of Imperative Programs using Max-SMT. In: FMCAD, pp. 218–225 (2013)
26. Massé, D.: Policy Iteration-based Conditional Termination and Ranking Functions. In: McMillan, K.L., Rival, X. (eds.) VMCAI 2014. LNCS, vol. 8318, pp. 453–471. Springer, Heidelberg (2014)
27. Miné, A.: The Octagon Abstract Domain. Higher-Order and Symbolic Computation 19(1), 31–100 (2006)
28. Podelski, A., Rybalchenko, A.: A Complete Method for the Synthesis of Linear Ranking Functions. In: Steffen, B., Levi, G. (eds.) VMCAI 2004. LNCS, vol. 2937, pp. 239–251. Springer, Heidelberg (2004)
29. Sankaranarayanan, S., Ivančić, F., Shlyakhter, I., Gupta, A.: Static Analysis in Disjunctive Numerical Domains. In: Yi, K. (ed.) SAS 2006. LNCS, vol. 4134, pp. 3–17. Springer, Heidelberg (2006)
30. Urban, C.: The Abstract Domain of Segmented Ranking Functions. In: Logozzo, F., Fähndrich, M. (eds.) Static Analysis. LNCS, vol. 7935, pp. 43–62. Springer, Heidelberg (2013)
31. Urban, C., Miné, A.: An Abstract Domain to Infer Ordinal-Valued Ranking Functions. In: Shao, Z. (ed.) ESOP 2014. LNCS, vol. 8410, pp. 412–431. Springer, Heidelberg (2014)

Region-Based Selective Flow-Sensitive Pointer Analysis

Sen Ye, Yulei Sui, and Jingling Xue

Programming Languages and Compilers Group
School of Computer Science and Engineering, UNSW Australia

Abstract. We introduce a new region-based SELective Flow-Sensitive (SELFS) approach to inter-procedural pointer analysis for C that operates on the regions partitioned from a program. Flow-sensitivity is maintained between the regions but not inside, making traditional flow-insensitive and flow-sensitive as well as recent sparse flow-sensitive analyses all special instances of our SELFS framework. By separating region partitioning as an independent concern from the rest of the pointer analysis, SELFS facilitates the development of flow-sensitive variations with desired efficiency and precision tradeoffs by reusing existing pointer resolution algorithms. We also introduce a new unification-based approach for region partitioning to demonstrate the generality and flexibility of our SELFS framework, as evaluated using SPEC2000/2006 benchmarks in LLVM.

1 Introduction

Finding a right balance between efficiency and precision lies at the core of pointer analysis. A flow-insensitive analysis (FI), as formulated for C using Andersen's algorithm [2] in Figure 1(a), is fast but imprecise, because it ignores control flow and thus computes a single solution pt to the entire program. Here, $pt(v)$ gives the points-to set of a variable v. In contrast, a flow-sensitive analysis (FS), as formulated by solving a data-flow problem in Figure 1(b), makes the opposite tradeoff. By respecting control flow (`[S-OUTIN]`, `[S-INOUT1]` and `[S-INOUT2]`), separate solutions $pt[\overline{\ell}]$ and $pt[\underline{\ell}]$ at distinct program points $\overline{\ell}$ and $\underline{\ell}$ (the ones immediately before and after each ℓ-labeled statement) are computed and maintained. Preserving flow-sensitivity this way has two precision benefits. One is to track the values read at a location through the control flow. The other is to enable *strong updates*: if a location is definitely updated by an assignment, then the previous values at the location can be killed. In `[S-ADDROF]`, `[S-COPY]` and `[S-LOAD]`, p at $\underline{\ell}$ is strongly updated since $pt[\overline{\ell}](p)$ is killed. For any $q \neq p$, its points-to information is preserved (`[S-INOUT1]`). In `[S-STORE]`, o at $\underline{\ell}$ is strongly updated if o is a singleton, i.e., a concrete location uniquely pointed by p (`[S-STORE`^{SU}`]`) and weakly updated otherwise (`[S-STORE`^{WU}`]`). For a target o' not pointed by p, its points-to information remains unchanged (`[S-INOUT2]`).

Flow-sensitivity is beneficial for a wide range of clients such as bug detection [22,30,31,34], program verification [10,11] and change impact analysis [1,4]. As the size and complexity of software increases, how to achieve flow-sensitivity

M. Müller-Olm and H. Seidl (Eds.): SAS 2014, LNCS 8723, pp. 319–336, 2014.

$$\texttt{[I-ADDROF]}\ \frac{p = \&o}{\{o\} \subseteq pt(p)} \qquad \texttt{[I-COPY]}\ \frac{p = q}{pt(q) \subseteq pt(p)}$$

$$\texttt{[I-STORE]}\ \frac{*p = q \quad o \in pt(p)}{pt(q) \subseteq pt(o)} \qquad \texttt{[I-LOAD]}\ \frac{p = *q \quad o \in pt(q)}{pt(o) \subseteq pt(p)}$$

(a) FI: constraints for Andersen's algorithm (flow-insensitive)

$$\texttt{[S-ADDROF]}\ \frac{\ell\colon p = \&o}{\{o\} \subseteq pt[\underline{\ell}](p)} \qquad \texttt{[S-COPY]}\ \frac{\ell\colon p = q}{pt[\overline{\ell}](q) \subseteq pt[\underline{\ell}](p)}$$

$$\texttt{[S-STORE}^{SU/\boxed{WU}}\texttt{]}\ \frac{\ell\colon *p = q \quad o \in pt[\overline{\ell}](p)}{pt[\overline{\ell}](q) \subseteq pt[\underline{\ell}](o) \quad \boxed{pt[\overline{\ell}](o) \subseteq pt[\underline{\ell}](o)}}$$

$$\texttt{[S-LOAD]}\ \frac{\ell\colon p = *q \quad o \in pt[\overline{\ell}](q)}{pt[\overline{\ell}](o) \subseteq pt[\underline{\ell}](p)} \qquad \texttt{[S-OUTIN]}\ \frac{v \in \mathcal{V} \quad \ell' \in succ(\ell)}{pt[\underline{\ell}](v) \subseteq pt[\overline{\ell'}](v)}$$

$$\texttt{[S-INOUT1]}\ \frac{\ell\colon p = \_ \quad q \neq p}{pt[\overline{\ell}](q) \subseteq pt[\underline{\ell}](q)} \qquad \texttt{[S-INOUT2]}\ \frac{\ell\colon *p = \_ \quad o' \notin pt[\overline{\ell}](p)}{pt[\overline{\ell}](o') \subseteq pt[\underline{\ell}](o')}$$

$\mathcal{V}$: set of variables *succ*: mapping statements to control flow successors

(b) FS: constraints for data-flow (flow-sensitive)

Fig. 1. Two traditional pointer analyses, FI and FS, for C programs

exactly or approximately with desired efficiency and precision tradeoffs becomes attractive. The "sparse" approach [14,23,35] aims to achieve the same precision as FS but more scalably. The basic idea is to first over-approximate the points-to information in a program with a fast but imprecise pre-analysis and then refine it by propagating the points-to facts *sparsely* only along the pre-computed def-use chains instead of across all program points as FS does. Alternatively, the "strong-update" approach [21] sacrifices the precision of FS in order to gain better efficiency. The basic idea is to proceed flow-sensitively to perform the same strong updates as in FS but falls back to FI otherwise. Despite these recent advances on flow-sensitive analysis, balancing efficiency and precision remains challenging, partly due to the difficulty in orchestrating various algorithms used during the analysis and partly due to the desire to meet different clients' needs.

A program usually exhibits diverse characteristics in its different code regions, which should be handled with different efficiency and precision tradeoffs (to avoid under- or over-analysing). In this paper, we propose a new region-based SELective Flow-Sensitive (SELFS) approach to pointer analysis for C that operates on the regions partitioned from a program rather than individual statements as in [14,35]. Top-level pointers can be put in SSA form [8] without requiring pointer analysis. To track the value-flows of address-taken variables effectively, we will perform a pre-analysis to enable their sparse analysis as in [14,23,35], but on a region graph with its regions containing loads and stores. Each region is analysed flow-insensitively but flow-sensitivity is maintained across the regions.

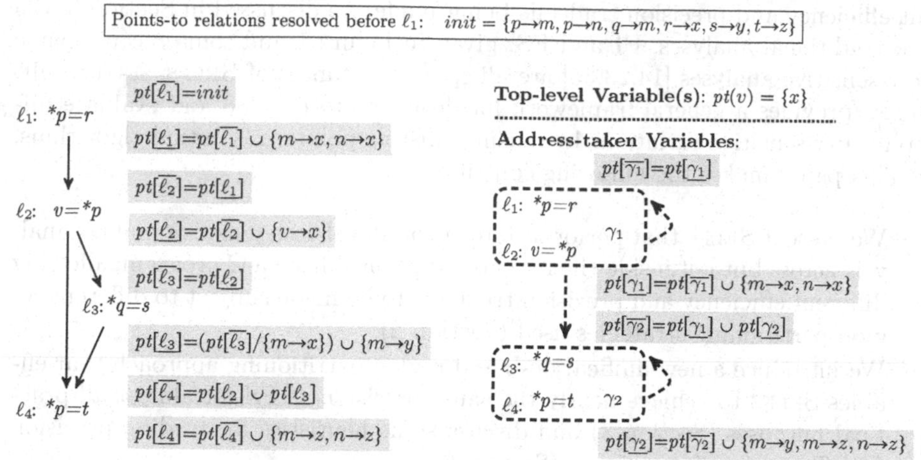

(a) Flow-sensitive analysis (b) The SELFS analysis

Fig. 2. An illustration of SELFS performed on regions γ_1 and γ_2 by preserving the precision of FS with respect to the reads from variables (with further details given in Figure 3 and Examples 1 – 3). The focus is on analysing the points-to relations for the top-level variable v and the two address-taken variables m (a singleton) and n, by assuming that the points-to relations in *init* are given. Here, $pt[\overline{\gamma}]$ ($pt[\underline{\gamma}]$), where γ is a region, is an analogue of $pt[\overline{\ell}]$ ($pt[\underline{\ell}]$), where ℓ is a statement.

Consider Figure 2, where the points-to relations in *init* are known before the code is analysed. Figure 2(a) depicts the points-to relations obtained by applying FS to the code. Note that a strong update on m (assumed to be a singleton) is performed at ℓ_3. Figure 2(b) gives the solution obtained by SELFS on a region graph (with two regions γ_1 and γ_2) to achieve more efficiently the same precision for reads from (but not necessarily for writes into) each variable. As p points to m and n, no strong update is possible at ℓ_1. Instead of flow-sensitively propagating the points-to relations from ℓ_1 to ℓ_2, both can be analysed flow-insensitively in region γ_1 without any precision loss for the reads from m and n at ℓ_2. Interestingly, even if a strong update is performed for m at ℓ_3, the points-to relations from ℓ_2 and ℓ_3 are merged on entry of ℓ_4, making any read from m at ℓ_4 (if any) as precise as if ℓ_3 and ℓ_4 are analysed together in γ_2 flow-insensitively. Note that SELFS has over-approximated the potential target of m at ℓ_3: $m \rightarrow y$ found by FS in Figure 2(a) with $m \rightarrow x$, $m \rightarrow y$ and $m \rightarrow z$ given in Figure 2(b). As argued in Section 3, preserving the precision for reads from all variables always preserves the alias information (among others). By operating at the granularity of regions rather than statements while maintaining flow-sensitivity across their edges (illustrated further in Figure 3), SELFS is expected to run faster.

Our SELFS analysis is also advantageous in that region partitioning is separated as an independent concern from the rest of the analysis. Different region partitions may lead to different degrees of flow-sensitivity, resulting in different efficiency and precision tradeoffs being made. As discussed in Section 3, the two traditional analyses, FI and FS, given in Figure 1 and some recent sparse flow-sensitive analyses [14,23,35] are all special instances of SELFS. As a result, SELFS provides a general framework for designers to develop and evaluate different flow-sensitive variations by reusing existing pointer resolution algorithms.

This paper makes the following contributions:

- We present SELFS that performs inter-procedural flow-sensitive pointer analysis across but not inside the regions partitioned from a C program, allowing different efficiency and precision tradeoffs to be made subject to different region partitioning strategies used (Section 2).
- We introduce a new unification-based region partitioning approach that enables SELFS to achieve nearly the same precision as FS for almost all practical purposes (Section 3) and discuss some heuristics for trading precision for efficiency in future work (Section 6).
- We have implemented SELFS in LLVM (version 3.3) and evaluated it using a total of 14 benchmarks selected from SPEC2000 and SPEC2006 (Section 4). SELFS can accelerate a state-of-the-art sparse yet precision-preserving version [14] of FS by 2.13X on average while maintaining the same precision for reads from variables, i.e., for all alias queries. In addition, the best speedups are observed at `h264ref` (7.45X) and `mesa` (6.08X).

2 The SELFS Analysis Framework

In this section, we present our SELFS analysis on a given region graph created from a program. In the next section, we describe some region partitioning strategies. Section 2.1 makes precise the canonical representation used for analysing C programs. Section 2.2 defines the region graphs operated on by SELFS. Section 2.3 formalises our region-based flow-sensitive pointer analysis.

2.1 Canonical Representation

In the pointer analysis literature, a C program is represented by a CFG (Control-Flow Graph) containing the four types of pointer-manipulating statements shown in Figure 1: $p = \&o$ (ADDROF), $p = q$ (COPY), $p = *q$ (LOAD) and $*p = q$ (STORE). More complex statements are decomposed into these basic ones. Passing arguments into and returning results from functions are modeled by copies. For a given ADDROF statement $p = \&o$, o is either a stack variable with its address taken or an abstract object dynamically created at an allocation site.

For simplicity, we adopt the convention of LLVM by separating the set $\mathcal{V}$ of all variables into two subsets, (1) $\mathcal{A}$ containing all possible targets, i.e., *address-taken variables* of a pointer and (2) $\mathcal{T}$ containing all *top-level variables*, where $\mathcal{V} = \mathcal{T} \cup \mathcal{A}$. For the four types of statements given, we have $p, q \in \mathcal{T}$ and $o \in \mathcal{A}$.

2.2 Region Graph

Our SELFS analysis operates on a region graph created from a program being analysed. Leveraging recent progress on sparse flow-sensitive analysis [14,23,35], we will perform a pre-analysis to both guide region partitioning and enable sparse analysis at the granularity of regions rather than individual statements.

To obtain a region graph from a program, top-level and address-taken variables are treated differently. In our SELFS framework, top-level variables are always analysed sparsely since they can be put in SSA without requiring pointer analysis. A top-level pointer that is defined multiple times is split into distinct versions after SSA conversion. All versions of a variable, say $q_{i_1}, \ldots, q_{i_n}$, that reach a joint point at the CFG are combined by introducing a new PHI statement, $q_j = \phi(q_{i_1}, \ldots, q_{i_n})$, where $q_j, q_{i_1}, \ldots, , q_{i_n} \in \mathcal{T}$, so that every version is defined once (statically). After SSA conversion, the *(direct) def-use chains* for all top-level variables are readily available. As a result, their points-to sets can be simply obtained flow-sensitively by performing a flow-insensitive analysis.

Unlike top-level variables, address-taken variables are read/written indirectly via top-level pointers at loads/stores and thus harder to analyse sparsely. Sparsity requires points-to information to be propagated along def-use chains but the *(indirect) def-use chains* for address-taken variables can only be computed using points-to information. To break the cycle, we perform a pre-analysis as in [7,14,23,30] to first over-approximate indirect def-use chains and then refine them by performing a data-flow analysis sparsely along such pre-computed def-use chains.

Note that an address-taken variable o accessed at a store represents a potential use of o if a weak update is performed ([S-STORE^{WU}] in Figure 1(b)). Due to space limitation, we refer to [14] on how to over-approximate indirect def-use chains (via a pre-analysis named AUX). The basic idea is to annotate a load $p = *q$ with a potential use of o for every o pointed by q and a store $*p = q$ with a potential use and def of o for every o pointed by p. Then indirect def-use chains can be built by putting all address-taken variables in SSA.

Therefore, SELFS keeps track of value flows for top-level variables in SSA explicitly along their (direct) def-use chains and refines value flows for address-taken variables along their pre-computed (indirect) def-chains in a region graph.

Definition 1 (Region Graph). *A region graph* $\mathcal{G}_{\text{rg}} = (\mathcal{N}_{\text{rg}}, \mathcal{E}_{\text{rg}})$ *for a program is a multi-edged directed graph.* $\mathcal{N}_{\text{rg}}$ *is a partition of the set of its loads and stores into regions.* $\mathcal{E}_{\text{rg}}$ *contains an edge* $\gamma_1 \xrightarrow{o} \gamma_2$ *labeled by an address-taken variable* $o \in \mathcal{A}$ *from* γ_1 *to* γ_2*, where* γ_1 *and* γ_2 *may be identical, if there is an indirect def-use chain for* o *from* γ_1 *to* γ_2 *computed by the pre-analysis.*

Example 1. Consider our example again in Figure 3. Figure 3(b) duplicates the region graph from Figure 2(b) except that its edges are now annotated explicitly with address-taken variables indicating their value flows. By Definition 1, these edges are added based on the statement-level indirect def-use chains obtained by pre-analysis, given in Figure 3(a). The presence of self-loop edge(s) in a region allows naturally the loads/stores inside to be analysed flow-insensitively. □

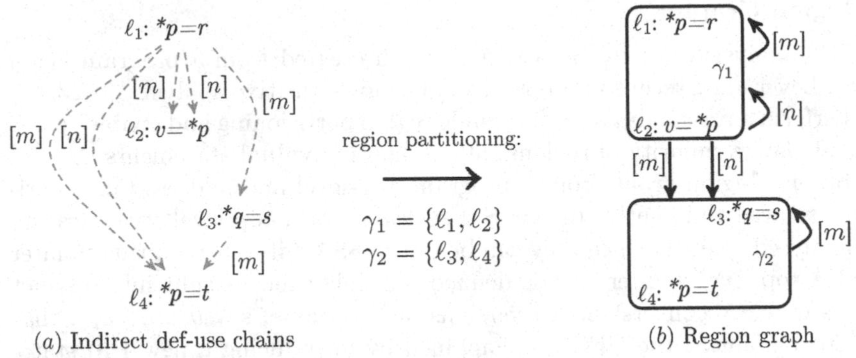

Fig. 3. The region graph in Figure 2(b) redrawn with all indirect def-use edges made explicit. The pre-analysis yields $p \rightarrow m$, $p \rightarrow n$ and $q \rightarrow m$ (included in *init* in Figure 2).

2.3 Region-Based Flow-Sensitivity

Figure 4 gives the inference rules used in our SELFS framework. Top-level variables are analysed as before except that they are now in SSA (`[R-PHI]`). Therefore, analysing the top-level variables in SSA flow-insensitively (`[R-ALLOC]` and `[R-COPY]`) as in FI gives rise to the flow-sensitive precision obtained as in FS. As a result, the points-to sets $pt(p)$ and $pt(q)$ of top-level pointers p and q are directly read off at a load (`[R-LOAD]`), a store (`[R-STORE]`), and in `[R-INOUT]`.

SELFS computes and maintains the points-to relations for address-taken variables sparsely in a region graph. Flow-sensitivity is maintained across the regions (along their indirect region-level def-use edges) but not inside. This implies that all statements in a region γ are handled flow-insensitively if $|\gamma| > 1$ and flow-sensitively otherwise (i.e., if $|\gamma| = 1$). As SELFS operates at the granularity of regions, the notation $pt[\overline{\gamma}]$ ($pt[\underline{\gamma}]$) for a region γ is an analogue of $pt[\overline{\ell}]$ ($pt[\underline{\ell}]$) for a statement ℓ, as already illustrated in Figure 2(b). For a region γ containing multiple statements, $pt[\underline{\gamma}]$ is the solution for all program points inside the region.

Below we explain the four rules, `[R-DU]`, `[R-INOUT]`, `[R-LOAD]` and `[R-STORE]`, used to compute the points-to relations for address-taken variables.

Together with `[R-INOUT]`, `[R-DU]` represents the sparse propagation of points-to relations for address-taken variables $o \in \mathcal{A}$ across their pre-computed def-use chains at the granularity of regions. In contrast, FS propagates such points-to relations blindly across the control flow (`[S-OUTIN]`, `[S-INOUT1]` and `[S-INOUT2]`).

In `[R-LOAD]`, $\gamma = \mathtt{selR}(\ell)$ is the region where the load at ℓ resides. No strong update is possible even if γ contains a store since $|\gamma| > 1$ will then hold. Regardless of how many statements that γ contains, the points-to set of o at the entry of γ is propagated into the points-to set of p: $pt[\overline{\gamma}](o) \subseteq pt(p)$, where $pt[\overline{\gamma}](o)$ contains the points-to relations that are (1) either received from its predecessors (`[R-DU]`) or (2) generated inside γ (due to a self-loop edge labeled by o when $|\gamma| > 1$), in which case, all statements inside γ are analysed flow-insensitively.

`[R-STORE]` is similar except that the points-to set of o indirectly accessed at a store is updated at the end of the region γ that contains the store. `[R-STORE`^{SU}`]`,

$$\texttt{[R-ADDROF]}\ \frac{\ell\colon p = \&o}{\{o\} \subseteq pt(p)} \qquad \texttt{[R-COPY]}\ \frac{\ell\colon p = q}{pt(q) \subseteq pt(p)} \qquad \texttt{[R-PHI]}\ \frac{\ell\colon p = \phi(\_, q, \_)}{pt(q) \subseteq pt(p)}$$

$$\texttt{[R-STORE}^{SU}/\boxed{WU}\texttt{]}\ \frac{\ell\colon *p = q \quad o \in pt(p) \quad \gamma = \texttt{selR}(\ell)}{pt(q) \subseteq pt[\underline{\gamma}](o) \quad \boxed{pt[\overline{\gamma}](o) \subseteq pt[\underline{\gamma}](o)}}$$

$$\texttt{[R-LOAD]}\ \frac{\ell\colon p = *q \quad o \in pt(q) \quad \gamma = \texttt{selR}(\ell)}{pt[\overline{\gamma}](o) \subseteq pt(p)} \qquad \texttt{[R-DU]}\ \frac{o \in \mathcal{A} \quad \gamma \xrightarrow{o} \gamma'}{pt[\underline{\gamma}](o) \subseteq pt[\overline{\gamma'}](o)}$$

$$\texttt{[R-INOUT]}\ \frac{\gamma \in \mathcal{N}_{\text{rg}} \quad o' \notin \{o \in pt(p) \mid (*p = q) \in \gamma\}}{pt[\overline{\gamma}](o') \subseteq pt[\underline{\gamma}](o')}$$

Fig. 4. Inference rules for SELFS (with top-level variables in SSA)

which is explained earlier in Section 1, comes into play only when $|\gamma| = 1$. Recall that SELFS only analyses single-statement regions flow-sensitively.

Example 2. Let us apply our inference rules to the region graph in Figure 3(b) to obtain the points-to relations given in Figure 2(b). As $|\gamma_1| = |\gamma_2| = 2$, [R-STORE^{SU}] cannot be applied. When γ_1 is processed, applying [R-STORE^{WU}] to ℓ_1 adds $m \rightarrow x$ and $n \rightarrow x$ to $pt[\underline{\gamma_1}]$ and applying [R-LOAD] to ℓ_2 yields $pt(v) = x$. Applying [R-DU] to the two self-loop edges $[m]$ and $[n]$ around γ_1 gives rise to $pt[\overline{\gamma_1}] = pt[\underline{\gamma_1}]$. Applying [R-DU] to the two edges $[m]$ and $[n]$ from γ_1 to γ_2, we obtain $pt[\overline{\gamma_2}] = \{m \rightarrow x, n \rightarrow x\}$.

When γ_2 is analysed, [R-STORE^{WU}] is applied to each store. So the points-to relations in $pt[\overline{\gamma_2}]$ are preserved in $pt[\underline{\gamma_2}]$. Then we add $m \rightarrow y$ generated at ℓ_3 and $m \rightarrow z$ and $n \rightarrow z$ at ℓ_4 to $pt[\underline{\gamma_2}]$. Next, applying [R-DU] to the self-loop $[m]$ on γ_2 causes $m \rightarrow y$ and $m \rightarrow z$ to be added to $pt[\overline{\gamma_2}]$. Finally, we obtain $pt[\overline{\gamma_2}] = \{m \rightarrow x, m \rightarrow y, m \rightarrow z, n \rightarrow x\}$ and $pt[\underline{\gamma_2}] = pt[\overline{\gamma_2}] \cup \{n \rightarrow z\}$. □

Theorem 1 (Soundness). SELFS *is sound if the pre-analysis used is.*

Proof Sketch. A sound pre-analysis over-approximates the indirect def-use chains used for constructing the edges in a region graph $\mathcal{G}_{\text{rg}}$. Essentially, SELFS combines FI and FS to refine such pre-computed def-use chains flow-sensitively ([R-DU] and [R-INOUT]) by performing strong updates ([R-STORE^{SU}]). □

Theorem 2 (Precision). *Suppose* FI *is used as the pre-analysis, Then* SELFS *lies between* FI *and* FS *in terms of precision.*

Proof Sketch. We can show that SELFS is no more precise than FS (with respect to each variable's points-to set) by observing the following facts: (1) performing the pre-analysis with FI gives rise to over-approximated indirect def-use chains (Theorem 1), (2) both analyses handle top-level pointers in exactly the same way except that SELFS does it sparsely in SSA ([R-ADDROF], [R-COPY] and [R-PHI]) and FS takes a data-flow approach ([S-ADDROF] and [S-COPY]), and (3) SELFS applies FS only to a region that contains one load or one store and FI to handle the remaining regions flow-insensitively. Thus, for every variable, the points-to set obtained by SELFS is no smaller than that obtained by FS.

To see that SELFS is no less precise than FI, we note that SELFS works by refining the points-to sets produced by FI (as the pre-analysis) through performing strong updates and maintaining inter-region flow-sensitivity. □

Finally, some prior representative analyses are special instances of SELFS, with the following changes made to SELFS (mainly to region partitioning):

FI in Figure 1(a): All loads and stores are in one region (and top-level variables are not in SSA if they are to be analysed also flow-insensitively).
[14]: Each region contains one load or one store (same precision as FS).
FS in Figure 1(b): Each region contains one statement and each inter-region edge represents control flow, labeled by all variables.
[21]: Each store is in its own region if it can be strongly updated and all the other stores and all the loads are in another region (less precise than FS).

3 Instantiating the SELFS Analysis

SELFS is sound (Theorem 1) and can easily achieve a precision between FI and FS on an arbitrary region graph $\mathcal{G}_{\text{rg}}$ (Theorem 2). Ideally, we should use a region graph $\mathcal{G}_{\text{rg}}$ that allows SELFS to attach the precision of FS at the efficiency of FI.

In this section, we introduce a new unification-based approach that allows SELFS to preserve the precision of FS with respect to the reads from all variables, thus making it nearly as precise as FS in practice. We also discuss how to relax this so-called strict load-precision-preserving approach to tolerate some precision loss in future work in Section 6. Our focus is on demonstrating the generality and flexibility of SELFS in allowing efficiency and precision tradeoffs to be made subject to region partitioning strategies used.

3.1 Load-Precision-Preserving Partitioning

As discussed in Section 2, SELFS degenerates into the sparse analysis [14] if SELFS operates on a region graph, denoted $\mathcal{G}_{\text{one}}$, such that each of its regions contains one load or one store. In this important special case, SELFS is significantly faster than FS while achieving the same precision as FS, but can still be costly for large programs, especially when field-sensitivity is considered. By merging small regions into larger ones, SELFS can run faster at some possible precision loss.

We introduce a partitioning strategy that works by unifying two regions into a larger one successively, starting from any given region graph, say $\mathcal{G}_{\text{one}}$. Some unification steps are applied online if they require the knowledge about whether a strong or weak update is performed at a store and some can otherwise be applied offline. Our rules are *load-precision-preserving* in the sense that every load behaves identically before and after each unification. Thus, for every load $\cdots = *q$, the points-to set of every target o pointed by q remains unchanged.

For almost all practical purposes, making all the loads precise is as good as making SELFS as precise as FS. First of all, the points-to set of every top-level pointer remains unchanged (since it is overwritten from either an ADDROF, a LOAD statement, or possibly via a sequence of COPY or PHI assignments). Thus, the precision for reads of q in $\cdots = q$ and $\cdots = *q$ is preserved. In addition, the alias information remains unchanged. This is because in our LLVM-like canonical representation, all aliases must be tested between top-level pointers. Similarly, all function pointers are reserved in the same way as they are all top-level.

However, some stores can be imprecise, but only when they are not read from later, as is the case of $*q = s$ illustrated in Figure 2(b) and revisited later in Example 3. Such stores are dead code and can thus be eliminated.

3.2 Unification

The following lemma gives a sufficient condition to make SELFS load-precision-preserving and motivates the development of our unification approach.

Lemma 1. *Let $\mathcal{G}_{rg}$ be a region graph with its two regions identified by γ_i and γ_j. Let $\mathcal{G}'_{rg}$ the resulting graph after γ_i and γ_j are unified (i.e., merged) into a new region $\gamma_{i,j}$. Let L be the set of all regions in $\mathcal{G}_{rg}$ such that each contains at least one load. Let L' be similarly defined for $\mathcal{G}'_{rg}$. Let $\pi : L \mapsto L'$ be defined such that $\pi(\gamma) = \gamma$ if $\gamma \notin \{\gamma_i, \gamma_j\}$ and $\pi(\gamma) = \gamma_{i,j}$ otherwise. If $\forall \gamma \in L : \mathrm{pt}[\overline{\gamma}] = \mathrm{pt}[\overline{\pi(\gamma)}]$ before and after the unification, then* SELFS *is load-precision-preserving.*

Proof. No strong update can be performed in a region γ that contains a load since that would imply $|\gamma| > 1$. For every region $\gamma \in L$, if $pt[\overline{\gamma}] = pt[\overline{\pi(\gamma)}]$, then $pt[\overline{\gamma}][o] = pt[\overline{\pi(\gamma)}][o]$ for every load $p = *q$ that appears in both γ and $\pi(\gamma)$, where $o \in pt(q)$ (`[R-LOAD]`). So SELFS is load-precision-preserving. □

This lemma is expensive to apply during the analysis. Guided by the basic idea behind, we have developed a conservative but simple unification approach. Each unification step operates on a small neighbourhood of the two regions being unified. Our approach is promising as it can be relaxed to allow different efficiency and precision tradeoffs to be made, as discussed in Section 6.

Definition 2 (Region Types). Given a region γ, $\tau(\gamma) = \mathsf{S}$ if a strong update can be performed inside (implying that γ contains a single store), $\tau(\gamma) = \mathsf{W}$ if a weak update can be performed inside, and $\tau(\gamma) = \mathsf{L}$ if γ contains loads only.

When unifying a region γ with another region in a region graph $\mathcal{G}_{rg} = (\mathcal{N}_{rg}, \mathcal{E}_{rg})$, we can identify the *potential* points-to relations generated by γ and the *potential* uses for the points-to relations generated by the two regions being unified directly from $\mathcal{G}_{rg}$. Below we write *rsucc* (*rpred*) to relate a region to its set of successors (predecessors) in a region graph.

– $GEN(\gamma) = \{o \mid \gamma \xrightarrow{o} \gamma', \gamma' \in \mathcal{N}_{rg}\}$ contains the address-taken variables potentially defined in γ (`[R-DU]`), which implies $GEN(\gamma) = \varnothing$ if $\tau(\gamma) = \mathsf{L}$.

- $USE(\gamma) = \{\gamma' \mid \gamma' \in rsucc(\gamma)\} \cup \{\gamma \mid \gamma \text{ contains a load}\}$ gives the set of potential uses for the points-to relations generated by γ and the region to be unified together. Note that $rsucc(\gamma) \supseteq \{\gamma\}$ if γ contains a store that produces values used by some other stores or some loads also contained in γ (Figure 3).
- $PRD(\gamma) = rpred(\gamma)$ gives the set of all potential defs for the points-to relations used in γ.

When merging two regions, we need to reason about the value flows for the address-taken variables potentially defined inside these two regions.

Definition 3 (Value-Flow Reachability). Let γ_i and γ_j be two regions in $\mathcal{G}_{rg} = (\mathcal{N}_{rg}, \mathcal{E}_{rg})$. We say that γ_j is *o-reachable* from γ_i, where $o \in \mathcal{A}$, and write $\gamma_i \overset{o}{\hookrightarrow} \gamma_j$ if there is either (1) an edge $\gamma_i \overset{o}{\rightarrow} \gamma_j \in \mathcal{E}_{rg}$ (*directly reachable*) or (2) a path $\gamma_i \overset{o}{\rightarrow} \gamma_1, \ldots, \gamma_n \overset{o}{\rightarrow} \gamma_j$ in $\mathcal{G}_{rg}$ (*indirectly reachable*) via one or more regions, $\gamma_1, \ldots, \gamma_n$, where $\tau(\gamma_k) = W$, for weakly updating o.

When two regions γ_i and γ_j are unified, all loads and stores in the resulting region are resolved flow-insensitively (since $|\gamma_i \cup \gamma_j| > 1$), even though a strong update is possible in either region before. The points-to relations flowing into both γ_i and γ_j from $PRD(\gamma_i)$ and $PRD(\gamma_j)$ are merged, preserved and propagated together with the points-to relations generated inside γ_i and γ_j to their uses in $USE(\gamma_i)$ and $USE(\gamma_j)$. In order to preserve the precision for loads, we can ensure conservatively that the same propagation happens before and after each unification (for loads). The presence of a strong update in γ_i or γ_j can be unification-preventing only when the killed values in γ_i or γ_j cannot already reach their uses in $USE(\gamma_i)$ and $USE(\gamma_j)$ before the unification.

Let us introduce some notational shorthand, where $R, R' \subseteq \mathcal{N}_{rg}$ and $O \subseteq \mathcal{A}$:

$$R \overset{O}{\hookrightarrow} R' =_{\text{def}} \forall o \in O : \forall \gamma \times \gamma' \in R \times R' : \gamma \overset{o}{\hookrightarrow} \gamma'$$

Theorem 3 (Load-Precision-Preserving Unification). *Unifying γ_i and γ_j will make* SELFS *load-precision-preserving if all the following conditions hold:*

C1 $\{\gamma_i\} \xhookrightarrow{GEN(\gamma_i)} USE(\gamma_j)$;
C2 $PRD(\gamma_i) \xhookrightarrow{GEN(\gamma_i)} USE(\gamma_i) \cup USE(\gamma_j)$;
C3 $\{\gamma_j\} \xhookrightarrow{GEN(\gamma_j)} USE(\gamma_i)$; *and*
C4 $PRD(\gamma_j) \xhookrightarrow{GEN(\gamma_j)} USE(\gamma_i) \cup USE(\gamma_j)$.

Proof Sketch. By unifying γ_i and γ_j, only the points-to relations reaching the regions in $USE(\gamma_i) \cup USE(\gamma_j)$ are affected. As is standard, SELFS is monotonic, implying that no strong update at a store is possible after the store has been weakly updated. Therefore, any indirect reachable path (Definition 3), once established, will remain unchanged. For reasons of symmetry, let us consider C1 and C2 only. C1 says that whatever γ_i generates (along its def-use edges) must be used not only by $USE(\gamma_i)$ (by construction) but also by $USE(\gamma_j)$. C2 says that even if some values are killed in γ_i due to a strong update, the killed values will still reach both $USE(\gamma_i)$ and $USE(\gamma_j)$ via a different path (without going through γ_i), rendering the values non-killable (effectively).

Let π be defined in Lemma 1. If C1 – C4 hold, then $\forall \gamma \in USE(\gamma_i) \cup USE(\gamma_j) : pt[\overline{\gamma}] = pt[\overline{\pi(\gamma)}]$. By Lemma 1, SELFS is load-precision-preserving. □

Example 3. Let us apply Theorem 3 to the example given in Figure 3, assuming initially that each statement is in its own region: $\gamma_1 = \{\ell_1\}$, $\gamma_2 = \{\ell_2\}$, $\gamma_3 = \{\ell_3\}$ and $\gamma_4 = \{\ell_4\}$. Let us try to unify γ_1 and γ_2. According to the region graph given in Figure 3(a), we have $GEN(\gamma_1) = \{m, n\}$, $GEN(\gamma_2) = \varnothing$. $USE(\gamma_1) = \{\gamma_2, \gamma_3, \gamma_4\}$, $USE(\gamma_2) = \{\gamma_2\}$, $PRD(\gamma_1) = \varnothing$ and $PRD(\gamma_2) = \{\gamma_1\}$. By Theorem 3, C1 – C4 are satisfied. So γ_1 and γ_2 are unifiable. We can also choose to unify γ_3 and γ_4 instead. Then $GEN(\gamma_3) = \{m\}$, $GEN(\gamma_4) = \varnothing$. $USE(\gamma_3) = \{\gamma_4\}$, $USE(\gamma_4) = \varnothing$, $PRD(\gamma_3) = \{\gamma_1\}$ and $PRD(\gamma_4) = \{\gamma_1, \gamma_3\}$. Note that $GEN(\gamma_4) = \varnothing$ because there are no outgoing def-use chains from ℓ_4. Again, C1 – C4 are satisfied, making γ_3 and γ_4 unifiable. By proceeding in either order, we will obtain the region graph shown in Figure 3(b).

Note that unifying γ_3 and γ_4 makes SELFS lose the precision at ℓ_3 as explained earlier. However, in this example, both ℓ_3 and ℓ_4 are dead code. If we add a load $\ell_5 : w = *q$ immediately after ℓ_3, which is in a new region $\gamma_5 = \{\ell_5\}$, there will be a new indirect def-use $\ell_3 \xrightarrow{m} \ell_5$ in Figure 3(a). In this case, γ_3 and γ_4 are no longer unifiable since $USE(\gamma_3) = \{\gamma_4, \gamma_5\}$. By treating γ_3 as γ_i in Theorem 3, C2 is violated since there is only one path from γ_1 to γ_5: $\gamma_1 \xrightarrow{m} \gamma_3 \xrightarrow{m} \gamma_5$, where a strong update is performed on m in γ_3. So γ_5 is not m-reachable from γ_1. In fact, merging γ_3 and γ_4 will cause the load $\ell_5 : w = *q$ to lose precision since the store at ℓ_3 will only be weakly updated afterwards. □

Figure 5 illustrates our unification approach further, by assuming that all indirect def-use chains are related to one address-taken variable, o. In Figure 5(d), if W_3 is S_3 (with a strong update to o inside), then the unification cannot be performed as L_{45} is not o-reachable from S_1 (the predecessor of S_2 and S_3). Otherwise, L_{45} may receive spurious points-to relations propagated from S_1. In Figure 5(h), S_1 and W_{2345} cannot be unified further because the predecessors of S_1 reach W_{2345} via only S_1 (where a strong update to o is performed).

4 Evaluation

We demonstrate the effectiveness of SELFS under our unification-based region partitioning strategy. The baseline is a state-of-the-art sparse yet precision-preserving version [14], denoted SFS, of FS given in Figure 1(b). We have selected 14 large C programs (totalling 672 KLOC) from SPEC CPU2000/CPU2006, with their characteristics given in Figure A.1. Our platform is a 2.00GHz Intel Xeon 32-core CPU running Ubuntu Linux with 64GB memory.

4.1 Methodology

As discussed in Section 2, SFS works on a region graph such that each region contains one single load or store. To apply our load-precision-preserving parti-

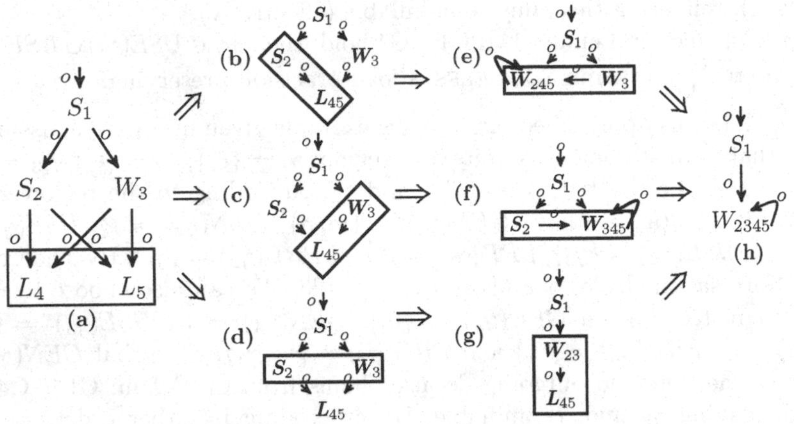

Fig. 5. Some possible unification sequences illustrated for a part of a region graph, by assuming that all indirect-use edges are related to one single address-taken variable, o. The type of a region is identified by S, W or L (Definition 2).

tioning in SELFS, we start with a region graph such that each load or store is in its own region. We then apply our unification-based approach to form larger regions. As a result, SELFS is load-precision-preserving (Theorem 3), resulting in the same precision for alias queries as SFS (among others). We repeat a process of picking a region randomly and trying to unify it with one of its predecessors, successors, and siblings in that order until no more unification is possible.

For efficiency reasons, we verify the four conditions in Theorem 3 during the SELFS analysis by restricting ourselves to the o-reachable paths (Definition 3) such that each of its intermediate nodes is one of the two regions to be unified. As a result, starting with Figure 5(a), we will accept Figures 5(c) and (d) but reject Figure 5(b). Finally, some unification steps are performed offline rather than online during the analysis if they do not require the knowledge about whether a store in a region (containing that store only) can be strongly updated or not.

4.2 Implementation

We have implemented SELFS in LLVM (version 3.3). The source files of each benchmark are compiled into bit-code files using clang and then linked together using llvm-link, with mem2reg being applied to promote memory into registers. We use FI, i.e., Andersen's analysis (using the constraint resolution techniques from [25,27]) as pre-analysis for building indirect def-use chains [14,30,31].

SELFS is field-sensitive. Each field of a struct is treated as a separate object, but arrays are considered monolithic. Positive weight cycles (PWCs) that arise from processing fields of struct objects are detected and collapsed [24]. Distinct allocation sites are modeled by distinct abstract objects as in [14,30,31].

Program	Size KLOC	Analysis Times (Secs)			SELFS' Regions (of L, S and W Types)				
		SFS	SELFS	Speedup	#L	#S	#W	#Avg	#Max
ammp	13.4	0.31	0.31	1.00	538	0	187	1.53	16
crafty	21.2	0.30	0.31	0.97	377	0	328	1.95	276
gcc	230.4	826.34	408.93	2.02	10690	294	6867	2.23	401
h264ref	51.6	40.84	5.48	7.45	3523	159	1460	1.94	128
hmmer	36.0	0.42	0.52	0.81	1170	59	487	1.59	56
mesa	61.3	1096.63	180.37	6.08	3801	0	2211	1.40	50
milc	15.0	0.28	0.26	1.08	566	8	253	1.69	66
parser	11.4	3.80	2.31	1.65	820	11	931	1.47	110
perlbmk	87.1	407.86	143.25	2.85	7514	513	4451	1.78	189
sjeng	13.9	0.07	0.19	0.37	463	0	524	1.50	14
sphinx3	25.1	1.16	1.23	0.94	953	14	598	1.98	42
twolf	20.5	1.07	1.02	1.05	1798	1	494	3.51	184
vortex	67.3	86.01	37.92	2.27	2369	198	2061	2.11	830
vpr	17.8	0.30	0.27	1.11	768	0	305	2.36	39

Fig. 6. Comparing SFS and SELFS

We have implemented SFS differently from that in [14]. In this paper, a program's call graph is built on the fly and points-to sets are represented using sparse bit vectors, for both SFS and SELFS, which are implemented in LLVM 3.3. In [14], implemented in LLVM 2.5, a program's call graph is pre-computed and points-to sets are represented using binary decision diagrams (BDDs).

4.3 Results and Analysis

As shown in Figure 6, SELFS is 2.13X faster than SFS on average under our load-precision-preserving partitioning strategy while maintaining the same precision for reads, i.e., for all alias queries in all the functions from a benchmark. The best speedups are achieved at `h264ref` (7.45X) and `mesa` (6.08X). Note that SELFS can go faster, approaching eventually the efficiency of FI, if increasingly larger regions are used. The analysis time of a benchmark, which excludes the time spent on pre-analysis, is the average of three runs.

Let us look at the results of the two analyses in more detail. SFS spends 2465.39 seconds to analyse all the benchmarks but SELFS finishes in 782.37 seconds. In Columns 6 – 10, we see the number of regions of each type as well as the average and maximum region sizes. The average region sizes range from 1.40 (`mesa`) to 3.51 (`twolf`). In `gcc`, `perlbmk` and `vortex`, each largest region ends up with 150+ loads or stores being resolved flow-insensitively, with the precision for all reads being preserved. This shows the great potential promised by SELFS in achieving load-precision-preserving flow-sensitive analysis in a region-based manner. With better tuned unification rules, better speedups are expected.

For relatively small program, such as `ammp`, `hmmer`, `milc` and `sjeng`, SELFS yields little or no performance benefits due to the overhead on region partition-

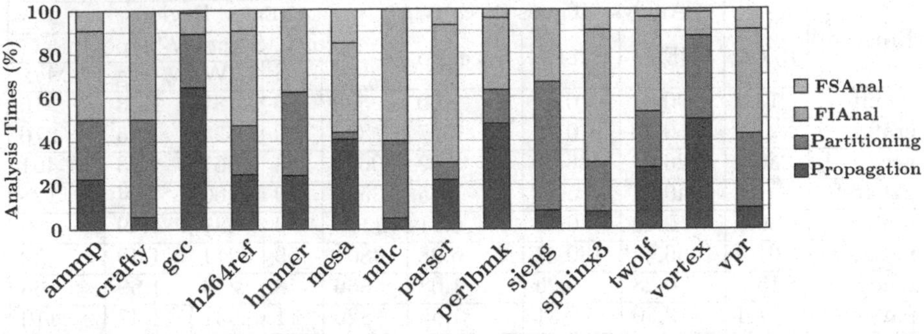

Fig. 7. Percentage distributions of SELFS' analysis time in a benchmark over "FSAnal" (the time for its flow-sensitive analysis), "FIAnal" (the time for its flow-insensitive analysis), "Partitioning" (the time on region partitioning), and "Propagation" (the time for propagating points-to facts across the indirect def-use chains in the region graph)

ing, as illustrated in Figure 7. However, for relatively larger ones, which contain more objects and more dense def-use chains to be dealt with flow-sensitively (Figure A.1), such as `gcc`, `mesa`, `perlbmk` and `vortex`, SELFS is beneficial. The best speedups are observed at `h264ref` (7.45X) and `mesa` (6.08X), because the times for propagating points-to facts across indirect def-use chains have been significantly reduced by 22.3X and 10.24X, respectively (Figure 8).

5 Related Work

Sparse Pointer Analysis. Sparse analysis, a recent improvement over the classic iterative data-flow approach, can achieve flow-sensitivity more efficiently by propagating points-to facts sparsely across pre-computed def-use chains [14,15,23,32,35]. Initially, sparsity was experimented with in [16,17] on a Sparse Evaluation Graph [5,26], a refined CFG with irrelevant nodes being removed. On various SSA form representations (e.g., factored SSA [6], HSSA [7] and partial SSA [20]), further progress was made later. The def-use chains for top-level pointers, once put in SSA, can be explicitly and precisely identified, giving rise to a so-called semi-sparse flow-sensitive analysis [15]. Recently, the idea of staged analysis [11,14] that uses pre-computed points-to information to bootstrap a later more precise analysis has been leveraged to make pointer analysis full-sparse for both top-level and address-taken variables [14,23,35].

Hybrid Analysis. The aim of hybrid-sensitive pointer analysis is to find a right balance between efficiency and precision. As a well-known example for mixing different flow-insensitive analyses, one-level approach [9] lies between Steensgaard's and Andersen's analyses (in terms of precision) by not applying its unification process to top-level pointers. For context-sensitivity, hybrid analysis has been used in Java to pick up the benefits of both call-site sensitivity and object sensitivity [19]. In [21], strong updates are performed for only singleton objects on top of a flow- and field-insensitive Andersen's analysis. Earlier [12,29], how to adjust the analysis precision according to clients' needs is discussed.

Program	Propagation Times (Secs)		Speedup
	SFS	SELFS	
ammp	0.13	0.05	2.60
crafty	0.02	0.01	2.00
gcc	741.42	270.32	2.74
h264ref	25.20	1.13	22.30
hmmer	0.11	0.09	1.22
mesa	719.97	70.31	10.24
milc	0.02	0.01	2.00
parser	2.65	0.43	6.16
perlbmk	285.90	68.96	4.15
sjeng	0.02	0.01	2.00
sphinx3	0.53	0.08	6.63
twolf	0.42	0.23	1.83
vortex	77.33	18.47	4.19
vpr	0.05	0.02	2.50

Fig. 8. Propagation times of SFS and SELFS for analysing the address-taken variables across their indirect def-use chains

Region-based Analysis. Region-based analysis, which partitions a program into different compilation units, was commonly used to explore locality and gain more opportunities for compiler optimisations, such as inlining [13,33], partial dead code elimination [3], and just-in-time optimisation [28]. In [36,37], programs are decomposed into different regions according to the alias relations and each region is solved independently. Same partition strategy was also adopted by [18] to speed up a flow- and context-sensitive pointer analysis.

6 Conclusion

We introduce a new region-based flow-sensitive pointer analysis, called SELFS, that allows efficiency and precision tradeoffs to be made subject to region partitioning strategies used. We have implemented SELFS in LLVM and demonstrated its effectiveness with a unification-based region partitioning strategy, by comparing it with a state-of-the-art flow-sensitive analysis. In addition, our unification-based approach is interesting in its own right as it leads to a particular analysis that is as precise as FS for almost all practical purposes.

In future work, we will develop a range of partitioning strategies to relax our unification-based approach. There is a lot of freedom in performing a precision-loss partitioning (Theorems 1 and 2). In order to be tunable and client-specific, a relaxed strategy can be designed along the following directions (among others). First, the user can identify parts of a program that require flow-sensitive analysis based on client analyses' needs (e.g., hot functions and major changes made during software development). Second, the user may request customised flow-sensitivity for some selected variables. Third, some stores can always be weakly updated (to enable more offline unification steps, for example). Finally, our unification approach can be relaxed to enable more regions to be merged without having to preserve the precision for all the loads.

Acknowledgments. The authors wish to thank the anonymous reviewers for their valuable comments. This work is supported by Australian Research Grants, DP110104628 and DP130101970, and a generous gift by Oracle Labs.

References

1. Acharya, M., Robinson, B.: Practical change impact analysis based on static program slicing for industrial software systems. In: ICSE 2011, pp. 746–755 (2011)
2. Andersen, L.O.: Program analysis and specialization for the C programming language. PhD Thesis, DIKU, University of Copenhagen (1994)
3. Cai, Q., Gao, L., Xue, J.: Region-based partial dead code elimination on predicated code. In: Duesterwald, E. (ed.) CC 2004. LNCS, vol. 2985, pp. 150–166. Springer, Heidelberg (2004)
4. Ceccarelli, M., Cerulo, L., Canfora, G., Di Penta, M.: In: ICSE 2010, pp. 163–166 (2010)
5. Choi, J.-D., Cytron, R., Ferrante, J.: Automatic construction of sparse data flow evaluation graphs. In: POPL 1991, pp. 55–66 (1991)
6. Choi, J.-D., Cytron, R., Ferrante, J.: On the efficient engineering of ambitious program analysis. IEEE Transactions on Software Engineering 20(2), 105–114 (1994)
7. Chow, F., Chan, S., Liu, S., Lo, R., Streich, M.: Effective representation of aliases and indirect memory operations in SSA form. In: Gyimóthy, T. (ed.) CC 1996. LNCS, vol. 1060, pp. 253–267. Springer, Heidelberg (1996)
8. Cytron, R., Ferrante, J., Rosen, B., Wegman, M., Zadeck, F.: Efficiently computing static single assignment form and the control dependence graph. ACM Transactions on Programming Languages and Systems 13(4), 451–490 (1991)
9. Das, M.: Unification-based pointer analysis with directional assignments. In: PLDI 2000, pp. 35–46 (2000)
10. Das, M., Lerner, S., Seigle, M.: ESP: Path-sensitive program verification in polynomial time. In: PLDI 2002, pp. 57–68 (2002)
11. Fink, S.J., Yahav, E., Dor, N., Ramalingam, G., Geay, E.: Effective typestate verification in the presence of aliasing. ACM Transactions on Software Engineering and Methodology 17(2), 1–34 (2008)
12. Guyer, S.Z., Lin, C.: Client-driven pointer analysis. In: Cousot, R. (ed.) SAS 2003. LNCS, vol. 2694, pp. 214–236. Springer, Heidelberg (2003)
13. Hank, R.E., Hwu, W.-M.W., Rau, B.R.: Region-based compilation: An introduction and motivation. In: MICRO 1995, pp. 158–168 (1995)
14. Hardekopf, B., Lin, C.: Flow-sensitive pointer analysis for millions of lines of code. In: CGO 2011, pp. 289–298 (2011)
15. Hardekopf, B., Lin, C.: Semi-sparse flow-sensitive pointer analysis. In: POPL 2009, pp. 226–238 (2009)
16. Hind, M., Burke, M., Carini, P., Choi, J.-D.: Interprocedural pointer alias analysis. ACM Transactions on Programming Languages and Systems 21(4), 848–894 (1999)
17. Hind, M., Pioli, A.: Assessing the effects of flow-sensitivity on pointer alias analyses. In: Levi, G. (ed.) SAS 1998. LNCS, vol. 1503, pp. 57–81. Springer, Heidelberg (1998)

18. Kahlon, V.: Bootstrapping: a technique for scalable flow and context-sensitive pointer alias analysis. In: PLDI 2008, pp. 249–259 (2008)
19. Kastrinis, G., Smaragdakis, Y.: Hybrid context-sensitivity for points-to analysis. In: PLDI 2013, pp. 423–434 (2013)
20. Lattner, C., Adve, V.: LLVM: A compilation framework for lifelong program analysis & transformation. In: CGO 2004, pp. 75–86 (2004)
21. Lhoták, O., Chung, K.-C.A.: Points-to analysis with efficient strong updates. In: POPL 2011, pp. 3–16 (2011)
22. Livshits, V.B., Lam, M.S.: Tracking pointers with path and context sensitivity for bug detection in c programs. In: FSE 2003, pp. 317–326 (2003)
23. Oh, H., Heo, K., Lee, W., Lee, W., Yi, K.: Design and implementation of sparse global analyses for C-like languages. In: PLDI 2012, pp. 229–238 (2012)
24. Pearce, D., Kelly, P., Hankin, C.: Efficient field-sensitive pointer analysis of C. ACM Transactions on Programming Languages and Systems 30(1) (2007)
25. Pereira, F., Berlin, D.: Wave propagation and deep propagation for pointer analysis. In: CGO 2009, pp. 126–135 (2009)
26. Ramalingam, G.: On sparse evaluation representations. Theoretical Computer Science 277(1), 119–147 (2002)
27. Rick Hank, R.R., Lee, L.: Implementing next generation points-to in Open64. In: Open64 Developers Forum
28. Suganuma, T., Yasue, T., Nakatani, T.: A region-based compilation technique for a Java just-in-time compiler. In: PLDI 2003, pp. 312–323 (2013)
29. Sui, Y., Li, Y., Xue, J.: Query-directed adaptive heap cloning for optimizing compilers. In: CGO 2013, pp. 1–11 (2013)
30. Sui, Y., Ye, D., Xue, J.: Static memory leak detection using full-sparse value-flow analysis. In: ISSTA 2012, pp. 254–264 (2012)
31. Sui, Y., Ye, D., Xue, J.: Detecting memory leaks statically with full-sparse value-flow analysis. IEEE Transactions on Software Engineering 40(2), 107–122 (2014)
32. Sui, Y., Ye, S., Xue, J., Yew, P.-C.: SPAS: Scalable path-sensitive pointer analysis on full-sparse SSA. In: Yang, H. (ed.) APLAS 2011. LNCS, vol. 7078, pp. 155–171. Springer, Heidelberg (2011)
33. Triantafyllis, S., Bridges, M.J., Raman, E., Ottoni, G., August, D.I.: A framework for unrestricted whole-program optimization. In: PLDI 2006, pp. 61–71 (2006)
34. Ye, D., Sui, Y., Xue, J.: Accelerating dynamic detection of uses of undefined variables with static value-flow analysis. In: CGO 2014, pp. 154–164 (2012)
35. Yu, H., Xue, J., Huo, W., Feng, X., Zhang, Z.: Level by level: making flow-and context-sensitive pointer analysis scalable for millions of lines of code. In: CGO 2010, pp. 218–229 (2010)
36. Zhang, S., Ryder, B.G., Landi, W.: Program decomposition for pointer aliasing: A step toward practical analyses. In: Gollmann, D. (ed.) FSE 1996. LNCS, vol. 1039, pp. 81–92. Springer, Heidelberg (1996)
37. Zhang, S., Ryder, B.G., Landi, W.A.: Experiments with combined analysis for pointer aliasing. In: PASTE 1998, pp. 11–18 (1998)

A Appendix

Program	Size	#Statement					#Ptrs	#Object				
	KLOC	AddrOf	Copy	Load	Store	Total		Glob.	Heap	Stk	Func	Total
ammp	13.4	702	6875	925	187	8689	29499	49	42	76	209	376
crafty	21.2	1632	9603	1011	367	12613	44744	457	33	70	147	707
gcc	230.4	8934	135332	32498	7832	184596	399377	1400	154	1018	2273	4845
h264ref	51.6	1829	27845	8324	1635	39633	114221	374	209	284	287	1154
hmmer	36	1195	7635	2083	581	11494	32415	42	376	89	155	662
mesa	61.3	2691	45447	6112	2298	56548	136415	35	322	465	1130	1952
milc	15	1104	8591	1138	263	11096	26437	92	63	203	270	628
parser	11.4	1417	6045	1626	964	10052	23417	174	114	42	353	683
perlbmk	87.1	4366	39602	17096	5154	66218	148231	415	28	458	1168	2069
sjeng	13.9	926	5579	848	632	7985	29624	214	14	119	173	520
sphinx3	25.1	1898	10169	2482	622	15171	36588	69	59	122	421	671
twolf	20.5	1371	14390	7526	506	23793	62430	304	192	116	212	824
vortex	67.3	6636	20408	6577	3185	36806	104218	739	29	1864	961	3593
vpr	17.8	1195	5703	2222	310	9430	28405	101	6	101	303	511

Fig. A.1. Program characteristics

Author Index